Lecture Notes in Computer Science

Edited by G. Goos and J. Hartmanis

368

H. Boral P. Faudemay (Eds.)

Database Machines

Sixth International Workshop, IWDM '89
Deauville, France, June 19–21, 1989
Proceedings

Springer-Verlag
Berlin Heidelberg New York London Paris Tokyo Hong Kong

Editorial Board

D. Barstow W. Brauer P. Brinch Hansen D. Gries D. Luckham
C. Moler A. Pnueli G. Seegmüller J. Stoer N. Wirth

Volume Editors

Haran Boral
MCC, 3500 West Balcones Center Drive
Austin TX 78759, USA

Pascal Faudemay
Laboratory MASI, University Paris 6
4 place Jussieu, F-75252 Paris cedex 05, France

CR Subject Classification (1987): H.2.6

ISBN 3-540-51324-8 Springer-Verlag Berlin Heidelberg New York
ISBN 0-387-51324-8 Springer-Verlag New York Berlin Heidelberg

This work is subject to copyright. All rights are reserved, whether the whole or part of the material is concerned, specifically the rights of translation, reprinting, re-use of illustrations, recitation, broadcasting, reproduction on microfilms or in other ways, and storage in data banks. Duplication of this publication or parts thereof is only permitted under the provisions of the German Copyright Law of September 9, 1965, in its version of June 24, 1985, and a copyright fee must always be paid. Violations fall under the prosecution act of the German Copyright Law.

© Springer-Verlag Berlin Heidelberg 1989
Printed in Germany

Printing and binding: Druckhaus Beltz, Hemsbach/Bergstr.
2145/3140-543210 – Printed on acid-free paper

Preface

This volume contains 24 papers presented at the Sixth International Workshop on Database Machines. The papers cover a wide spectrum of topics including: system architectures, storage structures, associative memory architectures, memory resident systems, deduction and retrospectives on maturing projects. The papers were selected from a total of 60 submissions from 8 countries. Our thanks go to the authors for writing excellent papers and for their efforts in meeting deadlines, to the MASI Laboratory (University UPMC Paris 6 & CNRS, France) for organizing and sponsoring the workshop, to the IEEE Computer Society and AFCET for their cooperation, to the Program Committee members for their thorough reviews and to Coila Sims of MCC for her help in preparing this volume.

April 1989

Haran Boral
Pascal Faudemay

Table of Contents

Architecture

An Object Flow Computer for Database Applications
  Herman Lam, Chiang Lee, Stanley Y. W. Su 1

Design and Implementation of KARDAMOM – A Set-oriented Data Flow
  Database Machine
  Günter von Bültzingsloewen, Cirano Iochpe, Rolf-Peter Liedtke,
  Ralf Kramer, Michael Schryro, Klaus R. Dittrich, Peter C. Lockemann 18

An Experiment on Response Time Scalability in Bubba
  Marc Smith, Bill Alexander, Haran Boral, George Copeland,
  Tom Keller, Herb Schwetman and Chii-Ren Young 34

Esprit Projects

Language Levels and Computational Model for a Parallel Database Accelerator
  Björn Bergsten, Michel Couprie, Rubén González-Rubio,
  Brigitté Kerherve and Mikal Ziane 58

A Graph Based Data Structure for Efficient Implementation of Main Memory
  DBMS's
  Philippe Pucheral and Jean-Marc Thevenin 73

Implementing PRISMA/DB in an OOPL
  Annita N. Wilschut, Paul W. P. J. Grefen, Peter M. G. Apers
  and Martin L. Kersten 97

Parallel Hashing and Sorting

Database Processing Models in Parallel Processing Systems
  Sakti Pramanik and Myoung Ho Kim 112

Parallel Sorting Methods for Large Data Volumes on a
  Hypercube Database Computer
  Bjørn Arild W. Baugstø and Jarle Fredrik Greipsland 127

Evaluation of 18-stage Pipeline Hardware Sorter
  Masaru Kitsuregawa and Weikang Yang 142

Pot-Pourri

A Parallel Container Model for Data Intensive Applications
  Setrag Khoshafian and Patrick Valduriez 156

Function Request Shipping in a Database Machine Environment
  Gary Hallmark 171

Special Function Unit for Statistical Aggregation Functions
  Mahdi Abdelguerfi 187

Associative Memories

Generic Associative Memory for Information Retrieval
  C. H. Ben Choi and Dik L. Lee 202

Design and Analysis of a Parallel VLSI String Search Algorithm
  Kuo Chu Lee and Victor W. Mak 215

Integrating Integrity Constraints With Database Filters Implemented in Hardware
  Manuel Penaloza and Esen Ozkarahan 230

Memory Resident Database Systems

Main Memory Database Research Directions
  Margaret H. Eich 251

Recovery Algorithms for Database Machines With Non-Volatile Main Memory
  Rakesh Agrawal and Hosagrahar V. Jagadish 269

An Intelligent Memory Transaction Engine
  Abhaya Asthana, Hosagrahar V. Jagadish and Scott C. Knauer 286

Deduction

A Parallel Transitive Closure Algorithm Using Hash-Based Clustering
  Jean-Pierre Cheiney and Christophe de Maindreville 301

A New Version of a Parallel Production System Machine, MANJI-II
  Jun Miyazaki, Kenji Takeda, Hideharu Amano and Hideo Aiso 317

A Parallel Processing Architecture for Real-Time Production Systems
With Truth Maintenance
  Satoshi Fujita, Reiji Aibara, Masafumi Yamashita and Tadashi Ae 331

Project Retrospectives

The Braunschweig Relational Database Machine Project Results
  Holger Herzog, Frank Hildebrandt, Hans-Otto Leilich, Peter Mertinatsch,
  Günter Stiege and Hans Christoph Zeidler 345

The Development of the CROSS8 and HC16-186 Parallel (Database) Computers
  Kjell Bratbergsengen and Torgrim Gjelsvik 359

Analysis of Some Experimental Results for the TDM
  Liming Meng 373

Author Index 387

An Object Flow Computer For Database Applications *

H. Lam **
C. Lee **
S.Y.W. Su ***

Database Systems Research and Development Center
CSE E470
University of Florida
Gainesville, Florida 32611
U.S.A.

Abstract

In the past two decades, a considerable amount of research exists which use hardware, firmware, and novel architectures to achieve the needed efficiency in implementing database management functions. However, most of the efforts have been directed toward developing database computers for supporting a relatively primitive data model, namely, the relational model. This paper presents the design and performance evaluation of an Object Flow Computer (OFC) for processing data modeled by an Object-oriented Semantic Association Model (OSAM*). The OFC allows high-level semantic constructs as seen by the users of a large data/knowledge base to be processed by hardware directly without many levels of transformations to a low-level data representation. It employs a vertically fragmented data storage structure and a two-phase processing strategy to process queries in order to avoid unnecessary transfer of a large amount of data from secondary storage and among processors. Also, a set of primitive operators is defined for the OFC. Depending on the performance requirement, these operators can be implemented in software or as special-purpose processors in the form of VLSI chips. Based on these primitive operators, a high-level database request can be decomposed and executed in parallel. Finally, the OFC combines a number of known database processing techniques such as query decomposition, pipelining mode of data processing, and data flow control strategy. Together with hardware/firmware support in the form of special-purpose processors, the OFC offers an integrated software/hardware solution to the very large database management problem.

---

*This research is supported by the Florida High Technology and Industry Council, grant number UPN 85100316.

** Department of Electrical Engineering

***Department of Electrical Engineering and Department of Computer and Information Sciences

1. Introduction

In the past two decades, a considerable amount of research exists which use hardware, firmware, and novel architectures to achieve the needed efficiency in implementing database management functions (See references in [HSI83, SU88a]). Despite the fact that much progress has been made, the continuous demand for increase in functionality and higher efficiency in database management systems (DBMSs) has diminished the value of past efforts. A database computer that has a significant performance improvement (one or two orders of improvement) over conventional systems is still a goal rather than a reality. The reasons for the past failure to reach the goal are as follows.

First, most researchers (including ourselves) developed database computers in the past for supporting a relatively primitive data model, namely, the relational model. The relational model captures very limited semantic constraints, does not support abstract data typing and the concept of inheritance, does not allow user-defined operations and knowledge rules, and lacks many other features provided by semantic data models or object-oriented data models. Furthermore, the normalization process required in the relational model forces data and their relationships to be unnecessarily scattered in a large number of relations. To relate the data in these relations, a large number of relational join and set operations need to be performed. No matter how database computer designers improve the performance of join and set operations, the frequency of performing these operations places a limit on the performance improvement of the existing database computers. The need for data models that are rich in semantics has become apparent in recent years as DBMSs are used for supporting engineering, scientific, and military applications. Semantic data models [CHE76, SMI77, MYL78, HAM81, SU88b] provide a number of general semantic constructs which allow users to conveniently model complex data and data relationships as well as semantic constraints. DBMSs using these models can operate more intelligently and provide the users with more functionalities. Recently, these DBMSs are further enhanced by incorporating object-oriented concepts into them [COP84, BAT84, GEM86, MAI86, ZDO86, ONT87, SU88b]. The object-oriented paradigm introduced by artificial intelligence and programming language communities possesses many desirable features, e.g. abstract data typing, inheritance, information hiding, etc., for capturing the structural properties and behavioral aspects of objects. For building future DBMSs, it is natural to combine the features of semantic modeling and the object-oriented paradigm into object-oriented semantic data models. However, in order to meet the efficiency requirement, high-level data manipulation functions provided by these powerful DBMSs must be directly supported by hardware.

The second reason is as follows. Generally speaking, query processing can be viewed as (1) identifying the objects of interest in a database, and (2) processing the descriptive data of these objects to produce the final result. We observe that these are indeed two distinct phases of query processing which are intermixed in the conventional processing strategies. Consequently, a large amount of (sometimes unnecessary) data is accessed from the database and repeatedly transmitted among the processors during the identification phase of query processing. Efficiency and reliability can be gained by making such distinction.

Lastly, most of the existing database computers use various hardware and software techniques in isolation; a natural tendency of a developing field. These techniques have not been fully integrated to take full advantage of the efficiencies offered by special-purpose hardware, multiprocessor architectures, and parallel processing algorithms. For example, the advanced parallel processing techniques such as query decomposition, data flow, pipelining, intermediate result sharing among concurrent queries used in [WON76, BOR80, JAR84, KIM84, SEL85, SU86, MIK88a, MIK88b] and the special-purpose processors used in [TAN80, BAN83, KIT84, LEE87] have not been combined and used to their full advantages.

This paper presents the design and evaluation of an Object Flow Computer (OFC), which directly supports an object-oriented semantic data model. High-level semantic constructs as seen by the users of a large data/knowledge base are processed by the OFC without many levels of transformations to a low-level data representation.

The OFC employs a vertically fragmented data storage structure and a novel two-phase query processing strategy which avoids unnecessary data transfers between the main memory and secondary storage and among processors. A set of primitive operators is defined for the OFC. Depending on the performance requirement, these operators can be implemented in software or as special-purpose processors in the form of VLSI chips. Based on these primitive operators, a high-level database request can be decomposed and executed in parallel. The OFC combines a number of known database processing techniques such as query decomposition, pipelined mode of data processing, and data flow control strategy. Together with the hardware/firmware support in the form of special-purpose processors, the OFC offers an integrated software/hardware solution to the very large database management problem.

This paper is organized as follows. Section 2 describes the general architecture of the Object Flow Computer. The primitive operations of this computer are defined. In Section 3, the use of the OFC to support an object-oriented semantic data model is described and a two-phase query processing strategy is presented. In Section 4, an evaluation of the OFC and the two-phase processing strategy using an analytical model is summarized. The summary and conclusion are given in Section 5.

2. The Object Flow Computer

The Object Flow Computer (OFC) is designed to directly support a high-level Object-oriented Semantic Association Model (OSAM*). We shall briefly describe the model through an example before presenting the architecture of the OFC.

2.1 Object-Oriented Semantic Association Model

Shown in Figure 1(a) is an example university database represented in the semantic diagram (S-diagram) representation of OSAM*. In OSAM*, application-world objects are grouped into entity classes (represented as rectangular boxes in Figure 1(a)) based on some common semantic properties. The expressive power of OSAM* lies in its capability to use various semantic association types to model the relationships among the object classes in an application-world. There are five semantic association types defined in OSAM*: Aggregation (A), Generalization (G), Interaction (I), Composition (C), and Cross-Product (X). In Figure 1(a), the entity class PERSON has two types of associations:

generalization (G) and aggregation (A). The generalization association is similar to the superclass-subclass concept of many O-O systems. In this example, the class PERSON is a generalization of the classes FACULTY and STUDENT. All the semantic properties PERSON (e.g. structural properties, operations, and rules) are inherited by FACULTY and STUDENT. The aggregation (A) association models the semantics that the SS# and Name characterize the objects of PERSON. The interaction (I) association of the class ADVISING models the fact that a faculty member can advise some students. This interaction is described by the attribute Startdate, which is modeled by an A association between ADVISING and Startdate. The I association of the class SECTION models the fact that a faculty may teach some course to some student. This interaction is characterized by Section#, Room#, and Textbook. For the description of the other associations and a more detailed description of OSAM*, refer to [SU88b].

2.2 Architecture of the Object Flow Computer

In OFC, the semantic diagram and the instances of its object classes are mapped into an internal storage structure which is in the form of generalized relations (G-relations). Structurally, a G-relation is an un-normalized relation in which an attribute of the G-relation does not have to be atomic and can itself be a G-relation. Semantically, the G-relation representation captures the required information to support an O-O semantic data model: the identification of an object (OID), the description of an object (attributes or instance variables), and the relationship (association) of an object to other objects. Correspondingly, the attributes of a G-relation in the OFC can be classified as follows: an object identifier (OID), a set of descriptive attributes, and a set of association attributes. An OID is a system-generated object identifier. It is used to uniquely identify an object with the system. The descriptive attributes contain data that describes the object and the association attributes contain information concerning the object's association with other objects.

In the OFC, the data in a G-relation is vertically partitioned and stored in a vertical fragmentation storage model. Selected G-relations corresponding to the database in Figure 1(a) are shown in Figure 1(b). This storage model is similar to the one introduced in [COP85, KHO88] for the relational model. However, the attributes of a relation in their model are fully fragmented, i.e. one fragment for each attribute. In the OFC, the fragmentation strategy is guided by the semantics of the data. More specifically, data in a G-relation is partitioned into a vertical fragment of descriptive attributes and a vertical fragment of association attributes. The corresponding OID's are stored with the fragmented data and are used to identify and relate the data in these two fragments. The data in these fragments are stored in the order of their OID's.

Each data fragment is stored in secondary storage and is assigned to a set of processing units, as shown in Figure 2(a), including a local controller (LC) and a number of special-function units (SFU's) which implement the various OFC operators. (The requirements for the OFC operators will be discussed in Section 2.3.) This set of SFU's can be implemented in software or as a set of VLSI chips as co-processors. A data fragment together with its associated set of SFU's is viewed as a <u>logical processing node</u>. Physically, the OFC consists of a network of physical processing nodes. Each physical node consists of a general-purpose processor and zero or more special-purpose co-processors. A set of logical nodes can be mapped onto a single physical node. Within a physical node, a common pool of SFU's can be time-shared by a number of data fragments stored in this physical node. In this manner, with a proper data and resource allocation, each logical processing node can effectively have its own set of SFU's.

Referring again to Figure 2(a), data within a processing node is staged into the main memory from the secondary storage and forms a pipeline of data blocks. The processing of the data (locally) by one or more processors associated with the data is automatically triggered when data arrives at the processors. As shown in Figure 2(b), the architecture of the OFC provides a general-purpose computing environment which is controlled by the Control Computer. The database needs are supported by the network of processing nodes (PN's) connected through an interconnection network.

2.3 Architecture of a Processing Node

A processing node consists of a vertical data fragment and its associated set of SFU's, each implementing an OFC operator. As shown in Figure 3, each SFU (represented by a circle) has an output pipe and one or more input pipes. The light arrows represent the controlling input pipes and the dark arrows represent the input pipes to be controlled. The SFU is activated when the required blocks of objects (represented by OID's) and/or their data have arrived and been staged into the input pipes. Results are transferred out of the SFU's output pipe when a full block of output objects or data has been produced. In the OFC, the object data is represented by an ordered pair (OID,v), where v is the value(s) of an (or a set of) attribute(s) and OID is the associated object identifier.

2.3.1 Primitive Operators in the Object Flow Computer

In the OFC, a number of database operations are distinguished: Selector (SL), Merge-Selector (MS), Sorter (SR), Merge-Sorter (MSR), Join (JN), Restricted-Join (RJ), Semi-Join (SJ), Restricted-Semi-Join (RSJ), set operators (Set-Intersection (SI), Set-Union (SU), Set-Difference (SD)), and Constructor (CN). These operations are introduced to account for the fact that the input data to a processor may have some useful characteristics (e.g., one of the input is in sort order). Thus, different algorithms can be employed to achieve better efficiency and can be implemented in hardware as distinct operators. The detailed description of these OFC operators is given in [LAM87, LEE88]. The descriptions of those operators that are used in this paper are given below:

<u>Selector (SL)</u>. The selector, illustrated in Figure 3(a), has one input pipe, holding blocks of pairs (OID,v). The braces, { }, represent a set or block of objects or data. This operator has a selection condition, C, specified on the attributes in v. If a pair (OID,v) of the input data satisfies the selection condition, then the associated object (represented by its OID) is included in the output. Alternatively, the attribute values v will also be included in the output. The selector is an OID order-preserving operator. That is, the output has the same OID order as the input.

<u>Merge-Selector (MS)</u>. As shown in Figure 3(b), the merge-selector has an input pipe holding blocks of data which consist of the pairs (<u>OID</u>,v) and an input pipe holding blocks of <u>OID's</u>. Both OID and OID' are ordered and are unique, as indicated by the underline

symbol. Processing begins when both pipes are full. The function of the MS operator is to select those ordered pairs (OID,v) whose OID value is contained in {OID'}. Since both inputs are in OID order, a simple merge process is used. The merge-selector is an OID order-preserving operator.

Join (JN). This is the regular join operation. As shown in Figure 3(c), the join operator performs a relational join operation on the two streams of data contained in the two input pipes. The join operation is based on the join condition, J, which can be defined over the identifiers (e.g., OID1 op OID2) or over the attributes (e.g., a op b), where "op" is any of the comparison operators. The output is the result of the join operation in the form of blocks of (OID1',OID2',a,b) or some projection of it. The join operator is not OID order-preserving.

Semi-join (SJ). The semi-join operator implements an operation similar to the semi-join operation that has been defined in the relational literature. In other words, it functions the same as the regular join operation except that there is no concatenation of the inputs and all the output data result from only one of the input file. The semi-join operator is shown in Figure 3(d). It has two input pipes: one containing data in the form of (OID,v) and the other containing a pipeline of objects {OID2} or value {v}. The join condition J can be defined over the OID's or v's. In the operation, the input {OID2} or {v} is used to select data from another input {(OID1,v)} based on the join condition. The output of a semi-join operation is (OID1',v) or any projection of it. The semi-join operation is not OID order-preserving.

Restricted-Semi-Join (RSJ). The restricted-semi-join has the same function as a semi-join operation except the following restrictions. First, the join condition is defined over OID's. Secondly, one of these two OID's to be joined must be ordered and unique, e.g., OID1 of Figure 3(e). Finally, an optional restriction is that the output has the same OID order as OID2. With this restriction, the restricted-semi-join operation is OID order-preserving with respect to OID2. This optional restriction is applied in the collection phase of a two-phase query processing strategy to be described in Section 3.1.

Constructor (CN). The constructor is used to populate a skeletal generalized relation (G-relation) with data. The inputs of the constructor are any number of input pipes containing data to be used for the construction, as shown in Figure 3(f). The data in these input pipes contain only values but no OID's. The construction of the G-relation is controlled by the skeletal G-relation [G] which contains a bit map of the resultant G-relation. A "1" in the skeletal G-relation corresponds to a value in the output G-relation and a "0" corresponds to an null value in the output G-relation. The output of the constructor is a fully populated G-relation. This operator is also essential in the collection phase of the two-phase query processing strategy.

3. Query Processing in the Object Flow Computer

In this section, an example is given to provide an overview of the processing scenario within an OFC in support of an object-oriented semantic data model. For this example, the following query is used to demonstrate the working of the Object Flow Computer:

For each faculty member who is in the College of Engineering and is advising students who are taking courses with section# >= 9000, retrieve the faculty member's name and specialty. Also retrieve the students' names and the course titles.

Before we proceed with the OFC processing, let us first illustrate the use of the relational data model (Figure 4) and a conventional query tree to process the query. The decomposed operations and the general flow of the execution of these operations for this query are specified in the query tree shown in Figure 5. Note that this query tree has been optimized so that all the projections and selections are at the bottom of the query tree and that only the necessary attributes required to process the query (i.e. those required in some selection or join conditions or in the output list) are carried up the query tree during execution. Also, the number of join operations are minimized. In spite of the optimization, the number of join operations in the query tree is substantial, due to the nature of the relational data model (normalization). Moreover, a large amount of data are carried along unnecessarily and transmitted and retransmitted among processors. For example, if a join operator near the root of the query tree has a low join-selectivity factor, then a potentially large amount of data (e.g. attribute values that are simply for output purpose such as Fac.specialty) will be carried along unnecessarily during the object identification phase and be eliminated by that join operator. The transfer of the unnecessary data from secondary storage to processor and among processors is very costly. To remedy this problem, a two-phase processing strategy is introduced in the next section.

3.1 The Two-Phase Processing Strategy

The OFC two-phase processing strategy is similar to the "pivot" strategy proposed in [KHO88]. The pivot strategy also uses tuple ID's (i.e. surrogates) in relating objects rather than using attribute values. The main difference is that in the pivot strategy, the intermediate results are maintained as binary relations. Consequently, a m-way join over a pre-determined pivot surrogate is necessary to obtain the final result. In the two-phase strategy described below, this m-way join is avoided by the construction of a skeletal G-relation during the processing of the query.

To illustrate the two-phase processing strategy of the OFC, the database in the form of _fragmented_ G-relations in Figure 1(b) is used. Recall that descriptive attributes describe the properties of an object, and association attributes contain information concerning the association of the object with other objects.

Query processing in the OFC is divided into two phases: _object identification_ phase which identifies objects of interest in the database and a _result-processing_ phase which processes the objects' descriptive data to produce the final result. As an illustration, the object identification phase and the result-processing phase for the example query are shown in Figure 6(a) and Figure 6(b), respectively, in the form of an _object flow tree_ (OFT). Like a conventional query tree, an OFT specifies the operations and the general flow of the execution of these operations, except that it is defined with respect to the fragmented G-relations and the object flow operators instead of relations and relational operators. The circles in the OFT represent object flow operators. As before, the light arrows represent controlling pipes and the dark arrows represent pipes to be controlled. The direction of the arrow specifies the direction of the flow. The braces, { }, represent a set or block of OID's or data.

The processing of the object identification phase begins at the bottom of the OFT. The selection operators (SL) are used to select objects from the descriptive G-relations. The selected objects, in the form of OID's, are then piped from one operator to another (RSJ, SJ, JN, etc.) and are used to select and relate to other objects (using association G-relations). During this process, a skeletal G-relation containing only OID's is gradually formed. In this example, the final skeletal G-relation at the root node contains three OID columns [(Fac_OID, Stud_OID, Cou_OID)]. Each OID represents an object that qualifies for the final result. The instances of the skeletal G-relation are piped out of the JN operator and serve as the input to the result-processing phase.

In the case of a retrieval query such as this example, the result- processing phase collects the descriptive data associated with the objects identified in the first phase. As shown in Figure 6(b), data are collected from fragmented descriptive G-relations using the RSJ operators. The RSJ operators in this phase will enforce the optional restriction mentioned in Section 2.3.1 so that output data preserve the same order with respect to their input OID's. Note that, by using these OID's, only the resultant data are retrieved. Finally, based on the skeletal G-relation, the CN operator uses the collected data to construct the final result.

In general, the two-phase query processing strategy can be used to perform system-defined operations such as retrieval, deletion, update, etc., as well as any user-defined operations. The key features of this query processing strategy are summarized below:

<u>Increase horizontal concurrency</u>. The high-level query is decomposed into an OFT of primitive operators. Operators at the same level of the tree can be executed in parallel, thus increasing the horizontal concurrency of the system. For example, the SL operators for G-relations D_DEPARTMENT and D_SECTION in the identification phase can operate in parallel and all the RSJ operators in the result-processing phase can operate in parallel.

Moreover, since files are vertically fragmented in the system, horizontal concurrency can be further increased. Note that the association G-relations are generally used in the identification phase (except for the initial selection) and descriptive G-relations are used in the result-processing phase. As a result, while the association part of a G-relation (e.g., A_FACULTY) is being processed in the first phase, the descriptive part (e.g., D_FACULTY) can be used in the second phase.

<u>Increase vertical concurrency</u>. Pipelining and object flow execution allow the operators at different levels of the OFT to be executed concurrently, thus increasing the vertical concurrency of the system. For example, the operators from the identification phase, SL, RSJ, SJ, JN, and the operators from the result-processing phase, RSJ and CN, form a 6-stage pipeline. These operators are all operating concurrently, each processing the block of objects or data that was transferred to it from the previous operator(s) in the pipe.

<u>Minimize the join operator</u>. The join operation is recognized to be the bottleneck operations in conventional database systems. Much work has been devoted to improve its performance. In the OFC, our proposed solution is to simply replace the join operation, when possible, with much more efficient specialized join operations (RJ, SJ, and RSJ). This is possible in the OFC because associations among objects are explicitly specified in

the object-oriented semantic data model and the "join" of these objects are generally through their OID's. As illustrated by our example, most of the join operations in the relational model implementation shown in Figure 5 are replaced by much more efficient RSJ and SJ operations.

   Minimize unnecessary data transfer. In a conventional data flow system, all attribute values of a relation are transferred into the main memory from the secondary storage whether or not they are relevant to a query (i.e., relations are not vertically fragmented). Also, by not distinguishing the identification phase from the result-processing phase of query processing, all attribute values that are included in the output project list and/or participate in any qualification condition in any part of the query tree are carried along and transmitted (and retransmitted) among the processors, even though they may eventually be eliminated by an operator further up in the query tree.

   In the OFC, objects in the form of OID's flow through the system and are used to select and relate objects during the first phase. Since an OID requires far fewer bytes to represent than an entire "tuple" in general (a 4-byte OID represents up to 2^{32} = 4G tuples), each block can hold much more OID's than tuples. The information contents of the blocks transferred among processors are much denser. Transfer of actual data is postponed until the second phase when the relevant objects have been identified. Thus, only the required data is transferred. This advantage is even more dramatic when complex objects are processed since they are defined in terms of many other objects, resulting in a large amount of data associated with them. Since a large amount of (sometimes unnecessary) data is not repeatedly transmitted through the network of pipelines, the reliability of the system is also increased.

4. Performance Comparisons

   In this section, the performance evaluation of the two-phase processing strategy of the OFC is presented. For this evaluation, the example query in Section 3 and Figure 6 is used. The result is compared with that produced by using the conventional strategy shown in Figure 5.

4.1 The Analytical Model and Performance Settings

   For comparison purpose, we assume ideal machines are used in both processing strategies. In other words, we assume that the query tree in Figure 5 and the object flow tree in Figure 6 are executed in a multiprocessor system, whose processors are interconnected in exactly the same manner as the trees. Therefore, no bus contention exists in these ideal machines. Each node (operator) of the trees is implemented by a processor in the corresponding position of an ideal machine. For fairness in comparison, all processors are assumed to be general-purpose processors. Each processor has a local memory of the same size and, if necessary, a private disk for storing intermediate result. We also assume that processing is in a pipelined fashion in both cases. Local I/O time of a processor is overlapped with its processing time. These times can also be overlapped with the time for communication with its predecessor(s) and successor(s). Note that this pipeline factor is not modeled in most of the evaluation models described in the literature. The reason that we take it into consideration is that pipelined processing is an efficient way of processing queries in a multiprocessor system. To assume no overlap among processors will only increase, in our favor, the difference in performances between the two processing strategies.

For join operations, we assume all ordinary and special joins are performed using a hybrid-hash based join algorithm presented in [DEW84], even though the OFC is designed to take advantage of the specialized join operators to speed up the query execution. The hybrid-hash join algorithm is used because it has been shown in [DEW84] that it outperforms other join algorithms in most cases. Any slower algorithms will again only enhance the comparison results in our favor. All base (G-)relations are assumed to have the same number of tuples. The number of attributes in a (G-)relation are shown in Figures 1 and 4. Each attribute contains the same number of bytes. All selection operations have an identical selectivity factor. All join operations also have an identical join factor. The parameters and their values used in the analysis are listed in Table 1.

The evaluation of query execution in a pipelined processing environment has been published in our previous work [MIK88a, MIK88b]. For convenience, we repeat here some relevant cost functions for the join operation that conceptually illustrate the pipeline effect in execution. In these equations, we assume i and j are the two inputs to a join processor k.

```
Nok = size of output data from processor k
    = (number of input i tuples)*(number of input j tuples)*join_factor

Tek = time at the completion of join in k
    = t_hash_stage + t_probe_stage

Trk = time at which the first data block is outputted from k
                        Tek - max(Tri,Trj)
    = max(Tri, Trj) + ------------------
                              Nok
```

where
```
    t_hash_stage  = max [input i response time,
                        input j response time +
                          max(total time to receive all input j data blocks,
                              time to build hash table for input j) ]

    t_probe_stage = max [input i response time + total time to receive all
                            input i data blocks - t_hash_stage,
                        total time to hash input i data (including load and
                            unload) and probe j hash table + a * t_idle,
                        communication time to transmit Nok output data +
                            a * t_idle]

    t_idle = input i response time - t_hash_stage
    a = 1 if t_idle > 0;   a = 0 if otherwise.
```

Note that in t_hash_stage and t_probe_stage, we have assumed the input j data arrives at processor k first (i.e., faster response time) and the hash table is built on input j data. In Tek, the costs of hash_stage and probe_stage are summed together because these two stages are executed sequentially. Inside each stage, there are parallel executions. Only the maximal cost in those parallel steps is included in the total execution cost. The detailed costs of hash and probe stages can be found in [DEW84]. These three equations for Nok, Tek, and Trk can be iteratively applied from the leaves of a query tree to the root to obtain the total query processing cost.

4.2 Results and Discussion

Based on the evaluation model, the total execution times for both processing strategies are determined by varying the relation size, attribute size, main memory size, page size, join factor, and selectivity factor. The detailed equations for the evaluation can be found in [LEE88]. The parameters and their values used in the analysis are listed in Table 1. The result is shown in Figure 7. For clarity, we also provide the exact values of selected points for each curve.

In Figure 7(a), the advantage of the two-phase processing strategy over the conventional strategy becomes evident as the relation size increases. When relation size reaches 100,000 tuples, two-phase processing is about 15 times faster than conventional strategy. On the other hand, when the relation size is small, these two strategies are comparable. The reason is that, in this case, the number of disk I/O's required for processing a query is the main determining factor. In other words, when the relation size is relatively small in comparison with the size of main memory, the cost of loading and transferring the small amount of unnecessary data during the object identification phase in the conventional strategy has less of an impact on the performance.

Figure 7(b) shows the comparison under the variation of attribute size. The advantage of the two-phase processing strategy over the conventional strategy again widens as the attribute size increases. This is to be expected because as the attribute size increases, the amount of the "unnecessary" data carried along in the object identification phase of the conventional strategy increases accordingly.

Note that variation of attribute size is equivalent to the variation of the number of attributes in a relation. Therefore, Figure 7(b) can also be used to represent the result of varying the number of attributes of a relation. Furthermore, Figure 7(b) can represent the result of varying the "complexity" of complex objects in a database. In both cases, the advantage of the two-phase processing strategy increases significantly as the number of attributes and/or the complexity of objects increase.

Figures 7(c) and 7(d) show that the total execution time decreases as the main memory size or page size increases. This is expected because in both cases the number of disk accesses decreases. However, at each point, the performance of the two-phase strategy is at least an order of magnitude better than the conventional strategy.

We also evaluate the effects of selectivity factor and join factor on performance within a range of selectivity factor (0.01 - 0.15) and join factor (0.00001 - 0.0001). The result shows that the two-phase strategy still significantly outperforms the conventional strategy. (Note that these two factors cannot be too large if a reasonable size of output is expected.)

In conclusion, the above evaluation results underscore a long-recognized fact that the I/O problem is one of the main bottlenecks in processing a very large database. Since the two-phase processing strategy is designed to minimize unnecessary data accesses and transfers, it can greatly improve the system performance and ease, if not alleviate, the I/O bottleneck problem.

5. Summary and Conclusion

In this paper, we presented the design and performance evaluation of an Object Flow Computer. Different from the past database computers, the OFC is designed to directly support a higher-level, object-oriented semantic data model. It employs a vertically fragmented data storage structure and a two-phase processing strategy to process queries to avoid unnecessary transfers of a large amount of data from secondary storage and among processors. Also, a set of primitive operators is defined for the OFC. As dictated by performance requirement, these operators can be implemented as special-purpose processors in the form of VLSI chips, as demonstrated in [LAM87, LAM89, LEE87]. Based on these primitive operators, a high-level database request can be decomposed and executed in parallel. Finally, the OFC combines a number of known database processing techniques such as query decomposition, pipelining mode of data processing, and data flow control strategy. Together with hardware/firmware support in the form of special-purpose processors, the OFC offers an integrated software/hardware solution to the very large database management problem.

REFERENCES

[BAN83] Bancilhon, F., Richard, P. and Scholl, M., "VERSO: The Relational Database Machine," *Advanced Database Machine Architecture*, D. Hsiao (ed.), Prentice-Hall, 1983, pp.1-18.

[BAT84] Batory, D. S., and Buchmann, A. P., "Molecular Objects, Abstract, Abstract Data Types and Data Models: A Framework," *Proc. International Conference on Very Large Data Bases*, 1984, pp. 172-184.

[BOR80] Boral, H., and DeWitt, D. J., "Design Considerations for Data-flow Database Machines," *Proc. ACM-SIGMOD*, Santa Monica, Calif., May 14-16, 1980, pp. 94-104.

[CHE76] Chen, P.P.S., "The Entity Relationship Model: Towards a Unified View of Data", *ACM Trans. on Database Systems*, No. 1, March, 1976.

[COP84] Copeland, G. and Maier, D., "Making Smalltalk a Database System", *Proc. ACM SIGMOD*, Boston, Mass., June, 1984.

[COP85] Copeland, G. P. and Khoshafian, S. N., "A Decomposition Storage Model," *Proc. ACM-SIGMOD*, Austin TX, May 28-31, 1985, pp.268-279.

[DEW84] DeWitt, D. J., Katz, R. H., Olken, F., Shapiro, L. D., Stonebraker, M. R., and Wood, D., "Implementation Techniques for Main Memory Database Systems," *Proc. ACM-SIGMOD*, 1984, pp. 1-8.

[GEM86] Servio Logic Development Corp., *Gemstone System: Programming in OPAL*, Beaverton, OR., 1986.

[HAM81] Hammer, M. and McLeod, D., "Database Description with SDM: A Semantic Database Model," *ACM TODS*, September 1981, pp. 351-386.

[HSI83] Hsiao, D. K., et al.,"The Implementation of a Multi-Backend Database System (MDBS): Part I- Software Engineering Strategies and Efforts Toward a Prototype MDBS," Chapter 10, *Advanced Database Machine Architecture*, D. K. Hsiao (ed.), Prentice-Hall, August, 1983.

[JAR84] Jarke, M., "Common Subexpression Isolation in Multiple Query Optimization," *Query Processing in Database Systems*, Eds. Kim, W., Reiner, D., and Batory, D., Springer Verlag, 1984.

[KHO88] Khoshafian, S., Valduriez, P., and Copeland, G., "Parallel Query Processing for Complex Objects," *Int'l Conf. Data Engineering*, L.A. Calif., Feb. 1-5, 1988, pp. 202-209.

[KIM84] Kim, W., Gajski, D., and Kuck, D., "A Parallel Pipelined Relational Query Processor," *ACM TODS*, June 1984.

[KIT84] Kitsuregawa, M., Tanaka, H., and Moto-oka, T., "Architecture and Performance of Relational Algebra Machine GRACE," *Proc. of the International Conference on Parallel Processing*, 1984.

[LAM87] Lam, H., Su, S.Y.W., Seeger, C., Lee, C., Eisenstadt, W.R., "A Special Function Unit for Database Operations within a Data-Control Flow System", *Proceedings of the 16th. International Conf. on Parallel Processing*, August 17-21, 1987, St. Charles, Illinois.

[LAM89] Lam, H., Lee, C., and Su, S.Y.W., "A Special Function Unit for Database Operations (SFU-DB): Design and Performance Evaluation", submitted to *IEEE Transactions on Computers*.

[LEE87] Lee, C., Su, S. Y. W., and Lam, H., "Algorithms for Sorting and Sort-based Database Operations Using a Special Function Unit," *5TH Int'l Workshop Database Machines*, Japan, Oct. 5-8, 1987, pp. 158-171.

[LEE88] Lee, C., "Evaluation of Query Processing in the Object Flow Computer", Technical Report, Database Systems Research and Development Center, University of Florida, October 1988.

[MAI86] Maier, D., et. al., "Development of an Object-Oriented DBMS", *Proc. of OOPSLA '86 Conference*, Sept. 29 - Oct. 2, Portland, Oregon, pp. 472-482.

[MIK88a] Mikkilineni, K.P. and Su, S.Y.W.,"An Evaluation of Relational Join Algorithms in a Pipelined Query Processing Environment," *IEEE Trans. on Software Engineering*, Vol. 14, No. 6, June 1988, pp. 838-848.

[MIK88b] Mikkilineni, K.P., Chow, Y.C. and Su, S.Y.W.,"Petri-Net Based Modelling and Evaluation of Pipelined Processing of Concurrent Database Queries", to appear in *IEEE Trans. on Software Engineering*.

[MYL78] Mylopoulos, J., Bernstein, P.A., Wong, H.K.T., "A Language Facility for Designing Interactive Database Intensive Applications", *Proc. ACM-SIGMOD*, Austin, Texas, May, 1978, pp. 144-156.

[ONT87] Ontologic, Inc., *Vbase Integrated Object System: Technical Overview*, Billerica, MA., 1987.

[SEL85] Sellis, T., and Shapiro, L., "Optimization of Extended Database Query Languages," *Proc. ACM SIGMOD*, May 1985.

[SMI77] Smith, J. and Smith, D., "Data Abstractions: Aggregation and Generalization," *Communications of ACM*, 20(6), June 1977, pp. 405-413.

[SU86] Su, S.Y.W., Mikkilineni, K.P., Liuzzi, R., and Chow, R., "A Distributed Query Processing Strategy Based on Decomposition, Pipelining, Intermediate Result Sharing Techniques,", *Proc. COMDEC*, 1986.

[SU88a] Su, S.Y.W., *Database Computers: Principles, Architectures, and Techniques*, McGraw-Hill Book Co., N.Y., 1988.

[SU88b] Su, S.Y.W., Krishnamurthy, V., and Lam, H., "An Object-oriented Semantic Association Model (OSAM*)", to appear in *A.I. in Industrial Engineering and Manufacturing: Theoretical Issues and Applications*, A. Kumara et. al. (eds.), American Institute of Industrial Engr., 1988.

[TAN80] Tanaka, Y., Noxaka, Y., Masuyama, A., "Pipeline Searching and Sorting Modules as Components of a Data Flow Database Computer," *Information Processing 80*, North-Holland Publishing Co., 1980, pp. 427-432.

[WON76] Wong, E., and Youssefi, K., "Decomposition - A Strategy for Query Processing," *ACM TODS*, September 1976.

[ZDO86] Zdonik, S.B. and Wegner, P., "Language and Methodology of Object-Oriented Database Environments", *Proc. of the 19th. Annual Hawaii International Conference on System Sciences*, Jan., 1986.

Table 1. Parameters and their values used in the evaluation.

System Parameters:

word - Word size 4 bytes.
main - Main memory size is 1 Mbytes.
page - Page size is 4 Kbytes.
macc - Time to access one word is 200 ns.
comp - Time to compare two 4-byte values is 800 ns.
hash - Time to hash a 4-byte value is 500 ns.
comm - Communication bandwidth is 10 Mbytes/sec.
disk_IO_ran - Operation time for a random disk IO is 20 ms.
disk_IO_seq - Operation time for a sequential disk IO is 5 ms.

Workload Parameters:

OID_size - Size of an object ID is 4 bytes.
attr_size - Size of an attribute is 20 bytes.
rel_size - Size of a relation is 100,000 tuples.
attr_per_tuple - The number of attributes of a tuple is determined by the query in the example.
sel_fac - Selectivity factor is 0.1.
jn_fac - Join (including special joins) factor is 0.0001.
F - Fudge factor is 1.2.

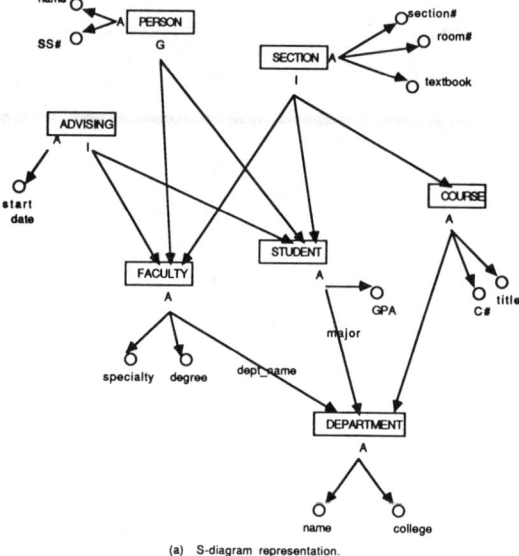

(a) S-diagram representation.

Figure 1. University database modeled in OSAM*.

Note: The condition $\sqrt{|R|*F} \leq |M|$ (see [DEW84]) must be satisfied for hybrid-hash join, where $|R|$ is the size of the relation R to be hashed and $|M|$ is the size of main memory. F is a fudge factor which accounts for the different types of increments, say, in hashing and sorting. For example, a hash table containing R will require a main memory size of at least $|R|*F$.

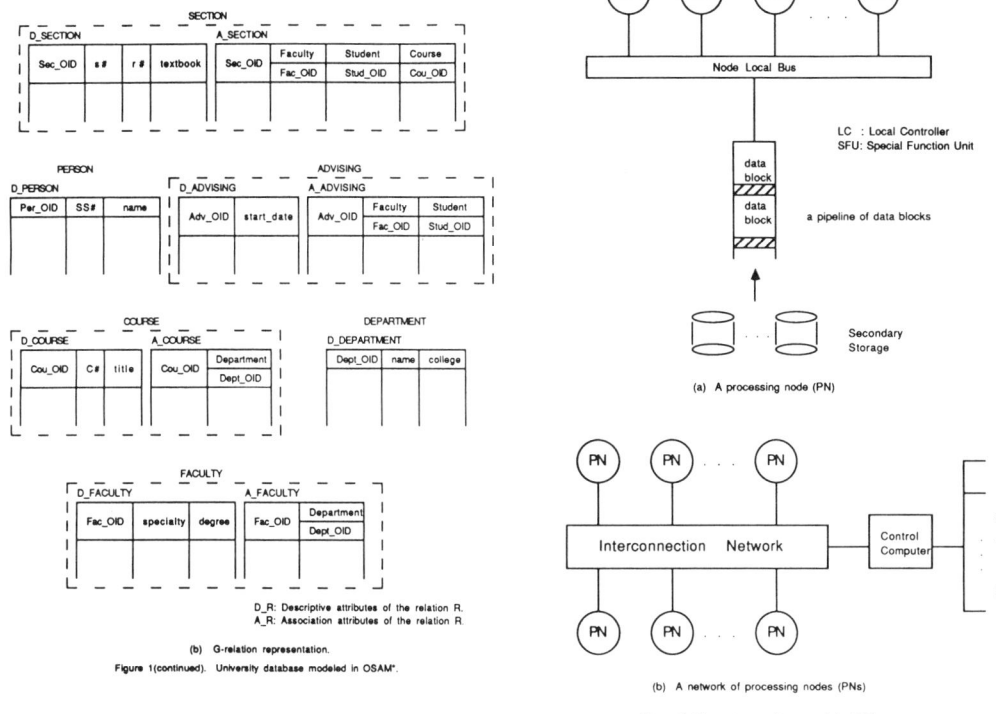

D_R: Descriptive attributes of the relation R.
A_R: Association attributes of the relation R.

(b) G-relation representation.

Figure 1(continued). University database modeled in OSAM*.

(a) A processing node (PN)

(b) A network of processing nodes (PNs)

Figure 2 The system architecture of the OFC

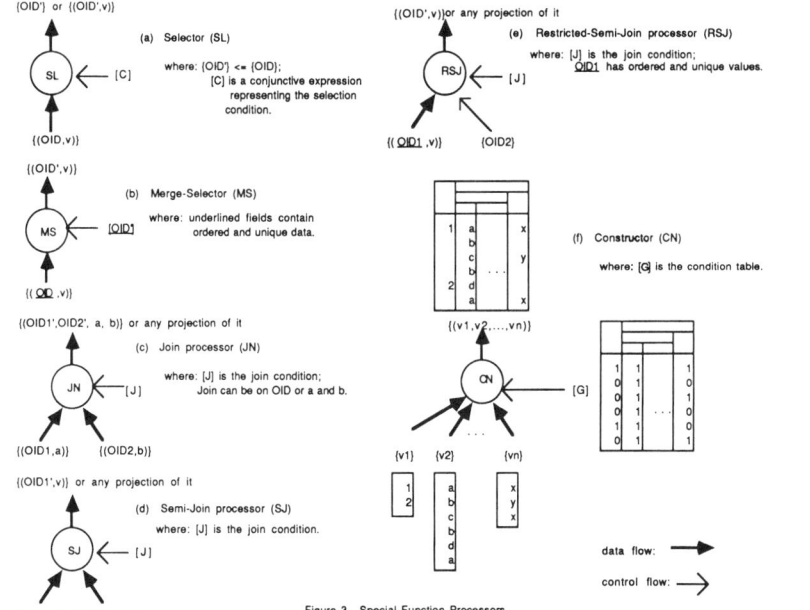

Figure 3. Special Function Processors.

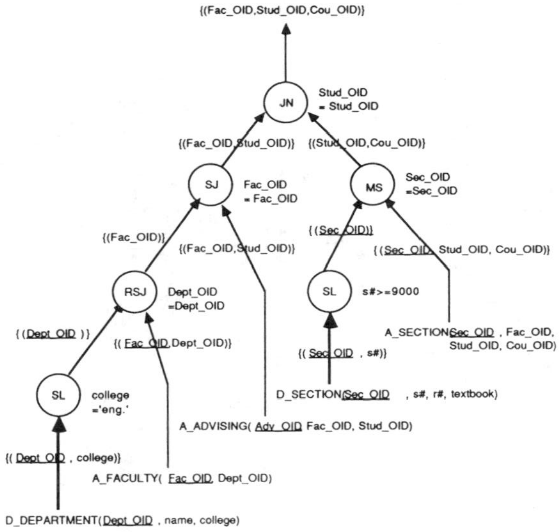

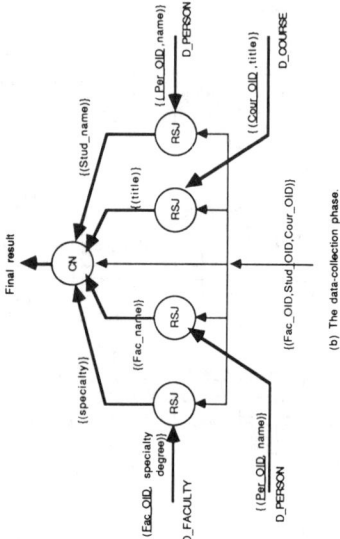

(a) The identification phase.

Figure 6. The object flow tree of the example query.

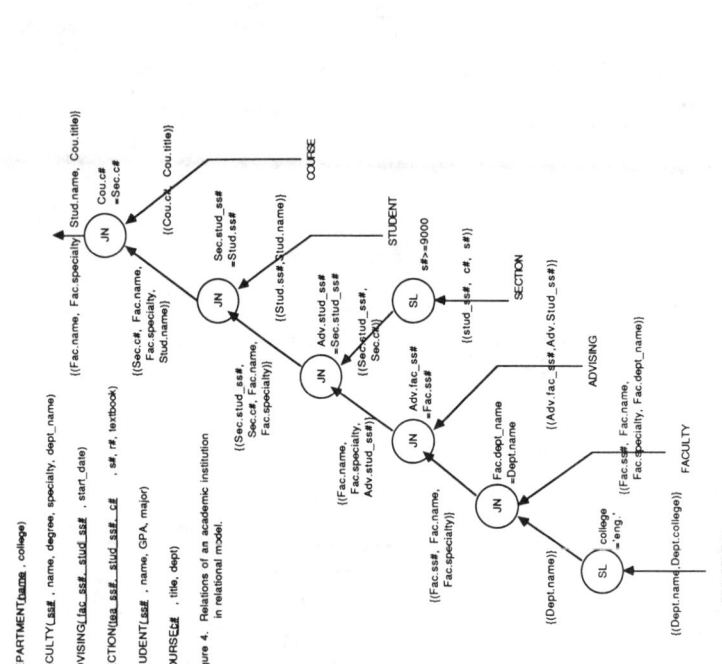

(b) The data-collection phase.

Figure 6(continued) The object flow tree of the example query.

DEPARTMENT(name, college)
FACULTY(ss#, name, degree, specialty, dept_name)
ADVISING(fac_ss#, stud_ss#, start_date)
SECTION(sec_ss#, stud_ss#, c#, s#, r#, textbook)
STUDENT(ss#, name, GPA, major)
COURSE(c#, title, dept)

Figure 4. Relations of an academic institution in relational model.

Figure 5. A conventional query tree - all necessary attributes are carried along during execution.

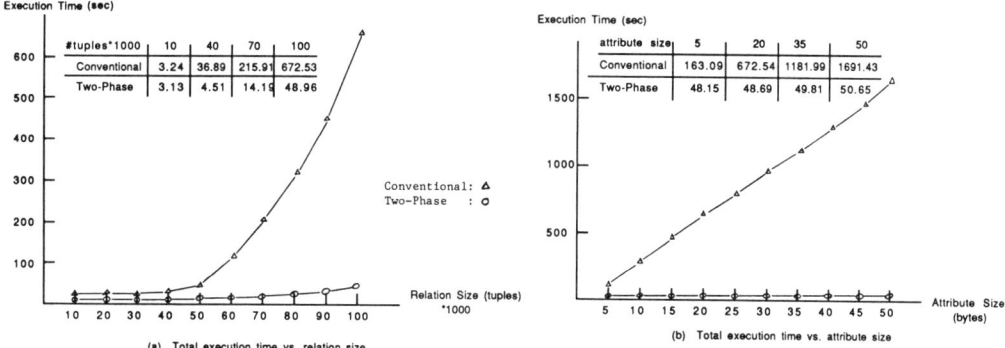

Figure 7 Performance comparisons of two processing strategies.

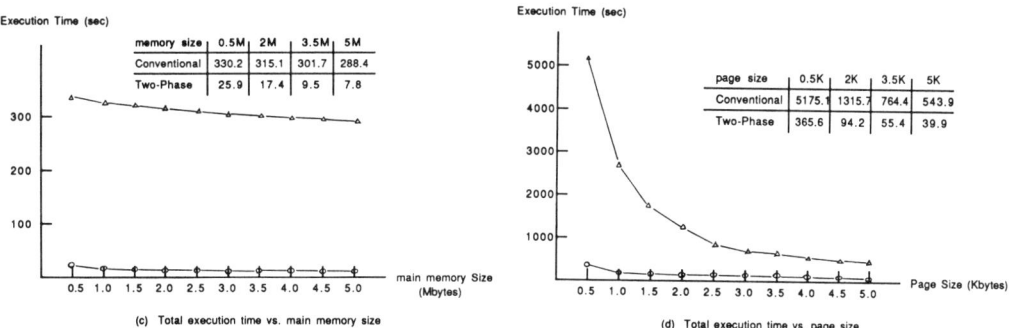

Figure 7(continued) Performance comparisons of two processing strategies.

Design and Implementation of KARDAMOM — A Set-oriented Data Flow Database Machine

Günter von Bültzingsloewen, Cirano Iochpe, Rolf-Peter Liedtke,
Ralf Kramer, Michael Schryro, Klaus R. Dittrich, Peter C. Lockemann

Forschungszentrum Informatik an der Universität Karlsruhe
Haid-und-Neu-Straße 10–14, D–7500 Karlsruhe 1
email: liedtke@ira.uka.de

Abstract: *Recently, several proposals for multiprocessor database machines have emerged. Most approaches focus upon the solution of the I/O-bottleneck or upon parallel algorithms for relational operations. Other crucial issues in such systems include communication between the software modules of the database management system which are distributed across the processors and efficient control of parallel query execution. In this paper, we argue that strictly set-oriented query execution and data flow control are appropriate mechanisms in order to minimize overheads for communication and control of execution. Then we give an overview of the design of the multiprocessor database machine KARDAMOM which integrates both concepts. An important feature is a two-level system architecture, where the upper level consists of those parts of the system which operate exclusively on tuple sets instead of pages. A dedicated storage manager is proposed which provides a uniform interface for the representation of tuple sets as well as for the exchange of tuple sets between different system components. Other important issues are related to query translation and optimization and to transaction management in a set-oriented environment.*

1 Introduction

An important part of recent research in database machines has been devoted to multiprocessor systems consisting of general purpose processors (instead of dedicated hardware). Much attention has been given to the problem of releaving the I/O-bottleneck [DeWi86, KhVa88]. There has been much work on parallel algorithms for relational operations, too, especially for the join operation [DeGe85, KTMo83]. However, other crucial issues in multiprocessor database machines have been widely neglected, most notably those related to communication between the software modules of the database management system which are distributed across the processors, and to the efficient control of parallel query execution.

Within the KARDAMOM project at FZI Karlsruhe, we are currently developing a multiprocessor database machine which attacks both issues. Strictly set-oriented query execution provides for reduced communication overhead and improved main memory utilization. Data flow control is used as an appropriate method for achieving a high degree of parallelism with minimal control overhead.

This paper gives an overview of the overall system design of the KARDAMOM database machine. It is designed as a multiprocessor database backend with a relational interface (SQL) which acts as a server to a host system running the application programs. The basic idea behind the software design is to decompose the database management system into a number of *functional components*, each implementing specific suboperations of transaction processing (relational algebra operations, software filtering, update, concurrrency control and recovery). The components are realized as processes that are mapped onto the processors of the multiprocessor system. The assignment of components to processors is handled in a very flexible way. It is possible to have only one single instance of some component mapped to some processor as well as to have several instances of other components which are replicated on several processors. Copies of the same component are able to process different operations (e.g. several centralized join operations originating from different database operations) or they can cooperate in processing a single operation (e.g. a distributed join operation originating from a single database operation). Thus we are able to obtain intra-transaction parallelism for reduced transaction response times as well as inter-transaction parallelism for increased throughput. Furthermore, the components can be replicated and distributed across the processors as demanded by the performance requirements of a special application.

The remainder of the paper is organized as follows. In section 2 we discuss the concepts of data flow and set-oriented query execution which are fundamental to our system design. In section 3 we give an overview of the system architecture and the functions of its main components. Section 4 deals with the important issues of query translation and generation of data flow programs. Section 5 explains in more detail how the different components interact when executing retrieval and update queries. Finally, section 6 concludes with an outlook on further research topics which have not been covered so far.

2 Basic Concepts

The design of the KARDAMOM database machine is based on two fundamental concepts. First, we use data flow control as the control mechanism for query execution. Second, query execution proceeds strictly set-oriented, i.e. operands and results consumed and produced by the functional components during query execution are represented as sets of tuples wherever applicable.

2.1 Data Flow Control

One of the most important goals in the design of a system with parallel execution capabilities is to exploit parallelism as much as possible with a minimum of control overhead. Data flow control is a mechanism which promises to achieve this goal and has already been proposed for database machines [Chan76, BoDe82, DeWi86, AlCo88]. As it is closely combined with set-oriented query execution in our approach, we discuss this method in some more detail.

When a query is decomposed into a set of operations, the degree of parallelism among them is only limited by data dependencies between them, as long as the availability of sufficient system resources is not considered. Data flow programs are a convenient means to capture such dependencies. Essentially, a data flow program is a directed acyclic graph, where the nodes represent operations and the arcs represent the flow of data between operations. Thus a precedence relation on the set of operations is defined by relating operations producing some output with those needing the output as input. Operations with no precedence relationship between them can potentially be executed in parallel. Hence, a data flow program expresses the potential parallelism within the set of operations into which a given query is decomposed.

When executing a data flow program it is not necessary to schedule all operations in advance and supervise the sequence of their execution. Instead, for each operation only the availability of its inputs and of a functional component for its execution have to be checked. Additionally, the system state at runtime can be taken into account (e.g. load distribution, processor utilization, priority of concurrent operations), in order to select an operation to be started. Thus, the degree of parallelism effectively achieved at runtime depends on the system load and the effective execution duration of the different operations of a data flow program.

Parallelism within a query can be increased in two ways [Chan76]. Certain operations may be split into sub-operations which operate on disjoint data partitions and thus can be executed independently and in parallel (node splitting; e.g. parallel join of hash buckets within a hashing join). The second method is to execute successive operations in a pipelined fashion. This is possible if the data dependence between them is not strict, i.e. if the second operation does not have to wait until it has received all data it needs but can already start execution when only the first portion of operand data has arrived (e.g. the partitioning phase of a hashing join can start when the first tuples qualified by a preceding selection are available).

2.2 Strictly Set-oriented Query Processing

Communication tends to be a major bottleneck in any distributed system. In a multiprocessor database backend three types of interfaces can be identified where transmission of data is necessary:

- As the database resides on disk storage data to be accessed have to be read from or written to disks via the I/O-interface.

- Data which are the output of some functional component and the input of some other component must be exchanged between them (along the arcs of data flow programs) and, if necessary, between the different processors the components are allocated to.

- Queries and their results must be transmitted between the host running the application and the database backend across the host/backend interface.

Assuming a given communication mechanism, two measures can be taken in order to reduce the communication overhead. First, the amount of data which are transmitted should be as small as possible. No needless or redundant information should be transmitted. Second, the number of messages for transmitting a given amount of data should be as small as reasonable in order to reduce the overhead of message processing.

Results of SQL queries usually consist of result relations constructed by relational algebra operations. Thus, it is guaranteed that no unnecessary information is transmitted at the host/backend interface. On the other hand, in order to minimize the number of messages, each message should contain a set of as many tuples as possible instead of only a single tuple. Conversely, tuples to be inserted should also be collected into sets and sent to the backend as a single message. Therefore, it is important to note that we extend the set-orientation which is already inherent to SQL queries to insertions.

Within the database backend itself, functional components execute mostly relational algebra operations. Intermediate results which are passed to other components according to the arcs of a data flow program will therefore typically be organized as relations. Messages should contain only the information belonging to these relations, i.e. only those tuples they consist of. As has been argued for the host/backend interface, tuples belonging to an intermediate result should be collected and transmitted to the receiver in bulk form. However, we make a restriction with respect to pipelining. In certain cases it is possible that an operation can already be started while the preceding operation producing its operands is still being executed. Then more parallelism can be achieved if the intermediate result is transmitted as a sequence of several messages each containing a subset of the result, instead of being transmitted as a whole. However, the trade-off between the gain of more parallelism on one side and the cost of increased communication overhead on the other needs to be explored in more detail.

In order to eliminate unnecessary information as early as possible, and as all communication within the database machine is based on tuple sets anyway, these should be generated as early as possible. Leaf nodes of data flow programs will usually include accesses to base relations, i.e. they will require I/O-operations. In order to construct tuple sets as results of accesses to base relations, we employ data filtering which is a well-known technique for database machines: relations are scanned sequentially and tuples are selected on the fly combined with projections, if required [BaSc80, FKTa86, Kies84, OzPe87]. The result is a set of tuples which qualify with respect to the selection predicate. This tuple set represents the desired type of data object for further manipulation and communication. We are going to explain this technique further in section 3.2.

In summary, we are able to keep the communication overhead low, if we use tuple sets as units of communication when intermediate or final results have to be transmitted. As a consequence, functional components internally operate on tuple sets as well. Hence, another advantage of this concept is an improved utilization of main memory, as only those data which are actually needed for further processing have to be stored.

3 Overview of The Architecture

Obviously, the KARDAMOM software architecture (see figure 1) is devised such that it reflects the set-oriented query execution method discussed in section 2.2. Functional components can be classified into components realizing the mapping between base relations for persistent storage and tuple sets for internal query processing and components working on tuple sets only. We refer to base relations defined in the schema as *physical objects* and to tuple sets as *logical objects*. Accordingly, the first group of components is called *physical layer* ($DBMS_{phys}$), the latter *logical layer* ($DBMS_{log}$). Each functional component is realized as a process. Additionally, we introduce a set-oriented memory manager providing functions for accessing and manipulating tuple sets representing operands and

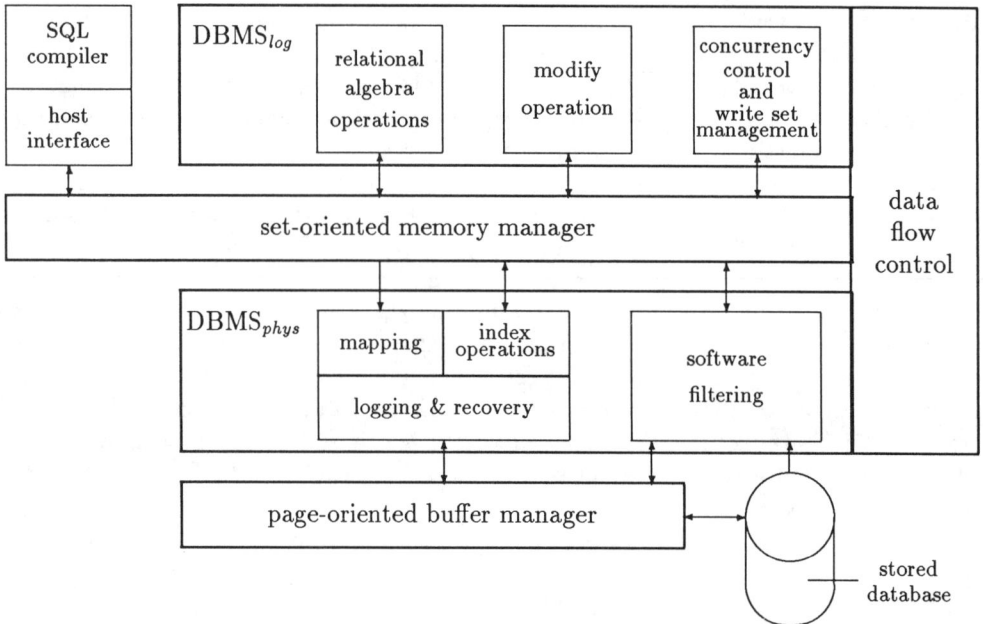

Figure 1: Software architecture of the KARDAMOM database machine

results of operations within data flow programs.

3.1 Hardware Architecture

The hardware of the database backend consists of a multiprocessor system which can be either of the "shared nothing" or the "shared memory" type [Ston85]. Processors are connected by a shared bus and have local disks attached to them. There may also be processors without disks. In case of a shared nothing system, processors have only local memories. However, it is possible to provide a global shared memory in addition to the local memory of each processor. In this case we have a shared memory architecture, which may offer performance advantages if message-oriented communication is replaced by communication via shared memory [BhSt88].

3.2 Physical Layer

The physical layer consists of those functional components which create logical objects from base relations and update base relations. As base relations are primarily held on secondary memory, $DBMS_{phys}$ has to manage and access secondary storage. As has been mentioned above, read access, i.e. the creation of logical objects, is accomplished by filtering. Instead of using dedicated filter processors which has proven to be impractical [BoDe83, GaSc85], we employ software filtering on the basis of general purpose processors. Using double buffering, I/O-operations overlap with the selection of qualified tuples (on-the-fly-filtering). Thus I/O waiting time is utilized for the execution of simple relational operations (selection, projection without elimination of duplicates). In order to keep up with I/O-transfer, the complexity of selection predicates must be limited. On the other hand, to minimize I/O-delays, relations should be stored contiguously on disk.

However, filtering may be time-consuming even if all pages of the relation are stored contiguously. Therefore, we provide some techniques to accelerate filtering. First, for highly selective queries filtering can be combined with indexing (in analogy to [Kies83]). Second, besides the parallelism which is inherent to the filter technique, more parallelism is introduced by distributing the database across several disks. Then disjoint partitions of the same relation can be searched in parallel, similar to Bubba [CABK88] or Gamma [DeWi86].

Write access to the stored database is performed only during or after commit of a transaction. It integrates *write sets*, i.e. logical objects containing tuples to be inserted, modified or deleted into the corresponding base relations by mapping them to pages. For this purpose, $DBMS_{phys}$ determines the pages where the appropriate tuples are located or have to be placed, respectively. These pages are loaded into the page-oriented buffer. Then the tuple sets reflecting the updates are mapped to the pages. This includes writing the new or updated tuples into the pages and modifying free-space lists, page mapping tables and possibly index data. Writing updated pages to disk is performed completely independently from the transaction causing the update. Hence, $DBMS_{phys}$ is an autonomous component and thus is able to implement optimizing strategies supporting efficient access of base relations. Nevertheless, typical transaction properties like persistence and atomicity have to be guaranteed. This is discussed in more detail in sections 5.4 and 5.5.

3.3 Logical Layer

$DBMS_{log}$ contains all functional components operating on tuple sets only. These are first the usual relational algebra operations like join, union etc., including also operations for the realization of node splitting, for example the partitioning necessary for parallel join algorithms [DeGe85].

Second, the logical layer contains operations which prepare updates. In order to make the logging mechanism simple and efficient all updates of a transaction are kept in a workspace local to it. According to the set-oriented query execution method updates are represented as tuple sets as well (so-called *write sets*). There are up to three write sets per base relation and transaction: an *insert set*, a *modify set* and a *delete set*, containing the tuples to be inserted, modified and deleted, respectively. For example, all insertions a transaction wants to perform on a base relation are collected in exactly one insert set. At commit write sets are forwarded to the mapping component of $DBMS_{phys}$.

As a transaction has to see its own changes, write sets have to be taken into consideration when a base relation is filtered. The result set of a filter operation must be checked against the corresponding write sets. Insert and modify sets are filtered, too, and the result is added to the first filter result. When a tuple selected from the base relation is also contained in the modify or delete set (in a different version), the version read from the base relation is discarded.

Finally, the logical layer realizes concurrency control on the logical level. The details of concurrency control are discussed in section 5.4.

3.4 Set-oriented Memory Manager

The set-oriented memory manager provides the workspace for the individual functional components. All data retrieved from base relations as well as those to be inserted are retained until they are transmitted to the host system or mapped to base relations. It provides a uniform functionality to manage and access tuple sets.

Furthermore, it is the task of the set-oriented memory manager to perform all transfers of tuple sets between functional components. This mechanism is somewhat different from the stream-oriented execution strategy used in Gamma [DeWi86]. Gamma is based on a pure shared nothing architecture with message based communication between the operator processes executing the nodes of a dataflow program. The set-oriented memory manager of KARDAMOM, however, creates the view of a single global memory which can be accessed by all functional components in a uniform way independent of the underlying hardware architecture. Thus we achieve a logically shared memory architecture which can be realised on top of a physically shared memory architecture as well as a physically shared nothing architecture (or a combination of both)(cf. section 3.1).

The advantage is that we are able to avoid copying of possibly large amounts of data whenever (physically) shared memory is available for transfer of intermediate results between functional components. This is the case if functional components are allocated to the same processor or to processors which share a common address space. Otherwise, the data must be transferred by messages. The set-oriented memory manager autonomously decides about the need of transferring tuple sets between address spaces and executes the transfers if necessary. As tuple sets are referenced by logical names, the communication mechanism chosen can remain completely transparent for the individual functional components.

Another advantage is that functional components need not be synchronized when they exchange intermediate results as it seems to be the case in Gamma. A result is created by some functional component within the set-oriented memory, and a component operating on the result subsequently can access it whenever it is appropriate, independent of which operation the creating component is executing at that time or whether that component still exists. However, this does not preclude pipelining since it is possible to break a single result into a number of packets of several tuples and to transfer them between the components separately. Thus communication by tuple streams is possible as well if desired.

More details on the set-oriented memory management can be found in [BLDi87].

3.5 Host Interface

The host interface provides the connection to the host system where application programs run which issue calls to the database system. The physical interconnection may be accomplished by a local area network or even by a shared bus. Transactions consisting of a sequence of queries (i.e. of SQL-statements) are precompiled to data flow programs (see section 4) which are stored in a module library in the database backend. Calls of queries are transmitted to the backend and initiate execution of the respective data flow programs. Results are transmitted back to the host after completion of the operation.

4 Query Translation and Optimization

4.1 Objective of Optimization

The general objective of query optimization is to find an efficient plan for the execution of a given query in a given system environment. Specific goals may be to minimize total processing cost or to minimize execution time. In centralized database systems, these objectives are largely equivalent, and optimizers attempt to minimize total processing cost. In a multiprocessor database machine, these objectives do not coincide as a higher degree of parallelism usually implies reduced execution times and increased total processing cost because of increased communication and control overhead.

The overall goal of our system design is to obtain increased throughput as well as reduced response times in a multiuser environment. Throughput is reduced if we increase the parallelism inside single queries because of increased processing overhead; average response time is usually reduced because of reduced execution time. However, in case of high resource utilization (high throughput) it may actually be increased as higher total processing cost may cause longer waiting times until a query can be executed. Hence, the optimization problem involves a tradeoff between execution time and total processing cost. Which combination leads to the desired throughput and response times depends on the load conditions and can only be determined at run time. Therefore, the optimizer should construct several alternative plans under the following objectives:

(1) Minimize total processing cost.

(2) Minimize execution time subject to a maximum x%-increase of total processing cost (for several values of x); or equivalently,

(2') Maximize the degree of parallelism (defined as the average number of processors used during the execution of the query) subject to a maximum x%-increase of total processing cost.

To choose an appropriate plan at runtime, we have to know more about the effects of increased total processing cost and reduced execution time on response time and throughput. In order to obtain this knowledge, simulation experiments or performance measurements should be performed, which examine query execution under several load conditions using the query execution plans determined by the optimizer.

4.2 Query Execution Plans

A query execution plan contains information about the operations to be executed, the order of operations and the assignment of operations to processors. It is essentially represented by a data flow program which does not contain executable code; instead, an operation is described by its type and several parameters (e.g. join attributes, filter predicate) which are interpreted at runtime by the functional component executing the operation.

The set of elementary operations includes operations of a relational algebra which is extended to cover the complete expressiveness of SQL [Bült87, Daya87], update operations

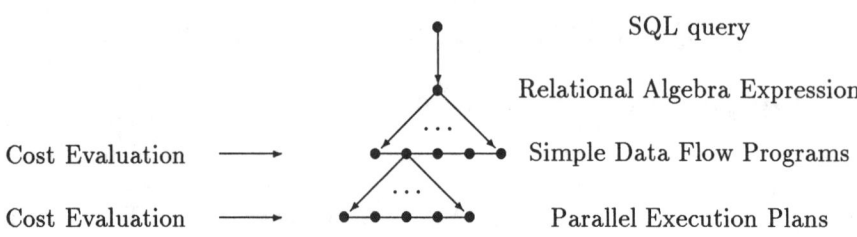

Figure 2: Generation of query execution plans

and operations for transaction management, especially concurrency control. A data flow program is thus a generalization of the operator tree of a relational algebra query. Parallel algorithms for the execution of relational algebra operations are described by several nodes of a data flow program. For example, a parallel hashing join consists of partitioning nodes, join nodes and a union node to combine the partial results.

In order to build a parallel execution plan, a data flow program is augmented by scheduling information: the processor where a node should be executed, and a priority list which defines an execution order among the nodes which are executable on a certain processor at a given time. The assignment to a processor has to be fixed only for nodes that access or manipulate (certain partitions of) base relations, as they reside on a disk attached to a certain processor. All other nodes can be collected into groups which are mapped to processors at runtime, at most one group to one processor.

4.3 Generation of Query Execution Plans

The generation of an optimal query execution plan is a complex (NP-hard) optimization problem. We use a *split-and-prune* search strategy [Pear 84] to solve this problem. It is similar to a decision tree, where with each decision a subset of potential solutions which are derivable from a certain partial solution is split into smaller subsets (or equivalently, a partial solution is extended in different ways). The decisions can be described formally using functional rules as in [LeFL88].

A query execution plan is constructed in three main steps, the last two steps performing the search according to the split-and-prune strategy (see figure 2):

(1) The SQL query is translated into an expression of an extended relational algebra. The expression is in a special normal form which defines an order of algebraic operations only as far as absolutely necessary, so that an optimal expression can be reached from this starting point. The translation has been developed starting from [Bült87], however avoiding unnecessarily complicated expressions. The expression is simplified using transformations which are known to produce better expressions (e.g. elimination of unnecessary joins).

(2) Starting from this normal from, algebraic expressions and methods for the execution of algebraic operations are generated using functional rules similar to [LeFL88]. Thus we generate simple data flow programs (single processor execution plans) which

contain no parallel algorithms for algebraic operations and no scheduling information. Among others, decisions have to be made regarding the ordering of join operations, the positioning of selections and aggregations, and the selection of methods for the execution of algebraic operations.

(3) Single processor execution plans are transformed into parallel execution plans by making two basic decisions: adding potential parallelism by node splitting or pipelining, and realising parallelism by associating processors and priorities with operations, thereby defining a schedule as in deterministic scheduling theory [Coff76]. The search can be limited, as we only have to add potential parallelism repeatedly to nodes on the critical path. Furthermore, a schedule can be constructed using a heuristic which has been proven to be useful in deterministic scheduling theory: critical path scheduling.

We expect that both degree of parallelism and processing cost will increase while we add potential parallelism in step (3). Hence we can finally choose an optimal processing plan for each increase in total cost we are interested in. Note that it is not sufficient to construct parallel execution plans only for the best simple data flow program as the parallelization overhead may differ.

5 Query Execution

5.1 Data Flow Control

Three kinds of processes are involved in data driven query execution: a load balancing component, operation schedulers (OS) and functional components (FC). To execute an SQL statement, these processes exchange messages as shown in figure 3.

The load balancing component receives a set of parallel execution plans for an SQL statement, selects one according to the load condition, and distributes the nodes of the underlying data flow program by sending them to operation schedulers (one on each processor) that implement data flow control. Besides the operation itself, a node contains information about successor nodes (which result is to be used as which operand of which node controlled by which operation scheduler), the firing rule (see below) and the priority (determined by the optimizer). The distribution is determined by associating a distinct processor with each group of nodes of the query execution plan.

The task of the operation schedulers is to realize the firing rule for the nodes they have received. It is usually fulfilled as soon as all operands needed for the execution of the operation are available. If the firing rule for an operation is fulfilled and a functional component implementing the operation is available, it can be sent to this component for execution. In case the firing rule is fulfilled for several operations of one or more data flow programs, the scheduler has to select one using the priorities.

In some cases, the operation scheduler can decide that an operation does not have to be executed; for example, if one of the operands of a join operation is the empty set, the result is the empty set, too; if a lock request has not been granted, the succeeding read access (like all other succeeding nodes) must not be executed. If such a condition is fulfilled, the results of the operation are directly computed by the operation scheduler.

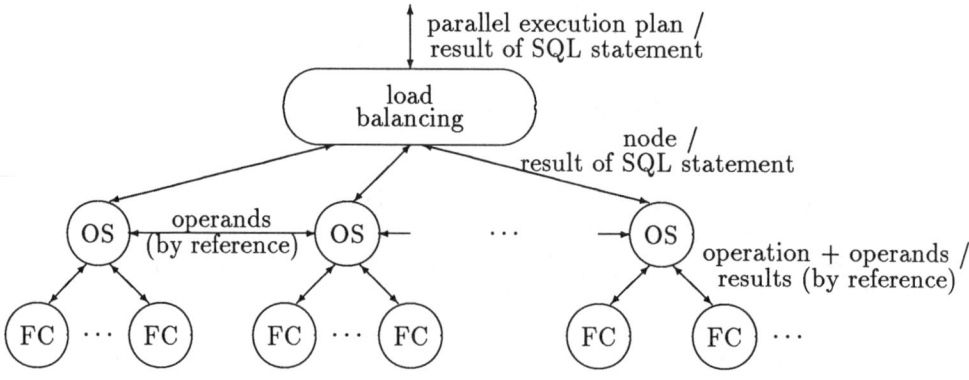

Figure 3: Data flow control

After an operation has been executed, the operation schedulers supervising succeeding nodes are informed that the corresponding operands are available. For the purpose of data flow control, operands are transmitted "by reference": the messages exchanged between functional components and operation schedulers contain logical names that can be interpreted by the set-oriented memory manager. The operands themselves are kept in the set-oriented memory and are requested by the functional components when needed.

5.2 Update Statements

Insertion, modification and deletion are prepared in the logical layer by manipulating the corresponding write sets which are not integrated into base relations before commit. The data flow programs shown in figure 4 illustrate the processing of updates. Every box represents an operation which is executed by one of the functional components; only the operations Filter and Commit belong to $DBMS_{phys}$ while all other operations belong to $DBMS_{log}$. Put operations PutInsert, PutModify and PutDelete are provided to integrate the logical objects (tuple sets) to be inserted, modified or deleted into the write sets of a transaction T for a relation R. For example, PutInsert adds a set of tuples submitted by the user to the insert set.

To perform a modification, the set of tuples to be modified is first selected by a Filter operation of $DBMS_{phys}$. The Modify operation modifies the tuples of this set according to the SQL update statement. Finally, PutModify integrates the modified tuples into the write sets: modified tuples which are contained in the insert or modify set are replaced by the new tuple versions; all other modified tuples are added to the modify set. Similarly, to perform a deletion, the set of tuples to be deleted is first selected by a Filter operation, whereupon PutDelete adds the tuples of this set to the delete set (if they are not contained in the insert set) and removes them from the modify and insert set (if necessary).

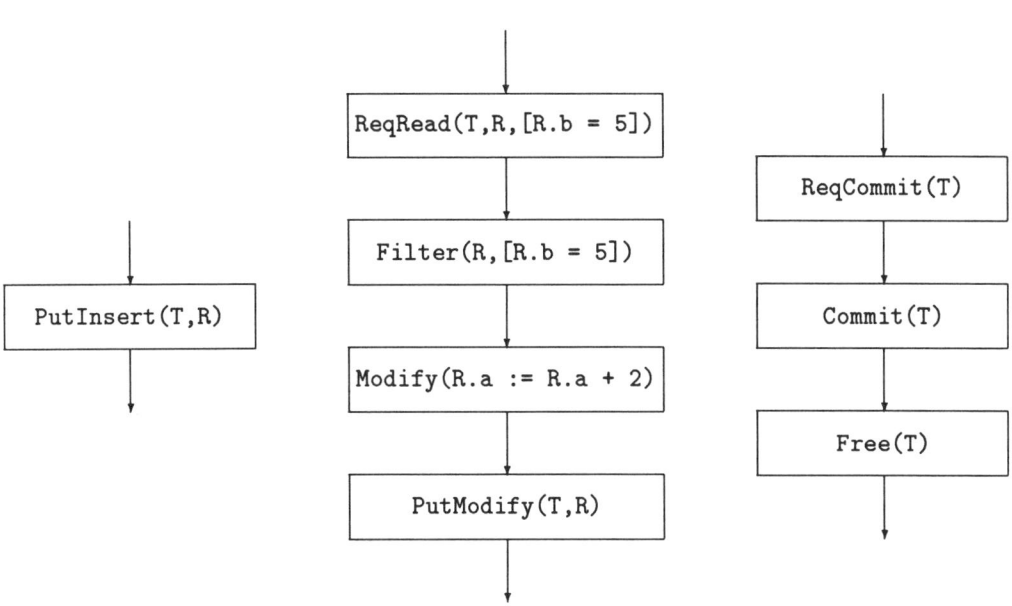

Figure 4: Data flow programs for insertion, modification and commit

5.3 Select Statements

As a transaction has to see its own changes, write sets have to be taken into consideration during read access of a base relation. Therefore the operation ReqRead determines the write sets corresponding to the read access. The Filter operation selects tuples not only from the base relation, but also from the corresponding insert and modify set. When a tuple selected from the base relation is also contained in the modify or delete set (in a different version), the version read from the base relation is discarded.

Complex select statements are compiled into data flow programs which contain, besides the operations ReqRead and Filter, relational algebra operations like union, join and aggregate. For example, to execute a join query, each of the operands of the join is computed as a set object by the operations ReqRead and Filter. The two operands are then combined by a Join operation. The algebraic operations are implemented using hash based algorithms [DeGe85].

We have also implemented a variant of the parallel Grace hash-join [DeGe85]. Here we have ReqRead, Filter, Partition and Hash operations operating in a pipelined fashion on partitions of the first relation to be joined. The Hash operations build hash tables for tuples of the first relation according to join attribute values. A second set of operations works also in a pipelined fashion on partitions of the second relation: ReqRead, Filter, Partition and Join. The Join operations probe the hash tables and build result tuples if matching tuples are found. The implementation of pipeling is based on set-oriented memory management: units of transmission are again set objects.

	T'		
		r	a	x
T	r	+	+: T→T'	–
	a	+: T'→T	o	o
	x	–	o	o

(+: no conflict; T→T': serialization condition;
−: conflict; o: no conflict test)

Figure 5: Compatibility matrix of the modified (r,a,x)-protocol

5.4 Concurrency Control

We use a two-level concurrency control mechanism which is distributed among $DBMS_{log}$ and $DBMS_{phys}$. $DBMS_{phys}$ ensures the atomicity of its operations using a conventional page-oriented concurrency control mechanism. $DBMS_{log}$ guarantees that transactions are serializable with respect to calls of operations of $DBMS_{phys}$ using a modification of precision locks [JBBa81] that is based on the (r,a,x)-protocol [Baye76] (see figure 5).

The basic idea of precision locks is to characterize a read lock by a predicate and a write lock by a write set containing inserted, modified or deleted tuples; this corresponds directly to the read and write operations of $DBMS_{phys}$. If tuples are always read before they are modified or deleted, this kind of concurrency control has to test read–write conflicts only. To do so, read predicates have to be applied to write sets.

r-locks are acquired by `ReqRead` operations, a-locks by `Put` operations. `ReqCommit` operations convert a-locks into x-locks. Direct conflicts result only from incompatibilities between r-locks and x-locks, i.e. if a read access of a current transaction collides with a write access of a transaction that wants to commit. Only these read-write conflicts have to be tested synchronously and may block transactions: the committing transaction has to be blocked until all transactions with a conflicting read-access have been finished; during the same time, transactions with a new conflicting read-access have to be blocked, too.

A collision between an r-lock and an a-lock leads to a serialization condition only, i.e. the reader has to finish before the writer may commit. Conflicting serialization conditions indicate that a deadlock will occur if the participating transactions try to commit. Hence, if a conflicting serialization condition is detected, one of the participating transactions has to be aborted. As explained in [BILD88], we can choose between a pessimistic and a more optimistic concurrency control mechanism, depending on the time when serializability is checked.

5.5 Commit Processing

After concurrency control has acquired x-locks for all write sets a transaction has prepared (`ReqCommit`), these are forwarded to the `Commit` operation of $DBMS_{phys}$. It collects the write sets together with the mapping operators which will be applied to them as well as the transaction identifier into a logical log record, and saves them as redo-information on the logical log file (LLog). The successful execution of this step guarantees that the transaction survives system crashes. Nevertheless it can yet be aborted by the system in case there is no more disk space where to map its write sets.

The write sets of the transaction are then mapped to database pages by the mapping component of $DBMS_{phys}$. If this activity ends successfully, the system information which was updated during the mapping process is written to the physical log file (PLog). Examples of system information include tuple-to-page mapping information, free-space lists, and index data. Depending on the result of the mapping, the commit component either writes a commit record to LLog (OK) or deletes the logical log record of the transaction from LLog ($\neg$OK). Finally all the locks held by the transaction are released (**Free**) and the user is informed about the outcome of the commit.

6 Conclusions

In this paper we have described the design of a multiprocessor database machine which is based upon set-oriented query execution under data flow control. These two concepts allow to reduce the communication and control overhead to a minimum. In order to allow parallel processing, the database management is decomposed into a number of functional components, each implementing specific suboperations of transaction processing. Set-oriented query execution implies a two-level architecture where components of the upper level operate exclusively on tuple sets instead of pages. All tuple sets are managed and accessed by means of the set-oriented manager which provides a uniform interface to all components. The functional components are coordinated by a data flow control mechanism which distributes and schedules the operations of the data flow programs into which SQL statements are compiled.

A one-processor version of the proposed architecture has been implemented within the KARDAMOM project at FZI Karlsruhe. Besides a performance evaluation of this first prototype, our future work will focus on problems arising in a multiprocessor architecture. The issues we want to explore in some detail include the following:

- As the optimization of SQL queries for parallel execution is a very complex search problem, we plan to investigate heuristics to prune the search space effectively.

- Another important topic are the strategies used by the load balancing component to choose an appropriate degree of parallelism (increase in processing cost) for the SQL queries to be executed and to distribute the nodes of the corresponding data flow program.

- Set-oriented memory management poses several further problems. These include communication between functional components which is needed to transmit set objects according to data flow. Another topic is a replacement strategy for the case that set objects cannot be kept in main memory due to space limitations.

- Our approach to transaction management allows to defer updates arbitrarily. Hence the choice of an appropriate point in time — with respect to synchronization of concurrent transactions — to map a set-oriented representation of an update result to the respective database pages is another important topic. It affects throughput as well as transaction response time.

- The database may be distributed across several disks to support parallel disk access. Here the problem arises to find out which distribution strategy is best, i.e. how relations should be partitioned and distributed to achieve a maximum of efficiency.

References

[AlCo88] W. Alexander, G. Copeland: Process and Dataflow Control in Distributed Data-Intensive Systems. Proc. ACM SIGMOD Int. Conf. on Management of Data, Chicago, June 1988

[BaSc80] F. Bancilhon, M. Scholl: Design of a Backend Processor for a Data Base Machine. Proc. ACM SIGMOD Int. Conf. on Management of Data, Los Angeles, May 1980

[Baye76] R. Bayer: Integrity, Concurrency and Recovery in Databases. Lecture Notes in Computer Science 44, Springer, 1976, pp. 79-106

[BhSt88] A. Bhide, M. Stonebraker: A Performance Comparison of Two Architectures for Fast Transaction Processing. Proc. 4th Int. Conf. on Data Engineering, Los Angeles, February 1988

[BILD88] G. v. Bültzingsloewen, C. Iochpe, R.-P. Liedtke, K.R. Dittrich, P.C. Lockemann: Two-Level Transaction Management in a Multiprocessor Database Machine. 3rd Int. Conf. on Data and Knowledge Bases, Jerusalem, 1988, pp. 374-386

[BLDi87] G. v. Bültzingsloewen, R.-P. Liedtke, K. R. Dittrich: Set-Oriented Memory Management In A Multiprocessor Database Machine. Proc. 5th Int. Workshop on Database Machines, Karuizawa, October 1987, pp. 611–625

[BoDe82] H. Boral, D.J. DeWitt: Applying Data Flow Techniques to Database Machines. IEEE Computer, August 1982, pp. 57–63

[BoDe83] H. Boral, D.J. DeWitt: Data Base Machines: An Idea Whose Time Has Passed? In: H.-O. Leilich, M. Missikoff (eds.): Database Machines. Int. Workshop, Munich, September 1983, Springer-Verlag, 1983

[Bült87] G. v. Bültzingsloewen: Translating and Optimizing SQL Queries Having Aggregates. Proc. 13th Int. Conf. on Very Large Data Bases, Brighton, September 1987

[CABK88] G. Copeland, W. Alexander, E. Boughter, Tom Keller: Data Placement In Bubba. Proc. ACM SIGMOD Int. Conf. on Management of Data, Chicago, June 1988, pp. 99–108

[Chan76] P.Y. Chang: Parallel Processing and Data Driven Implementation of a Relational Database System. Proc. of the 1976 Conf. of the ACM, pp. 314-318

[Coff76] E.G. Coffmann (ed.): Computer and Job-Shop Scheduling Theory. John Wiley & Sons, 1976

[Daya87] U. Dayal: Of Nests and Trees: A Unified Approach to Processing Queries That Contain Nested Subqueries, Aggregates, and Quantifiers. Proc. 13th Int. Conf. on Very Large Data Bases, Brighton, September 1987, pp. 197-208

[DeGe85] D.J. DeWitt, R. Gerber: Multiprocessor Hash-Based Join Algorithms. Proc. 11th Int. Conf. on Very Large Data Bases, Stockholm, 1985

[DeWi86] D.J. DeWitt et al.: GAMMA - A High Performance Dataflow Database Machine. Proc. 12th Int. Conf. on Very Large Data Bases, Kyoto, August 1986

[FKTa86] S. Fushimi, M. Kitsuregawa, H. Tanaka: An Overview of The System Software of A Parallel Relational Database Machine GRACE. Proc. 12th Int. Conf. on Very Large Data Bases, Kyoto, August 1986

[GaSc85] S. Gamerman, M. Scholl: Hardware versus Software Filtering: The VERSO Experience. Proc. 4th Int. Workshop on Database Machines, Grand Bahama Island, March 1985

[JaKo83] M. Jarke, J. Koch: Range Nesting: A Fast Method to Evaluate Quantified Queries. Proc. ACM SIGMOD, San Jose, May 1983, pp. 196-206

[JBBa81] J.R. Jordan, J. Banerjee, R.B. Batman: Precision Locks. Proc. ACM SIGMOD Int. Conf. on Management of Data, 1981

[KhVa88] S. Khoshafian, P. Valduriez: Parallel Execution Strategies for Declustered Databases. In: M. Kitsuregawa, H. Tanaka (eds.): Database Machines and Knowledge Base Machines. Proc. 5th Int. Workshop, Karuizawa/Japan, October 1987, Kluwer Academic Publishers, 1988, pp. 458–471

[Kies83] W. Kiessling: Database Systems for Computers with Intelligent Subsystems: Architecture, Algorithms, Optimization. Report TUM-I8307, Technical University of Munich, Institute of Computer Science, August 1983 (in German)

[Kies84] W. Kiessling: Tuneable Dynamic Filter Algorithms for High Performance Database Systems. Proc. Int. Workshop on High Level Language Computer Architecture, 1984, pp. 10–20

[KTMo83] M. Kitsuregawa, H. Tanaka, T. Moto-oka: Application of Hash To Data Base Machine and Its Architecture. New Generation Computing, Vol. 1, No. 1, 1983

[LeFL88] M.K. Lee, J.C. Freytag, G.M. Lohman: Implementing an Interpreter for Functional Rules in a Query Optimizer. IBM Research Report RJ 6125, March 1988

[OzPe87] E.A. Ozkarahan, M.A. Penaloza: On-the-Fly and Background Data Filtering System for Database Architectures. New Generation Computing, Vol. 5, No. 5, 1987, pp. 281–314

[Pear84] J. Pearl: Heuristics: Intelligent Search Strategies for Computer Problem Solving. Addison Wesley, 1984

[Ston85] M. Stonebraker: The Case for Shared Nothing. Proc. Int. Workshop on High Performance Transaction Systems, Pacific Grove, CA, Sept. 1985

[Ullm82] J.D. Ullman: Principles of Database Systems. 2nd Edition, Pitman, 1982

An Experiment on Response Time Scalability in Bubba

Marc Smith, Bill Alexander, Haran Boral, George Copeland,
Tom Keller, Herb Schwetman and Chii-Ren Young

MCC
3500 West Balcones Center Dr.
Austin, Texas 78759

Abstract

We describe results from an experiment that investigates the scalability of response time performance in shared-nothing systems, such as the Bubba parallel database machine. In particular, we show how--and how much--potential response time improvements for certain transaction types can be impaired in shared-nothing architectures by the increased cost of transaction startup, communication, and synchronization as the degree of execution parallelism is increased. We further show how these effects change under increased levels of concurrency and heterogeneity in the transaction workload. From the results, we conclude that although parallelism must be limited in some circumstances, in general the benefits of increased parallelism in shared-nothing systems exceed the costs.

1. Introduction

Parallel systems promise that, for many applications, performance will scale with the size of the system. As processors are added, the system's capacity for total work increases and more parallelism can be applied to each program, resulting in both throughput and response time improvements. When a high degree of scalability is required, as in Bubba [Boral 88], "shared-nothing" message-passing architectures are usually preferred over shared-memory and shared-disk architectures [Stonebraker 86].

However, a problem with shared-nothing systems is the cost of transaction startup, communication, and synchronization. As the number of nodes applied to a program increases, the number of processes and inter-process messages for that program increases. Also, it takes longer to start all the processes and to coordinate their completion. These negative effects of parallelism work against the performance improvements of parallelism.

Analytic models can give us accurate estimates of how parallelism affects throughput, and can also approximate average response times. However, more sophisticated models are required to fully understand the negative impact of the effects mentioned above.

Consequently, we designed and implemented an experiment on a 40-node Flex/32 multicomputer to determine empirically how response times scale with parallelism in a shared-nothing system, such as Bubba. The experiment is the first step in a large system scalability study. Empirical results from smaller "experimental vehicles" (EVs) will be used to validate detailed simulation models of much larger systems. Such models will be used to study scalability up to 1000 nodes [Smith 88, Boral 88].

A few previous experiments have investigated how performance scales with parallelism in shared-nothing systems.

- Scalability of Gamma's [DeWitt et al. 86] performance has been assessed using implementation benchmarks [DeWitt et al. 87, 88] and a validated simulation [Gerber 86, Gerber & DeWitt 87]. The analyses have been limited to single-user workloads, however. While single-user studies uncover important system inefficiencies, it is very difficult to extrapolate multi-user system performance from their results.

- NonStop SQL's performance on the Tandem architecture was evaluated in a multi-user Debit-Credit benchmark [Anon. et al. 85, Tandem 87, Tandem 88]. This study focused on throuput scalability, although specific response time requirements had to be met. The Debit-Credit transaction was not parallelized in this benchmark. Even if it had, Debit-Credit only has a fixed degree of parallelism (four single-tuple accesses). Thus, additional processors mainly help inter-transaction parallelism, but do little to alter parallelism (and response time) within an individual transaction.

- In [Bhide 88], a simulation study compares the performance of shared-nothing systems with shared-disk and "shared-everything" systems running an arbitrary multi-user workload. In order to be fair in the study, the same number of processors were used in each system, up to a limit of 5. Not surprisingly, shared-everything systems perform best in this low range; but larger systems of this type are quickly limited by memory and bus bandwidths (and are also less tolerant of faults).

We are instead interested in seeing how performance scales in larger shared-nothing configurations under different multi-user workloads.

The rest of the report describes this first experiment, which we called "E1". Section 2 defines the response time scalability study in the context of Bubba, and defines a measure of response time inflation within parallel transactions called "response time skew". Section 3 describes our experimental vehicle (EV) implemented on the Flex. Section 4 describes the design of the experiment on the EV. Sections 5, 6, and 7 describe experiment results for three different workload mixes: single transaction-at-a-time, multiple concurrent transactions of homogeneous type, and a heterogeneous mix of concurrent transactions. We show how system performance and response time skew changes under increased levels of concurrency and heterogeneity in the transaction workload. Finally, Section 8 summarizes our findings.

2. Background and Problem Definition

We use the Bubba architecture as a concrete example of a shared-nothing system, to provide a useful context for the experiment. We briefly describe relevant details of the Bubba architecture, and define E1 in those terms.

2.1. Bubba Overview

The overall hardware organization of Bubba is illustrated in Figure 2.1. It consists of a few "interface processors" (IPs), up to 1024 "intelligent repositories" (IRs) and a few "checkpoint-and-log IRs" (CIRs). All nodes are geographically close, so that an inexpensive hypercube interconnect provides ample bandwidth, short message latencies, and low error rates. Bubba is designed to use (fast) commodity hardware.

An IR contains a fragment of the database, and executes subtransactions pertaining to that fragment. Each IR has a disk with a controller, a communication processor, a hypercube link, and a main processor, which share a local memory. An IP receives

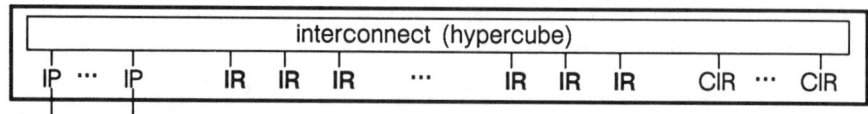

Figure 2.1: Overall Hardware Organization of Bubba

transaction programs and execution requests from one or more hosts and initiates processes that coordinate transaction execution. A CIR maintains on-line database checkpoints and logs for recovery. IR nodes are most relevant to E1.

Data is "declustered" (horizontally partitioned) across IRs to achieve parallelism and load balancing (e.g., [Teradata 85], [Livny et al. 87], [DeWitt et al. 86], [Tandem 87] and [Copeland et al. 88]). A "data placement" algorithm [Copeland et al. 88] decides how many IRs should be used to store each relation, using known or estimated statistics on access frequency and size. This number of IRs is called the "degree of declustering" (DD) of the relation. The algorithm then carefully chooses the specific IRs to be used as the "home" for each relation, so that the total IO and CPU load is balanced across all IRs. A small "global directory", replicated in each node, indicates the mapping of base relations to IRs. Tuples of each base relation are distributed across their home IRs by hashing on the tuple key values. In general, DD is not the same for all base relations.

A user transaction program in Bubba is expressed in FAD [Danforth et al. 87] and compiled into a dataflow program containing one or more "components" (program fragments) [Hart et al. 88]. To filter data as soon as possible, component code is loaded into the IRs that contain base data needed by the transaction, and executed there. Dataflow arcs indicate data dependence, and the transmission of partial results from one component to the next.

The dataflow programs are executed according to a dataflow execution strategy [Alexander & Copeland 88]. The main features of the strategy are:

- A transaction is executed as a parallel process distributed across the relevant IRs. Each IR runs a special purpose operating system ("BOS") that supports a multi-threaded process model (similar to Mach [Acceta et al. 86]). Light-weight "threads" of the process communicate by sending unacknowledged datagrams* to message queues of other threads. Each component is implemented by a set of parallel threads, one per IR in the component's home. Each thread executes the same component code on its fragment of the relation. Thus, (1) an individual component can be executed in parallel in several IRs due to declustering; (2) threads for different components in the same transaction can run concurrently, constrained only by dataflow dependencies; (3) multiple programs can be executed concurrently.

- Many components selectively access only one or a few tuples in a base relation according to input or derived key values. To avoid starting up processes on IRs that will not find data with these key values, Bubba "dynamically activates" component threads only in those IRs that are determined to be relevant by "associative routing". When the results of one component are used by another component to perform a selection or join, the global directory is used to partition the results according to their (foreign) key values so that each destination IR only receives requests for data in its

---

* Unacknowledged datagrams are used for efficiency. The message environment will be relatively error-free, so a simple timeout mechanism is used to detect lost messages.

fragment. Each subset is sent in a message to the corresponding destination IR. A process thread is dynamically activated by BOS when its first message arrives.

- Because of dynamic activation and associative routing, the IRs that will actually participate in the sending and receiving ends of a dataflow arc are determined only at run-time. "Dataflow control methods" are used to discover and inform each receiving thread how many messages to expect from senders [Alexander & Copeland 88]. The dataflow control methods in E1 are "set-at-a-time" (vs. pipelining) protocols; i.e., a thread blocks until the dataflow control protocol indicates that it has received *all* incoming messages.

- A "Transaction Coordinator" (TC) process for each transaction communicates with the user, loads and starts the transaction, and serves as the "master" in the distributed two-phase commit protocol. In all other respects, transaction execution is initiated and synchronized entirely by data flow. TCs usually run in IPs.

These concepts are illustrated with a simple dataflow graph in Figure 2.2. If the placement of Items and Orders overlaps (as in the example), threads 1 and 2 may run concurrently in the same IR(s), as shown.

As one can see, the parallel execution model we are investigating is non-trivial, and exhibits a high degree of asynchrony. E1 studies the net effect of this asynchrony on response time performance.

2.2. Experiment: Measure Response Time "Skew"

The response times of individual components obviously determine the response time of the transaction. There is parallelism both between components and within components in a transaction. Parallelism between components is determined by the dataflow graph, and is fairly static and independent of the system size. Parallelism within a component, however, scales up as the number of IRs in the component's home increases. In E1, we are mostly concerned with the latter's effects on response time.

Ideally, component response time would decrease proportionally to the degree of parallelism. That is, a component would execute about n times faster with n nodes than with 1 node. Of course, this is not the case. When a component is run as a set of parallel threads, the overall response time will be negatively impacted by the following effects:

1) *Uneven distribution of work.* The response time of a component is determined by the response time of its longest threads. A thread may be "long" because it has to do more work than the others because of an uneven distribution of tuples.

2) *Delays due to starting, synchronizing, communicating between, and terminating a set of parallel threads.* This delay is often proportional to the number of threads. For example, our communications system currently lacks a multicast mode, requiring identical copies of a message (e.g., "COMMIT") to be sent one-at-a-time. In fact, *multicast cannot always help*: when routing a set of values associatively to a group of IRs, the set is partitioned into different subsets which are sent in individual messages to their respective IRs, one after another.*

3) *Contention between concurrent threads from the same or other transactions.* Contention also increases a thread's response time. Contention is proportional to the multiprogramming level (*MPL*) at each node. The *MPL* is determined by the incoming workload, load balancing, and the degree of declustering--as we increase

---

* The entire set could be multicast to all nodes, and the data could be filtered at the receiving end, but this usually wastes bandwidth, and may involve nodes that would not normally be sent data.

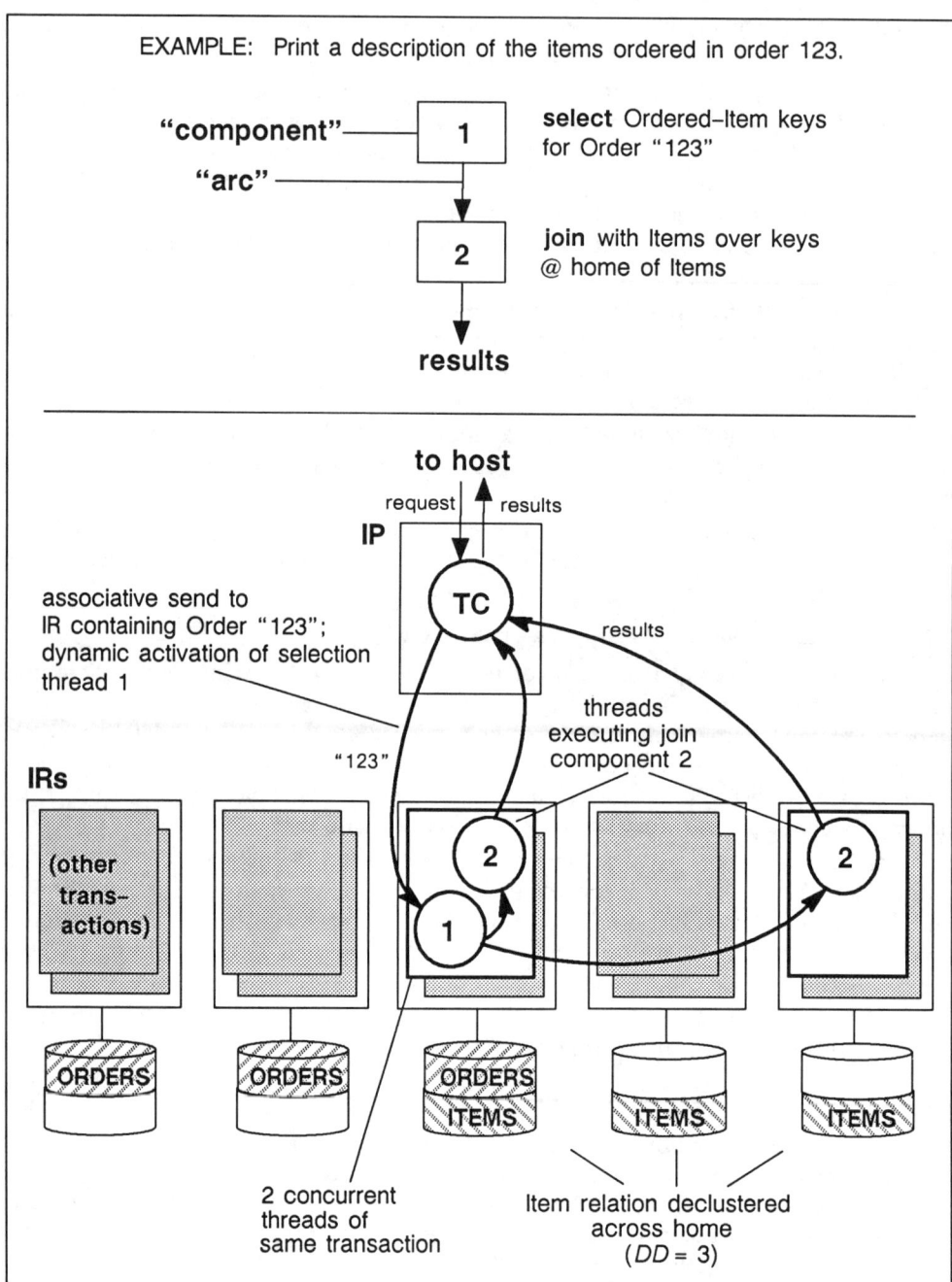

Figure 2.2. Dataflow Execution and Dynamic Activation in Bubba

the degree of declustering, the homes of base relations begin to overlap. Thus, each node is likely to be involved in more transactions.

While this is not an exhaustive list, we will see that these are very important factors that can cause component response time to worsen as parallelism is increased.

We define a measure for the negative effect of parallelism on component response time, called "(component) response time skew" (*RTSkew*). *RTSkew* compares the response time of a component (*ComponentRT*), executed by a parallel set of threads, to the average response time of the set of threads executing that component (*AvgThreadRT*):

$$RTSkew \equiv \frac{ComponentRT}{AvgThreadRT} \geq 1 \,. \qquad \text{(Eq. 1)}$$

These measures are illustrated in Figure 2.3. *ComponentRT* is defined to be the period between the time that the first thread starts and the time that the last thread stops. *AvgThreadRT* approximates the ideal response time of the threads, when the total work is distributed evenly across the threads. In the ideal case, the skew for a component would equal 1. As delays due to starting and stopping the threads increase, and as the variation in individual thread response times increases, the skew ratio becomes greater than 1. In E1, we measure a component's *StartDelay*, the time from when the first thread in the component starts until the last thread starts, and its *RTVariation*, the difference between the longest thread's response time (*MaxThreadRT*) and the average response time of the threads, to understand how start delays and response time variations contribute to skew.

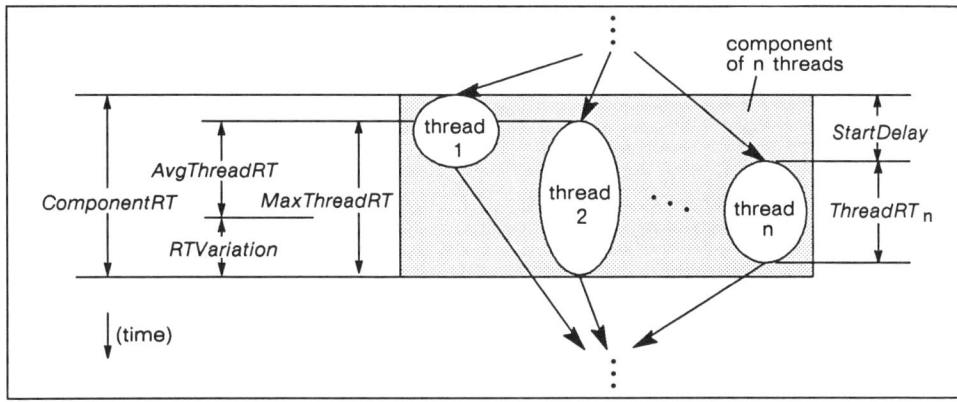

Figure 2.3. Response Times Within A Component

How do we control response time skew in a component? It appears that skew is influenced largely by *DD* and the multiprogramming level (*MPL*) of transactions in each IR. If so, we can control skew by controlling *DD* and *MPL*. The experiment attempts to discover how much each influences skew, and how badly skew affects response time.

3. The Experimental Vehicle

This section describes the experimental vehicle (EV) upon which E1 was built.

3.1. EV Hardware Implementation

E1 was implemented on a 40-processor Flex/32 multicomputer, illustrated in Figure 3.1. Each processor (with 16 MHz Motorola 68020, 68851 MMU, and 68881 FPU) has 6MB local memory, a 180 MB 5-1/4" CDC Wren III winchester disk, and a

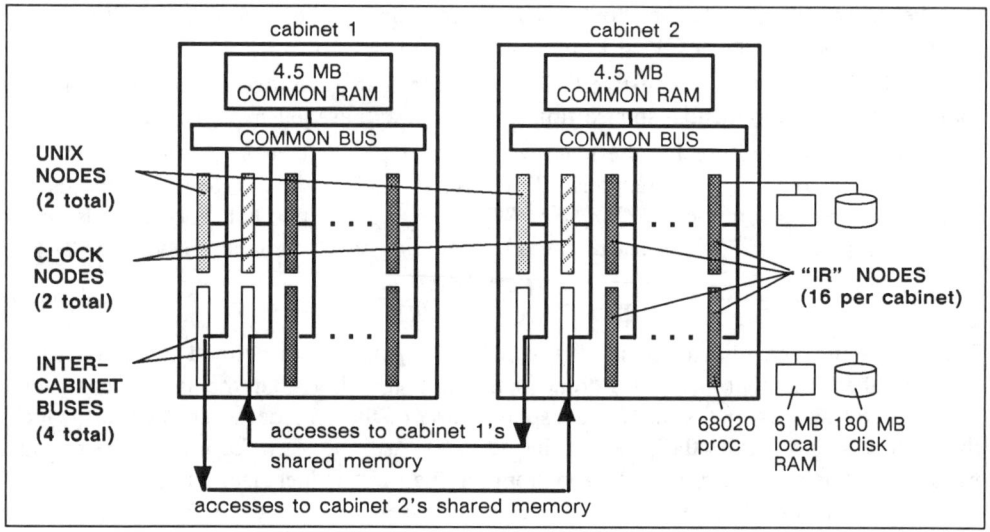

Figure 3.1. 40-node Flex/32 Configuration

high-performance ESDI disk controller. Two Flex cabinets house the 40 nodes.

Our interconnect is simulated using 9 MB of common memory as a "wire" to hold messages-in-transit. Nodes access the common memory only for messages. Common memory is partitioned so that each node has a dedicated buffer pool for outgoing messages, managed exclusively by that node without locks or critical sections. Thus, there are no "hot spots" in the message system.

Thirty-two of the 40 nodes were used to implement IRs. Rather than sacrifice separate nodes for IPs, we chose instead to run TC processes on IRs so that we would have as many IRs as possible (in Section 5 we shall see how this proved to be a mistake). Other nodes were used for experiment control and maintaining clock words in common memory for instrumentation. Four nodes' slots were given up for intercabinet buses.

3.2. EV Software Implementation

The distributed execution subsystem described in Section 2.1 was implemented according to the Bubba design specifications. This software included the global directory, dynamic thread activation, dataflow control, TC, and two-phase commit protocol.

The IR nodes in each cabinet ran the KEV database kernel [Wilkinson & Boral 87], the predecessor of BOS. KEV was modified to support the distributed process model described in Section 2.1, although its threads are "welter" rather than "light" weight. Response time costs of basic KEV operations are shown in Table 3.1.

The database system work at an IR was simulated using real CPU instructions, disk IOs, and messages. The use of simulation was opportunistic: we had already characterized the CPU, IO, and communication requirements for a set of transactions from an Order-Entry application workload scenario developed for an early Bubba queueing model, called FIRM [Boughter et al. 87]. FAD programs were "hand-compiled" into dataflow graphs describing the transaction components and dataflow dependencies. For a given program and a given data placement (*DD* was varied), the FIRM cost model [Alexander et al. 87] would estimate the total work that

Disk IO (1 KB blocks)	28 ms avg	includes disk driver overhead

Messages (128 bytes)
    inter-IR send
             recv
	
	0.65 ms
	 2.3 ms
		recv cost includes intercomputer-interrupt handling, scheduling of kernel message handler task, dynamic activation check, copying message body to local buffer & enqueueing, and scheduling of receiving thread

intra-IR send recv	0.93 ms 0.68 ms	send cost includes enqueueing message on receiver's queue, & scheduling receiving thread

Process Management
    thread create/activate
    thread delete
    thread switch
    system call overhead
	
	 2.5 ms
	 3.4 ms
	 0.20 ms
	 0.25 ms
		
		call & return

Table 3.1. Response Times of Basic KEV Operations

"real" Bubba database system code would do for each component, in terms of instruction counts (in the DBMS but not the OS), IOs, and messages. The dataflow graph and workload estimates were represented in tables.

A simulator was invoked whenever a component thread was dynamically activated. According to the component's entries in the workload tables, the simulator would

1) invoke a specified dataflow control protocol to receive data messages on each dataflow arc incident to the component;
2) perform a specified number of random read IOs;
3) spin for the number of estimated DBMS instructions (e.g., for index lookups, etc.);
4) save the ids of "updated" disk blocks in a transaction "workspace";
5) synthesize foreign key values to be associatively routed, partition them into subsets by consulting the global directory for each value, and call a specified dataflow control protocol to send the subsets to the destination IRs;
6) terminate the thread.

At commit time, the TC in charge of the transaction would activate a special commit thread in each IR that participated. This thread would rewrite the blocks listed in the transaction workspace, and carry out the "slave" end of the two-phase commit protocol. Since the TC does not actively control a transaction's execution, it must be told which IRs have participated in the transaction by the dataflow control protocols.

3.3. EV Instrumentation

To measure performance, the EV software (primarily KEV) was instrumented with a generic event trace mechanism. At run-time, trace calls generate records containing the event type, a timestamp, and any relevant state information, in a large buffer in the node's local memory. To avoid impacting experiment performance, we buffered entire experiment traces in each IR which were written out only at the end of the experiment.

4. The Experiment

This section describes the workloads measured in E1.

4.1. The Workload

Two transactions in the Order Entry application scenario, called Suggested-Order (SO) and Store-Layout (SL), have problematic response times in the shared-nothing architecture because their dataflow graphs contain components which have a variable degree of parallelism equal to *DD*. The other transactions in the scenario only contain components with fixed degrees of parallelism (like Debit-Credit), and their response times are independent of *DD* beyond a few nodes.

As it happens, SO and SL are both read-only queries, so concurrency control and logging were not needed for E1. (However, we expect concurrency control to play a large role in *RTSkew* for arbitrary workloads. This may be examined in a future experiment.)

4.1.1. Suggested-Order

The Suggested-Order (SO) transaction answers the query "given the current inventory and per-item sales histories for items in warehouse X, what items should warehouse X order today (both normal and rush orders)?" The logical dataflow graph for Suggested-Order is illustrated in Figure 4.1, and the physical dataflow graph is shown in Figure 4.2. Component 2 (C2) is of interest, since it executes in parallel across *DD* IRs.

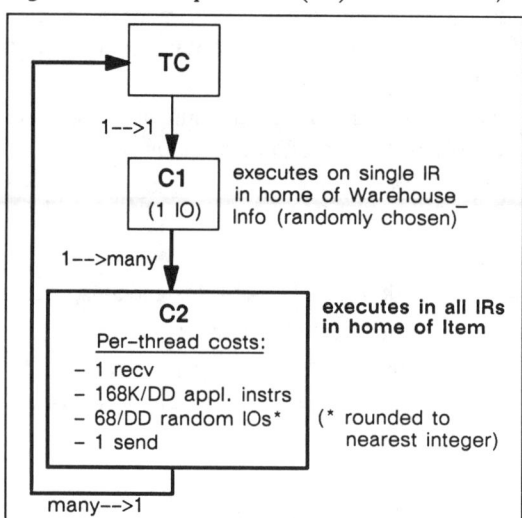 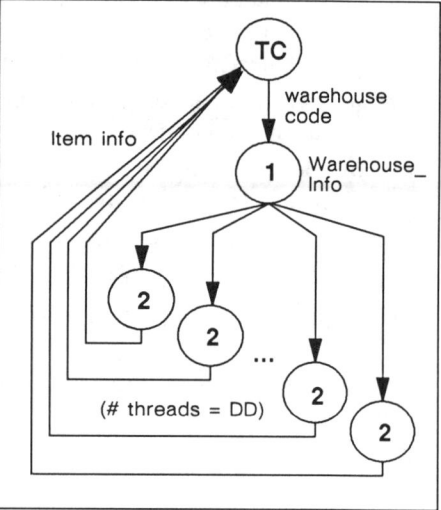

Figure 4.1. Logical Dataflow Graph for Suggested-Order

Figure 4.2. Physical Dataflow Graph for Suggested-Order

In the experiment, the TC routes a message containing a (simulated) transaction parameter to a random IR in the home of component C1. A dynamically activated C1 thread simulates a direct tuple fetch from a base relation by doing a random read IO on the local disk. The C1 thread then sends the (simulated) result in a message to each IR in the home of component C2. A C2 thread is dynamically activated in each of these IRs to simulate a full scan and semi-join by executing 168K/*DD* application instructions and 68/*DD* random IOs (amounts derived by the cost model for a 32-IR database, as discussed in Section 3.2). Each thread generates a result message and sends it to the TC, which merges the simulated results.

4.1.2. Store-Layout

The Store-Layout (SL) transaction answers the complex query, "Given the per-item sales histories for items in a customer (store) X in the season S, how many items should be stocked and how should they be arranged on store shelves to maximize profit?" The process dataflow graph is given in Figure 4.3, with the per-thread costs given in the component boxes. Components C3, C5, and C6 simulate parallel joins on base relations whose degree of declustering is *DD*.

The SL transaction is simulated much like SO as described above. However, SL is more complex in that the results of C3 and C5 are used in C6; each thread in C3 and C5 sends a message to each thread executing C6 resulting in $2(DD^2)$ messages (e.g., 32 messages for *DD*=4, and 2048 messages for *DD*=32). The quadratic number of messages is due to the normalized schema; if a the user were able to nest some of the base relations within others, the parallel join between C3, C5, and C6 could be simplified.

The final thread, C7, simulates a sort and repeated iteration over the results of C6 to compute the answer to the query (simulated by over 6 million dummy instructions!). No attempt was made to parallelize this component in E1.

4.2. Data Placement

We used a version of the data placement algorithm for Bubba described in [Copeland et al. 88] for our "data distribution" in E1. No data was actually stored on the IRs; only the mapping of base relations to IRs was needed for the global directory. The algorithm normally considers the size, "heat" (frequency of access), "temperature" (heat/size), and availability requirements of base relations when choosing *DD* for a relation. For E1, we modified the algorithm slightly in order to force each relation to be declustered to the same *DD*, specified as a parameter.*

We used five data placement configurations in E1, where *DD* = {4, 8, 16, 24, 32}. The Order-Entry schema was reduced to the seven base relations accessed by SO and SL. The data placement algorithm optimized the load balancing across all IRs for each *DD* assuming an arbitrary 2:1 mix of SO:SL transactions. While optimized for the 2:1 mix, the five placements illustrated in Figure 4.4 were used for all E1 runs.

4.3. Simplifications To The Simulation

In order to conduct a controlled experiment with few variables, the simulation included the following simplifications:

1) For simplicity and conservation of (precious) message buffer space, all simulated messages were implemented by real messages of small fixed size = 128 bytes. This yields an optimistic simulation of message delays.

2) All disk IOs were simulated by random IOs. This yields a pessimistic simulation for sequential scan times.

3) When a scan of *n* disk blocks was done in parallel by *DD* threads, each thread would perform *n/DD* IOs, where *n/DD* was rounded to the nearest integer. This yields an optimistic simulation of load balancing, since data distribution will usually be imperfect, i.e., each thread will have to perform a different number of IOs. Also, due to rounding, the total number of blocks scanned changes (slightly) for each *DD*.

4.4. Experiment Procedure

In the experiment, we executed streams of SO and SL transactions, 500 in each run,

---
* Although heat was not used to determine the degree of declustering for a relation, heat was still used to determine which IRs should store a relation, so that the cumulative heat was balanced across IRs.

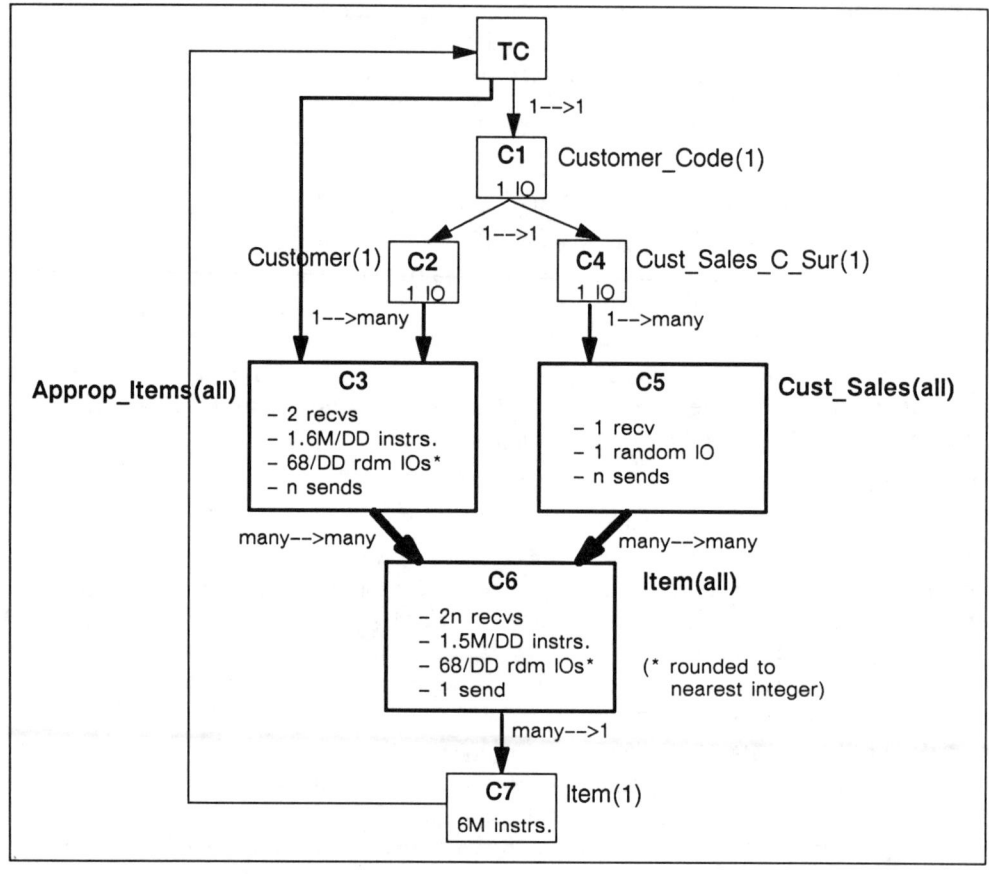

Figure 4.3. Logical Dataflow Graph for Store-Layout

on the 32-node EV using each of the five data placements, and measured the response times of individual threads. From the thread response times, we derived response times of components and transactions. By examining the response time distributions, and computing average response times, 90th percentile response times, and response time skew, we determined how RT scales with *DD*.

In the first set of runs, we ran transactions one-at-a-time (i.e., the "degree of multiprogramming in the system," or *DMP,* was 1) to observe the inherent response time performance of each transaction for each *DD*. These results are discussed in Section 5.

The next set of runs were designed to determine the effect of concurrency on response times. We varied the Poisson arrival rates for homogeneous SO and SL workloads up to some maximum level for each *DD*, and measured the relationship between response time vs. throughput and *MPL* after the fact. After finding the maximum sustainable throughput by trial and error, we ran the workloads at 0.5, 0.6, 0.7, 0.8, and 0.9 times the maximum. These results are presented in Section 6.

Finally, we conducted a set of runs with a 2:1 mix of concurrent SO and SL transactions, to observe response time characteristics under heterogeneous workloads. These results are discussed in Section 7.

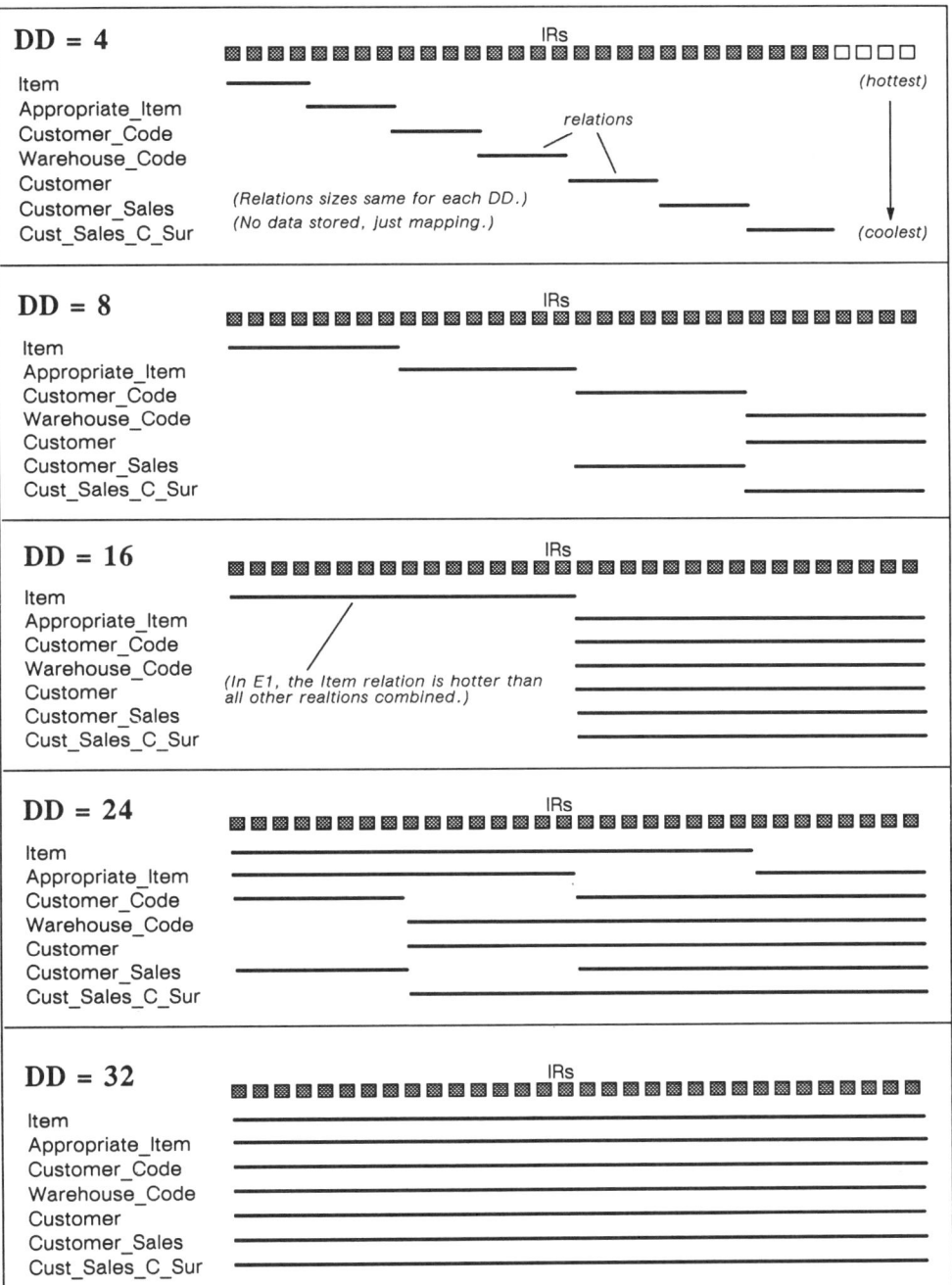

Figure 4.4. Data Placements for DD = {4, 8, 16, 24, 32}

5. Results: Single Transactions At A Time

In this section, we examine how each transaction behaves in a single user environment. We derive *ComponentRT* and *RTSkew* from the measured *ThreadRT*s as depicted in Figure 2.3, and *TransactionRT* (not depicted in Figure 2.3) from when the first thread in the first component starts to when the last thread in the last component stops.

5.1. Suggested-Order

Fundamentals of RT scaling. As Figures 5.1 and 5.2 show, *TransactionRT* of SO and *ComponentRT* of component C2 are not linear functions of the degree of parallelism, *DD*. Why? First, the average *ThreadRT* of C2 (curve T) is not linear in *DD*. *ThreadRT* decreases as a function of *DD* according to

$$c1 + c2/DD,$$

where $c1$ is the startup and termination cost per IR and $c2$ is the amount of work done by the component across all threads (68 IOs and 168K instructions in this case). Thus, the reduction in work per thread diminishes as *DD* is increased, which explains the diminishing returns on *ThreadRT* speedup as *DD* is increased. Second, as expected, *RTSkew* increases monotonically with *DD*. In the range *DD*=4 to 16, the speedup in *ThreadRT* increases faster than *RTSkew* increases, so there is a net speedup in *ComponentRT*. But in the range *DD*=16 to 32, *RTSkew* increases at a faster rate while *ThreadRT* speedup reaches a point of diminishing returns. At this point, *ComponentRT* begins to increase again. From Eq. 1, we have

$$ComponentRT = ThreadRT \cdot RTSkew.$$

That is, *RTSkew* represents a response time inflation factor much like "speedup" represents a response time improvement factor. As Figures 5.1 and 5.2 show, there is some optimum where the ratio of thread speedup to skew has been maximized, and in turn *ComponentRT* is minimized. This characterizes the fundamental tradeoff between the positive effect of parallelism (*ThreadRT* speedup) and the negative effect (*RTSkew*).

It may be surprising to see skew's apparently significant effect on performance at such a low *DD* (*DD*=16 is the optimum). However, first, SO is "small": at *DD*=32, each C2 thread only does 2 IOs. The relative impact of start and synchronization delays is much more significant than if the work per thread was higher. Second, there are only single transactions in the system at a time. Section 6 discusses reasons to increase *DD* beyond 16 to attain better overall performance with concurrent transactions.

Contributors to RT skew. We examined two factors that contribute to *RTSkew* in E1, *StartDelay* and *RTVariation*, illustrated in Figure 2.3. *StartDelay* measures the staggering of thread start times when a previous component activates the threads via a sequence of messages. *RTVariation* measures how much the longest *ThreadRT* (*MaxThreadRT*) differs from the average (*AvgThreadRT*).*

In the worst case, the longest thread in a component is also the last one started, and

$$ComponentRT = StartDelay + AvgThreadRT + RTVariation.$$

But in general, this is only an upper bound, and *StartDelay* and *RTVariation* are merely indicators that suggest their relative contribution to *RTSkew*.

Our analysis shows that *StartDelay* is the primary contributor to *RTSkew* in C2. *StartDelay* increases linearly in *DD*, since a separate message activates each C2 thread.

RTVariation for C2 is nearly constant in the range *DD*=4 to 16. There are only small

---
* Note that *RTVariation* is not the same as statistical variance.

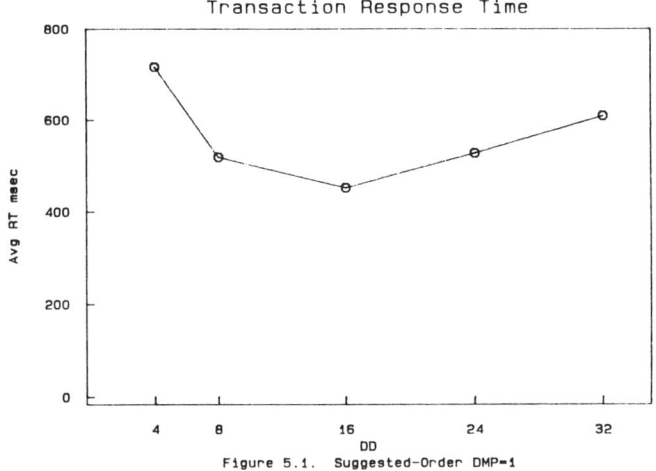

Figure 5.1. Suggested-Order DMP=1

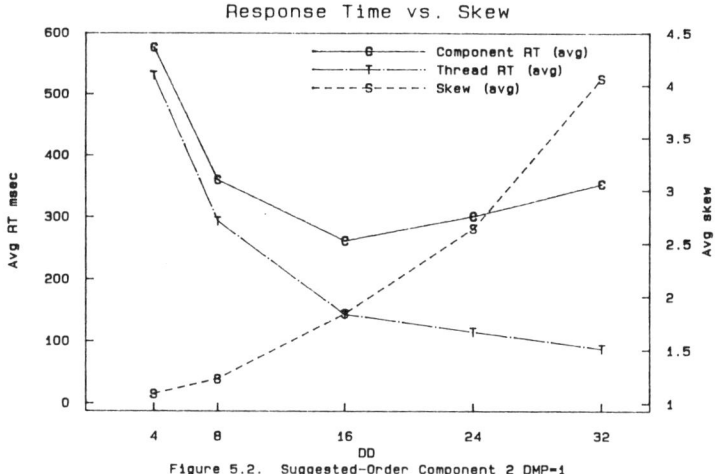

Figure 5.2. Suggested-Order Component 2 DMP=1

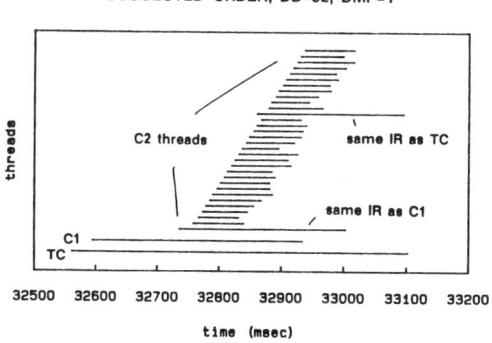

Figure 5.3.

variations in *ThreadRT*s due to blocking for the initial message, and random seek times.

But for *DD*=24 to 32, *RTVariation* increases substantially. Our analysis reveals the following cause. Whenever a thread executing C1 starts a "local" C2 thread on the same IR, the local C2 thread blocks until the C1 thread has finished (under a FCFS scheduling discipline). This extends the response time of the local C2 thread, and often the response time of the component. In E1, this only occurs in the cases of *DD*=24 and 32, where the data placement specifies that the homes of C1 and C2 are *overlapped* (partially for *DD*=24 and fully for *DD*=32). This overlap does not occur for *DD*=4, 8 or 16.

RTVariation could be reduced in this situation by adopting the rule that a node should send to itself last when sending a sequence of messages, such as when the C1 thread sends to the C2 threads. This would start work on the remote nodes as soon as possible, deferring new work on the local node until last. Intuitively, this seems like a reasonable idea, and it would certainly reduce or eliminate the *RTVariation* measured in the situation above. However, it is not likely to have any major net impact on *ComponentRT*, since the local C2 thread still cannot run until the C1 thread has finished. The idle time "saved" from *RTVariation* would simply be added to *StartDelay*. The interference due to multiprogramming on a single CPU is always there.

The time profile in Figure 5.3 illustrates the *ThreadRT*s of SO's threads for *DD*=32.

It would have been helpful to trace finer-grain system events like message arrivals and task switches, to help us characterize *RTVariation* in more detail. For instance, the blocking time due to thread interference described above could have been measured directly. Unfortunately, in the current setup, instrumentation overhead and buffer space limitations prevented us from tracing more than basic thread start and stop events.

An anomaly. Our decision to run the TC "threads" on the IRs resulted in multiprogramming interference similar to that described above, but was *worse* because the TC runs at a higher priority than component threads, preempting them. Fortunately, we determined from the trace that TC interference did not significantly impact the results.

5.2. Store-Layout

Tradeoff: Parallelism vs. messages. The SL *TransactionRT*s are plotted as a function of *DD* in Figure 5.4. The shape of the curve is "dampened" somewhat by the large, constant amount of work done by C7. In any case, we see that as we begin to increase *DD*, more work can be done in parallel, reducing response time. But as we continue to increase *DD*, the total number of messages sent between all threads in the transaction increases quadratically ($O(DD^2)$), resulting in more work per thread, and offsetting any CPU or IO savings per thread. Thus, for SL, the benefits of parallelism are best realized at low *DD*; *TransactionRT* increases rapidly as *DD* increases due to messages.

Tradeoff: Parallelism vs. multiprogramming interference. Figure 5.5 shows the *ThreadRT*, *ComponentRT*, and *RTSkew* curves for component C3. In contrast to Figure 5.2, the upturn in the *ThreadRT* curve T shows how the usual CPU and IO savings per thread is offset by increased message processing as *DD* increases.

RTSkew for C3 appears to "accelerate" as *DD* increases. Our analysis shows that while *StartDelay* remains linear in *DD*, *RTVariation* in C3 becomes very large--up to 4 times greater than *StartDelay*--as *DD* goes to 24 and 32. The main reason for this appears to be competition for the processors by threads of the transaction. For *DD*=24 and 32, the homes of C3, C5 and C6 threads overlap (cf. Figure 4.4) and an absence of dataflow dependencies allow these threads to execute concurrently on the same IRs,

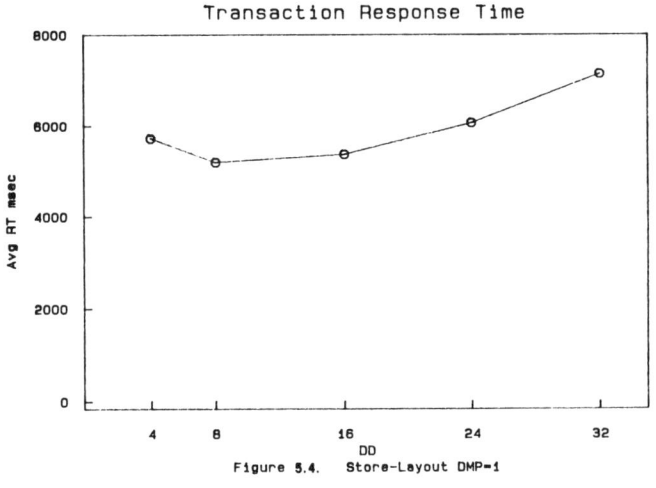

Figure 5.4. Store-Layout DMP=1

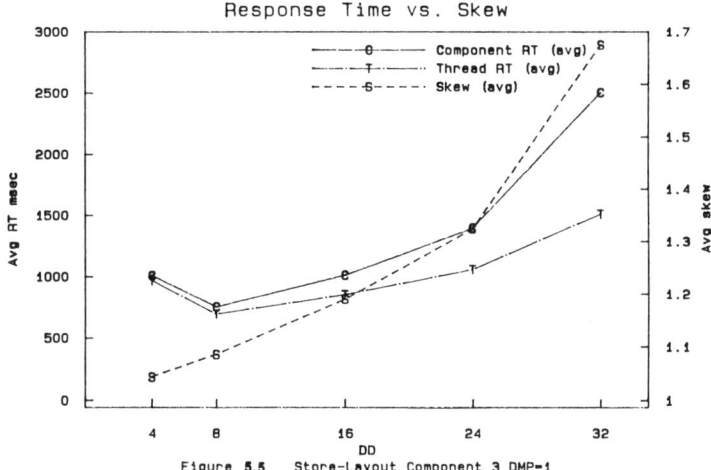

Figure 5.5. Store-Layout Component 3 DMP=1

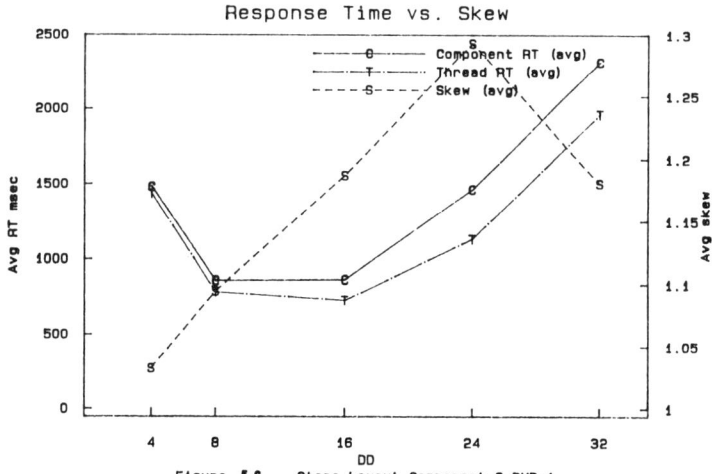

Figure 5.6. Store-Layout Component 6 DMP=1

resulting in interference and attendant delays. This is the same type of *intra-transaction* interference observed between C1 and C2 threads in SO.

Figure 5.6 shows the *ThreadRT*, *ComponentRT*, and *RTSkew* curves for C6. The *ThreadRT* and *ComponentRT* curves have the same shapes as C3's curves, for the same reasons. But, surprisingly, *RTSkew* falls from $DD=24$ to 32. The suspected reason is that the homes for competing components C3, C5 and C6 only *partially* overlap for $DD=24$, but fully overlap for $DD=32$. Thus, the C6 threads for $DD=32$ are uniformly hindered, with very little variation in *ThreadRT*s, while for $DD=24$, there is more variation since only some threads are hindered. Nevertheless, even though *RTSkew* is better for $DD=32$, the C6 threads are doing much more communication work, resulting in worse *ComponentRT*s.

The magnitude of *RTSkew* in C6 is less than that of C3 (and C5, not shown). (Perhaps this makes the drop in *RTSkew* between $DD=24$ and 32 described above appear overly dramatic.) In part, this is because of C6's position in the dataflow graph: since the set-at-a-time dataflow control protocols limit pipelining, C6 threads only run after the C3 and C5 threads have completed most of their work.

6. Results: Concurrent Transactions

To examine the effect of concurrency and multiprogramming on *TransactionRT*, we ran homogeneous SO and SL workloads for $DD=\{4, 8, 16, 24, 32\}$, varying the arrival rate up to the maximum sustainable for each DD, and measuring *ThreadRT*, *ComponentRT*, and *TransactionRT*; average CPU and disk utilizations, for the "worst" IRs and across the system; and an *estimate* of the *MPL* in the worst IR.*

6.1. Suggested Order

Tradeoff: throughput vs. RT skew. Figure 6.1 shows how the average *TransactionRT*s for SO vary as the arrival rates are increased for each DD. SO response times are determined by the response times of C2 (not shown). For reference, *TransactionRT*s for the previous $DMP=1$ case are plotted at TPS = 0.0. This puts the single-user results into perspective: the *TransactionRT* penalty for increased DD is relatively insignificant when the system is lightly-loaded. What really matters is how much DD can be increased to improve system throughput without significantly hurting response time.

Table 6.1 shows that disks (in the home of C2) are the bottleneck resources for $DD=4$ to 16, while CPUs (in the home of C2) become the bottleneck for $DD=24$ and 32, although the disks are still highly utilized. This improvement in system utilization is due to better load balancing as intended by full or nearly full declustering.

DD	TPS	CPU Util. (worst IR)	CPU Util. (system)	Disk Util. (worst IR)	Disk Util. (system)	Avg *MPL* (worst IR)
4	1.71	.30	.04	.97	.12	24.6
8	3.54	.40	.12	.92	.23	25.3
16	7.74	.71	.42	.90	.46	38.1
24	8.23	.91	.63	.73	.54	53.7
32	8.64	.99	.85	.73	.73	51.1

Table 6.1. SO Resource Utilizations

Figure 6.1 shows that, under low utilization, response times are best for $DD=16$. As

---
* Rather than sampling the MPL periodically over time, we instead sampled the number of existing threads in an IR each time a new thread was created. This method may actually yield a higher MPL number, especially when threads are created in bunches. Our "MPL" is a pessimistic estimate.

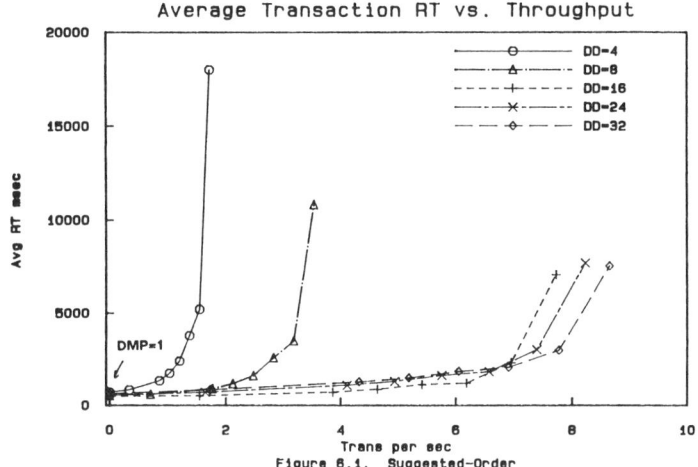

Figure 6.1. Suggested-Order

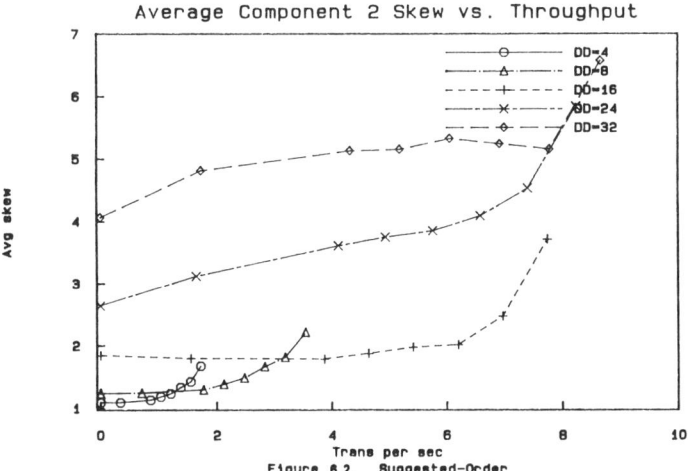

Figure 6.2. Suggested-Order

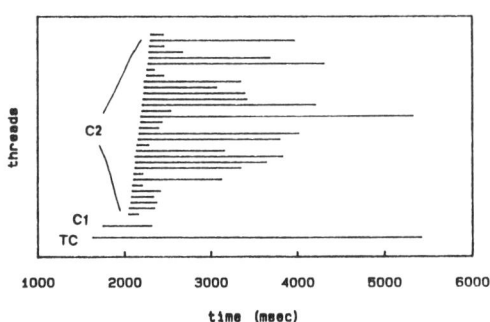

Figure 6.3.

discussed in Section 5.1, this is due to high *RTSkew* for *DD*=24 and 32. However, Figure 6.1 and Table 6.1 show that better load balancing at higher *DD* allows the system attain higher throughput, while maintaining reasonable response times. In this case, the costs of declustering (higher *RTSkew*) are not as important as the benefits (higher throughput).

MPL vs. RT skew. Figure 6.2 shows that *RTSkew* for C2 is "well-behaved": it remains fairly "flat" as the load (and *MPL*) increases until the system reaches saturation. Our analysis shows *RTVariation* contributes much more to *RTSkew* than *StartDelay* (perhaps by a few orders of magnitude). The widely varying *ThreadRTs* in the presence of competing concurrent transactions are evident in the time profile of Figure 6.3.

RT distributions vs. average. Many applications have response time requirements such as "90% of the transactions must finish within 1 second." If skew results in widely varying *ComponentRT* and *TransactionRT* distributions, throughput levels may need to be lowered drastically (by some scheduling policy) in order to meet the requirements. Fortunately, the 90th percentile response times for SO (see [Smith et al. 88]) indicate that throughput levels do not have to be reduced significantly to meet some *TransactionRT* guarantee. For example, in order to guarantee 90% of the transactions complete in less than 5 seconds, throughput must be reduced less than 5% of maximum.

6.2. Store-Layout

Tradeoff: Parallelism vs. messages (again). Figure 6.4 shows how the average *TransactionRTs* for SL vary as the arrival rates are increased for each *DD*. For reference, *TransactionRTs* for the *DMP*=1 case are plotted at TPS = 0.0. These curves are different from SO curves in that they show both response time and throughput suffer as *DD* is increased, due primarily to the $O(DD^2)$ messages per transaction. Table 6.2 shows that the bottleneck resource is always the CPU; for low *DD* it is because there is much application work per thread, while for high *DD*, most of the CPU cost is due to message handling. *DD*=16 has the best throughput and response time performance because it has the right balance of load balancing and number of messages. For *DD*=4 and 8, there are relatively few messages, but our analysis shows only 1/8 or 1/4 of the nodes are reasonably utilized (those executing C6). For *DD*=24 and 32, all the nodes are highly utilized, but only because they have many more messages to process. For *DD*=16, there are a moderate number of messages, and the data placement algorithm was able to assign relations to IRs to balance the total load over all IRs, not just 4 or 8.

DD	TPS	CPU Util. (worst IR)	CPU Util. (system)	Disk Util. (worst IR)	Disk Util. (system)	Avg *MPL* (worst IR)
4	0.49	.86	.14	.26	.07	65.5
8	0.78	.86	.30	.20	.11	36.3
16	0.80	.75	.59	.14	.13	21.3
24	0.52	.88	.61	.10	.08	30.5*
32	0.41	.98	.96	.07	.07	24.9

* The slight increase is probably an effect of partial home overlap for DD=24.

Table 6.2. SL Resource Utilizations

Tradeoff: Parallelism vs. multiprogramming interference (again). Components C3 and C5 exhibit similar behavior in the concurrent transaction workload: as *DD* increases from 4 to 16, their *ComponentRTs* (not shown) are almost unaffected as the arrival rate is increased from single-transaction-at-a-time to maximum throughput. In contrast, for

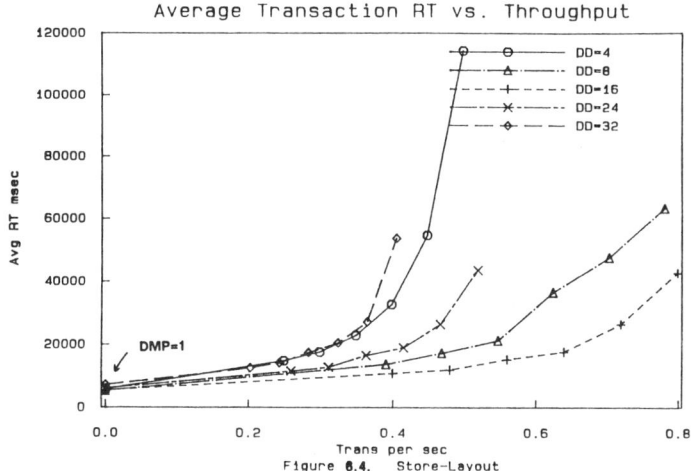

Figure 6.4. Store-Layout

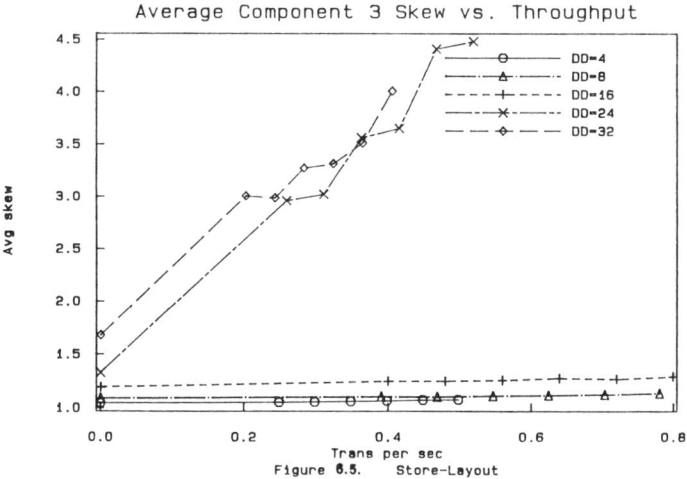

Figure 6.5. Store-Layout

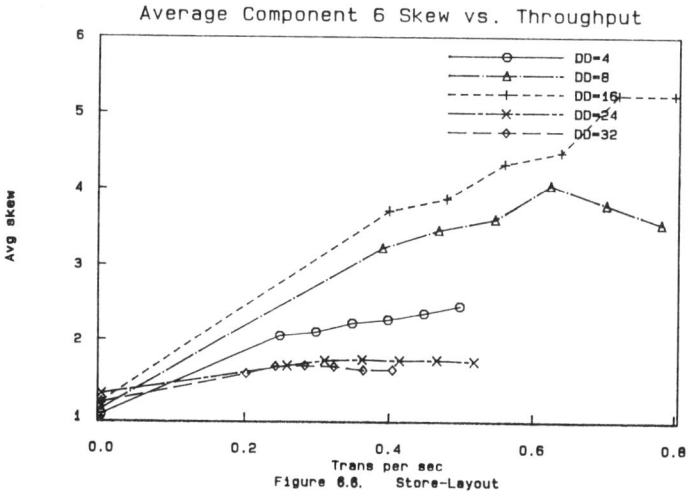

Figure 6.6. Store-Layout

DD=24 and 32, their *ComponentRT*s increase very rapidly as throughput increases, in part because the individual *ThreadRT*s increase (cf. Figure 5.5), but mainly because of the increase in *RTSkew*, shown for C3 in Figure 6.5. Our analysis shows that *RTVariation* is very high for DD=24 and 32, apparently from the contention between threads of the same transaction (cf. Section 5.2) as well as threads of other concurrent transactions, *particularly C6 threads*. C3 and C5 threads conflict with C6 threads for DD=24 and 32 because their homes overlap. The overlap effect is amplified because C6 is "the bottleneck component," as we will explain. Thus, even though the number of times a thread is switched (= number of receives and IOs) goes down as DD increases, each thread will have to wait longer to get the processor (E1 uses FCFS queueing) because of contention with other C6 threads.

Cost of receive operations. In the concurrent transaction case, C6 replaces C7 as the most significant contributor to SL *TransactionRT*. (The C6 *ComponentRT* vs. throughput curves, not shown, look almost identical to Figure 6.4.) Three possible reasons for this seem likely. First, the C6 threads may be started fairly early in the life of the transaction (by dynamic activation upon arrival of the first messages), but because of dataflow dependencies and limited pipelining in our dataflow control protocols, they are not allowed to proceed until C3 and C5 threads have finished their work and sent all of their messages. As a result, *ThreadRT* and *ComponentRT* include a lot of idle time (waiting for messages) that cannot currently be detected in the measurements. Note that this represents a type of "transaction skew" (not measured in E1) that accumulates over components in a transaction. Second, C6 does $2 \cdot DD$ blocking receive operations, each of which may result in a switch to another thread. As DD increases, the number of these switch points increases. As the queueing time per switch increases with contention, *ThreadRT* increases. Third, receive operations are more expensive than sends: receive operations may cause thread switching, while sends do not; receivers must process message interrupts; in the EV, receivers copy message bodies from senders' message queues, perhaps contending for the intercabinet link; and the receiver's OS must handle dynamic thread activation if necessary.

MPL vs. RT skew. Surprisingly, *RTSkew* curves for C6 in Figure 6.6 reveal that *RTSkew* is *lowest* for DD=24 and 32 and *highest* for DD=16. Our analysis shows that *RTVariation* in C6 is greater for DD=16 than for DD=32. But the measured *MPL* levels for DD=16 (Table 6.2) are actually lower at that point. This may be explained by the fact that for DD=4, 8, and 16, there is no overlap between C6 and any other SL components. Contention is *only* between threads of *other* transactions, whose threads are most likely to be *active*, as opposed to threads of the same transaction, whose threads may be blocked due to dataflow dependencies. In this situation the contention is probably higher for DD=16 even though the same number of threads may be present in an IR.

RT distributions vs. average. The 90th percentile *TransactionRT* curves for SL (see [Smith et al. 88]) have the same general shape as the average *TransactionRT* curves (Figure 6.5), but have increased slopes. The differential between the 90th percentile and average curves is still small: to meet a 90% *TransactionRT* requirement of 50 seconds (for example), the throughput rate must be reduced by about 15%.

7. Results: Heterogeneous Workload

To observe *RTSkew* in a heterogeneous mix of concurrent transactions, we performed a set of runs with a mix of about 2 SOs per SL (2:1). The choice of mix was largely arbitrary. In retrospect, it would have been better to strike a balance between the total amount of work generated by SO vs. SL transactions, to avoid significant biases in performance. A 10:1 ratio would have provided such a balance. Of course, the results in this section are specific to the 2:1 mix--other mixes will yield different results.

SL transactions dominate. The average *TransactionRT* vs. throughput curves for SO and SL (see [Smith et al. 88]) reveal the first of two main conclusions from the mixed workload study: in this mix, *TransactionRT*s for SO are *strongly influenced by the SL transactions*. The general shape and scale of the mix's SO curves look more like the SL curves of the homogeneous (Figure 6.5) and mixed workloads (not shown), rather than the SO curves in Figure 6.1! Given that *TransactionRT* for the SL transactions is an order of magnitude greater than the SO transactions in the homogeneous cases, and that the "main" SO and SL components (C2 and C6, respectively) always share the same relation home, it is not surprising that the SL transactions overwhelm the 2:1 mix, to the point that SO transactions resemble SL's performance.

Heterogeneity and RT skew. When comparing *RTSkew* (not shown) with that of the homogeneous workloads, we observed that the skew for SO C2 is much worse (up to 2 times as much), while the skew for SL C6 has decreased, but only very slightly.

More anomalies. Several anomalies in the measurements revealed the second main conclusion from the mixed runs: *the limited number of trials in each of our runs (500) was not adequate*. Since transaction types are chosen randomly by the driver process, there is not an exact 2:1 ratio of SO to SL transactions in the measured lot. Also, the simulated arrival process was Poisson, resulting in contractions (bursts) and expansions (lulls) in the input stream. Since the measurement interval was measured in units of transactions instead of time, one experiment run might capture a burst in the stream, with correspondingly poor *TransactionRT*, while another run with faster *average* arrival rate may capture an expanse in the input stream, with correspondingly better *TransactionRT*. As a result, the exact measurements in the mixed runs all have questionable accuracy. The accuracy can be improved if the measurement interval per run would be substantially increased (so that the "law of large numbers" would apply).

Nevertheless, it is clear from the measurements that *TransactionRT*s of small transactions like SO will be severely impacted by larger transactions like SL in a mix with high concentrations of the large transactions, because of high *RTSkew*. Moreover, the 90th percentile response times (not shown) are much worse for the mixed cases than for the homogeneous runs. Thus, depending on the mix, either substantial cuts in throughput or changes in the mix may be required to meet *TransactionRT* guarantees.

8. Conclusion

For a large class of simple transactions (which excludes SO and SL), individual response times are *not* strongly affected by increased parallelism. For example, Debit-Credit and other transactions in our Order-Entry scenario have fixed degrees of parallelism. If these types of transactions dominate the system workload[*], then increasing the degree of declustering can help throughput through inter-transaction parallelism, without significant response time penalties. For these workloads, more declustering means better performance [Tandem 88, Copeland et al. 88].

For simple parallel scan transactions like SO, E1 shows response time skew due to increased parallelism is much less troublesome than expected (at least for $DD \leq 32$). The

---

[*] In the full Order-Entry scenario, SO and SL only make up 0.4% of the workload, over time.

major aim of declustering, namely load balancing, seems to be more important to good system performance than the relatively small increases in response time due to skew.

For the complicated SL query, E1 shows performance is poor as *DD* is increased, which is in agreement with our analytic model [Copeland et al. 88]. But the problem is the number of messages required, not skew. The number of messages per query may be reduced by nesting base relations when possible, transforming large parallel joins into simpler programs that look more like parallel scans. In any event, large parallel transactions will require very efficient communications in a shared-nothing system; Bubba will have fast dedicated message processors and an efficient communications protocol. Finally, methods for parallelizing message sequences can reduce the CPU load as well as *StartDelay* effects: e.g., Gamma distributes message sequences in parallel down a logical binary-tree imposed on the nodes [Gerber 86, Gerber & DeWitt 87].

It would be advantageous to be able to predict the net effect of skew at the time *DD* is chosen for each relation during data placement. Unfortunately, making this prediction analytically does not appear to be easy. Heuristics can probably be developed with experience. One important data placement consideration is multiprogramming interference among components. It would be worthwhile to extend the data placement algorithm to detect the "affinity" of relations within and across transactions in the estimated workload, and put relations that may be used heavily at the same time on different sets of IRs.

We have seen the importance of limiting *MPL* and controlling the mix. It appears that skew is "well-behaved" for reasonable *MPL*, so that standard scheduling mechanisms should suffice. Since large transactions can *greatly* affect other transaction response times, it would be worthwhile to distinguish and segregate job classes.

It is not clear how skew would be affected if Bubba's "set-at-a-time" dataflow control protocols were replaced by schemes that allow more pipelining. On one hand, performance might be expected to improve due to the increased level of concurrency in a transaction. On the other hand, pipelining may increase the variation in response times due to increased levels of asynchronous activity, protocol complexity, and competition for the processor. This would make an excellent experiment! Another important experiment would be to study the effect of concurrency control on skew.

While E1's behavior was reasonably realistic, we decided not to validate a Bubba model against the hybrid simulation-and-implementation. Instead, we are replacing the simulated DBMS code in the EV with real code, including concurrency control and "fixes" for the anomalies discovered in E1. The new EV will also have a more robust instrumentation subsystem. Any models will be validated against this more realistic EV implementation. We reemphasize that modeling is critical to understanding response time scalability beyond 32 nodes, up to 1000.

Acknowledgements

Ellen Boughter and Chris Buckalew provided the data placement and workload tables for the simulation. Jerre Bowen, Larry Clay, Julieta Criollo, Ying Hung, Bonnie Kerola and Ned Nowotny implemented the E1 and KEV software on the Flex EV.

References

[Accetta et al. 86] Accetta, M., Baron, R., Bolosky, W., Golub, D., Rashid, R., Tevanian, A., Young, M., "Mach: a New Kernel Foundation For UNIX Development," *Proc. Of Summer Usenix* (July 1986).

[Alexander & Copeland 88] Alexander, W., Copeland, G., "Process and Dataflow Control In Distributed Data-Intensive Systems," *Proc. 1988 ACM SIGMOD Conference on Management of Data*, Chicago, June 1988.

[Alexander et al. 87] Alexander, W., Keller, T., Boughter, E., "A Workload Characterization Pipeline for Models of Parallel Systems," *Proc. 1987 ACM SIGMETRICS Conference on Measurement and Modeling of Computer Systems*, May 1987.

[Anon. et al. 85] Anon. et al., "A Measure of Transaction Processing Power," *Datamation*, Vol. 31, No. 7, April 1, 1985.

[Bhide 88] Bhide, A., "An Analysis of Three Transaction Processing Architectures," *Proc. of the 1988 Conference on Very Large Databases*, Los Angeles, Aug. 1988.

[Boral 88] Boral, H., "Parallelism in Bubba," *Proc. of the International Symposium on Databases in Parallel and Distributed Systems*, Austin, Texas, Dec., 1988.

[Boughter et al. 87] Boughter, E., Alexander, W., Keller, T., "A Tool for Performance-Driven Design of Parallel Systems," *Proc. of the 4th International Conference on Modelling Techniques and Tools for Computer Performance Evaluation*, Palma, Spain, Sept. 1988.

[Copeland et al. 88] Copeland, G., Alexander, W., Boughter, E., Keller, T., "Data Placement in Bubba," *Proc. 1988 ACM SIGMOD Conference on Management of Data*, Chicago, June 1988.

[Danforth et al. 87] Danforth, S., Valduriez, P., Khoshafian, S., "FAD - A Database Programming Language, Rev. 2," MCC Technical Report DB-151-85 (Rev.2), Sept. 1987 (a version has been submitted to ACM TODS).

[DeWitt et al. 86] DeWitt, D.J., Gerber, R., Graefe, G., Heytens, M., Kumar, K., Muralikrishna, M., "GAMMA - A High Performance Dataflow Database Machine," *Proc. of the 1986 Conference on Very Large Databases*, Tokyo, Japan, Aug. 1986.

[DeWitt et al. 87] DeWitt, D.J., Ghandeharizadeh, S., Schneider, D., Jauhari, R., Muralikrishna, M., Sharma, A., "A Single-User Evaluation of the Gamma Database Machine," *Proc. of the 5th Int'l Workshop on Database Machines*, Karuizawa, Japan, Oct. 1987.

[DeWitt et al. 88] DeWitt, D.J., Ghandeharizadeh, S., Schneider, D., "A Performance Analysis of the Gamma Database Machine," *Proc. 1988 ACM SIGMOD Conference on Management of Data*, Chicago, June 1988.

[Gerber 86] Gerber, R.H., "Dataflow Query Processing Using Multiprocessor Hash-Partitioned Algorithms," Ph.D. Thesis, Computer Sciences Technical Report #672, Univ. of Wisconsin-Madison, Oct. 1986.

[Gerber & DeWitt 87] Gerber, R.H., and DeWitt, D.J., "The Impact of Hardware and Software Alternatives on the Performance of the Gamma Database Machine," Computer Sciences Technical Report #708, Univ. of Wisconsin-Madison, July 1987.

[Hart et al. 88] Hart, B., Danforth, S., Valduriez, P., "Parallelizing FAD, A Database Programming Language," *Proc. of the International Symposium on Databases in Parallel and Distributed Systems*, Austin, Texas, Dec., 1988.

[Livny et al. 87] Livny, M., Khoshafian, S., Boral, H., "Multi-Disk Management Algorithms," *Proc. 1987 ACM SIGMETRICS Conference on Measurement and Modeling of Computer Systems*, May 1987.

[Smith 88] Smith, M., "An Experimental Vehicle for Parallel Database Machine Design," MCC Technical Report ACA-ST-076-88, Feb. 1988.

[Smith et al. 88] Smith, M., Alexander, S., Boral, H., Copeland, G., Keller, T., Schwetman, H., Young, C.-R., "An Experiment on Response Time Scalability in Bubba," MCC Technical Report ACA-ST-379-88, Nov. 1988.

[Stonebraker 86] Stonebraker, M., "The Case For Shared Nothing," *Database Engineering*, Vol. 9, No. 1, 1986.

[Tandem 87] The Tandem Database Group, "NonStop SQL, A Distributed, High-Performance, High-Availability Implementation of SQL," *Proc. of 2nd International Workshop on High Performance Transaction Systems*, Asilomar, CA, Sept. 1987.

[Tandem 88] The Tandem Performance Group, "A Benchmark of NonStop SQL on the Debit Credit Transaction," *Proc. 1988 ACM SIGMOD Conference on Management of Data*, Chicago. June 1988.

[Teradata 85] "DBC/1012 Data Base Computer System Manual, Release 1.3," *C10-0001-01, Teradata Corp.*, Los Angeles, Feb. 1985.

[Wilkinson & Boral 87] Wilkinson, K., Boral, H., "KEV-A Kernel for Bubba," *Proc. of the 5th Int'l Workshop on Database Machines*, Karuizawa, Japan, Oct. 1987.

Language Levels and Computational Model for a Parallel Database Accelerator[1]

Björn Bergsten[1], Michel Couprie[2], Rubén González-Rubio[1]*,
Brigitte Kerhervé[3]**, Mikal Ziane[1]

(1) Centre de Recherche Bull, 68 Route de Versailles, 78430 Louveciennes France
(2) ESIEE, 2 Boulevard Blaise Pascal, B.P 99, 93162 Noisy -Le-Grand France
(3) INFOSYS, 15 rue Anatole France, 92800 Puteaux France
(*) *current address* : Université de Sherbrooke, Sherbrooke Québec, Canada, J1K2R1
(**)*current address* : ENST, 46 rue Barrault 75013 Paris France

Abstract

In this paper, we present the language levels and the computational model supported by DDC (Delta Driven Computer). DDC is a parallel system dedicated to process classical and deductive database applications. The original approach of this system comes both from the language levels and the computational model. Our objective was to define languages and a computational model particularly adapted to parallelism. We chose an intermediate language which allows a logical representation of database queries. The computational model favours or-parallelism and pipelined execution of users's programs. It also processes classical relational operations and deductive operations in a uniform way. We present here a general overview of the accelerator and we focus on the language levels and the computational model.

1. Introduction

Nowadays, it is recognized that database systems are important in business applications. The relational model is currently used in many database systems because it provides simple and powerful features. However, it is insufficient to support new applications which are emerging, e.g. Computer Aided Design, Office Automation, and Knowledge Base Systems. Database systems will evolve taking into account two major requirements: efficiency and new functionalities. Some ways to improve efficiency are parallelism, compilation, and I/O reduction. Furthermore new methods and algorithms must be integrated within the systems to support new requirements e.g. deduction, object-oriented systems, and interfaces with programming languages.

---

[1]This research project was developed at BULL research Center and is partially financed by projects 415 and 956 of the European Strategic Program of Research and Development in Information Technology (ESPRIT).

The objective of our project [Gon 87] was to design an efficient database accelerator able to support new applications. We focused on the architecture of this system and on the languages to be supported. We chose a parallel architecture because we think that to improve efficiency of a system, parallelism is a good approach. We were also concerned by the definition of languages. One of them had to allow classical database manipulation but also new types of manipulation as deduction. We chose a language in which database manipulation are transformed into a logical representation. The other language had to be parallel in order to be executed on the parallel architecture of the accelerator.

The proposed hardware architecture consists of two systems: one is a general purpose host computer and the other is *DDC (Delta Driven Computer)*, a parallel system which plays the role of a database accelerator. We use parallelism, compilation and I/O reduction to improve the efficiency of a database system and we propose a language called *VIM* [Pug 85] which is able to handle deduction. Parallelism comes from both: the architecture and the computational model. DDC is a multiprocessor system with distributed memory. Program execution is done following an original computational model called *Delta-Driven* which is parallel. DDC manipulates relations, which are distributed among processors, in a way that each processor can work independently on a part of a relation. Data manipulation in DDC is done through VIM, a production rule language, which is a declarative language where parallelism is *implicit*. By compilation VIM programs are transformed into *DDCL (Delta Driven Computer Language)* programs where parallelism is *explicit.*.

This paper is organized as follows. In section 2, we present an overview of the DDC. In section 3, we present the VIM language and in section 4, its associated computational model. In section 5 we show how we map the computational model onto the architecture. In section 6, we illustrate this mapping by a complete example and we present some performance results obtained on our parallel prototype. In section 7, we conclude.

2. An Overview of the DDC

DDC Delta Driven Computer is a multiprocessor system with distributed memory. The machine executes VIM programs in sequence. A VIM program corresponds to a Database query (see section 3). The execution of a VIM program is done in parallel, following a new computational model called Delta-Driven. A VIM program is compiled into a DDCL program in order to be executed in DDC. DDCL is considered as the assembly language of each node. More details on DDCL can be found in [Ber 88]

The physical architecture of the DDC [Gon 88] machine consists of a set of nodes, linked by an internal communication system, and without shared memory, see figure 1. All the nodes are identical, consisting of a Processor, a Communication device and a Memory: P-C-M triple. This architecture is very simple, it is justified by the performance and the flexibility. We already talked about increasing performance by exploiting parallelism. By flexibility we mean that when it is necessary to augment the throughput or the capacity of the system, it must be done in an easy way, for instance by just adding new nodes into the system. This architecture has also some advantages concerning fiability and availability but these subjects are out of our study scope. There are other database machines based on multiprocessors with distributed memory (also the term shared nothing architecture is used). They are Teradata DBC/1012 [Nec 85], GAMMA [Dew 86], MBDS [Dem 86], Tandem NonStop SQL [Tan 87] and Bubba [Wil 87]. Our approach differs from these approaches in the use of a computational model to process all kind of relational operations. In general, specific algorithms are dedicated to process each relational operation.

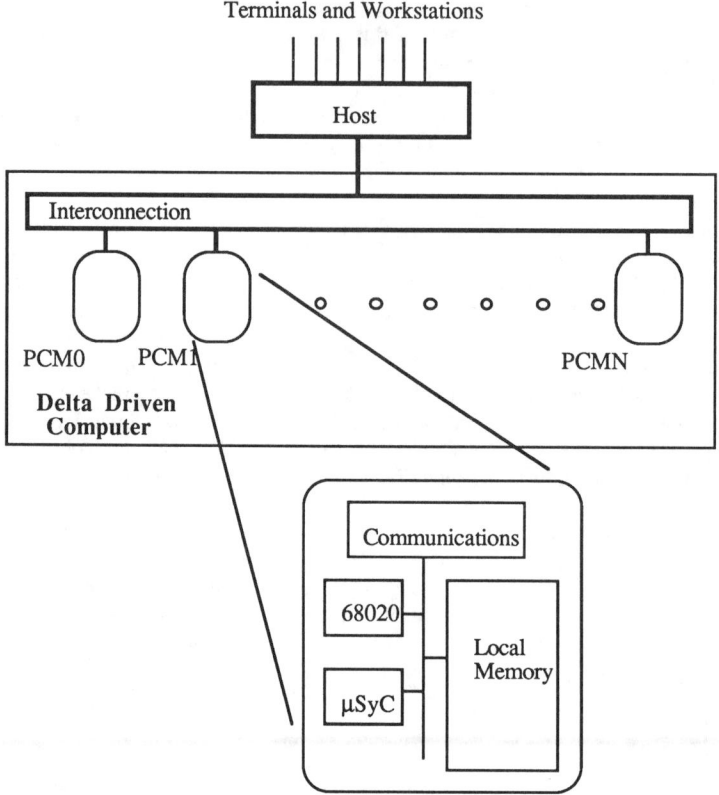

Figure 1. DDC Physical Architecture.

In every node of DDC, the 68020 processor will be helped by the coprocessor μSyC (microprogrammable Symbolic Coprocessor). It is a coprocessor dedicated to symbolic treatments in Database context and in Artificial Intelligence. μSyC is microprogrammable because we want to have an adaptable instruction set, which corresponds to DDCL. Its role is to assist the central processor to which it is connected, in executing specific operations faster than the central processor. The advantages of the association central processor, coprocessor are numerous : improvement of the performance, system modularity and parallelism. To these advantages μSyC combines the microprogrammation which gives the possibility to define new instructions for specific applications.

The functionalities of DDC are divided into two main layers: the language layer and the execution layer, see figure 2. The language layer provides user with interfaces and language compilation. Two languages are defined: VIM and DDCL. The execution layer is in charge of executing DDCL programs. It manages the local memory of each node, the internal representation of the relations and the communication process. It also controls the distributed termination of saturations. The execution layer stays in a receive-produce-send cycle until no more new facts are produced.

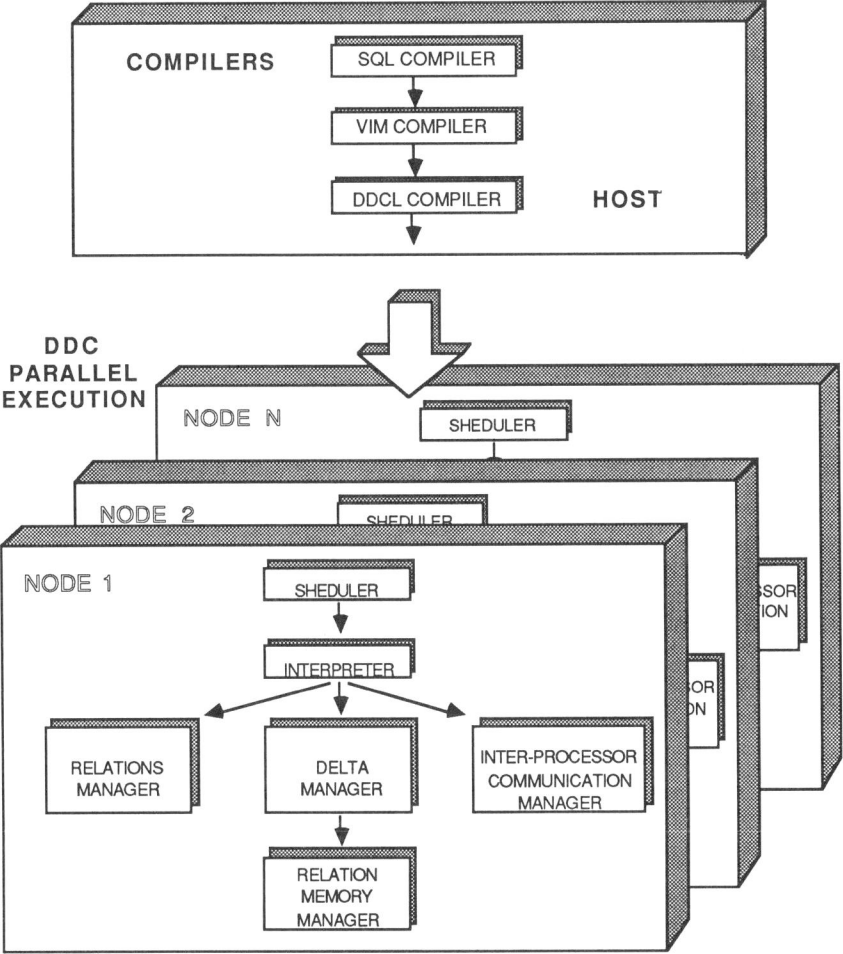

Figure 2 : DDC Functional Architecture.

Each node in DDC executes DDCL programs on data stored in its local memory. In order to efficiency execute these programs, we focus on the internal representation of the relations and on the algorithms for the DDCL primitives. In [Cou89] we studied several representations for the relations : compacted automata, B-trees or sorted indexes. For each of them we defined the corresponding algorithms which implement the DDCL primitives. The representation with compacted automata offers good performance and we are currently working on extending this representation to all types of data. Nevertheless it seems necessary to offer several internal representations. This choice could be made by the compilers according to the manipulations on the data.

3. The Intermediate Language

In the functionnal architecture of DDC, we distinguished the language layer from the execution layer. In this section we are concerned with the language layer which contains the compilers for the languages supported by DDC. At the highest level we offer a SQL interface for classical manipulations of databases. A SQL command is compiled into a VIM program. During this phase of compilation several optimizations can be processed. In the present prototype the SQL to VIM compiler treates the subset of SQL which concerns the searching commands. This compiler shows us that this intermediate language is a good approach for database queries representation. As VIM is a production rule language, it allows to represent also deductive queries which are not supported by SQL. In this section we describe VIM and we show that we can easily express database queries.

VIM is a production rule language and a VIM rule must have one of the following forms:

$p => r_1, r_2, ... , r_n.$
$p, q => r_1, r_2, ... , r_n.$
$p, \text{not } q => r_1, r_2, ... , r_n.$

Where p, q and r_i are predicates. A predicate has the form:

$p(X_1, X_2 ... , X_n)$

Where X_i are variables or constants. In a VIM rule functional terms are not allowed. Predicates p and q are called hypotheses while predicates r_i are called conclusions. Variables occurring in conclusions are always instantiated in hypotheses. Variables are local to a rule and are similar to variables in logic programming. Note that in a rule, it is mandatory to have one or two hypotheses and there is at least one conclusion.

The semantic of a VIM rule is:"if all hypotheses are true, then produce (=>) in the database all conclusions". A hypothesis is true if it matches a fact in the database. Producing a conclusion means to add a new fact into the database. A fact corresponds to a tuple in a relation, producing a conclusion means to insert a new tuple into the corresponding relation.

A VIM program is a set of VIM rules which produces by saturation all possible facts from the facts in the database and rules. The result of a program is a set of deduced facts. The introduction of negative hypothesis, interpreted as "if this hypothesis is not confirmed" (negation by absence) causes problems in non-monotonic aspects of general programs. We accept only a class of programs, called *stratified programs* [Apt 86],where recursion "through" negation is disallowed. Stratified programs can be divided into a sequence of strata to be executed. That means that all negative hypothesis should always be produced in a precedent stratum. A VIM program is then divided into strata. Rules in a stratum are commutative, monotonic and can be executed in parallel.

VIM is relationally complete according to Codd [Cod 72] because it can express the five basic relational operations :

- Projection: "project p over attribute X".

    $p(X,Y) => r(X).$

- Selection: "select all tuples in p such that the second attribute is equal to "c" ".

    $p(X,"c") => r(X,"c").$

- Cartesian product: "Cartesian product of p and q".

    p(X),q(Y) => r(X,Y).

- Difference: "p minus q".

    p(X), not q(X) => r(X).

- Union: "p union q".

    p(X) => r(X).
    q(X) => r(X).

As VIM can also express recursion, DDC can support deductive applications which are not supported by classical database systems.

Two examples are shown below to illustrate the expressive power of VIM. The first example is a rather complex relational query, whereas the second is a deduction example.

Relational query. Suppose we have two relations *read(reader, book)* and *list(book)*. We want to find all the readers who have read at least all the books given in the relation *list*, this operation is called a relational division.

In VIM, we write:

    read(X,_), list(Y) => temp(X,Y).
    temp(X,Y), not read(X,Y) => no_good(X).
    read(X,_), not no_good(X) => solution(X).

In first rule *temp(X,Y)* corresponds to a cartesian product which contains all readers *read(X,_)* related with all books in *list(Y)*. In second rule *no_good* corresponds to tuples that are on *temp(X,Y)* but not in *read(X,Y)*. In third rule *solution(X)* corresponds to tuples that are on *read(X,_)* but not in *no_good(X)*. *solution(X)* corresponds to solutions of the query. As we will explain later, this program must be stratified because of the negation in the hypothesis.

The division example expressed in SQL is as follows.

```
select distinct reader
from read r1
where not exists
    (    select *
        from list
        where not exists
        (    select *
            from read
            where reader = r1.reader
            and book = list.book ))
```

This query could be paraphrased as: Retrieve (with elimination of duplicate) all readers from relation read {...*select distinct reader from read r1*...} such as there does not exist {...*where not exits*...} any book from relation list {...*(select * from list*...} they haven't read {...*where not exists (select * from read where reader = r1.reader and book = list.book))*}.

Deduction. We have the relation *parent(father-name, child-name)* and we want to compute all descendants of people given in relation *descendant_of(name)*. In VIM we have:

descendant_of(X), parent(X,Y) => descendant_of(Y), solution(Y).

This rule means that if we want to compute all descendants of X and if X is parent of Y, then the solution is Y and all the descendants of Y, and so on. This query could not be expressed in SQL.

4. The Computational Model

The Delta-Driven computational model is the model according to which the saturation of a VIM program is executed. For a VIM program, saturation means the production of all possible conclusions by applying rules on data until no more new data are produced.

To execute a saturation we consider that rules consume and produce streams of tuples. A tuple produced or consumed by a rule is called a *Delta*. If a Delta does not exist in the database, we call it *WhiteDelta* otherwise we call it *BlackDelta*. BlackDeltas are dropped while WhiteDeltas are used to fire all the rules using them. This elimination of duplicates is part of the computational model and ensures against useless computation and guaranties termination. Saturation ends when no more WhiteDelta is produced. As the computation is driven by Delta streams we say that the model is Delta-Driven.

Executing a Rule. Following the computational model, it is possible to execute any type of VIM rule. This execution must be optmized by the VIM to DDCL compiler in order to avoid useless computation and useless communication. We detail here the execution model for each kind of VIM rules. Before studying the three forms of VIM rules, let us introduce some terminology. As we have said before, a VIM program is decomposed into strata, each of them containing one or several rules. The rules of a stratum are applied to process a saturation The execution of a rule depends on the state of the relations in the stratum: a relation could be empty or not before the corresponding saturation; it could be produced or not by this saturation. We call *basic relation* a relation which is not empty before the saturation. We call *deduced relation* a relation which is produced during the saturation. Some relations could be both *basic and deduced*. In all cases we distinguish the *basic part* of the relation (the one produced before the saturation processed in this stratum) and the *deduced part* (the one produced in the stratum we are considering). During the saturation, the deduced part of a relation p is the WhiteDeltas-p stream issued from VIM rules.

To simplify notation, we consider only VIM rules with a single conclusion.

Rule "p => r."

This rule is either a selection or a projection. If we consider that all tuples of p have to be tested by the selection criterion, then the idea is to apply the selection criterion on each tuple of the WhiteDelta stream. In order to process the selection or the projection, the basic part of p is transformed into a stream of WhiteDelta-p. In general, a projection produces duplicates (unless projection on key), in that case we eliminate duplicates on the BlackDelta-r stream.

Rule "p, not q => r."

As we mentionned before, we just consider stratified programs and thus we suppose here that q has been completely deduced in a previous stratum.

This means that q could not be deduced in the rule we consider. The general execution mechanism of this rule is very close to the first studied rule's one. We divide relation p into its basic part (basic-p) and its deduced part (the stream of WhiteDelta-p). Each tuple of this stream will be searched in q: if it is not found, then a BlackDelta-r is produced, otherwise not.

Rule "p, q => r."

This rule is either a cartesian product or a join (if p and q share a common variable). In this operation, each tuple of p which has a chance to join with a tuple of q must meet it only once. When this happens, a tuple r is sent in the BlackDelta-r stream. The problem with such a rule is to avoid that two tuples from p and q join twice. We can show that two tuples P and Q from relations p and q couldn't be joined twice if and only if the two couples of events (<store P in p>, <join P with q>) and (<store Q in q>, <join Q with p>) are mutually indivisible. By mutually indivisible, we mean that one of the two couples must be completely executed before the other. As a matter of fact, if these two couples are divisible, when P is produced and stored in p, it can be thus consumed both by <join Q with p> and by <join P with q>. In order to examine the indivisibility of these events, we consider all the combinations of the status of relations p and q. For each combination we give the execution strategy we adopt. Following combinations are examined:

case	p	q
1	B	B
2	B	D
3	B	B+D
4	D	D
5	D	B+D
6	B+D	B+D

where B stands for basic; D for deduced; B+D for basic and deduced.

We don't study the combinations ((D,B), (B+D,B) and (B+D,D)) because considering the commutativity of the rules, they are equivalent to cases 2, 3 and 5.

- Cases 1, 2 and 3: p is basic. In that case we transform the eventual basic part of q into WhiteDelta-q, this stream will be joined with p. As a rule consumes only one stream of delta, we need to store one of the two relations (here p) to be able to process the cartesian product or the join operation. The couples of events (<store P in p>, <join P with q>) and (<store Q in q>, <join Q with p>) are simplified into (<store P in p>) and (<join Q with p>) which, are of course, mutually indivisible.

In the other cases (4, 5, 6), both p and q are, at least, deduced. This means that we are obliged to store completely both relations: each produced tuple P will be joined with stored-q (union of the basic-q and the current computed deduced-q), and vice-versa for each produced tuple Q. As it is expensive to store relations, whenever it is possible (linear recursion), the compiler tries to produce first either p or q, and then compute the rule in an other stratum These rules comes therefore to one of the 3 first cases since at least one of the relations is basic.

- Cases 4 and 5: p is deduced, while q is deduced and possibly basic. This means that before the saturation, relation p is empty. We can thus consider that (<store Q in q>, <join Q with p>) are indivisible for all tuples Q of basic-q. All deduced tuples P will fire the two events (<store P in p>, <join P with q>), and vice-versa for the tuples Q of relation q. If we can't ensure that these two couples of events are mutually indivisible, then we disallowed this combination of the status of the relations.

- Case 6: p and q are both deduced and basic. To fall into the first three cases, we compute first the join between basic-p and basic-q. To do that, we can, for example, transform basic-p into a stream of WhiteDelta-p. Each tuple P of relation p of this stream will be joined with the relation q (which is still equal to basic-q). Again, it is essential to do this join before any tuple Q is produced. After that, we have the same constraints as in cases 4 and 5.

5. Mapping the Computational Model onto the Architecture

In this section, we show how the execution model is mapped onto DDC. This mapping depends essentially on how relations are distributed over the nodes. Thus we present first some strategies to distribute relations and we justify our choice. Then we present briefly the DDCL language.

Different mapping strategies. In the execution model, we defined implicitly two kinds of objects: actions and relations. An action is a sequence of code which consumes a stream of deltas, and can produce streams of deltas. Actions share relations which can grow or remain constant during a saturation.

We define a *wide execution* scheme as a program with a large number (say 10) of basic relations. We define a *deep execution* scheme as a program with a lot (say 5) of intermediate relations. To speed up wide execution scheme programs we need efficient or-parallelism. By efficient or-parallelism, we mean that the operations on all the basic relations must be executed in parallel whenever it is possible. To speed up deep execution scheme programs we need and-parallelism. That means that operations on relations must be pipelined as much as possible.

Two ways to parallelize our execution model are:

- to store each relation on a single node. This solution obtains good parallelism in some particular applications where the execution scheme is both deep and wide and when relations are small. Wide, because two (or more) different relational operations could be executed independently in parallel. Deep, because some relational operations could be pipelined executed. And finally, relations should be small because of the large amount of communication. These conditions are satisfied on programs with a lot of rules (deep execution scheme) and a lot of small relations (wide execution scheme). Applications of this type are some implementation of OPS5-like systems [Gup 84].

- to partition relations into buckets, one bucket per node. In this solution, we obtain good or-parallelism on the relational operation level. For example, a join operation is executed in all nodes in parallel while the first solution executes it on a single node. Bucket partitioning is used in other parallel database machines, as for exemple in GAMMA [Dew 86].

We can imagine a mixed solution where some relations are distributed over all nodes, while some others are stored completely on a single node. More generally, relations could be distributed on a certain number of nodes. This method is used in some database machines with a large number of nodes more than 100, as for exemple the MCC machine [Val 88].

The DDC strategy. In DDC, we have chosen the solution to partition relations into buckets, one bucket per node. First, because DDC is a Database accelerator and should be able to execute queries on large relations (need of efficient parallelization of relational operations). Second, DDC will not have more than 20 nodes, and we think that it is more efficient to distribute all relations over all nodes as we do, rather than distributing some relations over a subset of nodes, because the optimization techniques become difficult and therefore expensive in time.

Our approach is similar to this of GAMMA [Dew 86] in the sense that we also favour or-parallelism in executing the same operation in parallel on the buckets of the relation. Our approach is different since we also try to execute operations in pipe as much as possible. The parallel execution is based on the data distribution.

We distribute all relations by applying a hash function *h* on the first attribute. For example, relation p(X,Y) is distributed on the value of its attribute X. This means that p is partitioned into p0, p1, ... pn-1 (DDC has n nodes) such that pi contains all tuples <X,Y> where h(X)=i. Let p(X,Y) be a relation. If we want to distribute it on attribute Y (and not X), then we create a copy p-copy such that p-copy(Y,X) = p(X,Y).

With this data distribution, all rules presented in section 4 may be processed. An exception is the cartesian product where both relations are deduced.

6. A complete example

The following example shows how a complete VIM program is compiled into a DDCL program which will be executed in parallel by DDC. It illustrates the stratification, and various optimizations on the code. We here give the different optimizations applied to the DDCL program which lead us to a very compact code where the pipelined execution reduces the execution costs.
We consider again the relational division example:

    read(X,_), list(Y) => temp(X,Y).
    temp(X,Y), not read(X,Y) => no_good(X).
    read(X,_), not no_good(X) => solution(X).

Compilation

We suppose that *read* and *list* relations are loaded in DDC before the execution, then two strata are needed to execute this program: the first stratum contains the two first rules while the second stratum contains the last rule.

As we consider that both *read* and *list* are basic relations, in the first rule which is a cartesian product (p,q =>r), we fall in the case 1 we have studied before. So the compiler decides to transform the relation *list* into a stream of WhiteDelta-list by the following action:

    action regenerate-list():
        with select (list,<Y>) *map*
            message (ALL,WhiteDelta-list,<Y>)
        endmap
    endaction

The WhiteDelta-list stream is broadcasted to all nodes such as each tuple of this stream will encounter each tuple of relation *read* in the action WhiteDelat-list:

    action WhiteDelta-list(<Y>):
        with select (read,<X>) *map*
            message (NODE,BlackDelta-temp,<X,Y>)
        endmap
    endaction

The action BlackDelta-temp eliminates duplicates of the cartesian product, that means that it transforms the BlackDelta-temp stream into a WhiteDelta-temp stream:

```
action BlackDelta-temp(<X,Y>):
    if new_add (temp,<X,Y>) then
        message (NODE,WhiteDelta-temp,<X,Y>)
    endif
endaction
```

The WhiteDelta-temp are searched in the basic-read relation in order to generate the *no_good* relation (second rule):

```
action WhiteDelta-temp(<X,Y>):
    if not search (read,<X,Y>) then
        message (NODE,BlackDelta-no_good,<X>)
    endif
endaction
```

The last action of the first saturation eliminates duplicates of the relation *no_good*:

```
action BlackDelta-no_good(<X>):
    new_add (no_good,<X>)
endaction
```

To fire the second saturation, we regenerate the relation *read* by the following action,

```
action regenerate-read(X):
    with select (read,<X>) map
        message (NODE,WhiteDelta-read,<X>)
    endmap
endaction
```

Each tuple of the WhiteDelta-read stream is searched in the no_good relation. If it does not appear in no_good then it is a solution:

```
action WhiteDelta-read(<X>):
    if not search (no_good,<X>) then
        message (NODE,BlackDelta-solution,<X>)
    endif
endaction
```

The last action eliminates the duplicates of the solution:

```
action BlackDelta-solution(<X>):
    if new_add (solution,<X>) then
        message (HOST,solution,<X>)
    endif
endaction
```

<u>first optimization</u>: in some operations it is not necessary to eliminate duplicates, thus the relation is not stored in memory.

The action BlackDelta-temp becomes:

>   *action* BlackDelta-temp(<X,Y>):
>   *message* (NODE,WhiteDelta-temp,<X,Y>)
>   *endaction*

The action BlackDelta-solution becomes:

>   *action* BlackDelta-solution(<X>):
>   *message* (HOST,solution,<X>)
>   *endaction*

second optimization: every time a stream of BlackDeltas or WhiteDeltas is sent to the current node (message with option NODE such that the hash function gives always the current node), the primitive message is replaced by the code of the action which should consume the message.

In the DDCL code of the division, we can apply this second optimization several times:

- the action BlackDelta-no_good is executed in the action WhiteDelta-temp;
- the action WhiteDelta-temp is executed in the action BlackDelta-temp;
- the action BlackDelta-temp is executed in the action WhiteDelta-list;
- the action BlackDelta-solution is executed in the action WhiteDelta-read;
- the action WhiteDelta-read is executed in the action regenerate-read.

The DDCL code becomes:

first saturation:

>   *action* regenerate-list():
>   *with* select (list,<Y>) *map*
>   *message* (ALL,WhiteDelta-list,<Y>)
>   *endmap*
>   *endaction*
>
>   *action* WhiteDelta-list(<Y>):
>   *with* select (read,<X>) *map*
>   *if not* search (read,<X,Y>) *then*
>   new_add (no_good,<X>)
>   *endif*
>   *endmap*
>   *endaction*

second saturation

>   *action* regenerate-read(X):
>   *with* select (read,<X>) *map*
>   *if not* search (no_good,<X>) *then*
>   *message* (HOST,solution,<X>)
>   *endif*
>   *endmap*
>   *endaction*

These two steps of optimization give us a very short code where operations are pipelined as much as possible.

Exhibition of the parallelism. The first DDC prototype has been developed on a BULL SPS7, a multi-processor machine using a multi-processor configuration of UNIX. At the present time, a four processors configuration is used and we work with the UNIX communication tools for interprocessor communication. Each PCM node is simulated by a UNIX process locked on a physical processor.

Up to now, to simplify our presentation, we considered that the relations read and list were loaded in the local memory of the nodes. In these measures we are also interested in the work of the host which is in charge of input output primitives. Thus in this example two new rules are added to manage the relation loading in the nodes and the treatment of the results. The program becomes:

> input "read_file"(X,Y) => read(X,Y)
> -----
> input "list_file"(Y) => list(Y)
> read(X,_), list(Y) => temp(X,Y).
> temp(X,Y), not read(X,Y) => no_good(X).
> -----
> read(X,_), not no_good(X) => output "solution-file" solution(X).

The different strata are delimited by "-----". The first two rules load the relation *read* and *list* in the memory of the nodes while the last rule writes the solution in the file *"solution-file"*
We study the activity of the nodes of DDC during the execution of the division program for 1000 tuples. The first figure shows the activity of two nodes and the host while the second one shows the activity of four nodes and the host. The different strata appear in the figure. The first stratum is the one during which the host sends tuples from the relation *read* to all the other nodes. In the second stratum, the host sends the *list* relation while the nodes execute the rules 3 and 4. During the third stratum, the nodes calculate the solution and send it to the host which writes them in the solution file.

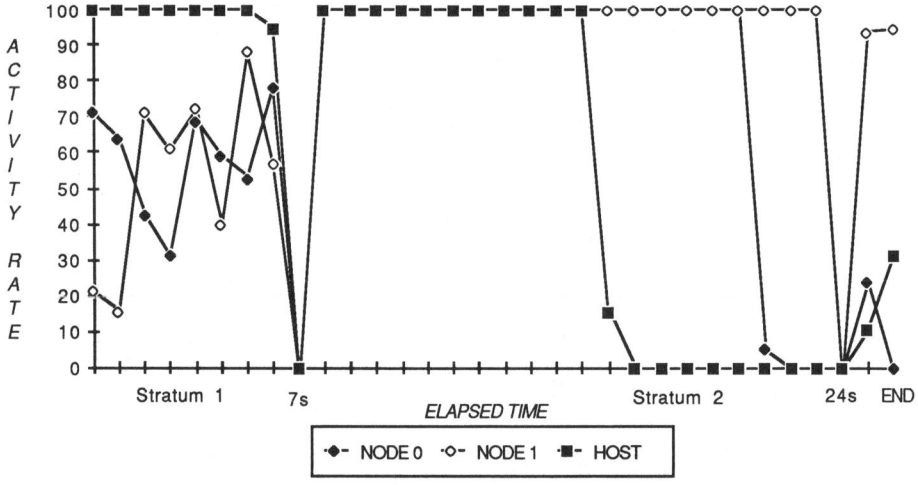

Figure 3 a. DDC Nodes Activity, 2 PCMs and the Host.

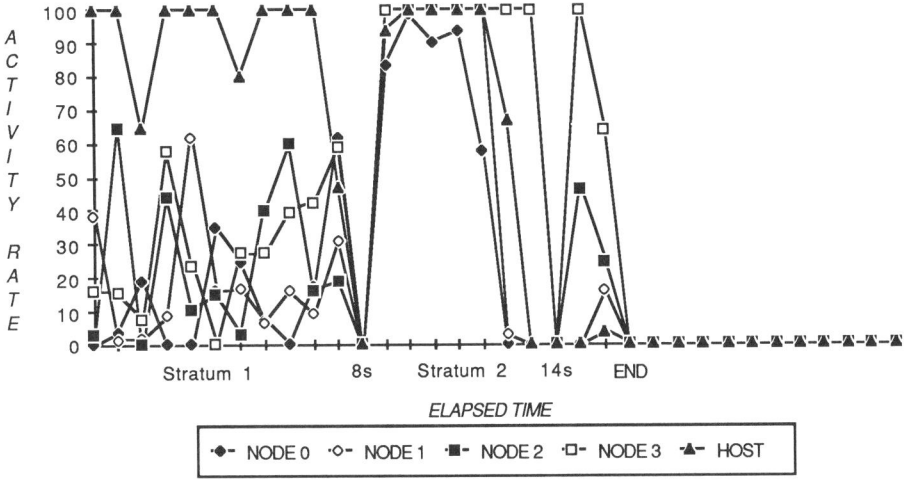

Figure 3 b. DDC Nodes Activity, 4 PCMs and the Host.

Stratum 1: (0-7s in fig.3a; 0-8s in fig.3b)
In both cases the activity rate of the host is about 100% since it sends tuples from the *read* file to the other nodes. In the figure 3a the two nodes are working at 50% while in the figure 3b they work at 50%. This fact is due to the data distribution which is made according to the number of nodes. In the first case a node receives around 50% of the relation while in the other case it receives only around 25% of the relation.

Stratum 2: (7-24s in fig.3a; 8-14s in fig.3b)
With 2 nodes, the execution time is 17seconds, while it is only 6 seconds with 4 nodes. This amazing speed-up cannot be explained only by the parallelism, but also by the hash join technique which is implicitely used in the computational model.

Stratum 3: (24-26s in fig.3a; 14-17s in fig.3b)
This stratum, which produces the solution, is very short and the nodes and the host are working at about 20%.

7. Conclusion

In this paper, we have presented DDC a parallel database accelerator. This accelerator is dedicated to process classical and deductive databases applications. Its physical architecture consists of a set of nodes, linked by an internal communication system and without shared memory. Its functionnal architecture is divided into two main layers : the language layer and the execution layer. The key of our approach is the set of different languages levels we have defined. Our intermediate language called VIM can suport logical languages and database languages. This language is a production rule language which is compiled into DDCL the assembly language of our machine. In DDCL is expressed the Delta Driven computational model. This computational model allows us to process saturations on data flows, and thus to execute classical relational operations as well as deductive operations.

References

[Apt 86]   Apt K., Blair H., Walker A.: "Towards a Theory of Declarative Knowledge". Proc. Workshop on Foundations of Deductive Databases and Logic Programming, Washington D.C., pp 546-629, 1988.

[Ber 88]   Bergsten B., Gonzalez-Rubio R., Kerhervé B., Rohmer J.: "An advanced Database Accelerator". IEEE Micro October 1988.

[Cod 72]   Codd E. C.: "Relational Completeness of Database Sublanguages". Database Systems, Computer Sciences Symposia. Vol 6. Englewood Cliffs. N. J. Prentice-Hall 1972.

[Cou 88]   Couprie M., Bergsten B., Gonzalez-Rubio R. "Languages and Algorithms for a Memory-based Parallel Relational Engine". Internal report CRG Bull 1988.

[Dem 86]   Demurjian S., Hisiao D., Menon J.: "A Multi-Backend Database System for Performance Gains, Capacity Growth and Harware Upgrade". Int. Conf. on Data Engieering. Los Angeles. February. 1986.

[Dew 86]   DeWitt D.J., Gerber R.H., Graefe G., Heytens M. L., Kumar K. B., Muralikrishna M.: "GAMMA - A High Performance Dataflow Database Machine". VLDB. Kyoto. August 1986.

[Gon 87]   Gonzalez-Rubio R., Bradier A., Rohmer J.: "An overview of DDC: Delta Driven Computer". PARLE Conference. Eindhoven, 1987. (also: rapport de recherche Bull DSG/CRG/86017).

[Gon 88]   Gonzalez-Rubio R., Couprie M.: "DDC: Delta Driven Computer and μSyC: Microprogrammable Symbolic Coprocessor". EUROMICRO 88. Zurich. September 1988.

[Gup 84]   Gupta A.: "Implementing OPS5 Production Systems on DADO" Report CMU-CS-84-115. 1985.

[Nec 85]   Neches P. M.: "The Anatomy of a Data Base Computer System". COMPCON. San Francisco. February. 1985.

[Pug 85]   Pugin J. M.: "BOUM: An Instantiation of the (PS)2 Concept". 5èmes Journeées Internationales Systèmes Experts. Avignon. 1985.

[Tan 87]   Tandem Database Group.: "NonStop SQL, a Distributed High-Performance, High Availability Implementation of SQL". Int Workshop on High Performance Transaction Systems. Asilomar. September. 1987.

[Val 88] Valduriez P. "Parallel Recursive Query Processing in a Share Nothing Server" Quatrièmes journées bases de données avancées, Benodet. March 1988.

[Wil 87]   Wilkinson K., Boral H.: "KEV: the Operating System Kernel of Bubba". Int Workshop on Database Machines. Karuizawa. October. 1987.

A GRAPH BASED DATA STRUCTURE FOR EFFICIENT IMPLEMENTATION OF MAIN MEMORY DBMS's

Philippe PUCHERAL[*], Jean-Marc THEVENIN[**]

[*]Laboratoire MASI, Université Paris 6
4, place Jussieu, 75005 Paris, France

[**]INRIA France
BP. 105, 78153 Le Chesnay, France
Network address theven@madonna.inria.fr

Abstract

Considering that in future DBMS's it will be possible to hold the active database in main memory, a new physical database organization is proposed. This organization aims two objectives: be compact and decomposable such as the active database always fits in main memory and speed up extended relational algebra in term of CPU time. Tuples and indices are integrated in a unique data structure called DBGraph. Tuples and values are stored separately and constitute the vertices of the DBGraph. Edges between tuples and values are maintained using OID's in order to constitute a bipartite graph. This graph precompiles selection, join and transitive closure operations. Set oriented execution of relational algebra is generated using a breadth first traversal of this graph while pipeline execution is produced using a depth first traversal. The two strategies lead to the same temporal complexity. Storage cost evaluations demonstrate the compactness of the DBGraph structure. Performance evaluations show that in a main memory context transitive closure on DBGraph outperforms transitive closure on join indices, still considered as one of the best algorithm.

I INTRODUCTION

Upon the last years, technological progress raised up the idea that future DBMS's would have very large main memories. Therefore, the hypothesis that the complete database or the active database fit in main memory, becomes more realistic. The active database is defined as the subset of the database accessed by the current set of queries. This assumption has two main consequences on DBMS's design. First, transaction management must be redefined. Crash recovery when the primary copy of the database resides in main memory, constitutes the principal field of investigation in this area [DeWi84, Garc84, Eich87, Lehm87]. Secondly, the bottleneck of the system is no more the I/O but

---

This work has been supported by the ISIDE Esprit Project n°1133

the CPU time required to perform an operation. Then, physical database organization and query evaluation must be reconsidered to take advantage of this context [DeWi84, Amma85, Lehm86b, Naka87].

This paper focuses on physical database organization for efficient implementation of a Main Memory DBMS (MMDBS). The main objective is to speed up software execution of relational operations when the active database fits in main memory. In this context, data structures which precompile relational operations providing direct access to tuples in memory are well adapted. Indeed, inverted data structures are no more limited by I/O. The second objective is to ensure compactness of data structures and efficient space utilization. It is a critical issue to ensure that the active database and all necessary indices fit in main memory.

Recent studies for MMDBS have been concentrated on efficient space utilization. Classical index structures have been reconsidered in this way. Although it is shown in [DeWi84] that AVL-Tree run faster that B-Tree in a main memory context, B-Tree will be prefered considering their compactness. The T-Tree index structure, merging the advantages of B-tree and AVL-Tree, was introduced in [Lehm86a]. A more radical approach [Amma85] uses as indices, arrays of tuple identifiers (TID's) pointing to tuples containing the indexed values. These arrays are simply sorted on the pointed values. Such a compaction allows to index each attribute of a relation. Some work was also dedicated to reduce the space occupancy of temporary results in order to save main memory for permanent data [Amma85, Bitt86, Lehm86b]. Finally, vertical partitionning [Hamm79] is well suited to fetch in memory only the relevant data for a given query.

Several kinds of indices can be added to a classical database organization to precompile relational operations. Inverted indices are widely used to perform selection. A generalized access path structure introduced in [Haer78] uses multi-relation indices which associate for each value one TID list per linked relation. Such indices are interesting for they can be used as well for selections as for precompiling joins. Specialized indices, called join indices, have been proposed in [Vald87] to prejoin relations. A join index materializes links between two relations with a table of two columns containing TID's linking tuples matching together. It was demonstrated that join indices lead to very efficient execution of join and transitive closure operations. These proposals satisfy the performance requirements of a MMDBS. Nevertheless, such indices suffer from the fact they are defined apart from the database architecture and then introduce extra storage and update costs. Furthermore, their use on temporary results is not obvious.

In order to get compact precompiling structures, some approaches integrate indices in the database storage architecture. These approaches store domain values apart from relations such that any domain value is stored only once [Miss82, Amma85]. In [Miss82], relations are not directly stored for they can be materialized through multi-relation domain indices. This organization favors join on basic relations but projection and operations on temporary results become critical. In [Amm85], relations and indices contain only pointers to domain values. Such approaches are well suited for MMDBS as they allow to store links between tuples and values in a very compact way with a reduced extra cost of update. Nevertheless query evaluation seems less efficient than with join indices since some links are not directly represented.

In this paper we propose an integrated database storage organization to precompile extended relational algebra in a compact way. This architecture is based on a bipartite graph data structure called DBGraph. The whole database is stored as a DBGraph. This DBGraph contains a set of tuple vertices, a set of value vertices and edges connecting these two sets. Tuples are connected by one edge to each of their attribute values instead of containing directly these values. Domain values are also connected by one edge to each tuple referencing them for one of its attributes. Temporary results are linked to the tuples of basic relations from which they are extracted using temporary edges. Thus, they can be mapped onto the DBGraph in a uniform and compact way.

Selection, join on basic or temporary relations and transitive closure are speed up in a similar way by a simple traversal of this DBGraph. Selections are performed using edges between values and tuples. Links between tuples matching together for a Join R⊗S are established using edges linking tuples of R to values then edges linking values to tuples of S. Finally, the transitive closure of a relation is equivalent to the transitive closure of a sub-part of the DBGraph. As temporary results are linked to tuples of basic relations, they determine a set of entry vertices in the DBGraph which can be exploited by any operator. Depending on the graph traversal strategy applied on the DBGraph, a set oriented or a pipeline evaluation of a query can be produced. Pipeline evaluation suppress the need of temporary results. Finally, a DBGraph presents as good properties in term of storage cost as in term of performances. Their compactness is mainly due to the fact that any value is stored only once and that the same edges are used to precompile all operations. Furthermore, it is possible to partition the DBGraph in order to fetch in memory only the subpart of the DBGraph relevant for a query.

The main features of a DBGraph can be summarized as follows: (i) it is compact and decomposable, (ii) precompiles the queries expressed in extended relational algebra, (iii) preserves its properties with temporary results and (iv) the queries can be evaluated in a set oriented or a pipeline way with a same level of performances.

The remainder of the paper is organized as follows. The DBGraph notion is formally introduced in section II. Then, two ways to perform extended relational queries on a DBGraph are studied in section III. An efficient and compact implementation of a DBGraph is proposed in section IV. A storage cost evaluation compares this implementation of a DBGraph versus a Flat File organization in the same section. Finally, performances of a query execution are evaluated in section V. Summary and future works are given in section VI.

II MAPPING DATABASE INTO DBGRAPH

The introduction of a graph formalism, to define the proposed physical database organization, offers numerous advantages. First, all relational operators can be expressed in a simple and uniform way by a combination of basic graph traversal primitives, independently of the physical DBGraph implementation. It ensures a clean description of all algorithms and a high modularity of the corresponding code. Moreover, SQL queries can be directly compiled into DBGraph traversal primitives following various strategies. For instance, set oriented or pipeline execution of a same query can be produced using two different well known graph traversal algorithms (respectively breadth first search and depth first search). The graph theory results allow to compare the temporal complexity of both strategies. Finally, recursive processes such as the transitive closure operation can be expressed on a graph in a very natural way. Graph theory principles ensure the correct termination of such processes.

In this section, the DBGraph concept is primarily defined. Then, we show how selection and join operators can be expressed on a DBGraph.

II.1 DBGraph definition

For the sake of clarity, we introduce notations for entities manipulated in the sequel of the paper. A database DB is defined as a set of relations denoted R and S (only two relations will be useful in the following) and a set of value domains denoted Dj. The schema of a relation is an aggregation of attributes where r.k denotes the kth attribute of the relation R and $t_{r.k}$ denotes the value of this attribute for the tuple t. We note T the set of all tuples of a database DB and V the set of all domain values of a database DB. Finally, Tr (resp. Ts) denotes the subset of T vertices holding the tuples of relation R (resp. S).

We can define an isomorphism between a database DB and a graph, called DBGraph. A DBGraph is a bipartite graph containing a set of tuple vertices, a set of value vertices and valued edges connecting these two sets, as detailled figure 1. The set of tuple vertices holds all the tuples of DB and the set of value vertices holds all the domain values of DB. Each edge (t, v, r.k) of the DBGraph is an indirected valued edge connecting a tuple vertex t to a value vertex v. The valuation r.k of this edge specifies that the tuple t belongs to the relation R, that the value of the kth attribute of t is v and consequently that the domain of v is the domain of the attribute r.k. Then a tuple vertex is linked by an edge to each of its attribute value and a value vertex is linked by an edge to each tuple which references it for one of its attributes. The notion of DBGraph can be more formally defined as follows:

Definition: DBGraph

The DBGraph of a database DB is a valued bipartite graph G(X,A) where X=(T,V) is the set of vertices of G, A is the set of edges of G and the edge $(t, v, r.k) \in A$ iff $t \in T$, $v \in V$ and $t_{r.k} = v$.

Properties: A DBGraph is bipartite since T and V form a partition of X and there is not any edge connecting two vertices of T or two vertices of V. Then, each traversal of the DBGraph gives an alternance of tuples and values. Each couple of tuples, of the same or of different relations, having the same value for one of their attribute are connected by a path of length two. Finally, the relations form a partition of T and the value domains Dj form a partition of V.

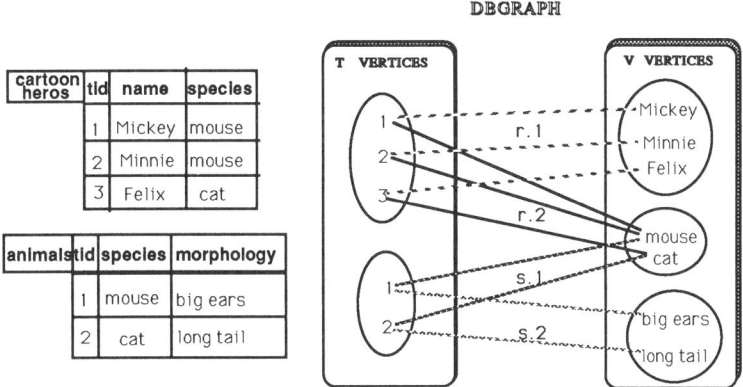

For the sake of clarity, tuples are identified by a TID and the relation Cartoon_Heros (resp. Animals) is denoted by R (resp. S) to standardize valuations of edges.

Figure 1: instance of a DBGraph

II.2 Querying a DBGraph

In the sequel, we consider all queries expressed on a database DB by a composition of the Select operator σ_Q (where Q denotes the selection qualification), the Project operator π_P (where P denotes the attribute list of projection) and the equi-Join operator $\otimes_M$ (where M denotes the equi-join predicate), defined in the usual way. Queries involving transitive closure operator are treated in a separate section since transitive closure appears as a special combination of the other relational operators. Aggregate functions and inequi-join operations are not discussed as DBGraph does not provide any optimization of these functions. The select and join operators can be expressed on a DBGraph as follows:

• *select operator:*

The select operator σ_Q applied on a DBGraph, determines the subset T_σ of T containing all tuples of a given relation R which satisfies the qualification Q. To simplify, we assume that Q is a simple comparison predicate (r.k θ c) where c is a constant and θ is the comparator. Then T_σ contains all tuple vertices connected to a value satisfying the qualification Q, by an edge valued by r.k. The select operator is then expressed as follows:

$T_\sigma = \sigma_Q(T)$ where $T_\sigma = \{t \in T / (v \, \theta \, c) \text{ is true and } (t, v, r.k) \in A\}$

The extension of Q to conjunctions and/or disjunctions of predicates is handled performing unions and/or intersections of the T_σ sets corresponding to each predicate.

- *join operator:*

    The join operator applied on Tr and Ts determines the set $T_\otimes$ of couple of vertices corresponding to tuples matching together according to the join predicate (r.k=s.l). The DBGraph properties implie that these tuple vertices are connected by a path of length two, as expressed below.

    $T_\otimes = \otimes_M(Tr, Ts)$ where $T_\otimes = \{(t1,t2) \mid t1 \in Tr, t2 \in Ts$
    and $(t1, v, r.k) \in A, (t2, v, s.l) \in A\}$

For a query QR, these two operators determine a subset of pertinent vertices in the DBGraph which allows to construct the result. This set can be reached in the DBGraph using two different strategies. The select and join operators defined earlier are set oriented. They induce consequently a traversal of a DBGraph from sets of vertices to sets of vertices in a similar manner as a *breadth first search* strategy [Sedg84]. On the other hand, the same set of pertinent vertices can be reached using a *depth first search* strategy [Gibb85]. This second strategy consists to evaluate complete paths of a graph one by one. Such traversal of the DBGraph is equivalent to a pipeline execution of a relational query and does not generate any temporary result.

III STRATEGIES TO TRAVERSE A DBGRAPH

In this section, set oriented strategy and pipeline strategy are detailed and compared. For set oriented strategy, specific traversal primitives are first defined. Then selection, join and transitive closure algorithms are expressed on basic relations using these primitives. The management of temporary relations introduced by this strategy is discussed. Finally, pipeline evaluation of a query on a DBGraph is proposed as a good candidate strategy.

III.1 Set oriented traversal primitives

Two basic primitives are defined to navigate in a DBGraph G(X,A) with X=(T,V).

- *succ_val primitive:*

    This primitive delivers the subset T_r' ($T_r' \, T_r$) containing the tuples of a given relation R whose k^{th} attribute value belongs to a given set of values V' (V' V). Thus, It is an application from V to T which determines the subset of T vertices connected to V' vertices by edges valued by r.k.

    $T_r' = succ\_val(V', r.k)$ where $T_r' = \{t \in T \mid v \in V' \text{ and } (t, v, r.k) \in A\}$.

• *succ_tup primitive:*
This primitive performs the projection of a given tuple t of a relation R on its kth attribute.

$v = succ\_tup(t, r.k)$ where $v \in V$ and $(t, v, r.k) \in A$.

Combinations of these two primitives are allowed since their results and entry parameters are compatible together. As these primitives are set oriented, their combination determines a *breadth first traversal* of the DBGraph.

III.2 Select and join algorithms

We have previously shown how select and join operators can be formally expressed on a DBGraph. We give now a transcription of these operators in term of traversal primitives. Queries involving select and join operators will thus be interpreted as a sequence of traversal primitives.

• *Select algorithm on DBGraph:*

The DBGraph leads to an execution of the select operation similar to that performed using inverted indices. The set of values satisfying the selection criteria is first determined. Then the matching tuples are obtained applying the succ_val primitive to this set of values.

> **Function** $\sigma_Q(Tr) : T_\sigma$
> /* Tr denotes the subset of T vertices holding the tuples of the relation R */
> /* Q is a comparison predicate $(r.k \; \theta \; c)$ */
> **begin**
> $V' := Select_Q(V);$
> $T_\sigma := succ\_val(V', r.k);$
> **end**

The function $Select_Q(V)$ builts the set $V' = \{v \in V \; / \; (v \; \theta \; c) = true\}$. This function can be optimized using indices on V as it will be detailed in section IV. The extension of Q to complex qualifications is obvious as discussed section II.2.

• *Join algorithm on DBGraph:*

Let us consider a join predicate M on the form (r.k=s.l) where r.k and s.l vary on the same domain Dj. A first strategy to perform the join consists first to sequentially scan the domain Dj. Then, for each value of this domain, two successive applications of the succ_val primitives allow to reach the subsets T_r' and T_s' where T_r' (resp. T_s') contains the tuples of R (resp. S) connected to this value by an edge valued by their join attribute. Finally, a cartesian product (Tr' X Ts') is performed since all tuples of T_r' match with all tuples of T_s'.

Function $\otimes 1_M(Tr,Ts) : T_\otimes$
/* Tr (resp. Ts) is the subset of T vertices holding the tuples of relation R (resp. S) */
begin
$\quad T_\otimes := \emptyset;$
$\quad$ **for each** $v \in Dj$ **do**
$\quad\quad T_r' := succ\_val(v, r.k);$
$\quad\quad T_s' := succ\_val(v, s.l);$
$\quad\quad T_{temp} := T_r' \times T_s';$
$\quad\quad T_\otimes := T_\otimes \cup T_{temp};$
$\quad$ **end for**
end

As domains are shared by several relations, Card(Dj) can be high in comparison to Card(T_r) or Card(T_s), where Card denotes the cardinal of a set. A second join algorithm, based on a different traversal of the DBGraph, runs faster than the previous one in this particular case. This second algorithm consists to first sequentially scan the smallest relation to join. Then, the join attribute value of each tuple of this relation is retrieved through the succ_tup primitive. Finally, a succ_val primitive is applied to reach the subset T_s' of tuples of S having this same value for their join attribute.

Function $\otimes 2_M(Tr,Ts): T_\otimes$
/* We assume Card(Tr) < Card(Ts) < Card(Dj) */
begin
$\quad T_\otimes := \emptyset;$
$\quad$ **for each** $t \in T_r$ **do**
$\quad\quad v := succ\_tup(t, r.k);$
$\quad\quad T_s' := succ\_val(v, s.l);$
$\quad\quad T_{temp} := t \times T_s';$
$\quad\quad T_\otimes := T_\otimes \cup T_{temp};$
$\quad$ **end for**
end

In both algorithms, the union $T_\otimes \cup T_{temp}$ can be advantageously replaced by a concatenation since generation of duplicates in $T_\otimes$ is impossible. A DBGraph precompiles join operations in a similar way as join indices since comparisons between tuples are avoided during all the operation. The join is reduced to traverse links in main memory. Numerous comparisons with join indices will be introduced in the sequel of this paper. Indeed, the use of join indices is currently considered as one of the most convenient way to speed up join and transitive closure operations using direct links between tuples.

III.3 Transitive closure on a DBGraph

Recently, the database community has manifested a strong interest in efficient evaluation of recursively defined relations [Hens84, Banc86]. The most popular approach to reach this goal is to define dedicated operators to compute the transitive closure (called TC) of a relation [Han86, Gard86]. TC algorithms are now central algorithms in KBMS's.

Computing the TC of a relation R on attributes r.k and r.l consists to add in R all tuples deductible by a transitive application of joins (for clarity, R is assumed binary). In other words, if $t1_{r.l}=t2_{r.k}$, a new tuple $(t1_{r.k},t2_{r.l})$ must be deduced and added in R. For instance, if t1=(a,b) and t2=(b,c) then the tuple (a,c) is generated. When a recursively defined relation is queried, only the relevant sub-set of its TC is built. For instance, let us consider the academic example of the Ancestor relation, recursively defined from the Parent basic relation as follows:

$$\text{Parent }(X,Y) \longrightarrow \text{Ancestor }(X,Y)$$
$$\text{Parent }(X,Z) \wedge \text{Ancestor }(Z,Y) \longrightarrow \text{Ancestor }(X,Y)$$

The retrieval of all John ancestors, expressed as Ancestor (*,John) does not imply the generation of the whole Ancestor relation. The problem is solved by pushing up selection before processing recursion [Hens84, Gard86]. The corresponding TC algorithm can be computed by a loop of relational operators, as follows :

```
Function TC_Q(R):TCR
    /* compute the TC of R according to the initial query selection Q */
    /* and store the result in TCR */
    begin
        ΔR := π_P(σ_Q(R));              /* σ_Q is applied to the basic relation */
        TCR := ΔR;                       /* before processing recursion */
        while ΔR ≠ ∅, do
            ΔR := π_P( ⊗_M(ΔR,R));       /* M= (Δr.l=r.k) and P= (Δr.k, r.l) */
            ΔR := ΔR - TCR;
            TCR := TCR ∪ ΔR;
        end while
    end
```

The difference ΔR := ΔR - TCR is mandatory to avoid TC program to loop forever in case of cyclic data (e.g sequence of R tuples like (a,b), (b,c), (c,a)). Numerous proposals have been made to optimize this algorithm: reduction of the number of loops [Ioan86], propagation of temporary results by join waves [Han86], speed up joins in the loop using join indices [Vald86].

A more natural and efficient way to elaborate the transitive closure of a relation consists to compute the TC of the sub-part of the DBGraph corresponding to this relation. To make the recursion easier to express, we introduce the notion of Relation_Closure_Graph (denoted RCGraph) which is directly derived from the DBGraph notion. The RCGraph of R on attributes r.k and r.l is a graph in which vertices represent tuples of R and two vertices t1 and t2 are connected by an edge (t1, t2) if the corresponding tuples match together according to the auto-join predicate (r.k=r.l). This RCGraph remain always virtual and traversals of a RCGraph are translated on the corresponding DBGraph using the classical *succ_val* and *succ_tup* primitives. In fact, each edge connecting two tuples in the RCGraph corresponds to a path of length two in the DBGraph, as detailled figure 2.

Definition: Relation_Closure_Graph

The RCGraph G'(Tr,Ar) of a relation R on attributes r.k and r.l is a virtual graph derived from the DBGraph G(X,A) with X=(T,V) as follows : Tr is the subset of T vertices holding the tuples of relation R and (t1, t2) ∈ Ar iff t1, t2 ∈ Tr and (t1, v, r.k) ∈ A, (t2, v, r.l) ∈ A.

Properties: Two vertices ti and tj of G'(Tr,Ar) are transitively connected if there exists a path (ti<—>tk, tk<—>tl, ..., tn<—>tj) ∈ Ar. Thence, there is a direct mapping between the TC of R and the TC of its RCGraph.

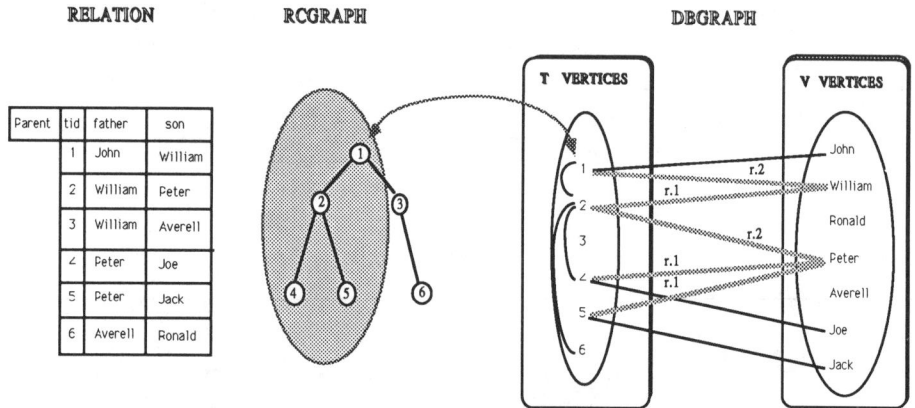

The relation Parent is denoted by R to standardize valuations of edges. To simplify the figure, only the edges belonging to vertices of the encircled subpart of the RCGraph are represented in the DBGraph. The grey edges of the DBGraph materialize the virtual edges of this subpart of the RCGraph. These virtual edges are also represented between the T vertices for clarity.

Figure 2: Mapping between a RCGraph and a DBGraph

Transitive closure algorithm on RCGraph:

The query selection on the recursive relation determines a set T_r' of entry vertices in the RCGraph. According to this initial selection, the TC of the RCGraph consists, for each t of T_r', to find all vertices (called the descendants of t) reachable from t by a path. A visited vertex is marked to avoid going twice through the same path. Marking technics are widely used to prevent infinite looping of graph traversal algorithms in case of cyclic data. The costly difference operation needed by the previous TC algorithm is then avoided. The result of each RCGraph traversal is a spanning tree of root t over the descendants of t. A new primitive is introduced to perform such a traversal on a RCGraph(Tr,Ar):

- *neighbor_tup primitive:*

    This primitive delivers the set NT of vertices directly connected (i.e. by only one edge) to the non marked vertices of an entry set T_r' ($T_r' \subset Tr$). Vertices of NT are then marked and not anymore considered for graph traversal.

    NT = neighbor_tup(T_r') where NT = {t'∈ Tr / t∈ T_r' and (t, t') ∈ Ar and mark(t)=false}

    Note that parameter and result of *neighbor_tup* are homogeneous. Thus, a recursive application of this primitive is valid.

As the *neighbor_tup* primitive is set oriented, it defines a traversal of a RCGraph from sets of vertices to sets of vertices using a *breadth first search (BFS)* strategy. Such closure algorithm is well known in graph theory and [Sedg84] demonstrates that this algorithm stops and is of temporal complexity O(m) (where m=Card(Ar)). A RCGraph traversal for each element t of T_r' is accomplished using the following algorithm:

Function BFS(t):Desc
      /* *Desc is the set of descendants of t* */
      begin
            $\Delta Desc := neighbor\_tup(t)$;
            $Desc := \Delta Desc$;
            while $\Delta Desc \neq \emptyset$, *do*
                  $\Delta Desc := neighbor\_tup(\Delta Desc)$;
                  $Desc := Desc \cup \Delta Desc$;
            end while
      end

The difference operation between ΔDesc and Desc is unnecessary while cycles in data are avoided by marking all visited vertices and the union Desc∪ΔDesc can be replaced by a concatenation. Recall that the RCGraph notion remain always virtual. Then, the BSF function is translated on the original DBGraph in term of *succ_val* and *succ_tup* primitives.

This TC algorithm yields excellent performances in a main memory environment due to the fact that the DBGraph pre-compiles the whole TC operation. Section 5 shows that graph traversal outperforms all others methods when the sub-part of the DBGraph corresponding to the RCGraph fits entirely in main memory. Nevertheless, the behaviour of this algorithm is rapidly degraded if this hypothesis is not satisfied. The physical storage of the DBGraph has especially been studied to allow incremental loading of the pertinent sub-part (for a query) of a DBGraph. Note that DBGraph is a well suited support for a wide family of recursive processes. All processes expressed as traversal recursion [Rose86] can be speed up using a DBGraph structure.

III.4 Dealing with temporary results

Join operations are generally speed up by the use of clustered or inverted indices on join attributes, join indices [Vald87] or multi-relations indices [Haer78]. Nevertheless, it is often difficult or even impossible to apply such indices on temporary relations. As we consider that join are frequently preceded by a selection on one (or the two) relation to be join, this limitation is severe. Solutions are proposed in [Vald87] to ensure the validity of join indices after selections. Selections produce a list of TID's corresponding to the relevant tuples. This list is then semi-joined with the join index in order to produce a new valid join index on temporary relations.

The DBGraph storage of relations allows a much more efficient resolution of this problem. As temporary results contain only links to tuples of basic relations from which they are extracted, they represent a simple extension of a DBGraph. Temporary results are represented as a set of temporary vertices connected with the corresponding T vertices via temporary edges. The degree (number of edges) of a temporary vertex is equal to the number of basic tuples involved in this temporary result. For instance, if the temporary result is issued from selection (resp. join), each temporary vertex is connected with a unique vertex (resp. two vertices) of T, as illustrated figure 3.

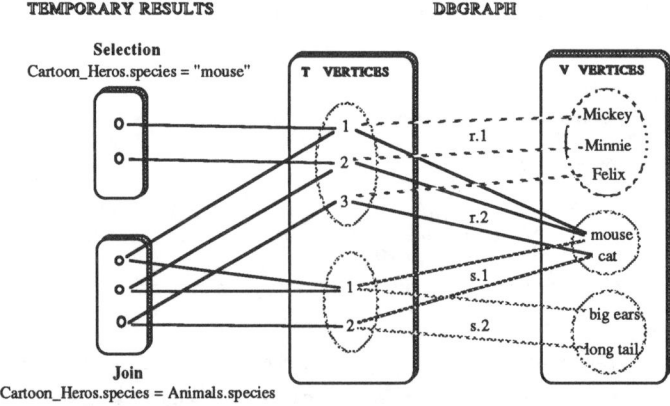

Figure 3: temporary result from a selection and from a join

This representation of temporary results presents three major advantages. First, temporary results are as compact as possible since they do not contain any value. It is on prime importance in MMDBS since it enforces the hypothesis that the active database fit in main memory. Secondly, project operations are posponed at the end of the query evaluation. The query optimizer is then discharged of the task to generate projections on non relevant attributes before join operations. This task has been proved to be time consuming in [Amma85]. Finally, temporary results preserve links to basic tuples. Then, a temporary result determines a set of entry vertices in the DBGraph which can be directly exploited by any operator. Consequently, join of temporary relations are speed up in a similar way as join of basic relations by a simple DBGraph traversal. Note however that a supplementary edge must be traversed for each element of the temporary result in order to reach the corresponding basic tuples.

III.5 Pipeline strategy versus set oriented strategy

A same query can be evaluated using a breadth-first traversal or a depth-first traversal of the DBGraph. The first strategy provides a set oriented execution of relational algebra when the second one produces *one tuple at a time* such as a pipeline strategy. Pipeline strategy has already been implemented in some relational systems. The pipeline strategy offers two major advantages. Temporary results have no more to be generated then main memory stands only for permanent data. In addition, tuples already produced can be displayed while query processing is still in progress. Nevertheless, pipeline execution is limited to the subpart of a query involving selection, join and projection operators since difference, intersection, aggregate and sort operators are purely set oriented. Furthermore, computing a join in a pipeline way without specialized structures can provide as low performances as those of a Nested Loop join algorithm.

The pipeline execution of a query on a DBGraph is informally introduced below. Let us consider a generic query QR on the form ($\sigma_Q R1 \wedge R1 \otimes R2 \wedge R2 \otimes R3 \wedge ... \wedge Rn\text{-}1 \otimes Rn$). The number of joins in

QR determines the length of a *pertinent path* connecting a tuple of R1 to a tuple of Rn and the corresponding join predicates determine the successive valuations of edges belonging to this path. A *pertinent path* covers all vertices needed to produce one tuple of the query result. The pipeline evaluation of the query QR starts by a selection on R1 which determines a set of entry value vertices in the DBGraph. Each value constitutes the root of one or more paths in the DBGraph. These paths are explored one after the other and a result tuple is generated at each time that the extremity of a *pertinent path* is reached. Backtrack is applied at the extremity of each pertinent path or when a path fails.

When selections in QR are applied on several relations, they can be handled in two ways. One solution is to apply first selections in a set oriented way. Selected vertices of the corresponding relations are marked. Then, non marked vertices are not considered during the *pertinent paths* exploration. A second solution consists to check the selection criteria for each tuple vertex reached during the *pertinent paths* exploration. Queries involving successive joins on the form (R1⊗R2 ∧ R1⊗R3... R1⊗Rn) are more complex to evaluate. A simple depth first traversal is no more suited as several paths must be explored in parallel. Evaluation of such queries remain possible with good performances but the method is more complex to implement.

It is shown in [Gibb85] that the temporal complexity of a depth-first search is O(max(n,m)) (where n=Card(X) and m=Card(A)). Then DBGraph appears well suited for the pipeline evaluation of such queries since depth-first traversal yields similar performances as breadth-first traversal (O(m)). Breadth first traversal and depth first traversal are summarized figure 4 for a query expressed by a selection followed by a join.

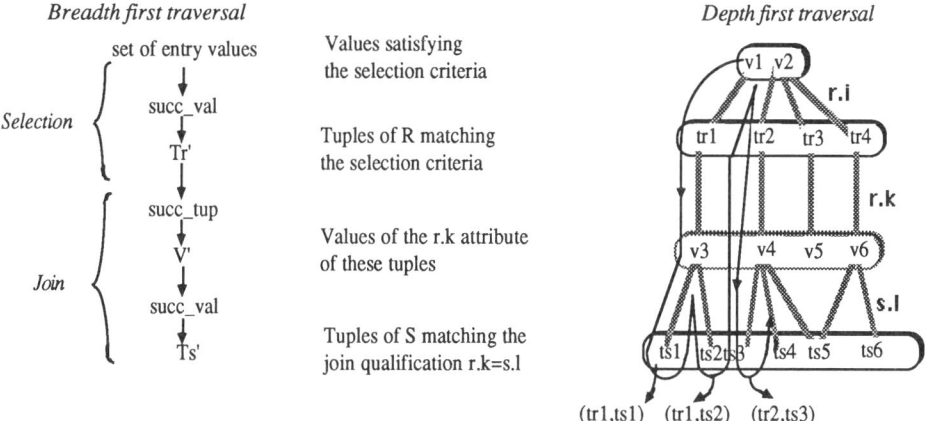

A selection is first applied on attribute i of the relation R followed by a join r.k=s.l. A *pertinent path* for this query owns three edges with the successive valuations r.i, r.k, s.l. To clarify the figure, only a subset of candidate paths is represented. Four tuples of R (tr1 to tr4) satisfies the selection criteria and three tuples of R match with six tuples of S (ts1 to ts6) giving seven tuples in the result denoted by (tr1,ts1), (tr1,ts2), (tr2,ts3) ...

Figure 4: BFS and DFS strategies on a DBGraph

IV IMPLEMENTATION OF A DBGRAPH

IV.1 Physical implementation

Numerous physical representations of graphs can be found in the litterature. We detail below a particular implementation of a DBGraph(X,A) where X=(T,V), well adapted to MMDBS.

Domain values are stored only once to preserve compact data structures. As the D_j domains form a partition of V, all values varying on the same domain can be clustered in a separate segment. Thus, it is possible to load the values of one domain independantly of the others and to take advantage of vertical partitionning. For the same reasons, tuples of one relation R are stored in one segment as the relations form a partition of T. Each object stored in a segment has a unique and invariant identifier called OID. Then, tuples and values can be referenced by OID's. Indices speed up selections on domain values. The index structure can be any one recommanded for MMDBS [Lehm86b]. Its particularity is to contain only OID's referencing the key values stored in the domain [Amma85]. In case of variable length keys, the gain in term of storage cost is important.

In the formal description of a DBGraph, edges of A are not oriented and may be traversed in both directions. In the implementation, an edge (t, v, r.k) is split in two arcs (oriented edges) materialized by OID's. The OID corresponding to an arc (v—>t) is stored in an inverted list attached to the value v. The valuation r.k of this arc is represented by the fact that inverted lists are subdivided in as much sublists as there is attributes r.k varying on the value domain. The valuation r.k of the arc (t—>v) is represented by the fact that the tuple t belongs to the segment of relation R and that the corresponding OID is stored in place of the kth attribute. Then, valuations of arcs are implicit and do not compromize the compactness of a DBGraph.

In summary, tuples of permanent relations are implemented via arrays of OID's and values are stored with collections of inverted sublists of OID's. The shortest way to store the inverted sublists is to put them one after the other behind the corresponding value, as in [Haer78]. We did not choose this solution for we want to be able to fetch in memory the inverted sublists corresponding to one attribute r.k independently of the others. Thus, in accordance with the vertical partitionning strategy adopted for domain values, all the inverted sublists corresponding to attribute r.k are stored in one segment. Domain values are followed by an array, called sublist array, containing OID's referencing the sublists. It contains one entry per attribute r.k varying on the domain and is indexed by r.k. Inverted lists corresponding to key attributes contain only one OID. In this case, many space is saved storing the OID directly in the sublist array. The physical implementation of a DBGraph is represented figure 5.

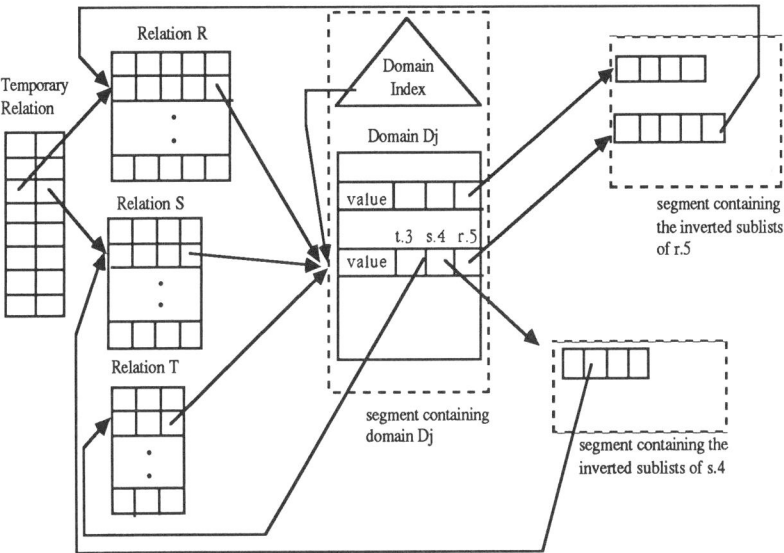

The temporary result is issued from a join between R and S.
The attribute t.3 is assumed to be a key attribute

Figure 5: physical implementation of a DBGraph

IV.2 Storage cost evaluation

Flat file organization (FF) and DBGraph organization (DBG) are evaluated in term of storage cost. For the sake of simplicity we assume for DBG that domain index are stored as array of OID sorted on the referenced values, like in [Amm85]. In a similar way, FF indices are supposed to be stored as arrays of couples (value, TID) sorted on the values. In the sequel, p denotes the size of an OID or a TID. We assume also that all domains of a DBGraph are indexed in order to speed up relational queries in all cases.

Given one domain containing N values with an average length l and a attributes varying on this domain with an average cardinality C for each relation, the storage cost of the corresponding subpart of the DBGraph yields:

$Cost\ (DBG) = N\ (\ l + ap\ )$ /* size of the domain segment containing N values */
  /* with their corresponding sublist array */
  $+ aCp$ /* size of a segments containing all inverted sublists */
  /* of one attribute */
  $+ aCp$ /* size of a columns of OID in the relations */
  $+ Np$ /* size of the domain index */

$= aC\ (\ 2p + \dfrac{N}{aC}(\ l + p\ (\ a+1\ )\ )$

For a Flat File organization using k indices, let an evaluation for the storage cost be as follows:

$$Cost(FF_k) = aCl \quad \text{/* size of } a \text{ columns of values in the relations */}$$
$$+ k(C(l+p)) \quad \text{/* size of } k \text{ indices */}$$
$$= aC(l + k/a(l+p))$$

In order to compare the storage cost of the two methods, we introduce the concept of domain selectivity that can be formalized as follows:

$$S = \frac{\text{number of domain values}}{\text{number of attribute values varying on the domain}} = \frac{N}{aC}$$

Then the difference between the two methods in term of storage cost depends on four parameters: S, l, a and k. The cost equality is expressed by the following equation:

$$Cost(FF_k) = Cost(DBG)$$

$$aC(l + k/a(l+p)) = aC(2P + S(l + p(a+1)))$$

$$S = \frac{l + k/a(l+p) - 2p}{l + p(a+1)}$$

In case there is no index for the flat file organization ($k = 0$), we get:

$$S = \frac{l - 2p}{l + p(a+1)} = 1 - \frac{p(a+3)}{l - p(a+1)}$$

Comparisons between FF without index and DBG are summarized figure 6 in a similar way as in [Miss82]. The plotted curves indicates the most efficient organization according to different values of S and l parameters. Average length of values l is expressed in units of a on the abscissa.

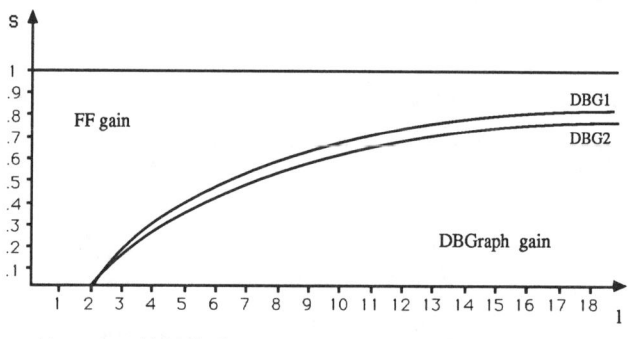

l is expressed in unit of p.
Values of the dependant variable: k=0.
Curve DBG1 corresponds to a=1, and curve DBG2 corresponds to a=2.

Figure 6: DBGraph versus Flat File organization without index

Each curve devides the plan in a gain region for FF and a gain region for DBGraph. They show that DBGraph is generally more space consuming than flat file organization without index. This extra-cost diminishes when domain selectivity decreases (S becomes low) or l increases. Thus, DBGraph should not introduce an extra-cost for domain containing enumerated types. For domain containing short key attributes like numbers, the extra-cost is compensated by two facts: all joins, generally performed on key attributes, will be speed-up by the DBGraph and S can be low as several relations share the same set of keys. Furthermore, the evaluation do not take into account that inverted sublists for key attributes are directly stored in the sublist array. It is also important to point out that losts due to high domain selectivities or short values on several attributes can be balanced by large gains obtained on a few enumerated type domains. It can be show that for relation schemas introduced in the Wisconsin benchmark [Bitt83], a DBGraph organization is well-suited. Defining a new attribute on a domain implies to add a new entry on the sublist array of each value of this domain. To preserve efficient storage, the new attribute range of values should have a wide intersection with the values already defined in the domain, which decreases the domain selectivity. This phenomena is shown by a comparison of the three curves.

Figure 7 gives a comparison of DBGraph versus flat file organization using one join index or k selection indices (with $k=0$, 1 or 2) for a domain holding two attributes. To simplify the evaluation of join indices size, we consider join on a key attribute such as at most one tuple of the second relation matches with each tuple of the first relation. It is a favorable case for join indices. The space occupancy of a flat file organization including join indices is evaluated according to the following formula:

$Cost\ (FF_{kj}) = Cost(FF_k)$ /* size of FF organization using k selection indices */
$\qquad\qquad\qquad + j\ (C\ 2p\ )$ /* size of j join indices containing C rows of two TID's */

Then the equivalence between DBGraph and flat files with join and selection indices in term of storage cost is given by the following formula:

$Cost\ (FF_{kj}) = Cost\ (DBG)$

$aC\ (l + k/a\ (l + p) + 2jp/a\ ) = aC\ (2p + S(l + p(a + 1)))$

$$S = \frac{l + k/a\ (l + p) + 2jp/a - 2p}{l + p(a + 1)} \qquad \text{with a=2, k=0 and j=1, we get} \qquad S = \frac{l - p}{l + 3p}$$

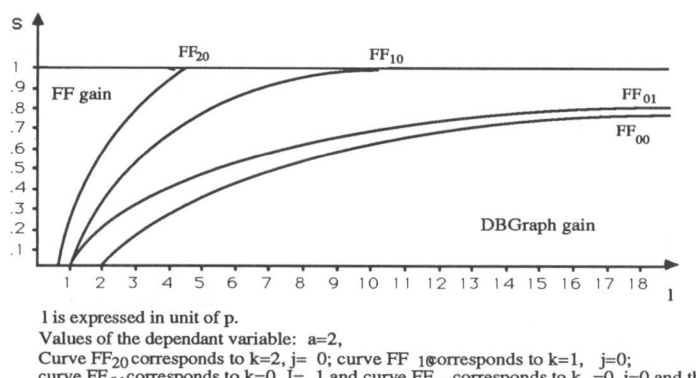

l is expressed in unit of p.
Values of the dependant variable: a=2,
Curve FF_{20} corresponds to k=2, j= 0; curve FF_{10} corresponds to k=1, j=0;
curve FF_{01} corresponds to k=0, J= 1 and curve FF_{00} corresponds to k =0, j=0 and then is equivalent to curve DBG2

Figure 7: DBGraph versus Flat file organization with indices

It appears clearly that DBGraph becomes rapidly the best candidate organization as soon as indices are added in the flat file schema. As the number of indices determines the performances of software queries evaluation in a main memory context, the superiority of a DBGraph organization is obvious. The extra-cost involved by selection index is strongly dependent of value lenght l. Comparing curves FF_{01} and FF_{10} show that selection indices are much more space consuming than join indices. This is mainly due to the fact that join indices contains only TID's instead of values. For the same reasons, the gap between FF_{01} and FF_{00} curves decreases progressively as l increases since TID size can then be neglected in regard to value size.

IV.3 Updating DBGraph and concurrency control handling

Updating a tuple in a DBGraph consists to delete links with old values and to create links with new values for each updated attribute. In most cases values are shared by several attributes. Then insertion (resp. suppression) of one link just incure one update in the corresponding inverted sublist. When values are not shared, three pages must be updated in order to update the domain index, insert (resp. suppress) the value in the domain and create (resp. delete) the corresponding inverted sublist. This scattering of data, due to the partitionning of the DBGraph, could introduce undesirable I/O. Mecanisms of differed updates on disk, generally used in MMDBS [Garc84] [DeWi84], are well adapted to avoid this drawbrack.

Insertion and suppression of links in a DBGraph have the same complexity and are quite simple. This property is interesting if we make the comparison with join indices. At each insertion of a new tuple in a relation, join index maintenance requires to select all tuples of the other relation matching with this tuple. It is argued that this overhead incured by join indices can be shared largely with referencial integrity checking in case of join on foreign keys. Nevertheless, there is still an overhead while the DBGraph precompiles the referencial integrity checking as well as selection and join operations.

As all operations are performed on the DBGraph, there could be heavy contention on that structure. We envision to suppress lock maintenance on domain indices using a multi-level transaction protocol [Weik84]. This proposal is based on the fact that logical operations on indices (such as insert a new value) commute whereas operations on their physical structure (such as node splitting in a B-Tree) do not commute. The multi-level transaction protocol allow to temporarily lock indices during the update in order to ensure the logical operation atomicity then to release these locks at the logical operation end. Therefore contention on indices is solved but phantom problems [Eswa76] appear. Considering that each entity addressable with an OID can be locked and that values are stored separately from the domain indices, phantoms can be avoided in DBGraphs locking domain values or inverted sublists during the whole transaction. Then, only the minimal subpart of the domain index remain locked after the update. It could be a response to the critical problem of locking indices [Baye77].

V PERFORMANCE EVALUATIONS

For the sake of conciseness, TC algorithm is the only one evaluated in details since transitive closure is expressed as a combination of the other operators. Selection algorithm on DBGraph yields the same level of performances as classical methods using inverted indices. Its efficiency is determinated by the index structure chosen to perform the $Select_Q(V)$ operation, which is independent of the DBGraph structure themselves. Thus, selection algorithm is not further detailed. The first join algorithm on DBGraph $\otimes 1_M(R,S)$ is linear in Card(Dj) as the second one $\otimes 2_M(R,S)$ is linear in Card(R), where R is the smallest relation to be joined. The DBGraph structure pre-compiles join operations in a similar way as join indices whose effectiveness has no more to be proved [Vald87]. The major difference is that join index provides direct links between tuples matching together as DBGraph provides only transitive links. Then join on permanent relations runs faster with join indices but the gap is minor considering the main memory context. In compensation DBGraph is more efficient to perform join on temporary results, as temporary result determines a set of entry vertices in the DBGraph which can be directly exploited by the join operator. On the contrary, the use of join indices on temporary results requires costly transformations as detailed section III.4. The Project operator constitutes the main drawback of the DBGraph structure. It requires one access to each value belonging to the attribute list of projection. This drawback is balanced by the fact that projections are posponed at the end of query evaluation and then performed only once.

According to the main memory environment, evaluations of TC algorithms are expressed in CPU time. Relation_Closure_Graph traversal is compared to join loops on join index which is considered as one of the most efficient TC algorithm [Vald86]. Execution time of the original selection and time to compose the final result will be neglected as they are constant and independant of the two methods. We use in the evaluation parameters from [Banc86], well suited to model different types of graphs:

di = in degree of a node, giving the average number of edges entering a node,
do = out degree of a node, giving the average number of edges going out a node,
h = height of the graph, giving the longest path in the graph.

Thus, a genealogical tree in which any parent has three childrens and any child has two parents will be defined by $di=2$, $do=3$, h=number of generations. The expansion factor, modeling the average number of vertices accessed at each iteration of a breadth first traversal, is defined by $E = di / do$. For the join loops method, E is an approximation of join selectivity at each iteration. Other parameters used in the evaluation are the following :

$t=$	$Card(R)$ where R is the input relation of the TC algorithm,
$\sigma=$	selectivity factor of the initial selection applied to R,
$t*do =$	estimation of the cardinal of the auto-join index of relation R,
$a=$	access time for one word in main memory,
$c=$	time needed for comparing two OID's.

V.1 Cost of TC on join index

The TC algorithm on join index is derived from the basic TC algorithm detailled section III.3. Loops of joins are directly applied on join index instead of being applied on relations. We assume the join index to be sorted according to the column upon which the selection applies. It is the most favorable case as each successor of a vertex can then be found in $\log_2 n$ index access (n being the join index cardinal) instead of n/2 access if the index where not sorted. To always guarantee this favorable case, it is proposed in [Vald87] to maintain two copy of the join index on disk , each one sorted on a different column. At each iteration of the internal loop of the TC algorithm, the cardinal of ΔR is multiplied by the expansion factor E during the join $\Delta R:=\otimes_M(\Delta R, R)$. Before processing recursion, ΔR is initialized using $\sigma*t$ elements resulting from the initial selection applied on R. At iteration i-1, ΔR is thus composed of $\sigma*t*E^{i-1}$ elements where E^{i-1} denotes $E*E*...*E$ (i-1) times.

Then, the ith iteration of TC algorithm on join index may be splitted in four steps :

(i) Performing the join $\Delta R:=\otimes_M(\Delta R,R)$ requires $\sigma t*E^{i-1}$ searches on the join index. As a search requires $\log_2 t*do$ reads and comparisons (the join index is sorted),the resulting cost is:
$$Join\_Cost = [\sigma*t*E^{i-1} * log2(t*do)] (a+c).$$

(ii) The result of step (i) contains $\sigma*t*E^{i-1}*E$ elements. Writing this intermediate result requires:
$$Write\_Cost = \sigma*t*E^i*a.$$

(iii) This result must be sorted before processing the difference and union operations. It yields:
$$Sort\_Cost = [\sigma*t*E^i*log2(\sigma*t*E^i)] (2a+c).$$

(iv) Union between the intermediate result ΔR and the recursive relation TCR being built (TCR is assumed to be sorted as the union of two sorted relations gives a sorted relation). At each iteration, TCR is augmented of $\sigma*t*E^i$ elements. Thus, TCR contains $\Sigma_{k=1 \text{ to } i-1} (\sigma*t*E^k)$ elements at iteration (i-1). Difference and union are performed with a simple scan of ΔR and TCR, which yields :

$$Union\_Diff\_Cost = 2*[\ \sigma*t*E^i + \Sigma_{k=1 \text{ to } i-1}\ \sigma*t*E^k\ ]\ (2a+c).$$

Finally, the global cost of the TC algorithm using Join Index (JI) for all iterations is :

$$JI\_Cost = \Sigma_{i = 1 \text{ to } h} (\ Join\_Cost + Write\_Cost + Sort\_Cost + Union\_Diff\_Cost\ ).$$

V.2 Cost of TC on Closure_Graph

The evaluation of the graph traversal consists in applying the BFS function to each element of the input set σ*t of vertices. The *neighbor_tup* primitive will be called h times during a BFS execution. At each application of the form $N_t = neighbor\_tup(N_t)$, the size of N_t is multiplied by the expansion factor E. Thence, at the ith iteration, the *neighbor_tup* primitive is applied on a set containing E^{i-1} vertices (materialized by OID's) and returns a set containing E^i vertices. For each of the E^{i-1} vertices, the *neighbor_tup* primitive performs three accesses to get the tuple (vertex) from its OID (due to the implementation of OID's), two more accesses to verify that the vertex is not yet marked and to mark it, one access to read the concerned attribute identifier (OID corresponding to an arc t—>v) of that tuple, then three accesses to get the attribute value in the domain, and finally two accesses to get the corresponding inverted sublist. Thus, the retrieval of all successors of a given vertex using the *neighbor_tup* primitive requires 11 memory accesses. In summary, an execution of the BSF function for the h iterations requires:

$$BSF\_COST = \Sigma_{i=1 \text{ to } h} (11*E^{i-1})$$

As the BSF function is applied to each element of the input set σ*t, the total cost of the graph traversal approach appears to be:

$$GT\_COST = 11* \sigma*t* \Sigma_{i=1 \text{ to } h} E^{i-1}$$

V.3 Comparison of costs

Figure 8 displays graphical comparisons for typical values of parameters E, σ, t, h. The obtained results are given in memory access numbers (i.e., c is set equals to 2a). For the sake of clarity, the curves are represented as continuous although h can only be given natural number values.

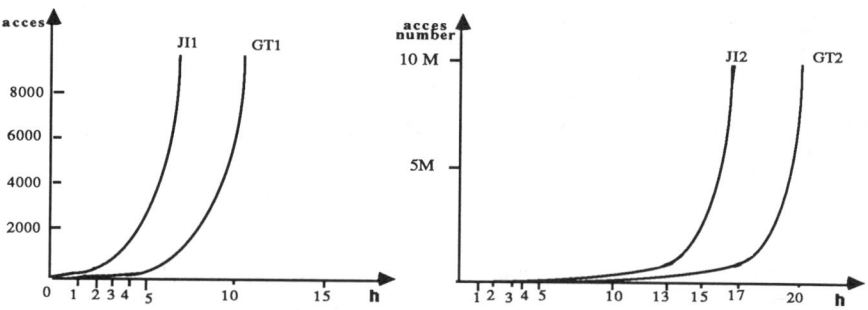

Values of the dependant variables : E=2, σt=1, t=10.000
JI and GT curves are plotted on two different scales to compare both curves for all values of h.

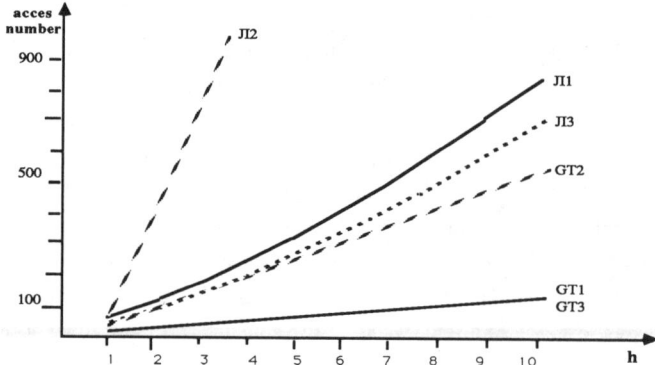

Values of the dependant variables : E=1.
Bold curves (JI1 and GT1) : correspond to σt=1, t=10.000.
Hached curves (JI2 and GT2) : correspond to σt=4, t=10.000.
Dotted curve (JI3) : correspond to σt=1, t=1000. The GT curve is invariant in function of t.

Figure 8: Performance variations of JI and GT algorithms

Analysis of these curves yields several remarks. First, algorithms JI and GT behave exponentially in function of h when E is greater than 1. This natural result derives from the fact that the number of accessed vertices at each iteration increases exponentially. Note however that GT algorithm is more "resistant" than JI algorithm as its exponential factor is smaller. Secondly, the GT algorithm is linear when E = 1 while the JI algorithm is linear only if E=1 and σt=1. When σt is greater than 1, the logarithmic cost of sorting intermediate results must be added to the JI algorithm evaluation. Finally, JI algorithm does not have constant performances in function of t. Indeed, the size of the join index, given by t*do, determines the cost of each index search.

In summary, it appears that the GT algorithm outperforms the JI algorithm. This is mainly due to the fact that the DBGraph structure pre-compiles the whole TC operation. The strongest advantages of the GT algorithm appearing through the evaluation are the simplicity of detecting cyclic data and the direct access without scan and comparison to the successors or predecessors of a vertex.

VI SUMMARY AND FUTURE WORK

Considering that in future DBMS's it will be possible to hold the active database in main memory, a new physical database organization has been proposed. Tuples and indices are integrated in a unique data structure called DBGraph. This data structure aims two objectives: be compact and decomposable such as the active database always fits in main memory and speed up extended relational algebra in term of CPU time.

In a DBGraph, tuples and values are stored separately. Links between tuples and values are maintained using OID's in order to constitute a bipartite graph. This graph precompiles selection, join and transitive closure operations. Two strategies where described to traverse this graph in order to answer a relational query. Set oriented execution of relational algebra is generated using a breadth first search strategy while pipeline execution is produced using a depth first search strategy. As the two strategies lead to the same temporal complexity, the second one is recommended for it minimizes the storage cost of temporary results even if it is more complex to implement.

Storage cost evaluations have demonstrated the compactness of a DBGraph. Compared to a flat file organization without any index, a DBGraph is more costly for short values with high domain selectivity but more compact in other cases. When adding indices in flat file organization, DBGraph appears to be the best candidate even for short values. Finally, it is easy to partition the DBGraph in small segments in order to take advantage of vertical partitionning. This enforces the probability that active database fits in main memory.

Performance evaluations show that transitive closure on DBGraph outperforms transitive closure on join indices and more generally that DBGraph is well suited to support recursive processing. For the sake of conciseness, other operators where not evaluated in detail since the transitive closure operator is expressed as a composition of the other relational operators. Performance gains using DBGraph should be similar to those obtained using indices for selection and join indices for join on basic relations. Furthermore DBGraph speeds up operations on temporary results in a similar way as on basic relations. Finally DBGraph are much easier to update than join indices.

As all operations are performed on the DBGraph, there could be heavy contention on that structure. A solution has been introduced to avoid this drawback. It could be a response to the critical problem of locking indices. Future works should be done in this area.

Aknowledgements
The authors wish to thank Karima Bennis, Michel Freville and Sylvie Renard for fruitful discussions and for their active participation in prototyping the DBGraph organization.

REFERENCES

[Amma85]   Ammann A. C., Hanrahan M. B., and Krishnamurthy R., "Design of a Memory Resident DBMS", Proc. of IEEE COMPCON 1985.
[Banc86]   Bancilhon F. : "An Amateur's Introduction to Recursive Query Processing Strategies", ACM SIGMOD Proc., May 1986, Austin, Texas.
[Baye77]   Bayer R., Schkolnick M., "Concurrency of Operations on B-Trees", Acta Informatica, 9, 1977.
[Bern87]   Bernstein P.A., Hadlacos, Goodman N., "Concurrency Control and Recovery in Database Systems", Addison-Wesley Ed., 1987.
[Bitt83]   Bitton D., DeWitt D. J., Turbyfill C., "Benchmarking Database Systems: a Systematic Approach", Proc. of the 9th int. Conf. on VLDB, Florence, Nov. 1983.
[Bitt86]   Bitton D., Turbyfill C., "Performance Evaluation of Main Memory Database Systems", Cornell University, TR 86-731.
[Dewi84]   DeWitt D., Katz R., Olken F., Shapiro L., Stonebraker M., Wodd D., "Implementation Techniques for Main Memory Database Systems", Proc. of SIGMOD, Boston, June 1984.
[Eich87]   Eich M. H., "MARS: The Design of a Main Memory Database Machine", 5th IWDM Proc., Karuizawa, Oct. 1987.
[Eswa76]   Eswaran K. P., Gray J. N., Lorie R., Traiger L. L., "The Notion of Consistency and Predicate Locks in a Database System", Proc. of ACM, V19, No 11, Nov 1976.
[Garc84]   Garcia Molina H., Lipton R.J., Valdes J. "A Massive Memory Machine", Proc. IEEE COMPCON 1984.
[Gard86]   Gardarin G., de Maindreville C. : "Evaluation of Database Recursive Programs as Recurrent Function Series", ACM SIGMOD Proc., Austin, May 1986.
[Gibb85]   Gibbons A., "Algorithmic graph theory", book, Cambridge University Press, 1985.
[Haerd78] Haerder T., "Implementing a Generalised Access Path Structure for a Relational Database", Proc. of ACM TODS, Vol. 3, No 3, Sept 1978.
[Hamm79]   Hammer M., Niamir B.,"A Heuristic approach to attribute partitioning", Proc. of ACM SIGMOD, 1979.
[Han85]   Han J., Lu H., "Some Performance Results on Recursive Query Processing in Relational Database Systems", Proc. Data Engineering Conf., Los Angeles, February 1986.
[Hens84]   Henschen L.J., Naqvi S.A., "On compiling queries in recursive first-order databases", JACM, Vol. 31, N° 1, Jan. 1984.
[Ioan86]   Ioannidis Y. E., "On the Computation of the Transitive Closure of Relational Operators", Proc. of 12th int. Conf. on VLDB, Kyoto, August 1986.
[Lehm86a] Lehman T. J., Carey M.J., "A Study of Index Structure for Main Memory Database Management Systems", Proc. of 12th int. Conf. on VLDB, Kyoto, August 1986.
[Lehm86b] Lehman T. J., Carey M.J., "Query Processing in Main Memory Database Management Systems", ACM SIGMOD Proc., Austin, May 1986.
[Lehm87]   Lehman T. J., Carey M.J., "A Recovery Algorithm for a High-Performance Memory-Resident Database System", Proc. of ACM SIGMOD, San Francisco, May 1987.
[Miss82]   Missikov M., "A Domain Based Internal Schema for Relational Database Machines", ACM SIGMOD Proc., New-York, June 1982.
[Naka87]   Nakano R., Kiyama M., "MACH: Much Faster Associative Machine", 5th IWDM Proc., Karuizawa, Oct. 1987.
[Rose86]   Rosenthal A. , Heiler S., Dayal U., Manola F., "Traversal Recursion : A Practical Approach to Supporting Recursive Applications", ACM SIGMOD Proc., Austin, May 1986.
[Sedg84]   Sedgewick R. : " Algorithms" , Book, Addison-Wesley Pub., 1984.
[Seli79]   Selinger P. G., Astrahan M. M., Chamberlin D. D., Lorie P. A., Price T. G., "Access Path Selection in a Relational Database Management System", Proc. of ACM SIGMOD, Boston, 1979.
[Vald86]   Valduriez P., Boral H., "Evaluation of Recursive Queries Using Join Indices",Proc. 1st International Conference on Expert Database Systems, Charleston, 1986.
[Vald87]   Valduriez P., "Join Indices", Proc. of ACM TODS, Vol. 12, No 2, June 87.
[Weik84]   Weikum G., Schek H., "Architectural Issues of Transaction Management in Multi-Layered Systems", Proc. of the 10th int. Conf. on VLDB, Singapore, Aug. 1984.

Implementing PRISMA/DB in an OOPL *

Annita N. Wilschut   Paul W.P.J. Grefen   Peter M.G. Apers
University of Twente

Martin L. Kersten
Centre for Mathematics and Computer Science

Abstract

PRISMA/DB is implemented in a parallel object-oriented language to gain insight in the usage of parallelism. This environment allows us to experiment with parallelism by simply changing the allocation of objects to the processors of the PRISMA machine. These objects are obtained by a strictly modular design of PRISMA/DB. Communication between the objects is required to cooperatively handle the various tasks, but it limits the potential for parallelism. From this approach, we hope to gain a better understanding of parallelism, which can be used to enhance the performance of PRISMA/DB.

1 Introduction

The PRISMA project is a large scale research effort in which the development of a multi-computer and the implementation of non-trivial applications on top of this multi-computer are research issues. The project comprises the development of parallel hardware, the implementation of an operating system, the implementation of a parallel object-oriented language, and the implementation of applications, such as a database management system and an expert system shell, in this language. In this paper, we discuss our experiences with the implementation of a main memory DBMS (PRISMA/DB) in the parallel object-oriented language, called POOL [Amer88].

Because the hardware, the operating system, the language implementation, and the DBMS are developed in parallel, many design decisions in PRISMA/DB were taken without knowledge of the performance behavior of the underlying system. The potential for parallel execution, a phenomenon that is not yet well-understood, makes it even harder to obtain a DBMS architecture that fully exploits the capacity of the multi-computer system. To alleviate the problems, we have heavily used the facilities in POOL to set up PRISMA/DB in a *modular* way as a set of rather independent objects (processes), which each perform certain tasks, such as query processing, concurrency control, etc. This

---

*The work reported in this document was conducted as part of the PRISMA project, a joint effort with Philips Research Eindhoven, partially supported by the Dutch "Stimuleringsprojectteam Informaticaonderzoek (SPIN)".

modular design leads to potential *parallelism* between those objects. On the other hand, *communication* between the objects is needed to synchronize the global query handling process. This communication may reduce the potential parallelism. Also, communication between different processors may cause a large amount of network traffic with obvious consequences for the performance of the system. Hence, both modularization and communication influence the potential for parallelism.

When splitting up PRISMA/DB into functional components, it is not clear what grain size to choose and which tasks to execute in parallel. Our approach is to design PRISMA/DB in a strictly modular way into gradually smaller objects. The language POOL allows us to dynamically control the allocation of objects to processors. In this way, we can decide which objects can execute in parallel and which messages really have to go over the network. As a first approach, objects that form a functional component of PRISMA/DB, such as a parser or a query optimizer, are allocated to the same processor. As soon as the multi-computer system is available, we intend to experiment with the allocation of objects to study parallelism and to enhance the performance.

The paper is organized as follows. The remainder of this section gives an overview of the architecture of PRISMA/DB and a short introduction to the object-oriented language POOL. Sections 2, 3, and 4 deal with modularity, communication, and parallelism and their interaction. Section 5 is about the possibilities we have to experiment with the architecture of PRISMA/DB when the multi-computer system is available.

1.1 An overview of PRISMA/DB

PRISMA/DB is a database mangement system with the following features:

- *Main memory* storage of the entire database. Main memory storage improves performance, because no disk I/O is needed for retrieval. Furthermore the design of the data manager becomes simpler, because there is only one level in the storage hierarchy. Secondary storage is used only for logging and back-up to enable recovery.

- *Distribution* of relations allows parallelism in the execution of simple ralational operations like a selection or a join. By dynamically allocating fragments of relations to different processors, performance is gained.

- Support of two user interface languages: *standard SQL* as data definition and data manipulation language, and a logic retrieval language called *PRISMAlog* [Hout88], which is comparable with languages like Datalog and LDL [Morr86] [Tsur86]. An implementation of the SQL standard has been chosen to accommodate existing application environments relatively easy. A logic programming interface is chosen to have the possibility to integrate data and knowledge processing on the PRISMA machine.

The system has a modular structure with well-defined interfaces. An important role in these interfaces is played by the internal language XRA (eXtended Relational Algebra), which is a relational algebra extended with recursion, iteration, and transaction and session management. This language provides a uniform way to express queries throughout the whole DBMS. The architecture of PRISMA/DB is sketched in figure 1. For a

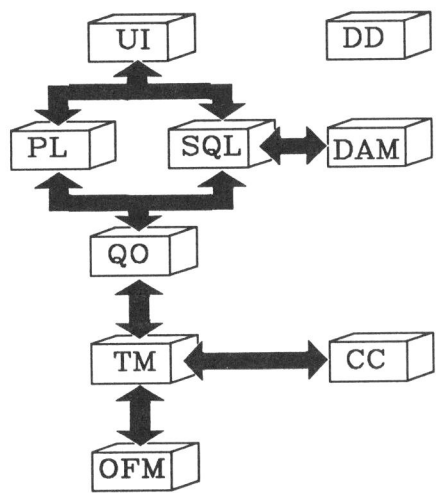

Figure 1: Architecture of PRISMA/DB

comparison with other systems we refer to [Kers87]. The components of PRISMA/DB are briefly described below.

The *Data Dictionary* (DD) is the central storage of all system information. The *Data Allocation Manager* (DAM) constructs fragmentation and allocation schemes for relations. The *Concurrency Controller* (CC) is responsible for the serializability of concurrent transactions; currently a standard two-phase locking protocol with exclusive and shared locks is used, because such a protocol has proven to perform well [Care88]. The locking granularity is that of relation fragments.

The *User Interface* (UI) is the terminal server between user and one of the parsers. The *SQL Parser* (SQL) translates SQL programs into XRA. The *PRISMAlog Parser* (PL) translates PRISMAlog programs into XRA. In particular, the parser translates the prolog-like recursion of PRISMAlog into μ-calculus expressions in XRA [Aper86b] [Aper86c].

The *Query Optimizer* (QO) deals with fragmentation transparency, removal of views, translation of μ-calculus expressions into iterations and transitive closure expressions, and, of course, the traditional optimization of queries.

The *Transaction Manager* (TM) manages the execution of schedules produced by the query optimizer. This involves requesting locks from the CC, creation of new OFMs to store intermediate results and controlling the OFMs involved in the execution of a transaction.

A *One-Fragment Manager* (OFM) controls a single fragment in the database. The OFMs form the smallest granularity for parallelism. There is a separate manager for each fragment, because this approach allows us to generate specilized OFMs to control a specific schema or to execute a specific XRA operation.

The components listed above can be divided into two groups: permanent and temporary components. The permanent components are the Data Dictionary, the Data Allocation Manager, the Concurrency Controller, and the One-Fragment Managers that manage the fragments of the permanent relations in the database; they are created when the DBMS is initialized and they remain accessible during the lifetime of the DBMS. The temporary components are created dynamically to support user sessions and transactions during a session. For example, for each user session a new User Interface is created. For each language session within a user session, either a SQL or a PRISMAlog parser and a Query Optimizer are created. Finally, for each transaction within a language session, a new Transaction Manager is created; this TM controls the creation of temporary One-Fragment Managers for the management of intermediate results of queries. These temporary objects are garbage collected, when not needed anymore.

1.2 The implementation language POOL-X

POOL stands for Parallel Object-Oriented Language [Amer87] [Amer88]. Our DBMS has been implemented in POOL-X, an extended version of POOL which has specially been designed for the implementation of a DBMS. POOL-X has many features in common with other object-oriented languages; inheritance, however, is not supported, because the semantics of the concept inheritance is not yet fully understood. Below we will highlight the most important features of the language.

POOL-X is a *strongly typed* object-oriented language. *Objects* are the basic building blocks in the language. They are instances of *Classes*. All objects in one Class have the same data and routines acting on these data. Objects can be *created dynamically*. Conceptually, objects are independent, active entities; objects behave as processes. Hence, parallelism can be modeled simply by creating objects.

Class definitions are grouped into *Units*. A Unit is a functionally coherent part of a system. A Unit consists of two parts: The *Specification Unit* describes the features of the Classes in the Unit that are visible to other Units. The *Implementation Unit* contains the implementation of the Classes in the Unit; the implementation details are not visible to other Units.

Objects *communicate* by sending each other messages. A receiver will only accept a message if it has explicitly stated that it is ready for it. While performing the action requested in the message, the receiver may send messages to other objects or even to the sender of the original message.

POOL-X messages come in two sorts: synchronous and asynchronous. When a *synchronous* message is sent, the sender is blocked, until an answer arrives. When an *asynchronous* message is sent, the sender just goes on with its own activities after sending the message.

The language POOL-X is designed for programming a multi-computer system. Objects are, by default, allocated to some processor by the operating system. POOL-X provides *allocation pragma's* that overrule the default allocation. Using these pragma's the DBMS programmmer can control the allocation of objects to processors, and thus influence the parallelism within the DBMS.

2 Modularity

When building a large and complex system, one should split up the system into a number of functionally independent modules with precisely defined interfaces. There are two aspects to this: firstly, the architecture of the system should have a structure that makes

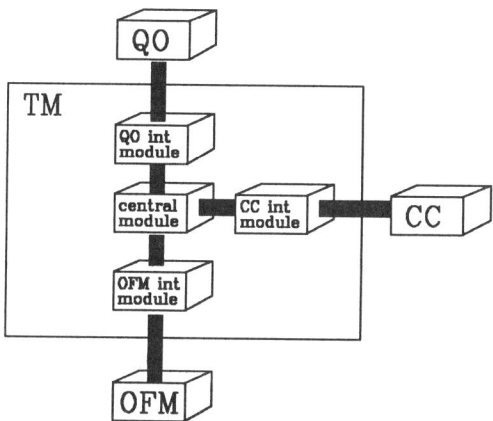

Figure 2: Transaction Manager Architecture

a modular decomposition feasible; secondly, the implementation language should provide thorough support for constructing a modular system. These two aspects are discussed in the following two subsections. Furthermore, the modular structure of a system has a great impact on the communication structure within the system and, consequently, on the possibilities for exploiting parallelism. These issues are addressed in sections 3 and 4.

2.1 Designing a modular DBMS

PRISMA/DB is designed according to a strictly modular approach. Applying this approach to all design levels resulted in the following hierarchical structure of the system.

At the highest level we identify the *components* of PRISMA/DB as described in section 1. These components make up the architecture of the DBMS at the highest level of abstraction.

One level lower, we use a modular structure to describe the internal architecture of each component. The component is further decomposed into a number of *modules* each having a well-defined functionality. As an example, the Transaction Manager is split up into the following four modules (figure 2):

- the Query Optimizer Interface Module, which takes care of some preprocessing tasks on incoming queries;
- the Central Module, which does all central administration and synchronisation of (sub)queries;
- the Concurrency Control Unit Interface Module, which does the local lock administration and handles the two-phase locking protocol;
- the One-Fragment Manager Interface Module, which takes care of the actual execution of queries, the transport of data between One-Fragment Managers, the two-phase commit protocol, and the integrity constraint handling.

At the lowest level we have the internal structure of modules; here we find local data structures for instance.

2.2 Implementing a modular system in POOL

Modularity can be viewed at a number of abstraction levels. POOL provides three abstraction levels to do so.

- At the highest level is the notion of System, consisting of an entire application.
- At the second level the language provides the notion of Units. As described before, a Unit is a functionaly coherent piece of software with a strictly defined interface to the outside world. As such it is a good tool to model modularity at the highest abstraction level of the system being implemented.
- Below the unit level, POOL provides the notion of Classes. A Class can be seen as an active abstract data type. As such, it can be used to model modularity on lower abstraction levels and to provide data abstraction.

It can be concluded here, that POOL provides the means for a well-structured architecture of a system into three layers, supported by the notions of System, Unit, and Class. If one wants to add more layers to the system hierarchy, POOL does not offer language support in the sense of scoping (nesting of Units or Classes is not allowed). The notion of Classes however, is a good aid for well-structured program design. So a multi-level hierarchical structure of the application must both rely on the language facilities as on good programming discipline. To conclude, we should keep in mind that one of the goals of modularization is to make explicit where potential parallelism is available.

3 Communication in PRISMA/DB

In the preceding section, we have seen that PRISMA/DB can be viewed as a collection of fairly independent components (objects). On the one hand, these objects all have their internal activity; on the other hand, several components have to cooperatively handle the global processes such as query processing. The latter requires communication between the components.

To keep the design of the global communication structure manageable, the communication between the components (and also on the lower levels of the system) should comply with the following restrictions: The *communication protocol* must be *well-defined*, otherwise it is hard to agree on it. The communication must be *correct* in the sense that it may not result in deadlock or livelock problems. The communication may not have more negative impact on the amount of possible parallelism than necessary; this means that no unnecessary serialization of processes may be caused by communication protocol. This last aspect of communication is dealt with in the next section.

In this section, we first make the distinction between interfaces and protocols. Secondly, we discuss our strategy to handle the complexity of the communication protocols. Thirdly, we give an example of a communication protocol. Finally, some protocol problems are discussed.

3.1 Interfaces and Protocols

As stated in the introduction on POOL, objects are grouped into Classes. All objects belonging to one Class have the same external interface, which is specified in the specification of the Class. The *interface* between an object of Class A and an object of Class B consists of the set of messages A can send to B and vice versa.

It is possible that the interface between two objects contains synchronous messages in two directions. If no agreement exists on the protocol that should be used, the two objects could simultaneously start sending a synchronous message to each other, which would leave them waiting for answer for ever. We use the word *protocol* for an agreement on how the interface should be used. It is clear that a good protocol is needed to let the components of PRISMA/DB work cooperatively and to prevent the problems mentioned above. POOL supplies a formal way to specify interfaces; there is, however, no way to formalize protocols on a higher abstraction level than the code in the Implementation Units, which makes reasoning about their correctness (e.g. deadlock freedom) difficult.

3.2 Communication driven software engineering

For PRISMA/DB we decided to implement the communication protocols before actually implementing the components. The primary reason for this is, as stated above, that getting the protocols right is extremely important. This is even more so in our situation, where PRISMA/DB is implemented by a group of people working at 2 different locations. Integrating the work of several people may cause many problems, due to all sorts of misunderstanding. By integrating the "empty shells" of the components before adding internal functionality to them, we expected to have fewer problems at integration time. This approach has already proven to work. Assembling our very first working DBMS from its functional components only took less than a week.

The second reason for our strategy is a modeling one. The typical activity of a component can be described by the following pseudo-code:

```
initialize;
WHILE still_work_to_do
DO wait_for_request;
   receive_request;
   handle_request;      %% may include sending answer
                        %% or sending messages
                        %% to other objects
   internal_administration;
OD
```

As shown by code, the communication layer is the top layer of each component. Therefore, it seems natural to start here.

In PRISMA/DB we can distinguish various types of communication. Firstly, queries have to be transported through the system. A User Interface, a Parser, a Query Optimizer, a Transaction Manager, and some One-Fragment Managers each work on query execution; so, queries have to be sent down this chain of components. Secondly, if an error occurs during query execution, an error message has to be sent in opposite direction through the chain of components. Finally, all sorts of control messages have to be sent through the system (e.g. information from the data dictionary may be asked, the transaction manager has to request locks on fragments from the concurrency controller, transactions need a two-phase commit protocol to guarantee atomic execution of transactions).

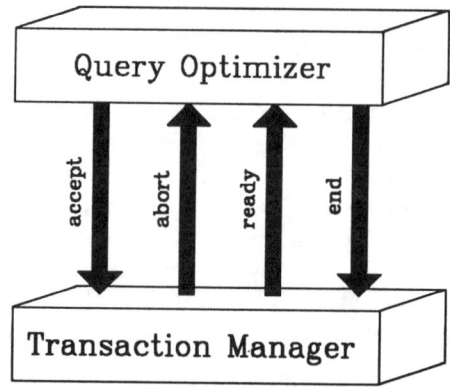

Figure 3: Interface between Query Optimizer and Transaction Manager

We use a uniform protocol for query and error handling, between all components involved, which reduces the number of different interfaces in the system. As an example, the protocol between the query optimizer and the transaction manager is described in the next subsection. Each type of control information needs its own protocol. The same issues are important in all these protocols, however, so one example will give a good idea of the communication in PRISMA/DB.

3.3 An example protocol

The interface between the query optimizer and the transaction manager consists of 4 methods (see figure 3).

- The query optimizer (QO) can send an optimized query to the transaction manager (TM), using the method *accept*.
- The TM can tell the QO that the transaction is aborted (due to some error or a concurrency control problem) using the method *abort*.
- The TM can tell the QO that the execution of a transaction is ready using the method *ready*.
- The QO can tell the TM that the transaction is ready using the method *end*.

These methods are asynchronous.

The protocol over (and rationale behind) this interface is as follows. In the normal flow of control (without errors or concurrency problems) the QO will (after creating a TM) start sending optimized parts of a transaction to the TM. The last statement of every transaction is "commit" or "abort", so the TM knows when a transaction ends. The QO may never use a method *accept* of the TM anymore after sending a "commit" or "abort" (also using *accept*).

If nothing ever went wrong, an interface consisting of one method would do here. But unfortunately errors do occur. In case of an error, the TM sends an *abort* message to the QO, which may still be busy optimizing the rest of the query. Some parts of the query may be on their way from the QO to the TM, while the *abort* message is sent in the opposite direction. The TM will have to wait for these messages before it can terminate.

For this reason the method *end* is added to the interface. *End* has to be the last message from the QO to the TM.

On the other hand, the QO must know when the execution of a transaction is ready, because it could get an *abort* message from the TM while the transaction is still executing. The TM sends a *ready* message to the QO after succesful completion of the transaction, so the QO knows no *abort* can come from this transaction anymore.

3.4 A protocol problem

The various protocols between objects have been designed in the way stated above. We are confident that all individual protocols are fine. But, if all protocols between the components are depicted in one picture, a complex structure emerges. Research was done in modeling the communication protocols in the DBMS as a Petri-net. This approach appeared infeasible though, because of the size of the resulting Petri-net, and because of the fact that if-then-else statements cannot properly be modeled in a Petri-net [Voor89]. Though this is considered a serious problem, it turns out that system deadlocks do not seem to occur anymore after an initial phase.

4 Parallelism

4.1 A simple taxonomy of parallelism in a DBMS

Before giving a discussion on parallelism, we start with a simple taxonomy of the forms of parallelism. Three different forms can be identified (figure 4):

multi-tasking By multi-tasking we mean the ability of a system to execute several independent transactions at the same time. This concept is closely related to the multi-tasking notion in operating systems.

pipe-lining The execution of a transaction is performed in a number of consecutive stages: parsing, query optimization, interpretation of the schedules, and execution at the lowest level of the DBMS. If a transaction is broken into pieces that are sent one after another through the consecutive stages of processing in such a way that several components are working simultaneously, we speak of pipe-lining.

task spreading If the processing of a (sub)transaction at a certain level is decomposed into a number of sub-processes that are executed at the same time, we speak of task spreading. Task spreading involves three steps: firstly, splitting the task into subtasks, creating processes for the execution of the subtasks, and sending the subtasks to the appropriate objects; next, parallel execution of the subtasks; finaly, sending the results of the subtasks to a central process and creating the final result.

We can identify two types of task-spreading (see for example [Kahn87]):

and-parallelism The result of the task is made up out of the results of all subtasks. Hence the task can be completed after all subtasks are completed.

or-parallelism The result of the task is made up out of the result of one or more subtasks. Hence the task may be completed before completion of all subtasks.

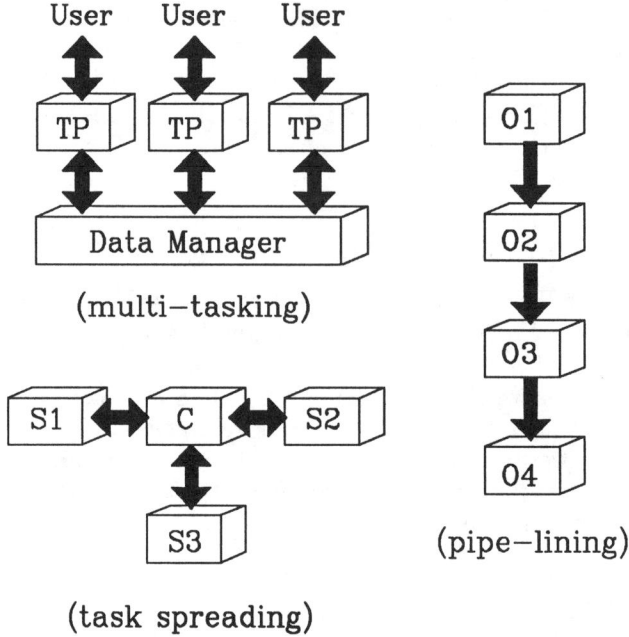

Figure 4: Forms of parallelism

Note that these concepts can be applied in a sort of recurrent way: within a subtask at certain level of the DBMS we can have pipe-lining again. A related description of parallelism in a DBMS can be found in [Bora85].

4.2 Modeling parallelism in POOL

The language POOL gives much freedom in exploiting parallelism. New parallel processes can be created by simply creating new objects each having their own local process. To make use of parallelism, however, we have to synchronize all these processes is some way. This can be achieved in two ways: the creation of new objects and the communication between objects. We briefly discuss this for the various forms of parallelism.

multi-tasking Each task is executed by a collection of POOL objects. The objects belonging to one task communicate with each other; there is no communication between objects that belong to different tasks. Note that all tasks use the central resources of the system, which are objects too. Therefore, the communication between an object O_1 belonging to a task and an object O_2 belonging to a central resource, should be designed in such a way, that O_1 cannot block or delay O_2. For this reason, synchronous method calls from O_2 to O_1 should not be used.

pipe-lining In pipe-lining the objects (processes) are arranged into a sequence $O_1 \cdots O_n$. Each object O_i in principle only needs to send messages to its successor in the pipe-line O_{i+1}. Because we want the objects to execute independent of each other in time, we need both non-blocking communication and some means of message buffering between O_i and O_{i+1}; both concepts are offered by POOL asynchronous methods. The most natural way of creating a pipe-line is by letting an object O_i create its successor O_{i+1}.

task spreading Task spreading needs a coordinating object, say C. Defining n as the number of subtasks, this objects creates objects $S_1 \cdots S_n$ for carrying out the subtasks. After creation, each S_i gets its task via an asynchronous method from C. Upon completion of its task, each S_i sends its result to C. Note that synchronous communication between C and S_i is not suitable since this would not allow C to go on after having activated the first subtask.

4.3 Parallelism in PRISMA/DB

Looking at the architecture of PRISMA/DB at the highest abstraction level (the component level), we can easily identify all three forms of parallelism.

The *multi-tasking* occurs where several autonomous global query processes are running at the same time. A global query process consists of a User Interface, a Parser, a Query Optimizer, a Transaction Manager, and a set of One-Fragment Managers to hold intermediate results. All global query processes are independent of each other apart from sharing the same central resources of PRISMA/DB.

Pipe-lining is found in the sequence of components in the global query process as decribed above. Parts of transactions are transported and processed in a pipe-line manner through the various levels of the transaction processor. Further, pipe-lining is used in processing query trees at the One-Fragment Manager level. Here a Transaction Manager builds an execution structure out of OFM's to process intermediate results and channels for tuple transport. The layout of this structure is the same as that of the query tree. Processing is done in a data flow manner, resulting in a high degree of pipe-lining between the levels of the query tree.

Task spreading is possible at all levels of PRISMA/DB, so also within every component. It should only be used for computation-intensive work, however. The most obvious use here is at the lowest level, where the data storage is handled. Instead of having one manager for all the data in the entire database, we chose to have separate managers for fragments of relations. Each One-Fragment Manager process can be thought of as a subtask of the data manager task. Task spreading may also occur in a single component; an example could be the Query Optimizer, where we could split up the optimization process into a number of sub-processes each doing part of the optimization.

When looking at task spreading in a DBMS we notice that or-parallelism can hardly be ever used. An example of possible or-parallelism can be found in the standard two-phase commit protocol (see [Date83]). When we execute the local pre-commit decisions in parallel at the One Fragment Manager level, we can use or-parallelism in deciding about global commit; this is possible because a single negative pre-commit decision always results in a global abort. Note however, that we gain only in an abort situation here.

4.4 Logical versus operational parallelism

When talking about parallelism it is important to distinguish between two concepts:

logical parallelism By logical parallelism we mean the parallelism that we model into the software system; this is closely related to the modular structure chosen for the system. The amount of potential parallelism here is only limited by the number of processes (objects) existing at the same time.

operational parallelism As soon as we execute a system on real hardware, it is obvious that there cannot be more processes running in parallel than there are processors in the system. The number of active processes running concurrently is called operational parallelism. It should be clear that the possible amount of parallelism here is limited both by the available number of processors and by the amount of logical parallelism.

Developing a large system in POOL gives the freedom to look at these two appearances of parallelism in truly independent steps. When designing system, attention is paid to logical parallelism only; concern is focused on a good software structure, the underlying hardware is not important. In a second stage of the development process, the allocation pragma's in POOL can be used to bind the various processes (objects) to processors in the system. By grouping objects on the various processors in the system, we determine which processes will be running in operational parallelism (on different processors) and which not (on the same processor).

Determining a good allocation of the objects of PRISMA/DB is difficult. Therefore, we need a great deal of experimenting with the allocation to obtain a high degree of parallelism and thus a good performance. This problem is discussed in the next section.

5 Experiments

As stated before, we plan to do experiments to gain understanding of the behavior of parallel systems. If the ratio between transmission costs and the costs for local processing is unknown, it is hard to decide whether sending some amount of work to another node for parallel execution will speed up some process as a whole.

The section on modularity showed the possibilities for a modular design of the database system in POOL. This modular design makes it possible to experiment with the allocation of components and to move certain subtasks from one component to another. The section on parallelism explains that logical and operational parallelism are independent in POOL. So, the design for the PRISMA database can be made with all sorts of possible parallelism in mind, from very coarse (e.g. multi-tasking) to very fine (e.g. task spreading in the optimization of one query). The possibility to move subtasks and to change the parallelism gives us a nice opportunity to experiment with the database system, to gain knowledge on parallel execution of programs and to get the best possible performance from our system. Below some examples of possible experiments are given.

5.1 Sequential versus Parallel execution of queries

Consider the following Relational Algebra expression:

$$(\sigma_{3="PRISMA"} EMPLOYEE) \bowtie_{5=1} (\pi_{1,6} CITY)$$

Calculating the result of this expression requires the calculation of a selection and a projection, and after those of a join. The selection, the projection and the join are each executed by a separate OFM. There are several schemes to organize this calculation.

- The calculation can be done sequentially on one processor. In this case there are no transmission costs, but the processor has to be shared among three OFMs. This scheme can only be chosen if the OFMs for base relations *EMPLOYEE* and *CITY* reside on the same processor.

- The calculation of the selection and the projection can be done in parallel on two nodes followed by the join on one of the two nodes that are already involved. In this case, the result of either the projection or the selection has to be sent to the other node.

- The calculation of the selection and the projection can be done in parallel on two nodes followed by the join on a third node. This gives an extra possibility for parallelism: the result of the selection and the projection can be pipe-lined to the join. In this case both the result of the selection and the result of the projection have to be sent to another node.

It is not at all clear which of the three schemes is most efficient. If the transmission overhead is high, the first one is probably best. The implementation of PRISMA/DB in POOL gives the possibilty to experiment. Going from one scheme to another only involves changing some allocation pragmas. Nothing else in the program has to be changed; the potential for parallel execution is available, but it does not need to be exploited. Once the behavior of such executions is understood, the query optimizer can be programmed to dynamically generate the right allocation pragma's.

5.2 An experiment with the boundary between components

As shown in figure 1, there is an interface between the Transaction Manager and the Concurrency Controller. In general, a TM is located on another node than the CC. If a TM wants to use the same fragment several times, it may repeatedly request the same lock. This strategy is simple for the TM: it does not have to do its own lock administration. Every use of a fragment requires transmission of a request over the network though. On the other hand, the TM may have its local lock administration. Before requesting a lock, it finds out whether it already holds a lock on the fragment. If so, no request needs to be sent over the network; if not, the lock has to be requested from the CC. This strategy saves transmission costs at the expense of some local overhead in the TM.

The implementation of the system in POOL gives us the possibilty to postpone the decision on such issues until after implementing the system. In the modular design it is easy to switch between the two ways of handling the problem. Our current implementation has a local lock administration in the TM. The central module of the TM has an interface with its lock administrator. It does not take much time to eliminate this object from the TM and adjust the interface of the CC to what the central TM expects from its local lock administration. Nothing has to be changed to the the central TM or to the main part of the CC.

These two examples show that the object-oriented approach allows us to postpone some of the design decisions or to changed them quite easily.

6 Conclusions and a Look into the Future

Currently we have a first prototype of PRISMA/DB running on an interpreter on a sequential machine. The status of this prototype shows that it is well possible to implement a complex DBMS in a modern (and even experimental) object-oriented language. POOL-X offers a programming environment that makes implementation of complex parallel processes possible in a reasonably short time. The parallel object-oriented programming environment has shown to be a good basis for modeling modularity, communication, and parallelism into a complex system. One of the strong points, is the flexibility of the system, which allows us to experiment with the architecture to study parallelism and to enhance the performance.

Our major concern at this time is the performance of the system on the target machine, which is still being developed. The high level features of POOL-X may cause some loss of performance when a straight-forward implementation of the language is used. Therefore, we expect that the performance of PRISMA/DB on the multi-processor machine will highly depend on the optimization qualities of a POOL-X compiler. However, we are confident that with the modular structure of PRISMA/DB, it is relatively easy to tune or adjust the system at a later step in this project.

Acknowledgements

We wish to thank the project members for providing a challenging environment and productive cooperation with the teams from Philips Research Laboratories Eindhoven, the University of Amsterdam and the Centre for Mathematics and Computer Science Amsterdam in the development of our DBMS. In particular, we wish to thank dr. A.J.Nijman for bringing academia and industry together, dr. H.H.Eggenhuisen for providing good project management and for stimulating the interaction between the various subprojects, P.America for his work on the definition of POOL-X, M.Beemster and J.v.d.Spek for their work on the realization of the POOL-X interpreter and finally the other members of the database group for their cooperation.

References

[Amer87]   P. America, *An introduction to object-oriented programming*, Doc.nr. 364, Esprit Project 415A, Philips Research Laboratories, Eindhoven, The Netherlands, 1987.

[Amer88]   P. America, *Language definition of POOL-X*, Doc.nr. 350, PRISMA Project, Philips Research Laboratories, Eindhoven, The Netherlands, 1988.

[Aper86a] P.M.G. Apers, J.A. Bergstra, H.H. Eggenhuisen, L.O. Hertzberger, M.L. Kersten, P.J.F. Lucas, A.J. Nijman, G. Rozenberg, *A Highly Parallel Machine for Data and Knowledge Base Management: PRISMA*, Doc.nr. 1, PRISMA Project, Philips Research Laboratories, Eindhoven, The Netherlands, 1988.

[Aper86b] P.M.G. Apers, M.A.W. Houtsma, F. Brandse, *Extending a Relational Interface with Recursion*, Proceedings of the 6th Advanced Database Symposium, Tokyo, Japan, 1986.

[Aper86c] P.M.G. Apers, M.A.W. Houtsma, F. Brandse, *Processing Recursive Queries in Relational Algebra*, in Data and Knowledge (DS-2), Ed. R.A.Meersman, A.C.Sernadas, Elsevier Science Publishers, IFIP, 1988.

[Aper88]   P.M.G. Apers, M.L. Kersten, H.C.M. Oerlemans, *PRISMA Database Machine: A Distributed, Main-Memory Approach*, Proceedings of the International Conference on Extending Database Technology, Venice, Italy, 1988.

[Bora85] H. Boral, S. Redfield, *Database Machine Morphology*, Proceedings of the 11th International Conference On Very Large Data Bases, Stockholm, Sweden, 1985.

[Care88] M.J. Carey, M. Livny, *Distributed Concurrency Control Performance: A Study of Algorithms, Distribution and Replication*, Proceedings of the 14th International Conference on Very Large Data Bases, Los Angeles, USA, 1988.

[Date83] C.J. Date, *An Introduction to Data Base Systems Part II*, Addison Wesley, 1983.

[Hout88] M.A.W. Houtsma, H.J.A. van Kuyk, J. Flokstra, P.M.G. Apers, M.L. Kersten, *A Logic Query Language and its Algebraic Optimization for a Multiprocessor Database Machine*, Memorandum INF-88-52, University of Twente, 1988.

[Kahn87] K. Kahn, E.D. Tribble, M.S. Miller, D.G. Bobrow, *Vulcan: Logical Concurrent Objects*, Research Directions in Object-Oriented Programming, MIT Press, Cambridge, Massachusetts, 1987.

[Kers87] M.L. Kersten, P.M.G. Apers, M.A.W. Houtsma, H.J.A. van Kuijk, R.L.W. van de Weg, *A Distributed, Main Memory Database Machine*, Proceedings of the 5th International Workshop on Database Machines, Karuizawa, Japan, 1987.

[Morr86] K. Morris, J.D. Ullman, A.V. Gelder, *Design overview of the NAIL! system*, Stanford University, STAN-CS-86-1108 Stanford, CA, 1986.

[Tsur86] S. Tsur, C. Zaniolo, *LDL: A Logic-Based Data-Language*, Proceedings of the 12th International Conference on Very Large Databases, Kyoto, Japan, 1986.

[Voor89] L.v.d.Voort, *A qualitative analysis of the Prisma/DB Empty Shell*, Centre for Mathematics and Computer Science, Amsterdam, The Netherlands, 1989.

Database Processing Models in Parallel Processing Systems

Sakti Pramanik
&
Myoung Ho Kim

Michigan State University
Computer Science Department
East Lansing, MI 48824-1027

Abstract

This paper investigates database processing in parallel processing systems. The objective is to maximize throughput and minimize response time through conflict free data accesses. We propose abstract models as a general framework, and then present two specific parallel processing strategies for two common types of database applications. One is optimal file distribution for partial match queries, and the other is a multidirectory hashing scheme where database accesses are based on primary keys. We show that these proposed parallel processing strategies perform better than those proposed earlier. This work presents a new basis on which design of parallel processing database systems for various applications can be facilitated more systematically.

1. Introduction

There will be many applications for large databases that cannot be performed in an acceptable response time by current database systems. Since one of the most significant ways of improving performance is through parallelism, the importance of parallel processing in database systems has been increasingly recognized. Parallel processing in database systems can increase throughput and minimize response time through concurrent data accesses as well as processing data in parallel. However, parallel processing by itself does not necessarily lead to high performance. Some of the reasons are attributed to overhead due to interprocessor communication, remote memory accesses and data access conflicts. External I/O traffic has also shown to be a serious performance bottleneck [2, 11]. There have been numerous works on improving performance of database systems by specialized software/hardware techniques [4, 8, 10]. Our objective here is to investigate database processing for general purpose parallel processing systems.

The remainder of this paper is organized as follows. In section 2 we propose abstract parallel processing models for database systems. In section 3 we describe optimal file distribution for partial match queries. In section 4 we propose a multidirectory hashing scheme for queries based on primary keys. Section 5 contains concluding remarks.

This work was supported in part by National Science Foundation Grant No. CCR-8706069, and Naval Research Laboratory Grant No. N00014-87-K-2022.

2. Abstract Database Processing Models

In this section we describe high level abstraction of database processing for parallel processing systems. The objective of this abstraction is to define a framework which can be the basis of more specific implementation.

2.1. General Model for Database Parallel Processing Systems

We propose an abstract model for parallel processing of database systems. This is shown in Figure 1. The model is based on distributing data and access structures to enhance concurrency.

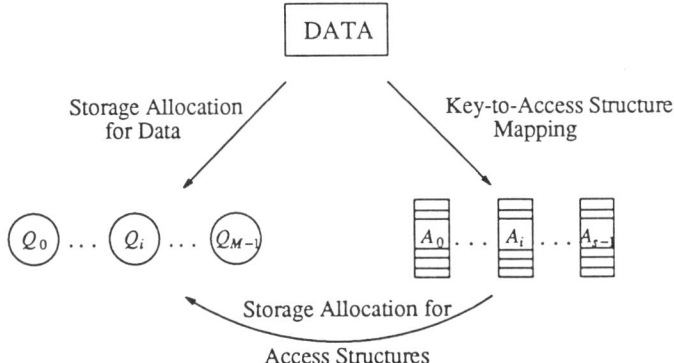

Figure 1. General parallel processing model for database systems

In the figure, Q_i's represent a set of parallel access nodes. These can be main memory modules or disks, depending on the parallel processing environment. A_i's denote a set of access structures. As shown in the figure, there are three mappings that are important for concurrent processing. They are (1) storage allocation for data, (2) storage allocation for access structures and (3) key to access structure mapping.

Storage allocation for data, and storage allocation for access structures determine the physical access concurrency among the nodes. In parallel processing systems, the speed mismatch between computation and data access time becomes a more serious problem than in the uniprocessor system due to data access conflict if data are not appropriately distributed over access nodes. Since database applications in general require many data accesses with relatively less computation, degradation of system performanc due to inappropriate storage allocation scheme may be more significant in database applications than in others.

In addition to physical memory access conflict, there are other sources of conflict for concurrent accessing of data. This means that even though two data are stored in different access nodes, access concurrency can still be reduced. One such source is the lock contention because the data in the same locking entity cannot be accessed concurrently when that entity is locked. Unfortunately, most access structures have critical parts which frequently need to be locked, e.g., root node in the tree type index and directory size dependent variables in dynamic hashing. Thus, in order to achieve high concurrency multiple independent access structures need to be constructed for each relation to reduce the amount of sharing for critical shared variables. By multiple access structures for each relation, we mean that a set of records pertaining to one relation is partitioned horizontally and each subset of partition contributes to each independent access structure. Thus, we need an appropriate mapping from a set of keys to a set of access structures. Key to access structure mapping determines logical access concurrency while storage allocation schemes for data and access structure determine physical access concurrency.

For many applications we can simplify the general model such that only a group of data which are stored in the same access node, say Q_i, contributes to a unique subset of access structures, say A_j to A_l which are also constructed in the same access node. By this approach storage allocation strategy for data and access structures can be treated integratedly, and the complexity of processing models can also be reduced. Two stage parallel processing model presented in the next section is based on this idea.

2.2. Two Stage Parallel Processing Model for Database Systems

The proposed two stage parallel processing model for database systems is shown in Figure 2. In the figure, the first stage, H1, is called *Data Distribution* algorithm and the second stage, H2, is called *Data Construction* algorithm.

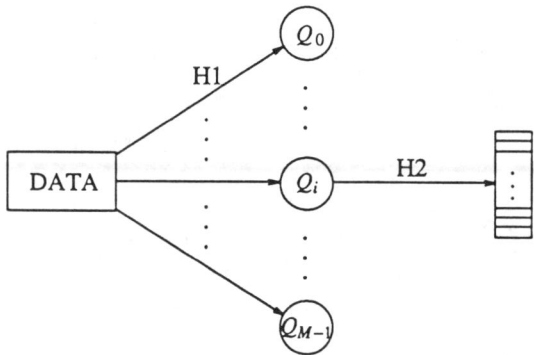

Figure 2. Two stage parallel processing model for database systems

The data distribution algorithm, which is the same as data storage allocation in the general model, determines how the data is appropriately distributed to the parallel access nodes so that access concurrency is maximized between the access nodes. The data construction algorithm, on the other hand, determines an appropriate data structure to minimize access time.

A data distribution algorithm can be a functional mapping which depends only on data values. For example, if node addresses are determined by hashed values of input data, the distribution algorithm is a mapping which is independent of time or other system parameters. Since data accesses are content-based for most database applications, it is advantageous to make a data distribution algorithm functional depending only on data values.

Let D be a set of data and $Z_M = \{0, 1, \ldots, M-1\}$ be a set of parallel access nodes. Let a data distribution algorithm be a function from D to Z_M. Since actual data are usually unevenly distributed in the data domain, data distribution algorithms are commonly designed based on hashed values which are evenly distributed in a hash address space. Thus, we define data distribution algorithm H1 as a composition of two functions, $H1^{(1)}$ and $H1^{(2)}$, such that $H1^{(1)}$ is a mapping from D to T and $H1^{(2)}$ is a mapping from T to Z_M, where T is the set of hash values. Figure 3 shows two level implementation of H1 in the model of Figure 2.

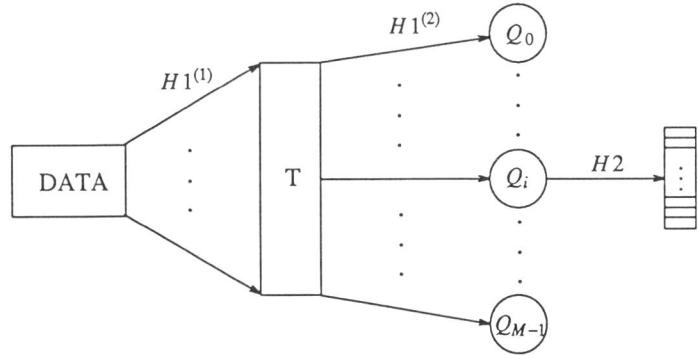

Figure 3. Two level implementation of H1 for the two stage model

Let H2 be a hash-based data construction algorithm and LD be a set of entries in all the local directories generated by H2 for a given file system. If there exists one-to-one correspondence between T and LD, T is called a *real global directory*. Otherwise, it is called a *virtual global directory*. When T is a real global directory, the set of all the local directories can be thought of as a partition of T. $H1^{(1)}$ is usually static because the use of dynamic hashing for $H1^{(1)}$ will cause significant overhead due to internode data movement. However, static hashing scheme for $H1^{(1)}$ may result in sparse local directories or long overflow chains. These problems can be avoided by using a virtual global directory, where the actual local directory is determined by H2. The use of real/virtual global directory is illustrated in section 3.2.

3. Parallel Processing Strategies for Partial Match Retrieval Type Queries

In this section we present parallel processing strategies for partial match queries. Partial match queries are queries where some of the attributes are specified, hence a set of qualified records need to be retrieved. For example, query q = [Age = *, Department = "mathematics", State = "Ohio"] is a partial match query, where * denotes a don't care condition.

It has been shown in [9] that multikey hashing is effective for partial match retrieval type applications. Multikey hash function, H, for a file with n fields is a set of n functions $\{H_1, \cdots, H_n\}$ such that given a record $r = <r_1, \cdots, r_n>$, $H(r) = <H_1(r_1), \cdots, H_n(r_n)>$. $H(r)$ is called a bucket. The main objective of this section is to maximize access concurrency for partial match queries by distributing buckets in multikey hashing.

3.1. Data Distribution Algorithm For Partial Match Queries

There are a few heuristic methods for distributing data in partial match queries. Du, et al. have proposed the Disk Modulo (DM) distribution method based on modulo arithmetic [3]. The DM distribution method is simple and elegant but does not work in many cases. For example, it may not give optimal distribution if some of the field sizes are less than the given number of devices. The Generalized Disk Modulo (GDM) distribution method has also been proposed in [3] to overcome this problem. Though this method gives a sufficient condition to achieve optimal distribution, no general method has been given to find the optimal distribution parameters. Several useful properties of these modulo based distribution methods have also been given in [12].

We propose Fieldwise eXclusive-or (FX) distribution methods which give better performance for a wider range of partial match queries than existing methods. The FX distribution methods use bitwise exclusive-or operation on the field values which are computed by multikey hashing. Field transformation techniques are developed to extend the scope of optimality.

Before describing the FX distribution method, it is necessary to introduce some notations as well as relevant definitions and assumptions.

Definition :
- $f_i = \{0, 1, \ldots, F_i-1\}$, where F_i denotes $|f_i|$.
- M denotes the number of parallel devices.
- N is the set of all natural numbers including 0.
- Z_M is the set of all integers from 0 to M-1.
- $(a_{m-1} \ldots a_0)_B$ is a binary notation of an integer, where a_i is a binary digit.

$|f_i|$ is assumed to be a power of 2 which is common for hash directory files for partitioned hashing schemes [1]. The number of devices M is also assumed to be a power of 2.

Definition : Let $R(q)$ be the set of qualified buckets for partial match query q in a given file system. A distribution method is called *strict optimal* for partial match query q in that file system if each device has no more than $\lceil |R(q)|/M \rceil$ buckets. When a distribution method is strict optimal for all possible partial match queries in a given file system, it is called *perfect optimal* for that file system.

Definition : [+] denotes exclusive-or operation between two bits. We will use the same notation [+] to denote exclusive-or operation between integers and sets of integers as follows. When $X = (a_{m-1} \ldots a_0)_B$ and $Y = (b_{m-1} \ldots b_0)_B$ are two integers, X [+] $Y = (a_{m-1}$ [+] $b_{m-1} \ldots a_0$ [+] $b_0)_B$. If X is an integer and $Y = \{y_1, \ldots, y_L\}$ is a set of integers, X [+] Y is defined as $\{X$ [+] $y_i \mid y_i \in Y\}$. If both $X = \{x_1, \ldots, x_K\}$ and $Y = \{y_1, \ldots, y_L\}$ are sets of integers, X [+] Y is defined as $\{x_i$ [+] $y_j \mid x_i \in X, y_j \in Y\}$

For example, if $X_1 = 2, Y_1 = 3$ and $Y_2 = \{0, 1, 2, 3\}$, then X_1 [+] $Y_1 = 1$ and X_1 [+] $Y_2 = \{0, 1, 2, 3\}$.

Definition : $\overset{n}{\underset{i=1}{[+]}}(Y_i) = Y_1$ [+] Y_2 [+] $Y_3 \cdots$ [+] Y_n.

Note that $\overset{n}{\underset{i=1}{[+]}}$ is a shorthand notation for performing exclusive-or operation between sets of integers $Y_1, Y_2, \ldots, Y_n$.

With respect to the two stage model of Figure 3, a multikey hash function corresponds to $H1^{(1)}$ and the FX distribution method presented in the following sections corresponds to $H1^{(2)}$.

3.1.1. Basic FX Distribution Method

Let $f_1 \times f_2 \times ... \times f_n$ be the set of all buckets. The Basic FX distribution method allocates bucket $<J_1, ..., J_n>$ into device $T_M \left[\sum_{j=1}^{n} (J_j) \right]$, where $T_M : N \rightarrow Z_M$ is a function which returns the rightmost $\log_2 M$ bits of domain values, and $J_j \in f_j$ for $j = 1, ..., n$.

Example 1. Figure 4 shows the bucket distribution by the Basic FX distribution method, where $f_1 = \{0, 1\}$, $f_2 = \{0, 1, 2, 3, 4, 5, 6, 7\}$ and $M = 4$. In the figure, binary numbers are used for field values and decimal numbers are used for Device No (This convention will be used in all the examples of the FX distribution method).

f_1	f_2	Device No
000	000	0
000	001	1
000	010	2
000	011	3
000	100	0
000	101	1
000	110	2
000	111	3
001	000	1
001	001	0
001	010	3
001	011	2
001	100	1
001	101	0
001	110	3
001	111	2

Figure 4. Basic FX distribution

As shown in Figure 4, the Basic FX distribution method is strict optimal for any partial match query in this file system. For example, if f_1 value is $(001)_B$ and f_2 is unspecified, then we have to access eight buckets $<(001)_B,(000)_B>, ..., <(001)_B,(111)_B>$. Since each device has two qualified buckets for this partial match query, the Basic FX distribution method is strict optimal for this query.

Theorem 1. The Basic FX distribution method is strict optimal for any partial match query in which the number of unspecified fields is 0 or 1.

Proof: Given in [6]. □

Theorem 2. For any partial match query which has two or more unspecified fields, the Basic FX

distribution method is strict optimal, if there exists at least one unspecified field i such that $F_i \geq M$.
Proof: Given in [6]. □

Theorem 1 and 2 show general characteristics of exclusive-or operation for optimal distribution. However, the Basic FX distribution method does not give optimal distribution for partial match queries with 2 or more unspecified fields, when the size of none of the unspecified fields is greater than or equal to M. For example, when M = 16 and all others are the same as in Example 1, the distribution is not optimal if both fields are unspecified. Thus, in the next section we propose field transformation techniques for the fields whose sizes are less than the given number of devices.

3.1.2. Extended FX Distribution Method

Let $f_1 \times f_2 \times \ldots \times f_n$ be the set of all buckets. The Extended FX distribution method allocates bucket $<J_1,\ldots,J_n>, J_j \in f_j$ for $j = 1, \ldots, n$, into device $T_M\left[\underset{j=1}{\overset{n}{[+]}}(X_j(J_j))\right]$, where

i) if $|f_j| \geq M$, X_j is the identity function,
ii) if $|f_j| < M$, X_j is an element of set of injective (one-to-one) functions whose domains are f_j and ranges are Z_M.

X_j is called field transformation function.

When X_j is the identity function for all $j = 1,\ldots,n$, the Extended FX distribution method reduces to the Basic FX distribution method. It is easy to see that Theorem 1 and Theorem 2 also hold for the Extended FX distribution method.

By the above definition, a field transformation function can be any one-to-one function. However, we are only interested in field transformation functions by which we can achieve strict optimal distribution for various types of partial match queries for which the Basic FX distribution method does not give strict optimal distribution. Since the fields whose sizes are no less than the given number of devices do not cause any problem, from now on we will focus only on the fields whose sizes are less than M. We will simply call the FX distribution method instead of the Extended FX distribution method.

The field transformation functions developed for the FX distribution method are as follows.

Definition : Let $f_l = \{0, \ldots, F_l-1\}$.
(1) $I : N \rightarrow N$ is the identity function.
(2) When $|f_l| < M$, $U^{M, |f_l|} : f_l \rightarrow Z_M$ is a function such that $U^{M, |f_l|}(l) = l*M/|f_l|$.
(3) When $|f_l| < M$, for $x = 1, \ldots, y$ in which y is a maximum integer such that $|f_l|^y < M$, $IU_x^{M, |f_l|} : f_l \rightarrow Z_M$ is a function such that $IU_x^{M, |f_l|}(l) = l\ [+]\ \left[\underset{k=1}{\overset{x}{[+]}} l*M/|f_l|^k\right]$.

Note that the function $IU_x^{M, |f_l|}$ is a general notation for functions $IU_1^{M, |f_l|}, IU_2^{M, |f_l|}, \ldots$, etc.

Example 2. When $f_1 = \{0, 1, 2, 3, 4, 5, 6, 7\}, f_2 = \{0, 1\}$ and M = 16, $U^{16,8}(f_1) = \{0, 2, 4, 6, 8, 10,$

12, 14}, $IU_1{}^{16,8}(f_1) = \{0, 3, 6, 5, 12, 15, 10, 9\}$, $IU_2{}^{16,2}(f_2) = \{0, 13\}$ and $IU_3{}^{16,2}(f_2) = \{0, 15\}$.

We have defined basic transformation functions, I, $U^{M,|f_i|}$, $IU_1{}^{M,|f_i|}$, ... , $IU_x{}^{M,|f_i|}$ which will be used in various combinations for optimal data distribution. For example, for any values of $|f_i|$, $|f_j|$ and M, it will be shown that the FX distribution method distributes ordered 2-tuples in $I(f_i) \times U^{M,|f_j|}(f_j)$ optimally. Because of notational complexity, we will leave out the superscripts M, $|f_i|$ from transformation functions whenever there is no ambiguity.

Theorem 3. When there are only two fields i, j and the given number of devices is M such that $F_j < M$, the FX distribution method with $I(f_i)$ and $U(f_j)$ is perfect optimal.
Proof: Given in [6]. □

Theorem 4. When there are only two fields i, j and the given number of devices is M such that $F_j{}^x < M$ for some positive integer x, the FX distribution method with $I(f_i)$ and $IU_x(f_j)$ is perfect optimal.
Proof: Given in [5]. □

Example 3. Let $f_1 = \{0, 1, 2, 3\}$, $f_2 = \{0, 1, 2, 3\}$ and M = 16. Figure 5 shows the bucket distribution by the FX distribution method with $I(f_1)$ and $IU_1(f_2)$, where $IU_1(f_2) = \{0, 5, 10, 15\}$.

$I(f_1)$	$IU_1(f_2)$	Device No
0000	0000	0
0000	0101	5
0000	1010	10
0000	1111	15
0001	0000	1
0001	0101	4
0001	1010	11
0001	1111	14
0010	0000	2
0010	0101	7
0010	1010	8
0010	1111	13
0011	0000	3
0011	0101	6
0011	1010	9
0011	1111	12

Figure 5. FX distribution with I and IU_1 transformation

Theorem 5. When there are only two fields j, k and the given number of devices is M such that $F_j < M$ and $F_k{}^x < M$ for some positive integer x, the FX distribution method with $U(f_j)$ and $IU_x(f_k)$ is perfect optimal.
Proof: Given in [5]. □

Example 4. Let $f_1 = \{0, 1, 2, 3\}$, $f_2 = \{0, 1, 2, 3\}$ and M = 16. Figure 6 shows the bucket distribution by the FX distribution method with $U(f_1)$ and $IU_1(f_2)$, where $U(f_1) = \{0, 4, 8, 12\}$ and $IU_1(f_2) = \{0, 5, 10, 15\}$.

$U(f_1)$	$IU_1(f_2)$	Device No
0000	0000	0
0000	0101	5
0000	1010	10
0000	1111	15
0100	0000	4
0100	0101	1
0100	1010	14
0100	1111	11
1000	0000	8
1000	0101	13
1000	1010	2
1000	1111	7
1100	0000	12
1100	0101	9
1100	1010	6
1100	1111	3

Figure 6. FX distribution with U and IU_1 transformation

Theorem 6. When there are only l fields, $i1, i2, \dots, il$ such that $F_{il} \geq F_{i(l-1)} \geq \dots \geq F_{i1}$ and $F_{il}^l < M$ for the given number of devices M, the FX distribution method with $IU_1(f_{i1}), \dots, IU_l(f_{il})$ is perfect optimal.
Proof: Given in [5]. □

Theorem 7. When there are only three fields i, j, k and the given number of devices is M such that $F_j < M$ and $F_k^x < M$ for some positive integer x which is greater than 1, the FX distribution method with $I(f_i)$, $U(f_j)$ and $IU_x(f_k)$ is perfect optimal, if either (i) there are at least 2 fields r and s such that $r, s \in \{i, j, k\}$ and $F_r F_s \geq M$ or (ii) $F_k \geq F_j$.
Proof: The proof for $x = 2$ is given in [6]. Refer to [5] for the complete proof. □

It is unfortunate that the FX distribution method does not always guarantee perfect optimal distribution when the number of fields whose sizes are less than M, is greater than or equal to 4 in general. In fact, it has been shown in [12] that when the number of fields whose sizes are less than the given number of devices, is greater than or equal to 4, there is no method which always guarantees perfect optimal distribution. However, even for these cases we will show through performance experiments that the FX distribution method still gives near optimal distribution for most partial match queries.

3.1.3. Performance Comparisons to Other Distribution Methods

In this section we compare the performance of the FX distribution method with those of the DM and GDM distribution methods for some typical file systems. Figure 7 shows the percentage of strict optimal distribution for all possible partial match queries in files with ten fields. In the figures X-coordinate denotes the number of fields whose sizes are less than the given number of devices, and Y-coordinate denotes the percentage of partial match queries for which the distribution is strict optimal. DM denotes DM distribution and FX denotes FX distribution. Here, results are computed from sufficient conditions given for each method. Since no general method has been given to determine the existence of parameter values for optimal distribution in the GDM distribution method, in Figure 7 we compare the FX distribution method to the DM distribution method only. Figure 7-(a) shows the case when for any two fields r and s whose sizes are less than the given number of devices M, $F_r F_s \geq M$. Figure 7-(b) is the case when for any two fields r and s whose sizes are less than the given number of devices M, $F_r F_s < M$, but for any three fields r, s and t whose sizes are less than M, $F_r F_s F_t \geq M$.

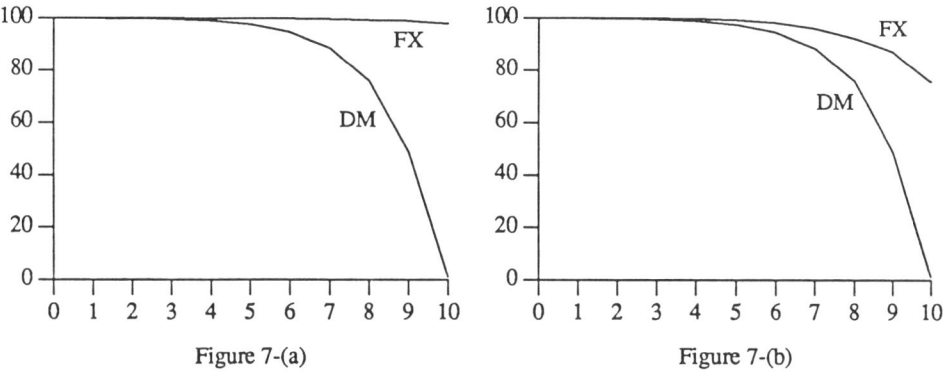

Figure 7-(a)   Figure 7-(b)

These results show that the FX distribution method gives high probability of strict optimal distribution for partial match queries in typical file systems. We also give results of performance experiments on average response time of the FX, DM and GDM distribution method as follows.

When systems are configured such that data retrieval time for any device is almost the same, the response time for a partial match query is determined by the device which has the largest number of qualified buckets. Thus, the largest response size defined below is one way of measuring response time of various distribution methods.

Definition : When $r_i(q)$ denotes the number of qualified buckets in device i for a partial match query q, the *largest response size* for the query q is defined as $MAX(r_1(q), r_2(q), \cdots, r_{M-1}(q))$.

Table 1-(a) through 1-(d) show the largest response size of the DM, GDM and FX distribution method for various cases. The first column denotes the number of unspecified fields in partial match queries. The value in each entry denotes the average of largest response sizes from all possible partial match queries for that entry.

For the GDM distribution method, we have used seven different sets of multiplication parameters. These sets are GDM1 : 3, 11, 23,37, 49, 53 and GDM2 : 5, 9, 31, 37, 53, 59 and GDM3 : 41, 43, 47, 51, 53, 57 and GDM4 : 3, 5, 7, 11, 13, 17 and GDM5 : 3, 7, 13, 43, 51, 57 and GDM6 : 2, 3, 5, 7, 11, 13 and GDM7 : 2, 5, 11, 43, 51, 57. Here, sets of parameters in GDM1, GDM2, GDM3, GDM4 and GDM5 are chosen based on [3], i.e., relative prime to the given number of devices. GDM6 and GDM7 have been used to include other cases. For the FX distribution method, field transformation functions applied in each experiment are as follows.

Table 1-(a) : $<I, U, IU_2, IU_3, I, IU_1>$, Table 1-(b) : $<I, U, IU_1, I, U, IU_1>$,

Table 1-(c) : $<IU_4, U, IU_3, I, IU_1, IU_2>$, Table 1-(d) : $<U, IU_1, IU_3, IU_4, I, IU_2>$

Here, the sequence of transformation functions corresponds to the sequence of fields to which these transformation functions are applied. Heuristics based on the given theorems have been used to choose these transformation functions.

DM	GDM1	GDM2	GDM3	GDM4	GDM5	GDM6	GDM7	FX	Optimal
2	2.1	1.3	1.7	1.4	1.3	1.5	1.3	1.5	1.1	1.0
3	4.4	2.2	3.1	2.2	2.2	2.4	2.3	2.6	1.6	1.2
4	10.3	4.4	6.2	4.3	4.2	4.7	4.5	5.1	3.0	2.7
5	22.3	8.7	12.3	8.2	8.2	9.2	9.0	10.7	6.7	6.7
6	52.0	18.0	26.0	17.0	18.0	19.0	20.0	22.0	16.0	16.0

Table 1-(a). $F_1 = F_2 = F_3 = F_4 = 2$, $F_5 = F_6 = 4$ and $M = 16$.

DM	GDM1	GDM2	GDM3	GDM4	GDM5	GDM6	GDM7	FX	Optimal
2	8.0	2.4	2.8	2.4	2.1	2.9	2.1	2.2	2.4	1.0
3	48.0	10.7	11.8	10.6	9.9	12.4	10.2	10.3	8.0	8.0
4	344.0	69.0	73.3	67.5	67.1	75.4	68.3	68.1	64.0	64.0
5	2460.0	522.3	531.3	517.3	516.2	538.2	520.5	517.0	512.0	512.0
6	18152.0	4115.0	4148.0	4102.0	4102.0	4146.0	4114.0	4102.0	4096.0	4096.0

Table 1-(b). $F_1 = F_2 = F_3 = F_4 = F_5 = F_6 = 8$ and $M = 64$.

DM	GDM1	GDM2	GDM3	GDM4	GDM5	GDM6	GDM7	FX	Optimal
2	4.1	1.2	1.3	1.3	1.2	1.2	1.0	1.4	1.0	1.0
3	17.8	2.8	3.1	2.7	2.5	3.0	2.6	2.9	1.9	1.5
4	81.9	9.6	9.2	8.7	8.2	9.9	8.9	8.8	6.5	6.3
5	351.3	35.3	33.5	32.8	32.2	35.0	35.8	31.8	29.3	29.3
6	1456.0	142.0	134.0	133.0	132.0	135.0	145.0	131.0	128.0	128.0

Table 1-(c). $F_1 = 2$, $F_2 = F_3 = 4$, $F_4 = F_5 = F_6 = 8$ and $M = 128$.

The tables show that except for the first row in Table 1-(b), the FX distribution method gives smaller largest-response-size than all the other methods. The FX distribution method is also very close to optimal. It should also be noted that there may exist a set of multiplication parameters by which the

	DM	GDM1	GDM2	GDM3	GDM4	GDM5	GDM6	GDM7	FX	Optimal
2	4.3	1.1	1.1	1.2	1.0	1.1	1.1	1.1	1.0	1.0
3	17.6	1.8	2.0	1.9	2.2	1.8	2.6	1.9	1.4	1.0
4	79.2	5.2	5.1	4.8	6.7	5.0	8.2	4.9	3.7	2.7
5	352.0	18.2	17.3	16.8	26.7	17.5	34.2	17.3	14.7	13.3
6	1592.0	73.0	72.0	70.0	119.0	71.0	155.0	69.0	64.0	64.0

Table 1-(d). $F_1 = F_2 = F_3 = F_4 = 4$, $F_5 = F_6 = 8$ and $M = 256$.

GDM distribution method gives better performance than those of GDM1, GDM2, ..., GDM7 in the tables. However, even though such set of parameters exist, those can only be found by trial and error method.

The FX distribution method has also an advantage of short CPU computation time over the GDM distribution method. In the FX distribution method, since the multipliers for U and IU_x functions are power of 2, multiplication can be substituted by shift operation. Note that this is not possible in the GDM distribution method because multipliers in the GDM distribution method are usually chosen from prime or odd numbers. Since computation time of exclusive-or and shift operations is much shorter than that of multiplication operation, the FX distribution method is faster than the GDM distribution method. The DM distribution method is faster than the FX distribution method, but as shown in Table 1, the DM distribution method is not suitable for a large number of parallel devices.

3.2. Data Construction Algorithms For Partial Match Queries

We describe two approaches of data construction based on the usage of multikey hash directory. Multikey hashing for a given file with n fields produce a subset of T, where $T = f_1 \times f_2 \times ... \times f_n$. As described in section 2, T can be used as either a real global directory or a virtual global directory.

3.2.1. Data Construction Based on Real Global Directory

Let $GD = [0..F_1-1, ... , 0..F_n-1]$ be a multi-dimensional array in which the range of the i-th dimension is $0..F_i-1$. This is the same range of multikey hashing for field i. Here, GD serves as a real global directory. Each element of GD contains the address of a bucket. When the directory is centralized, the problem is trivial. When the directory is distributed among the access nodes, an appropriate data construction method is given in [5].

When a multikey hash function $\Theta 1$ is used for a file V, using T as a real global directory is advantageous if for most $t \in T$, $\Theta 1^{-1}(t) \in V$ with reasonable average chain length. However, an appropriate $\Theta 1$ may not be easily determined for dynamic files. Hence, the real global directory may be very sparse or may have long overflow chain. Note that applying dynamic hash function for $\Theta 1$ will cause significant overhead due to internode data movement. The virtual global directory approach described below can avoid this problem.

3.2.2. Data Construction Based on Virtual Global Directory

The idea of the virtual global directory is to use one more hash function $\Theta 2$ which is local in each device. Let $<J_1, \ldots, J_n>$ be an ordered n-tuple produced by multikey hash function $\Theta 1$ for some record. The local hash function $\Theta 2$ uses this ordered n-tuple as an input key for its local directory. Since $\Theta 2$ does not affect data distribution, dynamic hash functions can be used as $\Theta 2$. When T is used as a virtual global directory, only the local directories physically exist. Each local directory can dynamically grow and shrink while the virtual global directory is static.

This two-level mapping data construction is more flexible than the real global directory because the storage utilization of directories is not affected by $\Theta 1$, and dynamic hash function for local directories can handle dynamic files. One disadvantage of the virtual global directory approach is that it may cause more probings to find qualified records than in the real global directory. This is because different ordered n-tuples produced by $\Theta 1$ can be mapped into the same local directory entry by $\Theta 2$.

4. Multidirectory Hashing for Key Access Applications

In this section we present another application of the two stage abstract model. This application is for random access file systems and is based on the multidirectory hashing scheme [7]. Multidirectory hashing is a class of hashing schemes where a set of directories are used for a single relation. Each one of the directories can be of different size and it grows and shrinks dynamically.

4.1. Construction of Multidirectory Hashing

The algorithm for the proposed multidirectory hashing is as follows.

(1) The hash address is partitioned into two parts. One part is used for directory number and the other part is used for locating the record within a local directory.

(2) Each directory of multidirectory hashing is created based on a hashing method.

Figure 8 shows the address mapping scheme of the proposed multidirectory hashing. This figure also shows relationship between the functions of this model and those of the two stage model in Figure 3. Note that the proposed multidirectory hashing is based on the virtual global directory approach.

4.2. Performance Comparison for Multidirectory Hashing

We show the results of performance experiments based on memory requirement for achieving near optimal response time (i.e., one access for a record and one key comparison). Figure 9 is the case when 5000 unique key values are inserted into the file. In the figure the directory size for the multidirectory hashing corresponds to the total size of all the directories. We can see the total directory size decreases considerably with increasing number of directories.

The lower bound on response time can be achieved in multidirectory hashing with much less memory requirement than in single directory hashing. On the other hand, the throughput increases considerably by concurrent processing of multiple directories. Since multiple independent directories reduce

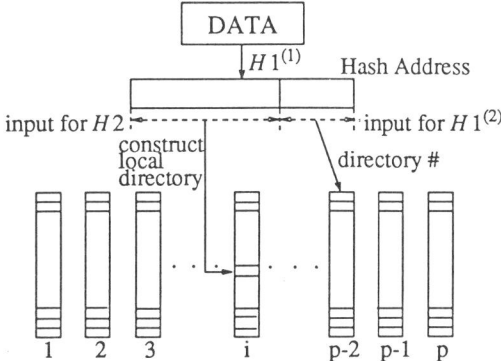

Figure 8. Hash address mapping in multidirectory hashing

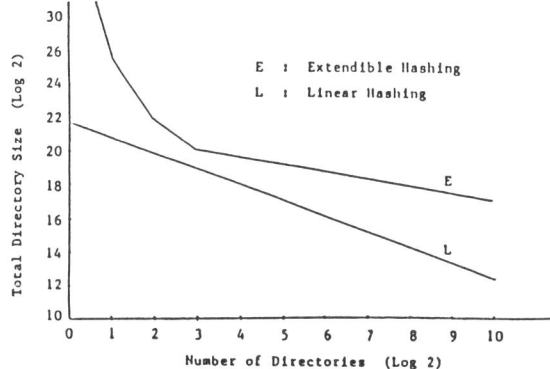

Figure 9. Total directory size in multidirectory hashing

the amount of sharing for critical shared variables which are necessary for most dynamic hashing schemes, we can guarantee much less lock conflict data accesses in multidirectory hashing than in single directory hashing.

5. Conclusion

We have presented abstract parallel processing models for database systems and investigated several design issues for parallel database systems. We have applied these abstract models to two common types of database applications which are partial match queries and key accessed main memory databases. First, for optimal file distribution for partial match queries the FX distribution method have been presented. The optimality conditions for the FX distribution method are given through theorems. We have compared the FX distribution method with others and have shown the performance improvement of the proposed distribution method. Two data construction approaches based on the real and virtual global directory are also described. Second, we have proposed a multidirectory hashing scheme which enhances concurrent accesses to a single file. We have shown that the memory requirement for near optimal response time in multidirectory hashing is much less than that in single directory hashing.

Acknowledgement

The authors would like to thank Hsiao-Yu Chou for the simulation results of Figure 9.

6. References

[1] Aho, A.V. and Ullman, J.D., "Optimal Partial-Match Retrieval When Fields Are Independently Specified," *ACM Trans. Database Systems*, vol. 4 no. 2 , June 1979, pp. 168-179.

[2] Boral, H. and Dewitt, D.J., "Database Machines : An Idea Whose Time Has Passed? A Critique of the Future of Database Machines," *Database machines*, Leilich, H.O. and Missikoff, M., eds., Springer-Verlag, 1983, pp. 166-187.

[3] Du, H.C. and Sobolewski, J.S., "Disk Allocation for Cartesian Product Files on Multiple-Disk Systems," *ACM Trans. Database Systems*, vol. 7 no. 1, March 1982, pp. 82-101.

[4] Kakuta,T., Miyazaki,N., Shibayama,S., Yokota,H. and Murakami,K.,"The Design and Implementation of Relational Database Machine Delta," *Database Machines, Fourth International Workshop*, March 1985, pp. 13-34.

[5] Kim, M.H., "Data Distribution Strategies for Parallel Database Accesses", Ph.D. dissertation, Computer Science Department, Michigan State University, 1989.

[6] Kim, M.H. and Pramanik, S., "Optimal File Distribution For Partial Match Retrieval," *Proc. ACM SIGMOD Conf.*, 1988, pp. 173-182.

[7] Pramanik, S. and Chou, H.-Y., "Performance of Multi Directory Hashing," Technical Report, Computer Science Department, Michigan State University, Oct. 10, 1987.

[8] Pramanik, S. and Kim, M.H., "Parallel Processing of Large Node B-trees," *IEEE Trans. on Computers* (to be published).

[9] Rothnie,J.B.Jr. and Lozano,T.,"Attribute based file organization in a paged memory environment," *Comm. ACM*, vol.17, no.2, 1974, pp. 63-69.

[10] Su, S.Y.W., L.H. Nguyen, A. Eman and G. J. Lipovski, "The Architectural Features and Implementation Techniques of multicell CASSM," *IEEE Trans. on Computers*, June 1979, pp. 430-445.

[11] Stone, H., "Parallel Querying of Large Databases : A Case Study," *IEEE Computer*, Oct. 1987, pp. 11-21.

[12] Sung, Y.Y., "Performance Analysis of Disk Modulo Allocation Method for Cartesian Product Files," *IEEE Trans. on Software Eng.*, Vol. SE-13, No. 9, Sept. 1987, pp. 1018-1026 .

Parallel Sorting Methods for Large Data Volumes on a Hypercube Database Computer

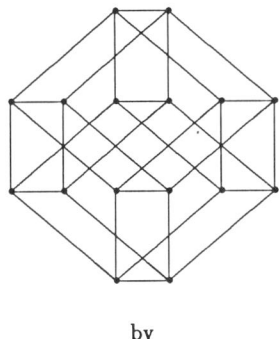

by

Bjørn Arild W. Baugstø and Jarle Fredrik Greipsland

Division of Computer Systems and Telematics
The Norwegian Institute of Technology
University of Trondheim

Abstract

Sorting is one of the basic operations in any database system. In this paper we present two external sorting algorithms for hypercube database computers. The methods are based on partitioning of data according to partition values obtained through sampling of the data. One of the algorithms which is implemented at the HC16 database computer designed at The Norwegian Institute of Technology, is described in detail together with a performance evaluation and a presentation of some test results.

1 Introduction

Sorting was one of the first non-numeric tasks assigned to computers. Since then numerous sorting algorithms have emerged both for internal sorting (using main memory only) and external sorting (using secondary storage like disks). For the last decade a lot of attention has been paid to parallel computers and parallel algorithms, and consequently parallel sorting schemes for different parallel architectures have appeared. This paper which is based on a project work done by the authors [Greip88] and a diploma thesis by one of the authors [Baug89], describes various sorting algorithms for a parallel database computer designed at The Norwegian Institute of Technology.

2 The topology of hypercubes

Initially we review some basic concepts of hypercubes. For a more thorough treatment of the subject, the readers will have to turn elsewhere. The hypercube is originally a mathematical term and the name is derived from the hypercube being a generalized cube. We shall think of the hypercube as a network topology, a way of connecting nodes (in our case computers). The edges between the nodes are of course communication lines.

It is common practice to refer to the dimension of a hypercube. If P is the number of nodes and D is the dimension, we have $P = 2^D$. A node is connected to one neighbour in each dimension. This means D lines are leading out from a node to neighbour nodes. A node is said to be either at coordinate 0 or 1 in each dimension. Node 1011, for instance, is at coordinate 1 in dimension 1,2 and 4 while at coordinate 0 in the 3rd dimension. The binary address of a node differs in one bit-position only from the addresses of its adjacent nodes. Node 0000, for instance, is adjacent to 0001, 0010, 0100 and 1000. These concepts are illustrated further in figure 1.

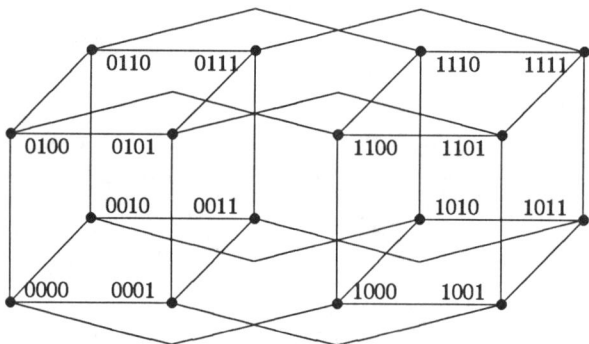

Figure 1: Hypercube of 4 dimensions.

Communication between two arbitrary nodes may have to rely upon other nodes as transit nodes in the transmission process. This is the price we have to pay for not having a fully connected network. The latter communication scheme, however, is not feasible for a large number of nodes. As described in [Brat80] the hypercubic interconnection scheme is a satisfactory compromise.

3 The HC16-186 parallel database computer

The advent of powerful inexpensive microprocessors and hard disks has made it economically feasible to get super high performance tying many of these components together. The HC16-186, designed at The Norwegian Institute of Technology, is an experimental database computer using a hypercubic network connecting 16 single board microcomputers, each complete with memory, SCSI-port to a hard disk controller, a 65 MB Winchester disk and a port to the combined interconnection network and host. The single board computer is running an Intel 80186 processor at a clock frequency of 10 MHz and contains 1 MB of main memory with no wait states.

The interconnection network is based upon dual port RAM chips, distinguishing the HC16-186 from most other hypercubic computers. The link between two nodes (two single board computers) is in essence a dual port RAM with 2 KB memory. Two nodes communicate through reading from and writing to their mutual dual port RAM. This yields a theoretical maximum for the neighbour communication data rate of 2.5 MB/s. In addition to internode communication, there is a dual port RAM link between each node and the host computer, an IBM AT compatible computer. The programs are free to use the dual port RAMs the way most suitable for the particular application, but there are also available communication routines both in assembly and C, hiding the details of the communication process for the programmer.

For secondary storage there is a Seagate ST227N disk at each node capable of storing 65 MB. For the entire hypercube this means a storing capacity of 1040 MB. Average access time for the disk is 40 ms and the nominal transfer rate is 798 KB/s. Positioning to a neighbouring cylinder takes 8 ms and rotation time is 16.67 ms. With the SCSI-port and SCSI-controller we are able to run the disk with an interleave factor of 1:1.

For more details about HC16-186 see [Brat89] (also presented at IWDM'89).

4 Sorting records in a relational database

The sorting algorithms described in this paper are designed to sort tuples or records in a relational database, but could obviously be used for other purposes as well. The sort is supposed to work in connection with other relational database operations like join, selection, projection, division, union, difference and intersection. The implementation of these operations on a parallel computer are described in [Baru87],[Brat87] and [DeWi85]

The relation to be sorted is horizontally partitioned into P subrelations (one subrelation pr. node). Normally, we are dealing with approximately equal partitions, but the sorting algorithm should work with uneven partitions as well. After the sort we have a horizontally partitioned relation where the subrelations are sorted and the smallest record (according to the sorting key) of node i is larger than the largest record of node $i-1$ for $0 < i < P$. The sort is not required to yield a perfect distribution (equal partition), but should come close to it since an uneven distribution will lead to varying execution times among the nodes for the operations following the sort.

5 Internal sorting on hypercubes

Several internal sorting schemes for hypercubes are described in the literature ([Brat88], [Seid88], [Yaman87]). So far, however, we have found no paper dealing with external sorting on hypercubes (i.e. hypercubes where there is a disk at each node).

Although external sorting is the main theme of this paper, we shall, as an introduction, briefly outline one particular internal sorting scheme which we have called hyperquicksort. The algorithm earns its name by being the well-known quicksort running in parallel on a hypercube. In the first stage of the algorithm, the subrelation at each node is sorted using one of the sequential sorting schemes, like quicksort. In the next stage an estimate of the median is used to partition the records at each node. Each node in the lower half of the hypercube (coordinate 0 in most significant dimension) exchanges records with its neighbour in the upper half (coordinate 1 in most significant dimension). After the exchange all records with keys smaller or equal to the estimated median reside in the lower half while those records with keys larger than the estimated median reside in the upper half. This process of estimating the median and partitioning the records is continued recursively for a total of D steps, keeping the records sorted locally at each node.

The description above is based on [Brat88]. Similar algorithms are given elsewhere (under varying names) [Seid88], so it is perhaps more appropriate to talk about a class of algorithms. The existing variants mainly stem from different methods employed to estimate the median.

6 Estimating partitioning values

The hyperquicksort algorithm revealed a common feature for all of the sorting algorithm we have assessed, namely the need for partitioning values. In hyperquicksort we were interested in the median, but more generally we are looking for the $P-1$ partitioning values that are splitting the volume into P equally sized parts.

Y. Yamane and R. Take of Fujitsu Laboratories also faced this problem. They suggested a parallel algorithm which finds the partitioning values for the equal partition. After a local sort of the keys at each node, the algorithm establishes the Kth smallest key through a parallel equivalent of a binary search. More specifically we have $O(log_2 n)$ iterations of 4 steps (where n is the total number of keys): i) Proposing local candidates, ii) selecting a global candidate, iii) assessing the global candidate and iv) making a conclusion. $P-1$ search processes run in parallel to establish all the partitioning values. For the details see [Yaman87].

The above method is constructed with internal sorting in mind. For external sorting where all keys can not be loaded into main memory, we would have a lot of disk activity making the method rather inefficient. Realizing this, Yaman asks at the end of his paper if there exists an efficient method for establishing partitioning values in the case of external sorting. We think estimated partitioning values is a solution to this problem. Allowing some variation in the lengths of the subrelations after the sort is complete, we can avoid the expensive operation of finding the exact partition. There is one important justification for this choice: The parallel relational database operations based on the hashing method, do not leave us with perfectly equal subrelations to be sorted, so we don't think it is absolutely necessary for the sorting algorithm to yield this perfect partition either. Obviously, there has to be a trade-off between the time consumption and the desired accuracy of the partitioning values.

In our original work [Greip88] we assessed several methods for estimating partitioning keys. We concluded that a technique based on sampling was the best choice. In other words we do not make use of the entire data volume in the process of finding partitioning values; only a certain percentage of the records at a node are sampled for this purpose. Making sure that all sampled keys fit into main memory, we can employ the method outlined above to find the exact partitioning values among the sampled keys and use them as our estimated partitioning values for the entire volume of records. This strategy also works well for uneven distributions of records initially, since the number of samples from one particular node is proportional to its number of records.

The sampling method can be used in different ways depending on which external sorting algorithm is chosen. The sampling may be performed after the local sort. With a sampling percentage of 4, for instance, every 25th record of the sorted records is sampled leaving a sorted set of samples at each node. When sorting large data volumes, one usually generates sorted subfiles, which are then subsequently merged into one sorted file (see below). In some cases it is then convenient to sample the subfiles rather than the resulting sorted file. This method, which is closely related to the first one, leaves us with a number of sorted sequences of sampled keys which are then merged prior to the parallel search for partitioning values. Alternatively, the sampling phase may come prior to the local sort. With uniformly distributed keys we can sample the first 4 percent of the records (assuming a sampling percentage of 4). This may however lead astray when some prearrangement exists among the records, for example sorted or partly sorted records locally at each node. As a precaution, the keys should be sampled from an appropriate number of blocks evenly spread throughout the file.

As might be expected, the two former alternative yields better estimates than the latter using the same sampling percentage. In other words this means we have to sample more keys to achieve an acceptable level of accuracy, when records are not sorted prior to the sampling. In both [Greip88] and [Baug89] there is a more extensive discussion of the sampling technique. In this paper we have chosen not to make an issue out of the optimal sampling percentage, and we have run all our tests with a sampling percentage of 2.

7 External sorting on hypercubes

7.1 External sorting on a single processor computer

The standard approach to external sorting is the sort-merge algorithms. The idea behind these algorithms is to generate sorted files (often called runs) from the unsorted data and then merge these files, in one or more steps, into a single sorted file (see figure 2). Moving from internal sorting to external sorting we find that the factors determining the running time of a program change magnitude. It is no longer necessarily the comparison time that dominates the total running time. We must also take into account the time for accessing records on secondary storage.

When generating sorted files, one usually employs a tournament tree (often modified into a *tree of losers*). The program uses a reservoir in main memory, which is kept filled with records. The tree of losers algorithm finds the record with the smallest key that is larger than the key of the last record written to the current run (output file), and writes it to the current output file. When no such record exists in the reservoir, a new run is started. In this way the algorithm generates sorted runs, with an average length of twice the size of the reservoir.

In the next phase, the sorted runs are merged together into one file. Depending on the type of mass storage device(s) used, there are various ways of handling this merge. Based on device characteristics, an optimal number of runs to merge in each step can be obtained. Using this number, a balanced tree of real and empty imaginary runs can be derived. The runs are then merged according to this tree.

This family of singleprocessor algorithms is thoroughly described by several authors, e.g. in [Knuth73] and [Aho83]. The same principles can be used for external sorting on a multiprocessor as well (see below).

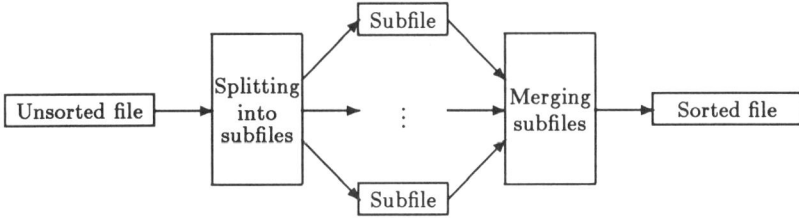

Figure 2: External sorting on uniprocessor

7.2 Why not use hyperquicksort as an external sorting algorithm?

An attempt to use the hyperquicksort approach on an external sorting problem has one main disadvantage. As described earlier in this text, each node maintains a sorted table of records. With large data volumes this table has to be located on disk. This means that a record, temporarily, will be stored on disk at each node it is passing through in the exhange steps of the algorithm. As we shall see in the next two algorithms, we can do with less disk accesses. Due to these unnecessary disk accesses we have discarded hyperquicksort in our search for good external sorting algorithms.

7.3 Local sort after reallocation (Algorithm 1)

Analyzing various algorithms, we observe that there are essentially two classes. In class one we have an initial local sort at each node followed by a reallocation phase achieving a globally sorted data volume. In class two the records are first distributed to their destination nodes and then sorted locally at these nodes. Looking at hyperquicksort, we see that it fits into the first class. In the remaining part of this section we shall describe an algorithm that belongs to the second class.

The algorithm is based on three distinct phases. First the partitioning values are calculated, then the records are reallocated to their destination nodes, and finally the records residing at each node are sorted locally.

Phase 1 The process of estimating partitioning values is described in a previous section. The exact partitioning values of a sampled set of records are used as the estimated partitioning values for the entire data volume. Thus we logically split the data volume into P portions of approximately equal size.

Phase 2 In this phase the records are transmitted to their destination nodes. Each node reads its local file, compares the key field(s) of the records with the obtained partitioning values and sends the records to the appropriate target nodes. (Note that a record on its way may pass through several other nodes in the hypercube network). Concurrently, each node receives records from other nodes. These records, and those which happened to be at their destination node initially, are inserted into a tree of losers. Using this tree, sorted intermediate files are generated. This method uses less disk accesses, than what would have been the case if the records were to be stored on disk before being sent through the tree of losers.

Phase 3 At this point all records reside at their destination nodes. It just remains to merge the sorted runs into one sorted file. This can be done without any communication with the other nodes, and hence a standard merge algorithm can be employed.

During the reallocation of phase 2, the local file can be read in any order since the records are reallocated prior to the local sort. A sequential read constitutes one obvious possibility. If the records happen to be sorted (or nearly so) at each node prior to the sort (with the keys belonging to the same domain), the sorting turns out to be rather inefficient for such a sequential read. Each node will in turn be the target node for records from all nodes, and the speed will depend on the processing and receiving capacity of one node. In other words each node will in turn make up the system bottleneck. To ensure an evenly distributed load on the network for this particular case also (which by no means is the average one), we can split the blocks of the file into P intervals and read blocks from these intervals in turn during reallocation (each node starting from a different interval). This strategy which requires a direct access file system, does not implicate an increase in access time compared to the sequential alternative. Since we in both cases have to write the sorted runs to disk in addition to reading the unsorted file, we do not benefit from a sequential access to the unsorted file. On an average the read/write head of the disk has to be moved just as much for both methods.

To reduce the overhead associated with the communication, several records can be combined into one larger message. We keep P buffers where records are copied to when reading the unsorted file. When a buffer is full, we have a message ready for transmission to the corresponding target node. At reception a message is disassembled and the records are inserted into the tree of losers. Whether this strategy results in a speed gain or not, is determined by the characteristics of the communication system. For our test programs on HC16-186 we have used this approach with the message size corresponding to the size of one dual port RAM channel.

7.4 Local sort prior to reallocation (Algorithm 2)

An initial local sort presents some problems to the subsequent reallocation phase. Each node has P sorted streams of records (one for each of the P nodes, according to the intervals determined by the partitioning values). These sorted streams are distributed throughout the network and then merged at the destination nodes. In such a merge process a node depends on receiving a record from one particular node before it can go on. Since one dual port RAM has to be shared between several streams, a node may either deadlock waiting for a message that will never arrive because the dual port RAM channel is full, or it will have to receive messages not required at the time and buffer them somewhere, until it finally gets the awaited record. To put an upper bound on the buffer space needed, we can use the protocol of the following algorithm:

1. Sorted runs are generated locally, using a tree of losers, and estimated partitioning values are determined from keys sampled from the sorted runs.

2. The sorted runs are merged. Instead of generating one sorted file at each node, we generate as many files as there are nodes in the cube. Each file contains the records that will be sent to one specific node (according to the partitioning values).

3. The sorted subfiles are reallocated and merged at the destination nodes. To limit the buffer space to main memory only, we make use of request messages. When a node needs a record in its merge process, it sends a request message to the node in question asking for a block of records. Concurrently with its own merge process, a node therefore has to provide for the distribution of requested blocks of records.

Reading the entire data volume from disk and writing it back is referred to as one pass of the data. In algorithm 2 we have three passes compared to the two passes of algorithm 1. Although algorithm 1 needs some disk operations to estimate the partitioning values, there is more disk activity associated with algorithm 2. On the other hand we have managed to separate the two most CPU-demanding operations, generating sorted runs and reallocating records, and we should expect to get better partitioning values due to the way the sampling is performed. Tests on HC16-186 for both alternatives show that the running time of algorithm 1 is somewhat better than that of algorithm 2. For the rest of this paper we shall concentrate on algorithm 1.

8 Performance evaluation

In this section we analyze the performance of algorithm 1. There are two obvious bottleneck candidates: The disk transfer and the local system bus. The bus is used during transfer of data between memory and disk, during relocation of data between nodes, during local moves of data between I/O-buffer and record working storage and during general program execution. The disk transfer is modelled in terms of rotations needed for reading/writing the data volume, including rotations lost due to moving the read/write head of the disk. During lost rotations and between sectors the bus is free for other activities. With asynchronous file system calls we are thus able to overlap the disk operations with the other operations. In the analysis, which follows the principles of Bratbergsengen's analysis of the relational algebra operations ([Brat87], [Brat89]), we estimate T_{bus}, the time consumption for the operations requiring bus access, and T_{disk}, the disk time, to determine which is the bottleneck. The analysis gives a relatively crude estimate of the execution time of the sorting algorithm, but, nevertheless, we think it is able to point out bottlenecks and the effect of faster microprocessors or disks.

In the analysis we use the following symbols:

P	= number of nodes.	D	= dimension of the hypercube.
N	= number of records.	L	= record length.
K	= key length (10 bytes).	α	= key length / record length.
V	= operand volume $(N \cdot L)$.	t_c	= avg. comparison time (45µs).
β	= sampling percentage.	t_b	= memory access time pr. byte (200 ns).

The bus load due to transfer between SCSI-port and buffer in primary memory is modelled through t_d, the time needed to transfer one byte. For HC16-186 the bus is dedicated to this transfer one sector at a time, giving a t_d of 1.067 µs.

In addittition to the bus load caused by moving data between dual port RAMS and main memory, there is also an overhead associated with the communication system. CPU-service is required at transmission, transit and reception. The average number of dimensions a message has to cross is $\frac{D}{2}$. This means $\frac{D}{2}+1$ moves are necessary. In our communication system we have introduced an extra buffer stage both at transmission and reception, releasing the space occupied in the dual port RAMs as quickly as possible to optimize the throughput. Calculating an overhead t_{ovh} pr. move, this means we have an overhead of $\left(\frac{D}{2}+3\right) \cdot t_{ovh}$ pr. message, where t_{ovh} is measured to 150 µs.

Throughout the analysis we refer to handling times. These are CPU activities associated with a record or a block of records. The handling times are of a complex nature and are only estimated very roughly.

Disktimes are estimated in terms of the number of rotations needed. A cylinder containns 6 tracks with 26 sectors of 512 bytes each. Our test programs have been run with a block size, V_{blk} of 31 sectors (i.e. $V_{blk} = 31 \cdot 512 = 15872$ bytes). In other words there are 5 blocks pr. cylinder. The disk time for reading/writing V bytes is then calculated as follows:

$$T_{disk} = \frac{V}{P} \cdot t_{rot} \cdot \frac{A}{V_{blk}}$$

where t_{rot} (16.67 ms) is time pr. disk rotation and A is the average number of rotations needed for reading or writing one block. We assume the volume is distributed evenly among the P nodes to be read/written in parallel.

The factor A will of course vary according to the characteristics of the disk operations. As yet, the file system of HC16-186 offers sequential disk operations only. We have therefore run our tests with uniformly distributed keys, allowing us to read the sampled keys sequentially from the start of the file (see comments in section 6). This means a factor $A_{seq} = \left(\frac{31}{26}+1\right) = 2.19$, since one rotation is lost between two commands for a sequential read on the same cylinder and one rotation is lost between two cylinders (cylinder to cylinder positioning takes 8 ms).

In phase 2 the read/write head of the disk is involved in longer moves, switching between the reading of the unsorted file and the writing of the sorted runs (both sequential operations). Assuming that the unsorted file and the sorted runs are allocated contigously on the disk and that the writing is performed at the same rate as the reading, we have that for each block read or written the disk head has to be moved a number of cylinders corresponding to the data volume sorted, i.e. $\frac{V}{P} \cdot \frac{1}{5 \cdot V_{blk}}$ cylinders. During the merging of phase 3, we also operate within an area of the disk that is twice the volume to be sorted. The moving of the read/write head is not as systematic as in phase 2, but as an average we can calculate the same positioning time, giving a common factor, A_{mul}, for both phase 2 and 3:

$$A_{mul} = \frac{t_{pmin} + \frac{t_{pmax}-t_{pmin}}{S_{max}} \cdot \frac{1}{5 \cdot V_{blk}} \cdot \frac{V}{P} + \frac{1}{2} \cdot t_{rot}}{t_{rot}} + \frac{31}{26}$$

In the above formula we have estimated the positioning time as a linear function of the minimum positioning time (t_{pmin}=8 ms), the maximum positioning time (t_{pmax}=95 ms) and the total number of cylinders (S_{max}=820). Latency time is of course $\frac{1}{2} \cdot t_{rot}$, while $\frac{31}{26}$ is the number of rotations for the actual transfer.

8.1 Phase 1

Only $V \cdot \beta$ of the data volume is read during the sampling process. Since virtually no processing of the samples takes place, this operation will be I/O-bound with the following disk time:

$$T_{disk}^1 = \frac{V \cdot \beta}{P} \cdot t_{rot} \cdot \frac{A_{seq}}{V_{blk}}$$

Next the partitioning values are found through the parallel search process described in section 6 (using main memory only). The analysis is based upon the one given in [Yaman87], adopting it to our particular model. We shall not examine the details here, just bring the result. The running time of this phase constitutes a small part of the total running time, and we have chosen to concentrate on phase 2 and 3 where the actual sorting takes place.

Total time consumption for the parallel search is:

$$
\begin{aligned}
T^1_{bus} &= \tfrac{12}{7} \cdot \tfrac{N}{P} \cdot \beta \cdot log_2(\tfrac{N}{P} \cdot \beta) \cdot t_c && \text{quicksort of samples} \\
&+ log_2(N \cdot \beta) \cdot \left(\tfrac{12}{7} \cdot P \cdot log_2 P + log_2(\tfrac{N}{P} \cdot \beta) \right) \cdot t_c && \text{comparisons during search} \\
&+ log_2(N \cdot \beta) \cdot [4 \cdot L \cdot \alpha + 12] \cdot P \cdot (\tfrac{D}{2} + 3) \cdot t_b && \text{moving data} \\
&+ log_2(N \cdot \beta) \cdot 4 \cdot P \cdot (\tfrac{D}{2} + 3) \cdot t_{ovh} && \text{communication overhead}
\end{aligned}
$$

For the factor of $\tfrac{12}{7}$ see [Knuth73]. Estimated total time for phase 1 is $T_1 = T^1_{disk} + T^1_{bus}$, since the two operations do not overlap.

8.2 Phase 2

Disk time for phase 2 is

$$ T^2_{disk} = 2 \cdot \frac{V}{P} \cdot t_{rot} \cdot \frac{A_{mul}}{V_{blk}} $$

since the entire data volume is read once and written once. For the sake of simplicity, we have assumed an equal partition in the analysis, i.e. the volume is equally divided between the nodes.

To calculate T^2_{bus}, we first estimate the bus load caused by moving data. During reallocation each byte of a message is moved $\tfrac{D}{2} + 3$ times, each move implying two memory accesses, a load and a store. In addition data has to be moved from workspace (area occupied by tree of losers) to the outbuffers for the sorted subfiles. Moving data from infile buffer to workspace is only necessary for those records staying at the node (an average of $\tfrac{1}{P}$). The remaining records are to be distributed to other nodes and are copied directly from the file buffers to the sendbuffer of the communication system (accounted for in the formula for reallocation). The resulting time consumption is:

$$ (\tfrac{D}{2} + 3) \cdot 2 \cdot \frac{V}{P} \cdot t_b + (1 + \tfrac{1}{P}) \cdot 2 \cdot \frac{V}{P} \cdot t_b = (D + 8 + \tfrac{2}{P}) \cdot \frac{V}{P} \cdot t_b $$

A significant portion of the time in this phase is spent in the tree of losers. If M bytes is available for the tree (670000 in our case), there is space for $\tfrac{M}{L}$ records. Each node inserts $\tfrac{N}{P}$ records and then drains $\tfrac{M}{L}$ records in the end (provided there are enough records to fill the entire tree). For an insertion we need $\lceil log_2 \tfrac{M}{L} \rceil$ comparisons to determine the record's proper place in the tree and 1 comparison to decide whether a new run should be started. When draining the tree in the end, this latter comparison is not required. Calculating a handling time t_{h1} (estimated to 20 μs) besides the actual comparison time, we get the following load:

$$ \left((\lceil log_2 \tfrac{M}{L} \rceil + 1) \cdot n + \tfrac{M}{L} \cdot \lceil log_2 \tfrac{M}{L} \rceil \right) \cdot (t_c + t_{h1}) $$

As already mentioned, records are combined into larger messages, filling as much as possible of a dual port RAM channel. If R denotes the number of bytes available in the channel (990 bytes in our case), we have $\lfloor \tfrac{R}{L} \rfloor$ records pr. message. In the analysis we calculate a general handling time t_{h2} (roughly estimated to 2000 μs) pr. message. This is an administration cost that can be attributed to reallocating a block of records, especially assembling and disassembling the message.

Altogether, we get the following formula for T^2_{bus}:

$$\begin{aligned}
T_{bus}^2 &= 2 \cdot \tfrac{V}{P} \cdot t_d & \text{to/from SCSI-port} \\
&+ (D + \tfrac{2}{P} + 8) \cdot \tfrac{V}{P} \cdot t_b & \text{moving data} \\
&+ \tfrac{1}{\lfloor \tfrac{R}{L} \rfloor} \cdot (\tfrac{D}{2} + 3) \cdot \tfrac{N}{P} \cdot t_{ovh} & \text{communication overhead} \\
&+ \left((\lceil \log_2 \tfrac{M}{L} \rceil + 1) \cdot \tfrac{N}{P} + \tfrac{M}{L} \cdot \lceil \log_2 \tfrac{M}{L} \rceil \right) \cdot (t_c + t_{h1}) & \text{tree of losers} \\
&+ D \cdot \tfrac{N}{P} \cdot t_c & \text{deciding destination node} \\
&+ \tfrac{1}{\lfloor \tfrac{R}{L} \rfloor} \cdot \tfrac{N}{P} \cdot t_{h2} & \text{message handling}
\end{aligned}$$

Estimated running time for phase 2 is then calculated as $T_2 = max(T_{disk}^2, T_{bus}^2)$. As figure 3 shows, CPU or bus capacity is the bottleneck (this situation will also be referred to as CPU-bound) for all practical record lengths.

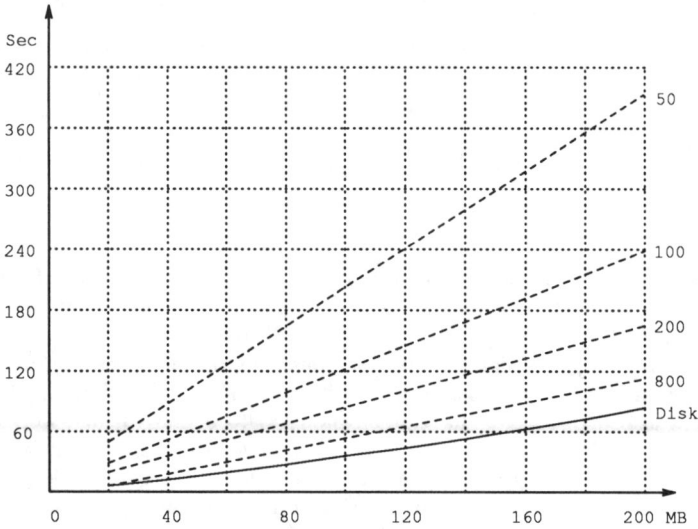

Figure 3: T_{bus}^2 and T_{disk}^2 as a function of operand volume and record length (T_{disk}^2 only dependent on volume). The maximum of T_{disk}^2 and T_{bus}^2 (for the appropriate record length) gives the estimated execution time of phase 2.

8.3 Phase 3

Disk time for phase 3 is

$$T_{disk}^3 = 2 \cdot \frac{V}{P} \cdot t_{rot} \cdot \frac{A_{mul}}{V_{blk}}$$

The tree of losers technique employed in phase 2 leaves us with files of average size $\frac{2 \cdot M}{L}$ records to be merged in phase 3. In other words there are $\lceil \frac{V}{2 \cdot M \cdot P} \rceil$ files at each node. We use a tree of losers for the merge phase as well and obtain the following bus load (assuming there are at least two files and that all files are merged in one go):

$$\begin{aligned}
T_{bus}^3 &= 2 \cdot \tfrac{V}{P} \cdot t_d & \text{to/from SCSI-port} \\
&+ 2 \cdot \tfrac{V}{P} \cdot t_b & \text{from infile buffers to outfile buffer} \\
&+ \left\lceil \log_2 \lceil \tfrac{V}{2 \cdot M \cdot P} \rceil \right\rceil \cdot \tfrac{N}{P} \cdot (t_c + t_{h1}) & \text{tree of losers}
\end{aligned}$$

This gives an estimated running time $T_3 = max(T_{disk}^3, T_{bus}^3)$. Figure 4 indicates that the merge phase is I/O-bound except for small record lengths (for the data volumes shown in figure 4).

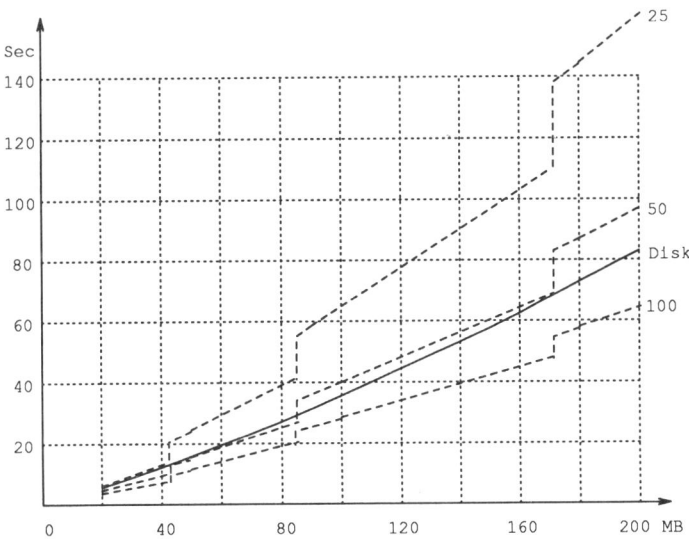

Figure 4: T^3_{bus} and T^3_{disk} as a function of operand volume and record length (T^3_{disk} only dependent on volume). The maximum of T^3_{disk} and T^3_{bus} (for the appropriate record length) gives the estimated execution time of phase 3.

9 Results

In this section we present the results from our tests of algorithm 1. Each node has the same number of records prior to the sort. The combined data volume of all nodes is referred to as the operand volume. All tests are run with a sampling percentage of 2 and a uniformly distributed 10 byte key. Since the sampling technique does not yield a perfect partition, running time for the merge phase will differ slightly from node to node. The measured times below are the times for the last node to finish. Figure 5 shows the measured running time for the algorithm as a function of data volume and record length. Keeping the data volume fixed, we see that the running time grows as the record length is decreased. This should come as no surprise after the performance evaluation of the last section where we found that phase 2 was heavily CPU-bound for all record lengths used in our tests.

We would like to emphasize one particular result from figure 5, namely the sort of 1 million 100 byte records (10 byte key), i.e. 100 MB. This is the sort benchmark as defined by Anon. et al. in [Anon85]. Our sorting algorithm ran this benchmark in 3 minutes, which we think is a good result compared to the relatively low cost of our hypercube database computer. Anon states in his paper that running times for commercial systems in practice range from 10 minutes and upwards.

Figure 6 illustrates how much time is spent in the different phases of the algorithm. As can be seen, the process of estimating the partitioning values constitutes a very small part of the total running time. Most of the running time can be attributed to phase 2 which performs the major part of the sorting job. In figure 5 it may look as though the running time is linear with respect to the operand volume. A closer examination reveals that this is not quite so. The running time for the merging of phase 3 grows slightly faster than a linear function. This can be observed from figure 6, but would be even more apparent for volumes beyond those shown in the figures (especially when files have to be merged in more than one go).

Figure 7 shows the estimated and measured running time for a sort of 100 byte records in the same diagram. As can be seen, the estimated time is somewhat less than the

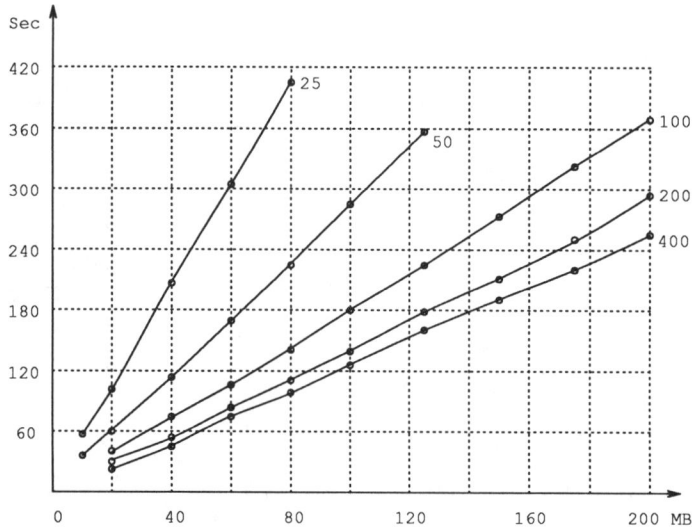

Figure 5: Measured run times as a function of operand volume and record length. Record length is written to each curve

corresponding measured one, with the deviation 'proportional' to the data volume. The same tendency is observed for other record lengths as well. This is to be expected since the models used in the performance evaluation are relatively simple, seeking to model the most important components, not every aspect down to the least detail. Nevertheless we think the analysis is useful, for instance to predict the effect of hardware changes. From the calculations and the test results it is clearly seen that CPU or bus capacity is the bottleneck. In our next database computer we plan to use a 20 MHz Intel 80386 as the node processor. This processor is in general 4 times faster than the 80186 used today. Bus capacity is 8 times larger. At the same time main memory is expanded to 4 MB and a dual port RAM to 4 KB. Using the same disks, we get an estimated running time of 71 seconds for the sort benchmark when the necessary changes are made to the parameters of the model. Conservatively, this means we expect a running time below 90 seconds. The improvement stems mainly from phase 2 which will then be I/O-bound. For a hypothetical HC32-186 we estimate the running time of the standard 100 MB test to 84 s. Based on these estimates we expect a HC16-386 (hypercube, 16 nodes, Intel 80386 processors) to perform slightly better (on sorting) than a HC32-186 (hypercube, 32 nodes, Intel 80186 processors).

As multiprocessor computers were introduced, it became of interest to investigate the speedup factor achieved moving programs from uniprocessors to multiprocessors. We define this factor as $\frac{T_1}{T_n}$ where T_1 is the execution time for one processor and T_n for n cooperating processors. In the following table we have listed the speedup factors for our algorithm on HC16-186 ($n = 2, 4, 8, 16$), both estimated and measured. Time is in seconds, the datavolume is 20 MB and record length is 100 byte.

Nodes		1	2	4	8	16
Estimated	Time	397	235	119	63	36
	Speedup		1.69	3.32	6.26	11.14
Measured	Time	481	266	143	77	39
	Speedup		1.81	3.36	6.27	12.4

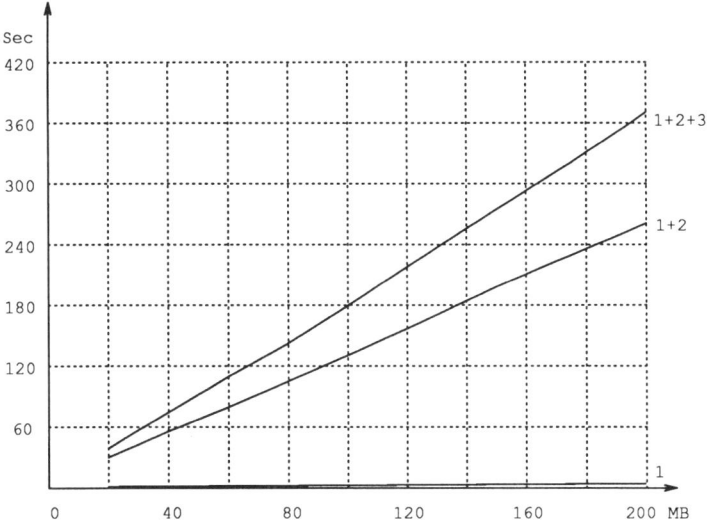

Figure 6: An illustration of how much time is spent in phase 1,2 and 3 respectively for a record length of 100 bytes.

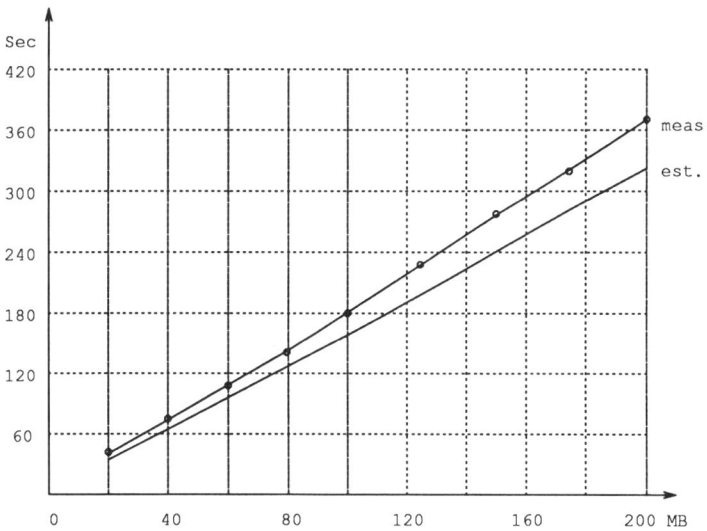

Figure 7: Estimated and measured run times for a record length of 100 byte.

10 Future work

High reliability is required from a database system, implying that problems caused by failing nodes is a very important issue in connection with multiprocessor database machines. These problems are examined in [Gudm88], a distribution strategy based on duplication of data is suggested. This means that data must be stored in at least two copies on the disks of two different nodes. When an error occurs, the failing node must be isolated and the data existing in only one copy reduplicated. We intend to modify our sorting algorithm to work under the conditions described above, employing the routing technique outlined in [Torb88b] for the communication (This is a modified version of e-cube routing handling failed processors). As a matter of fact, Algorithm 1 is not constrained to hypercube computers alone, and it might be of interest to see how the algorithm performs with other topologies.

11 Acknowledgements

The authors would like to thank Prof. Kjell Bratbergsengen and Øystein Torbjørnsen for their support during the project work spring 1988 and for their valuable comments on this paper. We would also like to express our gratitude to Torgrim Gjelsvik for his advice on more harware related topics.

References

[Aho83]   Alfred V. Aho, John E. Hopcroft and Jeffrey D. Ullman: *Data Structures and Algorithms*, Addison Wesley Publishing Company, Inc. 1983.

[Akl85]   Selim G. Akl: *Parallell Sorting Algorithms*, Academic Press, Inc. 1985.

[Anon85] Anon. et al.: *A Measure of Transaction Processing Power*, Datamation, April 1985.

[Baru87] C. K. Baru, O. Frieder, D. Kandlur and M. Segal: *Join on a Cube: Analysis, Simulation and Implementation*, Fifth International Workshop on Database Machines, Karuizawa, 1987.

[Baug89] Bjørn Arild Wangenstein Baugstø: *Parallelle Sorteringsmetoder for Store Datamengder i en Hyperkubisk Databasemaskin*, Division of Computer Systems and Telematics, The Norwegian Institute of Technology, University of Trondheim, (diploma thesis, in Norwegian).

[Brat80] Kjell Bratbergsengen, Rune Larsen, Oddvar Risnes and Terje Aandalen: *A Neighbor Connected Processor Network for Performing Relational Algebra Operations*, The Fifth Workshop on Computer Architecture for Non-numeric Processing, Pacific Grove, Ca, March 1980, SIGMOD Vol. X No. 4.

[Brat84] Kjell Bratbergsengen: *Hashing Methods and Relational Algebra Operations*, The 10th Conference on Very Large Data Bases, Singapore August 1984.

[Brat87] Kjell Bratbergsengen: *Algebra Operations on a Parallel Computer - Performance Evaluation*, Fifth International Workshop on Database Machines, Karuizawa, 1987.

[Brat88] Kjell Bratbergsengen: *Hyperkuben* Division of Computer Systems and Telematics, The Norwegian Institute of Technology, N-7034 Trondheim. March 1988 (in Norwegian).

[Brat89]   Kjell Bratbergsengen and Torgrim Gjelsvik: *The Development of the CROSS8 and HC16-186 Parallel (Database) Computers*, Division of Computer Systems and Telematics, The Norwegian Institute of Technology, N-7034 Trondheim.

[DeWi85]   David DeWitt and Robert Gerber: *Multiprocessor Hash-Based Join Algorithms*, The 11th Conference on Very Large Data Bases, Stockholm Aug. 1985.

[Greip88] Jarle F. Greipsland og Bjørn Arild W. Baugstø: *Sortering i hyperkuber*, Project work during spring 1988, May 1988 (in Norwegian), Division of Computer Systems and Telematics, The Norwegian Institute of Technology, University of Trondheim.

[Gudm88]   Kjetil Gudmundsen: *Strategies for Making a Fault Tolerant Database Management System on HC-16*, Division of Computer Systems and Telematics, The Norwegian Institute of Technology, University of Trondheim, 1988.

[Knuth73] Donald E. Knuth: *Sorting and Searching. The Art of Computer Programming*, Addison-Wesley Publishing Company, Inc. 1973.

[Meno86]   Jai Menon: *Sorting and Join Algorithms for Multiprocessor Database Machines*, Database Machines, Modern Trends and Applications, Springer Verlag.

[Seid88]   Steven R. Seidel and William L. George: *Binsorting on Hypercubes with d-Port Communication*, Department of Computer Science, Michigan Technological University, Houghton, ACM 1988.

[Torb88a] Øystein Torbjørnsen: *Turbo-C for the HC-16 Computer*, Working paper no. 43, Division of Computing Systems and Telematics, The Norwegian Institute of Technology, August 1988.

[Torb88b] Øystein Torbjørnsen: *Communication in a Failsoft Hypercube Database Machine*, Division of Computer Systems and Telematics, The Norwegian Institute of Technology, University of Trondheim, 1988.

[Yaman87] Y. Yamane and R. Take: *Parallell Partition Sort for Database Machines*, Fifth International Workshop on Database Machines, Karuizawa, 1987.

Evaluation of 18-stage Pipeline Hardware Sorter

Masaru Kitsuregawa, Weikang Yang
Institute of Industrial Science, The University of Tokyo

Shinya Fushimi
Mitsubishi Electric Corp.

ABSTRACT

Since the sorting is one of the most fundamental and frequently used operation in the current computer system, we have so far developed a high speed hardware sorter.

In this paper, we present the results of the performance evaluation of the 18-stage pipeline hardware sorter. One of the key features of our sorter is its employment of novel "*string length tuning*" algorithm, by which any length of records can be sorted very efficiently. The sorter can sort 256K records at one time. The sorting speed is 4 Mbytes/sec. Its memory capacity is 8 Mbytes. This practical scale sorting machine is connected to the system bus of a host computer through the bus adapter. Incorporating the sorter as a device in the operating system, we have evaluated its performance. The sorter showed much higher performance than the software sort utility on the host machine.

We are now making a sorting element board into a VLSI sort chip. The future plan is also briefly presented.

1. Introduction

Sorting is one of the most fundamental operation and used very frequently in the computer system. Several research efforts has been devoted to improve the sorting speed. Many efficient algorithms have been developed so far. In addition to the software approach, advances in hardware technology stimulates the development of specialized hardware sorter.

In database application where large amount of data is handled, the data is stored in the disks and is staged onto main memory from disks as needed. This data transfer time becomes a large overhead time. One solution is to utilize this data transfer time for sorting. Several types of O(N) time sorter, which can sort the data stream in O(N) time keeping up with its flow, has been proposed so far such as pipeline bubble sorter[1], parallel enumeration sorter[2], pipeline heap sorter[3] and pipeline merge sorter[4]. Several database machines such as RDBM[5],GRACE[6], DELTA[7] and IDP[8] incorporate a hardware sorter as a key function unit.

In 1982, we constructed one stage of a pipeline merge sorter[9]. The objective was to clarify the memory management mechanism and to understand its hardware complexity. Its sorting speed attained 3.0 Mbytes/sec. Through the hardware implementation we learned several design problems.

One of the most severe problem we faced is on record length. Generally we lose some flexibilities at the expense of the high performance when some function is implemented by hardware. As for sorting, the length of record is the most crucial parameter. The hardware sorter can sort very efficiently the records of a given length determined by hardware. Its performance deteriorates largely, however, when the length of the input record is different from the predetermined length. For this problem, we proposed the "*String Length Tuning*" (SLT) Algorithm in [10].

In 1987, we constructed the 18 stage pipeline hardware sorter of practical scale which implements SLT algorithm[11]. Thereafter the sorter was connected to the system bus of the host computer through a bus adapter in order to clarify the difficulty to incorporate such special device into a current computer system and also to evaluate its performance precisely under the control of an operating system.

In this paper we present the evaluation results of the hardware sorter. Section 2 gives the system overview of the sorter. In section 3 the SLT algorithm is briefly described, and it is shown how SLT is effective in our sorter. Section 4 describes the experimental environment for performance measurements. The process of activating the sorter and the flow of the data steam is explained. Section 5 gives the measurement results of performance evaluation. Our future plan for VLSI based sorting memory is described in section 6. Section 7 concludes the paper.

2. Development of 18-stage Pipeline Hardware Sorter

We adopted a pipeline merge sort algorithm for our sorter extended with elaborate memory management mechanism, named SLT.

Fig.1 shows the logical organization of the pipeline merge sorter, where $n(=\log_2 N)$ identical sort elements are connected linearly.

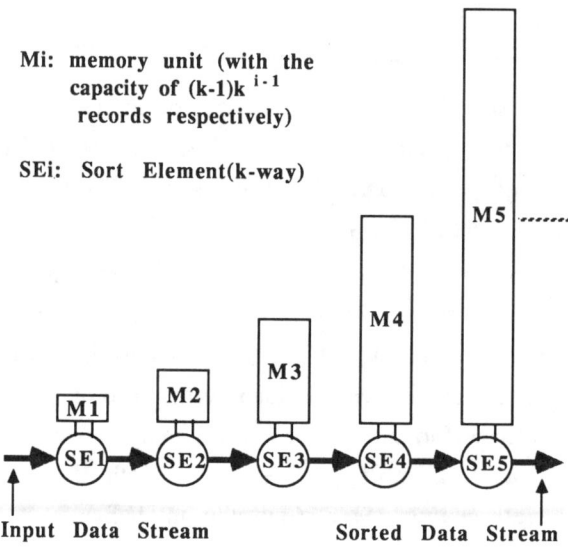

Fig.1 Organization of pipeline merge sorter

N is the total number of the records. The i-th sort element has a memory bank with the capacity of 2^{i-1} records. Each sort element does the 2-way merge operation. It is done in a pipelined manner. The sorting data stream is led into the first SE of the sorter. The i-th sort element SE_i receives sorted strings consisting of 2^{i-1} records, sent from SE_{i-1} or from input of the sorter, and merges them in pairs to generate strings of 2^i records and then outputs it into the next sort element SE_{i+1}. After all the data stream is input to the first stage of the sorter, the sorted data stream consisting of 2^n records is output from the last SE. To perform the 2-way merge sort operation, the SE loads the first string of the merge pair to its local data memory. When the second string of the same merge pair arrives, it starts the merge processing, compares two records from two strings, and outputs the larger or smaller record to its output port. This process continues until all the data stream is passed.

In the pipeline merge sorter, the total sorting time is $2N+\log_2 N-1$. This is the sum of data transfer time for input/output to/from the sorter plus the output delay. The output delay is the time taken between the arrival of last record in the sorting data stream to the first SE and the first appearance of output from the last SE. The delay is the transfer time through $\log_2 N-1$ pipeline segments. In our implementation, the pipeline segment is a word, and the sorting delay in a 18-stage sorter is only several micro seconds.

Fig.2 shows the organization of the pilot system we have implemented. The system consists of 28 boards, that is, eighteen sort element boards which have 64 Kbytes on board memory and ten extra memory boards. Total memory capacity is 8 Mbytes. Since the system has 18 elements, it can sort 2^{18}, 256K records at one time. Each sort element processes one word (two bytes) with three clock pulses (two memory reads for two merging operands and one memory write for input operand). Thus the system works in a word level pipeline manner. The merging processing is controlled by an horizontally microprogrammed control unit. The sorting speed is 4 Mbytes per second.

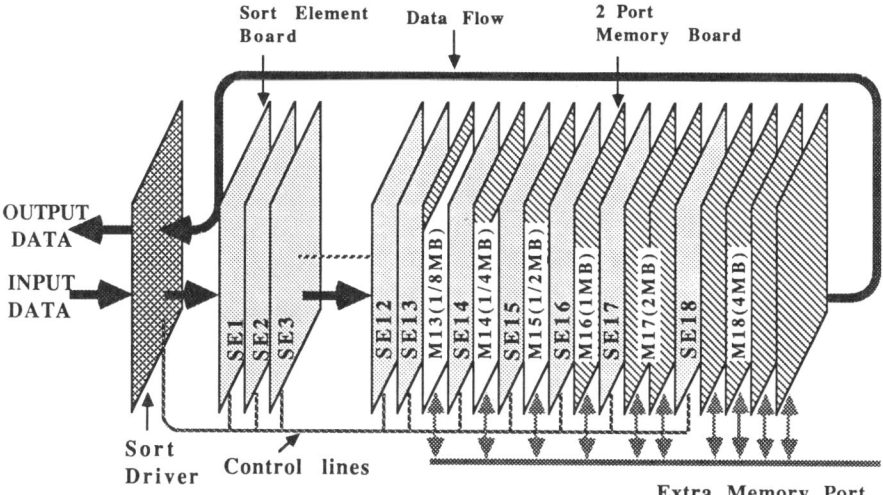

Fig.2 Implementation view of the pipeline merge sorter

3. String Length Tuning Algorithm and Its Effectiveness

One of the most distinct features of our sorter is its employment of the string length tuning algorithm(SLT). The detailed description of the algorithm is given in [10]. Here we show its effectiveness in the current implementation.

SLT is introduced to bring the flexibility for the record length. Since most of the previous designs assumed that the length of records is fixed, the efficiency decreased largely when the length of the actual record is different from the presumed length.

Suppose the sorter is designed to sort records having length L. Then we must take some higher control mechanism to sort the records with length $X(\neq L)$. If $X > L$, the first sort element cannot hold in the record due to insufficient memory space. The most simple algorithm is to skip the first elements until an element can hold the record in its memory and to make it work as a first element. With this ordinary algorithm, however, the memory efficiency is highly dependent on the length of the record. In the worst case, the memory utilization efficiency is about 50%. That is, the 8 Mbyte sorter with this ordinary algorithm can sort 8 Mbyte files for one record length but can only sort 4 Mbyte files for another record length. The sorting capacity changes depending on the record length, making the sorter hard to use.

The SLT algorithm changes the length of the string (sorted record sequence) dynamically, and attain very high memory utilization efficiency for any length of records. The basic idea is to make the first d sort elements, $SE_1,...,SE_d$, generate strings as long as possible that pack the (d+1)-th SE's memory. That is, (d+1)-th SE stores $\lfloor 2^d L/X \rfloor$ records, since it has the memory with the capacity of $2^d L$. We refer such d as Tuning Degree. For the details of SLT algorithm, please refer (10).

In Fig.3 memory usage pattern is shown for ordinary and SLT algorithms in the current implementation. It shows the effectiveness of SLT intuitively. To perform the SLT, the first d sort elements require some auxiliary memory. But the amount of this memory is guaranteed to be smaller than the record length of the currently sorted data file. In our implementation, the logical record length L is 32 bytes. Due to memory chip constraints, however, the first 12 elements have a 64 Kbyte memory. Thus, the $SE_1 \sim SE_{11}$ have surplus area. SLT just utilize these areas to generate largest strings to fit in the memory of SE_{12} and its successors that have no surplus memory, and to make the successors work at best condition of memory utilization.

After briefly describing the function of SLT algorithm above, now we show how to sort the files with arbitrary record length X in our sorter, and how much memory is really necessary in the $SE_1 \sim SE_d$.

Consider the situation such that a record whose length X is large and the first (i-1) SEs have to be skipped, thus merge sort operation starts at SE_i. We refer such X as R_i. The actual tuning degree is d-(i-1), for the record with length R_i. Each sort element

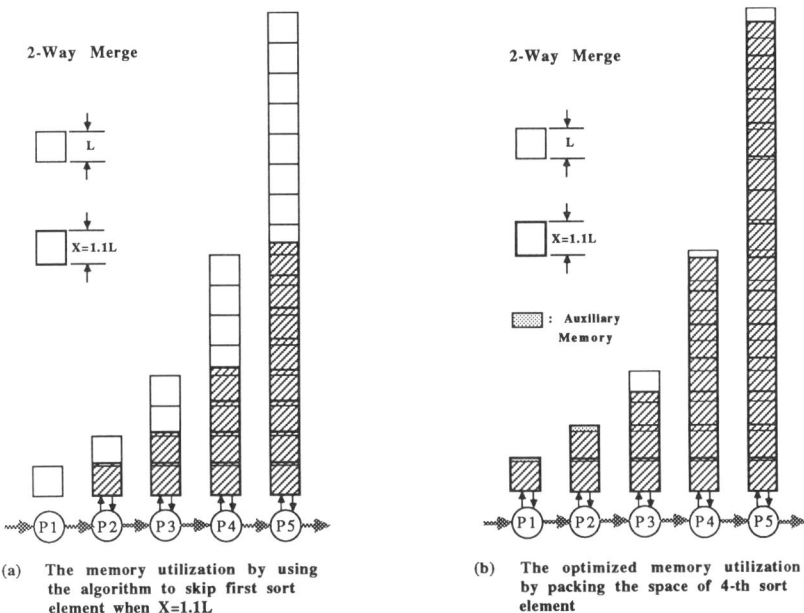

(a) The memory utilization by using the algorithm to skip first sort element when X=1.1L

(b) The optimized memory utilization by packing the space of 4-th sort element

Fig.3 Comparison of storage utilization efficiency between simple algorithm and String Length Tuning algorithm

must have space to hold an entire string, plus the space of one record. The latter space is required to work as a write buffer to store the input record. For the SE_j such as $j>d$, the memory capacity is $2^{j-1}L$. Since the memory space of the (d+1)-th sort element is the tuning target, the optimally tuned string length of SE_d, namely, the number of records of the output string from SE_d can be expressed as $\lfloor 2^d L/R_i \rfloor -1$. Generally, the value of this expression is between $2^{d-i}+1$ and 2^{d-i+1}. When R_i take its maximum value R_i^{max}, the equation shown below holds.

$$\lfloor 2^d L/R_i \rfloor -1 = (2^{d-i}+1).$$

By this expression, we can calculate the maximum record length when the i-th element works as the logically first. R_i^{max} for each i is derived as follows.

$$R_i^{max} = (2^d L)/(2^{d-i}+2).$$

The value of R_i^{max} for the index i depends on d and the system implementation parameter L.

The auxiliary memory required by the SLT is smaller than the record length. Next theorem shows the necessary memory of each sort element.

Theorem: The necessary memory of SE_i becomes maximum when it works as the logically first SE.

By this theorem, the required memory capacity of each SE_i is derived as $2R_i^{max}$.

The implemented system employs tuning degree 11. The R_i^{max} and the necessary memory capacity for each SE are shown in the table 1. With the R_i^{max}, we can calculate easily the number of skipping sort elements for a record length X.

Table 1. The sortable record length and the necessary capacity of each sort element

Sort Element	SE1	SE2	SE3	SE4	SE5	SE6	SE7	SE8	SE9	SE10	SE11
Logical mem. capacity ($2^{i-1}L$)	32	64	128	256	512	1K	2K	4K	8K	16K	32K
Sortable record length (R_i^{max})	62	126	254	504	992	1926	3640	6552	10922	16384	21844
Necessary mem. capacity	124	252	508	1008	1984	3852	7280	13104	21844	32768	43688

Now we show how effective SLT is by comparing the capacity of the sorter between ordinary and SLT methods. In Fig.4 the horizontal axis denotes the length of the record. The vertical axis denotes the maximum file size the sorter can sort. Without SLT, sort capacity changes largely depending on the record length. In our sorter, on the other hand, SLT mechanism is adopted and its memory space is fully utilized for records of any length, especially from 30 bytes to 4 Kbytes. Fig.5 shows the number of records the sorter can sort for each record length, which changes smoothly and ideally by introducing SLT.

4. Environment for Performance Evaluation

4.1. Connection of the sorter to the host machine

The sorter as a bare hardware can sort the records at the speed of 4.0 Mbytes per second. We thought that the system level performance is more important than this bare performance. We constructed an evaluation environment shown in Fig.6. In any special purpose processor, its driving environment is as much important as the processor itself. Software environment influences also very much the performance of the total system.

In Fig.6, SBA is a system bus adapter which consists of an 8 bit micro-processor, buffer memory, and a DMA control unit.

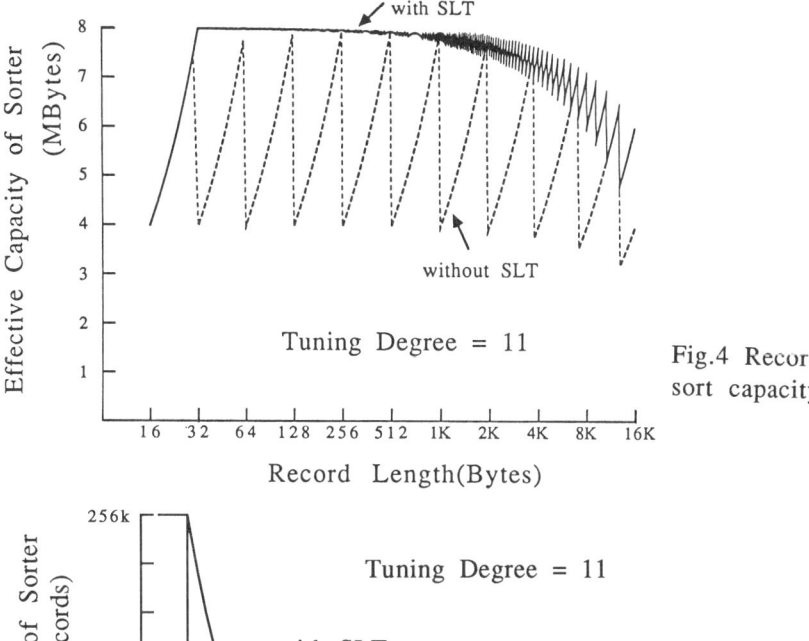

Fig.4 Record length versus sort capacity in Mbytes

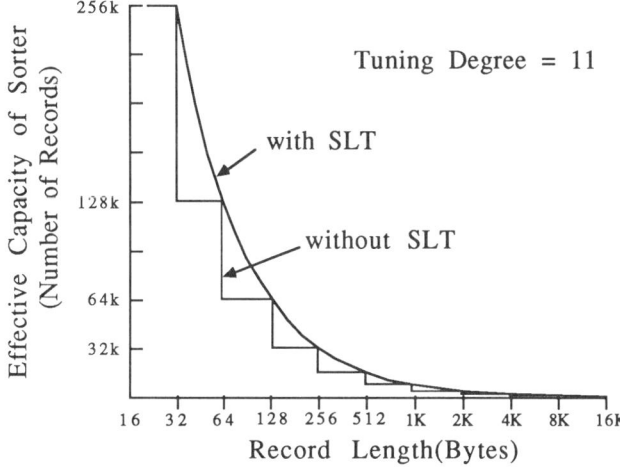

Fig.5 Record length versus sort capacity in record number

The detailed architecture is shown in Fig.7. It transfers data between the main memory of host computer and the sort unit. The I/O handler of the operating system on the host machine manages the I/O operation for the sorter. Once the SIO(start IO) instruction is issued by host, the microprocessor (MC68121 on the figure) on SBA interprets the CCW and invokes its sort operation. Fig.8 shows the I/O instructions.

In the current implementation, we use the disk driver instead of making a special driver in order to minimize the development time. Thus, I/O instructions for disks are inherited, but interpreted in the slightly different manner (e.g., write operation is interpreted in two ways) Sharing the driver with disks also makes it possible to write sorter-based sort utility using asynchronous disk I/O interface offered by the underlying operating system. The program which uses the sorter can leave for next processing

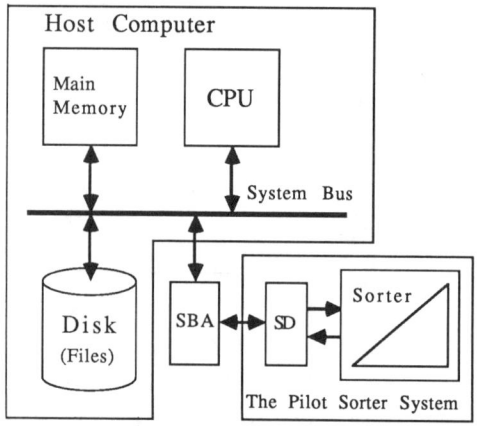

Fig.6 Experimental environment of the hardware sorter

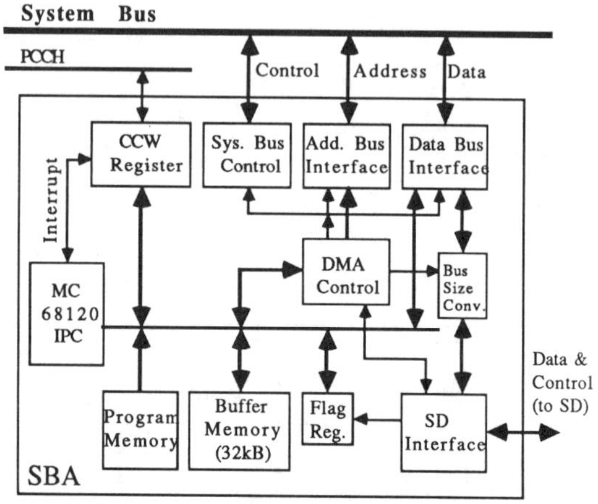

Fig.7 Architecture of system bus adaptor

SBA: System Bus Adaptor
SD: Sort Driver

PCCH: Program Control Channel   CCW: Channel Command Word
SD: Sort Driver

without waiting for the end of I/O to/from sorter.

Combining asynchronous I/O mechanism both for sorter and disks, we can construct the sorting program which utilizes the hardware sorter. The program uses double-buffering technique based on asynchronous I/O in several ways. In the first phase in which original data are read from disk and forwarded to sorter, disk data are transferred to one buffer while the sorter inputs data from another buffer, which has been filled with the data previously transferred from disk. We continue this operation by exchanging the roles of buffers until the file in disk is moved to sorter. The vice versa operation is executed in the second phase in which sorted data are read from sorter and written back to disk. It is easy to see that this program can fully overlap data transfer to/from sorter with that to/from disks.

Instruction	Operation	
SIO	Write	Sorter Reset
		Sorter Write
	Read	Sorter Read
TIO	Device Check	
CIO	SBA Reset	
AKIT	Acknowledge Interrupt	

Fig.8 The I/O instructions

4.2. Flow of the data stream

The data stream is supplied to SBA by a sequence of SIO instructions. In an ordinary device such as a disk, SIO is a unit of the data transfer. In our sort system, the data is given/taken to/from SBA with several SIOs, since it is not possible to handle such large amount of data as 8 Mbytes in single SIO instruction. Fig.9 shows the overview of the data movement among host machine, SBA and sort unit. SBA manages its current status shown in Fig.10.

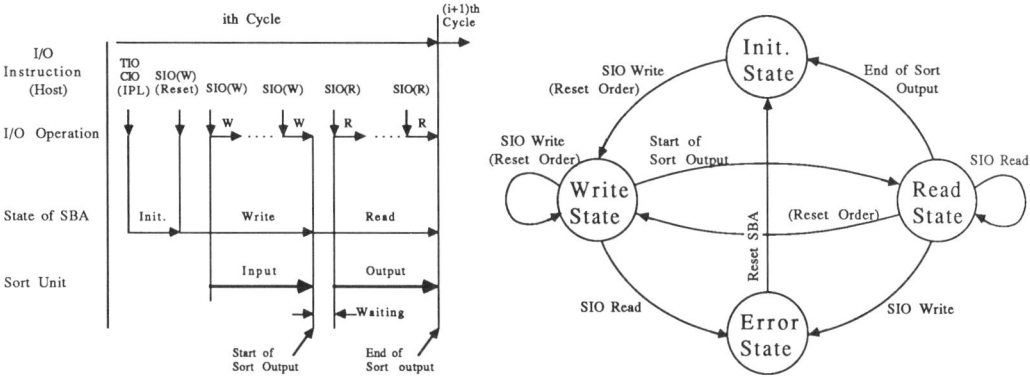

Fig.9 I/O operation sequence

Fig.10 Internal state transition of system bus adapter

By IPL, SBA is in the initial state. When a reset order is issued, SBA goes to write state where data is transferred from the host machine to the sorter. When the sorter detects the end of data flag which is embedded in the data stream, SBA is notified to move to read state where the sorted data is taken from the sorter to the main memory of the host machine. If the SBA receives the incorrect order, it sends an error status to the host.

The cost of incorporation of the hardware sorter to the host machine was not so large than we expected, although the system is not complete yet. The hardware volume of the SBA is relatively small. The interpreter for SIO on the microprocessor of the SBA is also very small.

5. Performance Evaluation

In order to clarify the performance of the hardware sorter in an actual environment, we did the following benchmark test. We measured the time to sort the file on the disk. The records of a file on the disk are at first transferred to the sorter through the main memory of the host machine. The sorted records are then written back to the disk again through the main memory of the host machine.

Let the capacity of the file be N (bytes), the data transfer rate from disk to main memory be h_d (bytes/sec), the data transfer rate from main memory to SBA is h_s (bytes/sec), the unit of data transfer be M (bytes), and the overhead time for one SIO operation be α (sec). SBA is designed to handle the data transfer rate of 4 Mbytes/sec. The system bus bandwidth is much higher than 4 Mbytes/sec. On the other hand, physical peak speed of data transfer of the disk is 1.2 Mbytes/sec, which is much lower than that of the sorter. The rate becomes even worse when it is measured under the operating system due to several overheads. The system bus bandwidth is much higher than h_d+h_s. Therefore the data transfer time from the disk to the sorter is determined by the transfer time from the disk to the main memory, with which the time from main memory to the sorter is overlapped. Thus the total sort time is expressed as

$$T=2(M/h_d+2\alpha)N/M$$

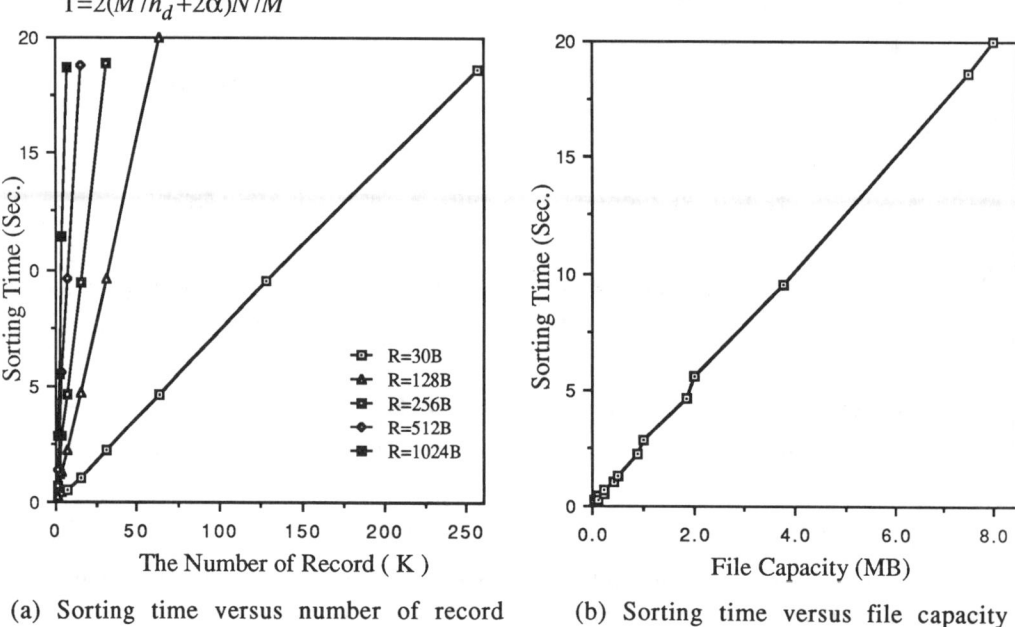

(a) Sorting time versus number of record   (b) Sorting time versus file capacity

Fig.11 Performance evaluation results

Fig.11(a) shows the measurement results. The horizontal and vertical axis denote the number of records and the sorting time respectively. The parameter R is the record length. For any record length, sorting time is linearly dependent on the number of records due to the O(N) sorting time complexity of the pipeline merge sort algorithm.

Actually the sorting time dose not depend on the record length, as suggested in Fig.11(b). Since the sorter works assuming the whole record body as a key, the volume of the file that is the product of the record length and the number of record determines the sorting time.

In order to fully utilize hardware sorter, we have to reduce the time spent in the 2nd term, namely SIO overhead time, $2\alpha N/M$. Fig.12 shows the sorting time varying with the size of the buffer on main memory. By employing the buffer of appropriate size, we can decrease the interrupt overhead time and use the sorter very efficiently.

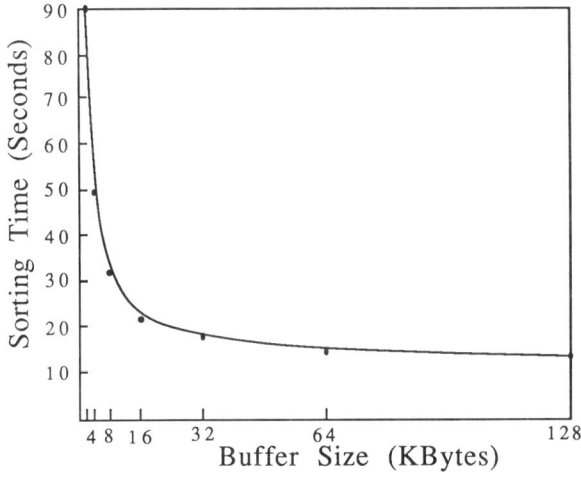

Fig.12 Sorting time dependecy on buffer size

In this experimental environment, we use the ordinary SMD disk drive whose data transfer rate is 1.2Mbytes/sec. So the disk becomes a bottleneck rather than the sorter itself. In current mainframe, however, higher performance disks with the transfer rate such as 3.0 or 4.5 Mbytes/sec are used, where our sorter would be better utilized.

Comparing with the software sort utility in the host machine, the hardware sorter showed 25 times higher performance when the file of 8 Mbytes with the record length 30 Bytes is sorted. The comparison is not necessarily fair since the software utility does not use 8 Mbyte memory space although the main memory of the machine is 8 Mbytes. More precise evaluation is left for the future work. In this hardware sorter, sorting time is determined solely by the volume of the file, whereas the time is dependent on the number of the records of the file with the sort software. Given the capacity of the file constant, the shorter the record length the more powerful the hardware sorter becomes.

With the relatively small cost for connecting the sorter to the host machine, we attained much higher performance in comparison with the conventional sort utility.

A Parallel Container Model
for Data Intensive Applications

Setrag Khoshafian
Ashton Tate
Walnut Creek, California

Patrick Valduriez
MCC
Austin, Texas

Abstract

Existing parallel programming languages do not capture the execution model of data intensive applications with declustered (horizontally partitioned) databases. A parallel model with concurrent containers storing persistent objects of the same type is proposed and discussed. Communication among the containers is through messages, which incorporate object identifiers and function abstractions. Restricting container assignment to particular types of objects (shared objects and set elements) is also discussed. Finally, the model is extended to incorporate result containers and container message variables.

1. Introduction

A number of computational models have been proposed for capturing parallelism and concurrency in a programming language. The most notable of these attempts include Hoare's communicating sequential processes [Hoare 1978], Hewitt's Actors [Hewitt et al. 1973] and McCarthy's 'pure' Lisp (functional) [McCarthy 1959]. Each of these approaches provides a certain amount of expressiveness in capturing the inherent parallelism in application domains. However, none seems to capture the execution environment of data intensive applications, with databases distributed across multiple independent execution units, in a direct and intuitive way. The generic "shared nothing" architecture of such systems is shown in Figure 1, where each node is an independent processing unit, including one or more CPU's, RAM, and disk. The persistent database is *declustered* [Livny et al. 1987] (equivalently termed "distributed", "horizontally partitioned" [Reiss 1978], or "horizontally fragmented") across these nodes according to a placement strategy which attempts to maintain load balancing [Copeland et al. 1988].

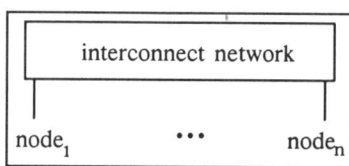

Figure 1: Parallel Database Machine Architecture

To reduce the size and number of data and communication messages, an efficient strategy is to "execute where the data is" [Khoshafian and Valduriez 1987a] . In other words programs are sent to the nodes which contain data to execute locally (contrast this, for example, with dataflow machines where the data is sent to the operation nodes). The strategy is used in numerous database machines including Bubba [Boral 1988], Gamma [DeWitt et al. 1986], and Grace [Kitsuregawa et al. 1983]. In these systems, the user accesses the database through a high level interface (e.g., SQL [Date 1987]). The user programs are subsequently interpreted or compiled to run on the parallel machine. This approach prevents the users from programming the parallel machine directly, because users are not provided with a simple and expressive parallel language integrated with the object model.

An example of a more recent parallel language for a database machine is the POOL parallel object oriented language of the PRISMA database machine [Kersten et al. 1987]. An extension of this language, POOL-X provides primitives for constructing objects of the object model (e.g., tuples). It also provides the means for placing objects in nodes. Our container model resembles POOL in these aspects, although our constructs are more tightly integrated with the object model and can be thought of as an extension of the database management system's data manipulation language (vs. an implementation language extended with object modeling primitives).

To further motivate the container approach, consider the following. One of the most frequently used operation in data intensive applications is a "filter" applying to every element of a distributed set. Assume the database consists of a number of relations (where each relation is a set of flat tuples) and there is a directory which maps a relation with a predicate onto a set of nodes. Conceptually, the directory is a two level index with a major clustering on relation name and a minor clustering on some attribute of the relation. Figure 2 provides an example of a directory. Suppose we want to locate the elements in relation Employee with cluster value 3299. The first level index on set name maps the name Employee onto the cluster value index for relation Employee. Then this second level index further maps the cluster value 3299 onto node number j. Now, if we want to retrieve, say, the name and address of every employee, we must execute the projection on nodes 1 through n. If we want to retrieve the tuple of the employee with number 3210, only node j needs to be involved.

We can see from this simple example that what gets (or should get) activated is selectively that sub-set of the relation which has pertinent data. There could be several such sub-sets on a node, each belonging to a different relation. However, these sub-sets are independent from one another and can be thought of as "executing" filters and other operations concurrently. Also, note that the elements of the sub-sets persist between different program invocations.

The *container model,* proposed in this paper, attempts to capture such an execution environment in simple but expressive parallel programming constructs. Containers are independent execution units which contain sub-sets of persistent objects of the same type. Containers communicate through asynchronous messages. The messages consist of the code to be executed by a container, as well as the identifiers of the objects to which the message pertains.

So far, we restricted our discussion to the relational model, where the persistent database consists of "flat" relations (i.e., sets of tuples with no nesting). The container model is integrated in a more general object model based on the FAD [Bancilhon et al. 1987] database language. The

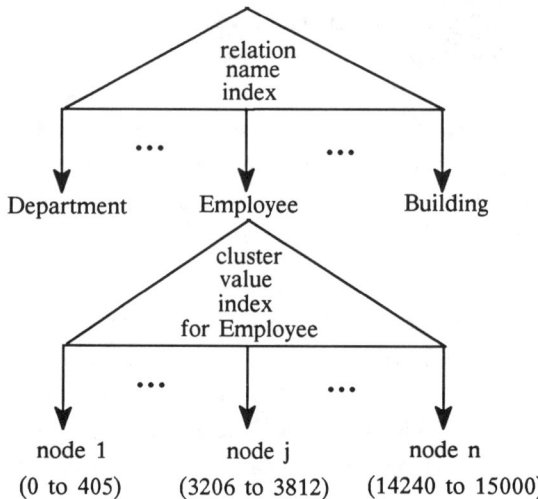

Figure 2: Global Directory Example

objects are built with set and tuple object constructors with arbitrary nestings of tuples within sets or sets within tuples. Furthermore, the object model supports the strong notion of object identity [Khoshafian and Copeland 1986]. This means that the uniqueness of objects is determined independent of content or addressability. It also means that the object space is a graph (vs. a tree in "value" base models [Ullman 1987]). With the container model, we can traverse the graph structured object space partitioned and distributed across multiple nodes, through simple message constructs sent to the concurrent container. Referential sharing of objects [Khoshafian and Valduriez 1987b], where the same object might have more than one parent in the graph structured space, do not pose any difficulties.

The rest of the paper is organized as follows. In Section 2 we introduce the object model which provides a context for the container model. In Section 3 we present the container model, which is the crux of this paper. Section 4 gives our conclusions and some directions for future research.

2. The Object Model

The primary contribution of this paper is the introduction of the container model, which captures the concurrency and execution environment of parallel shared nothing architectures for data intensive applications. However, the container model is defined with respect to a persistent object space. We thus need to define the objects in the model. Furthermore, to better understand the examples and the messages executed by the containers, we need to have a persistent programming language. The object model is that of the database programming language FAD [Bancilhon et al. 1987]. The constructs of the container model will be integrated with FAD in the subsequent sections. In the rest of this section, we give the basic definition of the object spaces, as well as the programming constructs which are used in the examples.

2.1 Objects

Objects are built with the "set" and "tuple" object constructors, on top of a layer of atoms (integers, floats, strings, etc.). Assuming that we have a set of identifiers, I, a set of attribute names N, and a set of atomic types A, each object is defined as a triple

[Id, Type, State]

where Id is in I, Type is either *set*, *tuple*, or *atomic* and

(1) If Type is atomic, then State is an atomic value (e.g., the integer 5, or the string "boy").

(2) If Type is *tuple*, then the State is
$$[a_1: i_1, ..., a_n: i_n]$$
where each a_i is an attribute name and each i_j is an identifier.

(3) If Type is *set*, State is
$$\{i_1, .., i_n\}$$
where each i_j is an identifier.

The identifier of an object O is retrieved through an "^" infix operator, O^Id. Similarly, the Type of the object is retrieved through O^Type.

2.2 Operators

In this paper we use the following basic operators and predicates:

(1) For atomic objects:
Arithmetic operators (e.g., integer or float '+', '*', etc.).
Comparators: *equal*(O_1, O_2), *lessthan*(O_1, O_2), *greaterthan*(O_1, O_2).
Update: *assign*(O_1, O_2) replaces the state of O_1, by the State of O_2.

(2) For tuples:
Extract: T•A, where T is a tuple object and A is an attribute name is the A attribute value of T.
Update: *tupleassign*(T, A, O) modifies the A attribute value of T to O.

(3) For sets: *insert*(Set, e) updates Set, inserting the object e into it.

Besides the basic operators and predicates, we have constructors which build more complex operators and predicates from simpler ones. Constructors take functions as input. We specify these argument functions through a lambda abstraction mechanism [Pingali and Kathail 84], which we denote by **fun**. Therefore, if x is a variable and e is an expression where x is free

fun(x) e

denotes a function, a predicate or an update abstraction having x as an input variable and and whose result is the object denoted by the expression e. Of course x is bound in fun(x) e and we adopt the usual convention concerning scoping.

The most frequently used constructor is *filter* which is defined as follows:

filter(f, Set$_1$, ..., Set$_n$) where f is an n-ary operator abstraction, and Set$_1$,, .., Set$_n$ are set objects, is a set equal to

$$\{f(x_1, ..., x_n) \mid x_1 \in Set_1, ..., x_n \in Set_n\}$$

We also have two other constructs which are used in our examples:

if <Predicate> *then* <expr$_1$>
  else <expr$_2$>

which, as usual, executes the then-clause exp$_1$ if the Predicate is TRUE; else expr$_2$ is executed.

do (expr$_1$, expr$_2$, ..., expr$_n$)

executes the expressions expr$_1$, ..., expr$_n$ in the given order.

2.3 The Persistent Space

The object space is partitioned between a *transient* and *persistent* object spaces. The persistent space persists after program termination, and subsequent programs manipulate the same persistent object space. The approach here is very similar to other persistent programming languages such as PS-Algol [Atkinson et al, 1983]. There is a reserved word **database** (or **db**) representing a handle to an object which defines the persistent object space. More specifically, the persistent object space is the collection of all objects which are *reachable* from the **database** root, where reachability from an object O is defined as follows:

(i) O is reachable from itself.

(ii) if S is a set object reachable from O whose state is $\{i_1, ..., i_n\}$ then each object with identity i_j is readable from O.

(iii) if T is a tuple object reachable from O and A an attribute of T then T•A is reachable from O.

As usual, a schema must be specified for the persistent database. We define this schema through a rooted graph [Kuper and Vardi 1984, 1985; Hull 1987] as follows:

Definition: A directed graph G is a couple (V, E) where V is a set nodes and E is a set of edges. An edge from node v to node w is denoted <v, w>; v is the *tail* of the edge and w is the *head* of the edge. An *in-edge* of a node w is an edge <v, w>. In-edges of a node are said to be *incident to* the node. An *out-edge* of a node v is an edge <v, w>. Out-edges of a node are said to be *incident from* the node.

The (immediate) successors of a node v are defined by the set:

$$suc(v) = \{w \mid w \in V, <v, w> \in E\}$$

The (immediate) predecessors of a node v are defined by:

$$pred(v) = \{u \mid u \in V, <u, v> \in E\}$$

A graph is *rooted* if there exists a distinguished node, *root*, such that:

(i) $pred(root) = \emptyset$

(ii) every node is reachable from root

In the following a • node denotes a tuple, and a * node denotes a set

Definition: A *schema* is a triple (S, μ, λ), where S is a *rooted directed graph*, μ is a *structuring function* and λ is a *labeling function*.

The domain of μ is the nodes of S and its range is $\{\bullet, *\} \cup A$, such that (1) each node which is mapped to an element of A, has no out-edges and (2) each * node has exactly one out-edge.

The labeling function λ maps each edge incident from a • node to an attribute name in N, such that different attribute names are assigned to different incident edges of the same node. For a more formal and extended description of the schema representation see [Khoshafian and Briggs 1988]. Figure 3 gives an example of a **db** schema for an order entry application involving items and warehouses.

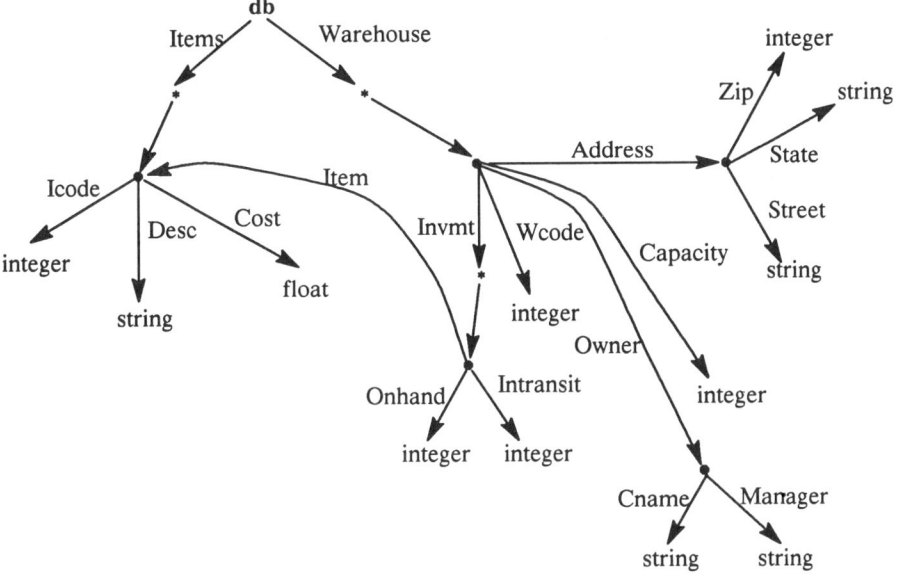

Figure 3: Example of a Database Object

We define the interpretation of the schema nodes as finite subsets of the object space *OS*. OS denotes the set of all objects built on top of the atomic objects, using set and tuple object constructors.

Definition: An *instance* of a schema is a function F from V (the set of nodes of the schema) to $p^{fin}(OS)$ (the set of finite sub-sets of objects [Hull 1987]), such that:

(1) if v∈V is a set node, then F(v) is a set of sets; if v∈V is a tuple node then F(v) is a set of tuples; if v∈V is an atomic node then F(v) is a set of atomic objects.

(2) if v≠w, then F(v) and F(w) are disjoint.

(3) if v is an atomic node labeled B, then the value of e is in dom(B) for each e in F(v).

(4) if v is a tuple node •; $v_1, ... v_n$ are the successors of v and the edge from v to v_i is labeled a_i, then $t.a_i$ is in $F(v_i)$ (i=1, ..., n), for each t in F(v).

(5) if v is a set node *, and w is the successor of v, then for each s in F(v), s is a subset of F(w).

3. The Container Model

3.1 Overview

The generic architecture of our underlying system consists of a number of independent nodes. The persistent object space is distributed across these nodes according to some prescribed placement strategy [Khoshafian and Valduriez 1987a; Copeland et al. 1988]. The basic execution strategy is to "execute where the data is". In other words, an operator that manipulates a particular persistent object must execute in the node which stores the object. Although several database machines (e.g., the DBC/1012 [Teradata 1983]) use a similar technique, there are few expressive programming paradigms which capture this model. Examples of other more general purpose parallel "shared nothing" architectures [Stonebraker 1986] include INTEL's iPSC [INTEL 1985] and Floating Point Systems (FPS) T/Series computers [Frankel 1986]. The container model is applicable to these machines as well.

It is true that one can utilize the Actor model [Agha 1987], or CSP [Hoare 1978] for that matter, to encode the concurrency of data intensive algorithms. However, neither of these models capture the execution strategies of data intensive applications running on shared nothing architectures in an intuitive and direct way. The interesting features such as "replacements", "tasks", and "guards", provided by these models are mostly unnecessary and do not directly represent or capture the efficient algorithms of massive data filtering, partial matching, joins, projects, etc..

Therefore, we propose the *container* model, which attempts to provide direct expressions of the concurrent execution of the nodes storing declustered persistent sets. To further motivate the container model's construct, the following observations are important. First, each node might contain a number of CPU's, which could operate in parallel on different objects. Second, in many cases, the same operator is applied to all (or many) objects of the same Type. Third, since the underlying architecture is shared nothing and loosely coupled, communication is through messages (vs. shared variables). Fourth, the "sub-sets" of a declustered set are *not* objects of the object space. Declustered partitioning is strictly a placement strategy.

3.2 Container Definition

Containers are built up from objects of the same type.

Definition: a *container* is a collection $C = <O_1, ..., O_n>$ of objects such that
$O_1\hat{}Type = O_2\hat{}Type = ... = O_n\hat{}Type$.

We say each O_i *resides* in C. The set of all container identifiers will be indicated by SC. Each container has its own processing power and the objects that reside in the container constitute the container's persistent memory. A container is either *dormant* or *active*. Initially a container is dormant. It becomes active when it receives a container-message (discussed below).

The concurrent execution model of containers is similar to other concurrent object-oriented models, including Actors [Agha 1987], ABCL/1 [Yonezawa et al. 1987] and Orient 84/K [Ishikawa and Tokoro 1987]. However, unlike these models, the concurrency is restricted to containers storing sub-sets of persistent objects (vs. all objects of the object space).

In a shared nothing architecture, each node will host a number of containers and thus the underlying hardware will transmit the messages to the appropriate containers. If there are more containers than CPU's, the containers will time share. Figure 4 gives the overall picture of containers in nodes of a parallel shared nothing architecture.

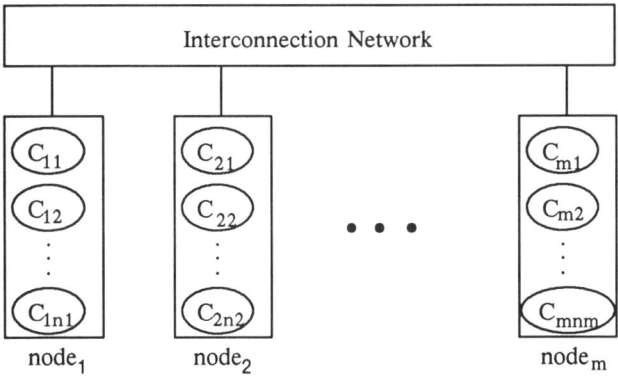

Figure 4: Containers in a Parallel Database Machine

An object can reside in exactly *one* container. The distribution of objects into containers is defined through a placement *function* as follows:

Definition: A *placer* is a function P from I (the set of identifiers) to C (the set of containers) such that an object O resides in container C if and only if P(O^Id) = C.

All containers execute concurrently. There is a container message queue associated with each container. A container gets the next message from the queue and executes it. Container messages are defined as follows:

Definition: A *container-message* is a couple *(ArgumentIndicator, Abstraction)* where ArgumentIndicator is either a "*" or a collection <i1, ..., in> of identifiers. The Abstraction is of the form *fun(x) e* where the only free variable in e is x. If the ArgumentIndicator is "*" then the abstraction is applied to every object residing in the container. Otherwise, the abstraction is applied to objects with identifiers i_1, ..., i_n, which should all be residing in the container.

Container messages are sent through sends which take as argument a container identifier (an element of SC) and a container message.

Definition: A **send** operator is given by *send* (C, Message) where C is in SC and Message is a container message whose arguments should all reside in the container C.

Figure 5 illustrates the container model. Each message either updates the container's persistent memory (i.e., the objects residing in the container) or queries the residing objects or both. A message might also generate messages to other containers.

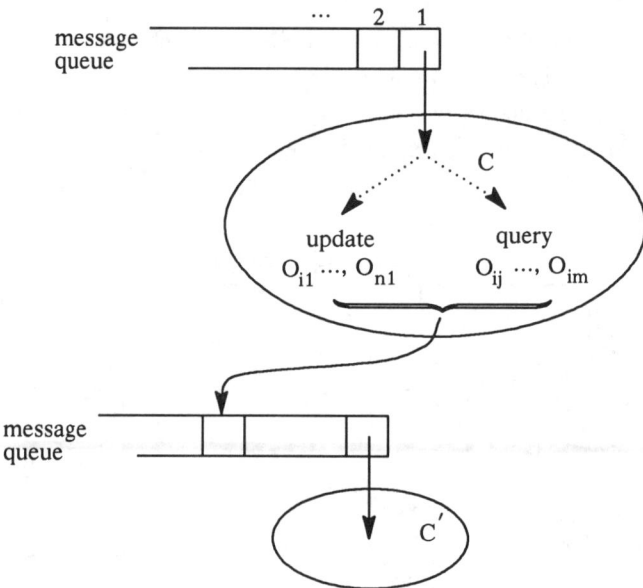

Figure 5: The Container Model

3.3 Container Manipulation

The proposed container model is general and flexible. For instance, it allows the placement of the different attributes of a tuple in different containers. However, the programs traversing the persistent complex object need to perform a send for every object accessed. For example, the program to raise the costs of items by 10% is:

send (P(**db**.Items^Id), (**db**.Items^Id, fun(x)
       filter (fun(y) send (P(y^Id), (y^Id, fun(z)
                      send(P(z.cost^Id), (z.cost^Id, fun(v) assign(v, v*1.1)))),
         x)))

In many cases, most of the sends are to objects within the same node, since the sub-objects reside in containers on the same node as the containers of the parents. In other words, the tuple and atomic sub-objects are typically stored in the same node as their first predecessor which is an element of a set.

Therefore, we can restrict the container model and require that set elements only be assigned containers. The sub-objects which are reachable from the set element *without* traversing an intermediate set object can be accessed directly without any sends. The previous example becomes

filter (fun(x) send (P(x^Id), (x^Id, fun(y)
                  tupleassign(y, cost, y.cost*1.1))),
       db.Items)

Unfortunately, due to referentially shared objects [Khoshafian and Valduriez 1987b], the solution does not work in general. More specifically, the same atomic or tuple object can be shared by several set elements. As a simple example, consider the schema in Figure 6 of a Persons database.

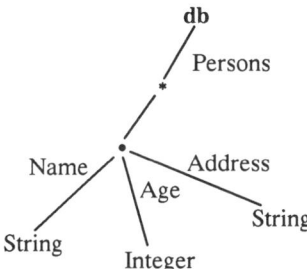

Figure 6: Example of Database Schema

Since we have the possibility that several people would always live in the same address ("shared" residence), we cannot directly access the Address attribute from the tuple representing a person. In the underlying implementation, shared objects such as the Address attribute, are either replicated or stored with one of the parents, with pointer references in the other parents of the shared object. Replication is rather expensive in both storage and update cost. In our model, storing the object with one of the parents amounts to mapping the containers of the parent and the shared object onto the same node. Therefore, we need a mechanism for distinguishing between "shareable" and "non-shareable" persistent objects. We accomplish this through annotations of the **db** schema.

Definition: A node in a conceptual schema has *non-shareable* instances if an element in an instance of the node cannot be the attribute value of two distinct tuples, or the element of two distinct sets, or the element of a set and the attribute value of a tuple.

Thus, if Name and Age of a person are non-shareable but Address *is* shareable, we can indicate this through annotations of the schema as in Figure 7.

Therefore, all the objects which are reachable from an element of a set through tuple nodes can be accessed directly (i.e., without sends) *provided* all the intermediate nodes have non-shareability annotations in the schema.

More generally, if in the **database** schema v is a shareable node (i.e., v does *not* have a non-shareable annotation) or if v's predecessor is a '*' node (i.e., instances of v are elements of sets)

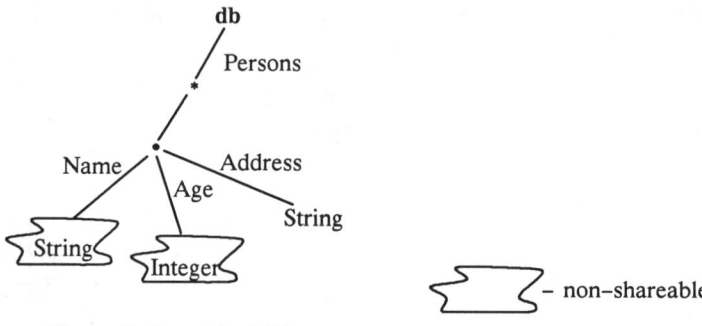

Figure 7: Annotated Schema

then all the objects reachable from an instance of v through non-shareable tuple nodes can be accessed directly.

3.4 Result Container

The previous examples performed updates to the persistent database. Needless to say, the model must also support database queries. Typically, a program will have a dataflow diagram consisting of all the activated containers and the container messages as in Figure 8.

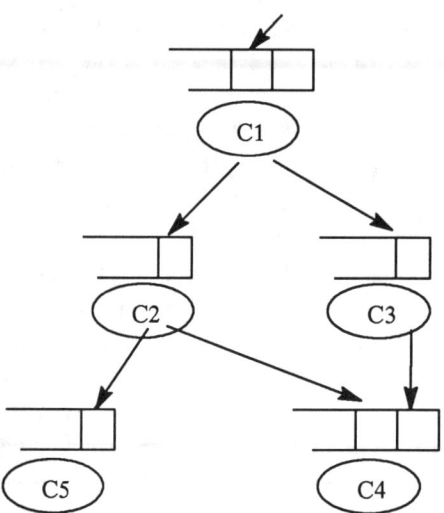

Figure 8: Example of Message Flow Within Containers

The result of the program must be returned to the user. Since the result cannot reside in a container, we introduce the handle **result** which stands for the identifier of a "logical" container. We can then send to the **result** container to accumulate the program's result.

For example, to obtain the item codes and descriptions of all items which are stored in warehouses located in Texas we have:

```
filter (    fun(x) send (P(x^Id),  (x^Id, fun(y)
                if (eq(y.Address.State, "Texas") then
                    filter ( fun(z) send (P(z.Item^Id), (z.Item^Id, fun(v)
                                    send(result, (*,
                                                [Icode:copy(w.Icode),
                                                 Desc:copy(w.Desc)]))))),
                            y.Invnt))),
            db.Warehouse)
```

3.5 Identifier Collections

So far in all of our examples the argument indicator of a container message was an individual element of the container. In many cases, messages might be replicated since more than one recipient of the same operation can reside in the same container.

If the same message has to be sent to *all* the elements of a persistent set, we introduce the operator *send–all* which takes as arguments a Set object and a message Abstraction and sends the abstraction to all containers of the set:

   send–all(Set, Abstraction)

This instruction is equivalent to:

   filter (fun(x) send(P(x^Id), (x^Id, Abstraction)), Set)

Using this operator, the previous example becomes more compact:

```
send-all (db.Warehouse, fun(x)
            if (eq(x.Address.State,"Texas") then
            send-all (x.Invnt, fun(y)
                send (result, (*,
                                [Icode:copy(y.Icode),
                                 Desc:copy(y.Desc)]))))))
```

3.6 Container Message Variables

We introduce container variables which enable us to construct container messages which are applicable to a sub–set of the objects residing in a container. In many cases, a message applies to a sub–set of the objects residing in a container. The abstraction in container messages apply to the objects without 'memory': there are no global variables. Thus, we cannot accumulate identifier sub–sets based on quantification. We define a container message as a quadruple:

   (ArgumentIndicator, MessageVariableAssignments, Abstraction, LastOp)

where ArgumentIndicator is as before, MessageVariableAssignments is a list

   $<X_1$ is e_1, X is e_2, ..., X_n is $e_n>$

where the X_i's are variable names and the assignments are performed sequentially. Therefore e_1 is an operator without free variables, the only permissible free variable in e_2 is X_1, in e_3 is X_1 and X_2 and so on. Also, the permissible free variables in e of the abstraction

Abstraction ≡ fun(x) e

are $X_1, ..., X_n$.

Finally, the LastOp is an operator where the only free variables are $X_1, ..., X_n$. This operator is executed *after* the Abstraction is applied to all the objects in the container indicated by the ArgumentIndicator. This resembles the postprocessing section of messages in POOL [America 1987].

Message variables and Last Operators can also be incorporated in send-all messages (when ArgumentIndicator is, by default, all the objects residing in the container).

For example, assuming that the warehouse owners are shared and the query is to retrieve the Manager's of warehouse owners with capacity > 100, an efficient program is:

```
send-all (db.Warehouse,
    let C = { } in
    fun(x) if( gt(x.capacity, 100)) then
        let IC =TRUE in
        do (   filter ( fun(y) if (equal(y.Cont, P(x.Owner^Id))) then
                            do (  insert(y.Ids, x.Owner^Id),
                                  assign(IC, FALSE)),
                    C),
            if IC then insert (C, [Cont: P(x.Owner^Id), Ids: {x.Owner^Id}])),
        filter(  fun(y) send (y.Cont, (y.Ids, fun(z)
                            send (result, (*, copy(z.Manager))))),
            C))
```

4. Conclusion

In this paper we have proposed some constructs for programming parallel shared nothing architectures for data intensive applications. The model is based on the notion of concurrent containers where a homogeneous sub-set of the persistent database resides. We showed how containers could be integrated in a powerful data model which supports arbitrary complex objects, using set and tuple object constructors. The model also supports the strong notion of object identity and the object identities to containers. Thus, such general and powerful object spaces are easily handled. We also argued for a restriction on the container model, where containers are assigned to elements of sets or shareable objects. This simplifies the code and renders it more readable, at the expense of some generality.

The container model could be used either to program a parallel database machine directly or as a target language from a high level interface language compiled onto the proposed model. The underlying premise of the container model is that it closely captures the execution environment and strategies of parallel database machines and naturally integrates with a complex data model. Of course this claim needs to be quantified through analyzing the overhead of supporting and implementing the container semantics. Other areas of future work include the following.

First, container concurrency should be integrated with a transaction model where concurrent (and possibly conflicting) transactions update the persistent database. One approach is to let each message also incorporate a transaction identifier. We can then use conventional concurrency control schemes, such as two-phase locking, to lock the objects accessed in the message on behalf of the transaction. Distributed concurrency control strategies, such as global deadlock detection or timeout mechanism, should be used to commit or abort a transaction. The technology is well known, and we believe distributed transactions could easily be integrated in the container model.

The second open issue is the assignment of containers to objects. That is, we need a mechanism for specifying the placer function. The most natural place for this is at object creation time. In other words, whenever a persistent object (a persistent set element or a shareable object in the constrained model) is created, the user must also specify containers for the newly created object. To support load balancing, it will be useful to provide primitives which modify the placer function (i.e., move objects among containers).

References

[Agha 1987] G. Agha, *ACTORS: A Model of Concurrent Computation in Distributed Systems*, MIT Press, 1987.

[America 1987] P. America, "POOL_T: a Parallel Object Oriented Language", in *Object Oriented Concurrent Programming*, Eds. A. Yonezawa and M. Tokoro, MIT Press, 1987.

[Atkinson et al. 1983] M.P. Atkinson, P.J. Bailey, W.P. Cockshott, K.J. Chisholm, R. Morrison, "An Approach to Persistent Programming", *Computer Journal*, Vol. 26, November 1983.

[Bancilhon et al. 1987] F. Bancilhon, T. Briggs, S. Khoshafian, P. Valduriez, "FAD: A Simple and Powerful Database Language", VLDB Conf., September 1987.

[Boral 1988] H. Boral, "Parallelism in Bubba", Int. Sump. on Databases in Parallel and Distributed Systems, Austin, Texas, December 1988.

[Copeland et al. 1988] G. Copeland, W. Alexander, E. Boughter, T. Keller, "Data Placement in Bubba", SIGMOD Conf., 1988.

[DeWitt et al. 1986] D. DeWitt et al, "GAMMA: A High Performance Dataflow Database Machine", VLDB Conf., August 1986.

[Frenkel 1986] K.A. Frenkel, "Evaluating Two Massively Parallel Machines", *Communications of the ACM*, Vol. 29, No. 8, 1986.

[Hewitt et al 1973] C. Hewitt, P. Bishop, R. Steiter, "A Universal Modular Actor Formalism for Artificial Intelligence", 3rd Int. Joint Conf. on Artificial Intelligence, August 1983.

[Hoare 1978] C.A.R. Hoare, "Communicating Sequential Processes", *CACM*, Vol. 21, No. 8, August 1978.

[Hull 1987] R. Hull, "A Survey of Theoretical Research on Typed Complex Database Objects", J. Paradaens, (Ed.), *Databases*, Academic Press (London) 1987.

[INTEL 1985] INTEL Corporation, iPSC Data Sheet, Order No. 2801 01-001, 1985.

[Ishikawa and Tokoro 1987] Y. Ishikawa and M. Tokoro, "Orient84/K: An Object-Oriented Concurrent Programming Language for Knowledge Representation", *Object-Oriented Concurrent Programming*, MIT Press, Cambridge, 1987.

[Kersten et al. 1987] M.L. Kersten et al., "A Distributed, Main-Memory Database Machine", IWDM, Karuizawa, Japan October 1987.

[Khoshafian and Briggs 1988] *"Schema Design and Mapping Strategies for Persistent Object Models,"* S. Khoshafian and T. Briggs, Information and Software Technology, December, 1988.

[Khoshafian and Copeland 1986] *"Object Identity"*, S. Khoshafian and G. Copeland, 1st Int. Conf. on OOPSLA, Portland, Oregon, October 1986.

[Khoshafian and Valduriez 1987a] S. Khoshafian and P. Valduriez, *"Parallel Execution Strategies for Declustered Databases"*, IWDM, Karuizawa, Japan, October 1987.

[Khoshafian and Valduriez 1987b] S. Khoshafian and P. Valduriez, *"Persistence, Sharing and Object Orienation: a database perspective"*, Int. Workshop on Database Programming Languages, Roscoff, France, September 1987.

[Kitsuregawa et al. 1983] M. Kitsuregawa, H. Tanaka, T. Moto-oka, "Application of Hash to Database Machine and its Architecture", *New Generation Computing*, Vol. 1, No. 1, 1983.

[Kuper and Vardi 1984] G.M. Kuper and M.Y. Vardi, "A New Approach to Database Logic", ACM Int. Symp. on PODS, Waterloo, April 1984.

[Kuper and Vardi 1985] G.M. Kuper and M.Y. Vardi, "On The Expressive Power of the Logic Data Model", SIGMOD, Austin, Texas, 1985.

[Livny et al. 1987] M. Livny, S. Khoshafian, H. Boral, "Multi-disk Management Algorithms", SIGMETRICS Conf., 1987.

[McCarthy 1959] J. McCarthy, "Recursive Functions of Symbolic Expressions and their Computation by Machine", Memo 8, MIT, March 1959.

[Pingali and Kathail 1984] K. Pingali and V. Kathail, "An Introduction to Lambda Calculus", Laboratory for Computer Sciences, MIT, July 1984.

[Teradata 1983] Teradata Corporation, *DBC/1012 Data Base Computer Concepts & Facilities*, Teradata Corp. Doc. No. CO2-0001-00, 1983.

[Yonezawa et al. 1987] A. Yonezawa, E. Shibayama, T. Takada, and Y. Honda, "Modelling and Programming in an Object-Oriented Concurrent Language ABCL/1", *Object-Oriented Concurrent Programming*, MIT Press, Cambridge, 1987.

Function Request Shipping in a Database Machine Environment

Gary Hallmark[*]
IBM Almaden Research Center

Abstract

In ARBRE, a multiprocessor shared nothing database machine, parts of a single transaction must execute at several processing sites. The code fragments which implement the transaction must somehow come to exist at the necessary sites; they must be linked and loaded; and each must be invoked by a coordinator or subordinate transaction thread. We call this mechanism function request shipping, or FRS. The primary concerns in FRS are about the code that implements the function: its language, representation, transport, and execution. We present three alternative mechanisms for code transport and execution: piggyback, callback, and shared disk. The performance of these mechanisms, with and without code caching, was measured on the ARBRE prototype. The results indicate that the method of choice depends on both the cache hit ratio and the size of the code fragments.

1 Introduction

Every database machine that does not permit database data to reside in shared memory or on shared disk ("shared nothing" [Sto86]) must have a mechanism to distribute the work of a single transaction to multiple processing sites. We call such a mechanism function request shipping, or FRS. Because shared everything and shared disk architectures need no FRS mechanism, FRS must be efficient in order for a shared nothing architecture to be competitive in the realm of high performance transaction processing. An FRS mechanism must send few messages and support intra-transaction parallelism so that locks are held for short periods of time. For data-intensive applications, FRS efficiency is of little concern. Rather, it must be powerful enough to express parallel query processing algorithms and flexible enough to experiment with new ones. In the

---
[*]Author's address: Oracle Corporation, Belmont, CA

ARBRE [1] prototype [LDH*89], we want an FRS mechanism which supports both high performance transaction processing and highly parallel query processing.

A traditional FRS technology, the synchronous remote procedure call (RPC)[BN84], is easy to use but inadequate because it does not support parallelism and requires too many messages. In RPC, a client process "calls" a remote procedure by sending a request message with the procedure arguments to an anonymous server process that performs the actual call. The server then sends the result of the call back to the client. The client process blocks until the result message is received. RPC can be extended to let the client issue multiple calls in parallel (multiRPC) and then iterate over the multiple replies [SS86]. The RPC model can also be extended to avoid requiring the client to send n request messages and receive n replies in order to invoke n procedures at one remote server. Instead, the client could send one request containing a code fragment that when evaluated calls the n procedures and combines the results. The client can then receive one reply with the combined results. This improvement over RPC is called remote evaluation (REV) [Sta86].

Our FRS mechanism generalizes REV in the same way that multiRPC generalizes RPC. In so doing, we obtain parallel remote evaluation with a small number of messages. The query optimizer is responsible for splitting a transaction into code fragments suitable for FRS. The optimizer produces at least two code fragments. The transaction coordinator process executes one, and the host process executes the other. Subordinate processes execute additional fragments at the request of the coordinator or at the request of other subordinates. We couple FRS with distributed transactions to provide at-most-once execution semantics [LS83]. We do not support nested transactions–if any process fails the entire transaction is aborted.

This paper investigates alternative methods of implementing FRS. We must resolve five orthogonal issues; whether to

1. use a general purpose language or a special purpose language,

2. compile the language or interpret it,

3. piggyback the code on the request message, callback for the code, or load the code from a shared disk [2],

4. cache the code at the servers, and

5. have one process (*e.g.* the coordinator) issue all function requests or allow subordinates to be FRS clients as well as FRS servers.

---

[1] Almaden Research Backend Relational Engine
[2] We do not assume shared disks for database data.

Alternatives for all the issues are discussed. In addition, all alternatives for issues 3 and 4 have been prototyped in ARBRE, and we present performance measurements.

The paper is structured as follows. Section 2 discusses alternatives for an FRS language and its representation. Section 3 enumerates three methods for code transport and invocation, and mentions the benefits of code caching. Section 4 relates our experience with compiled C++ as an FRS language and representation. Section 5 presents measured performance of the code transport methods listed in Section 3. Section 6 shows our measured transaction overhead, and suggests possible improvements. Section 7 discusses related work.

2 FRS Language and Representation

The FRS code defines the interface between the output of the query optimizer and the input to the database machine run time environment. In ARBRE, we have concentrated on prototyping the run time environment and developing algorithms and strategies to exercise it. For now we optimize and code query evaluation plans by hand. Consequently, we are biased toward an FRS language suitable for programming. One issue when choosing an FRS language is whether to use an existing, general purpose language or to design a special purpose one. A second issue is FRS code representation: whether to interpret or compile this language. We discuss these two issues in turn.

2.1 General Purpose versus Special Purpose

Deciding whether to use a general purpose language or to develop a special purpose language depends on the set of available programming languages and programming environments, the requirements imposed by the database machine, and the need for flexibility.

Language design is a slow, arduous process. If the database machine is to be used to process complex queries with intra-transaction parallelism, then constructs for parallelism and dataflow must be designed [SS86,BBKV87]. For transaction processing, traditional imperative constructs should also be available. If new algorithms, such as new join methods, are to be written in the language, a considerable amount of control and synchronization machinery must be designed. The requirements for the language can easily become a moving target. Design and implementation of other components of the database machine, *e.g.* communication and scheduling, may depend on the completion of the language design, thus serializing the overall project. It is easier to design and refine flexible abstractions in an existing language than to design and refine new language constructs and semantics.

A general purpose language has existing tools, such as a debugger and a compiler or an interpreter, which if reused may save development time. On the other hand, reuse of existing tools may cause problems. Invoking a language compiler as part of the query compilation and optimization process may lead to unacceptably long response times for *ad hoc* query processing. Integrating an existing interpreter into the run time environment of the database machine may be difficult.

A special purpose language may have constructs at a high level of abstraction, so that less code needs to be written to express a query evaluation plan. This may increase its efficiency, and reduce the size of its representation. This translates into fewer network packets for code transport. It may be possible to restrict the power of a special language in order to guarantee safety properties, which is important for human query optimizers, or buggy software ones.

In ARBRE, we decided to use an existing language. We needed flexibility for experimentation, and wanted to attack the difficult problems of parallel algorithm design and testing without the additional difficulties of language design. When our repertoire of algorithms and techniques stabilizes and when we no longer need to hand-code query evaluation plans, the task of designing a special purpose language should be more manageable.

2.2 Compilation versus Interpretation

Deciding whether to compile or interpret the FRS language involves another set of trade-offs. Compiling the FRS language, whether general purpose or specific, may produce better run time performance, especially if the code contains inner loops, such as complex predicates. Also, a compiler for a special purpose language may attempt sophisticated optimizations such as partial evaluation and parallelization [HDV88]. On the other hand, this may increase both space overhead and query compilation time.

Interpretation can yield good performance if most operators are high level. Moreover, an interpreted FRS mechanism may simplify debugging, avoid dynamic linking, support heterogeneity, and decrease communication by reducing code size [Fal87].

In ARBRE, we preferred an interpreted FRS language, perhaps with compiler support for critical inner loops, such as search predicates. However, we chose C++ as our FRS language and we wanted to reuse the existing C++ preprocessor and C compiler. Later in the paper we discuss the rationale for choosing C++ and the ramifications of choosing compilation.

3 Code Transport and Execution

For a client to execute a function at a remote server, the client must send a function request message to the server, and the server must have the FRS code which implements the function. We considered three methods of code transport:

- **piggyback**–the code is sent from the client to the server along with the function request message,
- **callback**–the code is not sent with the function request; the server will request the code if it is not already present, and
- **shared disk**–the operating system dynamically loads the code.

With the piggyback method, the code is always sent with the request. The code may be large in size, however, and cause the request message to require several network packets. With the callback method, the callback could be to the client, or to a code server. With the shared disk method, we let the operating system (MVS) link the code and load it dynamically from a shared disk. By considering the performance of the existing shared disk method, we can better judge the performance of the two network-based transport methods.

Caching the FRS code at the server may improve performance of all three alternatives mentioned above because dynamic code relocation is avoided if the already relocated code is cached. In addition, any packet reassembly overhead is avoided. A cache hit in the callback method makes the callback unnecessary. A hit in the shared disk method saves a disk access. A hit in the piggyback method, however, means that duplicate code was shipped. Reassembly and relocation overhead is avoided, but network bandwidth is not reduced.

Callback or shared disk may be better than piggyback for frequently executed transactions because with a large cache, the chance of a cache hit is high. Callback or shared disk may also be better than piggyback for *ad hoc* transactions if multiple clients issue the same function request to the same server in the same transaction. This situation can occur in a secondary index retrieval, for example, if two subordinates each scan a different part of the index and both request a third subordinate to retrieve records from the base table. This situation cannot occur if only one process issues all function requests.

In ARBRE we initially designed and implemented a piggyback scheme with no caching. However, the FRS code compilation produced larger sized code than we expected. Eventually we prototyped all three methods, each with FRS code caching which can be disabled for the purpose of measurement.

4 Implementation Experience

Our goals and background prompted us to adopt an existing general purpose language for FRS. Our first goal in ARBRE was to define an FRS language which supported hand-coding and experimentation with distributed algorithms. Second, we wanted a code representation which would achieve good performance for transaction processing and inner loops of queries. Third, we wanted a prototype that was quick to implement. Finally, none of the researchers working in the ARBRE group is an expert in language design.

By deciding not to develop a new language, we had to choose an existing language. Because much of the prototype is coded in C++, we chose to use C++ as the FRS code. The strong typing made it less error-prone to hand-code distributed algorithms, and the notion of a class made it possible to encapsulate services which the FRS code would invoke. Unfortunately, compilation was slow, code segments were large, debugging FRS code was difficult, and exceptions and storage management mechanisms were missing and had to implemented.

4.1 Design Details

Implementation of FRS using C++ was reasonably straightforward. In this section we briefly sketch the design of the server interface, the client interface, and the portable compiler output interface.

All procedures exported to FRS code at a server are accessed indirectly through a vector of function pointers called the *export vector*. Each FRS server contains a copy of the vector and code for each of the procedures available to the FRS code. C++ inline functions act as stubs, hiding this level of indirection from the caller.

For example, suppose we want to use FRS to invoke a function which computes the Euclidean distance between a point in the plane and the origin. This function will invoke two exported procedures: square() and the sqrt(). The distance function is written as a normal C++ function, but our implementation requires it to be a separate compilation unit.

```
# include "stubs.h"
float distance(float x, float y) {
    return sqrt(square(x), square(y));
}
```

The header file changes the usual interpretation of the square() and sqrt() function calls by defining them to be indirect calls through the export vector. Following is the pseudocode that implements stubs.h. Note that liberties have been taken with C++ typechecking in the interest of clarity.

```
typedef AnyFunction ...                       // ignore type of function
AnyFunction exportVector[] = { square, sqrt }; // initialize the vector
inline float square(float a) { return exportVector[0](a); }
inline float sqrt(float a) { return exportVector[1](a); }
```

A programmer providing a new procedure simply appends its address to the export vector, and provides a stub to call the new procedure indirectly through the vector. This process could and should be automated, but so far we have just provided macros to make the manual process less error prone.

The advantage of the indirection through the export vector is that only its starting address needs to be resolved to accomplish dynamic linking. We trade the time needed to perform the extra level of indirection per call for a simple, space-efficient dynamic linking method. Our export vector has about 150 entries, but a typical FRS code segment uses less than one-fourth of them.

The FRS mechanism is encapsulated at the client by two C++ classes, FRSrequest and FRSeval. An FRSrequest object has the following components:

- destination site,
- name of the FRS code (*e.g.* distance), or actual code if piggybacking is used, and
- arguments to the code (*e.g.* x,y).

FRSrequest arguments can be FRS code, so that function requests may issue other function requests. For example, the host may send subordinate code as arguments to the function request to the coordinator.

An FRSeval object has operations to send multiple FRSrequests to their respective destinations, to wait on their completions one-by-one, and to retrieve their results. The client may do other work in parallel with the servers before the first completion, and after each completion. In multiRPC [SS86], the client can provide a handler function to be called after each RPC completes. Thus the client can do no work in parallel with the servers before the first completion; we allow this extra flexibility.

Because we initially designed a piggyback code transport mechanism, the function request and the code, if any, are sent over a virtual circuit. There is a virtual circuit between each pair of processing sites in ARBRE that is shared by all FRS invocations between the two sites. When a site crashes and recovers, new virtual circuits are created automatically on demand.

Our FRS prototype runs on both the System/370 under the MVS operating system and on the RT PC under the AIX operating system. To provide portability, we defined a common representation for the FRS code. The representation consists of a header followed by relocatable machine code. The header contains offsets into the code that must be patched to make the code executable, followed by the locations of three entry points: a static class initializer, a static class destructor, and the main entry point. Three kinds of locations in the code must be patched:

- locations that must point to the base of the export table,
- locations that refer to other locations in the code (this section is empty if PC-relative addressing is used), and
- locations that point to static data areas.

The shared disk method of code transport relies on the MVS dynamic loader to perform code relocation and initialization of static data areas, and therefore is not portable. MVS has no dynamic linker; the compiled FRS code is prelinked with a small function which finds and returns the address of the export vector at run time.

The piggyback and callback FRS methods are portable. A small translation program must be written that converts the compiler output (*e.g.* a.out format on AIX and TEXT format on MVS) to our common representation. Our FRS code representation does not yet include debugging information.

4.2 Problems Encountered

Our experience with this FRS prototype implementation highlighted several problems. The time to compile even a trivial FRS code segment is quite high – about a minute on an IBM RT PC. One reason for this is that all the stubs are in one header file, and this entire file must be included in each FRS code compilation. Another is that our implementation supports only a one-to-one mapping between FRS code and compilation units, so that the time needed to process the stubs header file is not amortized over the compilation of several FRS code segments. Some compilers and environments support the notion of a "prime" file–a saved disk image of the content of the compiler's internal tables. If we could prime the stubs file, the compilation process would speed-up dramatically. However, without a true C++ compiler, this is impossible.

The space occupied by a trivial FRS code segment is also quite high. A compiled null code segment consumes 900 bytes in our 370 implementation, and over 1000 bytes on the RT. This is due to three factors. First, the C++ translator changes some of the inline stub functions to static functions (if a pointer to a stub function is needed, for example). Second, the C++ translator and C compiler do a poor job of eliminating dead code, so that unused non-inline stubs appear in the compiler output. Finally, our compilers tend to optimize for execution speed, rather than memory space. This is especially true when compiling for a RISC machine. A better stub generator or a better inlining mechanism would ameliorate the first two factors. A compiler switch to optimize for space would address the third.

Debugging compiled FRS code is difficult unless the FRS code contains debugging information and the debugger knows how to find it. Our portable FRS code representation does not currently support debugging. Consequently, the AIX debugger is able to place a breakpoint in the server code, but not in the FRS code itself. For example, we could set a breakpoint on or in the square() function, but not on entry to distance(). If the operating system is used to link and relocate FRS code, then it is possible to debug the FRS code directly. Unfortunately, MVS does not provide a symbolic debugger. We therefore rely heavily on print statements.

The absence of an exception mechanism and automatic garbage collection made it difficult to recover cleanly from an aborted transaction. We did not want FRS code to be responsible for checking return codes and properly releasing resources. Instead, we carefully designed and implemented the exported C++ class constructors and destructors which manage resources to perform the resource allocation and deallocation automatically. This works well as long as the FRS code runs to completion–C++ guarantees that destructors are called, and the service implementer guarantees that resources are returned. In order to manage the exceptional cases, we implemented a non-local return facility that unwinds nested function calls and returns control outside of the FRS code. We imposed an additional burden on the service implementers– resource management class constructors must register their corresponding destructors with the unwind mechanism, so that they can be invoked during the unwinding process. In this way, the class destructor is guaranteed to be invoked whether or not there is an exception.

Most of the problems mentioned above were anticipated during the design of the prototype, at least to some degree. We were surprised by the dramatic time and space overheads that the preprocessor/compiler combination imposed. We also found that an implementation of an exception mechanism without compiler support will incur a significant amount of run time overhead even if no exceptions are raised. Even with these problems, we feel we made a good choice given our goals and constraints.

5 Performance Evaluation

We supported just one FRS language and representation alternative (compiled C++), but we implemented and measured all three FRS transport mechanisms: piggybacking, callback, and shared disk, all with the option of code caching. We ran several experiments to evaluate their cost. In order to help decouple the choice of language from the choice of transport mechanism, the execution time of the FRS code was not measured in these experiments. However, the time to perform linking and relocation on the code was measured. Two code sizes are considered: small (1000 bytes) and large (10,000 bytes). The code itself was taken from real transactions, but short-circuited so as not to be executed.

The benchmark consists of an FRS client running alone on one network node, repeatedly shipping a function request to one server running alone on a different network node. The cost of transaction management is not measured.

The nodes are IBM 4381 computers, each of which is a two-way multiprocessor running the MVS/XA operating system. In these experiments, only one processor per node is used. The network is implemented by channel-to-channel connections through a 3088 control unit. The basic communication software is a high-performance datagram package that uses low overhead I/O channel programming techniques. We added a custom virtual circuit and pacing layer on top of the datagram package. The network packet size is $2K$ bytes. The unit of disk transfer can be as large as $32K$ bytes.

In all experiments, three quantities were measured per function request: elapsed time, client CPU time, and server CPU time. The measurement technique was informal. In each experiment a few hundred function requests were issued as part of the same transaction on a warm system. Averages for the three quantities were computed. Each such triplet of averages was computed separately ten times. After discarding at most one or two aberrant averages, we observed the remaining averages to be in close agreement.

	small code size (1000 bytes) times, ms					
	hit			miss		
Method	elapsed	client	server	elapsed	client	server
piggyback	6.3	2.7	2.6	6.3	2.7	2.6
callback	6.0	2.7	2.5	12.2	5.3	5.0
shared disk	6.2	2.7	2.6	33.5	2.7	7.9

	large code size (10,000 bytes) times, ms					
	hit			miss		
Method	elapsed	client	server	elapsed	client	server
piggyback	21.7	9.4	11.0	22.1	9.4	11.9
callback	6.0	2.7	2.5	28.0	11.9	14.4
shared disk	6.2	2.7	2.6	50.0	2.7	9.2

As can be seen from the above tables, the choice of method depends on the FRS code, the cache hit ratio, and a trade-off of throughput versus response time. Caching is relevant for small code sizes only if callback or shared disk is used. For large code sizes, the benefit of a cache with the piggyback method is minimal, but is pronounced for other methods. Unless the hit ratio is small, callback or shared disk look like a win for large code. For small code, or a very low hit ratio, piggybacking wins because it performs well without a cache, thus avoiding memory use and management complexity. With a low hit ratio and large code, shared disk uses fewest CPU cycles, but has the longest response time because of I/O latency. These observations are summarized in the following table, which lists the desirable FRS transport methods as a function of hit ratio, code size, and throughput versus response time. The methods are abbreviated by their first initial, and mentioned in order of preference.

FRS method performance, summary				
	throughput		response time	
hit	code size		code size	
ratio	small	large	small	large
high	p,c,s	s,c	p,c,s	c,s
low	p	s,p,c	p	p,c

6 Transaction Management

Performance of FRS is interesting only if it contributes appreciably to the overall response time and throughput of a database machine. Thus, it is uninteresting for data intensive queries. If the cost of transaction management dwarfs the cost of FRS, studying FRS in detail is uninteresting for transaction processing as well. This turns out not to be the case. In ARBRE, we reuse the SQL/DS [IBM] transaction manager for each site, and augment it with a distributed transaction manager. In addition to the FRS time, we measured 6 ms elapsed time, and 2.6 ms CPU time, per remote subordinate, for a read-only transaction with the presumed abort protocol [MLO86]. The elapsed time includes a round trip message for the prepare phase. Both times include the time for the database begin work and prepare. An update transaction is more costly, because SQL/DS forces a log record for the subordinates.

Recently, other systems have pushed transaction management into the operating system [HMSC88,STP*87] or language run time system [LCJS87] for better performance. High performance transaction processing in a shared nothing environment would benefit from further improvements in FRS, or from closer integration of transaction management and FRS.

7 Related Work

We have structured our work on FRS mechanisms for database machines according to five orthogonal categories. We explored trade-offs in choosing an FRS language and its representation, identified three methods of FRS code transport, and measured their performance with and without caching on a working prototype. In our FRS mechanism a distributed transaction may have several FRS clients, and that piggybacking the code in this case may result in a server receiving duplicate code. We now review related work in the context of our categorization.

Remote evaluation (REV) [Sta86] improves upon RPC by allowing the composition of remote calls, along with other program logic, without requiring a message pair for each remote procedure called. The REV design provides transactions but not parallel remote evaluation. Code is always piggybacked on the request message. Caching was mentioned but was not implemented. The relative merits of interpretation versus compilation are discussed, but not the merits of general purpose languages versus special purpose ones.

The network command language (NCL) [Fal87] uses interpreted Lisp as an FRS language to achieve a heterogeneous networked file system. Code is always piggybacked on the request message–there is no caching. Support for parallelism and transactions are provided at individual nodes, but not across the network. Bulk data is transferred as part of the function request and reply. In ARBRE, we use separate virtual circuits to transfer bulk data, so that two subordinates may exchange bulk data without either subordinate issuing a function request to the other.

The FAD dataflow language at MCC is the interface language to the Bubba database machine [BBKV87]. The FAD optimizer produces a number of code fragments, one executed by the coordinator, the others executed by subordinates. These fragments are called PFAD, an acronym for parallel FAD, [HDV88] and are interpreted. Two alternatives for FRS code (*i.e.* PFAD) transport are discussed in [AC88b]: preloading and dynamic loading. With preloading, code is explicitly cached at the sever site, so a function request never needs a callback. Preloading could be implemented by piggyback FRS from a coordinator to all potential subordinates. Dynamic loading, on the other hand, corresponds to callback FRS from subordinate to subordinate. Here, the callback is to the coordinator and the function request is implicitly contained in the first data message. A related concept, thread activation, is also discussed. In preactivation, a server process is allocated to the function request immediately. With dynamic activation, a server process is not allocated until the first data message arrives. In ARBRE, we always use preactivation.

Another MCC paper [KV87] also talks about preloading (they call it *ER*, for execute at repository) and dynamic loading. With this variation of dynamic loading, piggyback FRS is used from subordinate to subordinate, instead of callback. As we showed before, this may result in the receipt of multiple copies of the same code at the same server.

Yet another MCC paper [AC88a] investigates several dataflow control mechanisms using analytic and simulation models. Dataflow control is the problem of determining when each dataflow operator has received all messages it will ever receive from other dataflow operators, so that it may terminate. Our FRS mechanism does not address the problem of dataflow control. For data-intensive transactions in ARBRE we use FRS to implement dataflow operators and a separate mechanism (point-to-point) for dataflow communication and control. The performance of FRS is important only for control-intensive transactions.

In the Gamma database machine [DGG*86], a (software) query compiler produces code fragments that represent a parallel query execution plan. Piggyback FRS is used. The bulk of the FRS code is interpreted but search predicates are compiled.

8 Conclusions

FRS is important for high performance transaction processing and parallel query processing in a shared nothing database machine. We have discussed trade-offs for custom languages versus general purpose languages and compilation versus interpretation. We implemented the combination taking the least effort in our environment: compiling C++. This combination has proved flexible for experimentation with new algorithms because changing an algorithm means recompiling the FRS code, not rebuilding the runtime system. On the other hand, slow compilation and lack of support for debugging were drawbacks.

As a target language for an automatic query optimizer, perhaps the flexibility of a general purpose language is not needed. Certainly the time and space overhead of compilation should be reduced. On the other hand, optimizers and query languages are being extended to support object-oriented databases [LMP87,SR86]. A general purpose target language may better accommodate the extensions.

Three FRS transport methods–piggyback, callback and shared disk–were investigated empirically. No clear winner emerged–the choice depends primarily on code size and cache hit ratios, and secondarily on simplicity and a throughput versus response time trade-off. Conventional operating system support for dynamic loading suffices for many applications and facilitates debugging, but requires a shared disk.

9 Acknowledgements

The author gratefully acknowledges the comments and criticism received on early drafts of this paper from the other members of ARBRE: Raymond Lorie, Jean-Jacques Daudenarde, Jim Stamos, and Honesty Young.

References

[AC88a] William Alexander and George Copeland. Comparison of dataflow control techniques in distributed data-intensive systems. In *Proceedings of the 1988 ACM SIGMETRICS Conference on Measurement and Modeling of Computer Systems*, pages 157–166, May 1988.

[AC88b] William Alexander and George Copeland. Process and dataflow control in distributed data-intensive systems. In *Proceedings, ACM-SIGMOD International Conference on Management of Data*, pages 90–98, ACM, June 1988.

[BBKV87] F. Bancilhon, T. Briggs, S. Khoshafian, and P. Valduriez. Fad, a powerful and simple database language. In *Proceedings of the 13th International Conference on Very Large Data Bases*, pages 97–105, Brighton, England, September 1-4 1987.

[BN84] A. D. Birrell and B. J. Nelson. Implementing remote procedure calls. *ACM Transactions on Computer Systems*, 2(1):39–59, February 1984.

[DGG*86] David J. DeWitt, Robert H. Gerber, Goetz Graefe, Michael L. Heytens, Krishna B. Kumar, and M. Muralikrishna. Gamma–a high performance dataflow database machine. In *Proceedings of the 12th International Conference on Very Large Data Bases*, pages 228–237, August 1986.

[Fal87] Joseph R. Falcone. A programmable interface language for heterogeneous distributed systems. *ACM Transactions on Computer Systems*, 5(4):330–351, November 1987.

[HDV88] Brian Hart, Scott Danforth, and Patrick Valduriez. *Parallelizing a Database Programming Language*. Technical Report ACA-ST-257-88, Microelectronics and Computer Technology Corporation, Austin, TX 78759, August 1988.

[HMSC88] Roger Haskin, Yoni Malachi, Wayne Sawdon, and Gregory Chan. Recovery management in quicksilver. *ACM Transactions on Computer Systems*, 6(1):82–108, February 1988.

[IBM] IBM Corporation. *SQL/Data System General Information*. IBM Form No. GH24-5012.

[KV87] Setrag Khoshafian and Patrick Valduriez. Parallel execution strategies for declustered databases. In Matsura Kitsuregawa, editor, *5th International Workshop on Database Machines*, pages 626–639, Kluwer Academic Publishers, Japan, October 1987.

[LCJS87] Barbara Liskov, Dorothy Curtis, Paul Johnson, and Robert Scheifler. Implementation of Argus. In *Proceedings of the Eleventh ACM Symposium on Operating Systems Principles*, pages 111–122, November 1987.

[LDH*89] Raymond Lorie, Jean-Jacques Daudenarde, Gary Hallmark, James Stamos, and Honesty Young. Adding intra-transaction parallelism to an existing dbms: early experience. *IEEE Data Engineering Bulletin*, 12(1):2–8, March 1989.

[LMP87] Bruce Lindsay, John McPherson, and Hamid Pirahesh. A data management extension architecture. In *Proceedings, ACM-SIGMOD International Conference on Management of Data*, pages 220–226, May 27–29 1987.

[LS83] B. Liskov and R. Scheifler. Guardians and actions: linguistic support for robust, distributed programs. *ACM Transactions on Programming Languages and Systems*, 5(3):381–404, July 1983.

[MLO86] C. Mohan, B. Lindsay, and R. Obermarck. Transaction management in the R* distributed database management sysytem. *ACM Transactions on Database Systems*, 11(4):378–396, December 1986.

[SR86] M. Stonebraker and L. Rowe. The design of postgres. In *Proceedings, ACM-SIGMOD International Conference on Management of Data*, May 1986. Washington, D.C.

[SS86] M. Satyanarayanan and Ellen H. Siegal. *MultiRPC: A Parallel Remote Procedure Call Mechanism*. Technical Report CMU-CS-86-139, Carnegie Mellon University, Department of Computer Science, Pittsburgh, PA, August 1986.

[Sta86] James W. Stamos. *Remote Evaluation*. PhD thesis, Massachusetts Institute of Technology, MIT Laboratory for Computer Science, Cambridge, MA, January 1986. Also available as MIT technical report number MIT-LCS-TR-354.

[Sto86] Michael Stonebraker. The case for shared nothing. *IEEE Database Engineering Bulletin*, 9(1):4–9, March 1986.

[STP*87] A. Z. Spector, D. Thompson, R. F. Pausch, J. L. Eppinger, D. Duchamp, R. Draves, D. S. Daniels, and J. J. Bloch. *Camelot: A Distributed Transaction Facility for Mach and the Internet – An Interim Report.* Technical Report CMU-CS-87-129, Carnegie Mellon University, June 17 1987.

SPECIAL FUNCTION UNIT FOR
STATISTICAL AGGREGATION
FUNCTIONS[1]

MAHDI ABDELGUERFI
Department of Electrical Engineering
University of Detroit
4001 W. McNichols Detroit, MI 48221

ABSTRACT — This paper presents the design of a special purpose MOS processing unit for statistical aggregation functions such as SUM, COUNT, and AVERAGE. Tuples are input to and output from the proposed unit in parallel, one bit at a time. The processing of tuples is completely overlapped with their I/O time. The function unit is composed of a number of identical bit-serial structures operating in parallel. The architecture and VLSI implementation of the proposed unit is considered. The performance of the proposed design is compared with the implementation of statistical aggregation functions on the parallel pipelined relational query processor described in [1]. The comparative analysis shows that our approach performs significantly better than that of [1].

INDEX TERMS — Database Machines, Statistical Aggregation Functions, Parallel Processing, Bit-Serial Architecture, Odd-even Network, VLSI.

I. INTRODUCTION

Advances in VLSI technology have opened up new horizons for the design of high speed, reliable, and cost efficient algorithmically specialized processors. Since it is now possible to lay hundreds of thousands of transistors on a single chip, algorithms for a number of complex problems [9,10] can be efficiently implemented on one or few VLSI chips. For these designs to be efficient, they must satisfy conditions such as regular layout, simple control, and limited number of interconnections. One complex problem which plays an important role in database machines is the implementation of statistical aggregation function such as SUM, COUNT, and AVERAGE[2].

In [1] the design of a parallel and pipelined query processor is presented. In this processsor tuples are processed in parallel one bit at a time. Statistical aggregation functions are implemented in three steps (Figure 1). The relation is first sorted and then fed to an aggregation unit. The resulting relation is then sent to a duplicate marker.

---

[1]This work was supported in part by a faculty development award from FEDERAL MOGHUL corporation.

[2]The remaining two statistical aggregation functions MIN and MAX are computationally inexpensive and will not be considered in this paper.

In this paper, a SIMD architecture is utilized to perform the statistical aggregation functions. In contrast with the approach of [1], in our approach, the sorting, aggregation and duplicate marking are all performed concurrently. Also, in [1] three different network topologies are used to perform statistical aggregation functions. In our approach one network topology and one type one processing element (PE) are used to implement these functions.

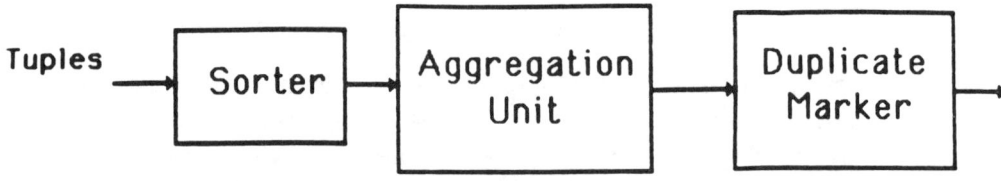

Figure.1 Implementation of Aggregation Functions on the Query Processor of [1].

The architecture of the proposed design is composed of several identical processing elements connected according to the odd-even network topology [2]. The processing elements operate on tuples bit by bit. As a result, this system is referred to as parallel bit-level pipelined architecture [3,4]. The main advantage of this approach is that the memory requirement of each PE is very small and is independent of the input size. The input operands are processed one bit at a time, hence, the amount of hardware in each PE is reduced. As a result, a large number of PE's can be integrated on a single VLSI chip. The proposed design has several features that are suitable for VLSI implementation:

1) Simple PE's — The system is composed of one type of simple processing element. Each PE operates on data bit by bit. Thus, the design and verification of the circuit will be easy.

2) Overlap of Data I/O and processing — The data processing time is completely overlapped with the inputting and outputting of data to and from the PE.

3) Static Interconnection Network — For ease of implementation a static interconnection between the different PE's is preferred as compared to a dynamic network. This will allow the system to process several data streams in a pipelined manner.

4) High throughput — This is achieved by the use of several bit-serial PE's operating in parallel.

5) Low pin count — This property results from the inputting and outputting of operands one bit at a time to and from the PE's.

6) The design is independent of the tuple size.

7) Limited interconnection requirement — This is acheived by using bit serial computation.

The odd-even network topology has been used to design several special purpose processing units. In [2], Batcher uses this topology to design sorting network. In [5], this structure is used for speech coding. In [6], the same topology is used to implement relational database operations. In this paper, we show that a processing unit based on the odd-even network topology can efficiently perform statistical aggregation functions.

II. SYSTEM ORGANIZATION

The efficient processing of statistical aggregation functions is an important factor that makes a database realistic as these operations are known to be CPU bounded. This section describes how these operations are realized on an odd-even network unit.

The processing of statistical aggregation functions involves in general two columns of the relation: GROUP BY column (C_g) and AGGREGATION column (C_a). In our approach a mark bit (M_b) is associated with each tuple. At each step, a number of tuples are simultaneously compared in the processing unit and their respective mark bits are manipulated according to the result of the comparisons. The mark bits are utilized to identify the qualified tuples. Figure 2 illustrates the process of performing SUM, COUNT, and AVERAGE on eight (8) reduced tuples (only the columns of interest are shown). It is noted that all reduced tuples are input to the processing unit with mark bits set to 1. During the process of performing SUM and AVERAGE a new column, called the sum column (C_s) is generated. Each value in C_s gives the sum of all C_a values corresponding to a distinct C_g value. Also, in the process of performing COUNT and AVERAGE a new column referred to as count column "C_c" is generated. Each C_c value gives the number of occurence of a distinct value in the GROUP BY column. Qualified tuples are output with a mark bit set to 1. Thus, disqualified tuples can be filtered out by examining their respective mark bits.

It can be seen that the AVERAGE function is a combination of both SUM and COUNT operations. In the following we will concentrate on the design of a SUM processing unit. It will be shown that the same unit can perform efficiently the two remaining operations.

II THE SUM ALGORITHM AND ITS VLSI IMPLEMENTATION

II.1 The Algorithm and its VLSI Implementation

An n-input processing unit for the SUM operation is composed of $[\frac{n(\log^2 n - \log n + 4)}{4} - 1]$ identical PE's[3] connected according to the odd-even even network topology. "n" reduced tuples are processed by the unit in

---

[3]Throughout this paper log refers to $\log_2$.

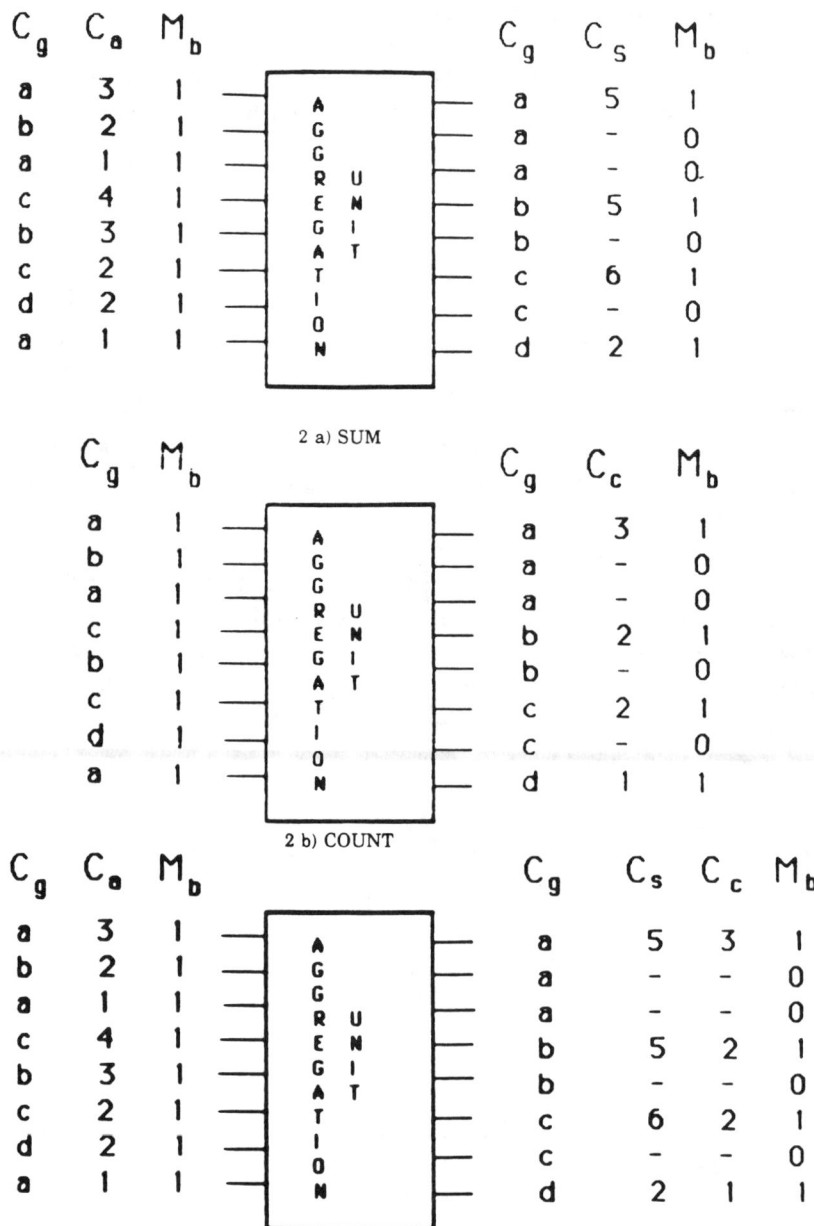

Figure.2 Implementation of SUM, COUNT, and AVERAGE.

$$\frac{\log n(\log n + 1)}{2}$$ steps. The algorithm to be implemented by each PE (Figure 3) is shown in appendix 1. Figure 4 shows an example in which an 4-input SUM unit is used to process a sequence of 4 reduced tuples.

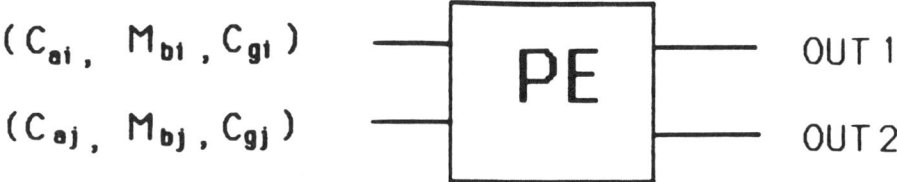

Figure.3 A PE.

In Figure 5 a block diagram of a PE is shown. The PE contains five flags (Fi,Fj,F1,F2,F3), a Control Circuit (CC), a serial adder, and a Bit Manipulation Circuit (BMC). It is recalled that the reduced tuples are input, processed, and output one bit at a time. First, the two GROUP BY values $G_{gm} = \{ C_{gm}^1 C_{gm}^2 ... C_{gm}^k \}$, m =i,j, are input to the PE bit by bit starting from the MSB's (C_{gi}^k, C_{gj}^k). "k" represents the number of bits in the binary representation of the group by values. Next, the mark bits M_{bi} and M_{bj} are input followed by the aggregate values $C_{am} = \{ C_{am}^p C_{am}^{p-1} ... C_{am}^1 \}$, m = i,j. It is noted that unlike the GROUP BY values, the aggregate

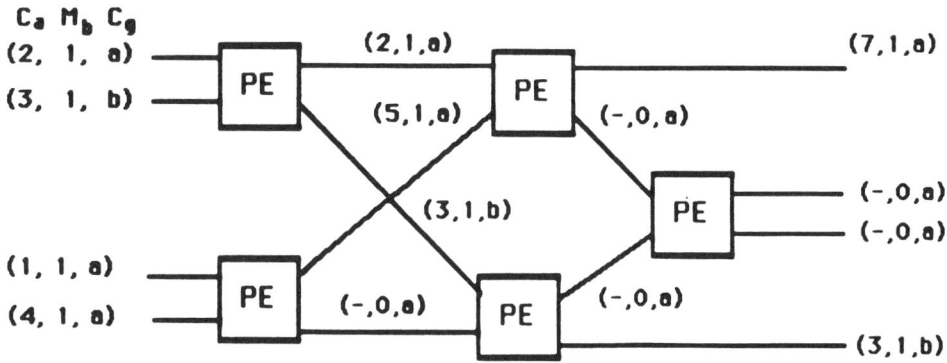

Figure.4 An Example

values are input starting from the LSB's (C_{ai}^1, C_{aj}^1). "p" is the number of bits in the binary representation of aggregate values. Note that the GROUP BY values comparison, the manipulation of mark bits, and the summation of aggregate values are completely overlapped with the inputting and outputting of the reduced tuples to and from the PE's.

Two control signal s_1 and s_2 are used for control and synchronization. The control signal s_1, is a start signal, it is applied to all PE's of stage M, $1 \leq M \leq \frac{\log n (\log n + 1)}{2}$, at time instant t_{M-1}. At time instant t_M, PE's of column M reset their five flags and begin the processing of the two reduced tuples present at their inputs. The control signal s_2 is used to indicate the completion of GROUP BY values comparison. This signal is applied to PE's of column M at time instant t_{k+M}. At the same time instant, the mark bits are input to the PE of stage M. From time instant t_{k+M+1} to $t_{k+M+p+1}$, the aggregate values are input to the PE's of column M.

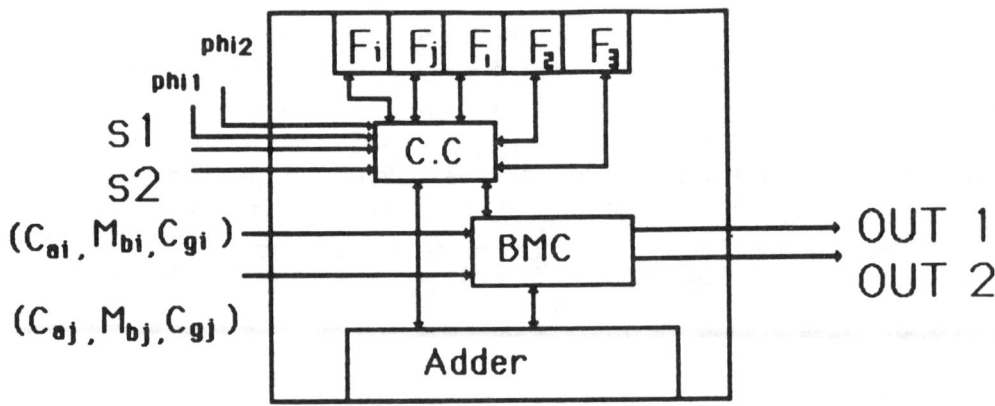

Figure.5 Block Diagram of a PE.

The serial adder is used to compute the count sum ($S = C_{ai} + C_{aj}$). The BMC computes the value of out_1 and out_2 as a function of the result of the GROUP BY values comparison, the mark bits value, and the sum S. The flags F_i and F_j are used to store the mark bits M_i and M_j. The flag F_3 is set by the control signal s_2. This flag when set indicates that GROUP BY values comparison has been completed. Finally, flags F_1 and F_2 are used to store the outcome of the comparison.

Next, the VLSI implementation of a processing element using MOS technology [7] is considered. A two-phase non-overlapping synchronous clock scheme is employed as shown in Figure 6. The mark bit M_{bi} (M_{bj}) is input to F_i (F_j) when both Phi_1 and s_2 are high. Flag F_3 is set by s_2 during Phi_1. The flag F_1 (F_2) is set during GROUP BY values comparison ($F_3 = 0$) when $C_{gi} \neq C_{gj}$ ($C_{gi} < C_{gj}$). The two outputs $out_m = \{ O_m^1, O_m^2 ... O_m^{k+p+1} \}$, $m = 1,2$, are determined by the BMU. The L-th output bits O_m^L, $m = 1,2$, $1 \leq L \leq k+p+1$, are computed as follows[4]:

$$O_1^L = \begin{cases} (G_i^{k-L+1} \overline{F_2} + G_j^{k-L+1} F_2) F_1 + \overline{F_1}(G_i^{k-L+1} + G_j^{k-L+1}) & \text{(GROUP BY values comparison phase } F_3=0) \\ & 1 \leq L \leq k, \\ (Mi + Mj)\overline{F_1} + (Mi \overline{F_2} + Mj F_2) F_1, & L=k+1, \text{(mark bit manipulation } F_3 = 1) \\ (C_i^{L-k-1} \overline{F_2} + C_j^{L-k-1} F_2) F_1 + (Ci Fi \overline{Fj} + S Fi Fj + C_j^{L-k-1} \overline{Fi})\overline{F_1}, \\ L > k+1, \text{(SUMming phase)} \end{cases}$$

$$O_2^L = \begin{cases} (G_i^{k-L-1} F_2 + G_j^{k-L+1} \overline{F_2}) F_1 + \overline{F_1}(G_i^{k-L+1} G_j^{k-L+1}) & , 1 \leq L \leq k \\ (Mi F_2 + Mj \overline{F_2}) F_1, & L = k+1 \\ (C_j^{L-k-1} \overline{F_2} + C_i^{L-k-1} F_2) F_1 + C_i^{L-k-1} \overline{F_1}, & L>k+1 \end{cases}$$

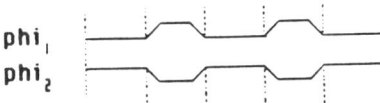

Figure.6 Timing waveforms

The nMOS layout of a PE is shown in Figure 7.

II.2. Implementing COUNT and AVERAGE Using the SUM Unit

The COUNT and AVERAGE functions can be implemented using the SUM unit. For the COUNT operation each reduced tuple will be input to the SUM unit with a Ca value set equal to 1. An example is shown in Figure 8. The AVERAGE operation is a combination of both SUM and COUNT. The AVERAGE operation is performed in the following manner. To each reduced tuple (Cg, Mb, Ca), we attach a new attribute value Cc. This attribute value is set initially to 1. The augmented tuple (Cg, Mb, Ca, Cc) is input one bit at a time to the SUM unit. The Cc value is input immediately following the inputting of the Ca values. The first (k+1) bits output from the SUM unit represent a GROUP BY value followed by a mark bit. The next "p" bits output from the unit represent a Cs value. Finally, the remaining output bits represent a Cc value.

---

[4]Without loss of generality, we assume that the Cs values can also be represented using p bits.

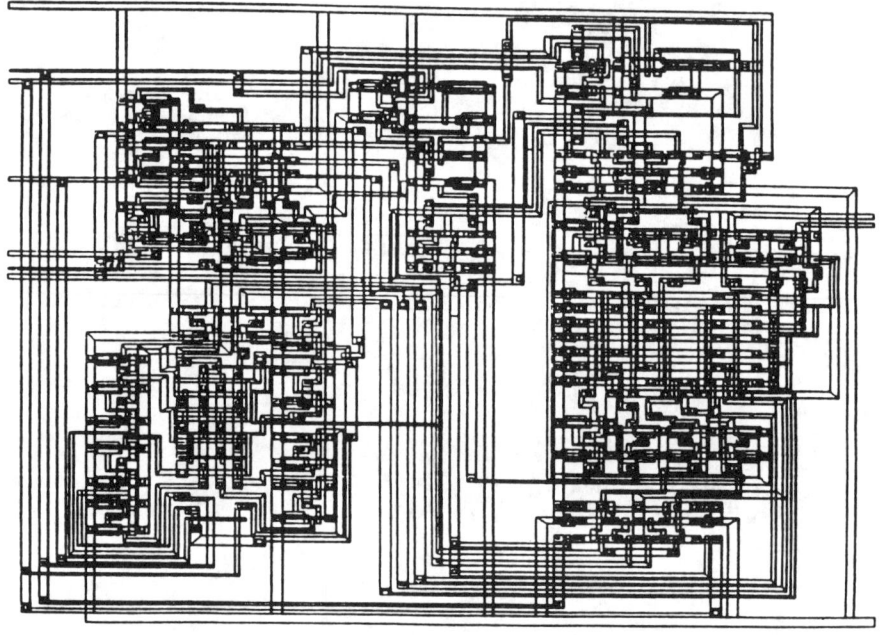

Figure.7 Layout of a PE.

III. COMPARATIVE ANALYSIS

In this section, the performance of our design is compared with that of the Parallel pipelined relational query processor described in [1]. In the comparative analysis the relevant parameters are:

k = number of bits in the binary representation of the GROUP BY values representation

p = number of bits in the binary representation of the aggregate values

r = time (in seconds) to manipulate and pass one bit to the neighboring PE n = number of inputs in the SUM unit

In our implementation, the processing of the reduced tuples is completely overlapped with the inputting and outputting of the reduced tuples to and from the SUM unit. Since the longest path in an n-input SUM unit is $\frac{\log n(\log n + 1)}{2}$ processing "n" tuples will take

$$T(n) = [\frac{\log n(\log n + 1)}{2} + (k+p+1)]r$$

Note that our approach allows for the pipelined processing for different streams of tuples (different relations)[5]. Suppose that "m" relations each composed of "n" tuples are to be processed by the SUM unit. The processing of these m relations in a pipelined manner will reduce the processing time from "mT(n)" to "T(n)+(m − 1)(k+p+1)r". The processing time is therefore reduced by $(\frac{m-1}{2})\log n(\log n + 1)r$ seconds.

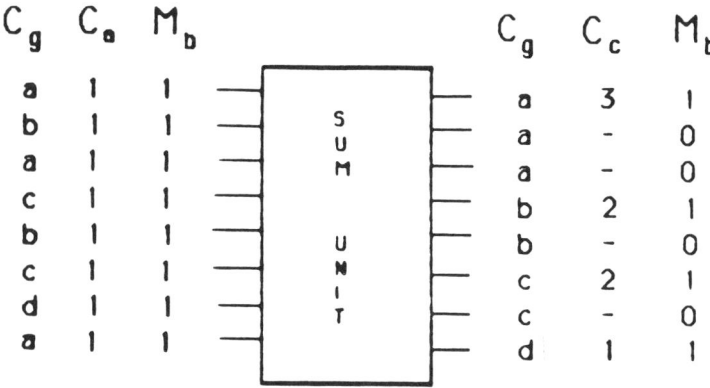

Figure.8 Using the SUM Unit to Implement COUNT.

The SUM algorithm we have described was internal. That is, the number of reduced tuples to be processed was assumed to be no larger than the number of inputs (n) of the SUM unit. In general, an entire relation cannot be processed internally by an odd-even based SUM unit (because of area and pin count limitations). Figure 9 shows how to obtain a 2n-input SUM unit from a number of n-input SUM units. This method is very useful to increase

---

[5]Note that the flags of each PE in the first column should be initialized immediately after the completion of the inputting of each relation. This is done by reapplying the reset signal s1.

the internal processing capability of a SUM unit. However, since VLSI chips are of fixed size and the number of tuples is very large, the application of the above method is impaired by financial as well as technological constraints. When the number of tuples is too large to be processed internally by a SUM unit, an external VLSI algorithm is the most practical solution. It is recalled that an external VLSI algorithm is one that allows a chip (or a set of chips) of fixed size to process an input set of any size [8]. One approach to this problem is based on an iterative use of a SUM unit of fixed size. The proposed algorithm is based on successively merging SUMmed sets of reduced tuples of increasingly larger size.

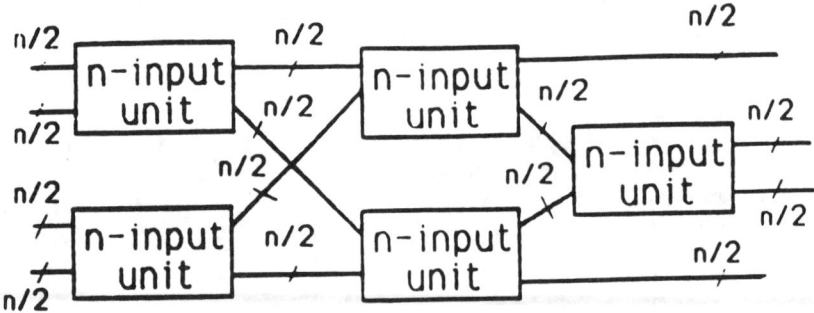

Figure.9 Designing a 2n-Input SUM Unit.

The external VLSI algorithm will use a SUM unit of fixed size (n-inputs) to process in an iterative manner a set of reduced tuple whose number[6] N is larger than n. Towards this end, a new control signal "MERGE" is added to the SUM unit. The new control signal allows an n-input SUM unit to have two operating modes. In the first mode (MERGE=0) the unit performs the internal algorithm described in section II. In the second operating mode (MERGE=1), the unit will merge two SUMmed sets of size $\frac{n}{2}$ each in $\log n$ steps. Figure 10 shows a 4-input SUM unit with a MERGE control signal.

The external algorithm is divided into two steps. During the first step the MERGE signal is reset to zero and the SUM unit is used to generate N/n SUMmed sets of size n each. When the N/n sets are processed in a pipelined manner the duration of this step is

---

[6]Without loss of generality N is assumed to be a multiple of n.

$$[\frac{\log n(\log n + 1)}{2} + \frac{N}{n}(k+p+1)]r$$

In the second step, the SUM unit is used as an $(\frac{n}{2} - X - \frac{n}{2})$ 2-way merger by setting the MERGE signal to 1. The second step requires $\log\frac{N}{n}$ phases. During the i-th phase, $1 \le i \le \log\frac{N}{n}$, $(1/2)^{i-1}\frac{N}{n}$ sets of $2^{i-1}n$ SUMmed reduced tuples are converted to $(1/2)^{i}\frac{N}{n}$ sets of $2^{i}n$ reduced tuples

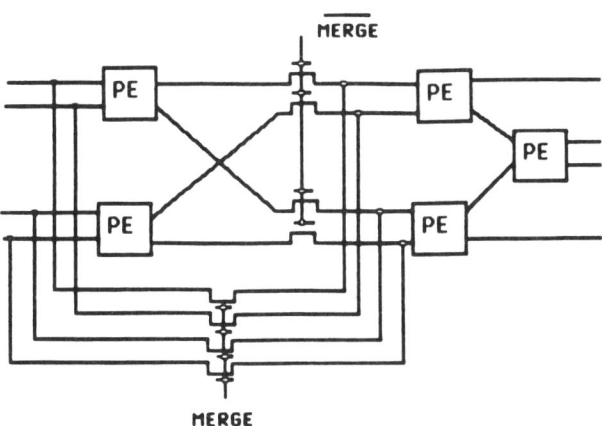

Figure.10 A 4-Input SUM Unit With a Merge Signal.

tuples each. Pipelining the $\log(N/n)$ phases will yield the following time duration

$$[\frac{\log n(\log n + 1)}{2} + \frac{N}{n}(\sum_{i=1}^{\log N/n}((2^{i+1}-1)/2^{i})(k+p+1))]r$$

$$= [\log n + (2\frac{N}{n}\text{-log}\frac{N}{n} - \frac{N}{n} + 1)(k+p+1)]r$$

The overall duration of the external algorithm is

$$T(n,N) = \left[\frac{\log n(\log n + 1)}{2} + \log n + (2\frac{N}{n}\log\frac{N}{n} + 1)(k+p+1)\right]r$$

In [1] a VLSI query processor is described. In this processor tuples are input in a bit serial, tuple parallel fashion. Unlike our approach statistical aggregation function are performed on presorted relations. An (nxn) sorter is used to sort internally n tuples and can also be used as a (nXn) 2-way merger. "n(3n-1)" bit-serial PE's are needed to design an (nXn) sorter. The longest path in the sorter consists of (2n-1) stages. The time needed to sort n tuples is

$$(k + p + 2n - 1)r$$

The duration of merging two sorted list of n tuples each is the same as that of sorting n tuples. The time needed to sort $N \geq n$ tuples can be computed using an approach similar to the one used to compute T(n,N). First the $\frac{N}{n}$ sets of n tuples each are sorted. Next, the unit is used as an (nXn) 2-way merger. The overall duration of the sorting is (see [1])

$$\frac{N}{n}(k+p+2n-1)(1+\log\frac{N}{n})r$$

The sorted relation is then input to the aggregation unit. An n-input aggregation unit is composed of logn stages and requires nlogn PE's. Processing N tuples will require about

$$\frac{N}{n}[k + p + \log n]r$$

The third step is the process of assigning a mark bit to each reduced tuple so that duplicates can be removed. This is done using an n-input duplicate checker. An n-input duplicate checker is composed of (2n-1) PE's organized in two (2) stages (see [1]). Processing N tuples will require about

$$\frac{N}{n}[k + p + 3]r$$

The overall duration of performing SUM is thus

$$D(n,N) = [(k+p+2n-1)(1+\log\frac{N}{n}) + (k+p+\log n) + (k+p+3)]\frac{N}{n}r$$

A comparative analysis is shown in Table 1. It can be seen that the odd-even based approach is significantly faster than the approach of [1]. For example, when $N/n = 2^{10}$ and $n = 64$, our approach is 5.5 times faster. It can be seen that the performance gap increases as n is increased. For instance for $N/n = 2^{10}$ the speed up is 1.69 for $n = 32$ and 2.85 when n is increased to 64. Note also that the performance gap decreases as the ratio N/n is increased.

Table 1

Comparative Analysis $\dfrac{T(n,N)}{D(n,N)}$ for $p=k=16$ bits.

n	$\dfrac{N}{n}=2^4$	$\dfrac{N}{n}=2^8$	$\dfrac{N}{n}=2^{10}$	$\dfrac{N}{n}=2^{12}$	$\dfrac{N}{n}=2^{14}$
16	1.50	1.20	1.16	1.12	1.10
32	2.05	1.75	1.69	1.65	1.62
64	3.50	2.96	2.85	2.78	2.72

IV. SUMMARY

This paper describes a special purpose parallel bit-level pipelined processing unit for statistical aggregate functions. The architecture is based on the odd-even network topology. The proposed unit is composed of a number of identical bit-serial processing elements operating in parallel. The VLSI implementation of the special purpose unit is considered. A comparative performance analysis with the Parallel Pipelined Query Processor described in [1], shows that our approach presents significant performance improvements.

ACKNOWLEGMENTS

The author gratefully acknowledges support for writing this paper from Federal Moghul Corporation under a faculty development award. The author would also like to express his sincere appreciation to S. Khalaf and A.K. Sood for their many helpful suggestions, and to the referees for helpful comments on the presentation of the paper.

APPENDIX 1

Procedure SUM [$(C_{ai}, M_{bi}, C_{gi}), (C_{aj}, M_{bj}, C_{gj})$]

// Two reduced tuples (C_{ai}, M_{bi}, C_{gi}) and (C_{aj}, M_{bj}, C_{gj}) are input to a SUM processing element //

1. Begin
2.   If $C_{gi} > C_{gj}$ then
3.   Begin $out_1 \leftarrow (C_{ai}, M_{bi}, C_{gi})$, $out_2 \leftarrow (C_{gj}, M_{bj}, C_{gj})$, end;
4.   If $C_{gi} < C_{gj}$ then
5.   begin $out_1 \leftarrow (C_{aj}, M_{bj}, C_{gj})$, $out_2 \leftarrow (C_{ai}, M_{bi}, C_{gi})$, end;
6.   If $C_{gi} = C_{gj}$ then
7.   begin
8.   If $M_{bi} \wedge M_{bj} = 1$ then[7]
9.   begin $out_1 \leftarrow (C_{ai}+C_{aj}, M_{bi}, C_{gi})$ $out_2 \leftarrow (-, 0, C_{gj})$, end;
10.   If $M_{bi} \wedge \overline{M_{bj}} = 1$ then
11.   begin $out_1 \leftarrow (C_{ai}, M_{bi}, C_{gi})$, $out_2 \leftarrow (-, M_{bj}, C_{gj})$, end;
12.   else
13.   begin $out_1 \leftarrow (C_{aj}, M_{bj}, C_{gj})$, $out_2 \leftarrow (C_{ai}, M_{bi}, C_{gi})$, end;
14.   End
15. End // Outputs SUMmed //

V. REFERENCES

[1] Won Kim, et al, "A Parallel Pipelined Relational Query Processor", *ACM Trans. on Database Systems*, Vol.9, No.2, June 1984, pp.214–242.

[2] Batcher, K.E., "Sorting Network and Their Applications," AFIPS Proc. Spring Joint Comput. Conf., Vol. 32, April, 1968, pp. 307–314.

---

[7] Throughout this paper $\wedge$ refers to the logical AND.

[3] Batcher, K.E., "Bit-Serial Parallel Processing Systems," *IEEE Trans. Comput.*, C-31, 1982, pp. 377–384.

[4] Hatamian, M., Cash, G.L., "Parallel Bit-Level Pipelined VLSI Designs for High-Speed Signal Processing," *Proc. of the IEEE*, Vol. 75, No. 9, September, 1987, pp. 1192–1202.

[5] Mohan, S., Sood, A.K., "A Multiprocessor Architecture for the (M,L)-Algorithm Suitable for VLSI Implementation," *IEEE Trans. on Comm.*, Vol. COM-39, No. 12, December, 1986, pp. 1218–1226.

[6] Sood, A.K., Abdelguerfi, M., Shu, W., "Hardware Implementation of Relational Algebra Operations," in **Database Machines: Modern Trends and Applications**, Nato ASI, Series F, Springer Verlag, 1986, pp. 341–380.

[7] Mead, C., Conway, L., *Introduction to VLSI Systems*, Reading, Massachsetts: Addison-Wesley, 1980.

[8] Bonucelli, M.A., et al., "External Sorting in VLSI", *IEEE Trans. on Comp.*, Vol. C-33, N0. 10, oct. 84, pp. 931–934.

[9] Abdelguerfi, M., et al., "Parallel Bit-Level Pipelined VLSI Design for the Histogramming Operation," *IEEE Computer Conference on Vision and Pattern Recognition*, Univ. of Michigan, June 1988, pp.945–950.

[10] Abdelguerfi, M., Sood, A.K.,"A Bus Connected Cellular Array Unit For Relational Database Machines," in **Database Machines and Knowledge Base Machines**, edited by Kitsuregawa, M. and Tanaka, H., Kluwer Academic Publishers, 1988, pp.188–201.

Generic Associative Memory for Information Retrieval

C.H. Ben CHOI
Dept. of Electrical Engineering

Dik L. LEE
Dept. of Computer & Information Science

The Ohio State University
Columbus, Ohio 43210

ABSTRACT

The design of a general purpose associative memory is described. Its applications on Prolog clause indexing and on Relational database search/retrieval operations are explored. This associative memory can perform parallel search for multi-word strings or records, and then retrieve any number of pointers or data. It can be used as a standard RAM for random read/write operations, and as a conventional associative memory for relational search and pattern matching.

I. Introduction

Associative Memory, alternatively known as Content Addressable Memory, differs from regular memory in the way the stored data are retrieved. Data stored in associative memory are addressed by their contents, not by their physical locations. The major advantage of associative memory over RAM is its ability to perform parallel search and pattern matching. This ability makes associative memory preferable in many applications, such as image processing [1], database system [2], and Artificial Intelligent computers [3; 4; 5; 6].

A conventional associative memory is structured in the form of an array (see Fig. 1). Each word has its own comparison circuit and a tag bit which is used to store the result of the comparison corresponding to that word. In a search operation, all the words in the associative

---

Research is supported by NSF Grant IRI-881064.
Any opinions, findings, and conclusions or recommendations expressed in this paper are those of the authors and do not necessarily reflect the views of the National Science Foundation.

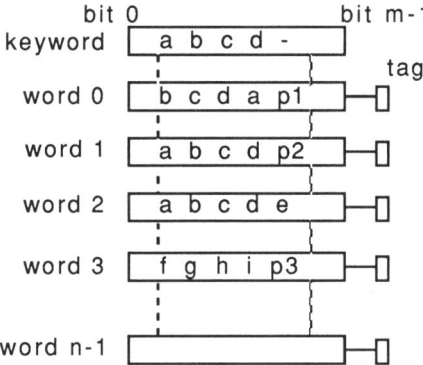

Fig. 1. A conventional associative memory.

memory are compared with a keyword simultaneously. And, the results are stored in the corresponding tag bits. The tag bits indicate which word(s) matches the keyword. The matched words can be read sequentially using a multiple response resolver [2; 7].

Although words and bits of a conventional associative memory are arranged in the form of an array, there is no way to tell whether one word is next to the other or not. This is because each word is independent and isolated from other words. This independence and isolation poses two limitations to a conventional associative memory. A conventional associative memory cannot be used to search a multi-word string that requires storage space of more than one word. Similarly, it cannot be used to retrieve a multi-word string. The example shown in (Fig. 1) illustrates these two limitations. Although the string "abcdefghi" is stored in word 2 and word 3, there is no way to search for that string. The reasons are that the string requires storage space of more than one word, and there are no mechanism in the conventional associative memory to tell whether one word is next to the other or not. The same reasons apply to the retrieval of multi-word string.

A conventional associative memory can be use as a table look-up device, but these two limitations make the table look-up device inflexible. A keyword "abcd_", for example, can be searched (where the bits represented by '_' are not used for comparison) (see Fig. 1). Word 1 matches the keyword. It is retrieved, and p2 can be used as an address to a record stored elsewhere. Since only one keyword can be searched, the number of bits in one word (m in this example) determines the maximum length of both the keyword and the pointer. However, sometimes a long keyword and a long pointer is required, sometimes a relatively short one is

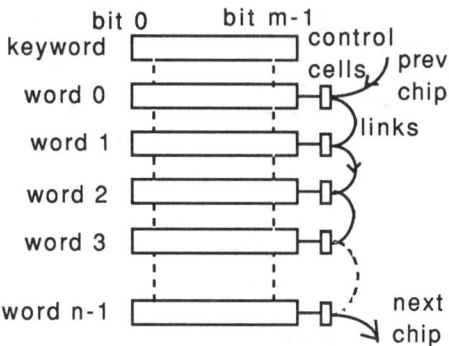

Fig. 2. Link-words association in GAM.

sufficient. For general purpose applications, one cannot decide what the maximum length of a word should be. If the bit length is too long, only a few words can be implemented in an associative memory. If it is too short, the associative memory may not meet the requirement of many applications.

In order to make an associative memory suitable for general purpose applications, several designs have been proposed, attempting to make associative memory perform the multi-word string search and retrieval. However, these designs pose their own limitations. One design limits the string length to eight words [8]. Another design requires all the strings stored in the memory to have same length. Also, the address of the first word of each string needs to be known before the search [9].

The design of a general purpose associative memory called GAM (Generic Associative memory) is discussed in this paper. The design is motivated by recognizing the need to handle in a flexible manner multi-word string comparison and to retrieve multi-word data associated with the matched strings. GAM implements both functions with a unique link mechanism. The control cells (see Fig. 2) not only serve as tag bits but link each word to its next word. With this link mechanism, the associative memory can search a string or a record with any number of words, and can then retrieve from the memory any number of pointers or data associated with the matched records (limited by the total memory space in all the connected memory chips). GAM can also be used as a standard RAM for random read/write operations, and as a conventional associative memory for relational search and pattern matching.

In Section II, we first outline two applications of this specially design associative memory, namely, Prolog clause indexing and Relational database search-retrieval operations. In Section III, we define the input and output lines of a GAM chip, followed by a discussion on the modes of operations in Section IV. In Section V, we describe the circuit design and implementation, while the evaluation is given in Section VI. Finally, we give a conclusion of our work and suggest future research.

II. Applications of GAM

The ability of GAM to perform parallel search/retrieval of multi-word string makes GAM an excellent device for Prolog clause indexing and for Relational database search/retrieval operations. These two applications of GAM are outlined as follows.

A. Prolog Clause Indexing

A Prolog program consists of a finite set of clauses which are facts, rules, and queries [10]. In the execution of a Prolog program, the unification engine needs to find the right clauses to unify. This is usually done by compiling the Prolog program and by using a hash table. For example, in Warren Abstract Machine's instructions set, *try*, *retry*, and *trust* instructions, followed by clause addresses, and *switch_on* instructions, followed by pointers to a hash table, are used to index the clauses [11]. The compiled program usually lacks the flexibility for modification. Every time one modifies the program, the program has to be recompiled. An interpreter is usually more suitable for dynamic environment, such as during the development of a Prolog Program. With the help of GAM, a unification engine can directly interpret the source program with reasonable speed.

There are two ways we can use GAM for Prolog clause indexing. If a Prolog program can be completely stored in GAM chips, GAM can directly search all the clauses and retrieve the matched ones. Consider the example shown in Program 1. A Prolog program is stored in GAM,

.father(peter,john).male(john).father(peter,marry).female(marry)
.**son**(*X,Y):-father(Y,X),male(X)*.daughter(X,Y):-father(Y,X),female(X).

Program 1. Complete program search.

one clause after another as shown. Each character is stored in one eight-bit word in GAM. The clause boundaries are designated with a special character. In the examples, we use a period for convenience. Given a query, son(Who,peter), GAM searches the keyword .son(and then retrieves its arguments and its clause body, X,Y):-father(Y,X),male(X). Similarly, given a query, daughter(marry,peter), GAM searches the keyword .daughter(and then retrieve, X,Y):-father(Y,X),female(X). A unification engine can then use the retrieved data to finish the unification process.

In case the whole Prolog program cannot be stored in GAM. The name of each clause head followed by a pointer will be stored in GAM, while the arguments and the clause bodies are stored in standard RAM (see Program 2). GAM can perform parallel search on the names of the clause head and then retrieve the corresponding pointers which are the addresses of the arguments and the clause bodies. A unification engine can then use the retrieved pointers to access the RAM and to complete the unification process. A detailed description of how GAM can perform these parallel search and retrieval is given in Section IV.

B. Relational Database Search/Retrieval

For relational database applications, GAM can perform parallel search of a key attribute and then retrieve the next attribute in a way similar to that for Prolog clause indexing. Furthermore, it can be programed to do relational searches, such as finding the records which are greater than, greater than or equal to, or less than, some specified value. Several algorithms for doing such relational searches were described in detail in [12]. Although those algorithms were designed for single keyword search, they could be extended to do multi-word string search for GAM.

IN GAM	IN RAM
.father(p1	p1: peter,john).
.male(p2	p2: john).
.father(p3	p3: peter,marry). .female(p4
	p4: marry).
.son(p5	p5: X,Y :- father(Y,X), male(X).
.daughter(p6	p6: X,Y:- father(Y,X), female(X).

Program 2. Program in GAM and RAM.

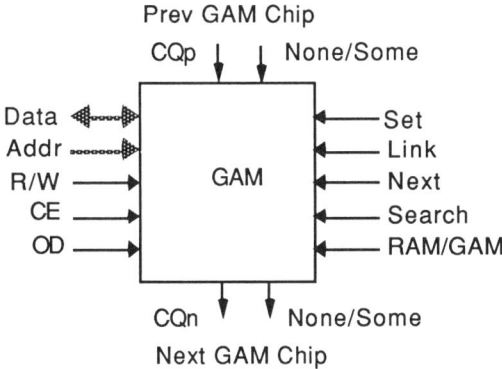

Fig. 3. GAM Chip (Inputs & Outputs)

III. Input/Output Lines of GAM Chip

Beginning from this Section, the design and operations of GAM are discussed. The input and output lines of a GAM chip are defined in this Section.

Fig. 3 shows the input and output lines of a GAM chip. Data, R/W, Addr, CE, and OD are the input and output lines used in a standard RAM. Set, Link, Next, Search, and RAM/GAM are the control lines used for associative search. CQp and None/Some are the lines which are used to concatenate several GAM chips. None/Some is also the signal line which tells whether there are no matched word or some matched words.

The control lines are defined as follows: Set turns on all control bits to prepare GAM for associative search. Link prepares GAM to search the next word during a multi-word string search, and it sets up a read-pointer, which is realized by a control bit, to point to the next word during a multi-word string retrieval. Next updates the read-pointer to point to the next string that also matches the key string. If more than one string matches the key string, this command allows all the data or pointers corresponding to those strings to be retrieved. Search enables GAM for parallel search and pattern matching. RAM/GAM selects GAM chip to act as a standard RAM or to act as associative memory.

```
                            ->time
             . A b c (      <-data
             SMLMLMLMLMLRNRN <-commands
           . 110000000000000
         m 101000000000000
         n 100000000000000
         ( 100000000000000
         p 1-000000000000000
         . 11-000000000000
         A 101100000000000
         b 100011000000000
         c 100000110000000
         ( 100000001100000  first
         p 1-0000000011000  <-read
         . 11-000000000000
         x 101000000000000
         y 100000000000000
         ( 100000000000000
         p 1-000000000000000
         . 11-000000000000
         A 101100000000000
         b 100011000000000
         c 100000110000000
         ( 100000001100000  next
         p 1-0000000011110  <-read

         ^-memory words  ^-control bits
```

Fig. 4. GAM operation example. (p is pointer, - is unknow 1 or 0)
(commands: Set, Match, Link, Read, Next)

IV. Modes of Operations

GAM can perform three major modes of operations, namely, standard RAM mode, Single-Word Associative mode, and Link-Words Associative mode.

In standard RAM mode, GAM functions the same way as RAM. This mode provides GAM simple interfacing to disk drive controller, DMA channels, and conventional processors (eg., for data loading and unloading).

In Single-Word Associative mode, GAM functions in the same way as a conventional associative memory. In this mode, the search procedure, in its simplest case, is a three-step process. First, the keyword is loaded into the Comparand register. Secondly, a Search command is given. Finally, the None/Some output line will tell whether there are some words in the GAM matched the keyword.

The Single-Word Associative mode is described in more detail as follows. First, the keyword is loaded into the m-bits Comparand register. Each bit of the keyword can be masked ON or OFF by the corresponding bit in the Mask register (the keyword shown in Fig. 2 consists of Comparand and Mask registers). Only the ON bits of the keyword will be compared. All the words in the GAM are compared with the Comparand register concurrently. The results of the comparison are stored in the Control Cells (see Fig. 2). The matched words can then be read out or written over, one at a time, using the Next command. The None/Some output line signals either "None" matched word or "Some" matched words.

In Link-Words Associative mode, GAM can perform parallel search/retrieval of multi-word strings. In this mode, the search procedure, in its simplest case, is outlined as follows: The key string is entered, one character at a time, into GAM. A Search command is issued after each character. A Link command is given after each Search command, except for the last one. After all the characters of the key string have been entered, the None/Some line will tell whether there are some strings in the GAM which match the key string.

For example, consider the Prolog program shown in Program 2. Given a query, father(Who,marry), GAM is used to search the string ".father(", and to retrieve both the pointers p1 and p3. The first character '.' is loaded into the Comparand register. A Search command is given. Then, a Link command is given. The second character 'f' is next loaded into the register. A Search command followed by a Link command is given. This process continues until the last character is encountered. The last character '(' is again loaded into the register and a Search command issued. At this point, the None/Some output line will tell there are some strings in the GAM that matched the string ".father(". A Link command will set a Read-pointer pointing to p1. Then, a Read command is given. As a result, the pointer p1 is retrieved. A Next command is then issued, which sets the Read-pointer pointed to p3. Finally, a Read command will retrieve the pointer p3.

The detailed control signals of the Link-Words Associative mode are described in the following example. Fig. 4 shows an example for searching a string, .Abc(, and retrieving the pointers, p's. GAM contains the words shown in the first column of the figure. The Mask register is loaded with all 1's. The first row in the figure shows the data stored in the Comparand register in the corresponding steps. The second row in the figure shows the commands in every step of the operations.

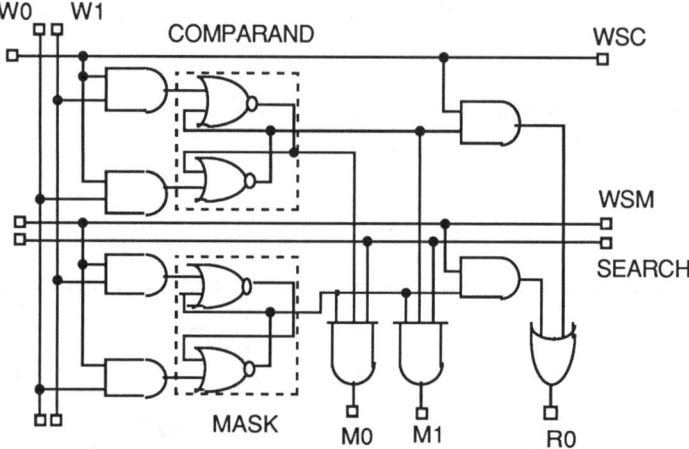

Fig. 5. Comparand and mask cell.

The first command to the GAM chip is Set, which sets all the Control Cells to 1's (second column in Fig. 4). The character '.' is loaded into the Comparand register. A Search (Match) command is then given. All the Control bits corresponding to the mismatches will be reset to 0's (third column). A Link command is then given. As the result all Control bits are shifted one word position down, with the first Control bits set to 0. The character 'A' is then loaded into the Comparand register. A Search (Match) command followed by a Link command are then given. The cycle repeats till the last character.

Then, a Read command is given and the data pointed by the First-Read (see Fig. 4) will be read out. The command Next is then given. As a result the Control bit corresponding to the First-Read position will be set to 0. And, the position of the Read-pointer will be updated. Now, the Read-pointer points to the Next-Read position. The None/Some output line will signal that there is still another match. A second Read command is then given, and the data pointed to by the Next-Read will be read out. A second Next command is given. After that, the None/Some line will signal no more matches.

V. Circuit Design and Implementation

The gate-level circuit design to accomplish the modes of operations is described in this Section.

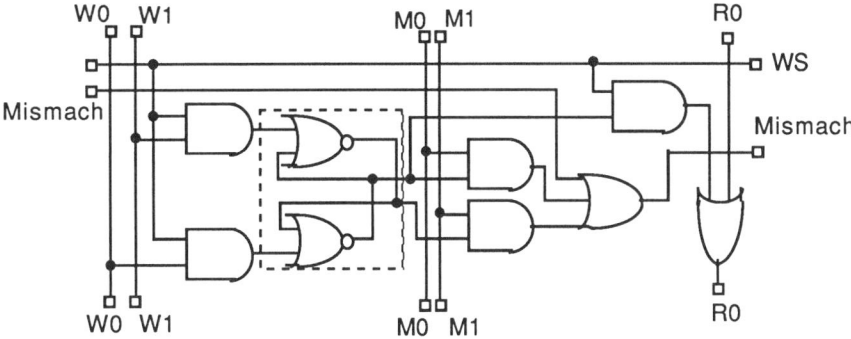

Fig. 6. Associative cell.

Each bit in the keyword (see Fig. 2) consists of a Comparand and Mask cells. The circuit to implement the Comparand and Mask cells is shown in Fig. 5. This cell can be read or written using the same method as used in standard RAM. They provide the masked comparand bit M0 and M1 to all the associative memory cells in the corresponding column.

Each bit in word 0 to word n-1 (see Fig. 2) is realized by an Associative cell. The Associative cell shown in Fig. 6 is a basic associative memory cell [13]. With a few minor modification on the control circuit, the associative cell can be implemented with 9 transistors on VLSI or LSI as shown in Fig. 7 [8; 9; 14; 15].

The GAM Control Cell (see Fig. 8) [16] which realizes all three modes of operations transpires to be amazingly simple. Only 10 gates are needed for each control cell. All the control signals to the Control Cell, namely, Link, Set, Next, and RAM/GAM, are positive pulses and no two control pulses can be given at the same time.

To realize the RAM/GAM selection, the gate O1 with the control line RAM/GAM is used. While all other control lines are pulled low, a positive pulse to RAM/GAM control line will reset all the control bits to 0's. The word select lines can then be used to select the word to be read or written in the same way as in a standard RAM. While the RAM/GAM is pulled low, Set control line can be used to set all the control bits to 1's which will make the GAM ready for associative search.

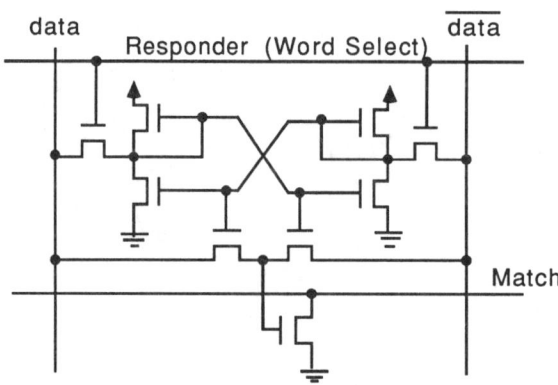

Fig. 7. A 9-transistor associative cell.

To realize the Link command, the gates A1, A2, the memory cell, and the Link control line act like a shift register. All the control bits are shifted down one position in the Link operation. The bit in the previous control cell is shifted down to the present control cell while the bit in the present control cell is shifted down to the next one.

To realize the None/Some signal line and the Read-pointer, gates A3, A4, which are connected to the previous and the next control cells, act like a priority encoder. The Read-pointer is pointed to the highest priority word which is the word to be read out or written over. To realize the Next command, the gate A5 and the Next control line will reset the memory cell which is selected by the Read-pointer. As a result the Read-pointer will point to the next matched word.

VI. Evaluation

The circuit design of GAM has been verified by using a simulation program called LogicWork run on a Mac II. In string search operations, the speed up of this associative memory over a conventional computer with RAM is proportional to the number of words stored in the memory. For example, suppose that there are 100 words stored in the memory, and the search key is 5 words. Also, assume that the same search algorithm is used in both systems. The associative memory described here requires 10 steps while the conventional computer with RAM requires more than 100 steps. If the number of words stored in the memory is now increased to 500 words. GAM still requires 10 steps. But, the conventional computer now requires more than 500 steps. In this example, if the access time of GAM is 1.5 times that of RAM, the overall speed up of GAM over RAM is over 33 times.

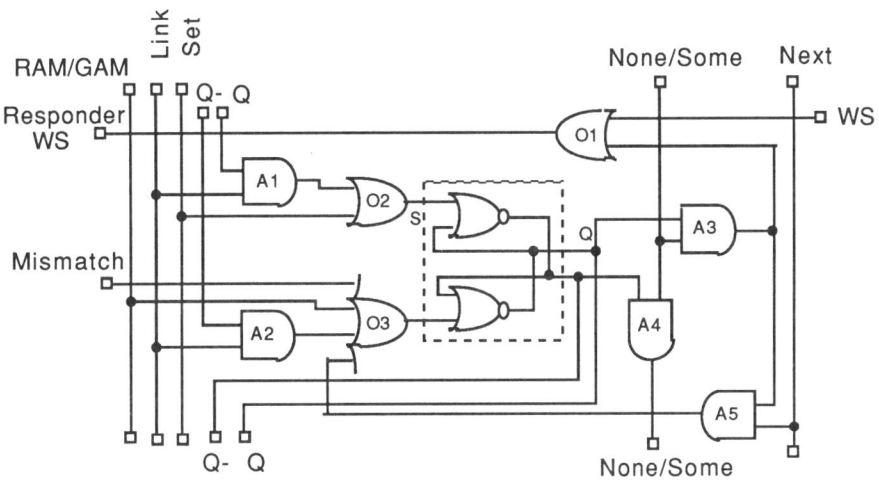

Fig. 8. GAM control cell

VII. Conclusions and Future Work

The design and applications of an associative memory called GAM, which can perform parallel search/retrieval of multi-word string, were described. GAM can also function as a standard RAM and as a conventional associative memory. These features make GAM suitable for general purpose applications, as well as an excellent device for Prolog clause indexing and Relational database search/retrieval operations. We are incorporating GAM to our Prolog Knowledge-Base Computer (PKBC) which is being designed as a symbolic multi-processor system with hardware support for unification. Our future research includes the design of a unification engine for performing full unification. The unification engine is based on a pattern matching device developed for complex pattern matching [17]. We need to extend it to handle such things as variables and structures and to incorporate it with GAM which can best serve as a clause indexing device.

References

[1] Char, Jois Malathi, Vladimir Cherkassky, Harry Wechsler, and George Lee Zimmerman, "Distributed and Fault-Tolerant Computation for Retrieval Tasks Using Distributed Associative Memories," IEEE Transactions on Computers, Vol. 37, No. 4, Pages 484-490, April, 1988.

[2] Lee, Dik Lun, "A Distributed Multiple-Response Resolver for Value-ordered Retrieval," Proc. 12th Annual International Symposium on Computer Architecture, Pages 258-265, June, 1985.

[3] Robinson, Ian, "A Prolog Processor Based on a Pattern Matching Memory Device," Proc. International Conference on Logic Programming, Pages 172-179, 1986.

[4] Anderson, Judy M., William S. Coates, Alan L. Davis, Robert W. Hon, Ian N. Robinson, Shane V. Robison, and Kenneth S. Stevens, "The Architecture of FAIM-1," Computer, Pages 55-65, January, 1987.

[5] Moldovan, Dan I. and Yu-Wen Tung, "SNAP: A VLSI Architecture for Artificial Intelligence Processing," Journal of Parallel and Distributed Computing 2, 109-131, 1985.

[6] Naganuma, Jiro, Takeshi Ogura, Shin-Ichiro Yamada, and Takashi Kimura, "High-Speed CAM-Based Architecture for a Prolog Machine (ASCA)," IEEE Transactions on Computers, Vol. 37, No. 11, pages 1375-1383, November 1988.

[7] Lee, Dik Lun, and Lochouskey, Fred, "Text Retrieval Machines," in Office Automation, D. Tsichritzis, ed., Spring Verley, New York, N.Y., pages 339-375, 1985.

[8] Ogura, Takeshi, Shin-ichiro Yamada, and Junzo Yamada, "A 20Kb CMOS Associative Memory LSI for Artificial Intelligence Machines," IEEE International Conference on Computer Design, Page 574-577, 1986.

[9] Adams, Stuart J., Mary Jane Irwin, and Robert M. Owens, "A Parallel General Purpose CAM Architecture," Advance Research in VLSI, Pages 51-71, 1986.

[10] Sterling, Leon and Ehud Shapiro, The Art of Prolog. The MIT Press, Cambridge, Massachusetts, 1986.

[11] Warren, David H.D., "An Abstract Prolog Instruction Set," Technical Note 309, SRI International, October, 1983.

[12] Foster, Caxton C., Content Addressable Parallel Processors. Van Nostrand Reinhold Co., New York, pages 57-102, 1976.

[13] Foster, Caxton C., Content Addressable Parallel Processors. Van Nostrand Reinhold Co., New York, page 15, 1976.

[14] Robinson, Phillip, "The SUM: An AI Coprocessor," Byte, Pages 169-180, June, 1985.

[15] Kokubu, Akio, Minoru Kuroda and Tatsumi Furuya, "Orthogenal Memory A step Toward Realization of Large Capacity Associative Memory," VLSI 85, E.Horbst (editor) Elsevier Science Publisher B.V. (North-Holland), 1986.

[16] Choi, C.H. Ben, "Parallel Distributed Computer Architecture and General Associative Memory for Artificial Intelligent Processing," Master thesis, Dept. of Electrical Engineering, The Ohio State University, Columbus Ohio, 1988.

[17] Lee, D.L. ALTEP - A cellular processor for high-speed pattern matching. New Generation Computing, Vol. 4, No. 3, pages 225-244, Sept., 1986.

Design and Analysis of a Parallel VLSI String Search Algorithm

K. C. Lee   V. W. Mak

Bellcore
445 South Street
Morristown, New Jersey 07960-1910
U. S. A.

Abstract

String searching is one of the basic operations in many areas of non-numeric processing. In this paper, we propose a parallel VLSI string search algorithm called the Data Parallel Pattern Matching (DPPM) algorithm. The DPPM algorithm can efficiently utilize the high degree of integration of VLSI technology to attain very high speed processing through parallelism. The DPPM algorithm serially broadcasts and compares the pattern to a block of data in parallel. Performance of the DPPM has been evaluated both analytically and experimentally. Based on the simulation statistics and timing analysis on the hardware prototype, a search rate of multiple gigabytes per second is achievable using 2 μm CMOS technology.

1 Introduction

Given a data string and a pattern, the problem of string searching is to find *all* occurrences of the pattern in the data string. String searching is one of the basic operations in many areas of non-numeric processing, such as text retrieval in database applications.

Reducing the time required to search a large text database has been an active area of research for the past decade. Many different software and hardware algorithms have been proposed and implemented [Boy77] [Knu77] [Fos80] [Cur83] [Hal83] [Has83] [Tak87]. All of these algorithms examine the characters in the data string sequentially. Their search rates[1] are then constrained by the single character comparison speed of the implementation. Furthermore, many of these algorithms exhibit large numbers of redundant comparisons.

In this paper, we propose a parallel VLSI string search algorithm called the Data Parallel Pattern Matching (DPPM) algorithm. The DPPM algorithm differs from other

---
[1] Number of characters searched in one second.

algorithms in that it serially broadcasts and compares each character in the pattern to a block of characters of the data string in parallel. As soon as a mismatch between the current data block and any character of the pattern is detected, the current data block is discarded to eliminate any subsequent redundant comparisons.

Performance of the DPPM has been evaluated both analytically and experimentally. Based on the simulation statistics and timing analysis on the hardware prototype, a search rate of multiple gigabytes per second is achievable using 2 μm CMOS technology. The DPPM algorithm can efficiently utilize the high degree of integration of VLSI technology to attain very high speed processing through parallelism.

The remainder of the paper is organized as follows. After a discussion of previous work in section 2, we present the DPPM algorithm in section 3. Section 4 discusses the technology issue in implementing data broadcasting in VLSI, and describes the VLSI implementation of the DPPM engine prototype. Section 5 introduces a simple analytical performance model for the DPPM algorithm. Section 6 describes the simulation experiment conducted to evaluate its actual performance on a large text database. A conclusion is given at the end of this paper.

2 Previous Work

The two most well known software algorithms in string searching are the KMP algorithm [Knu77] and the Boyer-Moore algorithm [Boy77]. Both algorithms exploit on the characteristics of the pattern to improve the search speed. The search rates of these software approaches are limited by the speed of the underlying processor and by the sequential nature of the character by character comparison operation.

Haskin and Hollaar [Has83] proposed mapping of the Finite State Automaton (FSA) onto custom hardware. The FSA approach is very efficient for sequential input data. However, its search rate is also limited by the character by character comparison in state transition.

[Fos80] [Cur83] [Hal83] and [Tak87] proposed using comparator arrays [Mea76] to improve search performance by comparing different pairs of characters simultaneously. In [Fos80], data string and pattern characters are moving in opposite directions. At any clock cycle, only half of the cells in the systolic array are actually doing useful computation, therefore half of the physical hardware is wasted.

In [Cur83] [Hal83] and [Tak87], the pattern is pre-loaded into the comparator array.

Each character of the data string is broadcast serially to the array, and comparison results are generated simultaneously. Since a string search operation on text databases exhibits very low selectivity, comparisons beyond the first few characters of the pattern are usually unnecessary. Thus, most of the comparisons with the last few characters of the pattern are redundant.

3 The DPPM Algorithm

The DPPM algorithm proposed in this paper also uses the comparator array to parallelize search operations. Instead of serially broadcasting the data string characters to a comparator array containing the pattern as in previous approaches, the DPPM algorithm serially broadcasts the pattern characters to a comparator array containing a block of the data string on a demand-driven basis. The algorithm can also detect multiple occurrences of the pattern without any backtracking of the data string even if they are overlapped or across a block boundary.

Let Blk[1:b] be the current data block of size b characters, and Pat[1:p] be the pattern of length p. Conceptually, the DPPM algorithm serially broadcasts each pattern character to a block of the data string. If the pattern character matches with any of the characters in the block, the next pattern character is broadcast in the next comparison cycle. If at any cycle, no match is found between the current pattern character and the data block, the data block is discarded and the search continues with the next block. A partial match occurs when Pat[i], i > p, matches with the last data block character Blk[b]. This partial match information is stored and used in the next block to continue the search by comparing Pat[i+1] to the first data block character Blk[1].

Pseudo code of the control flow of the DPPM algorithm is shown in Figure 1. The description below follows closely with the pseudo code. DC[1:p] is a bit-vector indicating the *don't care* positions in the pattern. DC[i] is set if there is a *don't care* at Pat[i]. Mask[1:b] controls the activation of the comparator array based on the results of the previous comparison cycle. If Pat[1] matches Blk[i] in the first comparison cycle, then Mask[i+1] is set in the next comparison cycle enabling the comparison between Pat[2] and Blk[i+1]. T[1:b] holds the results of the comparator array. Vin[2:p] and Vout[1:p-1] hold the partial match information from the previous block and the current block, respectively. Vin[i] is set if there is a partial match in the previous block up to and including the character Pat[i-1]. Vout[i] is set if there is a partial match up to and including the character Pat[i] in the current block.

For each block of the data string, Mask is initially set to be all TRUE, enabling all comparators for the entire block. Vout is initialized to be all FALSE. Then each pattern character Pat[i], $1 \leq i \leq p$, is serially broadcast to the comparator array and compared to the entire data block. If $i < p$, the broadcast character is not the last pattern character, the comparison result of Pat[i] and Blk[b] is stored in Vout so that any partial match can be continued in the next block. If $i = p$, the last pattern character is broadcast, any match in the current comparison cycle indicates that an occurrence of the pattern is found in the current block. The positions at which matches are detected are reported. Since the last pattern character is reached, no further comparison is necessary, and the current block can be discarded.

If Pat[i], $i < p$, matches with any of the first (b - 1) characters in the data block, we must continue the search with Pat[i+1] for the current block. The comparison result of Pat[i] and Blk[b] indicates only whether a partial match occurs in the current block, and does not require further comparison in the current block. If the search is continued with the current block, the Mask for the next comparison cycle is formed by shifting the comparison results of the current cycle. The first bit of the Mask is loaded from Vin[i+1] to continue any partial match from the previous block.

If no match is detected with the first (b - 1) characters, the algorithm checks to see if any partial match has to be continued for the rest of the pattern characters, Pat[(i+1):p]. If so, the first pattern character found will be broadcast in the next comparison cycle. In this case, only the first bit of the Mask is set. If no partial match is carried over from the previous block, the current block can be discarded.

The DPPM algorithm can be best illustrated using a simple example. Suppose we want to search for the pattern *abcd* in the data string *abadbbabcdee*. Figure 2 shows the operation of the DPPM algorithm using a block size of 4. The first block contains the characters *abad*. When compared to the first pattern character *a*, two matches are detected. The second pattern character *b* is then compared to the second and the fourth characters in the block. Since we have a match again at the second character, we compare the third character *c* with the third character in the block. This time, we do not have any match in the block, we can discard the current block and continue the search in the next block. This early mismatch detection mechanism avoids redundant comparisons and thus improves the search rate of the algorithm.

The next block contains the characters *bbab*. The pattern compares successfully up to

```
while (¬ End of Data String) do begin
    GetNextBlock(Blk);
    forall i from 1 to b do Mask[i] := TRUE;
    forall i from 1 to (p - 1) do Vout[i] := FALSE;
    i := 1;
    while i ≤ p do begin /* Comparison Cycle */
        forall j from 1 to b do
            T[j] := Mask[j] ∧ (DC[i] ∨ (Blk[j] = Pat[i]));
        if (i < p) then Vout[i] := T[b]
        else begin /* i = p: Report Match Found */
            forall j from 1 to b do
                if (T[j]) then Report Match at j;
            break;
        end;
        if (∨_{j=1}^{b-1} T[j]) then begin
            /* Prepare Mask for next comparison cycle */
            forall j from 2 to b do
                Mask[j] := T[j-1];
            Mask[1] := Vin[i+1];
            i := i + 1;
        end
        else if (∨_{j=i+1}^{p} Vin[j]) then begin
            /* Skip Unnecessary Pattern Characters */
            do i := i + 1 until (Vin[i]);
            Mask[1] := TRUE;
            forall j from 2 to b do Mask[j] := FALSE;
        end
        else /* Early Out */
            break;
    end
    forall i from 2 to p do Vin[i] := Vout[i-1];
end
```

Figure 1: Pseudo Code of the DPPM Algorithm

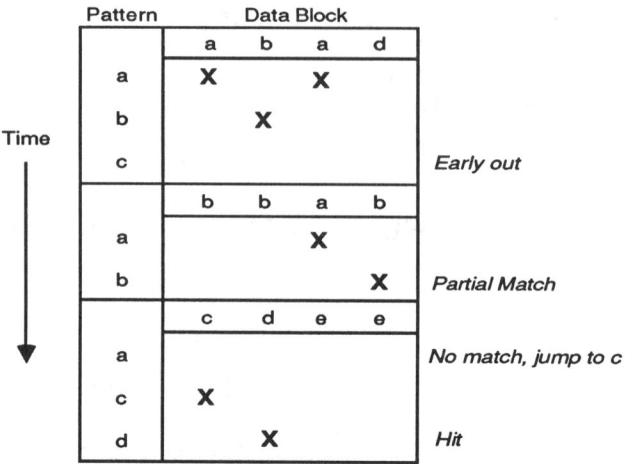

Figure 2: DPPM Example

the second character *b*. The end of the block is reached at this point, this partial match information is stored in Vout[2][2], and the current block is discarded.

The third block contains the characters *cdee*. The first pattern character *a* has no match with the block. Since Vin[3] is set, DPPM jumps to the third pattern character *c* and continues the search from there. Finally, a hit is detected with the fourth pattern character *d*.

Although not shown in this example, the DPPM algorithm can also detect multiple occurrences of the pattern even if they are overlapped. With the use of the Vin and Vout registers, partial match can be continued in the next block without any backtracking of the data string. Since the algorithm is independent of the block size, the search rate can be increased simply by increasing the block size, or the number of comparators. As a result, the DPPM algorithm can efficiently utilize the high degree of integration of VLSI technology to attain high speed processing through parallelism.

4 VLSI Implementation

The DPPM algorithm requires VLSI technology to implement broadcasting of pattern characters to many comparators simultaneously. Broadcasting requires a large fanout as well as long routing distance. It is therefore important to understand whether data broadcasting can be implemented effectively using current and emerging VLSI technology.

---

[2]This becomes Vin[3] in the next block.

The first design issue is whether the necessary degree of fanout can be achieved without introducing excessive delay. Using a block size of 1000, each bit of a pattern character has to be broadcast to 1000 gates. Using 2 μm CMOS technology, a typical gate capacitance is 20 fF, so the total input capacitance for 1000 gates is 20 pF. Assuming a typical gain factor of 50 μA/V^2, and output channel resistance of 10 KΩ, using the simplified RC model [Wes85], we can achieve a 1 ns delay for a buffering stage with a fanout of 4. With 5 cascaded buffer stages to achieve a fanout of 1000, a total delay of 5 ns is possible. This estimate matches very well with circuit simulation result using 2 μm CMOS technology. Using 2 μm BiCMOS [Kub88] technology, one BiCMOS gate can drive a load of 700 fF with 0.7 ns delay. This is equivalent to driving 35 gates in parallel. A fanout of 1000 can then be achieved in two cascaded buffer stages with a total delay of only 1.4 ns.

Propagation delay due to long routing distances can be minimized by using two layer metal routes. Since we are driving a large capacitive load using multiple stages of buffers, the propagation delay is dominated by the large input gate capacitance and high output channel resistance of the previous stage, the delay due to long metal run can be ignored in the timing analysis [Wes85].

The above analysis shows that with the large fanout capability of BiCMOS technology, together with two layer metal routes, data broadcasting in the DPPM algorithm can be implemented effectively. Even with 2 μm CMOS technology, data broadcasting can still be implemented with a reasonable propagation delay.

We are currently designing the VLSI implementation of the DPPM algorithm. Figure 3 shows the circuit block diagram of the DPPM engine. Before the actual search operation, the pattern, pattern length, and the *don't care* positions are first loaded into their corresponding registers. The data string is buffered and read one block at a time to the Block register. The comparator array performs the actual comparison between the pattern character and the data block. The results of the comparator array are ANDed with the Mask to form T. The first bit of the Mask is from the Vin register, and the last (b-1) bits are from the first (b-1) bits of T in the previous cycle. The last bit of T is stored in the Vout register.

The sequence controller controls the operation of the DPPM engine. By monitoring the values of T, the content of the Vin register, and the pattern length, the sequence controller decides for each cycle one of the following three actions:

1. Compare the next pattern character with the current block.

2. Discard the current block and continue the search with the next block.

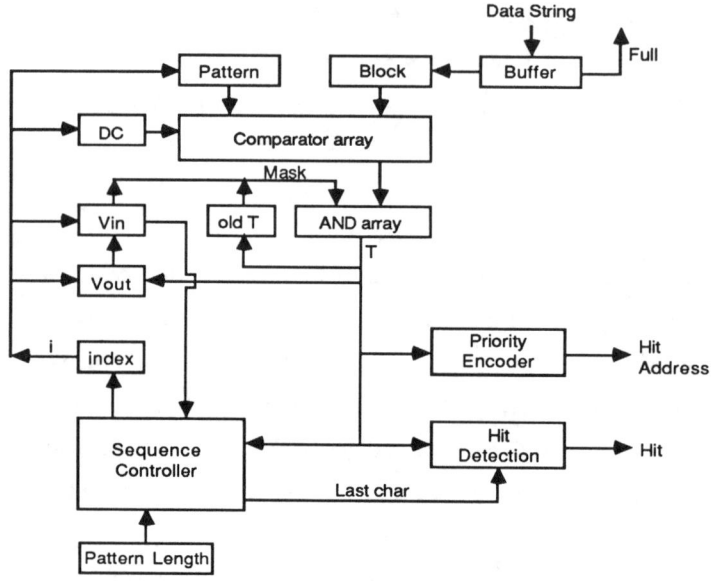

Figure 3: Circuit Block Diagram of the DPPM Engine

3. Jump to a pattern character to continue the partial match from previous block.

The sequence controller generates the value, i, which is used to index the pattern, don't care, Vin, and Vout registers. Each time a new data block is read, the first (p-1) bits of Vout is loaded into the last (p-1) bits of Vin. The first bit of Vin is always set.

The sequence controller also generates a *last character* signal when the last pattern character is reached. This signal is used by the hit detection unit which checks the values of T to report any hit in the search. The priority encoder produces the encoded addresses for all hit positions in the current block.

The critical path of the circuit is from the pattern register, through the comparator and AND arrays, to the priority encoder. Using 2 μm CMOS, the comparison cycle time is about 50 ns for a block size of 1000. This includes the broadcasting delay of 6 ns. If 1.2 μm CMOS is used, the cycle time will be approximately 33 ns. The estimated chip area of the DPPM engine for a block size of 128 is about 200 × 100 mil^2.

5 Performance Analysis

Performance of the DPPM algorithm depends on the block size used, the number of comparison cycles required per block, and the cycle time of the hardware. In this section, we present an approximate analysis of the performance of the DPPM algorithm. In order to simplify the analysis, we assume uniform distribution of characters in both the data string and the pattern. Using an approach similar to that in [Pra86], we model the string search process as detection of random events.

With a block size of b, we can assume that we have b independent comparisons of the pattern with the data block, with each starting at a different location. Let p be the pattern length, and m be the alphabet size of the character. Using the assumption of uniform distribution of characters, the probability of not finding the pattern in each comparison is

$$\alpha = 1 - \left(\frac{1}{m}\right)^p$$

Assuming the fact of not finding the pattern in one position of the data string does not affect the probability of not finding the pattern at a different position, then the probability of not finding the pattern for b consecutive comparisons is,

$$\beta = \alpha^b = \left(1 - \left(\frac{1}{m}\right)^p\right)^b$$

Therefore, the probability of finding a pattern with length p in b consecutive comparisons is,

$$\delta(p) = 1 - \beta = 1 - \left(1 - \left(\frac{1}{m}\right)^p\right)^b$$

$\delta(p)$ converges quickly to zero as p increases. The average number of comparison cycles per block is,

$$C = 1 + \sum_{i=1}^{p-1} \delta(i)$$

Let T be the comparison cycle time. The search rate at a block size of b, R_b, is defined as the number of characters that can be searched in one second,

$$R_b = \frac{b}{C \times T} \quad (1)$$

The speedup, S, of the DPPM algorithm is defined as,

$$S = \frac{R_b}{R_1}$$

Using 50 ns as the comparison cycle time, and a pattern length of 6, Figure 4 shows the search rate of the DPPM algorithm at different block sizes. The alphabet size, m, used in this case is 45 which corresponds to the case insensitive English alphabets, numbers and

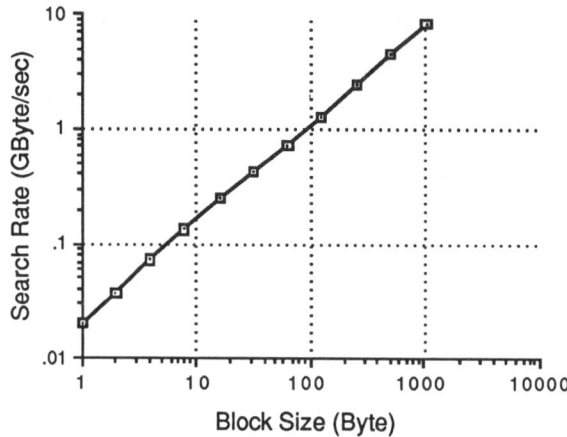

Figure 4: Search Rate of the DPPM Algorithm Using Analytical Results

a few common symbols.

6 Simulation Experiment

The analysis described in the previous section is only a simplified model of the actual performance of the DPPM algorithm. Exact analysis of the algorithm is very difficult because of the following two reasons:

1. Different characters have different frequencies of occurrence. For instance, **a**, **e**, and **s** occur more frequently than **q**, **x**, and **z** in the English language. The assumption of uniform distribution of characters in the data string or the pattern cannot be used in the analysis.

2. The occurrence of a character is not independent of its neighboring characters. Character groups like **ing**, **th**, and **un** occur frequently in the English language. This cross correlation property implies that we cannot treat the occurrence of a character in the input data string as an independent random event, and thus complicates the analysis.

The DPPM algorithm can be best evaluated by simulating its operation on a real text database. Under such an environment, we can estimate its performance, and can also gain insights into its behavior. The database chosen for this simulation experiment consists of the Associated Press wire news articles on August 2nd, 1988. The total size of the news article database is 4.4 MByte. All upper case characters in the database were converted to

Table 1: Test Patterns Used in the Simulation Experiment

about	after	again	against	almost
always	american	among	another	around
asked	because	become	before	being
better	between	business	called	children
could	course	didn't	don't	during
early	enough	every	first	found
general	given	going	government	great
group	himself	house	however	important
large	later	little	looked	might
national	never	night	nothing	number
often	order	other	people	place
point	possible	present	president	program
public	rather	right	school	second
several	should	since	small	social
something	state	states	still	system
their	there	these	things	think
those	though	thought	three	through
toward	under	united	until	water
where	which	while	white	within
without	world	would	years	young

lower case; case insensitive string searching was used in the experiment. The test patterns chosen for this simulation experiment are the 100 most frequent words in American English of at least five characters long (see Table 1) [Kuc67]. The pattern lengths vary from 5 to 10 characters with an average of 5.88 characters long. Use of these frequent words results in a conservative estimate of the algorithm's performance.

Figure 5 shows the average number of comparison cycles per block, C, measured at different block sizes. Although the pattern characters are serially compared to the data block, early mismatch detection allows the algorithm to search the next block as soon as a mismatch is detected. This feature is especially effective at smaller block sizes where the probabilities of matching the first few characters of the pattern are low. Without early mismatch detection, C should be equal to the average pattern length, in this case, 5.88. At larger block sizes, the probability of finding the pattern in the block is higher, thus the value of C also increases. If we keep increasing the block size, the value of C should approach the average pattern length asymptotically.

Using 50 ns as the comparison cycle time, T, Figure 6 shows the search rates, R_b, at different block sizes. Recall that increasing the block size requires proportionately more comparators on chip. At a block size of 16, the search rate is 212 MByte/sec. This rate matches the predicted optical disk transfer rate of 200 MByte/sec [Ber87]. At a

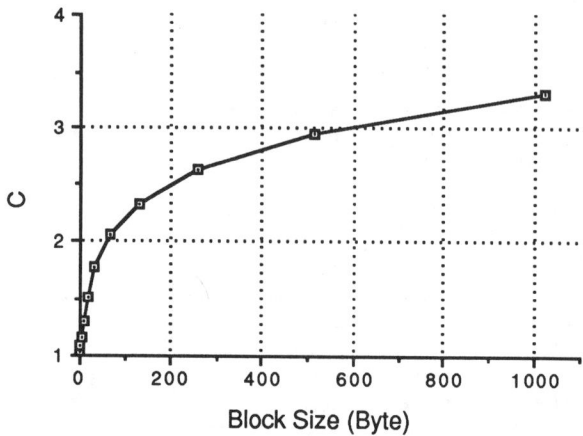

Figure 5: Average Number of Comparison Cycles per Block

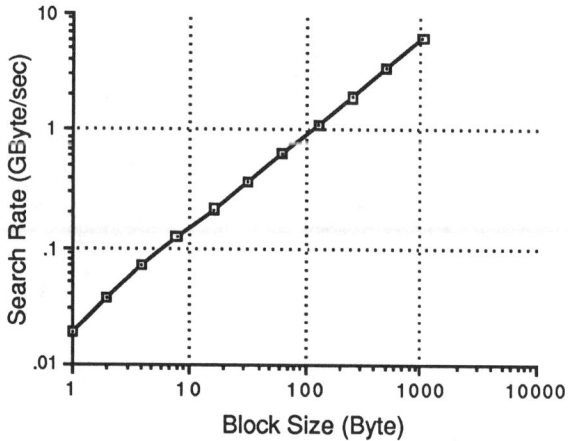

Figure 6: Search Rates at Different Block Sizes

block size of 128, the search rate reaches 1 GByte/sec. This rate is sufficient to handle existing memory bandwidth of supercomputers as well as data input from optical-fiber transmission systems in future communication networks.

Figure 7 shows the speedup, S, of the DPPM algorithm at different block sizes. The DPPM algorithm is indeed very scalable, and allows exploitation of a high degree of parallelism. Speedup can be obtained easily by increasing the size of the data block.

Intuitively, if the pattern is longer, more comparison cycles per block should be required in testing the pattern against the data string. However, this is not the case for the DPPM algorithm. Figure 8 shows the values of C for all patterns at a block size of 128. This figure indicates no strong correlation between the pattern length and C. This

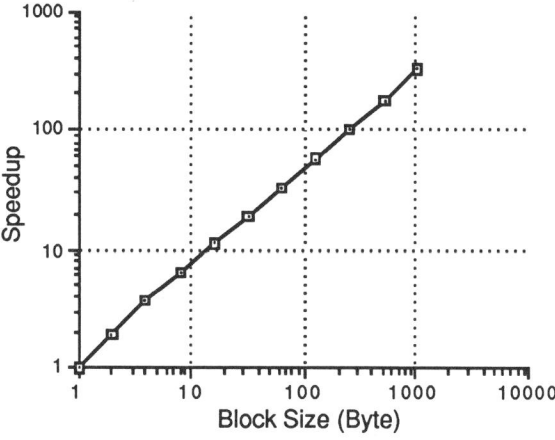

Figure 7: Speedup of the DPPM Algorithm

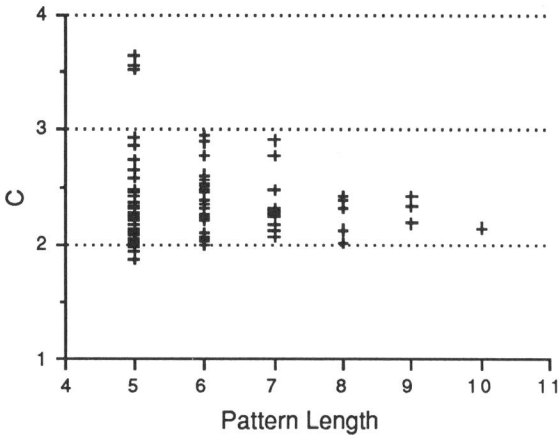

Figure 8: C for All Patterns at a Block Size of 128

insensitivity to the pattern length is due to the early mismatch detection in the DPPM algorithm. Since most blocks can be discarded after the first few characters, the length of the pattern has very little effect on C.

By the same token, the algorithm is also insensitive to the last few characters, or suffix, of the pattern. Using a block size of 128, the patterns *processes*, *processor*, and *processing* require essentially the same number of comparison cycles per block (see Table 2).

Since the result of a comparison cycle determines whether another comparison cycle is necessary for the current data block, performance of the algorithm is very sensitive to the pattern prefix. Patterns starting with frequently occurring prefixes (like th, st, and al) result in higher number of comparison cycles used. Consider the following three patterns:

Table 2: Effect of Different Pattern Suffixes on C

Pattern	C
processes	2.283
processing	2.282
processor	2.282

Table 3: Effect of Different Pattern Prefixes on C

Pattern	C
queue	1.160
dequeue	2.379
enqueue	2.579

queue, dequeue, and enqueue. Using a block size of 128, the DPPM algorithm has very different performance figures for them (Table 3). The pattern queue has twice the speed of searching the same database when compared to the patterns dequeue and enqueue. To take advantage of this prefix sensitivity property of the DPPM algorithm, we can speed up the search of the database by modifying the pattern used so that it starts with a less common prefix. Instead of searching for the pattern dequeue, we can use queue instead to speed up the search. However, the search result has less precision since all occurrences of the patterns queue and enqueue will also be found.

7 Conclusion

We have presented a novel parallel VLSI string search algorithm and its VLSI implementation. Performance of the DPPM algorithm has been evaluated by both an analytical technique and simulation. The results of the evaluation indicate that the algorithm has a high degree of parallelism and a search rate of over 1 GByte/sec is achievable using current and emerging VLSI technology. This search rate exceeds memory bandwidth of existing supercomputers and the transfer rate of future optical disk. It is also capable of handling the very high bandwidth of optical fiber transmission systems in the future. The design of a high performance subsystem for information retrieval of unformatted data based on an earlier version of the DPPM algorithm was reported in [Lee88].

Acknowledgment

We wish to thank G. Herman for his motivation in this project, O. Frieder for his many constructive comments during this research, J. Chao, W. Mansfield, and A. McAuley for their comments on this paper which greatly improve its presentation.

References

[Ber87] Berra, P. B. and Troullinos, N. B., "Optical Techniques and Data/Knowledge Base Machines," *IEEE Computer*, pp. 59–70, October, 1987.

[Boy77] Boyer, R. S. and Moore, J. H., "A Fast String Searching Algorithm," *Communications of the ACM*, vol. 20, no. 10, pp. 762–772, October, 1977.

[Cur83] Curry, T. and Mukhopadhyay, A., "Realization of Efficient Non-Numeric Operations Through VLSI," *Proceedings of VLSI '83*, 1983.

[Fos80] Foster, M. J. and Kung, H. T., "The Design of Special Purpose Chips," *IEEE Computer*, vol. 13, no. 1, pp. 26–40, January, 1980.

[Hal83] Halaas, A., "A Systolic VLSI Matrix for a Family of Fundamental Search Problem," *Integration VLSI Journal*, vol. 1, no. 4, pp. 269–282, December, 1983.

[Has83] Haskin, R. L. and Hollaar, L. A., "Operational Characteristics of a Hardware-based Pattern Matcher," *ACM Transactions on Database Systems*, vol. 8, no. 1, pp. 15–40, March, 1983.

[Knu77] Knuth, D. E., Morris, Jr., J. H., and Pratt, V. R., "Fast Pattern Matching in Strings," *SIAM J. Comput.*, vol. 6, no. 2, pp. 323–350, June, 1977.

[Kub88] Kubo, M., Masuda, I., Miyata, K. and Ogiue, K., "Perspective on BiCMOS VLSI's," *IEEE Journal of Solid-State Circuits*, vol. 23, no. 1, February, 1988.

[Kuc67] Kucera, H. and Nelson Francis, W., *Computational Analysis of Present-Day American English*, Brown University Press, Providence, 1967.

[Lee88] Lee, K. C., Frieder, O., and Mak, V., "A Parallel VLSI Architecture for Unformatted Data Processing," *Proceedings of International Symposium on Databases in Parallel and Distributed Systems*, pp. 80–86, December, 1988.

[Mea76] Mead, C. A., Pashley, R. D., Britton, L. D., Yoshiaki, T., and Snado, Jr., S. F., "128-Bit Multicomparator," *IEEE Journal of Solid-State Circuits*, vol. SC-11, no. 5, October, 1976.

[Pra86] Pramanick, S., "Performance Analysis of a Database Filter Search Hardware," *IEEE Transactions on Computers*, vol. C-35, no. 12, December, 1986.

[Tak87] Takahashi, K., Yamada, H., and Hirata, M., "Intelligent String Search Processor to Accelerate Text Information Retrieval," *Proceedings of Fifth International Workshop on Database Machines*, pp. 440–453, October, 1987.

[Wes85] Weste, N. and Eshraghian, K., *Principles of CMOS VLSI Design*, Addison-Wesley Publishing Company, 1985.

INTEGRATING INTEGRITY CONSTRAINTS WITH DATABASE FILTERS IMPLEMENTED IN HARDWARE

by

Manuel Penaloza and Esen Ozkarahan[1]

Computer Science Department
Arizona State University
Tempe, Arizona 85287-5406

Abstract

In an earlier study the concept of a filter chip for selection, projection, and join operations was presented. In this paper the filter concept is broadened to include database integrity constraints. The constraints are formalized in canonical forms. Several filter simplification techniques are described, and finally a filtering hardware architecture is presented.

1. Introduction

Preserving integrity is an important database management function. The integrity aspects of database modeling are represented in terms of integrity constraints (ICs). For preserving database consistency all changes to the database must constantly be monitored and integrity constraints enforced, rejecting illegal operations if necessary.

In an earlier paper [OzPe87] we presented the concept of a filter chip implementing database selection, projection, and join operations. In this paper we integrate integrity constraints as filters within a broaden concept of a "filter". The performance improvements achievable by the filter system were covered in [OzPe87]. A better performance improvement is expected in the filter implementation of ICs over the present software techniques.

Logic allows the formalization of facts, inference rules, ICs, and queries by means of first-order logic formulas. Logic has been used extensively to solve several database problems such as, the representation of incomplete information, the incorporation of more world knowledge (e.g., the representation of events) [REIT84], etc. In this paper we formalize different types of ICs using Horn clauses. Next, we define canonical filter expressions that allow the integration of ICs with the selection and projection operations. We then define several filter simplification techniques. Finally, we present a hardware organization for implementing filters.

---

[1] New address: The Penn State Univ., Behrend School of Business, Erie, PA 16509, USA

2. Formalization of Integrity Constraints

Integrity constraints (ICs) are a set of rules that any instance of the extensional database must obey. IC rules are classified as: *retrieval*, *update*, and *retrieval/update* constraints. Retrieval constraints prevent disclosure of private information from a relation. Update constraints prevent *inconsistency* of database state that may result from an update (delete, modify, or insert) operation. Retrieval/update constraints have the properties of the first two types of constraints. The types of ICs and their formalization by Horn clauses are given below. For each clause, only existential quantifiers are explicitly indicated. Also, the symbol "<==" will be used to denote implication in the IC clauses. This allows to make a distinction between an IC clause and a predicate definition. The relation on which integrity enforcement is applied will be referred to as a *primary relation*. The other relations used in an IC clause are referred to as *secondary relations*.

Restriction constraint.- This IC prevents a particular tuple attribute entry from being updated with a value that exceeds a lower or upper limit. A range limit for a tuple attribute is specified by two separate clauses. For example, the assertion "Every faculty salary must be less than 80000" is expressed by the clause:

$$LT(sal, 80000) \mathrel{<==} FAC(name, sal, dept) \qquad (2.1)$$

Join constraint.- This type of IC involves more than one relation. The IC makes sure that joined tuples exist or allowed to be inserted when the coexistence stipulation holds. For example, the statements (1) "Every faculty is associated with a department", and (2) "An individual cannot be the father and the mother of another person", are expressed as:

$$\exists d, chair(EQ(dept, d) \mathrel{<==} FAC(name, sal, dept) \land DEPT(d, chair)) \qquad (2.2)$$
$$\mathrel{<==} FATHER(x,y) \land MOTHER(x,y) \qquad (2.3)$$

Projection constraint.- This IC refers to the inaccessibility of one or more attributes of the relation to a database user. We introduce here the predicate $P\_U(user\_id, rel, attr, op)$. This relation (in this document we will use the words predicate and relation interchangeably) defines the operation *op* that a user with id *user_id* cannot perform on the attribute *attr* of the relation *rel*. The operation being checked in the constraint clause is indicated by *op* (i.e., retrieve, insert, modify, or delete). For example, the following assertion "Prevent user "xxx" from modifying any *s* value in relation FAC" is expressed as:

$$FAC(n,d) \mathrel{<==} FAC(n,s,d) \land P\_U("xxx", "FAC", "s", "m") \qquad (2.4)$$

Selection constraint.- This type of IC prevents a user from retrieving restricted tuples of a relation. For example, the following statement "Show only those tuples of relation FAC with s < 45000 or d="cs" to a user with id "uuu" is expressed by the following clause:

$$FAC(n,s,d) \mathrel{<==} FAC(n,s,d) \land \{ NE(user\_id, "uuu") $$
$$\lor [LT(s, 45000) \lor EQ(d, "cs")] \} \qquad (2.5)$$

Proj-Sel constraint.- This IC is the combination of projection and selection constraints. It allows a user access of a subset of the attributes of a relation if some conditions are satisfied. For example, the assertion "Prevent user with id "xyz" from changing "g" attribute entries of relation ST(s,n,g) when s>1000" is expressed as:

$$ST(s,n) <== ST(s,n,g) \wedge P\_U("xyz","FAC","g","m") \wedge GT(s,1000) \qquad (2.6)$$

Type constraint.-

This type of IC insures that attributes belong to the specified data types. The symbol τ identifies any of the valid data types. For example, the following clause defines the type for attribute "name" of relation FAC.

$$EQ(\tau_i,"name") <== FAC(name,sal,dept) \qquad (2.7)$$

Domain constraint.- This IC insures that the attribute entries of a relation belong to a specific database domain. We assume each domain is expressed by a unary predicate. For example, clauses (2.8) make sure that faculty names are valid names.

$$\exists nx(EQ(nx,name) <== FAC(name,sal,dept) \wedge NAMES(nx)) \qquad (2.8)$$

Dependency constraint.- This type of IC makes sure the relations follow the structural properties defined by their *functional* dependencies (FDs), *multivalued* dependencies (MVDs), and *join* dependencies. In addition to these three data dependencies, there exists several others, such as *embedded, mutual, transitive, subset, template, implied,* and *generalized transitive dependencies* [Fagi82]. This paper focuses on FDs and MVDs. Let R be a relation with n attributes, then the FD: $A_1 \rightarrow A_2$ and the MVD: $A_1 \rightarrow\rightarrow A_2$ are expressed by the formulas:

$$\text{FD:} \quad EQ(A_2,A'_2) <== R(A_1,A_2,A_3,...,A_n) \wedge R(A_1,A'_2,A'_3,...,A'_n) \qquad (2.9)$$
$$\text{MVD:} \quad R(A_1,A'_2,A_3,....,A_n) <==$$
$$R(A_1,A_2,A_3,...,A_n) \wedge R(A_1,A'_2,A'_3,...,A'_n) \qquad (2.10)$$

Key constraint.- The key of a relation can be defined as a constraint using the NE binary predicate with arguments as attribute names. In composite keys @ symbol expresses concatenation. For example, let R be a relation with five attributes and the key $A_1 A_2$, then we define the key constraint for R as follows:

$$NE(A_1@A_2,A'_1@A'_2) <== R(A_1, ... ,A_5) \wedge R(A'_1, ... ,A'_5) \qquad (2.11)$$

Dynamic constraint.- This type of constraint is used to indicate that a new entry for an attribute of a relation must be >, ≥, <, or ≤ the current value. A time variable is not required to indicate time precedence between the two entries. We assume that the relation that appears first in the clause body refers to: a) a set of temporary tuples that will be used to update the primary relation, or b) the primary relation stored on disk. The first case is assumed for any update operation, while the second case applies only for a retrieval operation. For example, the IC "any new salary for a STAFF member must be greater than the previous one stored in the database" is represented by the clause:

$$\exists s'(LT(s,s') <== STAFF(n,s,d) \land STAFF(n,s',d))) \qquad (2.12)$$

Inclusion constraint.- This constraint refers to attribute relationships within the same relation or among different relations. The values (entries) of one attribute are contained within the other. For example, if we have the relation schemas EMP(nme,sal,dno) and DEPT(dno,mgr), and if mgr⊆nme (nme is the set of employee names), then we can define the clause:

$$\exists nme(EQ(mgr,nme) <== DEPT(dept,mgr) \land EMP(nme,sal,dept)) \qquad (2.13)$$

Negation constraint.- This type of IC insures the unexistence of some facts in the database. For example, the assertion 'every foreign student admitted to the "ee" department must be a graduate student' can be expressed by the following IC using a headless clause:

$$<== STUDENT(name,"undergraduate","ee","foreign") \qquad (2.14)$$

Each of the ICs discussed thus far controls a primary relation when the specified operations are performed on the relation. Table 1 provides a summary of IC specifications by numbering the ICs with respect to their types. The single letters d, i, r, m are used to identify the operations *delete, insert, retrieve,* and *modify* in that order.

TABLE 1

Constraint-id	Constraint-type	operations
IC1	restriction	i, m
IC2	join	d, i, m
IC3	projection	d, i, m, r
IC4	selection	d, i, m, r
IC5	proj-sel	d, i, m, r
IC6	type	i, m
IC7	domain	i, m
IC8	dependency	i, m
IC9	key	i, m
IC10	dynamic	m
IC11	inclusion	i, m
IC12	negation	i, m

We start with the premise that each relation in a database has its own set of ICs. The ICs in Table 1 are used to regulate the flow of tuples of a relation in one or two directions: upward direction, for retrievals, or downward direction, for updates (up/down taken in the sense of out/in). We implement Integrity Constraints (ICs) as filters, since every tuple of a primary relation (P) must be filtered for the IC predicate. For each tuple of P being examined, an IC filter performs any of the following actions depending on the truth value of the filter conditions: (a) releases the entire tuple, (b) suppresses the tuple, and (c) releases a subset of the attribute values of a tuple. In general, an IC may use input tuples from one or more relations, one of which must be a primary relation, and performs two actions, corresponding to the TRUE or FALSE conditions of the IC predicate.

3. General Clause Format for Filter operations

Selection and projection operations are usually the first operations executed during query evaluation. Moreover, these operations have the characteristics of a filter, since they subset the data horizontally and vertically. We will refer to them as selection filters (SF) and projection filters (PF). Selection filters perform the actions of type (a) and (b) indicated in Section 2. Projection filters perform the actions of type (c) unconditionally. These two filters are relations, formed with tuples selected from the relation on which they operate. A formal definition of these two filters are given below.

DEFINITION (3.1). Selection Filter.- Let X be a horizontal fragmentation of relation P. X is generated by applying a set of conditions C on P. Let F_p be a filter on P. F_p is a *selection filter* iff $X \Longrightarrow F_p$.

DEFINITION (3.2). Projection Filter.- Let Y be a vertical fragmentation of relation P. Let att(Y) and att(P) indicate the set of attributes in Y and P respectively. F_p is a *projection filter* on P iff $att(Y) \subset att(P)$ and $Y \Longrightarrow F_p$.

Basically, any IC filter is either a selection or a projection filter. Inter-relation constraints such as "referential integrity" need the implementation of joins. However, as will be seen in the filter formulation (3.1), the filter formalism represents the end result of join which is an inter-relation mapping (i.e., selection). This is represented by the presence of secondary relations in the filter formulation. A filter without the presence of secondary relations reduces to a simple selection on a primary relation.

Conceptually, a selection IC filter generates two actions, but since action type (b) does not produce any tuple, we define it as one action filter. A projection IC filter prevents the release of some attributes whenever a condition is true, and always unconditionally releases the remaining attributes. Although a projection filter produces two actions, our next notation will provide a general form of expressing this filter by only one action.

Let $FILTER_{P,i}(\hat{p}[\hat{\omega}])$ be the <u>ith</u> IC filter applied to a primary relation P, where $\hat{p}$ is a vector representing the set of attributes of relation P that will be released by the filter, and $\hat{\omega}$ is the vector of the projection conditions that affect each attribute of P. Let $SC_{P,i}$ (SC stands for Selection Conditions) be the set of conditions associated with $FILTER_{P,i}$ that control the access to a tuple of P. Let PC_k (PC stands for Projection Condition) be a set of conditions that control the access to attribute <u>k</u> of P. The set of condition predicates in $SC_{P,i}$ are mostly expressed as a conjunction of simple conditions. $SC_{P,i}$ and PC_k are expressions whose evaluations are either T(RUE) or F(ALSE). Any IC filter on a primary relation P can be written in the following canonical form:

$SC_{P,i}$: $(\Pi_{\{Q\}})\ [\ C_{\{P,Q\}}\ ]$ $\qquad\qquad\qquad\qquad$ PC_k: $(\Pi_{\{Q\}})\ [\ C_{\{P,Q\}}\ ]$

$$FILTER_{P,i}(\hat{p}[PC])<n> \Longleftarrow P(\hat{p}) \wedge Q_1(\hat{q}_1) \wedge \ldots \wedge Q_M(\hat{q}_M)$$
$$\wedge\ EQ(SC_{P,i}, T) \qquad\qquad (3.1)$$

where:
Π_Q is a sequence of quantifiers for the attributes in the secondary relations,
$C_{\{P,Q\}}$ contains several simple conditions using attributes of P and Q, logical connectors, and binary predicates,
<n> a hexadecimal digit that identifies the operations on which the IC can be enforced,
$\hat{p}$ is the vector of attributes of P, each affected by a PC,
$\hat{q}_j$ is the vector of attributes of the secondary relation Q_j,
Q_j is the jth secondary input relation, and $1 \leq j \leq M$ (M: number of Q relations),
$1 \leq i \leq N$ (N: number of ICs attached to relation P).

In (3.1), PC is set to zero (i.e., set to False), when the attribute must be released unconditionally. On the other hand, if PC is set to one (i.e., True), it indicates that the attribute must not be released under any condition. This means that the filter becomes only a selection filter when PC is zero for all attributes. The parameter $\underline{n}$ in expression (3.1) is a 4-bit mask whose bits correspond to an operation in the set {d, i, m, r}. For example, suppose that the operations "delete" and "modify" are the only operations that need to be enforced for a certain filter. Then the value of $\underline{n}$ will be "1010" in binary or "A" in hexadecimal. Note that the relation controlled by the filter is the first predicate on the right hand side of the filter clause.

3.1. Examples

Each IC Horn clause may involve one or more relations. Then, it is necessary to define a separate filter expression for each of these relations. For example, clause (2.3) needs two filter expressions, one for FATHER relation, and the other for MOTHER relation. During the execution of a query, the primary relation in the filter definition represents (a) the stored relation if the query is for retrieval, or (b) the update tuples (e.g., the new tuple(s) to be inserted) in the case of an update query. To clarify our notation, we provide in the following the examples of some of the IC clauses of Section 2, and selection and projection operations using the filter expression (3.1).

EXAMPLE 1. Selection operation: "Select all faculties whose salaries are greater than 50000".

$SC_{FAC,1}$: $GT(s, 50000)$
$FILTER_{FAC,1}(n[0], s[0], d[0])<1> \Longleftarrow FAC(n,s,d) \wedge EQ(SC_{FAC,1}, T)$

The hexadecimal number 1 (i.e., 0001) signifies a retrieval operation.
The subscript 1 identifies the first IC defined for relation FAC.

EXAMPLE 2. Domain IC filter: "Make sure that faculty names are valid names". This example corresponds to clause (2.8).

$SC_{FAC,2} : (\exists n')[EQ(n,n')]$
$FILTER_{FAC,2}(n[0],s[0],d[0])<6> <== FAC(n,s,d) \wedge NAMES(n') \wedge EQ(SC_{FAC,2},T)$

The hex. number 6 represents the operations allowed on this IC filter (Refer to Table 1).
The subscript 2 identifies the second IC defined for relation FAC.

EXAMPLE 3. Dynamic IC filter: "Any new salary for a STAFF member must be greater than the previous one stored in the database". This example corresponds to clause (2.12).

$SC_{STAFF,2} : (\exists n',s',d')[EQ(n,n') \wedge GE(s,s') \wedge EQ(d,d')]$
$FILTER_{STAFF,2}(n[0],s[0],d[0])<6> <== STAFF(n,s,d) \wedge STAFF(n',s',d')$
$\wedge EQ(SC_{STAFF,2},T)$

The hex. number 6 represents the operations allowed on this IC filter (Refer to Table 1).

EXAMPLE 4. Projection operation: "Project r2 from R(r1,r2,r3)".

$FILTER_{R,1}(r1[1],r2[0],r3[1])<1> <== R(r1,r2,r3)$

The hexadecimal number 1 (i.e., 0001) signifies a retrieval operation.

EXAMPLE 5. Projection IC filter: Clause (2.4). Prevent user "xxx" from modifying any s value in relation FAC.

$PC_s : (\exists u,obj,op)[EQ(u,"xxx") \wedge EQ(rel,FAC) \wedge EQ(obj,"s") \wedge EQ(op,"m")]$
$FILTER_{FAC,2}(n[0],s[PC],d[0])<F> <== FAC(n,s,d) \wedge P\_U(u,obj,op)$

The hex. number F represents the operations allowed on this IC filter (Refer to Table 1).

EXAMPLE 6. A filter with SC and PC.

This is the most general case of a filter. This general filter is known here as the Proj/Sel filter. Let us assume we are given the constraint: "Select tuples of R(r1,r2,r3) when r3>120, and project attribute r1 if the user is 'abc'".

$PC_{r2} : (\exists u,obj,op)[EQ(u,"abc") \wedge EQ(obj,"r1") \wedge EQ(op,"r")]$
$SC_{R,3} : GT(r3,120)$
$FILTER_{R,3}(r1[PC],r2[0],r3[0])<F> <== R(r1,r2,r3) \wedge P\_U(u,obj,op) \wedge EQ(SC_{R,3},T)$

The hex. number F represents the operations allowed on this IC filter (Refer to Table 1).

4. Filter Classification

Some IC filters are subtypes of selection and projection filters. We introduce these subtypes in the following definitions. From now on, we will use the letter F to represent any filter, F_P, instead of $FILTER_{P,i}$ to represent the ith IC filter for a primary database relation P.

Null Filter.- F_p is a *null filter* (NF) on relation P iff $\emptyset \Longrightarrow F_p$.

Trivial Filter.- F_p is a *trivial filter* (TF) on relation P iff $P \Longrightarrow F_p$.

Primary Filter.- F_p is a *primary filter* (MF) on relation P iff it is defined without secondary relations.

Looped Filter.- F_p is a *looped filter* (LF) on relation P iff it is defined with one or more secondary relations, such that for every tuple in P to be filtered out, one, more, or all the tuples of the secondary relations must be searched.

Intrarelation Filter.- F_p is a *intrarelation filter* (IR) in relation P, iff it is a looped filter, and P also appears as one of the secondary relations. As an example, if attribute p1 is the key of the relation P(p1,p2), then its key constraint would be represented by the following filter expression:

SC_p : ALL(p1') $\wedge$ NE(p1,p1')
F_p <== P(p1,p2) $\wedge$ P(p1',p2') $\wedge$ EQ(SC_p,T)

where the first reference to P corresponds to the tuple to be updated.

Figure 1 shows a more complete filter classification that combines all the above definitions. This figure illustrates four main classes of filters: Null (NF), Trivial (TF), Selection (SF), and Projection (PF) filters. Some of these filters are further decomposed into subclasses, and subclasses of subclasses, and so on. Each connecting edge between a class and subclass is labelled with a symbol, indicating a filter subtype. These symbols are: N (null), T (trivial), P (projection), S (selection), I (intrarelation), L (looped), and M (primary). The terminal nodes represent eleven different types of filters.

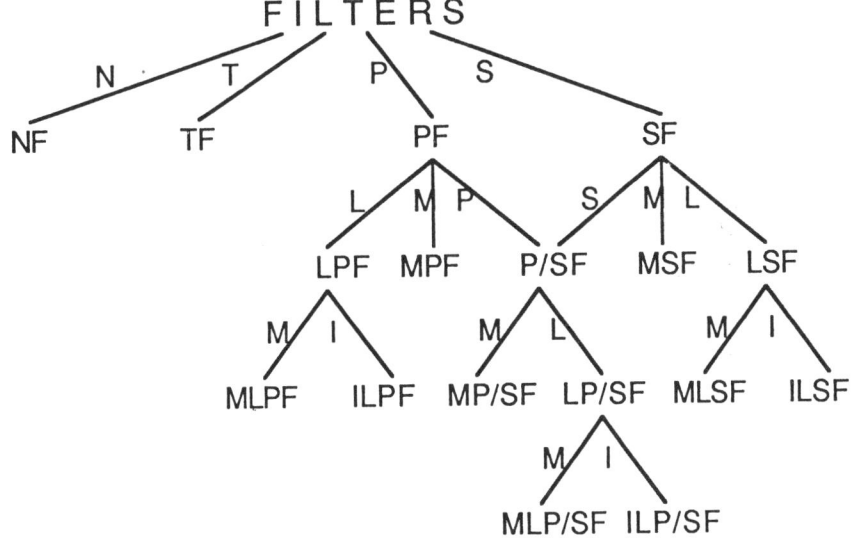

Figure 1. Filter Classification

For implementation purposes we need to reduce all the filters to either a selection filter or a projection filter. From Figure 1 we see that Proj/Sel filters must be decomposed into two complete and independent sets of filters. The following definition states the decomposition procedure.

DEFINITION (4.1). Let $F_{P,i}$ be a Proj/Sel filter for a relation P. This filter can be decomposed into a selection filter $F^s{}_{P,i}$ and a projection filter $F^P{}_{P,i}$, as follows:

$$SC_{P,i}: (\Pi_{\{Q\}}) [C_{\{P,Q\}}] \qquad\qquad PC_k: (\Pi_{\{Q\}}) [C_{\{P,Q\}}]$$

$$F^s{}_{P,i}(\hat{p}[\hat{o}])<n> <== P(\hat{p}) \wedge Q_1(\hat{q}_1) \wedge Q_2(\hat{q}_2) \wedge ... \wedge Q_q(\hat{q}_{qs}) \wedge EQ(SC_{P_i},T)$$

$$F^P{}_{P,i}(\hat{p}[PC])<n> <== P(\hat{p}) \wedge Q_{qs+1}(\hat{q}_{qs+1}) \wedge Q_{qs+2}(\hat{q}_{qs+2}) ... \wedge Q_M(\hat{q}_M)$$

where:
ô represents that each attribute of P has PC set to zero,
qs is the set of relevant Q relations for the selection filter,
the other parameters were defined in expression (3.1).

5. Filter and Projection Condition Representations

A selection condition (SC) or a projection condition (PC) is composed of several simple conditions $\underline{C}$, each of the form $\alpha\Theta\beta$, where α identifies an attribute of a primary relation. α could also be an attribute of a secondary relation or a database parameter stored in a register. The term β can be a constant (numeric or literal), an attribute of a primary relation, or an attribute of a secondary relation. The symbol Θ represents any of the binary comparators in the set $\{=, \neq, <, \leq, >, \geq\}$. Each condition $\underline{C}$ can be logically combined with another condition in SC (or PC) using logical connectors (NOT, AND, OR).

From this point on, we only use the term FC to refer to any SC or PC. A FC is represented as a binary condition tree, with several operative levels. Each level has at least one logical operation in it. From expression (3.1) an FC is in prenex form [BeB181] and written as $(\Pi_{\{Q\}})[C_{\{P,Q\}}]$. The first part of the expression consisting of quantifiers is called prefix, while the second part is called the matrix. The prefix is appended to the root of the condition tree. That is, it could be appended to a logical operator, or to a simple condition. The position of the quantifiers in the sequence determines the order in which they are used to simplify and/or evaluate the FC expression. That is, the quantifier closer to the root is evaluated or simplified first.

The condition tree has two types of nodes: (1) nonterminal nodes representing a logical connector or operator, and (2), terminal nodes representing simple conditions. Figure 2 shows a condition tree for the following FC expression, where P(p1,p2) is the primary relation, Q(m,s,t), R(n) are secondary relations, and a is a constant.

$$FC_p : (\forall R.n)(\exists Q.m, Q.s)[GE(P.p1,Q.m) \vee (LE(R.n,Q.s) \wedge GT(P.p2,a))]$$

6. Simplification and Evaluation of the Binary Condition Tree.

Usually, more than one IC filter is defined for each primary relation. Before we merge them, we discuss several strategies that simplify the expression of each FC. The simplification of an FC consists of finding an equivalent FC' expression such that if FC is true in old(D), then FC is also true in the new(D) iff the simplified FC' is true in the old(D). The old(D) and new(D) are the states of the database D, before and after the execution of the operation op. The new FC' tree is simplified by (1) possible existence of pairs of simple conditions where one of them is more restrictive than the other, (2) the information from the tuple to be inserted, deleted or modified; and (3) rearrangement of quantifiers (i.e., pushing them down the tree).

The objective is to find an FC', with one or more conditions, whose evaluation leads to a boolean value, making it easier to evaluate the entire FC and thus reducing access to the physical database storage. Several strategies have been presented in different papers [BeBl81, CMcS87, Koba84] that use syntactical transformations to reduce the evaluation complexity of an FC for any update operation. We assume simple updates, that is only a single tuple is used in an update operation. All these strategies make use of the fact that the database D is valid or consistent with FC in the current state. Therefore, it is not necessary to find Dop: new(D) in order to check if FC still holds in Dop. We need to check only if the incoming tuple satisfies FC or its equivalent, FC'.

6.1. Simplification of Restricted Condition Pairs.

An FC may have two conditions, where one is more restrictive than the other. Depending on the sequence pattern between these two conditions, the evaluation of the initial FC may always be False or True, regardless of the other conditions in FC. For example, let relation P(p1,p2) have an IC with conditions C_1: p1>5 and C_2: p1>3 among its set of conditions. C_1 is more restrictive than C_2 when $set(C_1) \subset set(C_2)$. The set(C) is the set of values of the attribute in C, satisfying this condition. From this

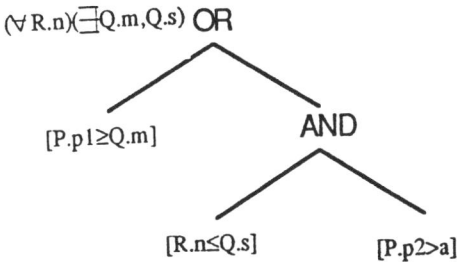

Figure 2. A Filter Condition (FC) tree

point on, we assume that the two conditions C_1 and C_2 belong to a particular FC, in which, C_1 is a more restrictive condition than C_2. Also, S represents the sequence of operations path between these two conditions.

When one or more restricted condition pairs (RCP) exist in an FC expression, then a reduction of FC is possible only if the sequence of operations between the conditions in a RCP is one of the two patterns: (1) "#+↓", or (2) ".↓#". The symbols "#", ".", "+", and "¬" represent any sequence of operations (or none), the operations AND, OR, and negation, respectively. The ↓ arrow indicates that the operation on its left is the operation of the subtree root common to both conditions of the RCP. The conditions C_1 and C_2 are at the left and right sides of any of these patterns. Each of the following FCs corresponds to one of the basic patterns. We also include the reduced FC expression and the operation sequence in the path between C_1 and C_2.

(1) " # + ↓ " pattern example: S: . ¬ + ↓   (# is " . ¬ ")
    FC_1: [¬(C_1 . C_x)] + C_2 FC'_1: TRUE

(2) " . ↓ # " pattern example: S: " . ↓ ¬ . + "   (# is " ¬ . + ")
    FC_2: C_1 . ¬[C_x . (C_2 + C_y)] FC'_2: C_1 . ¬(C_x)

Several other sequences of operations, besides the basic patterns, may enable the reduction of the initial FC. There exists a set of transformations, whenever applied to one of these sequences, will cause reduction to one of the basic patterns.

<u>Transformation 1.</u>- Any two operations that are both either a "+" or ".", and appear together in the sequence of operations S between C_1 and C_2, can be combined into one. The new sequence is equivalent to the initial sequence.

<u>Transformation 2.</u>- Any two negation operations that appear together in the sequence of operations S between C_1 and C_2 can be removed from S. The new sequence would be equivalent to the initial one.

<u>Transformation 3.</u>- Let S be the sequence of operations between C_1 and C_2. The following set of equivalent expressions can be used to reduce S into a S' sequence. As an example, the tree representation corresponding to step (c) is given in the following.

a) " . ¬ " ≡ " ¬ + "

b) " + ¬ " ≡ " ¬ . "

c) " . ↓ ¬ " ≡ " ¬ + ↓ "

d) " + ↓ ¬ " ≡ " ¬ . ↓ "

```
         AND                          NOT
         / \                           |
        C1  NOT        →              OR
            |                         / \
            C2                      NOT  C2
                                     |
                                     C1
```

case (c) of transformation 3.

LEMMA (6.1). Let C_1 and C_2 be two simple conditions included in an FC. Let C_1 be more restrictive than C_2. Then the following two definitions hold: (a) FALSE(C_2) → FALSE(C_1), and (b), TRUE(C_1) → TRUE(C_2)

The first expression says that if C_2 is FALSE (i.e., zero), then C_1 is also FALSE. Similarly, from the second expression we can deduce that C_2 is TRUE, only if C_1 is TRUE.

THEOREM (6.1). Let C_1 and C_2 be two simple conditions in a particular FC. Let C_1 be more restrictive than C_2. Then the two basic patterns " # + ↓ " and " . ↓ # " always lead to a reduction of the initial FC expression.

The sequence " . ¬ + ↓ ¬ + " is transformed into an equivalent sequence that results in a basic pattern. It is important to mention that these transformations are applied only in the direction toward the root of the tree, starting with the first operation of both extremes of a sequence.

" . ¬ + ↓ ¬ + " is transformed into:
" ¬ + + ↓ ¬ + # ", by transf. 3,
" ¬ + ↓ ¬ + # ", by transf. 1,
" . ↓ ¬ ¬ + # ", by transf. 3,
" . ↓ + # ", by transf. 2,
" . ↓ # ", by inserting "+" into #   (basic pattern).

We developed two algorithms for the two basic patterns (1) and (2) seen earlier. These algorithms have the objective of removing one of the conditions in the RCP, along with some other conditions of the FC subtree where C_1 and C_2 belong. Depending on the pattern found in the sequence of operations S, or by transformation of S, one of these algorithms is applicable to S. These algorithms are expressed in a pseudo-code. We assume that sequence S has been exposed to the transformation indicated above. Only the algorithm for pattern "#+↓" will be presented. The objective is to remove condition C_1 (note that we remove C_2 in the case of the pattern ".↓#") and some other conditions, depending on the operations in S. The algorithm for the other pattern can be written easily by modifying the following algorithm. The algorithm is as follows:

(1) PICK the first operation of S, and STORE it in *op*

(2) case *op*
    ".":   REMOVE the subtree whose root is *op*, SET *removed* = TRUE;
    "+":   REMOVE C_1 from the subtree whose root is *op*,
           SET *removed* = FALSE;
    "¬":   SET *op* = succ(*op*)   /*successor function*/
           IF *op* is "." THEN
               REMOVE ¬C_1, SET *removed* = FALSE;

                IF *op* is "+" THEN
                    REMOVE the subtree whose root is *op*,
                    SET *removed* = TRUE;
    (3) Set *flag* = TRUE

    (4) WHILE *removed*=TRUE and succ(*op*)="¬" or *op* is not the root
            SET *op* = succ(succ(*op*))
            IF *op* = "+" and *flag* = TRUE THEN
                REMOVE subtree whose root is *op*, SET *flag* = FALSE,
            ELSE IF *op* = "." and *flag* = FALSE THEN
                REMOVE subtree whose root is *op*, SET *flag* = TRUE,
            ELSE SET *removed* = FALSE;
        WEND;

    (5) IF entire tree is removed THEN SET *FC* = TRUE;

    (6) IF an operation (except "¬") has only one condition THEN
            PUSH up this condition to the next operation toward the root.

Let us for an example assume that the FC defined as $[\neg(C_1 \cdot C_x)] + C_2$. Then S is ".¬+↓". Using the algorithm, the execution of each step would be as follows:

(1) op = "."
(2) REMOVE ($C_1 \cdot C_x$). SET *removed* = TRUE.
(3) SET *flag* = TRUE.
(4) The while conditions are satisfied. Then SET op = "+". The conditions of the first IF are satisfied, therefore, the subtree whose root is "+" is removed. For this case, the whole tree is removed. Also, *flag* is set to FALSE.
(5) Because the whole FC tree is being removed, FC is set to TRUE. In other words, the FC is always true for any truth values of the conditions contained in FC. Therefore, the FC does not need to be evaluated.
(6) This step does not affect the value of the FC.

6.2. Identification of Irrelevant ICs

The identification of ICs that would be irrelevant for a given update avoids the evaluation of ICs that will not contribute to any integrity enforcement for the database. Therefore, it is important to identify the irrelevant ICs before any syntactical transformation is performed on the SC and/or PCs of an IC filter. The following four cases would identify irrelevant ICs during the update of a relation:

(1) The filter expression for an IC does not include the primary relation being updated.
(2) In a modification operation, neither the SC contains the attribute to be modified, nor the PC has a predicate on the attribute.

(3) In an insertion operation, the relation is quantified only by existential quantifiers.

(4) In a deletion operation, the relation is quantified only by universal quantifiers.

These four cases are presented in [CMcS87] as rules. The last two cases have been proven by Bernstein [BeBC80] and by Kobayashi [Koba84] using different approaches. An FC with aggregate predicates can also be tested to determine if it is irrelevant. For example, the IC with the FC expression: SUM(R.r1)≥500 can be removed from the set of IC filters when a tuple is inserted in relation R. Because old(D) |=FC, the sum of all entries for attribute r1 of R was already greater or equal to 500, and any new value for r1 (it must be positive) will not decrease the value for the aggregate function. Chan [CMcS87] has built a table to identify irrelevant aggregate expressions.

6.3. Simplification of the Condition Tree by Pushing down Quantifiers

The condition tree can be simplified by pushing down quantifiers, based on the following transformations:

(1) $(\forall P.\hat{p}')[C'_{\{P,Q\}}] \wedge (\forall P.\hat{p}'')[C''_{\{P,Q\}}] \equiv (\forall P.\hat{p}^*)[C'_{\{P,Q\}} \wedge C''_{\{P,Q\}}]$

(2) $(\exists P.\hat{p}^*)[C'_{\{P,Q\}} \vee C''_{\{P,Q\}}] \equiv (\exists P.\hat{p}')[C'_{\{P,Q\}}] \vee (\exists P.\hat{p}'')[C''_{\{P,Q\}}]$

(3) $(\Phi P.\hat{p}')[C'_{\{Q\}} \; op \; C''_{\{P,Q\}}] \equiv [C'_{\{Q\}}] \; op \; (\Phi P.\hat{p}')[C''_{\{P,Q\}}]$

where:

$\hat{p}'$, $\hat{p}''$, and $\hat{p}^*$ are the attribute vectors of P, and $\hat{p}^* = \hat{p}' \cup \hat{p}''$,

$C'_{\{P,Q\}}$, $C''_{\{P,Q\}}$, $C'_{\{Q\}}$ are the complex predicates that contain the primary and/or secondary relations,

op is one of the logical connector set {AND, OR},

Φ is an element of $\{ \forall, \exists \}$.

These transformations are the properties of predicate logic. Also, De Morgan's Law can be used to transform an original expression into another that corresponds to one of the above properties. For example, $(\exists P.\hat{p}^*)[\neg(C'_{\{P,Q\}} \wedge C''_{\{P,Q\}})]$ can be transformed to $(\exists P.\hat{p}^*)[(\neg C'_{\{P,Q\}}) \vee (\neg C''_{\{P,Q\}})]$. Finally, the last expression can be transformed to $(\exists P.\hat{p}')[\neg C'_{\{P,Q\}}] \vee (\exists P.\hat{p}'')[\neg C''_{\{P,Q\}}]$.

Figures 3.a-3.c show the simplification process carried out for the condition tree of Figure 2. The FC condition tree can be further simplified by using aggregate data, except in the case where a condition has the equal binary operator. Chan [CMcS87] has presented a table that allows to replace predicates called aggregate-substitutable by predicates with aggregate data. For example, Figure 3.d shows the final simplification condition tree using the substitution table.

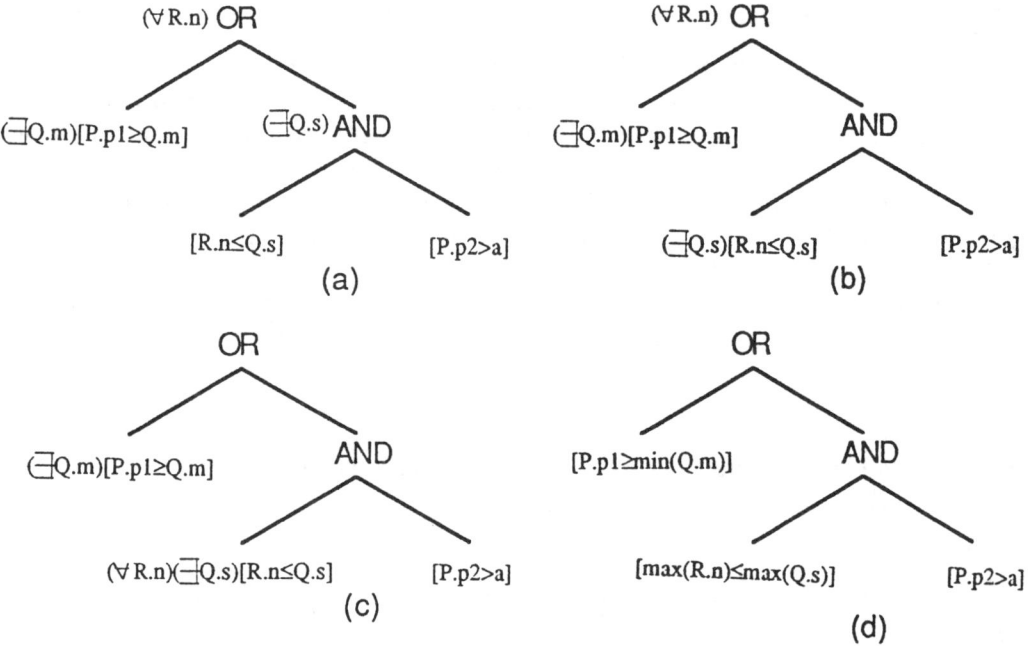

Figure 3. Simplification of an FC tree

7. Evaluation of Filters Associated with a Primary Relation

The simplification process discussed in the foregoing must be done before enforcement is performed. Furthermore, the transformations discussed in Section 7 can be done during database initialization, or when a new constraint is defined. Initially, the database manager defines the set of IC filters and keeps a separate group for each primary database relation. The following algorithm is executed during the initialization phase:

Step_1   Identify irrelevant ICs for insertion and deletion operations by looking at the FCs of the ICs. Update the parameter <n> in the filter expression, resetting the corresponding binary digit in n if the insertion or deletion operation does not need enforcement of this IC.

Step_2   Simplify each FC by identifying restricted condition pairs (RCPs).

Step_3   Simplify each FC by pushing down quantifiers and replacing some predicates with aggregate data.

During run-time access, some irrelevant filters might be detected in modification operations. That is, the attribute to be modified may not appear in the FC of an IC filter. Also, condition operands may be substituted with constants, such as the operands representing aggregate data. When all the ICs have been passed through the simplification mechanism, all the SCs for a primary relation must be "anded" together, leading to a global condition tree. Similarly, a global PC tree is built for each attribute of a primary relation. These global trees may include the selection and/or projection filters coming from the evaluation of a user query.

The evaluation of the global condition trees requires the maintenance of four aggregate data (i.e., for SUM, AVG., MAX, and MIN) for the attributes of each database relation. To avoid excessive access to physical database storage, we need to keep in a disk cache, the P-U relation, and several other relations that are projections of the stored relations (usually with one or two attributes) that are most frequently used in the SCs and PCs, particularly in conditions including the equal operator. We assume the existence of a disk cache large enough to store these projected relations. Relation P_U can be treated as a unary relation, by concatenating all the attributes into one. This is possible because all the attributes of P_U are of the alphanumeric type.

8. General Description of the Filter Processor

ICs and query filters require the evaluation of two main types of predicates expressed in SCs and PCs. The PC expressions are usually written in terms of the primary relations and the special relation P_U. Therefore, the filter processor (FP) needs two main subcomponents to evaluate them. They are the selection condition unit (SCU), and projection condition unit (PCU). The overall organization of the FP is shown in Figure 4, and described as follows:

(a) A RAM used as a disk cache, stores the secondary relations, including P_U. It is a multiport memory that enables parallel transmission of data to the SCU and

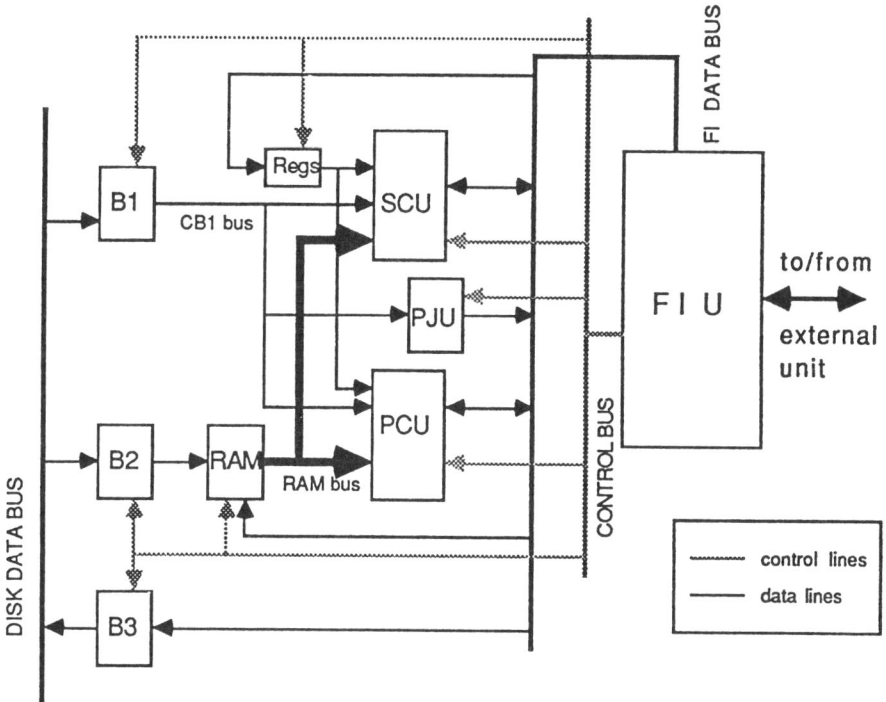

Figure 4. A general view of a Filter Processor

PCU circuits. Each relation is stored in one RAM module. Relations are assigned to modules such that space utilization is optimized. The relation information as to size, starting address, etc. is kept and maintained by the FIU. The disk cache is controlled by a special cache controller.

(b) A filter interface unit (FIU) that 1) controls the internal operation of the other FP components, 2) interfaces with an external device which sends/receives data to/from the FP, 3) decides whether the tuple or part of it must be released, 4) performs update or retrieval operations on the tuples not being filtered out, and 5) interfaces directly with disk devices (not shown in Figure 4). The FP can be seen as a powerful disk controller, where the FIU is implemented by a microprocessor.

(c) Buses consisting of data, address, and control buses. The control bus carries the control signal from the FIU to the components of the FP. The data buses consist of: 1) the external and bidirectional microprocessor FI bus that brings data to the SCU and PCU circuits, and receives data from the Projection Evaluator; 2) the bidirectional disk bus that allows flow of data from/to disks to/from other components; 3) one internal data bus for each RAM module, and 4) one internal data bus between the register bank and the SCU and PCU circuits. There are also other data lines (e.g., CB1 data bus) that are used to connect the disk buffers to other units. The address bus (not shown in Figure 4) is used to select the FP components.

(d) Data buffers that buffer data between disks and other units. B1 and B2 are data buffers which store data coming from the disk bus. The B3 buffer stores data sent to disks.

(e) A register bank called Regs which stores special data parameters that do not belong to the primary and secondary relations. Each register may be used as a condition argument. For example, the user identification and the operation being requested by the host are kept in two registers, before SCU and PCU are evaluated.

(f) A Projection unit (PJU) that performs the projection requested by the host. It eliminates duplicate tuples by use of a VLSI comparator array (VCA) [OzPe87].

9. The Architecture of the Filter and Projection Condition Units

The filter and projection condition units are composed of (a) an array of condition evaluator units (CEUs), (b) an array of logic evaluator units (LEUs), and (c) an array of registers which store the result of the LEU array. The CEUs evaluate the condition nodes, while the LEUs evaluate the operation nodes of the SC or PC binary tree. A description of these units is given in the next two subsections. The output of a CEU is the input of two LEUs. Also, the number of LEUs is one less than the number of CEUs. The connections among CEUs and LEUs are shown in Section 9.2 as part of an example of an FC tree evaluation.

9.1. Condition Evaluator Unit (CEU)

The evaluation of a simple condition in the FC binary tree is performed by a sequential circuit and controlled by a combinational logic. In order to evaluate each condition, the circuit is loaded with the information about the first operand, the type of the binary comparator used in the condition, the second operand, and additional control bits that indicate, among other things, whether the condition result must be negated (i.e., complemented). The types of conditions are: (1) $p_i \Theta c$, (2) $p_i \Theta p_j$, (3) $p_i \Theta q$, (4) $q \Theta c$, and (5) $r \Theta c$. The parameters p_i and p_j indicate two attributes of a primary relation, q is a secondary relation attribute, r is a register, c is a constant, and Θ is a binary comparator. The information for a condition (C) is stored in a *condition control word* and kept in the FIU.

Several registers inside each CEU buffer the data coming from the FIU, CB1, and RAM data buses. The loading of data in these registers is controlled internally by the CEU. The external control lines coming mainly from the FIU enter each CEU. Some of these control lines/signals are: (1) clock which synchronizes the operation of the CEUs, (2) start which is a broadcast signal coming from the FIU to indicate the start of the CEU evaluation, (3) load which indicates the time the data loading should begin in the CEU. This signal is propagated from a CEU to its neighbor. As soon as a CEU terminates the register loading, it sets the load line to high, (4) conn which indicates the connection of a CEU with its neighbor. The line is used for the evaluation of conditions controlled by a quantifier. A more complete description of the CEU is presented in [Pena88].

Each CEU is initially loaded with data coming from the condition registers of the FIU. Each CEU is evaluated when all the CEUs used in a query evaluation are loaded. This evaluation is performed in parallel as soon as the start signal goes to high. The CEU generates the match (MS) and end of evaluation (EOE) signals. CEU evaluation is terminated when EOE goes to high.

9.2. Logic Evaluator Unit (LEU)

Each LEU is a 1-bit processor that receives data input from 4 different sources, and generates 1-bit data output. The output depends on the operation executed by the processor, and it is propagated in three directions. Each LEU is connected to two CEUs and two LEU neighbors. Each LEU is a data-driven processor that communicates with these four units by means of control lines s_i, t_i, (for $1 \leq i \leq 6$). Figure 5.a shows the different inputs, outputs, and control lines for a LEU. Figure 5.b illustrates the different combinations of input values, along with the input code.

Control lines s_1 and s_2 correspond to the EOE signals generated from the left and right CEU connected to an LEU. Control lines t_1 or t_2 when high, issue a termination signal to the left and right CEU. of an LEU. The control lines t_3 or t_4 when high, indicate that any execution being performed on the left or right neighbor LEU must be terminated. The control lines t_5 or t_6 when high, indicate that the LEU is receiving a signal from either the left or right LEU neighbor, and must terminate execution. The

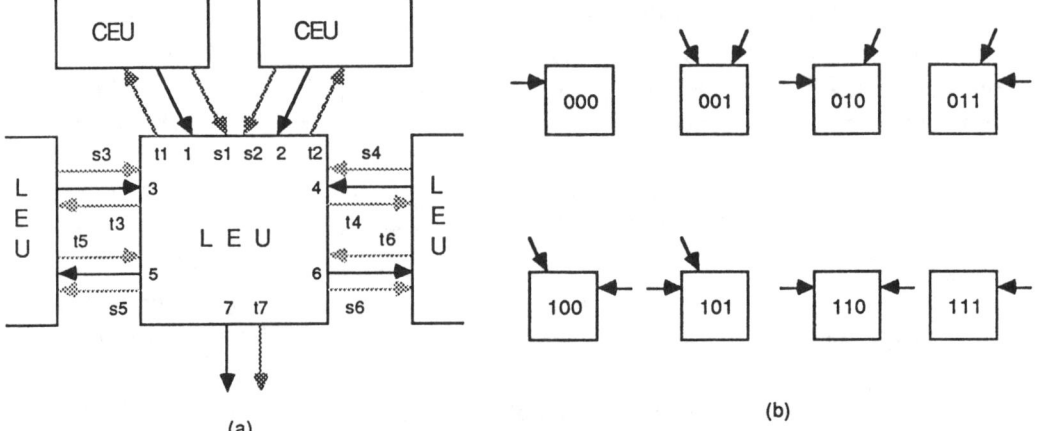

Figure 5. Different input/output combinations for a LEU

termination signal received by an LEU must be propagated to other units, and eventually may reach several CEUs. This set of termination signals is used to avoid unnecessary evaluation. There are two cases where evaluation of an LEU or CEU must be terminated:

(1) When one of the inputs to the LEU is false and a conjunction (i.e., "and") operation is evaluated by this processor.
(2) When one of the inputs to the LEU is true and a disjunction (i.e.. "or") operation is evaluated by this processor.

Control lines s_3 and s_4 indicate that the input is ready from the left and right LEU neighbor. Control lines s_5 and s_6 signal that the output is available to the left and right LEU neighbor. Finally, the additional control line s_7 indicates that output is available from the LEU to the outside register.

The operations the LEU may perform at a given time are given in Table 2. Another bit is needed to indicate whether the result of the operation must be negated. In total, 6 bits are used to control each LCU. The direction of the shift operation is represented by the negation bit. When high (i.e., one) the input 3 in the LEU will be transmitted to the right neighbor. Otherwise, the input 4 will be transmitted to the left neighbor. The shift operation is needed when the inputs for an operation in the tree are not available in a common LEU. All LEUs are executed asynchronously. Any LEU is executed as soon as the input values are available. A set of registers, eight bit wide, stores the results of all LEUs. Each register is addressable from the FIU.

The contents of the registers are transferred to the FIU. FIU will determine (by looking at the bit on which the result of the FC condition tree is indicated) if the evaluation of the FC from the FCU is true or false. In the case of the PCU, the registers' contents indicate the attributes that may be projected from a relation. The FIU will determine whether a projection issued by the user can be performed. We assume that the projection operation is rejected, if at least one attribute in the list of attributes to be projected cannot be accessed by a user.

TABLE 2		
symbol	code	description
-	00	processor does nothing
+	01	OR is performed
*	10	AND is performed
←	11	processor shifts input from one of its neighbors to the other

Figure 6 shows the evaluation of a condition tree. Only the data paths with no control lines are shown. Cx represents a condition with a quantifier. The shaded lines emanating from C1 in Figure 6.b represent a high impedance output. In this figure, the CEUs are labelled with the condition names taken from the tree. The binary tree must be transformed into a set of control bits that will determine the evaluation logic for the LEUs. The group of six bits for each LEU is shown in Figure 6.c. They are grouped in three sets called the input code, the operation code, and the negation bit (for complementing the processor output). The dash separating each group is used only for readability. A group of six zeroes represents an inactive LEU (e.g., LEU0).

The tree is evaluated logically in two phases, and the result will be available in LEU2. During the "first phase", LEU1 and LEU3 are evaluated while LEU2 is waiting for their completion. In "phase 2", LEU2 is the only active unit. It operates on the inputs coming from its neighbors and executes an "AND" followed by its complement.

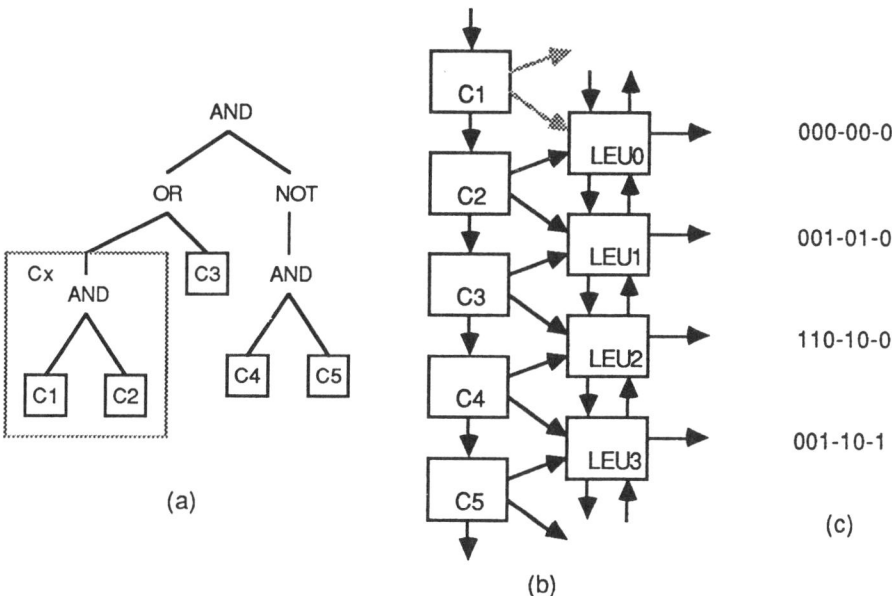

Figure 6. An example of a FC evaluation

To illustrate the use of the t signals let us suppose CEU3 completes evaluation before CEU2, and let EOE signal for CEU3 to be true (i.e., high). Since LEU1 will execute an "or", the result will be high no matter what value is returned by CEU2, therefore its execution terminates.

10. Conclusion

A carefully defined and cost effectively implemented filtering system for database operations inclusive of integrity constraints would improve system performance besides eliminating errors of software alternatives. A filtering formalism inclusive of its simplification is presented. An architecture is presented for implementation. Currently an extended performance study is under way to compare the proposed system with the software alternative of performing database operations and integrity enforcement.

REFERENCES

[BeBC80]   BERNSTEIN, P. A., BLAUSTEIN, B. T., AND CLARKE, E. M., "Fast Maintenance of Semantic Integrity Assertions using Redundant Aggregate Data", **Proc. of 6th Intl. Conf. on VLDB**, Montreal, Oct. 1980, pp. 126-136.

[BeBl81]   BERNSTEIN, P. A., AND BLAUSTEIN, B. T., "A simplification Algorithm for Integrity Assertions and Concrete Views", **Proc. of IEEE COMPSAC, Nov. 1981, pp. 90-99.**

[CMcS87]   CHAN, K. K., McDONELL, K. J., AND SRINIVASAN, B., "Performance Amelioration of Integrity Enforcement through Preprocessing", Technical Report No. 83, Monash University, 1987.

[Fagi82]   FAGIN, R., "Horn Clauses and Database Dependencies", **Journal of the ACM**, Vol. 29, No. 4, Oct. 1982, pp. 952-985.

[Koba84]   KOBAYASHI, I., "Validating Database Updates", **Information Systems**, Vol. 9, No. 1, 1984, Pergamon Press Ltd., pp. 1-17.

[OzPe87]   OZKARAHAN, E. A., AND PENALOZA, M. A., "On-the-Fly and Background Data Filtering System for Database Architectures", **New Generation Computing**, Vol. 5, No. 3, 1987, Springer-Verlag and Ohmsha Ltd.

[Pena88]   PENALOZA, M. A., "A Filter Architecture for the Evaluation of Integrity Constraints and Query Filters", **Technical Report** No. TR-88-022, Arizona State University, 1988.

[REIT84]   REITER, R., "Toward a Logical Reconstruction of Relational Database Theory", **Conceptual Modelling**, M. Brodie, J. Mylopoulos, and J. W. Schmidt, Eds. Springer-Verlag, Berling and New York, 1984.

MAIN MEMORY DATABASE RESEARCH DIRECTIONS *

MARGARET H. EICH

Department of Computer Science and Engineering
Southern Methodist University
Dallas, Texas 75275

ABSTRACT. The state of MMDB research with respect to some of the many unsolved problems is investigated. For MMDB systems to realize their full performance potential, the issues raised here must be addressed. We hope that this discussion will increase interest in main memory systems and stimulate future research activities.

1. INTRODUCTION

The study of *Main Memory Databases (MMDB)* has been ongoing for the past few years ([Ammann,1985], [DeWitt,1984], [Eich,1987a], [Garcia-Molina,1987a], [Gray,1983], [Hagmann,1986]). Several research projects have resulted in designs for MMDB systems: MARS ([Eich,1987b], [Eich,1988c]), MMM ([Garcia-Molina,1983], [Garcia-Molina,1984a]), MM-DBMS [Lehman,1986c], PRISMA [Kersten,1987]. At least two prototype systems have been built: SiDBM ([Leland,1985], [Leland,1987]) and MACH [Nakano,1987]. There are currently two commercially available MMDB systems: IMS/VS Fast Path [IBM,1978] and Office by Example (OBE) [Whang,1986]. The purpose of this paper is to investigate what we feel is the state of MMDB research with respect to some of the many unsolved problems associated with MMDB systems. For MMDB systems to realize their full performance potential the issues raised here must be addressed. We hope that this discussion will increase interest in main memory systems and spur more MMDB research activities.

In the following sections we first address the question as to what an MMDB system actually is. Next we explore several unsolved problems associated with architecture support, recovery, concurrency control, data structures, and query processing. We conclude the paper with our outlook for MMDB research and development in the future.

---

* This material is based in part upon work supported by the Texas Advanced Research Program (Advanced Technology Program) under Grant No. 2265 and by the National Science Foundation under Grant No. IRI-8713654.

2. MMDB DEFINITION

There exist at least four differing views as to what a Main Memory Database (MMDB) is:
1) All databases are stored in a semiconductor memory and thus require no I/O to access data. The main memory is large enough to hold all data.
2) Main memory is not necessarily large enough to store all data, but data is memory resident when accessed. The main memory copy is assumed to be the primary one.
3) Databases are permanently disk resident. Prior to executing a transaction, all required data is brought into memory. At transaction commit, any modified data must be downloaded to the disk.
4) Databases are permanently disk resident, but a large buffer or cache is assumed to exist in main memory. Through proper management of the buffer much of the I/O can be eliminated.

The first definition is perhaps the most extreme, while the last is the most liberal. Most recent MMDB research projects assume the first definition ([Eich,1987b], [Lehman,1986c], [Leland,1987], [Nakano,1987], [Salem,1986b]). IMS Fast Path and OBE employ the third one because of limited memory space and compatibility with existing DBMS software. The fourth view has attracted much research because performance gains can be realized simply due to the fact that fewer I/Os are required ([Copeland,1986], [Elhardt,1984], [Smith,1985]).

The definition of MMDB should not depend on the amount of I/O required to get to the data, but rather *where the database resides permanently*. Note that the first definition above requires no I/O to access the data. The last definition will also require no I/O in many cases. However, updates do require that the permanent database copy on disk be updated. The definition of MMDB should also not require any certain amount of main memory. It may be that a large cache system has more memory than a system of the second type. However, a database system of the second type assumes that the primary database copy is memory resident. Any data stored on secondary storage simply exists as a backup and need not necessarily be updated at transaction commit. It would be nice to assume that there is always enough memory to have all databases memory resident, however this is not realistic. So the first definition must (in large real life applications) be weakened to the second. We rule out the third and fourth definitions; these are not Main Memory Database systems. Instead, these are special cases of conventional database sytems where enough main memory exists to store all or major portions of active databases. In neither case is the main memory copy of the data viewed to be the "official" version of the database. In both cases, if the main memory contents are lost, they do not have to be recovered. This is the crucial issue: which version of the database must be recovered to a consistent state after a failure?

It is generally assumed that computer systems have a hierarchy of up to six memories [Baer,1980]. Following the notation discussed in Baer, this hierarchy applied to databases usually only includes the following four: cache (M_0), primary memory (M_1 or M_p), on-line storage (M_4), and off-line or archival (M_5). In conventional database systems the primary store is M_4, with M_5 used for recovery purposes, and M_0 and M_1 used only during processing.

In an MMDB system, the primary store is M_1, archival is M_4 and M_5, and M_0 is used only during processing. We therefore define a main memory database system as follows:

DEFINITION: A *Main Memory Database (MMDB)* is a database whose primary store is main memory, M_1.

What is important to the idea of MMDB is not the architecture used, but the perception of where data resides. Most of the problems associated with a conventional database system still exist with an MMDB system. However, conventional solutions to these problems may no longer apply or may be very poor solutions in the MMDB context.

Why is this definition of MMDB better than the four alternatives above? First of all, this definition does not make specific requirements on the available amount of main memory as with the first alternative nor does it predefine how/when the data is to be brought into main memory as does alternative three. A common complaint that we hear concerning MMDB systems is that they can never really be achieved because there will always be actual databases too large to fit into the available amount of main memory. This is a current reality which MMDB researchers must realize. Thus the MMDB definition must be able to handle the situation when main memory is not large enough to store all databases. With this assumption, MMDB systems must face the fact that at least some data has to be brought into M_1 from M_4. However, we don't feel that it is appropriate or advantageous for the MMDB definition to restrict when or how this occurs. This is a question of implementation and optimization. The second reason why our definition is better deals with actual implementation issues. Unless the database is viewed as primarily memory resident, transaction processing algorithms, data structures, optimization, recovery, and concurrency control issues will either function poorly or incorrectly. Techniques applicable for conventional databases are not usually the right ones for memory resident databases. Although our definition does not say anything about the size of main memory, unless it is large enough to store many databases and in fact at least large enough to store currently processed data (as in alternative 2) then it's use is questionable. Thus we assume an actual implementation of an MMDB must satisfy alternative two.

If there is not enough primary memory to store all databases, then what data should be memory resident? The *80/20 Rule* which indicates that a small amount of the database is accessed most of the time has become an accepted database principle [Bentley,1985]. This leads to the concept of a *hot set* or *hot spots* for a database ([Copeland,1986], [Gawlick,1985], [Sacco,1982]). The hot set is that small percentage of the database which is frequently accessed. Jim Gray has proposed *The Five Minute Rule*: "Pages referenced every five minutes should be memory resident" [Gray,1986]. If there is not enough main memory to store all data, then the Five Minute Rule says that at least the hot set should be memory resident.

Researchers frequently try to "justify" the use of MMDBs by discussing target applications ([Bitton,1986b], [Garcia-Molina,1984b]). As long as the current technologies for secondary storage devices and semiconductor memory remain the prevailing memory technologies, the need for MMDB sytems will exist. The well known *I/O bottleneck* associated with conventional database systems and DBMs will continue to be a problem. Similarly the availability of large cheap semiconductor main memories will increase. The questions should not be **WHY** use MMDB systems and what applications warrant them, but **WHY NOT** use MMDBs for all applications. The technology is available to dramatically increase database processing throughput, why not take advantage of it? It requires that database researchers and designers change their perception of databases. Why must we view databases as residing on secondary storage? Why must we continue to design database systems which require one I/O per database access? As pointed out by Hector Garcia-Molina, why is it relatively easy to spend hundreds of thousands of dollars on processing power but only a fraction of that on memory [Garcia-Molina,1984b]? Increased processing power does not necessarily improve database performance, but decreasing I/O certainly does. We must divorce ourselves from preconceived ideas of how databases function. To develop MMDB systems for the future, we must change how we think about databases.

3. ARCHITECTURAL SUPPORT

The purpose of this section is to investigate some of the architectural issues associated with MMDB systems. Figure 1 shows the MMDB model used in this paper. The MMDB is shown to be memory resident as is the DBMS and a log buffer. Due to the volatility of semiconductor memory, an *Archive Database* exists on secondary storage. The archive database is a complete image of some prior database state and is used solely for backing up main memory. Due to the volatility of main memory, all updates to main memory must be recorded on a *Log* located in some stable memory. Figure 1 shows the log on a secondary storage device, but it may actually exist in a nonvolatile main memory supported by a backup power supply, or in a combination of the two. During recovery processing, the log can be used to achieve UNDO and REDO processing and thus may contain *before Images (BFIM)* and/or *after images (AFIM)* of modified data. Together, the archive and log provide the ability to recover from a main memory failure.

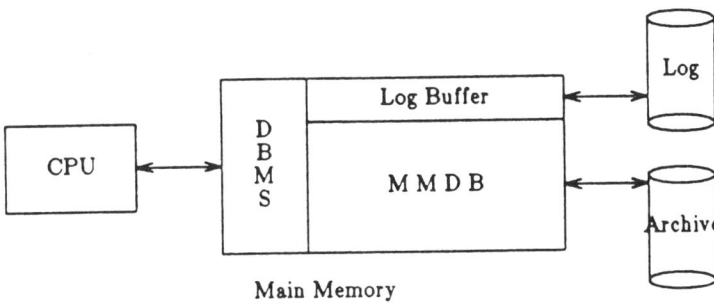

Fig. 1. - MMDB Model

3.1. Nonvolatile Main Memory

The availability of nonvolatile memory has been shown to be the one of the most important design decisions effecting transaction throughput in an MMDB system ([Eich,1987a], [Salem,1986b]). Transaction commit processing must guarantee that all database updates are placed in a nonvolatile memory. If all main memory is volatile, then a transaction can not commit until all updates have been placed on secondary storage. This I/O overhead directly effects the response time of the associated transaction. With enough nonvolatile memory to contain the log buffer, once log records have been written to the buffer in a nonvolatile memory then commit processing can complete.

A major problem associated with nonvolatile memory is how to implement it efficiently. There are several options available to realize a nonvolatile semiconductor memory [Eich,1988a]. A backup battery to conventional static RAM memories, *BBRAM (Battery Backup RAM)*, provides power in the case of problems with the AC input. There are several variations of the *Progammable Read Only Memory (PROM)*. These are the most used type of nonvolatile memory, but are not acceptable for an MMDB due to the fact that they cannot be updated as desired. The more versatile *EEPROMs (Electrically Erasable PROMs)* allow both erase and programming by the customer. However, there is a limit to the number of these operations which can be performed. To overcome some of the drawbacks of the EEPROM, the *NOVRAM (NOnVolatile RAM)* or *Shadow RAM* is becoming popular. A Shadow RAM consists of a static RAM and an EEPROM which completely duplicates the RAM. Most read/write cycles occur to the RAM, with data downloaded to the EEPROM if the power supply drops below some predefined threshold. We rule out Shadow RAM devices due to their limited size and probability that data could be lost because of the large transfer time from RAM to EEPROM. Unlike the PROM, the use of *bubble memories* would facilitate an unlimited number of reads and writes. When considering them for the MMDB environment one major problem is found: access time. The use of a *Universal Power Supply (UPS)* to provide power to an entire computer system provides an additional alternative to providing nonvolatile memory. The only currently viable alternatives for a nonvolatile memory in the MMDB environment are BBRAM and UPS.

Which of these approaches is the best? Neither is totally satisfactory. Due to the fact that UPS batteries must be recharged and that they provide only a short backup period, we feel that they have too great of a potential for failure. The limited size of BBRAM devices is not a major disadvantage since only the log buffer need be in nonvolatile memory. Likewise, the minimal increased access time has been shown to cause no performance problems [Eich,1988c]. Thus, based on the choices currently available, we feel that the BBRAM is the preferred option. However, the development of a reliable power supply which does not increase memory access time would be of great value to the development of MMDB systems.

3.2. Number of Processors

The use of nonvolatile memory eliminates the impact logging I/O has on transaction performance. An equally important architectural issue is the availability of separate logging/checkpointing processors ([Eich,1987a], [Salem,1986b]). The use of additional recovery processor(s) can reduce or eliminate the CPU overhead for logging. This can be of great importance when the CPU utilization is extremely high as in an MMDB system. A special HArdware LOgging (HALO) device has even been proposed [Garcia-Molina, 1983]. A potentially serious problem associated with the use of a recovery processor, however, is its lack of utilization. Recent simulation studies of the proposed MARS MMDB system have shown that a recovery processor devoted to checkpointing, logging, and recovery is consistently utilized at only 0%-2% [Eich,1988c]. This underutilization is due to the fact that the recovery processor performs mostly I/O operations and is continually requesting an I/O operation and then waiting for it to be completed. Future research must not only address the issue of number of processors, but also examine techniques to better balance the utilization of the processors. Even with adequate load balancing of two processors, it appears that the database processor would still be the bottleneck of the system. We are not convinced that this is a bad issue or even one that can be overcome if no database I/O is required. Future architectural design studies should be made to further examine the issues of number and distribution of processors.

3.3. Address Translation

An interesting problem which, to our knowledge, has not been investigated is that of address translation. At least two different approaches have been suggested ([Eich,1987b], [Lehman,1986c]), but both of these assume logical database addresses consist of levels of addresses (similar to the conventional segment/page/offset concept) and that traditional page tables are used to accomplish the translation to physical address. With this approach, address translation could become a bottleneck requiring more time than the database accesses. There are many questions to be examined to improve the translation process. Traditionally, a Translation Lookaside Buffer (TLB) or cache of recently used addresses is kept to speed up the translation process [Baer,1980]. These techniques work because of a high hit ratio caused by the strong locality of reference which exists within program execution. However, database programs do not always demonstrate any locality ([Effelsberg,1984], [Fernandez,1978],[Rodriques-Rosell,1976], [Stonebraker,1981]). We have to ask, then, will a cache or TLB really improve performance? What is the expected number of memory references required to perform an MMDB address translation? Much work is needed in this area.

3.4. Other Concerns

There are many other architectural issues which should be addressed to support MMDB systems. MMDB systems must not reside in a memory using a virtual memory scheme where the operating system has complete control over the paging techniques used. It has been shown that the use of a "long move" instruction can improve the performance of an MMDB system [Bitton,1987]. MMDB processing consists of many memory accesses, and copying of data between different memory locations. The ability to perform some of these instructions with "long" machine level instructions could improve performance and reduce address translation overhead. To also speed up database processing, the use of interleaved memories seems highly desirable.

Several other problems have been discussed by Garcia-Molina [Garcia-Molina,1987a]. Some paging mechanisms are not designed for large page tables, and spend too much time examining them. Because of excessive TLB faults, some programs may suffer performance degradation as the amount of main memory increases. Bus delays may eventually become a serious problem as memory sizes increase. Finally, current machines have a maximum physical address of 4 gigabytes assuming a 32 bit address. Certainly new processors or address techniques must be developed if larger MMDB systems are ever to be built.

4. MMDB RECOVERY ISSUES

The MMDB Recovery issues have been the most studied of all MMDB problems ([DeWitt,1984], [Eich,1986], [Eich,1987a], [Fan,1989], [Garcia-Molina,1983], [Hagmann,1986],

memory, they also are the most crucial to proper functioning in the MMDB system. In this section we confine ourselves to two recovery issues which we feel have not been adequately addressed: shadow memory and reloading.

4.1. Shadow Memory

The concept of shadow memory is not a new one ([Lorie,1977]). There are many advantages to the use of shadow memory for MMDBs: reduced log space, reduced MMDB accesses, faster reload processing, and reduced UNDO time [Eich,1988b]. Many of the concerns associated with the use of shadow memory in a conventional disk based system [Gray,1981], do not apply in the MMDB environment. We still must worry about how to address the shadow memory and determine whether the needed data is in the main memory or the shadow one. Another concern is the amount of space needed for the shadow memory. Gray has estimated 20% for System R shadow space [Gray,1981]. Salem has shown that shadow pages are too costly unless the shadow granules are small [Salem,1987a]. We envision much less space required for MMDB shadow memory because of the smaller size unit being shadowed and because of smart approaches which can be used for updating the MMDB (see below). A study based upon actual reference strings has indicated that the minimum cache size for the DB Cache is about 100 cache pages each of 200KB [Elhardt,1984]. A shadow memory containing only active dirty data with smaller shadow granules would be much less than this.

The following outlines how we propose handling updating of main memory and shadow memory in MARS to minimize the size of the shadow area. We assume that MM free space is indicated with special free space flags. Similar techniques would be used with a free space linked list:

Create:
    When creating a new relation, only the free space information which is changed needs to be updated in the shadow area. The actual data portion can be updated in main memory.

Insert:
    Update all information directly in main memory except for the free space flag. This flag value remains as is with the new data to be stored at that location updated in the shadow memory. The log, however, is updated with the complete AFIM. In the event of transaction failure, main memory remains in a valid state. With a successful transaction commit, only the new value to replace the flag need be changed.

Modify:
    The complete value to be changed must be updated in the shadow memory.

Delete:
    This is treated as a modify to the free space flag.

As can be seen, these approaches to updating can significantly reduce the space needed in the shadow memory.

4.2. Reload

Reloading is the process of restoring the MMDB from the archive and log. *Complete reloading* occurs when the MMDB is lost due to system failure caused by power outage, preventive maintenance, software errors, or hardware problems. We estimate that these types of failures will occur at the rate of about two per month [Gruenwald,1989]. *Partial reloading* is needed in the event of a main memory media failure or if the main memory is not large enough to store the complete database. There has been a lot of research into techniques for creating the data needed for recovery, but little into actual techniques for accomplishing the reloading. Even though a complete reload may occur infrequently, it is not an unimportant issue. Hagmann has examined the use of *fuzzy dumps* and *log compression* with estimates of recovering a one gigabyte database in 309 seconds [Hagmann,1986]. This seems to be a short time, but remember that this is added to the time the system is already down. Also, time has to be added to this to apply AFIMs from the log. In the 5 minutes to reload the entire database, at a transaction processing rate of 1000 trans/sec a backlog of 300,000 transactions has been created. The objective is not to load the data from the archive memory to main memory in the fastest possible manner. Rather, the objective is the best overall performance of the system as measured by response time and throughput. We break the problem of complete reload into the following: developing a priority scheme to reload based upon probably of use, determining how data on the archive memory should be stored, identifying the best length of time which the system can be down, and determining the optimum approach to apply log images needed to bring the system up to a consistent state [Gruenwald,1989]. We explore a few of these issues in the following paragraphs.

The reload process can be performed by prefetching entire databases before needed, prefetching needed pages, loading a database on demand, and loading pages as needed [Eich,1986]. Anticipatory I/O with conventional databases has been used [Smith,1978]. Its success depends on the database accesses being performed and the placement on disk. IMS/VS Fast Path [IBM,1978] and OBE [Ammann,1985] perform a demand loading for a database. The MM-DBMS reload technique assumes that after catalogs have been restored, the system is brought up, and reloading continues on a demand basis. If data is needed by a transaction, but is not memory resident, a demand load is performed [Lehman,1987b]. An abort of that transaction is then needed. Special reload transactions are created between regular transactions if time exists. We find the demand loading schemes to require too much overhead. The reload scheme must contain a demand piece since we can never successfully prefetch all data. However, if indeed hot spots in the database exist, reloading of these in a prefetch mode should reduce processing time of subsequent transactions. The concept of aborting a transaction if the needed data is not memory resident is totally unacceptable.

We propose a reload technique which uses both prefetch and demand loading. The lack of locality makes it difficult to predict what data will be needed first when reloading an MMDB after failure. Again we return to the hot set idea. We can use frequency of access to predict

is a high probability it will be referenced. We envision a reload priority based on the following:
1) Highest priority would be given to data which is actually needed immediately by transactions. These are the page faults created by executing transactions.
2) Next priority given to data needed by any transactions known to exist in the system. This would include transactions backlogged while the system is down and perhaps any executing when it went down.
3) Reload of any remaining pages of data would be performed based upon the access frequency priority.

Each of the lower level priority reloads can be preempted if any of the higher exist. The lowest level reload occurs in a background mode during transaction processing. The highest level is a page fault, while the middle level are prefetches of data as needed by waiting transactions. It is strongly possible that priorities may be modified based upon placement on the archive memory. For example, we may reload all data on any track with any data currently being loaded from it. Certainly this must be evaluated for its overall impact on throughput. We are only now beginning to define the concepts further [Gruenwald,1989].

A crucial issue with reloading is the technique used to bring the archive up to the most recent consistent state. This entails applying AFIMs from the log to the checkpoint found in the archive memory. The time required to apply these AFIM values depends on how often the archive memory is created and thus how much of the log must be read. With only creating a backup once a day, it has been estimated that simply reading the log would require about 24 minutes [Hagmann,1986]. Thus checkpoints or updates from the main memory to the archive memory must occur frequently. Based on the checkpointing technique used [Eich,1986], the archive may not even be in a transaction or action consistent state. After image values from the log must be applied to the correct locations to bring the database up to a consistent state. Most techniques proposed for this simply assume that the AFIM records for data must be applied in sequence to the reloaded data prior to first access. This puts a large burden on the recovery process, particularly if complete reloading is not performed at one time. Lehman has proposed a solution to this problem by maintaining log records at a partition level [Lehman,1987b]. Since the partition is also the unit of reload, when a partition is reloaded the log records can then be found and AFIMs applied. This process is time consuming since the log is still a sequential file and apparently all log records must be read to find those for the target partition. The use of a shadow memory seems, to us, to be an even better solution. During the reload process, the recovery processor reloads the needed AFIM values to the shadow memory [Eich,1987b]. This occurs in parallel to the database reload and all AFIM values must be applied to the shadow area before the database can be brought up. Once brought up, a special reload transaction is executed to apply the AFIM values to main memory. Note that this technique only requires that the log file be read once in sequence. Also, only the last AFIM value will finally be applied to the MMDB. This approach reduces the log processing and I/O overhead, but still does not require that the database be completely reload.

If main memory is not large enough to store the entire database we must be able to determine what subset should be reloaded. Certainly the same priority structure as defined above could be used. The subset to reload would then be based strictly on the available main memory space. Another approach would be to identify the hot set and to always have it memory resident. One technique to have the hot set memory resident is the *attribute-based buffering scheme* [Copeland,1986]. Based upon attribute frequency counts, these "hot" attributes are brought into the main memory buffer on demand. This kind of *vertical* locality has been recognized and accepted to occur in database systems and, many techniques for vertical partitioning have been proposed and justified ([Copeland,1986], [Cornell,1987], [Navathe,1984]). The use of vertical partitioning in the archive memory would for many applications require less I/O than a conventional horizontal storage structure. Thus, it appears likely that a storage organization based on vertical partitioning would allow the system to be brought up faster and ensure the execution of transactions sooner than conventional horizontal structures. We are currently investigating combining this technique with the concept of *disk striping* [Salem,1986a] to improve the overall MMDB system throughput. There are, however, two major problems associated with this approach: vertical partitioning may lead to greater fragmentation and thus more overall database pages, and there is time to reconstruct entire tuples from the partitioned attributes which increases the time to execute some types of database transactions. Overall system simulation experiments will be conducted to determine the best archive memory structure for overall system performance.

5. CONCURRENCY CONTROL

Since MMDB systems are aimed at high performance applications, techniques for facilitating the concurrent execution of transactions are warranted. Lehman has proposed the use of a two level hierarchical locking scheme [Lehman,1987a]. SiDBM and OBE use an optimistic approach ([Ammann,1985], [Leland,1985]). The PRISMA project assumes a two-phase locking technique [Kersten,1987]. Recently, an approach to MMDB concurrency control which relies on the use of extendible hashing has been proposed [Kumar,1988]. None of the published literature, however, justifies the choice of any of these techniques. We are aware of no systematic thorough investigation of the concurrency control problem in MMDB systems.

In a traditional disk resident database system, the cost to acquire a lock on a database entity is small compared to the overall retrieval cost. For a memory-resident database, however, the cost to acquire a lock and that to reference the entity are of the same order. Thus there is a question as to whether known concurrency control algorithms should be applied to main memory database systems [Salem,1986b]. We have recently conducted simulation experiments aimed at answering the question: Is concurrency control in an MMDB system needed? By examining the response time and throughput of both the MARS and MM-DBMS systems, we found that the serial execution of transactions consistently outperforms that when two-phase locking is used. The results are the same for both systems. We saw an improvement of about 5% in throughput without locking and a response time of almost 10 times higher with locking [Eich,1988c]. Similar results were obtained with different transaction mixes and different degrees of conflict. With all mixes, the response time without concurrency control was about 10 times better than the response time with concurrency control and 50% data sharing. The throughput without concurrency control was always better, but its superiority ranged from .8% to 19.6%.

These simulation experiments were based on the Wisconsin Benchmark transactions [Bitton,1983] which use relational algebra operations. Even though they included joins, there were no extremely long transactions which could cause a *Convoy Effect* problem. Several approaches have been suggested for avoiding the problems associated with these *long lived transactions* ([Garcia-Molina,1987b], [Salem,1987c], [Salem,1987d]). While these are approaches in the right direction, we feel that an investigation into more intelligent techniques are warranted. We are currently investigating the possibility of using several groups of concurrency control techniques. Transactions would be placed in a group based upon their processing requirements. Transactions would also be allowed to move between groups. Problems with approaches of this sort are the overhead. We must be able to prove the effectiveness of the approach.

6. DATA STRUCTURES

Data Structures used in conventional disk based database systems are usually designed to reduce the number of disk accesses. The idea is to quickly find the block where the data resides and to bring that block into main memory. Once brought into main memory, the entire block may need to be searched for the appropriate data. However, since the time to search the block in main memory is much less than the I/O time, this is no problem. Similar structures in MMDB systems may not be appropriate. Data structures used in main memory (such as AVL trees) typically contain smaller nodes with perhaps more levels in the tree than there are with secondary storage structures (such as B+ trees). In MMDB systems the objective is changed from reducing I/Os to efficient utilization of time and main memory space. Although transaction response time is crucial so is the memory utilization.

There has been much work in the area of MMDB data structures ([Ammann,1985], [DeWitt,1984], [Lehman,1986b]). SiDBM uses the AVL tree because of its fast search time [Leland,1985]. However, it has been found that B+ trees are preferable to AVL trees in MMDB systems due to the high percentage of the tree which must be memory resident for the tree to be competitive [DeWitt,1984]. The structure proposed by Ammann stores tuples as doubly linked lists [Ammann,1985]. An additional level of indirection is needed since the tuple scheme saves space if at least one third of the values are duplicates. However, the time to access the data and to reconstruct the tuples is greater. Lehman has proposed a new indexing structure, *T Tree*, designed specifically for use in MMDB systems [Lehman,1986b]. Basically, the T Tree is a binary tree with many elements in each node. Simulation experiments have shown that for unordered data a modified version of Linear Hashing was the best choice, while for ordered data the T Tree was best. These results were based upon time not memory utilization using index type operations rather than more general database operations. The question of what is to be optimized is thus raised. Unlike conventional systems where the number of I/Os is the crucial data structure issue, in MMDB systems we can't say whether space or time is the crucial issue.

While these results are interesting, much work remains. What is needed is a complete reevaluation of the objectives and techniques available for MMDB systems. Structures used in secondary storage databases are not necessarily advantageous. However, structures typically used for data structures internal to programs may not be the answer either because they are usually aimed at small amounts of data. Similarly we can not evaluate MMDB data structures by examining the indexing techniques separately. We must evaluate the entire main memory storage technique including placement of data within pages and even the address translation method. The address translation is itself a type of directory. Thus we have to contend with several levels of directories. The overall impact of these must be investigated. Since techniques for query processing also need to be reexamined, different structures for different processing techniques may be needed. This coordinated approach to examining data structures has been used in the design of the MACH machine [Nakano,1987]. The results are a complete encoding of all data. While this drastically reduces space requirements, it also increases the time. We are not endorsing the encoding structure used in the MACH design, but simply the technique of reevaluating and rethinking all aspects associated with data storage.

There are several additional concerns which need to be addressed with respect to MMDB data structures. Should pointers be physical addresses or logical addresses? Should data be pinned? The use of physical addresses would eliminate the extra level of addressing. Since reorganizing MMDB data does not have the benefits that it does with conventional databases, pinning may not be a problem. However, to take advantage of this would require special machine instructions using physical versus logical addresses. A compromise to the physical pinning is a type of "logical pinning". As has been proposed, data once stored at a logical address will not move ([Eich,1987b], [Lehman,1986c]). We do envision the use of pointers or links as techniques to handle variable length fields and joins [Lehman,1986c].

7. QUERY PROCESSING CONCERNS

Typical database processing algorithms are aimed at reducing the number of disk I/Os needed. As with data structures, this objective is not valid with MMDB systems. Fast algorithms which create large intermediate results may cause space problems in an MMDB system [Bitton,1986b]. Many people have examined techniques to perform relational database operations in the MMDB context ([DeWitt,1984], [Lehman,1986a], [Leland,1986], [Shapiro,1986]). Results indicate that hash join algorithms should perform well in most cases. Benchmarks of the OBE system, demonstrated the effectiveness of the pipelined join strategy [Bitton,1987]. Hashing has also been shown to be the technique of choice for duplicate elimination ([Bitton,1987], [Lehman,1986a]). Much remains in the area of algorithms, but a solid foundation has been made. In this section we concentrate on other query processing issues: temporary relations and optimization.

Typically, processing of relational query operations results in the creation of temporary relations. A major issue to be solved is the best approach to manage these temporary relations in an MMDB context. It has been proposed that instead of actually creating tuples, pointers to the source relations be created [Lehman,1986b]. The use of pointers for temporary relations in OBE has been evaluated and shown to be valid [Bitton,1987]. This saves space, but creates more overhead. This idea works well when selects or even joins are used to create the relations. What happens with temporary relations created by a series of more complex operations? We feel that a combination of the pointer approach and a more conventional approach seems warranted particularly if the temporary relation may become permanent. A related topic is that of using algorithms which avoid the creation of large intermediate relations. The pipelined join algorithm used in OBE avoids the creation of temporary relations [Bitton,1987].

How should query optimization in the MMDB context be performed? We identify two types of optimization:
1) *Query Optimization* - Determining the "best" processing strategy for a transaction.
2) *DBMS Optimization* - Optimizing the DBMS code itself to produce more efficient processing of the transactions.

With the first type of optimization, conventional disk based systems usually strive to reduce the number of disk I/Os required. With MMDB systems, the issue is much more complex. The objective of query optimization should not be reduction of I/Os (or equivalently memory references), but fast response times with reduction of memory space needed for temporary relations. With simple transactions the time spent performing query optimization could dominate the response time. Query optimization should only be performed with long running transactions. Recent simulation experiments pointed out that in many cases, the largest portion of CPU time for transactions was spent performing DBMS overhead activities such as preprocessing, commit processing, and concurrency control [Eich,1988c]. This points out the importance of performing DBMS optimization. This is crucial because this overhead applies

performance in an MMDB system than is query optimization.

8. CONCLUSIONS AND FUTURE DIRECTIONS

There are many unsolved problems in the MMDB area. While an MMDB system could be implemented without solving these problems, if the full potential for performance is to be achieved the issues discussed in this paper must be solved. We have examined only a few of these issues. Certainly there are many more which we were unable to include in this paper. A question of current interest to us is the impact of different data models on MMDB systems. For example, do they lend themselves better to object oriented database (OODB) systems rather than relational? Certainly many existing OODB systems load the entire database into memory prior to processing. Applications such as VLSI design and CAD/CAM usually require memory resident data.

We conclude by commenting on what we see is actually happening in the overall directions for database research. The recent interest in OODB research has forced database researchers into considering not only unformatted data but to also begin looking at procedures as data. Similarly, the concepts of abstract data type, monitors, and object oriented programming have forced the software engineering community to begin considering procedures and data together. The overall direction is heading towards a uniform view of data and process throughout all computer science areas. The differences between operating systems and databases become somewhat blurred when databases are memory resident. Thus we are witnessing the beginning of the coalescence of many different computer science disciplines. As database researchers we must be knowledgeable in the other disciplines if we are to take advantage of results previously derived in those areas and apply them to the needs of database sytems. This is particularly true in MMDB research.

9. REFERENCES

[Ammann,1985] Arthur C. Ammann, Maria Butrico Hanrahan, and Ravi Krishnamurthy, "Design of a Memory Resident DBMS," *Proceedings of the IEEE Spring Computer Conference,* 1985, pp. 54-57.

[Baer,1980] Jean-Loup Baer, *Computer Systems Architecture,* Computer Science Press, 1980.

[Bentley,1985] John Bentley, "Tricks of the Trade," *Communications of the ACM,* Vol. 28, No. 2, February 1985, pp. 138-141.

[Bitton,1983] Dina Bitton, David J. DeWitt, Carolyn Turbyfill, "Benchmarking Database Systems A Systematic Approach," University of Wisconsin-Madison Technical Report, December 1983.

[Bitton,1986b] Dina Bitton, "The Effect of Large Main Memory on Database Systems," *Proceedings of the ACM International Conference on Management of Data,* May 1986, pp. 337-339.

[Bitton,1987] Dina Bitton, Maria Butrico Hanrahan, and Carolyn Turbyfill, "Performance of Complex Queries in Main Memory Database Systems," *Proceedings of the IEEE Conference on Data Engineering,* February 1987.

[Copeland,1986] George P. Copeland, Setrag N. Khoshafian, Marc G. Smith, and Patrick Valduriez, "Buffering Schemes for Permanent Data," *Proceedings of the IEEE Data Engineering Conference*, 1986, pp. 214-221.

[Cornell,1987] D. Cornell and P. Yu, "A Vertical Partitioning Algorithm for Relational databases," *Proceedings of the IEEE Data Engineering Conference*, 1987, pp. 30-35.

[DeWitt,1984] David J. DeWitt, Randy H. Katz, Frank Olken, Leonard D. Shapiro, Michael R. Stonebraker, and David Wood, "Implementation Techniques for Main Memory Database Systems," *Proceedings of the 1984 SIGMOD Conference*, June 1984, pp. 1-8.

[Effelsberg,1984] Wolfgang Effelsberg and Mary E.S. Loomis, "Logical, Internal, and Physical Reference Behavior in CODASYL Database Systems," *ACM Transactions on Database Systems*, Vol. 9, No. 2, June 1984, pp. 187-213.

[Eich,1986] Margaret H. Eich, "Main Memory Database Recovery", *Proceedings of the 1986 ACM-IEEE Fall Joint Computer Conference*, November 2-6, 1986, pp. 1226-1232.

[Eich,1987a] Margaret H. Eich, "A Classification and Comparison of Main Memory Database Recovery Techniques," *Proceedings of the 1987 IEEE Database Engineering Conference*. (Earlier version available as SMU TR 86-CSE-15).

[Eich,1987b] Margaret H. Eich, "MARS: The Design of a Main Memory Database Machine," *Database Machines and Knowledge Base Machines*. Kluwer Academic Publishers, 1988, pp. 325-338.

[Eich,1988a] Margaret H. Eich and Wei-Li Sun, "Nonvolatile Main Memory: An Overview of Alternatives," Southern Methodist University Department of Computer Science Technical Report 88-CSE-6, January 1988.

[Eich,1988b] Margaret H. Eich, "MARS Shadow Memory: A Good Idea," Southern Methodist University Department of Computer Science Technical Report 88-CSE-7. February 1988.

[Eich,1988c] Margaret H. Eich, Chris Corti, Le Gruenwald, and Francisco Mariategui, "Main Memory Recoverable Database with Stable Log," August 1988, submitted to *IEEE Transactions on Knowledge and Data Engineering*.

[Elhardt,1984] Klaus Elhardt and Rudolf Bayer, "A Database Cache for High Performance and Fast Restart in Database Systems," *ACM Transactions on Database Systems*, Vol. 9, No. 4, December 1984, pp. 503-525.

[Fan,1989] Chinfeng Fan and Margaret H. Eich, "Performance Analysis of MARS Logging, Checkpointing, and Recovery," to appear in the *Proceedings of the Hawaii International Conference on System Sciences*, January 1989.

[Fernandez,1978] E. B. Fernandez, T. Lang, and C. Wood, "Effect of Replacement Algorithms on a Paged Buffer Database System," *IBM Journal of Research and Development*, Vol. 22, No. 2, March 1978, pp. 185-196.

[Garcia-Molina,1983] Hector Garcia-Molina, Richard J. Lipton, and Peter Honeyman, "A Massive Memory Database System," Princeton University Department of Electrical Engineering and Computer Science Technical Report, September 1983.

[Garcia-Molina,1984a] Hector Garcia-Molina, Richard J. Lipton, and Jacobo Valdes, "A Massive Memory Machine," *IEEE Transactions on Computers*, Vol. C-33, No. 5, May 1984, pp. 391-399.

[Garcia-Molina,1984b] Hector Garcia-Molina, Richard Cullingford, Peter Honeyman, and Richard Lipton, "The Case for Massive Memory," Princeton University Department of Electrical Engineering and Computer Science Technical Report 326, May 1984.

[Garcia-Molina,1987a] Hector Garcia-Molina, Arvin Park, and Lawrence R. Rogers, "Performance Through Memory," *Proceedings of the 1987 ACM SIGMETRICS Conference on Measurement and Modeling of Computer Systems*, May 1987, pp. 122-131.

[Garcia-Molina,1987b] Hector Garcia-Molina and Kenneth Salem, "SAGAS," *Proceedings of the ACM-SIGMOD International Conference on Management of Data*, May 1987.

[Gawlick,1985] Dieter Gawlick, "Processing 'Hot Spots' in High Performance Systems," *Proceedings of the IEEE Spring Computer Conference*,, 1985, pp.249-251.

[Gray,1981] Jim Gray, Paul McJones, Mike Blasgen, Bruce Lindsay, Raymond Lorie, Tom Price, Franco Putzolu, and Irving Traiger, "The Recovery Manager of the System R Database Manager," *Computing Surveys*, Vol. 13, No. 2, June 1981, pp.223-242.

[Gray,1983] Jim Gray, "Practical Problems in Data Management - A Position Paper," *Proceedings of the AMC-SIGMOD International Conference on Management of Data*, 1983, p. 3.

[Gray,1986] Jim Gray and Franco Putzolu, "The 5 Minute Rule for Trading Memory for Disc Accesses and the 5 Byte Rule for Trading Memory for CPU Time," Tandem Computers Technical Report 86.1, February 1986.

[Gruenwald,1989] "Recovery in the MARS Environment,", PhD Dissertation in preparation, SMU Department of Computer Science and Engineering, 1989.

[Hagmann,1986] Robert B. Hagmann, "A Crash Recovery Scheme for a Memory-Resident Database System," *IEEE Transactions on Computers*, Vol. C-35, No. 9, September 1986, pp.839-843.

[IBM,1978] IBM, *IMS/VS Version 1 Fast Path Feature General Information Manual*, GH20-9069-2, April 1978.

[Kersten,1987] Martin L. Kersten, Peter M.G. Apers, Maurice A.W. Houtsma, Erik J.A. van Kuyk, and Rob L.W. van de Weg, "A Distributed, Main-Memory Database Machine: Research Issues and a Preliminary Architecture," *Proceedings of the 5th International Workshop on Database Machines*, October 1987, pp. 496-511.

[Kumar,1988] Vijay Kumar, "A Concurrency Control Mechanism Based on Extendible Hashing for Main Memory Database Systems," University of Missouri-Kansas City Computer Science Technical Report, 1988.

[Lehman,1986a] Tobin J. Lehman and Michael J. Carey, "Query Processing in Main Memory Database Management Systems," *Proceedings of the ACM-SIGMOD International Conference on Management of Data*, May 1986, pp. 239-250.

[Lehman,1986b] Tobin J. Lehman and Michael J. Carey, "A Study of Index Structures for Main Memory Database Management Systems," *Proceedings of the International Conference on Very Large Data Bases*, 1986.

[Lehman,1986c] Tobin Jon Lehman, *Design and Performance Evaluation of a Main Memory Relational Database System*, PhD Dissertation University of Wisconsin-Madison, August 1986.

[Lehman,1987a] Tobin J. Lehman and Michael J. Carey, "Concurrency Control in Memory-Resident Database Systems," University of Wisconsin-Madison Computer Sciences Department Technical Report, February 1987.

[Lehman,1987b] Tobin J. Lehman and Michael J. Carey, "A Recovery Algorithm for a High-Performance Memory-Resident Database System," *Proceedings of the ACM-SIGMOD International Conference on Management of Data*, May 1987.

[Leland,1985] M.D.P. Leland and W.D. Roome, "The Silicon Database Machine," *Database Machines Fourth International Workshop*, Springer-Verlag, 1985, pp.169-189.

[Leland,1986] Mary Diane Palmer Leland, "Query Processing on the Silicon Database Machine," *Proceedings of the IEEE International Conference on Computer Design*, 1986, pp. 214-217.

[Leland,1987] Mary Diane Palmer Leland and William D. Roome, "The Silicon Database Machine: Rationale, Design, and Results,"
Proceedings of the 5th International Workshop on Database Machines, October 1987, pp. 454-467.

[Lorie,1977] Raymond A. Lorie, "Physical Integrity in a Large Segmented Database," *ACM Transactions on Database System*, Vol. 2, No. 1, March 1977, pp. 91-104.

[Nakano,1987] Ryohei Nakano and Minoru Kiyama, "MACH: Much Faster Associative Machine,"
Proceedings of the 5th International Workshop on Database Machines, October 1987, pp. 482-495.

[Navathe,1984] S. Navathe, S. Ceri, G. Wiederhold, and Y. Don, "Vertical Partitioning Algorithms for Database Design," *ACM Transactions on Database Systems*, Vol. 9, No. 4, December 1984, pp. 680-710

[Rodriques-Rosell,1976] Juan Rodriquez-Rosell, "Empirical Data Reference Behavior in Data Base Systems," *Computer*, November 1976, pp. 9-13.

[Sacco,1982] Giovanni Mario Sacco and Mario Schkolnick, "A Mechanism For Managing the Buffer Pool In A Relational Database System Using the Hot Set Model," *Proceedings of the 8th International Conference on Very Large Data Bases*, Mexico City, September 1982, pp. 257-262.

[Salem,1986a] Kenneth Salem and Hector Garcia-Molina, "Disk Striping," *Proceedings of the IEEE Data Engineering Conference*, 1986, pp. 336-342.

[Salem,1986b] Kenneth Salem and Hector Garcia-Molina, "Crash Recovery Mechanisms for Main Storage Database Systems," Princeton University Department of Computer Science technical report CS-TR-034-86, April 1986.

[Salem,1987a] Kenneth Salem and Hector Garcia-Molina, "Crash Recovery for Memory-Resident Databases," Princeton University Department of Computer Science Technical Report CS-TR-119-87, November 1987.

[Salem,1987b] Kenneth Salem and Hector Garcia-Molina, "Checkpointing Memory-Resident Databases," Princeton University Department of Computer Science Technical Report CS-TR-126-87, December 1987.

[Salem,1987c] Kenneth Salem and Hector Garcia-Molina, "The Correctness of Two Locking Protocols for Long-Lived Transactions," Department of Computer Science Princeton University Technical Report, July 1987.

[Salem,1987d] Kenneth Salem, Hector Garcia-Molina, and Rafael Alonso, "Altruistic Locking: A Strategy for Coping with Long Lived Transactions," *Proceedings of the International Workshop on High Performance Transaction Systems,* September 1987.

[Shapiro,1986] Leonard D. Shapiro, "Join Processing in Database Systems with Large Main Memories," *ACM Transactions on Database Systems,* Vol. 11, No. 3, September 1986, pp. 239-264.

[Smith,1978] Alan Jay Smith, "Sequentiality and Prefetching in Database Systems", *ACM Transactions on Database Systems,* Vol. 3, Vol. 3, September 1978, pp. 223-247.

[Smith,1985] Alan Jay Smith, "Disk Cache - Miss Ratio Analysis and Design Considerations," *ACM Transactions on Computer Systems,* Vol. 3, No. 3, August 1985, pp. 161-203.

[Stonebraker,1981] Michael Stonebraker, "Operating System Support for Database Management," *Communications of the ACM,* Vol. 24, No. 7, 1981, pp. 412-418.

[Whang,1986] K. Whang, A. Ammann, T. Bolmarcich, et al., "Office-By-Example, An Integrated Office System and Database Manager," IBM T.J. Watson Research Center Report RC 11966, June 1986.

RECOVERY ALGORITHMS FOR DATABASE MACHINES WITH NON-VOLATILE MAIN MEMORY

Rakesh Agrawal
H. V. Jagadish

AT&T Bell Laboratories
Murray Hill, New Jersey 07974

ABSTRACT

We consider a hypothetical database machine in which the main memory is non-volatile, and present recovery algorithms for such a machine. These algorithms are considerably simpler and more efficient than classical recovery algorithms.

1. INTRODUCTION

We consider a hypothetical database machine whose main memory is *non-volatile*, and study its implications for the recovery subsystem, since that is the aspect of database systems most impacted by the volatility of today's memory systems. We emphasize that we are assuming that the *whole* main memory is non-volatile, in contrast with some of the earlier studies [1,7,18] that stressed the desirability of some non-volatile random-access memory in addition to the volatile main memory. However, we do not assume that the whole database can fit in main memory, and assume that it has been stored on disks.

The immediate impetus for this work is the recent introduction of Ferroelectric Random Access Memories (FRAMs) [4,5,13] that show promise of becoming a DRAM replacement in the not too distant future. FRAMs appear to solve at least the first two of the following problems with EEPROMs, the current hallmark of non-volatile random access memories:

  i. It takes several orders of magnitude longer to erase and write EEPROMs compared to DRAMs.
  ii. The circuitry in an EEPROM cell is complex making it impossible to achieve the density, and hence the low cost, of DRAMs.
  iii. The contents of an EEPROM cell can only be written a limited number of times before wear-out begins to cause loss of data.

There are indications that FRAMs are headed in the direction of ameliorating the third problem as well.

Even if FRAMs do not live up to their promise, and even if the historical trends in ROM technology fail to produce alternatives with similar or better characteristics, there is still the possibility of using Uninterruptible Power Supplies (UPS). The case for UPSs has been eloquently made in [7]. Battery backup today costs roughly one dollar for every megabyte-hour. With a less than 1% cost overhead, the contents of memory can be made to survive a 2 hour power failure. The commercial use of battery backup in high-end systems corroborates this analysis.

We do not argue in this paper the feasibility or economics of non-volatile main memory. Instead, we take non-volatile main memory as given, and develop recovery algorithms applicable to a database machine endowed with non-volatile main memory. We assume that two-phase locking [10] is being used for concurrency control, as it is currently regarded to be the concurrency control algorithm of choice [3]. We only consider recovery from transaction and system failures, and assume that mirroring [10], for example, is used to recover from media failures.

In Section 2, we review the fundamental recovery principles that provide the basis for developing non-volatile main memory recovery algorithms in Section 3. In Section 3, we first present an algorithm that is applicable only if page-level locking is used, and then present a different algorithm that is applicable even if tuple-level locking is employed. The best features of the two algorithms are then combined into a hybrid algorithm. Finally, we present an algorithm that is appropriate if the past states of a database must be preserved. In Section 4, we present a cost model for evaluating the performance of the proposed algorithms, and develop cost equations for them. The performance evaluation is presented in

Section 5. We conclude with some final remarks in Section 6.

We assume familiarity with the basic notions of transactions, recovery, and concurrency control; see [6, 10, 12] for a tutorial introduction to these concepts.

2. RECOVERY PRINCIPLES

In this section, we review the fundamental recovery principles that we use in developing recovery algorithms for non-volatile main memory systems. These principles have been distilled from the classical recovery algorithms for volatile memory systems: logging [10], shadows [2, 15] and differential files [2, 17]. A somewhat different framework for understanding recovery algorithms has been presented in [12].

The recovery component of the transaction management system ensures, irrespective of any intervening system failures, that
  i. updates of an aborted or failed transaction are not visible to other transactions, and
  ii. updates of a committed transaction persist.

The first property is *failure atomicity* and the second is *durability of updates*.

Failure Atomicity: To ensure failure atomicity, it is necessary that the state of the database when the transaction began be preserved till the transaction commits. When a transaction updates an object, there are two basic choices:
  i. First record the old state of the object, and then update the object. The old state of an object is referred to as the *before-image* of the object. The before-image can be a complete image or differential information.
  ii. Make a copy of the object and then update the copy. The original object is referred to as the *shadow*. The updated copy can be a complete image or differential information.

In the event of a transaction failure, if a recovery algorithm makes the first choice, it has to restore the objects updated by the transaction to their original state by applying before-images. In the second case, the consistent state can be recovered by simply discarding the updated copies and reinstalling the shadow copies. Once the transaction commits, the undo information (before-images or shadows) is no longer required, and can be discarded.[1]

Durability of Updates: To make the updates of a transaction durable, there are two options:
  i. Updated objects are written to disk before committing the transaction.
  ii. Updated objects are not written to disk, but the information differentiating the updated version from the disk version is written to disk in a different location. This information is referred as the *after-image*.

If a recovery algorithm chooses the first option, no recovery action is required after system failure for the committed transactions. If the second option is chosen, after-images have to be applied to the copy on the disk to recover from system failure. After-images are required only until the copy on the disk has been updated. One may, however, choose not to discard after-images, but instead use them to represent the consistent database state. The state of an object in that case is obtained by applying some operations on the original state of the object and its after-images.

Overwriting: When overwriting an object on disk by an updated copy, the system may fail while this write is in progress. One option is to never overwrite. The alternative is to follow the discipline:
  i. If the updated copy belongs to an uncommitted transaction, there must be a before-image of the committed version on disk.
  ii. If the updated copy belongs to a committed transaction, there must be an image of the updated copy (after-image) on the disk.

---

[1]. Unless required for some other reason, such as preservation of past states.

Examples: Recovery algorithms differ in the choices they make for failure atomicity, durability of updates, and overwriting of objects. We illustrate by considering the three classical recovery algorithms: logging, shadows, and differential files.

In the case of logging [10], before-images are used for failure atomicity. After-images, which are forced to a log on the disk before committing a transaction, are used to ensure the durability of updates. An object is updated on disk by overwriting, but a before-image is first written to the log.

In the case of shadows [2, 15], failure atomicity is achieved by updating copies of the object (usually complete copies) and retaining original versions as shadows. All updated objects are forced to disk before committing a transaction to realize durability of updates. Objects on the disk are never updated by overwriting; rather, the updates of a transaction are committed by "atomically" swapping pointers from the shadow versions to the updated versions in the disk at the time of committing the transaction.

In the case of differential files [2, 17], only the copies of the objects are updated to effect failure atomicity (updates are usually maintained as differentials). Updated objects are forced to disk before committing a transaction to realize durability of updates. Objects on the disk are never overwritten; rather, the differential updates (after-images) are written to a separate location. The state of an object is retrieved by applying operations on the base version and differential updates.

2.1 Non-Volatile Main Memory

The primary advantage of non-volatile memory is that disks need no longer be the only repository for the "true" database state; it can be maintained in the main memory as well.[2] This implies that once a transaction has been committed by the system, it never needs to be redone, and hence a recovery algorithm does not have to account for the durability of updates. Another advantage of non-volatile memory is that the objects on disk may be overwritten without providing for failure during the write, as the memory copy automatically provides the backup copy (provided only the disk copy of the object being updated is affected, should an overwrite failure occur).

The recovery algorithms that we develop in the next section exploit these features of non-volatile main memory.

3. NEW RECOVERY ALGORITHMS

We now present non-volatile main memory recovery algorithms.

3.1 Algorithm 1: A Page-Level Algorithm

The first recovery algorithm uses shadows at a page level to realize failure atomicity, but unlike the classical shadow scheme, committed updated pages are written in-place.[3] We call a main memory updated page *dirty* if the transaction updating it has not committed, and *clean* if the transaction has committed.

We first assume that the main memory is large enough to accommodate all uncommitted pages of the currently active transactions. We then extend the algorithm to the case when these pages do not fit in main memory.

Processing of a Transaction

1. When a transaction begins, write[4] to a *transaction-list* a record containing the transaction identifier, its status, and a pointer. The status is initially set to *uncommitted*. The pointer is to a list of pages accessed by the transaction. The transaction-list is maintained in main memory.

---

2. This idea is similar to Elhardt and Bayer's notion in [9] where the data pages in the database cache and on disk together represent the current state of the database.
3. This algorithm can also be viewed as an adaptation of the recovery algorithm presented in [9] for non-volatile main memory systems.
4. We assume that the transaction-list is maintained as a circular buffer. System failure in the middle of an addition to a transaction-list cannot affect correctness if one updates the end marker after the complete record has been added to the list. Space allocated to the records for transactions that have been *forgotten* or *aborted* is re-used. We do not discuss issues related to the management of the transaction-list in presence of long transactions.

2. To read a data page, the transaction obtains a read lock on the corresponding page number, and checks if the page exists in memory; if not, the page is read from disk and the memory copy is marked clean.
3. To update a data page, the transaction obtains a write lock on the corresponding page number. If this page has not previously been updated by the transaction[5], it must have a clean copy in the memory (assuming a page is read before it can be written). If an in-memory clean page is different from its disk copy, the transaction makes a copy of the page, marks it dirty, and updates the copy; otherwise, the transaction changes the status of the in-memory page to dirty and updates it. Thus, the shadow could either be on disk or in memory. The same dirty copy is used for repeated updates of the same page by the same transaction.
4. If a clean page must move out of memory to make room for a new page, and it is different from the disk copy of the page, it is written back to disk in-place, overwriting the previous disk copy.

Commit Processing

1. Change the status of the transaction in the transaction-list to *committed*.
2. For each page updated by the transaction
   - if there is a clean copy of this page in main memory, discard the clean copy
   - change the status of the dirty copy to clean.
3. Release all locks held by the transaction[6].
4. Discard the list of pages accessed by the transaction.
5. Change the status of the transaction in the transaction-list to *forgotten*.

Recovery

Transaction Abort:
1. Discard dirty pages updated by the transaction.
2. Release all locks held by the transaction.
3. Discard the list of pages accessed by the transaction.
4. Change the status of the transaction in the transaction-list to *aborted*.

System Failure:
1. For each transaction in the transaction-list with the status *uncommitted*, perform a transaction abort[7].
2. For each transaction in the transaction-list with the status *committed*, perform steps 2 through 5 of the commit processing.

3.1.1 Correctness

If C represents the set of page numbers of the of committed pages in memory and D represents the set of page numbers on disk, the set $C \cup (D - C)$ represents the consistent database. The access discipline, which requires checking the set of clean pages in the memory prior to fetching a page from disk, ensures that the consistent database is accessed. Dirty pages remain unavailable to other transactions due to locks on the corresponding page numbers. At no time, are there two clean copies of a page in the memory because the earlier clean copy is discarded before the status of page is changed from being dirty to clean.

---

5. No other transaction can be concurrently updating this page, as we assume page-level locking.
6. All read locks may be released as soon as a transaction has issued the commit. The write lock on a page can be released immediately after its state has been changed from being dirty to clean.
7. We assume that the transactions uncommitted at the time of system failure are aborted and restarted. Since the main-memory is non-volatile, it may be possible that the process image and the execution state of the active transactions is still available. In that case, instead of restarting these transactions from the beginning, they can be continued where they were at the time of system failure.

While a transaction is active, there is always a shadow (either on disk or in memory) for any page updated by the transaction. Thus, a transaction can be aborted by simply discarding the private copies of its data pages.

It is safe to discard any shadow copy and replace it with the new clean copy once the transaction has committed, since shadows are required only until the transaction commits.

It is safe to accept the commit request of a transaction as soon as it made, since the "after-images" of the pages updated by the transaction are all in non-volatile memory. Even if the system fails immediately after the status of the transaction has been changed to committed, the transaction list contains the addresses of the pages updated by the transaction, and their states can be changed to clean when the system comes back.

The recovery actions for abort processing and for recovery from a system failure are idempotent, and hence can be repeated if the system fails when recovery is in progress.

3.1.2 Extension

Now consider the case when the main memory is not sufficient to hold all the dirty pages of the concurrently active transactions, and a dirty page must be paged out. In this case, instead of writing the dirty page in-place on disk, the dirty page must be written in some free location on disk. At the time of commit processing, the page is read into memory and marked clean. It may then be retained in memory or used to overwrite the disk version.[8]

3.1.3 Assessment

This recovery algorithm most closely resembles the classical shadow algorithm. However, it overcomes major drawbacks of the classical algorithm:
- In the proposed algorithm, all updates on disk are done in-place, and hence a page table to map logical page numbers to physical disk addresses is not required. This obviates the need for extra I/O due to indirection through the page-table — the major performance impediment with the classical algorithm [2].
- Another major problem with the classical algorithm is that it does not preserve the physical adjacency of the logically adjacent pages [2, 11]. Due to disk updates being done in place in the proposed algorithm, the data clustering is preserved.
- The classical algorithm is a FORCE algorithm [12] in that before committing a transaction, all the pages updated by the transaction must be written to disk. The proposed algorithm is a ¬FORCE algorithm in that the disk copies of pages need not be replaced by their updated versions in the memory at the time of committing a transaction. Only when a memory copy has to be paged out to disk to make room for a new page in memory is the corresponding disk copy overwritten. This has the advantage that a hot page may be updated in memory by several transactions without ever being written to disk.
- The commit request of a transaction is accepted by the system as soon as the request is made by changing its status to committed in the transaction-list, which reduces the window of vulnerability. In the classical algorithm, there is a considerable time gap between a commit request and its acceptance, during which a precommit record is written and the pages updated by the transaction are written to disk [2]. If the system fails in this period, the transaction is aborted at the time of recovery.

Like [9, 14], this algorithm incurs zero I/O cost due to recovery if all the pages updated by active transactions could be accommodated in memory.

---

8. One may write the dirty page in-place on disk by first creating a shadow copy in some other free location of the disk. The advantage of this approach is that if the transaction commits, the true copy is already in place and the commit processing simply requires discarding the shadow. This alternative has been explored further in Section 5.2.

The major drawback of this algorithm is that it does not work correctly with tuple-level locking, and hence limits concurrency. Consider, for example, a situation in which transaction A wishes to update a tuple on a page, and transaction B wishes to update another tuple on the same page. If each transaction creates its own dirty copy of the page, then the transaction that commits earlier will have its update lost. If both transaction use the same dirty page, then we have problems if one transaction (say, A) commits and the other aborts after having updated this page. A may mark the page clean including the update performed by B, or B may discard the page including any updates already performed by A.

3.2 Algorithm 2: A Tuple-Level Algorithm

Tuple-level locking can offer significant performance advantage over page-level locking [16]. We now present an algorithm that permits tuple-level locking.

This algorithm uses before-images at tuple level to realize failure atomicity. Like [9, 14], the before-images are maintained on a per transaction basis and are discarded after the transaction commits.

Unlike Algorithm 1, the main memory is not required to be large enough to be able to hold updated pages of all the active transactions. If an updated page has to be paged out to disk to make room for a new page in memory, it is written in-place on disk, even if it contains uncommitted updates. Such an overwriting is safe since the before-images are not discarded until the transaction commits.

Processing of a Transaction

1. When a transaction begins, write to a *transaction-list* a record containing the transaction identifier, its status, and a pointer. The status is initially set to *uncommitted*. The pointer points to a list of before-images of the tuples updated by the transaction.
2. Before reading or writing a tuple, obtain read or write lock respectively on the tuple.
3. When updating a tuple, first write the before-image of the tuple to the list of before-images. Then update the in-memory copy of the page the tuple is on.

Commit Processing

1. Change the status of the transaction in the transaction-list to *committed*.
2. Discard the before-images created by this transaction.
3. Release all locks held by the transaction.
4. Change the status of the transaction in the transaction-list to *forgotten*.

Recovery

Transaction Abort:
1. Undo the tuples updated by the transaction using the before-images (the corresponding data pages would be either in main memory or disk).
2. Discard the before-images created by this transaction.
3. Release all locks held by the transaction.
4. Change the status of the transaction in the transaction-list to *aborted*.

System Failure:
1. For each uncommitted transaction in the transaction-list, perform a transaction abort.
2. For each committed but not forgotten transaction, perform steps 2 through 4 of the commit processing.

3.2.1 Correctness

While a transaction is active, the before-image of any tuple updated by the transaction is maintained. Thus, a transaction can be aborted by restoring a consistent version of the updated tuples using their before-images. Before-images are required only until the transaction commits, and it is safe to discard them once the transaction has committed.

The commit request of a transaction can be accepted as soon as it is made since the tuples updated by the transaction are all in non-volatile memory. For the same reason, no transaction redo is required at the time of recovery from system failure.

If a system failure occurs during transaction abort, the undo may be repeated for some of the updates performed by the transaction. Such a repeated undo poses no problems provided that the undo information is kept in the form of before-images and not in the form of a compensation operation whose repetitions can get the database to a state different than the starting one.

3.2.2 Assessment

This algorithm can be compared with the classical logging algorithm. Some of the advantages of this algorithm over the classical logging algorithm are:
- This algorithm requires no checkpointing [10, 11].
- The log is *ephemeral*, being discarded as soon as the transaction commits, and hence no I/Os are required to write log records (provided that the before-images of all concurrently active transactions can fit in memory).
- The transaction commit is accepted as soon as the commit request is made. However, in the case of classical logging, the write ahead protocol [10, 11] requires all the log records for the transaction to be flushed to disk before committing the transaction.

As is the case with Algorithm 1, this algorithm also incurs zero I/O recovery cost if enough memory is available. However, the memory requirements are somewhat larger, as we now need memory large enough not only to hold the uncommitted updated pages, but also the before-images of updated tuples.

In terms of CPU cost, if a committed page is found in memory, this algorithm works better since the entire page need not have a fresh copy made as in the case of Algorithm 1. A copy of only the tuple (or differential information) is created as the before-image. However, if the page is brought from disk, Algorithm 1 works better, as it can simply update the memory copy of the page, whereas this algorithm has to additionally create before-images. The exact tradeoff depends on the degree of locality in data references.

3.3 Algorithm 3: A Hybrid Algorithm

We presented two algorithms above, one that used the page as the unit of copying and recovery, and another that used the tuple as the unit. The page is the natural unit to use when data is disk-resident, while a tuple copy is much cheaper when data is memory-resident. In this section, we present a hybrid algorithm that combines the best features of the two algorithms.

The basic idea is that when a page is read from disk, the disk version can act as shadow to recover from transaction aborts as in Algorithm 1. On the other hand, when the page of interest is found in memory, rather than making a fresh copy of the entire page as in Algorithm 1, before-images are created only of the tuples updated as in Algorithm 2.

We first assume page-level locking, and then discuss how the algorithm can be extended to tuple-level locking.

Processing of a Transaction

1. When a transaction begins, write to a *transaction-list* a record containing the transaction identifier, its status, and two pointers. The status is initially set to *uncommitted*. The first pointer points to a list of before-images of updated tuples, and the second to a list of dirty pages. Both the lists are initially empty.
2. To read a tuple, the transaction obtains a read lock on the corresponding page number, and checks if the page exists in memory; if not, the page is read from disk and the memory copy is marked clean.
3. To update a tuple, the transaction obtains a write lock on the corresponding page number.
4. If the page to be updated is clean but different from its disk version, the transaction writes the before-image of the tuple to be updated to the list of before-images and then updates the page. The status of the page in this case is maintained as clean.
5. If the page to be updated is clean and is the same as the disk version, the transaction updates the page without creating a before-image. The page in this case is marked dirty and added to the list of dirty pages of the transaction.

6. If the page to be updated is dirty, the transaction updates the page without creating a before-image. The status of the page remains dirty.
7. If a clean page has to be moved out of memory to make room for a new page and it is different from its disk version, it is written in-place on disk. A dirty page must not be paged out. If it is necessary to page out a dirty page due to memory limitation, the strategy discussed in Section 3.1.2, as an extension to Algorithm 1, must be used.

Commit Processing
1. Change the status of the transaction in the transaction-list to *committed*.
2. For each dirty page updated by the transaction,
    - if there is a clean copy of this page in main memory, discard the clean copy
    - change the status of the dirty copy to clean.
3. Release all locks held by the transaction.
4. Discard before-images and the list of dirty pages.
5. Change the status of the transaction in the transaction-list to *forgotten*.

Recovery

Transaction Abort:
1. Discard each dirty page updated by the transaction.
2. Undo the updated tuples for which before-images have been created for this transaction.
3. Release all locks held by the transaction.
4. Discard before-images and the list of dirty pages.
5. Change the status of the transaction in the transaction-list to *aborted*.

System Failure:
1. For each uncommitted transaction in the transaction-list, perform a transaction abort.
2. For each committed but not forgotten transaction in the transaction-list, perform steps 2 through 5 of the commit processing.

3.3.1 Correctness

Follows directly from the correctness of the two previous algorithms.

3.3.2 Extension

So far, we had assumed page-level locking. The page-level locks are required only on those pages that are shadowed on disk at a page level. Tuple-locking may be used on the pages that have before-images maintained in ephemeral log. This lock combination should actually work quite well. The frequently accessed hot pages are likely to be in memory and likely to have tuple-level before-images created so that tuple-level locking is possible on these. Page-level locking is required on the less frequently used pages that have to be fetched from disk.

3.3.3 Assessment

This algorithm should perform better than the previous two algorithms in most of the operating region. Like them, it has zero I/O cost for recovery as long as the updated pages of active transactions can be accommodated in memory. In terms of CPU cost, when updating a page, if the memory copy has a shadow on disk, this is the one that is updated without requiring any copy; if not, before-images are created but a complete copy of the page is avoided.

3.4 Algorithm 4: Recovery with Preservation of Past States

Certain applications require access to past states of the database, besides the current state. We now present a recovery algorithm that is suitable for tuple-level locking and also preserves past states. This algorithm is similar to Algorithm 2, except that before-images are stored on the same page as the updated tuple, and before-images are not discarded after the transaction commits. Tuples on data pages are organized to leave room for before-images. A before-image contains differential information of only those attributes of the tuple that have been updated. The past state of a tuple can be recovered by starting with the current state and applying differential before-images to it.[9]

Processing of a Transaction

1. When a transaction begins, write to a *transaction-list* a record containing the transaction identifier, its status, and a pointer. The status is initially set to *uncommitted*. The pointer points to a list of tuples updated by the transaction.
2. Before reading or writing a tuple, obtain read or write lock respectively on the tuple.
3. For updating a tuple, first create a differential before-image on the same page as the tuple, create a pointer from this before-image to the previous before-image of the tuple if any, make the tuple point to this before-image, and then update the tuple. The before-image also contains the transaction identifier. The tuple id is also added to the list of updated tuples for the transaction. The page may have to be locked in the exclusive mode while a tuple is being updated.
4. If a page has to be paged out to disk to make room for a new page in memory, write it in-place on disk, even if it contains uncommitted updates.
5. Old before-images can be archived by an asynchronous process (similar to the vacuum cleaner process in POSTGRES [18]) as the space on a page starts filling up.

Commit Processing

1. Change the status of the transaction in the transaction-list to *committed*.
2. Release all locks held by the transaction.
3. Discard the list of updated tuples for the transaction.
4. Change the status of the transaction in the transaction-list to *forgotten*.

Recovery

Transaction Abort:
1. For each tuple updated by this transaction, restore the previous state by applying the before-image created by the transaction. The before-image is then discarded by resetting the pointer from the tuple to the prior before-image.
2. Release all locks held by the transaction.
3. Discard the list of updated tuples for the transaction.
4. Change the status of the transaction in the transaction-list to *aborted*.

System Failure:
1. For each uncommitted transaction in the transaction-list, perform a transaction abort.
2. For each committed but not forgotten transaction in the transaction-list, perform steps 2 through 4 of the commit processing.

3.4.1 Correctness

Correctness arguments for this algorithm are similar to that for Algorithm 2. Before-images of tuples updated by a transaction are retained in the non-volatile memory until the transaction commits, and hence updates by a failed transaction can be undone by applying before-images to the updated tuples. The commit request of a transaction can be accepted as soon as it made since the tuples updated by the transaction are all in non-volatile memory. For the same reason, no transaction redo is required at the time of recovery from system failure.

If the system fails while recovery from a transaction abort is in progress, the recovery can be continued after the system comes back. However, before applying a before-image to an updated tuple, one must check the transaction identifier stored with the before-image to ensure that this update was not already undone.

---

9. The POSTGRES data manager [18] also records changes to a tuple on the same page as the tuple. However, after-images are saved, and the base tuple remains unchanged. Accessing a tuple requires starting with the base tuple and applying all the after-images to arrive at the current value.

3.4.2 Assessment

This algorithm can be thought of as a differential file algorithm [2, 17]. However, this algorithm overcomes many drawbacks of the classical differential file algorithms:
- The major performance problem with the differential files is the cost of performing "set difference" between the differential and the base file [2]. In the proposed algorithm, the current copy of the tuple is kept in the front of the update chain, and hence no set-difference is required. The update chain for a tuple is maintained on the same page as the tuple, and this makes an access to a previous state a rather inexpensive in-memory operation.
- In the classical algorithm, after a transaction makes a commit request, all the differential records created by the transaction must be written to disk before the commit can be accepted [2] (it is a FORCE algorithm [12]). In the proposed algorithm, the commit request is accepted as soon as it is made.
- The classical algorithm requires periodic merger of differential files into base files. This merger is not necessary in the proposed algorithm as the latest copies of tuples are always available and the old before-images can be incrementally retired asynchronously.

The performance characteristics of this algorithm are similar to Algorithm 2. The only disadvantage of this algorithm is that sequential processing of a relation may require a larger number of I/O's since the size of the relation is likely to be larger. However, this algorithm offers better functionality than the previous three algorithms.

4. COST MODEL

To evaluate the performance of the proposed recovery algorithms, we use a simplified version of the incremental cost model proposed in [2]. The *overhead* imposed on a transaction by a recovery algorithm is used as the performance metric, and it can be modeled as

$$OX = p_{succ} * O_{succ} + p_{fail} * O_{fail}$$

where
- p_{succ} is the probability that the transaction succeeds,
- O_{succ} is the overhead incurred when a transaction succeeds,
- p_{fail} is the probability that the transaction fails (aborted by the system or user)
- O_{fail} is the overhead incurred when a transaction fails,
- and, $p_{succ} + p_{fail} = 1$.

We assume that a transaction reads N_r tuples, out of which N_u tuples are updated. We further assume that every tuple read by a transaction lies on a distinct page and a tuple is read or written only once, so that a transaction reads N_r pages and updates N_u of them. We assume that a transaction abort occurs when the transaction has read $N_r/2$ and updated $N_u/2$ tuples.

We represent by T_{io} the time to read/write a disk page. T_{page} represents the cpu time to process a page in memory, and T_{tup} the cpu time to process a tuple in memory. The actual values of these parameters depend on the physical characteristics of the disk and the processing unit.

In the rest of this section, we develop cost equations for O_{succ} and O_{fail} for the proposed recovery algorithms. For comparison, we also develop equations for the classical logging algorithm [10], regarded to be the best algorithm from a performance viewpoint [2]. In developing equations for O_{fail}, we only consider the overhead to recover from a transaction failure, as system failures are infrequent compared to transaction failures. In the next section, values will be assigned to the various parameters to evaluate the relative performance of the algorithms.

4.1 Classical Logging

Assumptions

1. The number of log pages generated by a transaction is a function of the number of tuples updated by the transaction, N_u, and is given by $l * N_u$, where l is a parameter that depends on the size of a disk page and the average amount of log created for an updated tuple.

2. Both updated data pages and log pages are flushed to disk to make room for new pages, while the transaction is still active. The parameter f determines the fraction of updated pages and log pages that are flushed at any time. Thus, when a transaction aborts, $f * N_u/2$ of its updated pages and $f * l * N_u/2$ of the log pages created by it would have migrated to disk (we had assumed that a transaction is aborted after it has updated $N_u/2$ pages). The parameter f depends on the memory size, the size of the transactions, the multiprogramming level, and the buffering policy.

3. Pages updated by a transaction are not forced to disk at the time of committing the transaction. Thus, a page may be updated many times in memory without being written to disk. Therefore, when a transaction aborts, all the pages updated by it must be undone, since the disk copies of these pages may be old.

4. No cost is assigned for writing tran-begin and commit/abort records for transactions. We assume group commit [8] and that the writes for these records can be piggybacked with other log records for the transaction, instead of incurring separate I/Os.

Cost Equations

O_{succ} = CPU cost of creating log $\{N_u * T_{tup}\}$
   + I/O cost of writing log $\{l * N_u * T_{io}\}$

O_{fail} = Overhead before the transaction abort + Cost of undo processing
  = CPU cost of creating log $\{N_u/2 * T_{tup}\}$
   + I/O cost of writing flushed log pages $\{f * l * N_u/2 * T_{io}\}$
   + I/O cost of reading flushed log pages for undo $\{f * l * N_u/2 * T_{io}\}$
   + I/O cost of reading flushed updated data pages for undo $\{f * N_u/2 * T_{io}\}$
   + CPU cost of undoing updated data pages $\{N_u/2 * T_{tup}\}$
   + I/O cost of overwriting corrupted data pages on disk $\{f * N_u/2 * T_{io}\}$

4.2 Algorithm 1

Assumptions

1. The probability that a page read by a transaction is present in memory is h. Thus, a transaction reads $(1 - h) * N_r$ pages from disk and $h * N_r$ pages from memory. We further assume that if a transaction finds a page in memory, then it is different from its copy on disk. Thus, the number of memory to memory page copies is given by $h * N_u$. The parameter h depends on the size of memory, the multiprogramming level, the size of the transactions, and their access pattern.

2. The number of dirty pages flushed to disk while the transaction is still active is determined by the parameter f, and is given by $f * N_u$. The parameter f depends on the memory size, the size of the transactions, the multiprogramming level, and the buffering policy.

3. The costs of updating the transaction list, discarding the list of pages accessed by a transaction, and updating the free list of disk pages are negligible.

Cost Equations

O_{succ} = CPU cost of memory to memory copy of updated pages $\{h * N_u * T_{page}\}$
   + I/O cost of writing flushed dirty pages $\{f * N_u * T_{io}\}$
   + I/O cost of reading flushed dirty pages at commit time $\{f * N_u * T_{io}\}$

O_{fail} = overhead before the transaction abort + cost of undo processing[10]
  = CPU cost of memory to memory copy of updated pages $\{h * N_u/2 * T_{tup}\}$
   + I/O cost of writing flushed dirty pages $\{f * N_u/2 * T_{io}\}$

---

10. The cost of undo processing is taken to be zero since it only involves updating the transaction list, discarding the list of pages accessed by the transaction, and freeing the dirty pages on disk.

4.3 Algorithm 2

Assumptions

1. Each update of a tuple gives rise to one before-image. Thus, a total of N_u tuple level operations are required to create before-images.

2. Data pages may be flushed to disk, to make room for new pages, while the transaction is still active. We assume that the before-images are never written to disk. The parameter f determines the fraction of updated pages that are flushed at any time. Thus, when a transaction aborts, $f * N_u/2$ of its updated pages would have migrated to disk. The parameter f depends on the memory size, size of transactions, multiprogramming level, and the buffering policy.

3. The costs of updating the transaction list and discarding before-images are negligible.

Cost Equations

O_{succ} = CPU cost of creating before-images $\{N_u * T_{tup}\}$

O_{fail} = overhead before the transaction abort + cost of undo processing
= CPU cost of creating before-images $\{N_u/2 * T_{tup}\}$
+ I/O cost of reading flushed updated data pages for undo $\{f * N_u/2 * T_{io}\}$
+ CPU cost of undoing updated data pages $\{N_u/2 * T_{tup}\}$[11]

4.4 Algorithm 3

Assumptions

1. If a transaction finds a page in memory, this page is different from its copy on disk, and h is the probability of finding a page in memory. Thus, a transaction updates $(1 - h) * N_u$ pages without creating their before-images, since they have been read from disk and the disk copies serve as shadows. Before-images are created for $h * N_u$ pages, since they have been found in memory and do not have shadows on disk. The parameter h depends on the size of memory, multiprogramming level, size of transactions, and their access pattern.

2. The number of uncommitted data pages, which have no before-images and are flushed to disk temporarily in a separate location till the transaction commits to make room for new pages, is determined by the parameter f_1, and is given by $f_1 * N_u$. The parameter f_1 depends on the memory size, size of transactions, multiprogramming level, and the buffering policy. It is upper-bounded by $(1 - h)$.

3. Updated data pages that have before-images may be flushed to disk in-place to make room for new pages, while the transaction is still active. The parameter f_2 determines the fraction of updated pages that are so flushed. Thus, when a transaction aborts, $f_2 * N_u/2$ of its updated pages with before-images would have migrated to disk. The parameter f_2 depends on the memory size, size of transactions, multiprogramming level, and the buffering policy. It is upper-bounded by h, the fraction of updated pages for which before-images are created. Before-images are not written to disk.

4. The costs of updating the transaction list, discarding before-images and the list of pages accessed by a transaction, and updating the free list of disk pages are negligible.

Cost Equations

O_{succ} = CPU cost of creating before-images $\{h * N_u * T_{tup}\}$
+ I/O cost of writing flushed uncommitted pages without before-images $\{f_1 * (1 - h) * N_u * T_{io}\}$
+ I/O cost of reading flushed uncommitted pages without before-images at commit time $\{f_1 * N_u * T_{io}\}$

---

11. The undone pages need not be written to disk since they are in non-volatile memory.

O_{fail} = overhead before the transaction abort + cost of undo processing
= CPU cost of creating before-images $\{h * N_u/2 * T_{tup}\}$
+ I/O cost of writing flushed uncommitted pages without before-images $\{f_1 * N_u/2 * T_{io}\}$
+ I/O cost of reading flushed updated data pages for undo with before-images $\{f_2 * N_u/2 * T_{io}\}$
+ CPU cost of undoing updated data pages with before-images $\{h * N_u/2 * T_{tup}\}$

4.5 Algorithm 4

Assumptions

1. Due to the differential before-images being kept on the same page as the current state of tuples, reading and writing the same number of tuples may require extra I/O effort, particularly if the transaction accesses records sequentially (in case of random access, this overhead would be zero). The extra I/O effort is a function of number of pages accessed by the transaction, and is determined by a parameter m. Thus, extra I/O effort in reading is $m * N_r * T_{io}$ and in writing $m * N_u * T_{io}$.

2. Each update of a tuple gives rise to one differential before-image, but on the same page. Thus, a total of N_u tuple level operations are required to create before-images.

3. Data pages (along with differential before-images) may be flushed to disk, to make room for new pages, while the transaction is still active. The parameter f determines the fraction of updated pages that are flushed at any time. Thus, when a transaction aborts, $f * N_u/2$ of its updated pages would have migrated to disk. f depends on the memory size, size of transactions, multiprogramming level, and the buffering policy.

4. The costs of updating the transaction list and discarding the list of pages accessed by the transaction are negligible.

Cost Equations

O_{succ} = CPU cost of creating differential before-images $\{N_u * T_{tup}\}$
+ Extra I/O cost in reading data pages $\{m * N_r * T_{io}\}$
+ Extra I/O cost in writing data pages $\{m * N_u * T_{io}\}$

O_{fail} = overhead before the transaction abort + cost of undo processing
= CPU cost of creating differential before-images $\{N_u/2 * T_{tup}\}$
+ Extra I/O cost in reading data pages $\{m * N_r/2 * T_{io}\}$
+ Extra I/O cost in writing data pages $\{m * N_u/2 * T_{io}\}$
+ I/O cost of reading flushed updated data pages for undo $\{f * N_u/2 * T_{io}\}$
+ CPU cost of undoing updated data pages $\{N_u/2 * T_{tup}\}$

5. PERFORMANCE EVALUATION

5.1 Parameter Values

We assume that the average time to process a tuple, T_{tup}, is 0.5 ms., and to process a page of approximately 10 tuples, T_{page}, is 5.0 ms. The average time to read or write a disk page, T_{io}, is 25 ms.

The parameter l is the fraction of a log page consumed in creating log record for one updated tuple. We take l to be 0.1, which is about 400 bytes of log information for a 4K page.

The parameter h is the fraction of pages read by a transaction for which valid copies are found in memory. h is affected by the size of memory and the size and number of concurrent transactions, but is primarily determined by the reference pattern of the transactions, a characteristic that is application-dependent. Applications with high locality will have a high h. We have varied h from 0 (no locality) to 1 (very high locality).

The parameter f is the fraction of updated pages forced to disk while the transaction is still active. If a system has as many as 1000 concurrent transactions, each transaction updating 5 pages, we require enough memory to store 5000 pages, or roughly 20 MBytes, not a very high number. Thus, the value of f is likely to be low. We evaluate algorithms for three values of f: 0, 0.1 and 0.2.

For Algorithm 3, f is divided into two components, f_1 and f_2, representing the fraction of updated pages that are forced out dirty and forced out clean, respectively. $f = f_1 + f_2$. The cost of forcing out a dirty page is significantly higher than the cost of forcing out a clean page. We assume that the paging system will force out dirty pages only if clean pages are not available. We can further assume that the number of clean pages available in memory is proportional to the hit ratio h. Therefore, f_2 is upper-bounded by h. For any given value of f, Algorithm 3 has been evaluated by assuming $f_2 = f$, if $f \le h$, and $f_2 = h$, with f_1 taking up the remainder, otherwise.

In real systems, most transactions succeed rather than fail. We assume p_{succ} to be 0.9, that is, 90% of the transactions succeed and 10% of them fail. By varying p_{succ}, we found that as p_{succ} is reduced, there is a slight improvement in the relative performance of Algorithm 1. Other than this small change, the relative performance of the algorithms was not sensitive to the actual values p_{succ} and p_{fail}, since the trends for the overhead of failed transactions are not very different from the trends for successful transactions. We have, therefore, presented performance numbers only for one value of p_{succ}.

Table 1 summarizes the values of the various parameters used in our evaluation:

TABLE 1. Parameter Values

Parameter	T_{io}	T_{page}	T_{tup}	l	h	f	p_{succ}	p_{fail}
Value	25 ms.	5 ms.	0.5 ms.	0.1	0, 0.1, 0.2, ..., 1.0	0, 0.1, 0.2	0.9	0.1

In assigning values to the parameters, we have made one simplification. We have taken the same values of f and h for different algorithms. However, the memory requirement for different algorithms is not the same, and this can affect the values of these parameters. Algorithm 2 requires more memory than Algorithm 1 to be able to retain its in-memory ephemeral before-images. Assuming the before-image of a page to be 10% of the page, the extra memory required is roughly 10% of the total storage for the updated pages of all concurrently active transactions. In the absence of this extra memory, h is likely to fall and f is likely to increase. However, the increase in f is likely to be considerably less than 10%, and has been ignored. The same argument applies to Algorithm 3, which is a hybrid between Algorithms 1 and 2.

5.2 Evaluation

The relative performance of the classical logging and Algorithms 1, 2 and 3 have been plotted in Figure 1. The first graph is for $f = 0$, the second for $f = 0.2$, and the third for $f = 0.3$. The Y axis in all of these graphs represent overhead per updated page measured in milliseconds, and h has been varied along X axis. We have not plotted curves for Algorithm 4 in this figure as its characteristics are identical to Algorithm 2 if we disregard the effect on reading and writing costs of data pages due to increase in file sizes (this would be true if transactions have a random access pattern). We discuss the trends for Algorithm 4 separately.

Both classical logging and Algorithm 2 are insensitive to h, since before-images are created for every updated page irrespective of whether the page was found in memory or had to be read from disk. However, Algorithms 1 and 3 are quite sensitive to h, and their overhead increases with increasing h. This may appear anomalous since one expects the performance of the system to get better as more pages are found in memory. Whereas the overall system performance does indeed get better with an increase in number of pages found in memory, the *overhead* due to Algorithm 1 and 3 increases as memory to memory copies may now be required to create shadows while earlier the copies on disk could be used as shadows.[12]

Algorithm 1 is an excellent algorithm for very low values of f, and low values of h. In fact, when $f = h = 0$, this algorithm has nearly zero overhead. However, as f or h increases, the performance suffers, and could become significantly worse than even classical logging. As h increases, memory to

---

12. The copying from disk is counted in the overhead as this copy would be required any way in the course of an execution of a transaction.

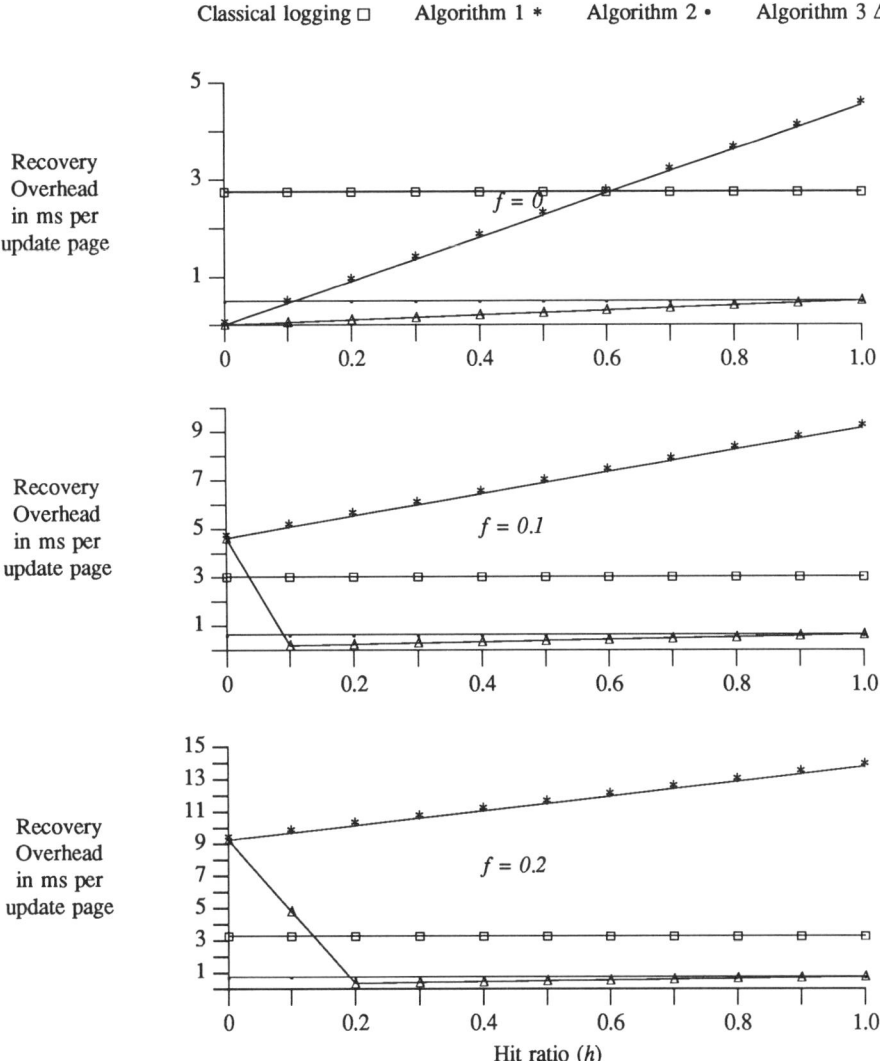

Figure 1. Recovery Overhead for Different Algorithms

memory copies to create shadows increase the overhead. As f increases, a larger fraction of dirty pages are forced to disk, and this writing cost together with the cost of reading them back at the time of commit increases the overhead. The latter problem can be ameliorated somewhat by the following strategy: Rather than write out a dirty page only to read it back again on commit, take a difference with the shadow (the shadow would either be in memory or on disk), retain the differential in memory, and then write the dirty page in-place on disk overwriting the shadow. For successful transactions, such a strategy would result in possibly one extra read I/O (if the shadow is not in memory) and CPU time to take difference with the shadow, rather than one write and a read I/O.

Algorithm 3 is identical to Algorithm 1 for $h = 0$, and identical to Algorithm 2 for $h = 1$. When h is 0, none of the pages is found in memory, and hence every memory page is updated using the corresponding disk copy as the shadow as in Algorithm 1. When h is 1, all pages are found in memory, and they are updated by creating before-images as in Algorithm 2. Algorithm 3 does best for intermediate values of h, attaining a minimum for $h = f$. When $h = f$, all the updated pages that are forced out to disk are the ones that are written in-place as their before-images are available in memory. When h is less than f, due to the forcing out of dirty pages without before-images that have to be written in a different place on disk, and have to be read back and reinstated in-place upon commit, the overhead becomes high.

What then is the algorithm of choice? Clearly, Algorithm 2 is uniformly better than the classical logging algorithm. The primary advantage of Algorithm 2 over classical logging is that the before-images in Algorithm 2 are ephemeral and don't have to be forced to disk for committing a transaction. Algorithm 1 can be useful if memory available is large and there is very little locality of reference. Otherwise, except for a very low locality together with very limited memory situation, Algorithm 3 performs best. In real systems, we expect medium or high locality and future systems are likely to have large rather than small memory. In a situation where memory is limited, the performance of Algorithm 3 can be improved by using the following strategies:

- As discussed above for Algorithm 1, for releasing memory occupied by a dirty page, create a differential before-image using the shadow and then write the dirty page in-place on disk. The shadow in this case would be on disk. This strategy would result in one extra read I/O and CPU time to take difference with the shadow, rather than one write and one read I/O.
- If f and h can be estimated for the application *a priori*, artificially raise h to become greater than f, by reading in pages from disk and then "pretending" they were found in memory. Thus, an updated page with before-images of uncommitted updates will always be available for paging out in-place, so that dirty pages without before-images never need be written out to disk.

With the above improvements, the left end of the curve for Algorithm 3 can be brought down to the level of Algorithm 2, making Algorithm 3 uniformly better.

Let us turn now to Algorithm 4. If pages are randomly accessed to render $m = 0$, the behavior of Algorithm 4 becomes identical to Algorithm 2, as observed before. We varied m to study its behavior for transactions whose access patterns exhibited varying degrees of sequentiality.[13] We assume that N_u is some fixed fraction of N_r to determine overhead per updated page. Table 2 shows the performance of Algorithm 4 for nonzero m, relative to its performance for $m = 0$, when it has the least overhead. f has been assumed to be zero. As expected, the cost of Algorithm 4 goes up sharply when a large number of tuples are read for every tuple updated, and when the cost of an access is high due to sequentiality. However, it ought be remembered that Algorithm 4 offers larger functionality than other algorithms.

TABLE 2. Additional Overhead Due to Saving Differential Images

$m =$ N_u/N_r	0.1	0.2	0.5	1.0
1.0	10.5	20.0	48.5	96.0
0.5	15.25	29.5	72.25	143.5
0.2	29.5	58.0	143.5	286.0
0.1	53.25	105.5	262.25	523.5

6. ACKNOWLEDGMENTS

We wish to thank Juan Andrade and Bruce Hillyer for carefully reading an earlier version of this paper and providing insightful comments.

---

13. Since no more than one page read is required per tuple, m is strictly less than 1.

REFERENCES

[1] R. Agrawal, "Concurrency Control and Recovery in Multiprocessor Database Machines: Design and Performance Evaluation", Computer Sciences Tech. Rep. #510, Univ. Wisconsin, Madison, Sept. 1983. Ph.D. Dissertation.

[2] R. Agrawal and D. J. DeWitt, "Integrated Concurrency Control and Recovery Mechanisms: Design and Performance Evaluation", *ACM Trans. Database Syst. 10*, 4 (Dec. 1985), 529-564.

[3] R. Agrawal, M. J. Carey and M. Livny, "Concurrency Control Performance Modeling: Alternatives and Implications", *ACM Trans. Database Syst. 12*, 4 (Dec. 1987), 609-654.

[4] S. Baker, "Ferroelectric Chips – Are Memories Made of This?", *VLSI System Design*, May 1988, 116-123.

[5] S. Baker, "Could Ferroelectric RAMS become the Golden Fleece", *Electronic Engineering Times*, Aug. 8, 1988, T20-T21.

[6] P. A. Bernstein and N. Goodman, "A Sophisticate's Introduction to Distributed Database Concurrency Control", *Proc. 8th Int'l Conf Very Large Data Bases*, Sept. 1982, 62-76.

[7] G. Copeland, R. Krishnamurthy and M. Smith, "The Case for Safe RAM", Tech. Rept. ACA-ST-080-88, MCC, Austin, Texas, Feb. 1988.

[8] D. J. DeWitt, R. Katz, F. Olken, D. Shapiro, M. Stonebraker and D. Wood, "Implementation Techniques for Main Memory Database Systems", *Proc. ACM-SIGMOD 1984 Int'l Conf. on Management of Data*, Boston, Mass., June 1984, 1-8.

[9] K. Elhardt and R. Bayer, "A Database Cache for High Performance and Fast Restart", *ACM Trans. Database Syst. 9*, 4 (Dec. 1984), 503-525.

[10] J. N. Gray, "Notes on Database Operating Systems", Rep. RJ1879, IBM Research Lab., San Jose, California, June 1978.

[11] J. N. Gray, P. R. McJones, B. G. Lindsay, M. W. Blasgen, R. A. Lorie, T. G. Price, F. Putzolu and I. L. Traiger, "The Recovery Manager of the System R Database Manager", *ACM Computing Surveys 13*, 2 (June 1981), 223-242.

[12] T. Haerder and A. Reuter, "Principles of Transaction-Oriented Database Recovery", *ACM Computing Surveys 15*, 4 (Dec. 1983), 287-318.

[13] R. Horton, "FRAM-ing Memories for Good", *Electronic Engineering Times*, Aug. 8, 1988, T22.

[14] IMS/VS Version 1, "FastPath Feature", General Information Manual, GH20-9069-2..

[15] R. A. Lorie, "Physical Integrity in a Large Segmented Database", *ACM Trans. Database Syst. 2*, 1 (March 1977), 91-104.

[16] D. R. Ries and M. R. Stonebraker, "Locking Granularity Revisited", *ACM Trans. Database Syst. 4*, 2 (June 1979), 210-227.

[17] D. G. Severance and G. M. Lohman, "Differential Files: Their Application to the Maintenance of Large Databases", *ACM Trans. Database Syst. 1*, 3 (Sept. 1976), 256-267.

[18] M. R. Stonebraker, "The Design of the POSTGRES Storage System", *Proc. 13th Int'l Conf. Very Large Data Bases*, Brighton, England, Sept. 1987, 289-300.

An Intelligent Memory Transaction Engine

Abhaya Asthana
H. V. Jagadish
Scott C. Knauer

AT&T Bell Laboratories
Murray Hill, New Jersey 07974

ABSTRACT

In this paper, we describe the structure and utilization of a high bandwidth, multi-ported, disk-sized memory system capable of storing, maintaining, and manipulating persistent shared data within it, independent of any external processing units. Up to thousands of active storage elements, each element having some storage and some associated processing logic, function independently or in groups to implement user-defined objects and data structures. Hundreds of transactions can concurrently be processed by mutually exclusive sets of elements. A fast response time is obtained due to the proximity of the processing with the memory, a specialized micro-architecture, and parallelism.

1. INTRODUCTION

Hardware support to speed up data access has been studied for quite some time now [13, 18, 19]. The basic idea has been to provide some intelligence at the disk head so that unnecessary disk accesses are minimized. These approaches have been able to provide only small factors of speed-up due to the limited intelligence possible at the disk head.

Special-purpose database machines have also been built. Performing a significant fraction of common database operations in hardware/firmware provides a performance benefit. The drawback is that the machine is special-purpose. It is not suited for running applications other than database, and there too, databases of a particular type. The viability of a database machine depends on its being suitable for other general-purpose computation as well[1].

The characteristics of data intensive applications can generically be considered to include a variety of pointer operations, field operations, pattern searching, and set operations, in addition to high bandwidth I/O. The rapid location of a named datum, through pattern matching, for example, has been studied extensively in the context of the design of large associative memories and systems based upon them. But more is possible. Once a datum is located, rather than move it to the requesting processor, one can also manipulate the datum at the point of storage itself. We would like, in particular, that the generic operations listed above be performed efficiently.

The price of semiconductor memory has been dropping rapidly (with the exception of a current glitch caused by governmental policies), and the feasibility of non-volatile main memory is now no longer in question [6]. The idea of a massive main memory being used to store databases has been explored in [8] and in [15]. It now appears virtually certain that completely silicon resident databases will soon become economically feasible for at least some

---

1. This is the positive statement equivalent to the negative statement in [11] regarding database machines.

interesting applications. An effective database machine should be able to function well over completely memory-resident databases, and also be able to efficiently support disks for larger databases.

With these concepts in mind, we designed SWIM (Structured Wafer-Scale Intelligent Memory) as a database and object-orientation accelerator that can be plugged in the back of any regular machine. The basic idea in SWIM is that enough intelligence is associated at the point of data storage to make it unnecessary for most data to be shipped to the main processor. The main processor would only serve to control and coordinate the operation of the memory units. Just as there is orders of magnitude difference between the access time from main memory and access time from disk, there is roughly an order of magnitude difference between the access time from cache and the access time from main memory. For applications that manipulate large data structures, effective use of a processor cache is usually difficult. Therefore, instead of a cache, which is a small memory attached to the processor, we attach a small special-purpose processor to the memory. This special-purpose processor has been designed to perform efficiently the pointer, field, and set operations mentioned above.

Existing systems, multiprocessor based or not, allow several concurrent transactions to be processed in a system for performance reasons. Much attention has also been focussed recently on exploiting parallelism within a single complex transaction. Parallel processing is a recognized way to speed-up operations that can conveniently be divided. Multiple processors have been suggested in the database context in [7, 17, 21]. SWIM's architecture is fundamentally that of an MIMD multiprocessor.

A SWIM system prototype is under construction. The hardware design is complete, and realization is in progress. The basic software architecture is in place, and a cycle-accurate simulator is available, but the data management code is yet to be written.

We begin with a quick overview of the SWIM architecture in Section 2. Section 3 is the heart of the paper. Here we present a discussion of the issues involved in building a data manager on SWIM, and show some of the design decisions we have made. In Section 4, we consider specific examples to give the reader an idea of the usage and performance of SWIM. We round off with some final remarks in Section 5.

2. OVERVIEW OF THE ARCHITECTURE

Figure 1 shows a conceptual view of the SWIM system. The memory system is composed of many small memory units, each called an Active Storage Element (ASE), embedded in a communication network. Each active storage element has microprogrammable processing logic associated with it allowing it to perform data manipulation operations locally. Simple and small objects can be stored and manipulated entirely within an ASE, while larger and more complex objects are stored within several ASEs, and are cooperatively managed. ASEs may operate independently or collectively. Furthermore, different groups of ASEs can operate simultaneously on different data structures, or sub-parts of a single data structure.

The global system architecture we envision is depicted in Figure 2. It is a shared-memory multiprocessor system, with SWIM constituting the memory subsystem for the multiprocessor. Any processor, Pi, can access the storage provided by SWIM via its associated memory port, called an Access Element. Additionally, a processor, Pi, could function as an I/O processor.

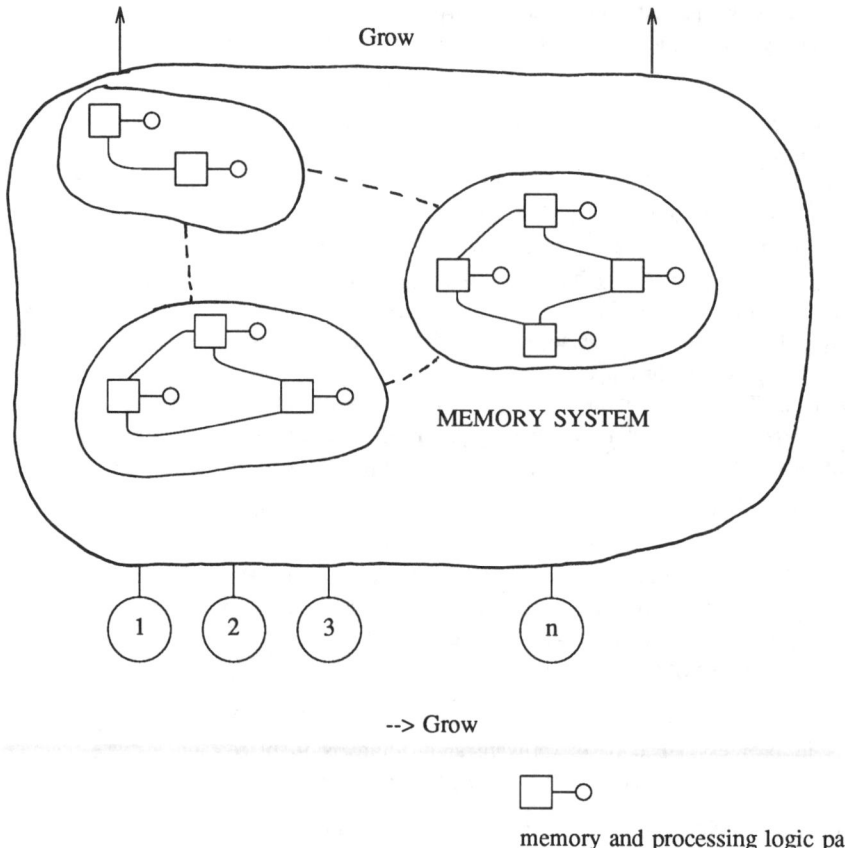

memory and processing logic pair

Figure 1. A Conceptual View of SWIM

A mass storage medium, such as high capacity magnetic or optical disk, could be added to the system for large databases or for archival purposes. The SWIM system itself is capable of paging data in and out of disk in parallel to, and with little interference in, other memory transactions. In fact, multiple disk drives could be used, as suggested in [14], for example. The availability of a large number of memory units permits many disk transfers to occur in parallel and permits a high I/O bandwidth.

SWIM is a parallel processing system in that the memory is divided into many small *Active Storage Elements* (ASE), operating in parallel. Groups of ASEs are interconnected via a Store Network, as shown in Figure 3, forming a *memory module* consisting of a two-dimensional grid of busses with switches at all the cross-points, as shown in Figure 3. One problem with most parallel processor implementations of database systems is that the interconnection network chosen has been a simple bus, with bandwidth on this bus becoming a performance bottleneck. The multiple bus structure internal to the Store Network will provide orders of magnitude more bandwidth for communication between ASEs. Each memory module also has some Control Logic for Accesses to Memory (CLAM). This logic performs several functions,

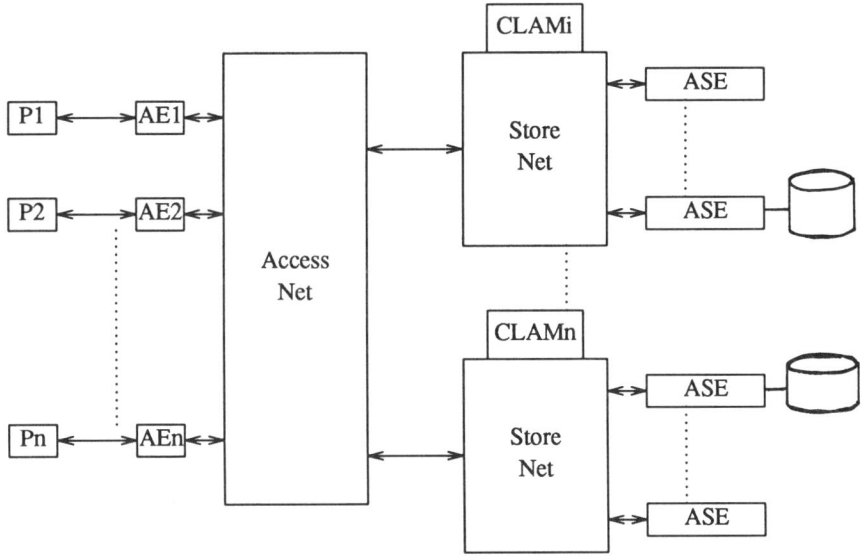

AEi: Access Element
CLAMi: Control Logic for Accesses to Memory
ASE: Active Storage Element

Figure 2. SWIM Architecture

mostly of a housekeeping nature. The Store Network also provides flexible and efficient communication between ASEs and the CLAM inside a memory module. Another important property of the Store Network is *disjointness*, that is, the ability to allow simultaneous communication between two or more sets of ASEs in a memory module. This property is consistent with our goal of being able to exploit the hitherto under-utilized memory bandwidth to the fullest.

Each ASE consists of five chips on a wafer circuit board, four memory chips, each 32K×8, and one logic chip, which includes the data structure manipulation logic, the micro-control store, and the communication facilities. Each bus is scaleable to 32 ASEs, for a total of 1024 ASEs in a memory module, with a storage capacity of 256 megabytes. In the absence of contention, a single packet, consisting of two 32-bit words of data, can be transmitted from one ASE to another in 200 nanoseconds. Communication across memory modules is significantly more expensive. We shall be concerned in this paper with the use of a single memory module.

3. BUILDING AN OBJECT DATA MANAGER FOR SWIM

3.1 Using SWIM

SWIM attempts to provide the *structured* view of memory that programs and human users would truly like to see. Figure 4 shows SWIM's view of memory: a processor sees memory

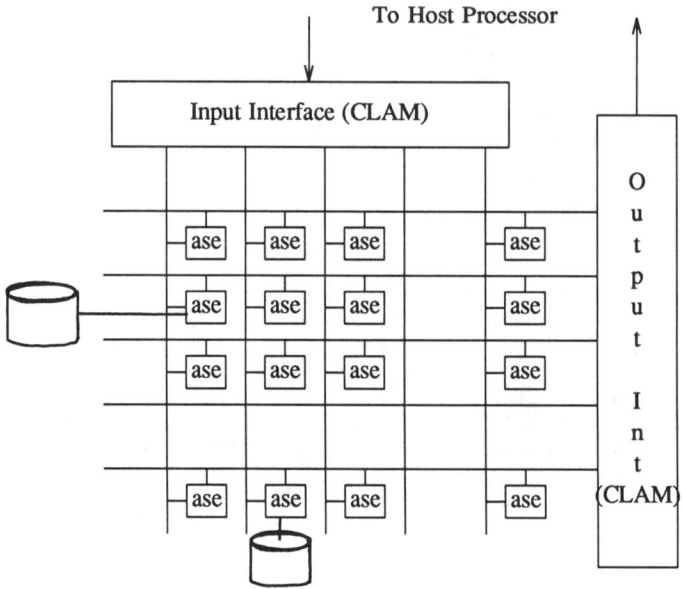

Figure 3. A Single SWIM Array and the Store Network

not as sequentially addressable linear memory but as a collection of data-structures, i.e. objects, that are created, manipulated, and accessed in any order simply by issuing the appropriate request to the memory system. A processor communicates with SWIM through *transactions*. Physically a transaction is a formatted set of bits (or a packet) that is transmitted from the processor to the SWIM system. A transaction consists of a *request* and a *reply*. A request could be a simple memory read operation or a more complex operation such as a relational join. A reply could be a "code" indicating the result of the requested operation, a value (or set of values), a pointer to a value, or an object identifier.

It is possible for a processor to issue transactions to SWIM one after another without waiting for the response from the previous transactions. SWIM would process these transactions and provide the responses required. Since some transactions may require more time than others, the responses may be out of order, and are identified by means of some transaction identifiers that the processor and SWIM agree upon.

It is our intent that SWIM be used as hardware support for an object-oriented software system such as (Concurrent) C++ [9, 20]. The structured objects supported by SWIM would be the types or classes mandated by the object-oriented software, with operations being associated with each object type. In specifying the object type, the user can select whether to implement the type in software, in SWIM microcode, or in some combination thereof. The user of the object type merely uses these pre-defined operations without being concerned about the SWIM microcode implementation details. The relationship between the software components and the SWIM system is shown in Figure 5. Operations on multiple objects are performed by initiating an operation on one object and having the microcode for this operation send messages that initiate corresponding "sub-operations" on the other objects involved. The

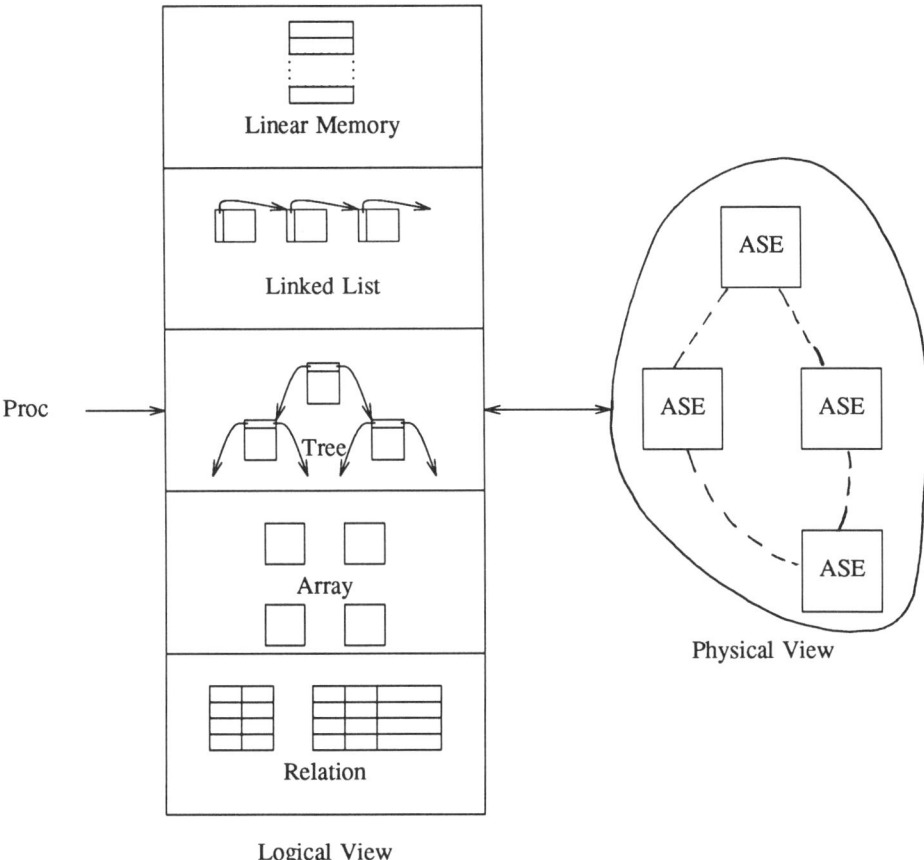

Figure 4. Processor's View of Structured Memory in SWIM

types of all the objects involved must be known to one another.

3.2 Object Management

SWIM supports persistent shared data in the hardware at the data structure level. As such, it naturally implements (at least a flat) object-oriented system, with encapsulation. Inheritance, the other major cornerstone of object-oriented systems, is not implemented in the hardware. Instead, where possible, inherited procedures are expanded at microcode compile time. Run-time downloading of microcode is possible for procedures that must be inherited at run time.

An object management system, similar to a conventional file system, is used to organize the data, and serves as the bottom layer of the object-oriented data manager. The SWIM interface to an object is similar to the standard UNIX® interface to the file system. Each data structure is treated like a sequential file in a traditional operating system. Once a user has determined a

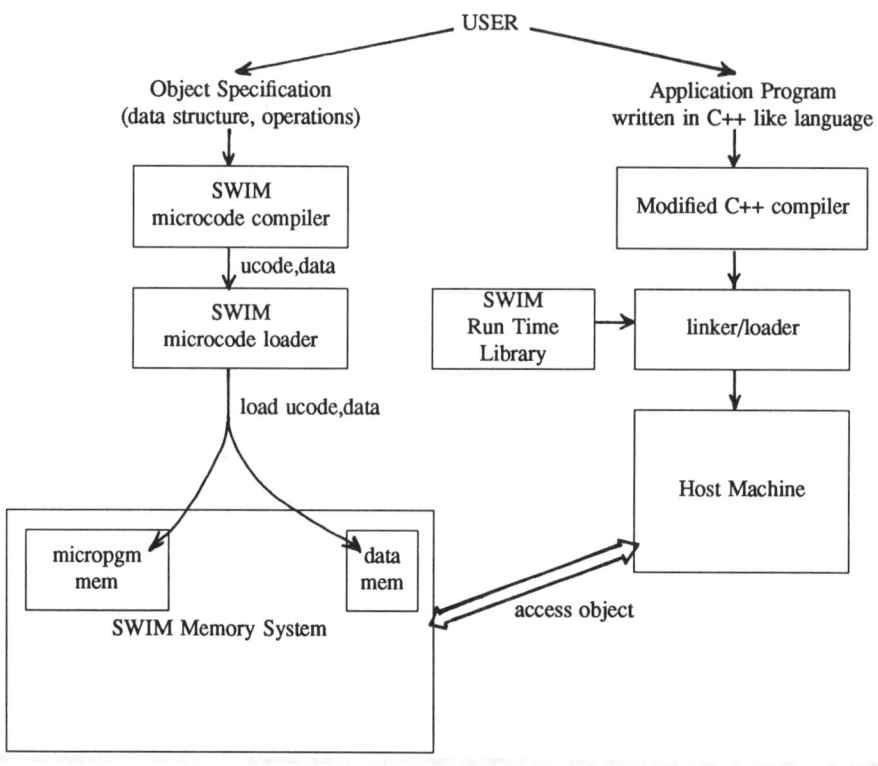

Figure 5. Code Compilation Path for a Computer System with SWIM

data structure that he wishes to access, he simply *opens* it and obtains an *object identifier* that can, subsequently, be used to access this object. The open operation ensures that the data structure of interest is in memory, paging it in if it is not; finds the ASE that has the data structure in it, and creates an identifier using the ASE address and the object identifier within the ASE. The permissions of the opening process are checked to ensure that the object is indeed accessible in the manner (read/write) intended. The inverse of open is *close*. Close simply records at the ASE that the object is now not to be referenced further. Multiple agents may open and close the same object concurrently, provided that such concurrent access is legitimate (for example, read only). An object that is opened by no one is called *passive* and is a candidate for paging out to disk when the need arises. (*Active* objects, those that are not passive, may also be paged out as in a virtual memory system. However, certain types of objects may have large paging costs, for example, when there are embedded pointers to other objects so that paging requires relocation. As such, the paging of active objects should be carefully controlled, and preferably avoided. In practical terms, if objects are properly defined, paging of active objects can be avoided if, in conventional terms, all pages affected by concurrently active transactions can be kept in memory).

An object directory system is used to locate or specify an object. This directory is structured like a directory in a traditional file system, as a tree with some additional "links". However, more sophisticated structuring is possible. The directory is itself an object managed by the system.

A new object, of an existing class, is created by a *create* command. Space is allocated in an ASE configured to handle the particular class of objects and an identifier returned to the user. Upon closing (performed automatically at the end of a program), such an object is deleted, unless it has previously been *saved* by naming it and creating a directory entry for it. Objects can be deleted, moved from one place in the directory to another, and so on, just as in a conventional file system.

An object oriented database application could run in this environment as a single program that manages concurrent access to a large number of objects. The primary service provided by such a program would be efficient searching and indexing mechanisms, and good paging strategies. The primitive directory system could also be supplanted. Beyond this, the structure of the object itself may be hidden from the user to the extent that it is intended to present the user with an abstraction.

3.3 Relational Databases

A characteristic of relational database applications is the requirement of handling large, relatively homogeneous sets of data in substantially similar ways. From the days of early associative processors, such as [4, 16], data parallelism has been suggested as a good technique to apply in this context. Today, the connection machine [10], appears to have a reasonable solution to the problem [12]. However, in parallel implementations of database machines, one has to worry about the I/O behavior [1]. The performance obtained from a large number of processors is likely to be limited by the I/O bandwidth obtainable. The intelligent use of indices is desirable.

In SWIM, even though hundreds of ASEs could be harnessed in parallel to answer a query, that is not the expected normal mode of operation. There are two basic "object" types: data pages (or horizontally partitioned relation fragments) and index pages. (Any semantic notion of objects that the user may have should be translated down to these basics for efficiency).

Query parsing and optimization are complex operations that are not data intensive. As such, they are performed in the main processor, and decomposed "primitive" queries posed to the SWIM system according to an access method selected by the main processor.

A significant cost in the use of indices is their maintenance as the data is updated. A major benefit of using SWIM is that this maintenance comes almost for free. When a query (or update) arrives, SWIM can immediately "return" with the response, and then reorganize the index in the background. Such background updating of index structures results in smaller latency to response, though not in greater throughput. Such a quick commitment of a transaction, prior to complete execution, is possible only if the system is able to guarantee atomic completion beyond the commit point. This guarantee can sometimes be given in the SWIM system.

3.4 Data Distribution

Whenever there are multiple locations at which data can be stored and processed, the question of data partitioning arises. This subject has been studied extensively in the context of distributed database design. These techniques do not apply in the SWIM context, in view of the small size of each processor and the extremely fast communication facility. On the one hand every ASE has memory for no more than 16 pages of 8K bytes each. On the other hand, 8 bytes is the standard minimum size communication between two ASEs, and such an 8 byte message can be transferred, register of transmitter to register of receiver in less than 200 nanoseconds. This speed is roughly 20 times typical disk transfer rates on a per byte basis, with the additional advantage that transfers here occur in 8 byte units rather than 8Kbyte units.

In consequence, locality of reference is good as long as the entire referenced data fits within the memory of one ASE. If more data is likely to be required by a transaction, it is usually faster to assign the excess to a different ASE where it can be found in memory through a quick message rather than having to wait for a disk transfer.

Two alternatives were considered for the placement of disks. We could have the disk drives be shared among all (or sets of many) ASEs. Or we could have dedicated disk drives, one to each (or at least some) ASE. The former is likely to give better disk I/O performance and make data placement issues disappear at least as far as the disk drives are concerned. However, it relies on a good switching network to enable the movement of pages of data from any ASE to any disk drive. While such a design is possible, it is against the SWIM philosophy of taking the computation to where the data is, in the belief that location transparency is likely to cause unacceptable performance penalties. We follow the latter alternative.

The heuristics for data distribution are that pages likely to be referenced together should be placed on the same drive, associated with the same ASE, provided that they are 16 or less in number. Once the threshold is crossed, it is better to split the co-referenced set of pages into two or more smaller sets and assign each to a different ASE. The problems are similar to those encountered in deciding what data should reside together on a page in an object-oriented database.

3.5 Transaction Migration and Concurrency

Each ASE behaves as a message-driven single context engine. The ASE has a notion of a transaction that is uninterruptible. Until one transaction is complete, no messages associated with other transactions will be received, though additional messages may be received by an executing transaction. There is no system support for the saving of contexts between transactions. Any state that one transaction wishes to leave for another must be done as part of the data structures stored at the ASE.

In the course of transaction execution at one ASE, messages may be sent to other ASEs, initiating the execution of transactions at these ASEs. The hardware supports asynchronous calls, though a particular application may wish to execute synchronous calls. (Note that even with synchronous calls, we really do not have the correct formal semantics for a *nested* transaction). The drawback of having a single-context engine wait for the sub-tasks to complete and return is that the engine has to remain idle while it waits, causing a loss of parallelism and hence performance.

A single user transaction will typically begin on one ASE, and then through the asynchronous initiation of procedures on other ASEs, *migrate* to other ASEs. It may or may not return to the initial ASE. All state associated with the "process" migrating is included in the message(s) initiating such migration. Thus a single user transaction could consist of multiple transactions on multiple ASEs. Each ASE transaction can be viewed as a primitive operation or method constituting the user transaction.

Multiple agents could issue transactions to SWIM at the same time. These agents could be different processes created under a single user program, different user processes on the same processor, or even completely unrelated processes on different processors. In fact, these processes need not even be resident on what we conventionally consider processors, but may include DMA units (that handle data transfer between SWIM and disks, used for overflow or back-up) and user terminals (including even Automated Teller Machines, for example). There is no serialization of transactions that are presented to SWIM. In fact, SWIM has a multiplexer (with some hardware buffering and conflict resolution) to permit multiple transactions to be received at the same time. As long as these transactions all refer to mutually disjoint data structures, even if they all be within the same SWIM system, parallel execution is possible. However, when two or more transactions that affect some data structures in common enter the system at the same time, there is danger of interference.

Provided that the user transaction is a single SWIM transaction, its atomicity is automatically preserved, since the ASE completes execution of one task before initiating the next one. When a user transaction translates into multiple atomic SWIM transactions, standard concurrency control techniques are required. For example, an atomic SWIM transaction can be used to "lock" an ASE or part of the data managed by an ASE, providing an application with the guarantee of no interference from other user transactions. The atomicity of user transactions is not guaranteed by SWIM but by the software written to translate user requests into SWIM transactions, and the concurrency control and deadlock prevention techniques adopted in the software. However, fairly high level atomic actions (especially compared to the primitive test-and-set provided on many machines) are directedly supported in the hardware to assist in this process.

3.6 Protection and Recovery

A transaction that aborts must undo any updates that have already been performed. We achieve this by performing in-place updates and maintaining an *ephemeral log* with each transaction. Upon commit this log is discarded. Upon transaction abort, the contents of the log are used to undo the updates. See [2] for details of this scheme. Upon any system failure, all currently active transactions can be aborted to bring everything to a consistent state.

A significant worry in using non-volatile main memory to store a database is that a software error could inadvertently clobber large parts of the database. The assumption in a traditional disk-based system is that the process of calling a device driver and paging material in and out of disk provides a reasonable "sanity check" and contains any damage within a small local region. In SWIM, since the processor does not directly access memory, but rather does so through the intermediary of some intelligence in the ASE, the same sort of "protection" against software errors is automatically achieved. Protection against power failure is through the use of non-volatile memory. If magnetic media are used, protection against media failure is through the standard techniques of mirroring, redundancy through logs, etc.

Protection against unauthorized access is normally not paid a lot of attention since it is assumed to be quite simple to do, given that the operating system is partitioning user space properly and protecting partitions zealously. A problem with the use of memory partitions for protection is that sharing becomes hard, and a lot of in-memory copying is often required. Since we have intelligence available to monitor each access to memory, we can now protect in the proper way at the level of an individual access. All read/write protection is provided by the ASE, and occurs transparently to the requesting processes on the main CPU.

4. EXAMPLES

In this section we consider two example applications to give the reader a flavor of the way in which SWIM is used, and the sort of performance benefits to be expected therefrom. The first example is a pattern search in a text file. We have actually implemented this on our cycle-accurate simulator, and present benchmarked performance numbers. This example is meant to give a thorough understanding of a simple problem. The second example is a thumbnail sketch of a transaction processing system. The code for this system is not in place yet; the example and performance estimates have been included to give an idea of how large applications may be ported to SWIM.

4.1 Pattern Search

Pattern searching through a text file is an important operation in many data management situations, such as in the case of bibliographic databases. Even in traditional databases, lexicographic comparisons are important for sorting, for performing selections based on fields that have not been indexed, and so forth. The operations involved in lexicographic comparison are similar to the ones for pattern matching described here.

Consider a text file stored across several ASEs using a two level tree structure. The root ASE maintains the pointers to all the leaf ASEs that store the data for the file. A search request, specifying the expression to be matched, is received by the root ASE. The search pattern could be an arbitrary text string with provisions for including wild card characters [*,?]. The root ASE sends messages to the leaf ASEs initiating the pattern search operation in all the ASEs in parallel. The root also designates one ASE to be the collator of the matches that are found, and relays the identity of this collator in the initiating messages sent to the leaves. From there on the search proceeds in parallel and the results are sent to the collator for storage or further processing. Note that the root ASE is free once it has initiated this parallel searching phase. Similarly, each text-file ASE is free when it completes searching through its portion of the file and hands off the matches to the collator.

For a search pattern that consists of only a few bytes, an 8 byte or 16 byte message from the root ASE may contain all the information necessary to initiate the pattern match at one of the parallel slave ASEs. Even if multiple point-to-point messages are used, the total time required for this purpose remains very small at under 200ns for an 8-byte message. Similarly, the effort to collate the matches is typically small. The bulk of the effort is in the actual pattern matching, where parallelism can be exploited.

Even aside from the parallelism, the pattern matching should proceed faster in a single ASE than on most full-sized regular general-purpose machines. One reason for this speed-up is the proximity of the processing to the data making every access look like a cache access, with no misses. A more important reason for the speed-up is that there are on average three separate conditions to be checked for each character (of the text file). Conditional branching is a well-known villain against performance in most machines. In a SWIM ASE, all three of these conditions can be checked simultaneously and the correct action taken, permitting one character examination every cycle. (See [5] for details). Similarly, there are comparison and control logic circuits specially devoted to speeding up the search operation in each ASE. Thus, overall, the specialized microarchitecture of the ASE provides a big win.

We benchmarked such a search transaction on our cycle-accurate simulator for the SWIM system. We used a file size of 2.66 Mbytes, and a 64Kbyte memory in each ASE, so that 41 ASEs were required to store the file. Since a pattern match search can take place on all the ASEs in parallel, one would expect a speed-up by a factor of almost 41 compared with a uniprocessor implementation. However, the results showed a speed-up by a factor of 5617 over an implementation of the same algorithm on a VAX 8650! Recall that the ASEs were designed to be able to perform one character search, of the form above, per cycle. We were able to get, in our benchmark, about 1.2 cycles/character search, which translates to about 60ns/character search time given our 50ns cycle time design goal. The corresponding number for the VAX 8650 was measured to be 8.25μs/character on a 55ns cycle time. Thus architectural improvements directly account for a speed-up by a factor of 137 for this particular application (which multiplied by 41 gives the total speed-up of 5617 observed).

4.2 Credit/Debit Transactions

As mentioned before, we have not yet written the software for this application, though fragments, such as a lock manager, have been written and simulated. As such, only rough performance estimates are possible, less reliable than the actual simulation numbers presented in the previous subsection. We present below our estimates of potential bottleneck points in the system and the limits they impose on the transaction rates that can be supported. A standard TP1 transaction [3] is assumed.

The architecture consists of specialized ASEs. There are *Transaction Manager* ASEs that maintain the data structures representing the state of the transaction and issue requests to other ASEs as appropriate. Several transactions share one *Transaction Manager*. There is one *Lock Manager* ASE that performs concurrency control. The remaining ASEs each manage some part of the database, and are responsible for queries to and updates on their respective fragments.

Each query first arrives at a transaction manager ASE, and is assigned a data structure there corresponding to its process (transaction) state. Sub-transactions are issued by the transaction manager, as appropriate, to obtain and release locks, read and update data, etc. Each of these sub-transactions goes directly to the relevant ASE, and is performed atomically. (We are ignoring any sequential processing that may also have to be run on such a system).

The processing for each transaction involves two index look-ups to locate the customer account, and one index look-up each to locate the teller and branch accounts. All transactions only update balances, with no insertions or deletions, so that the indices are never updated. Each of the account balance, teller balance and branch balance update involves obtaining a write lock, and modifying the balance in a recoverable way. A transaction may fail upon attempting to reduce an account balance below zero. Since indices are not updates, we will not consider index locks further, except to assume that two read locks are required.

Let us first look at the *Lock Manager* as a possible bottleneck. If a lock is available, it is immediately granted, and the process takes only 4 cycles. If the lock is not available at the time of request, the request is added to a wait-for graph, and cycles checked for[2]. It takes 3 cycles to cancel a pending request at the lock manager. It takes 2 cycles to release a lock, and 2 additional cycles to schedule a pending request. An "average" loop check requires 10 cycles. We assume that most loops involve no more than 2 transactions. Let the probability of successfully obtaining a requested lock with no waiting be p, a constant independent of the particular user transaction, of the particular data sought to be locked, and of the number of locks already obtained. If there is no deadlock, the number of cycles consumed is 20 for 5 locks (3 write locks and 2 read locks), plus an additional 12 per lock obtained after a delay. Then the number of ASE cycles of the *Lock Manager* consumed by a user transaction can be calculated to:

$20 + 12\times(\text{prob. of 1 request delayed}) + 12\times 2\times(\text{prob. of 2 requests delayed})$
$\quad\quad\quad + \cdots + 12\times 5\times(\text{prob. of 5 requests delayed}) =$
$20 + 60(1-p)p^4 + 240(1-p)^2 p^3 + 360(1-p)^3 p^2 + 240(1-p)^4 p + 60(1-p)^5$

For $p = 0.5$, the expression works out to 30.6 cycles, which require roughly 1.5µs, permitting a throughput of 650,000 transactions per second. Even if we assume $p = 0$, saying that no lock is ever granted without having to wait, we still require only 80 cycles per transaction at the lock manager, for a throughput of 250,000 transactions per second.

Looking at the network, per transaction there are roughly 20 short (8 byte) messages between ASEs and two longer messages, say 128 bytes each. There also is external input of 128 bytes and output of 128 bytes. This total message traffic works out to 136 packet transfers per transaction. Assuming a 1000 ASE SWIM system with 32 horizontal busses and 32 vertical busses, the total communication capacity of the system is 64 simultaneous packet transfers. Each transfer requires 100ns. Thus the maximum parallel transfer rate possible is 640 million packet transfers per second. Even assuming that a network loading of more than 20-25% could cause unacceptable delays in transmission, we still find the network capable of supporting 1 million transactions per second.

Let us examine concurrency at a hot page as a possible bottleneck. Assume a two-phase commit protocol with lock request on a hot page always being the last lock requested, so that the locks are all released immediately after this update has occurred. 4 cycles to get a lock, 2 cycles to release a lock, 8 cycles for the update, and 4 messages of 3 cycles each within the lock duration, gives a total time of 26 cycles, which at 50ns/cycle is 1.3µs. So the limit is 770,000 transactions per second if concurrency at a very hot page is the bottleneck.

---

2. In the simple credit-debit case, to minimize the amount of time for which locks are held on the more critical resources, the order of lock requests would be first the account record, then the teller record, and finally the branch record. If all transactions request locks in the same order, then deadlocks cannot arise in a two-phase locking scheme. As such no loop checks may be necessary, and our analysis here consequently overly pessimistic.

Now consider a cold page; one that is not in memory and has to paged from disk. The update time is not significant compared to the read in and write back. An ASE is kept busy for the duration of 1 page in and 1 page out, let us say roughly 40ms. One ASE is required for every 25 such "cold" updates per second. Assuming one such update per transaction, 400 ASEs devoted to cold pages can provide a throughput of 10,000 tps.

In summary, we find up until the 100 Ktps range, that the bottleneck in SWIM is not concurrent updates of hot pages (along with the associated recovery processing), is not the lock manager, and is not the communication network. The throughput is primarily limited by the ability to access well-partitioned data from disks attached to dedicated ASEs. In other words, the number of ASEs with attached drives is the limiting factor in the throughput that can be obtained. In other words the system can be scaled to achieve a desired performance level.

5. CONCLUSION

In this paper we have presented an overview of a memory transaction engine. Through the association of intelligence with semiconductor memory used for storage it becomes possible to build a memory transaction server with functionality and performance that were hitherto unknown. We have a fully functioning cycle-accurate simulator for this system and performance benchmarks on the simulator are very encouraging. Circuit design and layout are currently in progress. We conclude by highlighting the benefits of using SWIM as the basis for implementing database systems:

- A central theme in SWIM is to increase the memory functionality by storing in it not uninterpreted strings of bits but actual data structures that the memory can manipulate locally upon receiving requests from a processor. The most important consequence of this is that the processor to memory bandwidth requirement plummets as many low level memory accesses are replaced by a few high level commands concerning the structures.
- Data structure operations are now likely to complete sooner for several reasons. First, since the memory now physically adjoins the processing logic, access delays drop. Secondly, local data operations eliminate bus contention with other processors. Thirdly, a small, relatively specialized microprogrammable processor associated with each block of memory in SWIM can, through appropriate choice of architecture, out-perform a larger and more expensive general-purpose CPU for most memory operations. Finally, data parallelism can be exploited better.

REFERENCES

[1] R. Agrawal and D.J. DeWitt, "Whither Hundreds of Processors in a Database Machine," *Proc. Int'l Workshop High-Level Computer Architecture 84*, May 1984, 6.21-6.32.

[2] R. Agrawal and H. V. Jagadish, "Recovery Algorithms for Database Machines with Non-Volatile Main Memory," AT&T Bell Laboratories Technical Memorandum, 1989

[3] Anon, et al., "A Measure of Transaction Processing Power," *Datamation*, Apr. 1, 1985, 112-118.

[4] B. A. Crane *et al*, "PEPE Computer Architecture," in *IEEE CompCon*, 1972, 17-22.

[5] J. A. Chandross, H. V. Jagadish, and A. Asthana, "The Trap as a Control Flow Mechanism," *Proceedings of MICRO 21, the 21st Annual Workshop on Microprogramming and Micro-Architecture*, Dec. 1988.

[6] G. Copeland, R. Krishnamurthy, and M. Smith, "The Case for Safe RAM," Tech. Rept. ACA-ST-080-88, MCC, Austin, Texas, Feb. 1988

[7] D.J. DeWitt, "DIRECT - A Multiprocessor Organization for Supporting Relational Database Management Systems," *IEEE Trans. Computers*, C-28(6), June 1979, 395-406.

[8] H. Garcia-Molina, R. J. Lipton, and P. Honeyman, "A Massive Memory Database System," Technical Report #314, Dept. of Elec. Engg. and Comp. Sc., Princeton University, Sep. 1983

[9] N.H. Gehani and W.D. Roome, "Concurrent C," *Software—Practice & Experience*, 16(9), 1986, 821-844..

[10] D. Hillis, *The Connection Machine*, MIT Press, Cambridge, Mass., 1985.

[11] E. Neuhold and M. Stonebraker, "Future Directions in DBMS Research," Technical Report-88-001, Int'l Computer Science Inst., Berkeley, California, May 1988

[12] Craig Stanfill, presentation on, "Pattern Matching on the Connection Machine," *Third International Conference on Supercomputers*, Boston, MA, May 1988.

[13] Esen. A. Ozkarahan, Stewart A. Schuster, and K. C. Smith, "RAP - An Associative Processor for Data Base Management," in *Proceedings 1975 National Computer Conference*, vol. 44, AFIPS, 370-387.

[14] D. Patterson, G. Gibson, and R. H. Katz, "A Case for Redundant Arrays of Inexpensive Disks (RAID)," *Proc. ACM-SIGMOD 1988 Int'l Conf. on Management of Data*, Chicago, Illinois, June 1988.

[15] W.D. Roome and M.D.P. Leland, "The Silicon Database Machine: Rationale, Design, and Results," *Proc. 5th Int'l Workshop on Database Machines*, Karuizawa, Nagano, Japan, Oct. 1987.

[16] Jack A. Rudolph, "A Production Implementation of an Associative Array Processor - STARAN," in *Proceedings of the 1972 Fall Joint Computer Conference*, vol. 41, AFIPS, 229-241. Have this.

[17] David Elliot Shaw, "The Non-Von Supercomputer," Department of Computer Science, Columbia University, August 1982

[18] D. L. Slotnick, "Logic Per Track Devices," in *Advances in Computers*, vol. 10, Frantz Alt (ed.), Academic Press, New York, 1970, 291-296.

[19] David J. Stoves, "CAFS800: Some Principles and Practices," in *Proceedings of the 5th International Online Meeting, and Learned Information*, 1981. Paper Deals with CAFS.

[20] B. Stroustrup, *The C++ Programming Language*, Addison-Wesley., 1986.

[21] Stanley Y. W. Su, G. P. Copeland, and G. J. Lipovsky, "The Architectural Features of CASSM: A Cellular System for Non-Numeric Processing," in *Proceedings of the First Annual Symposium on Computer Architecture*, 1983, 121-128. Paper deals with CASSM.

A PARALLEL TRANSITIVE CLOSURE ALGORITHM USING HASH-BASED CLUSTERING

Jean-Pierre Cheiney *, Christophe de Maindreville **

* Ecole Nationale Supérieure des Télécommunications
46, rue Barrault 75013 Paris, France
** Institut National de la Recherche en Informatique et Automatique
Rocquencourt, BP 105, 78153 Le Chesnay Cedex, France

electronic addresses: cheiney@inf.enst.fr
maindrev@madonna.inria.fr

abstract

The importance of the performance problem brought about by the evaluation of recursive queries brings one to consider parallel execution strategies for the transitive closure operation. Such strategies constitute one of the keys to efficiency in a very large data base environment. In this paper we present a transitive closure algorithm. The innovative aspects of this algorithm concern: 1) the possibility of working with a reasonable amount of memory space without creating extra Inputs/Outputs; 2) the use of on-disk clustering accomplished by double hashing; and 3) the parallelization of the transitive closure operation. The processing time is reduced by a factor of p, where p is the number of processors allocated for the operation. Communication times remain limited; a cyclic organization eliminates the need for serialization of transfers. The evaluation shows the importance of the benefits of a parallel transitive closure execution.

1. introduction

The efficient implementation of a transitive closure operator today appears to be one of the keys to the evaluation of recursive queries in a deductive DBMS. Numerous algorithms have been proposed [BANC86], [VALD86], [AGRA87], [HAN88], [GARD88], [IOAN88]. However, if these algorithms are examined in an environment of very large relations, two aspects are uncovered that until now have received little attention:

- the first concerns taking into account the memory space available for the operation. Tuples under manipulation are generally assumed to be held in main memory; the possibility of multiple read-operations due to memory saturation is too often either treated optimistically or not even considered.

- the second concerns the parallelization of the transitive closure operation. Even though this is a solution for executing the operation within acceptable time limits, parallel algorithms are rarely proposed.

This situation is all the more surprising because a lot of these proposed algorithms use multiple joins, either directly or implicitly. However, all of the recent works on efficient join implementation show the advantages of parallel processing and the need for taking into consideration available memory space [DEWI84]. Indeed, this guarantees a parallel execution in a single read-operation of on-disk relations. After a period of defining operations and algorithms, we feel that today it is crucial, for the sake of execution efficiency, to study physical implementations, the use of clustering and access methods, and the unique advantages of multi-processor architectures [CHEI89].

Some recent papers approach the operator implementation problem by considering efficient transitive closure execution or using multi-processor architectures. [AGRA87] and [IOAN88] consider Input/Output minimization on direct algorithms (where transitive closure is considered as a problem of graphs). [VALD88a] proposes an execution of the operation in a parallel architecture. Transitive closure is executed in several passes and uses a two-way merge type operation from locally generated results. The relation is partitioned and, in n passes, with 2^n processor nodes, the total closure is calculated. However, the sequencing requires a coordinating node as well as a delicate balancing of overall system loading. [CHEI89] examines the efficient execution of a transitive closure that permits searches on a large number of rules.

In this paper we propose a multi-processor implementation of a transitive closure operator based on double hashing. This implementation aims to reconcile the processing of very large relations with acceptable response times. The framework is one of execution by join loops [BANC86]. Choosing a simple, well-known algorithm allows us to show more clearly the advantages of the "divide and conquer" strategy: the task is divided into a number of smaller tasks that can then be assigned to several processors. A very large transitive closure thus amounts to a collection of smaller operations. This decomposition provides:

i) the guarantee that each operation takes place in main memory without requiring extra read and write operations due to a lack of available memory space;

(ii) the assignment of the set of operations to several parallel processors, each of which performs the same task on a section of data (multiple backend operation).

We propose an algorithm based on double hashing of a binary relation to be joined, which is named "Double Hash Transitive Closure" (DHTC). This algorithm uses direct clustering of the relation to be joined without overburdening the memory for the linearization of the transitive closure operation, and can be directly implemented in a parallel structure. In a multi-processor arrangement with a multiple backend configuration [HSIA85] in which each processor performs the same relational operation, one can expect to achieve a reduction factor of p in the processing time of large transitive closures on on-disk clustering. Data transfers between processors are minimized and a cyclic organization eliminates the need for serialization of tasks caused by an occupied bus.

After this introduction, section 2 presents the basic concept of the algorithm applied for a general transitive closure denoted R*. Section 3 develops the parallel algorithm in a multi-processor architecture environment without shared memory. Finally, sections 4 and 5 present an evaluation of the algorithm, first from the point of view of memory space requirements, and then from the point of view of execution time. Section 6 concludes the paper.

2. a general algorithm for very large relations

In this paragraph we present the DHTC algorithm. The innovative aspects of the DHTC concern: 1) the possibility of working with a reasonable amount of memory space without creating too many Inputs/Outputs; 2) the use of on-disk clustering accomplished by double hashing; and 3) the parallelization of the transitive closure operation.

Using the same basic idea, a parallel algorithm is independently proposed in [VALD88b]. In fact, this algorithm does not use a clustering technique and re-hashes the new tuples during each iteration. In this paper, no consideration is given to the main memory size.

Most of the evaluations published on transitive closures use very optimistic hypotheses for analysing the number of Inputs/Outputs needed by the execution. Indeed, for algorithms that use join loops, it is generally supposed that join operations take place in main memory. Unless additional strategies are employed, this would call for a very large amount of memory space: if one considers a join loop algorithm, the memory has to be able to accomodate the largest possible ΔR generated during the processing, where ΔR is an intermediate relation in which newly generated tuples are stored in one iteration. As for the R pages, they are read one after the other. This hypothesis is especially overstated for certain distributions of the initial relation data. In addition, most algorithms use the set operations of union and difference for testing stop conditions. Such operations require sorts and suppression of duplicate tuples; furthermore, their efficient execution (i.e. calling for only one read operation of data from the disk) imposes severe constraints on available memory space.

When contemplating the manipulation of very large relations clustered on-disk, one can no longer consider the relation on which transitive closure is performed as a simple sequence of tuples. The main idea is to use clustering to reduce greatly the cost of the operation. Clustering characteristics, which are already largely used in the execution of other relational operators (selection, join, etc.) can likewise be exploited in transitive closure processing.

2.1. basic concept

Let us consider a binary relation R(X, Y) where X and Y are defined on the same domain D. The relation R defines a graph G, where a node is an element of D and an edge (x,y) denotes a tuple (x,y) of R. The transitive closure R* of the relation R consists of the transitive closure of its corresponding graph G, i.e. a tuple (x,y) is in R* iff there exists a path from x to y in G.

R is clustered on-disk. The size of this relation can be very large and thus, no optimistic hypothesis can be made regarding the comparison between this size and the size of available main memory. The join loop will be performed by a semi-naïve iterative algorithm [BANC86]. The major point we want to study is the limitation of Input/Output operations. In order to guarantee the linear aspect of the join operations, we want to reduce the size of the data which fits in main memory at a given time.

In an iterative algorithm, each iteration generates new tuples from R (stored on-disk) and ΔR tuples which were produced during the previous iteration. The latter may also possibly be re-written on the disk. During the initialization ΔR is composed of the set of R tuples. The generation of new tuples is based on joining the R relation with ΔR. In this configuration the use of a hash-based join algorithm is attractive [KITS83]: it permits efficient execution of the operator with reduced use of memory space [DEWI84]. In addition, the hash buckets used by the algorithm can correspond to an on-disk clustering of the relation. In order to use this possibility, the relation tuples are considered according to an on-disk clustering implemented with a hashing in n buckets, and the new ΔR tuples are considered as a set of n buckets that correspond to an identical hashing function.

Let's look at an iteration: with a hash-based join algorithm, each relation is divided into n buckets obtained by the same function applied to the join attribute. Only buckets having the same index are joined two by two, (buckets having different indices cannot join together). However, these algorithms are insufficient for executing a join loop because the result of one step must be rehashed according to a different attribute in order to form the usable buckets for the next step. Thus, if R is only hashed (and clustered) according to Y and ΔR according to X, the join resulting from a step permits only the joining of buckets where (R.Y) modulo n = (ΔR.X) modulo n ; but in order to form the ΔR tuples used in the next step, it is necessary to rehash the result according to the new value of X (the projection on the attributes R.X and ΔR.Y is immediately computed after the join).

Our proposal permits this rehashing to be avoided. The idea is to use a multi-attribute clustering technique which provides suitable hash buckets for each iteration. In order to do this, a *double-hashed* clustering of the relation R is performed. First R is hashed by a modulo function in n buckets according to the value of X; then each of these buckets is rehashed by the same function according to the value of Y. For example, one can use a Predicate Tree technique [GARD84] which guarantees a multi-attribute, dynamic hashing (necessary in the case of expansion). The tuples of the permanent relation R are thus hashed simultaneously according to the values of both X and Y. This technique allows the relation to be looked at according to two different partitionings [CHEI86]. The first (according to the value of Y) will be used for the join algorithm for hash buckets having the same index; the second (according to the value of X) will prevent the loss of the hash value information of each tuple according to the value of X and will thus avoid the need for a write-operation hashing during the following step.

The algorithm is illustrated on the following relation R:

R	X	Y
	1	2
	1	4
	2	3
	2	5
	4	2
	1	3

Y modulo2 ↓   0   1   ← X modulo2

	0	1
0	(4,2)	(1,2) (1,4)
1	(2,5) (2,3)	(1,3)

The relation is hashed in 4 buckets according to the values of X and Y. During initialization ΔR is composed entirely by R. Thanks to the on-disk double hashing, ΔR appears as 2 buckets (according to the values of X).

iteration 0

R	X	Y	
	4	2	bucket 00
	1	4	bucket 10
	1	2	
	2	3	bucket 01
	2	5	
	1	3	bucket 11

ΔR^0	X	Y	
bucket 0	4	2	
	2	3	
	2	5	
bucket1	1	2	
	1	4	
	1	3	

The first iteration of the algorithm will only perform joins between buckets 00, 10 of R and the bucket 0 of ΔR^0 on the one hand, and between buckets 10 and 11 of R and the bucket 1 of ΔR^0 on the other hand.

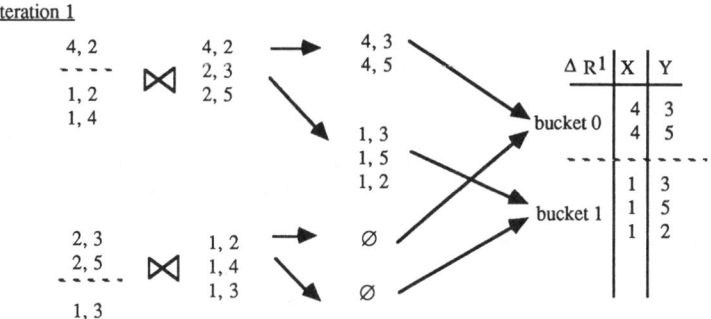

iteration 1

The results are stored directly in ΔR^1 without rehashing, according to the hash values of X which will be used during the following iteration. Iteration 2 can then proceed:

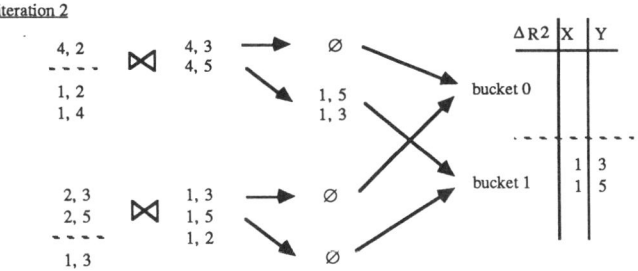

The stop condition is satisfied since no more new tuples are generated.

More generally, figure 1 represents, for the iteration p, the join between the buckets of index 3 of the R relation and the ΔR relation which has been obtained at the previous step. For this step, the join between the buckets of index 3 follows the join between the buckets of indices 0 to 2; it will be followed by the join between the buckets of index 4. The tuples of the ΔR relation which will be used at the next step are directly built without any rehashing, through accumulation of the tuples according to their hash values on X.

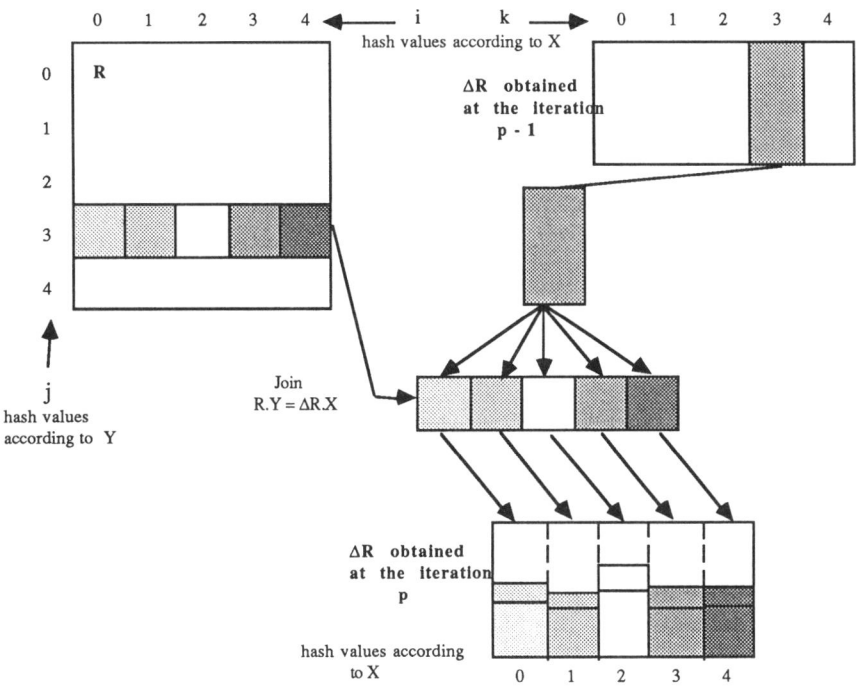

Figure 1: *Join loop with double hashing technique.*

2.2. Algorithm

We give in this section a more formal description of the algorithm.

- R is the permanent relation having the schema (X, Y)

- R is clustered on the two attributes X and Y. The hashing function used for this clustering is the same for both attributes; it is a modulo n function. The R relation is recursively hashed into n^2 buckets. First, it is hashed in n buckets according to the X attribute, and then, each one of these bucket is hashed into n buckets according to the Y attribute. The integer i represents the hash value for X and j represents the hash value for Y. $R = \cup_{ij} R_{ij}$ $0 \leq i \leq n-1, 0 \leq j \leq n-1$

- ΔR is a temporary relation composed of n buckets named k. ΔR_k store the tuples from ΔR having for k the hash value for the X attribute. $\Delta R = \cup_k \Delta R_k$ $0 \leq k \leq n-1$

    ΔR corresponds to one iteration of the construction of the transitive closure of R, denoted by R^*. The schema of this relation is (X, Y).

The join operation is assumed to include the projection that eliminates the join attribute. The join followed by the projection, i.e. the composition of R with S, will be denoted R∘S: $R \circ S = \Pi_{1,4} (R \bowtie_{2=3} S)$

```
function R* (R) : relation ;
  begin
     R* := R ;
     ΔR := R ;
     while ΔR contains new tuples do
        begin
           Z := ∅ ;
           for k :=0 to n-1 do
              for i:=0 to n-1 do
                 begin
                    RTik := ΔRk ° Rik ;
                    Zi := Zi ∪ RTik
                 end ;
           ΔR := ∪i Zi ;
           R* := R* ∪ ΔR
        end
  end ;
```

The Z ($\cup Z_i$) relation is necessary to stack all the tuples built in one iteration: ΔR has to be assigned to $\cup Z_i$ only when all the tuples of the previous generation are generated. In fact, the tuples of Z_i are obtained from the ΔR_k, with k between 0 and n-1.

The stop condition test and the elimination of redundant processing make it necessary to determine the existence of new tuples during each iteration. The determination of tuples must always be made in pairs. By the distributive property of the union operation, this condition can be determined separately on each hash bucket. The result is formed by an AND operation of the results evaluated on each bucket. Since the buckets are composed in order to be kept in main memory, the cost of the stop condition test is greatly minimized in the DHTC algorithm. We can take advantage of the partitioning of ΔR into several ΔR_k's, thanks to the double hashing.

3. parallel algorithm

The idea of decreasing execution times of relational operations by the intensive use of parallelism is very prevalent. Its effectiveness has been proven in numerous propositions and parallel implementations [KITS83], [DEWI86], [CHEI86]. The more recent data base machine architectures base their execution strategies around parallel algorithms. The multiple backend approach is very dominant [HSIA86]; besides the performance improvements, it provides other advantages such as reliability and possibilities for operating in a degraded mode. This approach lends itself to situations in which high-volume sequential processing is performed [GARD86], which is the case with transitive closures. One of the bases for this type of architecture is the division among the processors of the data to be processed. A simple, generally adopted way to perform this division is to form, using an appropriate function, as many hash buckets as there are processors available.

The DHTC algorithm is directly usable in such an environment. Thanks to the use of hashing, it lends itself naturally to parallelization. With a multiple backend configuration, as in [CHEI86], the join loop processing time can be divided by p, where p is the number of processors available.

The advantages of parallelization rest on the following principle: the initial relation is divided horizontally into several fragments, each of which is then processed by a separate processor. In an environment where memory is not shared ("shared nothing"), each processor processes the data from its own disk in its own memory. Each processor-memory-disk set can be viewed as a node in a network. In a centralized multi-processor architecture, the network consists simply of a bus, whereas with a divided configuration it consists of a veritable communication network. The main problem for parallel execution of a relational operation in general, and of a transitive closure in particular, is to give a maximum amount of local tasks to each processor while limiting data and message transfers at the same time. Unlike joins, the execution of a transitive closure cannot be totally "localized" by simple horizontal partitioning of the initial relation. In fact, tuples newly-produced in a particular node at a particular moment in the processing can be required by another node in order to continue the task. Transfers are thus absolutely necessary *during* execution of the transitive closure. However, inter-processor transfers can be limited to the smallest set necessary for each step.

We maintain the idea of a division of tuples among several nodes thanks to a partitioning by hashing on the attribute that will be the join attribute. The second hashing permits the composition of the buckets to be transferred in preparation for the next iteration. The sets of tuples exchanged between processors are minimized and formed directly. The bucket indices (i.e. the hash values) represent, for each bucket, the receiving node. Without extra processing or special messages, transfers are thus performed in a minimum of time. No extra synchronization or master node is necessary.

In a multiple backend configuration, each processor performs the same action. The data are divided into as many subsets as there are processors available for the operation. If each processor has its own disk (we shall assume, for simplicity's sake, such a configuration), the data are divided among these disks by hashing. At the outset, the relation R is distributed among as many sub-relations as there are processors. This division is calculated by hashing on the X attribute. Each sub-relation is rehashed locally according to the Y values. Overall, n^2 sub-buckets are to be dealt with (hashing in n buckets on the X attribute followed by rehashing of each bucket in n buckets on the Y attribute). If p processors are available, n = p is chosen.

Let p be the processor index; the buckets of index ip from R, i between 0 and n-1, will be clustered on the disk assigned to processor p (it is supposed that there is one disk per processor). The buckets of index p from the different ΔR's, produced during each step, are likewise distributed. In this way, for one iteration, the join of buckets R_{ip} and ΔR_p remains local to each processor. No transfers whatsoever are necessary per iteration for the processing of each step of an algorithm. The processing time during this phase of the algorithm is thus divided by the number of processors p. Actually, a non-uniformity in the hashing can considerably reduce this factor because the total time used is that of the slowest processor, i.e. the processor processing the largest volume of data. This problem, shared by all hashing methods, emphasizes the importance of a careful choice of the partitioning function.

The results from each join R_{ip} |X| ΔR_p must next be processed by processor i. Indeed, these tuples have the i hash value according to X; they form the ΔR_i sub-relation for the next iteration, which will be processed by processor i. A transfer is thus necessary. However, no rehashing has to be performed. The tuples destined for processor i are already stored in a specific sub-relation, thanks to the values from the second hashing. An initial version of the parallel algorithm can be given:

```
for each processor p do
    R*_p := R_p
    ΔR_p := R_p ;
    while ΔR_p contains new tuples do
        begin
            for i:=0 to p-1 do
                begin
                    Z_ip := ΔR_p ° R_ip ;
                    send Zip to node i
                end;
            receive (p-1) Z_pk ;        k=0..p-1, k≠p
            ΔR_p := ∪_k Z_pk ;          k= 0..p-1
            R_p* := R_p* ∪ ΔR_p
    end ;
```

The final result (R*) will be formed simply by the union of the different R^*_p's. It must be pointed out that this union does not require a suppression of duplicate tuples. Indeed, the sets to be combined are hash buckets and are thus necessarily disjoint.

In this algorithm, each processor awaits the arrival of all of the new tuples produced during one iteration in order to begin the next iteration (each of the p processors receives p-1 sub-relations coming from p-1 other nodes). A procedure that performs the "receive" function can easily take this role and verify that all the sub-relations have arrived.

One thing slows down this processing, however. A serialization, according to the order of write operations, can occur. In fact, if each processor p computes the buckets R_{ip} with the ordering (i:=0 to n), the serialization by the bus might slow down the entire computation: the processors compute all the buckets R_{ip} at the same time and try to send their results towards the same processor i (figure 2).

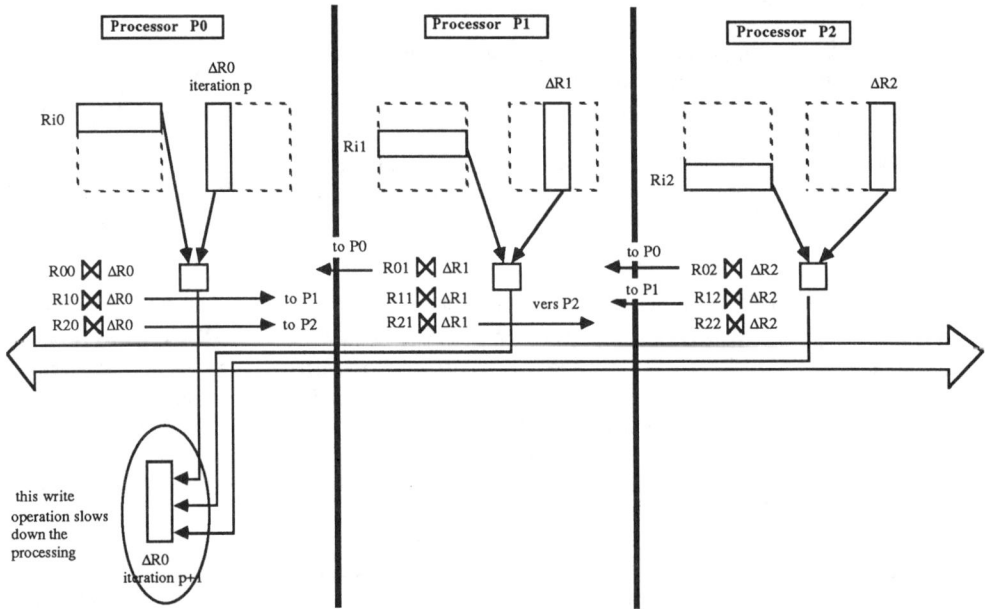

Figure 2: *inter-processor transfers and serialization according to order of write operations*

This problem can be solved by a cyclic organization of the data transfers. Each processor first computes the bucket R_{pp} and thus forms its own result. Then it computes the following bucket $(R_{(p+1)p})$ and transfers the result to the processor p+1. Thus, the data transfer is done in a cyclic way, each processor receiving one subrelation at a time, without a slow-down caused by simultaneous write operations in one node.

The algorithm is, for an iteration:

{parallel join loop}
    for each processor p do
        repeat
            i:=p ;
            $Z_{ip} := R_{ip} \circ \Delta R_p$;   {set of local joins}
            transfer Z_{ip} towards the disk used by the processor i ;
            i := (i+1) modulo p
        until i = p ;

The implementation can be further improved by pipelining the operations. Sub-relations transfered between nodes in fact don't need do be fully formed before being transfered. They can be transfered, page by page, as soon as they become available. Lost time due to possible loading imbalances between processors is thus minimized (such imbalances being due to a non-uniform hashing).

4. single read execution conditions

The evaluation of the algorithm brings out two critical elements: available memory size, and the cost of data transfers between processors. In order to simplify things, we shall first give the constraints on memory size which guarantee that each local operation remains linear. Then, since these conditions are not severe, we shall assume that they are satisfied and shall proceed to evaluate the time-performance of the algorithm.

4.1 Main memory size required for a single read execution in the case of a single processor

One difficult problem with large joins is making sure that their execution stays "linear"; each relation is read from disk only once. Therefore, this problem is very important with an iterative transitive closure algorithm, where a join is made in each iteration. The proposed algorithm reduces the memory requirement for a single read execution.

We use the following parameters to evaluate the main memory requirement:

|R| : size of R in pages ;
|M| : main memory size in pages ;
F   : uniformity ratio of hashing function .

Thus, when one relation R (size |R|) is hashed in n buckets, the size of the largest bucket (or sub-relation) is F. |R| / n.

Let n be the number of different hash values on X and Y. We want to determine the size of main memory required to guarantee one single read of the R relation, for each iteration.

During the join step, the buckets of identical hash values R and ΔR must join in main memory. The smallest sub-relation (ΔRj) stays in F. |R| / n pages (the Rij pages for one i value, are read one after another). In order to have full pages, we must keep n pages for Z. They correspond to the stacking of the produced tuples during an iteration (according to the Y hash values). These pages are written on disk as soon as they are full. R is hashed in n^2 buckets.

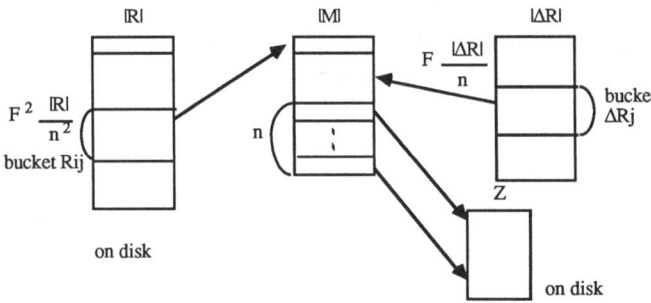

Figure 3: *"single read" join*

The condition is:

$|M| \geq F \cdot |\Delta R| / n + 1 + n$

With a cylindrical distribution of tuples [BANC86], the size of $|\Delta R|$ (new tuples generated during one step) can be considered equal to the size of the R relation. Thus, a sufficient condition is

$|M| \geq F/n \, |R| + 1 + n$

This condition is true when $(1 - |M|)^2 \geq 4 F \cdot |R|$. This constraint is easily met, it is:

$|M| \geq \sqrt{|R|}$ **condition 1**

The in-memory execution of each join loop step is guaranteed. If the memory is larger, the performance is improved because the Z result is kept in memory. The substitution of the old $|\Delta R|$ buckets by the new $|\Delta R|$ buckets is entirely performed in main memory. With this distribution, the relation has a maximum size $|R|$:

$|M| \geq F/n \, |R| + 1 + |R|$ let $|M| \geq (F/n + 1) |R| + 1$ **condition 2**

Condition 2 is harder to meet but guarantees an execution of the transitive closure in a single read.

4.2 multi-processor case

An overall memory size of $|B| = p \cdot |M|$ is presently available, where $|M|$ remains the local memory size available to a node in the network of processor-memory-disk sets. Since clustering is used, the hashing for partitioning is already done. At each node, the size of the sub-relations to be processed during each iteration is reduced, but the buckets remain the same as in the single-processor case. The memory size condition sought for is:

$|B| \geq p \sqrt{|R|}$ **condition 3**

We notice that the multi-processor configuration doesn't permit a reduction in local memory size. For a high number of processors, this situation brings about a significant increase in the cost of the architecture. However, if condition 3 is not true, it is possible to do a local re-hashing. This re-hashing implies two additional read-write operations. Indeed, they can be avoided by pipe-lining the transfers and the re-hashing [CHEI86]. On the other hand, it should be pointed out that each processor processes only one bucket out of the p buckets that form the relation R and the ΔR.

5. analysis and comparisons

This evaluation concerns the parallel processing of transitive closure. In this section we analyze the DHTC algorithm's performance and compare it to the performance of: 1) a simple iterative algorithm (Iterative Transitive Closure or ITC); and 2) Valduriez and Khoshafian's Parallel Transitive Closure (PTC) algorithm [VALD88a]. In order to make the comparison simpler, we shall use the same model and hypotheses as [VALD88a]. We thus assume that new tuples are uniformly produced, both by each processor and during each iteration of the join loop.

Likewise, we assume that the Input/Output times are identical for the three algorithms. This assumption is an optimistic hypothesis in favor of the ITC and PTC algorithms because they both require a large amount of memory space if on-disk re-read and re-write operations are to be avoided. In fact, the production time of new tuples taken into account in this evaluation includes both the processing and the necessary Inputs/Outputs. We consider this time as directly proportional to the number of new tuples produced, independent of the number of basic tuples processed (which are assumed to be read only once thanks to a sufficient amount of main memory). This hypothesis imposes much more substantial size requirements on the main memory for the ITC and PTC than for the DHTC.

5.1 response time

In the following analysis, we shall use the following parameters:

R : number of R tuples ;
Rnew : number of new tuples produced by the transitive closure ;
p : number of processors or nodes ;
d : number of join loop iterations ;

t : time to produce a new tuple ;
trf : time to transfer one tuple ;
msg : time to transfer one message ;

In this evaluation, we assume that the transfers do not saturate the network. The response time can be broken down into two parts: communication time and processing time. As for communication, messages between processors must be considered. These messages correspond to the operation of the algorithm's "send" and "receive" functions. Thus, the necessary time for transfering a bucket of n tuples equals n.trf + msg.

algorithme ITC

The ITC algorithm is performed by a single processor, after all the sub-relations on this node have been returned to their respective nodes of origin.

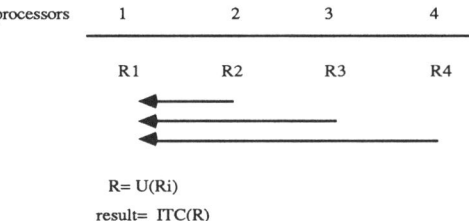

R= U(Ri)
result= ITC(R)

The response time consists of the communication time plus the processing time. The communication time corresponds to (p-1) times the transfer time of one sub-relation. In fact the serialization of transfers is inevitable here because one single node must receive all of the buckets. The communication time is thus:

$$(p-1)\left(\frac{R}{p}.trf + msg\right)$$

The processing time corresponds to the the production time of new tuples, i.e. simply : Rnew.t
The response time RT of the ITC algorithm is thus:

$$(p-1)\left(\frac{R}{p}.\text{trf} + \text{msg}\right) + \text{Rnew.t}$$

PTC algorithm

Valduriez and Koshafian give in [VALD88a] a complete evaluation of their algorithm. Let us recall that the PTC algorithm performs the transitive closure of a relation R distributed among p nodes, in $\log_2 p$ passes. During each pass, a "fusion" of two previous local results is performed. Redundant processing is avoided in this "fusion". With the same parameters, the number of tuples produced during each pass is [Rnew / ([$\log_2 p + 1$]] where [x] indicates the integer part of x. The sequence of processing and transfers is illustrated below:

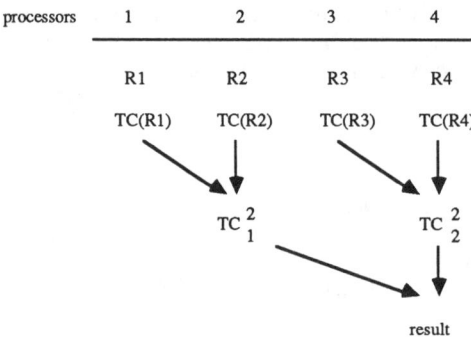

On the whole, the final cost is [VALD88a]:

$$RT(\text{ptc}) = \sum_{i=1}^{\log_2 p}\left(\left(\frac{R}{p}+\frac{2^{i-1}}{p}.DL\right).\text{trf} + \text{msg}\right) + \sum_{i=1}^{\log_2 p}\frac{2^{i-1}}{p}.DL.t$$

{ transfer time }　　　　　　{ processing time }

where DL is the number of new tuples produced in one pass.

DHTC algorithm

The number of new tuples generated during each iteration equals Rnew/d. Rnew/pd new tuples are generated in parallel per node and per iteration. These Rnew/pd tuples are seen in the form of p distinct sub-buckets which correspond to the p receiving nodes (actually p-1, since one sub-bucket stays where it is). The size of the sub-buckets sent is thus $Rnew/dp^2$. p of these buckets are sent together without serialization (cyclic organization). Overall, a small bucket of size $Rnew/dp^2$ is sent p times per iteration. It's this decomposition into small buckets that makes it possible to avoid the rehashing and the Inputs/Outputs.

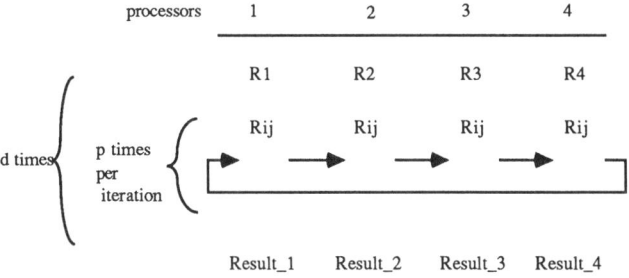

The transfer time of all the tuples together is thus:

$$p.d \left(\frac{Rnew}{d.p^2}.trf + msg \right)$$

With the hypothesis of uniformity, all the processors produce new tuples in parallel, and the processing time is divided by the number of active processors:

$$\frac{Rnew.t}{p}$$

Overall the expression for the response time is:

$$RT(dhtc) = \frac{Rnew}{p}.trf + p.d.msg + \frac{Rnew}{p}.t$$

5.2 performance comparisons

Two general remarks can be immediately formulated. First of all, it is noticed that DHTC requires more messages than the two other algorithms. This number equals the depth of the join loop times the number of parallel transfers during one iteration. Indeed, DHTC performs more transfers (hence the increased number of messages), but the buckets are smaller (hence the certainty of not having to write and re-read the buckets on-disk). And secondly, a close look allows one to notice that the result is localized differently according to the algorithm: for ITC and PTC, it's entirely located in one node, while for DHTC it's distributed in p disjoint buckets over p nodes. Two different architectures must therefore be considered. The first concerns a multiple backend operation, where each node constitutes a backend processor. A host processor submits the operation and receives the result. In this case, the response times mentioned in the previous section are directly applicable. The second concerns an operation where each node constitutes a site of a system. In this case, the result is requested at a particular site, and, for DHTC, the time to transfer the result to the final site must be added in. This case is of less interest for DHTC. This analysis will compare the performance of a multiple backend architecture implementing the three algorithms as well as the case of a utilization where the result is requested at a determined site.

The following values are chosen for the comparison:

$R = 1,000,000$ tuples $msg = 1ms$
$Rnew = 2,000,000$ tuples $trf = 5\ \mu s$
                              $t = 0,2\ ms$

The first curve shows the effect of the depth d of the join loop. It is noticed that this effect is only significant for a very large number of iterations and for a considerable number of processors. In current situations (up to 100 processors with depths of 100 loops), d is not a determining factor. We shall therefore neglect its effect in the rest of the evaluation and we shall choose an average value (d=100) for the comparisons.

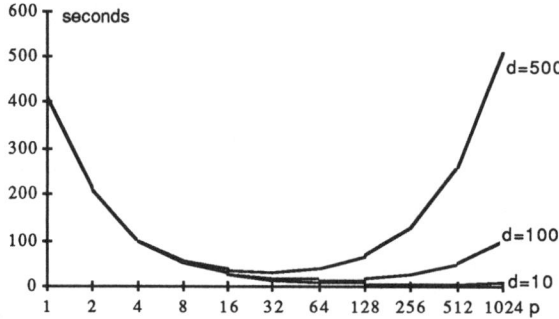

Figure 4: *effect of the depth of the join loop*

The figure below permits a visual comparison of the response times of ITC, PTC and DHTC as a function of the number of processors.

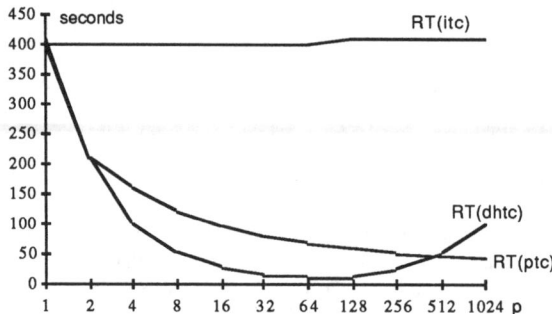

Figure 5: *performance as a function of the number of nodes (multiple backend configuration, Rnew=2,000,000)*

The elevated number of messages induced by the DHTC algorithm limits its possibilities when the number of processors becomes very large. The communication times between processors therefore become prohibitive. In fact, the message cost can be strongly reduced with, for example, new transputer-based machines [KUBL88]. A clear superiority is noticed however for the range in number of processors in current use. DHTC thus shows a performance improvement factor of two to four over PTC for a number of processors between 4 and 128, which are typical values in present multi-processor configurations.

In order to examine the performance of DHTC in an architecture where the result must be recomposed at a site, the transfer time for the (p-1) results available at the other sites can be added to RT(dhtc):

$$(p-1)\left(\frac{Rnew}{p}.trf + msg\right)$$

The response times in a utilization where the result is composed at a single site can therefore be plotted:

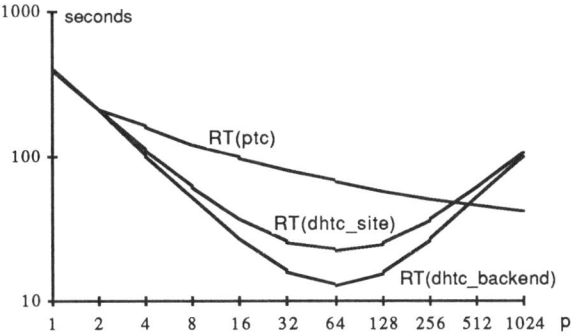

Figure 6: *performance as a function of the number of nodes*
(result at one site, Rnew=2,0000,000)

As anticipated, RT(dhtc_site) is less performant than RT(dhtc_backend); however DHTC remains better than PTC for all configurations in current use.

6. conclusions

We have presented in this paper a solution for efficiently implementing the transitive closure of a very large relation stored on-disk. The algorithm executes a join loop for which we propose an optimization based on clustering of the relations and parallelization. Thanks to a double hashing, the size of the sub-relations to be manipulated together in memory is reduced and a linearization of joins with substantially relaxed main memory size constraints can be guaranteed. The processing is divided into p parallel operations divided among p processors. This article goes only so far as to consider a semi-naïve algorithm for transitive closure. Our future research will consist of doing a more in-depth analysis of other possibilities for parallel executions.

7. references

[AGRA87] R. AGRAWAL, H.V. JAGADISH: *"Direct Algoritms for Computing The Transitive Closure of Database Relations"*, 13th VLDB, Brighton ,1987.

[BANC86] F.BANCILHON, R. RAMAKRISHNAN: *"An Amateur's Introduction To Recursive Query Processing Strategies"* , ACM SIGMOD, Washington, May 1986.

[CHEI86] J.P. CHEINEY, R. MICHEL, P. FAUDEMAY, J.M. THEVENIN : *"A Reliable Multiple Backend Using A Select-join Operator"*, 12th VLDB, Kyoto, Aug 1986.

[CHEI89] J.P. CHEINEY, C. DE MAINDREVILLE: *"Relational Storage and Efficient Retrieval of Rules in a Deductive DBMS"*, 5th Int. Conf. on Data Engineering, Los Angeles, 1989.

[DEWI84] D.J. DEWITT et al: *"Implementation Techniques for Main Memory Database Systems"*, ACM SIGMOD, Boston 1984.

[DEWI86] D.J. DEWITT et al: *"GAMMA- A Hight Performance Dataflow Database Machine"*, 12th VLDB, Kyoto, Aug 1986.

[GARD84] G. GARDARIN, P. VALDURIEZ, Y.VIEMONT: *"Predicate Trees: A Way for Optimizing Relational Queries"*, Computer Engineering Conf., Los Angeles, 1984.

[GARD86] G. GARDARIN: *"Efficient Processing of Very Large Databases : A Comparative Analysis of Architectures"* , IFIP, 1986.

[GARD88]   G. GARDARIN, P. PUCHERAL: *"A Graph Operator to Process Efficiently Linear Recursive Rules in Main Memory Oriented DBMS"*, 3rd Database Bresilian Symposium, Recife-Pernambuco, March 1988.

[HAN88]   J. HAN, G.QADAH, C. CHAOU: *"The Processing and Evaluation of Transitive Closure Queries"*, Proc. of EDBT, Venice, 1988.

[HSIA85]   D.K. HSIAO, S. DEMURJIAN: *"Benchmarking Database Systems in Multiple Backend Configuration"*, A Quatterly Bulletin of the IEEE Computer Society, Technical Comitee on Database Systems, V8, N°1, 1985.

[IOAN88]   Y. IOANNIDIS, R. RAMAKRISHNAN : *"Efficient Transitive Closure Algorithms"*, 14th VLDB, Los Angeles, 1988.

[KITS83]   M. KITSUREGAWA et al : *"Application of Hash to Database Machines"*, New Generation Computing, N°1, 1983.

[KUBL88]   F.D. KUBLER: *"Cluster Oriented Architecture for the Mapping of Parallel Processor Networks to High Performance Applications"*, Int. Conf. on Super Computing, St Malo, France, 1988.

[VALD86]   P. VALDURIEZ, H. BORAL: *"Evaluation of Recursive Queries Using Join Indices"*, Int. Conf. on Expert Database Systems, Charleston, South Carolina, April 1986.

[VALD88a]   P. VALDURIEZ, S. KHOSHAFIAN: *"Transitive Closure of Transitively Closed Relations"*, 2nd Int. Conf. on Expert Database Systems, Tysons Lorner, Virginia, April 1988.

[VALD88b]   P. VALDURIEZ, S KOSHAFIAN: *"Parallel Evaluation of the Transitive Closure of a Database Relation"*, Int. Journal of Parallel Programming, Vol 17, N°1, Feb. 1988.

A New Version of a Parallel Production System Machine, MANJI-II

Jun Miyazaki †, Kenji Takeda ‡, Hideharu Amano ‡, Hideo Aiso ‡

†Fuji Xerox System Technology Research Laboratory

3-57-6 Yoyogi, Shibuya-ku, Tokyo 151

JAPAN

Tel: +81 3 378 7290

‡Department of Electrical Engineering Keio University

3-14-1 Hiyoshi, Kohoku-ku, Yokohama 223

JAPAN

Tel: +81 44 62 1774

Abstract

Parallel systems for OPS5 have been developed. In such systems, parallel implementations of the Rete algorithm are adopted because the number of pattern matchings is minimized in the original algorithm. However, conventional approaches for parallel Rete algorithms require special hardware to cope with the dynamic process allocation and frequent communication. Dedicated machines are necessary for such methods.

In this paper, a new parallel execution method for general purpose multiprocessors is proposed. In this method, nodes in the Rete network are statically mapped onto a small number of processors (PUs) before execution. Since processes are not migrated and are not allocated dynamically, data structures can be designed so as to minimize the communication between PUs. Also the synchronization and process control can be simplified.

The key for the method is static mapping algorithms. Since the characteristics of the Rete network are completely different from the data dependency graph which is suitable for extracting inherent parallelism in general programming languages like FORTRAN, the conventional static mapping techniques cannot be applied. Some new mapping strategies are discussed and evaluated.

Although the method is utilized for most types of multiprocessors, an optimized architecture which is called MANJI-II is designed and proposed. MANJI-II supports quick transfer of tokens in the Rete network, by using a simple multicast mechanism, and non-cached shared memory. Although MANJI-II provides almost the same performance as that of dedicated architecture including the previous version of MANJI, the total cost of MANJI-II is extremely low.

1 Introduction

OPS5 [1] is one of the best established production systems and many application programs have been implemented. The Rete algorithm [2] is the fast rule matching algorithm for OPS5. This algorithm uses a kind of network which consists of the condition parts of rules. The network is well structured and eliminates redundant pattern matching as much as possible. However, when the number of rules becomes enlarged, especially over several thousands, execution time for rule matching becomes the main problem of the system. The Rete network has inherent parallelism, and parallel execution of the network has the potentiality of speeding up production systems.

Some systems and parallel algorithms have been proposed for the parallel execution of the Rete network. PSM [3] at Carnegie Mellon University and Distributed Rete algorithm machine [6] in Walterloo University are examples.

To make the best use of parallelism in the Rete algorithm in these machines, processes which correspond to nodes in the Rete network are allocated dynamically onto PUs [4]. To allocate processes quickly, these machines require special purpose hardware. However, high speed hardware schedulers are extremely expensive and hard to implement. Moreover, special data structures are needed to fit hardware schedulers. This makes the implementation of a parallel execution algorithm on general purpose multiprocessors difficult.

We started the MANJI project since 1986 to develop realistic architecture and algorithms for parallel execution of the Rete network. To eliminate the hardware scheduler, MANJI adopts a static mapping method for nodes in the Rete network. The first version of MANJI was proposed in [7] [8].

Although the hardware scheduler was eliminated in MANJI, a sophisticated communication mechanism was utilized, and the structure of MANJI is not sufficiently economical. The high performance of MANJI does not come from the parallel algorithm, but from the hardware of the communication mechanism.

Since the hardware of the communication mechanism is too complicated, we tried to improve the parallel algorithm before implementation of the real hardware. As a result, most of the hardware of MANJI appeared to be redundant. The refined parallel algorithm reduces communication drastically, so it can be implemented on the most types of multiprocessors. The next version, which is called MANJI-II, provides a simple architecture which is optimized to the algorithm.

This paper consists of 8 sections. In the next section we briefly introduce OPS5 and the Rete network. In section 3, the parallel execution policy is described. In section 4, static mapping algorithms are described. Section 5 explains the data structure for token passing and memory management. In section 6, the architecture for MANJI-II is introduced, and section 7 static mapping algorithms and the architecture are evaluated. Finally section 8 presents the conclusion.

2 OPS5 and the Rete network

2.1 OPS5

OPS5 is composed of three parts: the production memory (PM) which stores production rules; the working memory (WM) which stores the current status of the system; and the rule interpreter [1]. Rules have the form *(p rule name (condition part)) -- > (action part)*. Examples of rules are as follows:

(p rule1 (c1 ^attr1 10) (c2 $<x>$)   -- >   (modify 1 ^attr1 15))

(p rule2 (c1 ^attr1 10) (c3 $<y>$)   -- >   (remove 1))

OPS5 repeatedly executes the following three phases:

1) **Match Phase** Find all rule instantiations whose condition part matches the current WM. Form the conflict set by collecting matched rule instantiations.

2) **Conflict Resolution Phase** Select one of the instantiations from the conflict set.

3) **Act Phase** Update WM according to the action part of the selected rule.

OPS5 ends when there are no rules applicable in the Match phase.

2.2 The Rete network

The Rete algorithm is the fast rule matching algorithm in the Match phase for OPS5 [2]. The algorithm is executed on the Rete network. The Rete network memorizes past states of matching so as to avoid redundant matching as much as possible. If there are changes in WM at the Act phase, only these changes are sent as tokens to update the current state of WM stored in the network. Fig. 1 shows an example of the Rete network obtained by compiling the condition part of the two rule examples mentioned above. The Rete network consists of 4 kinds of nodes:

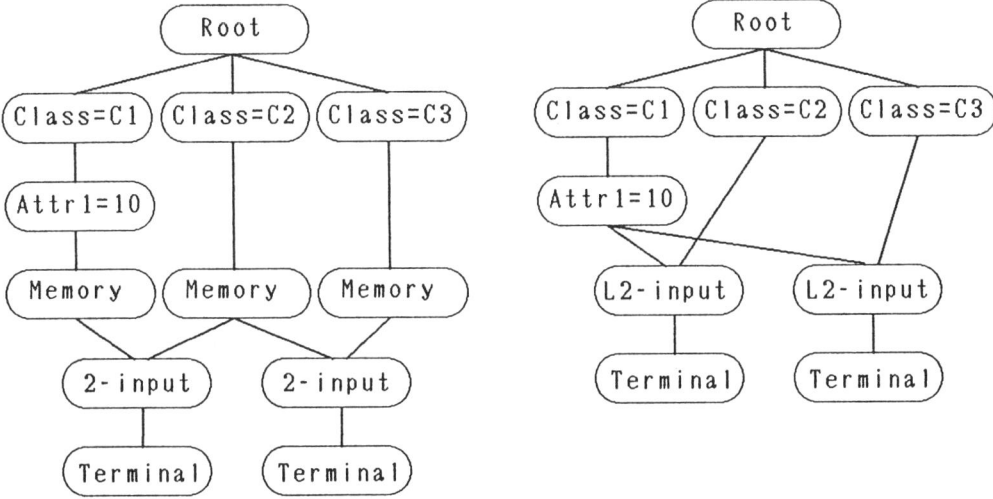

Fig. 1 Rete network   Fig. 2 Introduction of L2-input nodes

1) **Single-input nodes**: test constants as to whether reached tokens satisfy test conditions in Single-input nodes. If the test succeeds, Single-input nodes pass tokens to successors, else the tokens disappear.

2) **Memory nodes**: store tokens which reach these nodes, and update the contents of nodes according to the reached tokens. Memory nodes always are predecessors of 2-input nodes.

3) **2-input nodes**: compare tokens which are in the preceding left and right memory nodes. If there are tokens which matched, tokens are combined and sent to successors.

4) **Terminal nodes**: exist per rule. And if tokens have arrived at these nodes, the tokens and the rule name which correspond to these terminal nodes are listed on the conflict set as instantiations.

3 The Policy for the parallel execution method

The parallel Rete algorithm is designed based on the following policies:

1. The target machine is assumed to be bus connected multiprocessors which provide the shared memory. However, this algorithm can be applied to link connected multiprocessors without shared memory with a small modification.

2. Nodes in the Rete network are treated as processes and statically mapped onto the PUs.

3. The data sharing which causes bus transactions or synchronizations are eliminated as much as possible.

First, the concept of the memory nodes are modified according to policy 3. This modification is essential, as it influences the Rete network itself. Therefore, we will touch on this modification before describing the outline of the algorithm.

3.1 L2-input nodes

Memory nodes are shared by its direct successors, which are 2-input nodes. To extract as much inherent parallelism in the Rete network as possible, and to reduce the sharing of data, these successors have to access their preceding memory nodes in parallel. In order to maximize parallelism, these 2-input nodes must be mapped into different PUs and memory nodes have to be on shared memory space. However, this choice causes heavy bus congestion and performance degradation because a synchronization mechanism is needed to access memory nodes.

To avoid bus congestion and performance degradation, we prohibit the sharing of memory nodes by 2-input nodes. By this prohibition, each memory node is accessed by only one 2-input node, and each 2-input node can access each memory node in a 2-input node's local environment. Thus no synchronization mechanism is needed between memory nodes and 2-input nodes. And 2-input nodes and memory nodes can be regard as one combined node which we call a L2-input node. The network shown in Fig. 2 corresponds to Fig. 1.

3.2 Outline of the algorithm

Like the previous approaches to parallel production systems, the main target of the parallel execution is the Match phase. As the Match phase occupies up to 90% of the total execution time [3], the parallel execution of this phase is effective. Moreover the Conflict Resolution phase is executed in parallel and overlaps with the Action phase. The Act phase is executed basically sequentially, but tokens are input to the Match phase in a pipeline manner.

3.2.1 Parallel execution of the Match Phase

In the Match phase, the Rete network is executed in parallel. Tokens are transferred in a pipeline manner from the root node. Only pointers to tokens are transferred and real objects of tokens are shared by all PUs. Each process for a node begins when a token arrives.

1) **Processes in Single-input nodes** Single-input nodes act like filters for tokens. Tokens which satisfy the condition in Single-input nodes can pass through the node. If the condition is not satisfied, the tokens disappear.

2) **Processes in L2-input nodes** The process in an L2-input node has two stages. First, if a token has arrived at one of the input of an L2-input node, the contents of the memory which is attached to the input is updated. If the token indicates "add", the token is added to the memory, and if the token indicates "delete", the content of the memory is searched and the relevant token which is stored in the memory is deleted.

Second, every pair of tokens is found which match the condition of the L2-input node between reached tokens and tokens which are stored in the other side of memory. If there are matched pairs of tokens, new combined tokens are created from the tokens in each pair. These combined tokens are transferred to successor nodes.

3) **Processes in terminal nodes** If tokens reach the terminal nodes, tokens are stored in the memories of terminal nodes as instantiations of the conflict set. If tokens indicate "delete", tokens are deleted from the conflict set.

The Match phase ends when no token flows in the network.

3.2.2 Conflict Resolution Phase

The Conflict Resolution phase is executed in parallel in a process of elimination (that is in a "tournament"). In Fig. 3 terminal nodes are connected to parent conflict resolution nodes. Each node selects one instantiation and sends it to its parent. The instantiation which is selected at the top conflict resolution node is the real instantiation of the Conflict Resolution phase.

This method does not make one big conflict set which is shared by all the terminal nodes. Thus the conflict set does not have to be on the shared memory space, and no synchronization mechanisms are needed. Conflict resolution is not needed when the conflict set has not been changed, and in OPS5 only 0.5 % of the terminal nodes are activated in a recognize-act cycle [3]. Thus the distributed management of the conflict set results in reducing the number of comparisons, and the Conflict Resolution phase can be executed in parallel.

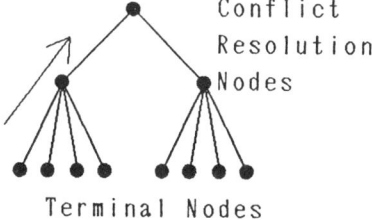

Fig. 3 Conflict resolution

3.2.3 Act Phase

The Act phase is executed sequentially by a special PU. This special PU is called the Action processor. The Action Processor keeps the action part of all rules in its local memory, and executes the action part of the rule which is selected in the Conflict Resolution phase. And the Action Processor produces tokens for the next recognize-act cycle.

The Act phase and the Match phase can be combined in a pipeline manner and tokens which are generated at the Act phase are input to the root node in the Rete network one after another.

4 Static Mapping

In the conventional approaches for parallel execution of the Rete network, processes which correspond to nodes in the network are dynamically allocated on PUs. Dynamic scheduling methods are suitable because the token flow in the Rete network is dynamically determined during execution. And this method is the best approach for extracting the relatively small inherent parallelism of the Rete network.

However, the granularity of processes in the Rete network is small and nodes must be frequently scheduled and allocated during execution. To schedule and allocate nodes at a high speed, special hardware is needed. For such a hardware scheduler, special data structures are also needed. Such hardware schedulers are extremely expensive and hard to implement. It is clear that such fast dynamic scheduling algorithms cannot be implemented on general multiprocessors. Thus, we introduce a static mapping method.

Although the execution of the Rete network is dynamically determined, a static mapping method is advantageous because the structure of the Rete network is not changed after compilation in most application programs, and the processing time for each node is almost predictable.

Although algorithms for static mapping methods are by nature an NP-complete problem, there are several research works on effective heuristic algorithms for numerical calculations [9]. In most cases, these algorithms adopt a policy that analyzes the data dependency and minimizes the critical paths between nodes. However, these approaches cannot be applied to the mapping algorithm for the Rete network for the following reasons:

a) An L2-input node can begin execution when one of tokens for the two inputs in L2-input nodes arrives, and does not have to wait for a token arrival at the other input of the L2-input node.

b) It often occurs that tokens are stopped in the middle of the network, and this causes token flow in parts of the network only.

For above reasons, if we design static mapping algorithms for the Rete network, the following points have to be considered:

a) The children of each node can be activated in parallel. In particular Single-input nodes near the root node have a large number of children. Thus each child should be mapped into different PUs.

b) In the early period of the Match phase, many Single-input nodes are activated. However, most of the tokens disappear until they reach the L2-input nodes, and only a few L2-inputs nodes are activated. On the other hand, an L2-input node often sends tokens to its children in a pipeline manner. Thus children can be activated in parallel with their parents. Moreover, it also sometimes occurs that the grandchildren of L2-input nodes can be activated in parallel with their grandparents.

c) The mapping algorithm must be simple enough to treat a large sized Rete network.

Taking into the above considerations, we developed an dedicated algorithm called **ENMA** (**E**qual opportunity for **N**eighbors **MA**pping). Unlike conventional algorithms based on the critical path scheduling, ENMA does not uses levels of paths, and tries to map grandparents, parents, child, and grandchildren to different PUs as much as possible.

ENMA algorithm

Step.0 Choose any node n_i ($i = 1$ to N, N is the number of nodes) in the Rete network.

Step.1 Evaluate the mapping state by calculating weight $PU_{weight}(i,j)$ of each PU_j ($j = 1$ to M, M is the number of PUs) for n_i.

$$PU_{weight}(i,j) = \sum_{(\text{distance of } n_i \text{ and } n_k \leq 2)\, \cap\, (n_k \text{ is mapped onto } PU_j)} weight(n_k)$$

Step.2 Select PU_p which has the least weight $PU_{weight}(i,p)$ and to which the least number of nodes are mapped.

Step.3 Map n_i to PU_p.

Fig. 4 shows the example of the weight for nodes at distance 1 and 2 from node G. The weight value for each node is determined by the characteristics of the parallel execution of the Rete network. In Fig. 4 parent

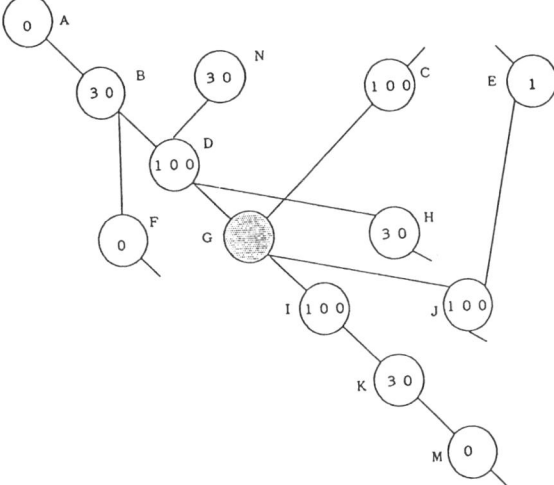

Fig. 4 Example of weight in ENMA

and children have the maximum weitht(100), because parents, children, and node G can be activated simultaneously, especially when nodes are L2-input nodes. Grandparents and grandchildren have the medium weight(30), because they have some possibility to be activated simultaneously with parents, children, and node G. The other nodes have the minimum weight(1) because there is no possibility to be activated simultaneously with the node G.

The order for mapping should be the same as the order of node generation. These algorithms are evaluated in section 7.

5 Data structure and memory management

In this section, the data structure for tokens and memory management for the data structure is described.

5.1 Elements in tokens

When WM is updated in the Act phase, tokens which correspond to changes in the WM are made. Fig. 4 shows the data structure for tokens. The contents of tokens are written into the Token Contents Table, and pointers to the Token Contents Table are input from the root node into the Rete network. The contents of the tokens contains the following information.

1) A flag for "add" or "delete" to WM

2) A time tag

3) Atoms : such as "c1", "attr1", or "10"

The Contents Table can never be changed after the Action processor generates tokens in the Action phase of 1 recognize-act cycle. However tokens are combined when they are processed through L2-input nodes.

5.2 Object-list

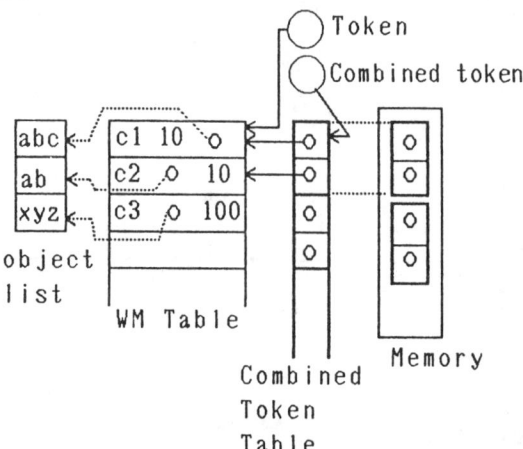

Fig. 5 Structure of token

The Token Contents Table does not store real strings for atoms in tokens, but the Object-list manages atoms (Fig. 5). In Object-list, duplications of entities are not allowed. The Token Contents Table maintains pointers to the Object-list, and thus string matchings are reduced to comparisons of pointers to Object-list. Numerical numbers are kept directly in the Token Contents Table.

5.3 Two stage token passing and a Combined Token Table

Tokens for single-input nodes and tokens for L2-input nodes are implemented in a different manner, and token passing has two stages.

A token for single-input nodes is a single word pointer for the Token Contents Table. It is called a fixed sized token. According to the features of the Rete network, it must be to transferred from one node to multiple nodes.

A token for L2-input nodes changes its size when it passes through an L2-input node. It is called a combined token. A combined token consists of several fixed size tokens, and a set of pointers for the Token Contents Table are stored in the Combined Token Table. Another pointer is used to point out the set of pointers in the Combined Token Table. In a usual Rete network, this type of token is transferred from one node to another.

5.4 Management of Combined Token Table

The Combined Token Table space is divided into the number of PUs. Each space is assigned to each PU, and a PU can write only in its own space. Each space is written to from the lower address, and does not overflow in general. Thus flags for showing the end of a reading from a PU is not needed, and no synchronization is needed. The Contents of it become unnecessary when a Match phase ends. When the next match phase begins, the Combined Token Table can be used from the first addresses.

Although a large space is assigned for Combined Token Table, if Combined Token Table becomes full, PUs resolve this condition by the following sequences:

1) Ask the other PUs to report spaces which have already finished reading their Combined Token Table.

2) By analyzing reports, waste space become clear.

3) Write into the waist space.

5.5 Simplification of Operating System

The simplest implementation of the parallel execution method mentioned above is realized by assigning 1 node to 1 process for the operating system on target machines. However processes for nodes in the Rete network are of small granularity, and communication between nodes is frequent, so process management becomes an overhead for the whole process. To avoid this overhead, it is better for each PU to have a simple node process management system and not to have complex operating systems.

The parallel execution method mentioned in this section does not need mutual exclusion operations, and each node can start processing when tokens arrive. While tokens are processed within nodes, there are no states which are waiting for token arrivals, and also no states which cannot transfer tokens to successors. Moreover, I/O operations are only processed in the Action processor. Thus, the node process management system can be simply constructed. The node process management system has queues for token communication and keeps the node process management list. The node management system repeatedly manages to fetch tokens from queues and to process nodes.

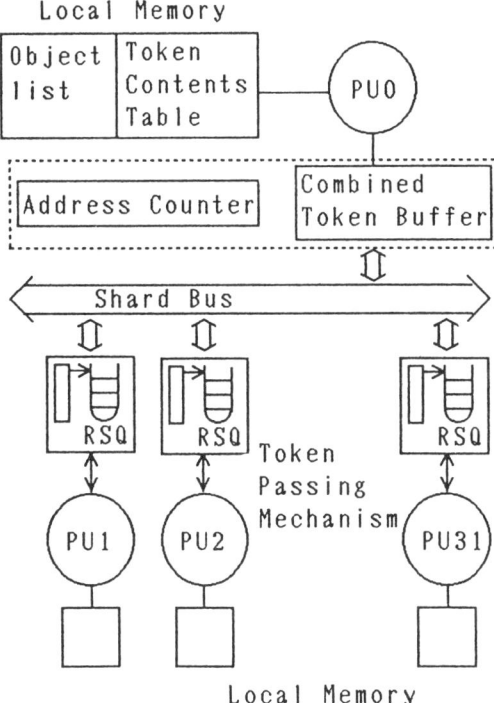

Fig. 6 Overview of MANJI-II

6 Architecture of MANJI-II

Since our implementation reduces the interaction between processors as much as possible, it can be applied to all multiprocessor systems which provide a shared memory. However, the transfer of tokens in the Rete network is still frequent and it will bottleneck the system. Therefore, we propose a new architecture named MANJI-II. Compared with the previous version MANJI, MANJI-II is designed so as to fit the implementation method and be far more cost effective.

6.1 Overview of the architecture

As shown in Fig. 6, MANJI-II consists of 32 high performance microprocessors connected with a simple shared bus. Compared with conventional general purpose multiprocessors, each PU provides a mechanism to transfer tokens but no cache memory. Instead of a large amount of shared memory, MANJI-II provides a small size a shared Message Buffer. All PUs are the same structure, except PU0, which is called Action processor. The Action processor executes the action part of rules and manages the shared Message Buffer, which is utilized to store the Combined Token Table. The data structures for our parallel match method shown in Fig. 5 are assigned to MANJI-II as follows:

a) **Object-list** Since matches are performed only between pointers on the Token Contents Table, Object-list is not accessed in the Match phase. In the Act phase, Object-list is updated only by the Action processor. Therefore, an Object-list is stored in the local memory of Action processor, and only pointers are broadcast to all other PUs during the Act phase.

b) **Token Contents Table** Although the Token Contents Table is accessed frequently in the Match phase to compare pointers, update is performed only in the Act phase. Therefore, the Token Contents Table is stored in local memory in each PU, and the updated pointer is broadcast from Action processor in the Act phase.

c) **Combined Token Table** This table is stored in the Message Buffer, which is managed by the Action processer. That is, this table is a shared data structure.

d) **Token** Tokens are transferred through the Token transfer mechanism attached to each PU.

e) **Memory nodes** Memory nodes are copied into the local memory of each PU from the Combined Token Table in the shared Message Buffer.

6.2 Mechanism for token passing

To transfer two stage token passing mentioned in section 3.2.1 efficiently, MANJI-II introduced two communication mechanisms: the Token transfer mechanism named RSQ (Receiver Selectable multicast with Queue), and the shared Message Buffer. RSQ is specialized for sending a single size data to multiple PUs, and Message Buffer is provided for one to one transfer of variable size data. As shown in Fig. 7, the fixed size token is directly transferred using RSQ. For the transfer of a combined token, a pointer for the Message Buffer is transferred using RSQ, and then the data block pointed to is transferred using Message Buffer.

6.3 Token transfer mechanism RSQ

There are two types of methods for transferring data from one to multiple PUs. One is the sender designate method. In this method, the sender PU constructs a message packet which includes the identifier of all the receivers in its header. Another method is receiver selectable. In this method, the receiver PUs select a message from the message identifier. The former method is advantageous if the receivers dynamically change. However, in this implementation nodes are statically assigned into PUs, and the latter method is suitable. In MANJI-II, a communication method named RSQ (Receiver Selectable multicast with Queue) is utilized to multicast fixed sized tokens. RSQ is based on a communication method RSM (Receiver Selectable Multicast) [10] which was originally proposed for scientific calculations, and utilized in the communication mechanism of the previous version of MANJI.

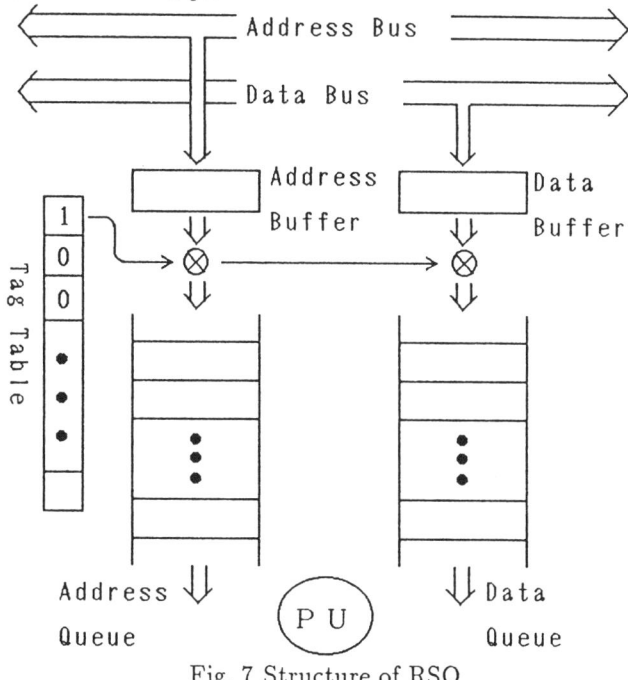

Fig. 7 Structure of RSQ

In RSQ, all PUs are connected with a bus and share a global address space, as shown in Fig. 7. The RSQ manager attached to each PU provides tag memory which indicates whether the data written in the address is needed or not. Since the same data is transferred to all output links of a node in the Rete network, a single address of the global address space is assigned to the output links. Address tags in the RSQ manager is set before calculation according to the information of the Rete network and its assignment. Data (pointer) written in an address is stored in the buffer when the address tags are referred to. If the data is judged to be necessary for the PU, the data is pushed into the queue with its address. Otherwise, the data is discarded. Each PU fetches the data from the queue, and performs the corresponding process.

Compared with RSM utilized in the previous version of MANJI, RSQ is simplified because the synchronization mechanism is omitted. Using this implementation, a token can never outrun the previously transferred one, and the synchronization mechanism in RSM is not needed. If nodes in the Rete network are appropriately mapped, the size of the queue in RSQ does not become large.

6.4 Message Buffer

The Message Buffer in MANJI-II is prepared for storing Combined Token Buffer. Since the Combined Token Buffer is utilized only once and then thrown away in one cycle, the buffer provides a hardware address counter which indicates the top of the unused region.

Combined tokens are transferred in the following manner. When a PU must send a Combined Token, it writes the set of pointers into the Message Buffer according to the address counter. This operation is performed indivisibly using a block transfer. The sender PU receives the top of the written address from the Message Buffer and transfers it using RSQ. After this operation, the address counter is incremented by the size of the Combined Token. The receiver PU fetches the pointer from the RSQ manager, and reads the Combined Token from the the Message Buffer. When a match phase is completed, the address counter of the Message Buffer is cleared.

6.5 Comparison of architectures

Table 1 shows a comparison of three types of architecture, that is, a typical general purpose multiprocessor like Balance/Symmetry or Multimax, the previous version of MANJI, and MANJI-II. The implementation described in this paper can be applied to all three architectures. Under the implementation, MANJI-II provides the highest performance/cost ratio. RSQ provides the same performance as RSM, and Message Buffer can work as effectively as VMRM in MANJI. The performance of MANJI-II is almost the same as that of MANJI, in spite of the economical hardware.

The hardware of RSQ is simple compared with the common snoop cache mechanism, and the amount of memory in the Message Buffer is much smaller than that of shared memory in general multiprocessors. Therefore, the architecture of MANJI-II is simple and economical, even when compared with general multiprocessors.

7 Evaluations

The implementation method described here is designed so as to reduce the communication and synchronization as much as possible. To make the effect of the method clear, the following evaluations are needed:

a) The static mapping method proposed here degrades parallelism compared with the dynamic mapping method. How does the degradation influences the performance?

b) The transfer of fixed sized tokens is still frequent and may cause bus congestion. How does the congestion degrades the performance?

For a realistic evaluation, we traced some practical programs written in OPS5 and registered the behavior of tokens in the Rete network. The programs used for evaluation are as follows:

1) **Arizuka expert system** 1036 rules
   An expert system to generate the input data file for the simulation of queuing systems.

2) **HANG-A expert system** 80 rules
   An expert system to diagnose a parallel machine $(SM)^2$-II[11].

3) **Disassembler for microprocessors** 125 rules
   A disassembler to generate mnemonics from the machine code of various types microprocessers.

These problems are practical, and consists of a satisfactorily large number of rules. In particular 1 provides the maximum grade of rules for the current programs written in OPS5.

Before simulation, the above programs executed for a sufficient amount of time, the pattern of sending tokens are registered. Then, the Rete network is mapped according to the mapping strategy described in Section 4, and the list of mapping information is generated. The simulation is performed using the information from the trace and the mapping.

7.1 Parallelism of Static Mapping

We simulated the performance of MANJI-II when the parallel execution method is implemented on it. In this simulation, bus congestion and overhead of the process switching, and the processing time for the operating system are considered. Fig. 8 shows the result of simulations using several mapping algorithms for the Arizuka expert system on MANJI-II. And it shows the average execution time for a Match phase, and the execution time is the relative value which sets a bus cycle as the unit time. We estimate execution time for each type of nodes through experimental implementation of the parallel execution method mentioned in this paper on transputer: for example, the processing time for Single-input nodes as four unit time.

In Fig. 8, We compare three static mapping algorithms and dynamic scheduling. The **level mapping** is the classical algorithm which tries to make the critical path to be processed in the shortest time as much as possible. ENMA is considered to use the pipeline effect by the tokens which pass through L2-input nodes one after another and to utilize the parallelism produced by one token as much as possible. The **random mapping** only maps nodes to PUs at random.

According to the results, ENMA shows the best performance among static mapping algorithms. The difference of execution time between dynamic scheduling and ENMA is within 10 %, in average. In this simulation scheduling time for the dynamic scheduling is not included. To allocate nodes dynamically within this time difference, a very fast hardware scheduler is necessary. Thus the static mapping algorithm described in this paper reasonably effective.

7.2 Evaluation of Performance

Fig. 9 shows the speedup ratio for the several sample programs when using ENMA static mapping. Broken lines show the ideal speedup which excludes the bus congestion, the overhead of the process switching, and overhead of the operating system. In programs with a small number of rules, the performance becomes saturated if the number of PUs is over 32. This shows that the loss of the performance is mainly caused by the small inherent parallelism of the evaluation program. This is easily observed by comparisons with the ideal speedup which is shown by the broken lines. According to these results, it is concluded that bus congestion and the overhead of process switching are within 10 %.

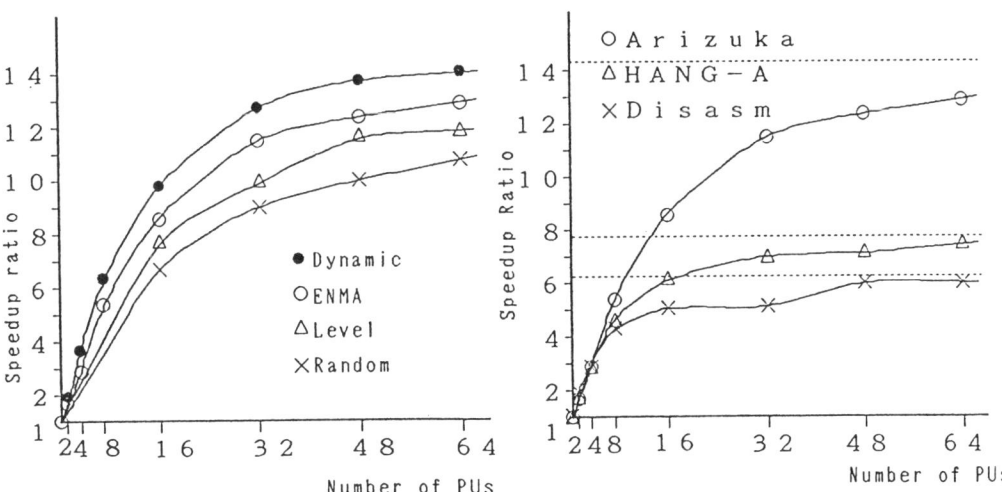

Fig. 8 Effect of static mapping

Fig. 9 Speedup ratio

8 Conclusion

In this paper, a parallel execution method for the Rete network was described. This method does not need hardware scheduler, but adopts static mapping algorithm of nodes. And in this method, the data structure for tokens passing was designed to eliminate synchronization mechanism and bus transaction as much as possible. By the evaluation, static mapping algorithm ENMA is reasonably effective when compared to dynamic scheduling. This parallel execution method can be implemented on general purpose multiprocessor systems. And this method was implemented on transputer system, which is the typical link connected multiprocessor, with a slightly modification.

To support the communication distinctive in this method, we introduced a special architecture MANJI-II. The communication mechanism in MANJI-II realized effective multicast and queues for token passing.

We are implementing this parallel execution method and the simulator of MANJI-II on the multiprocessor testbed system ATTEMPT [12].

References

[1] C.L.Forgy: OPS5 User's Manual, Dept. of Comp. Sci., Carnegie-Mellon Univ. (1981).

[2] C.L.Forgy: Rete: A fast algorithm for the many pattern/many object pattern match problem, Artificial Intelligence, vol. 19, pp. 17-37 (1982).

[3] A.Gupta, C.L.Forgy, A.Newell and R.Wedig: Parallel algorithms and architectures for rule-based systems, Proc. of 13th ISCA, pp. 28-37 (1986).

[4] A. Gupta, C. L. Forgy, D. Kalp, A. Newell, and M. Tambe: Parallel OPS5 on the Encore Multimax, ICPP, 1988, pp. 271-280

[5] A. Gupta, M. Tambe:Suitability of Message Passing Computers for Implementing Production Systems, AAAI 88, 1988, pp. 687-692

[6] M.A.Kelly, R.E.Seviora: A Multiprocessor Architecture for Production System Matching, AAAI, pp. 36-41 (1987).

[7] J.Miyazaki, H.Amano and H.Aiso: MANJI:An architecture for production systems, Proc. of 20th Hawaiian International Conference on System Sciences, vol. 1, pp. 236-244 (1987).

[8] J.Miyazaki, H.Amano, K.Takeda and H.Aiso: A shared memory architecture for MANJI production system machine, IWDM'87, pp. 517-531 (1987).

[9] H.Kasahara, S.Narita: Practical multiprocessor scheduling algorithms for efficient parallel processing, IEEE trans. on Comp., vol. c33 No11, pp. 1023-1029 (1984).

[10] H.Amano: RSM:A communication mechanism for multiprocessors, Proc. 2nd of International Conference on Computers and Applications, pp. 149-156 (1987).

[11] H.Amano, T.Boku, T.Kudoh and H.Aiso: $(SM)^2$-II: A new version of the Sparse Matrix Solving Machine, Proc. of 12th ISCA, pp. 100-107 (1985).

[12] H.Amano, T.Terasawa and T.Kudo: Cache with synchronization mechanism, To appear in IFIP CONGRESS'89

A PARALLEL PROCESSING ARCHITECTURE FOR REAL-TIME PRODUCTION SYSTEMS WITH TRUTH MAINTENANCE

Satoshi FUJITA, Reiji AIBARA, Masafumi YAMASHITA, and Tadashi AE

Faculty of Engineering, Hiroshima University

Saijo, Higashi-Hiroshima, 724 Japan

ABSTRACT

A production system is used widely to build various expert systems since it has many attractive properties. Thus it seems to be a natural trial to apply it to building a real-time system. Although much effort for the speedup of the production system has been made so far, still a serious problem to be solved remains: Because of the modification of data by an external event, the database may become inconsistent. Thus we have to check whether the action caused by an external event will keep the database consistent or not after each arrival of external event. However, the check which essentially searches for a data in the database inconsistent with the externally modified data, would be a fatal overhead of the real-time system.

In this paper, we show that the idea of truth maintenance in the nonmonotonic reasoning can be applied to keep the database consistent, and that the truth maintenance of the database can be achieved by each data keeping a short list called a foundation list. Next, we will propose an architecture based on three-dimensional integrated circuits (in short, 3-D IC) technology to execute the truth maintenance of the database effectively. The 3-D IC chip assumed here will be fabricated in the Integrated Circuit System Research Center of Hiroshima University.

1. INTRODUCTION

A production system is used widely to build various expert systems, since it has many attractive properties. Thus it seems to be a natural trial to apply it to building real-time systems.

The computation of a production system is a repetition of (1) the matching phase to search rule instances whose condition parts hold, (2) the conflict resolution phase to select the most adequate instance from the instances found in the matching phase, and (3) the action phase to execute the action part of the instance selected in the conflict resolution phase. The computation time is dominated by the matching phase, so many works have been done for obtaining an mechanism to execute the matching phase quickly. Forgy proposed an efficient pattern matching algorithm Rete [1] based on so-called the state-saving method [2]. By using this method, the matching operation for the whole database can be replaced by that for the data modified in the last action phase.

The state-saving method is really effective for the speedup of the matching phase (and hence will be used in our architecture as will be shown), however, still the following serious problem to be solved remains to build real-time production systems: A nature of a real-time system is the existence of external events. An external event is created outside the real-time system, arrives at the system and may modify the database. The system can not control the creation or the arrival timing of any external event. Hence, because of the nondeterminism of the modification timing of the database by an external event, the database may become inconsistent. (Whenever the data modified by an external event and a data in the database are inconsistent, we assume that it is the former that is correct, i.e., we modify the database so that the database is consistent with the former.) To make sure the consistency of the database, we have to test whether the modification keeps the database consistent or not after each arrival of external event. However, this test, even if it is possible, looks (and has been considered to be) time consuming and would become a fatal overhead of the system. This paper will treat this problem, provided the state-saving method.

In this paper, we assume that a real-time production system does not include negative statements. Namely, the negation of a data, which refers to the nonexistence of the data in the database, does not appear in any condition part and no remove data instruction appears in any action part. However, it does not mean that any data in the database will not be removed forever. Only an external event may remove a data from the database. This assumption reflects our position that the inference in the system be proceeded based on the monotonic reasoning and the only factor which breaks the monotonicity is the arrival of an external event. One of the fruits of this assumption is that no interference among rule instances occurs, which will hinder the parallel firing of rules [11]. This system starts with empty database. Then it is required that at any time any data in the database is derived using the rules from the data created directly by external events. We say the database is inconsistent if the database does not satisfy the above requirement. We also assume that the set of clusters forms a partially ordered set, where cluster C1 is smaller than cluster C2 if a data in C1 may be used when a data in C2 is created (by a rule). It is natural since it prohibits any cyclic dependency. (We use a term cluster instead of memory node in [1].) Under this assumption, we will show that the idea of truth maintenance in the nonmonotonic reasoning [3,4] can be applied to keep the database consistent, and that the truth maintenance of the database can be achieved by each data keeping a foundation list that keeps track of current reasons (i.e., data in the database) by which the data can be recreated. Next, to execute the truth maintenance of the database mentioned above effectively, we propose an architecture based on three-dimensional integrated circuits (in short, 3-D IC) technology [5-10]. The 3-D IC chip assumed here will be fabricated at the

Integrated Circuit System Research Center of Hiroshima University in a few years. The architecture performs a database search in parallel using the 3-D IC chip. The execution of the truth maintenance is quite effective since the consistency test essentially searches for a data inconsistent with a data modified by an external event.

In the following, Section 2 introduces a truth maintenance method to a real-time production system whose realization using 3-D IC technology is mentioned in Section 3. The effect and the realizability of the architecture is discussed in Section 4.

2. TRUTH MAINTENANCE METHOD FOR A REAL-TIME PRODUCTION SYSTEM

Consider the following simple passenger transportation problem. There are stations linearly connected by a railroad. (The stations are numbered from left to right.) A train carrying passengers runs from a station to one of the adjacent stations to load passengers having requested and waiting for the train at stations. A request is issued by a passenger and is accomplished only when the passenger gets on the train at the station, namely, the destination of the passenger is not considered here. The passenger transportation problem is the problem of controlling the movement of the train so that passengers waiting at stations can get on the train. The control must be done in a way that the train starts an action only if the action is required. We assume that the current train position (station name) is informed by a train position message from the train.

Consider a naive real-time production system to solve the passenger transportation problem. The requests by passengers and the train position messages constitute external events of the system. We assume that only one external event arrives at a time, and each data having already existed in the database is not added to it again by any rules and events. Figure 1 (a) describes the rules of the system. The data (req[i]=on) exists in the database if and only if a request has been issued at station i but not has been accomplished so far. The data (train_positionθi) where $\theta \in \{=,<,>\}$, represents the current position of the train.

Rules (1) and (2) make candidates of the next movement of the train (e.g., when there are data (req[4]=on) and (train_position<4) in the database, the request to the train (go_right_request) will be added to the database by rule (1)). Rule (3) informs the system of the fact that the train stays at one of the stations where passengers are waiting for. Thus the system can know the current status of the railroad by referring the database. We should note that although data (req[i]=on) and (train_positionθi) are updated outside the system by external events, each data about request (e.g., (go_right_request)) is created inside the system which **does not directly modified by any external events**. An action corresponding to one of the candidates is selected and executed by rules (4)-(6), however, the system requires an explicit truth maintenance to keep the database consistent, because there remains inconsistent data which can not directly modified by external events.

// Rules for Example 1 //

(1) **if** (req[i]=on) & (train_position<1) **then** make (go_right_request)
(2) **if** (req[i]=on) & (train_position<1) **then** make (go_left_request)
(3) **if** (req[i]=on) & (train_position<1) **then** make (stop_request)
(4) **if** (stop_request) **then** { stop to pick up passengers }
(5) **if** (go_left_request) **then** { go left to get passengers }
(6) **if** (go_right_request) **then** { go right to get passengers }

(a) A naive rule description for Example 1.

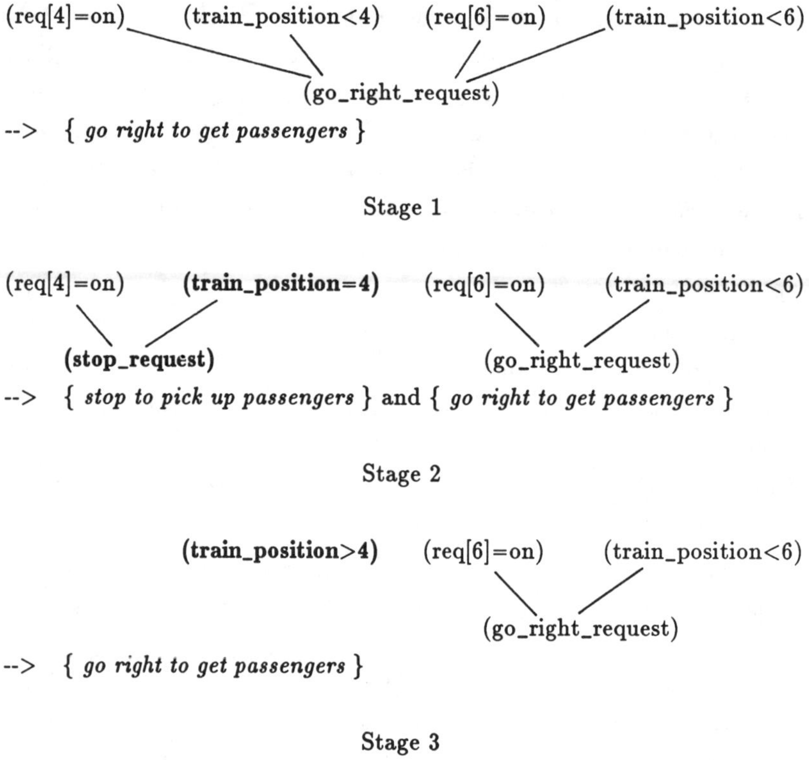

(req[4]=on)   (train_position<4)   (req[6]=on)   (train_position<6)
                    \   /
                  (go_right_request)
--> { go right to get passengers }

Stage 1

(req[4]=on)   **(train_position=4)**   (req[6]=on)   (train_position<6)
        \   /   \   /
     (stop_request)   (go_right_request)
--> { stop to pick up passengers } and { go right to get passengers }

Stage 2

(train_position>4)   (req[6]=on)   (train_position<6)
                                \   /
                             (go_right_request)
--> { go right to get passengers }

Stage 3

(b) A situation which requires truth maintenance.

Figure 1   Example 1.

Consider the case where passengers are waiting at Stations 4 and 6 and the train stays at station 2. Figure 1 (b) illustrates a series of ideal changes of the database starting from this situation (hereafter, call it Example 1). First (go_right_request) is created and then the train runs right due to this data in Stage 1. Next it arrives at station 4 and (stop_request) is created to pick up the passengers there in Stage 2. Finally, the train starts running right again to pick up the other passenger in Stage 3.

To make it possible, the system has to remove (stop_request) from and leave (go_right_request) to the database. One of the easiest solution for this problem is that whenever a request for the train accomplishes the system removes the request from the database. In Example 1, both (go_right_request) and (stop_request) are removed in Stage 2, and then (go_right_request) is recreated due to (req[6]=on) and (train_position<6). In a practical real-time system, such a recreation needs a considerably long time and, what is worse, it occurs frequently. This is a reason why we prohibit a system from containing negative statements. If we insist on our assumption, it is obvious that the system needs an external mechanism in order to remove meaningless data from the database, and if not, data such as (stop_request) or (go_right_request) can not be removed once they are created. We call this mechanism a truth maintenance, which is originally proposed for nonmonotonic reasoning [3,4]. It is true that this mechanism introduces new load to the system, but the load is lesser than that of the recreations of data mentioned above.

// A part of the database //
((req[4]=on), ϕ)   ((req[6]=on), ϕ)
((train_position<4), ϕ)   ((train_position<6), ϕ)
((go_right_request),   (((req[4]=on), (train_position<4)),
                                        ((req[6]=on), (train_position<6)))

(a) An example of foundation list (Stage 1 in Figure 1 (b)).

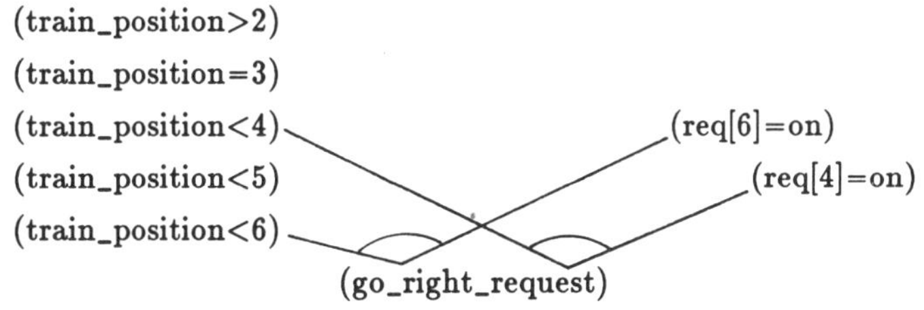

(train_position>1)
(train_position>2)
(train_position=3)
(train_position<4)   (req[6]=on)
(train_position<5)   (req[4]=on)
(train_position<6)
           (go_right_request)

(b) A data dependency graph caused by the foundation list at Stage 1.

Figure 2 Data structure in a real-time production system.

The truth maintenance mechanism should keep track on changes of the meaning of a data, i.e., the reason why the data exists in the database. In Example 1, the meaning of (go_right_request) changes in Stage 2, i.e., in Stage 1 passengers at two stations are waiting, while just one in State 3. For each data, we attach a foundation list to hold the meaning. An example of foundation lists is shown in Figure 2.

The foundation lists are used for truth maintenance in the following way. When a data is newly added to the database, all data, which are directly founded on the added data, are found by the database search (using an intelligent clustering method such as Rete [1]). Afterward, the foundation lists of them and added data are modified. If the added data has already existed in the database, foundation list of the data is modified so that it includes new foundation. These operation can be done in the matching phase. Conversely, when a data is deleted, all foundation lists which include the deleted data are modified, and if no foundation exists after the modification, the data itself is also deleted from the database. Note that this modification is applied recursively until no data is removed in the modification. We call this processing the truth maintenance phase. Figure 3 shows the difference between (a) a conventional production system model, and (b) a real-time production system

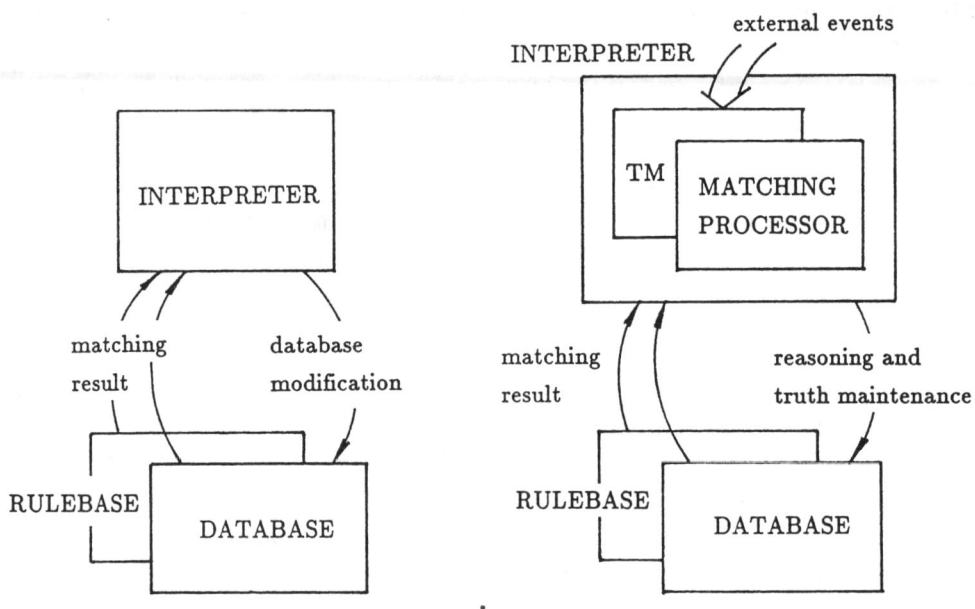

Figure 3 Models of production systems;
(a) conventional, and (b) a real-time production system.

model based on the truth maintenance. Since the set of clusters is a partially ordered set, these phases can be implemented easily.

Although the truth maintenance in a real-time system is reasonable, it might seem to be a reckless trial, since it requires much time for the search operation in both of the matching phase and the truth maintenance phase. To solve the problem, Section 3 will propose a parallel processing architecture by which both the matching phase and the truth maintenance phase can be executed effectively.

3. SYSTEM ARCHITECTURE USING 3-D IC

This section proposes an overlapped search architecture using 3-D IC technology for a real-time production system. 3.1 and 3.2 are concerned with parallel execution of the matching phase, and 3.3 mentions a parallel search in the truth maintenance phase.

3.1. Conventional architectures

When we start constructing a multiprocessor architecture which will support parallel execution of the matching phase, first of all we must decide how to divide the database and where to locate these pieces. DADO project [12,13] experiments divide the database into pieces and intersperse them on tree-structured DADO machine. This approach is certainly one solution; however, it wastes communication time due to the tree connected structure. On the other hand, the bus connected multiprocessor architecture is also applicable. PSM [2,14] and MANJI [15] distribute clusters (e.g., memory nodes in the Rete algorithm) of the database on each processor. They are originally proposed for the parallel matching. PSM applies cache technique effectively to realize dynamic allocation of the clusters, while MANJI allocates them on processors in static. The amount of communication among processors during the matching phase is small because of the locality of the database access in the Rete matching algorithm. Nevertheless, the amount of communication bottleneck, if the tuth maintenance mechanism is adopted, since it inevitably requires frequent global database access mainly due to the manipulation of foundation lists. Thus these architectures are not appropriate for our purpose.

3.2. Architecture using 3-D IC

No conventional multiprocessor architecture for production systems are appropriate for our real-time production system. It is mainly due to the narrow communication bandwidth between processors. One solution for this problem is that we apply direct memory access method on the architecture, however, it also causes a bus bottleneck if so many data (e.g., half of the memory space) should be transferred.

Three-dimensional common memory [5](in short, 3-D CM) is proposed to remove such communication bottleneck. It can support fast (e.g., in few machine cycles) memory-to-memory data transfer by using the direct inter-layer connection as in Figure 4. The development of 3-D CM, especially the optically interlayer-connected 3-D CM [10], is making steady progress at Integrated Circuit System Research Center of Hiroshima University. By using the 3-D CM, a common memory close to the ideal can be obtained [5].

Figure 5 shows an overview of the overlapped pattern matching model using 3-D CM for our real-time production system. Each processor (i.e., interpreter in Figure 3 (b)) connected to each layer performs the following procedure OLM. In procedure MATCH, we adopt a simplified (but Rete) state-saving matching algorithm by which the matching operation is clearly separated from the database modification, i.e., the matching phase does not execute any database modification. Procedure TM for truth maintenance is specified in the next section. Procedure TM starts on all processors at the same time, namely, when an external event arrives, a processor (e.g., the processor that earliest finishes the executing matching phase) declares the start of the truth maintenance phase to all other processors.

PROCEDURE OLM

// main routine //
1. initialize the database.
2. repeat step 3 while no external event arrives.
3. if s1=1 then execute procedure MATCH.

// interrupt handler //
4. if external events arrive, then execute procedure TM.
5. if the truth maintenance phase is started by the processor, execute procedure MATCH for newly added data.
6. go to step 2.

PROCEDURE MATCH

1. pick up one rule instance according to the scheduling strategy from the conflict set.
2. execute the selected instance and write the result on 3-D CM.
3. **send all data on its own memory plane** to the plane whose flag s1 is 0, and turn on the flag.
4. make the foundation list for the data written in step 2, modify all foundation lists to be corrected, and **send them** to the plane selected in step 3.
5. perform the matching operation using the conventional state-saving method, and return the result to the conflict set.

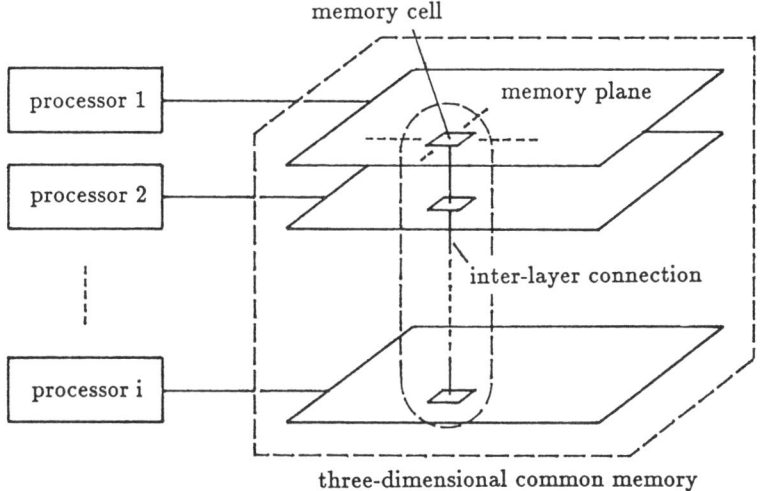

Figure 4 The three-dimensional common memory.

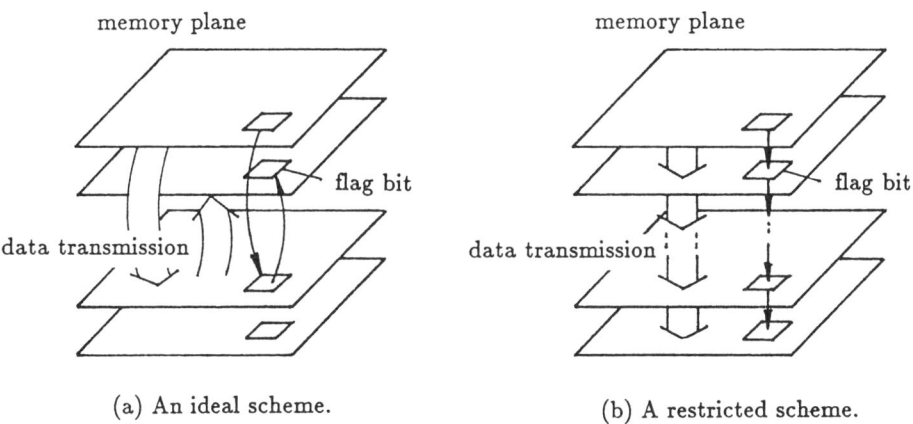

(a) An ideal scheme.

(b) A restricted scheme.

Figure 5 Inter-layer schemes of 3-D CM for overlapped matching; (a) an ideal scheme, and (b) a restricted scheme.

6.   turn off flag s1 on its own memory plane.

Note that the data transfer in steps 3 and 4 may be postponed if such plane does not exist. In such cases, the execution of step 6 must be frozen until these steps are accomplished.

In procedures OLM and MATCH, flag s1 is used to inform whether the data on the plane has a possibility to be referred to by its own processor (when s1=1) or not (when s1=0). Each processor whose flag s1 is 1 can start procedure MATCH if it idles, and therefore, the execution of steps 4 and 6 can be overlapped with the processing on other processors. Note that any processor referring to its own memory plane (i.e., s1=1) can not accept any data from other processors to perform the matching correctly. Hence so many data should be sent to the processor when it wishes to start other matching phase. The broad inter-layer bandwidth of 3-D CM is quite available for such data transmission. Figure 5 (a) shows an ideal scheme for the processing where the data transfer between any two layers is allowed, while (b) shows a limited scheme where the data transfer between only adjacent layers is allowed. The former can realize high throughput since any idle processors may accept data from any other processors. But it wastes larger space for the circuits than the scheme (b).

3.3. Parallel search for truth maintenance

By the architecture introduced in the last section, the truth maintenance phase can also be performed effectively in parallel.

Recall that we assumed that the set of data clusters is partially ordered. By the partial ordering, we can easily obtain a directed acyclic graph in which a node and an edge mean a cluster and their relation, respectively. Note that, in the graph, source clusters consist of data which might be modified by external events. Hence, we can accomplish truth maintenance by examining the foundation lists along to the acyclic directed graph from the roots to the leaves.

Consequently, by assigning the clusters to the processors in static, the examination of foundation lists can be executed in parallel. On the proposed model in Figure 5, each processor concurrently examines (and modifies) foundation lists of all data to be dealt with by the processor, referring to the whole database through 3-D CM.

The procedure TM can be specified as follows.

PROCEDURE TM

1.   repeat steps 2-4 while there remains data to be examined.

2. select one data from data clusters to be dealt with by the processor, s.t., any data in the foundation list have already been examined.
3. examine foundation of the data referring to the whole database and modify the foundation list.
4. if all foundations of the data have already been removed from the database, remove the data from the database.

Note that, in this procedure, 3-D CM is assumed to be used as a pure common memory, i.e., any data modification on a memory plane are immediately informed to any other planes in few machine cycles.

4. EVALUATION

4.1. Overlapped execution of the matching phase

This sub-section experimentally shows an effect of the ideal overlapped execution of the matching phase on a multiprocessor system. The architecture proposed in Section 3 realizes parallel execution of the matching phase ideally if the number of layers of 3-D IC is sufficiently large and the communication time between two layers is negligible.

An experiment is held on a multiprocessor system UNIP [16] using a parallel graph search program written by C language. UNIP adopts a bus connected multiprocessor architecture based on master-slave scheme. In this experiment, the database is distributed to each of local memories of slave processors but not fully duplicated, since the memory space is small (4Kbytes/processor). Namely, data transfer between any memory planes is not implemented here.

Figure 6 represents a result of experiments, i.e., the speedup of the matching phase when parallel execution of the matching phase is adopted. The saturation of the curve in ideal case is due to the limitation of parallelism in the search problem (about 6 in average). On actual experiment, the execution time is slower than the ideal case, which is caused by the long communication time on UNIP (15 msec/action, which corresponds to 3.6Kbytes/sec). Hence, if sufficiently fast communication time (e.g., 100Mbytes/sec) can be obtained, the parallel execution is so effective for speedup of the matching phase. (A result of software simulation is represented by a broken line in the figure.) The advantage is caused by that the time for database modification (i.e., steps 1 to 3 in procedure MATCH) is sufficiently smaller than that for database reference (i.e., steps 4 to 6 in procedure MATCH).

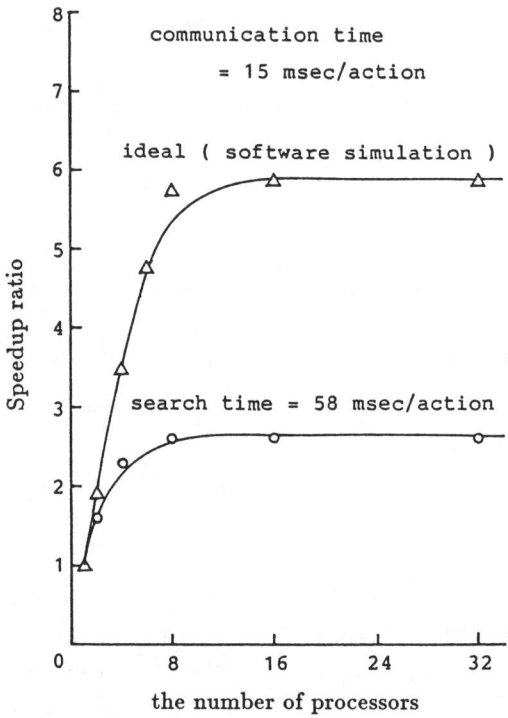

Figure 6   An effect of the overlapped matching.

4.2. Parallel search for truth maintenance

Figure 6 also shows an effect of our architecture on truth maintenance phase, since the truth maintenance is really a parallel search problem.

Although this experiment supposes simple AND graph in which every data modification directly influences adjacent (i.e., children) data, we would apply more ingeneous graph search algorithm for actual AND-OR graph search problems. For example, we may perform truth maintenance not for each database modification but using a lazy evaluation technique. Such implementations can reduce the load of database search, which makes the execution of the operation more effectively. Anyway, the broad inter-layer bandwidth of ideal 3-D CM has a possibility to make the execution of truth maintenance practical, since it is expected to achieve a speedup proportional to the number of processors.

4.3. Realizability

It requires much advanced technologies to fabricate 3-D CM assumed here. Although no actual 3-D CM chip is obtained so far, several simulation results have already been obtained by a group of device engineers [10].

By their report, a 3-D CM chip of 4 or 5 layers whose density is about 1Kbits/layer will be fabricated in a few years. In their design rule (2 micron NMOS rule is used), the size of a memory cell for 3-D CM is 5 or 10 times of that for conventional static RAM. The number of layers could be increased up to ten by an extend of current fabrication technology, which will be improved by some new techniques. The cycle time (or the access time) of the memory is not clear so far, however, plane-to-plane data transmission within one machine cycle (approximately, 5 nsec) can be accomplished by wired (or optical) inter-layer connections.

5. REMARKS

In this paper, we have introduced the truth maintenance method for a real-time production system, and proposed an overlapped search architecture using 3-D IC for the production system. This architecture supports both of (1) parallel firing on production systems and (2) parallel search for truth maintenance.

We should examine the following problems further;

(a) performance estimation of 3-D CM in the proposed architecture based on concrete physical parameters, and

(b) estimation of the availability in actual real-time environments.

Acknowledgements

The authors wish to express their thanks to research staffs of Integrated Circuit System Research Center of Hiroshima University, especially, Director and Professor M. Hirose and Professor M. Yamanishi for their helpful advices on the device fabrication technology, and Mr. T. Takeuchi for his simulation works on UNIP.

REFERENCES

[1] C.L. Forgy, "Rete: A Fast Algorithm for the Many Pattern/Many Object Pattern Match Problem," *Artificial Intelligence*, 19, pp.17-37 (1982).

[2] A. Gupta, et al., "Parallel Algorithms and Architectures for Rule-Based Systems," *Proc. 13th ISCA*, pp.10-19 (June 1986).

[3] J. Doyle, "A truth maintenance system," *Artificial Intelligence*, 12, pp.231-272 (1979).

[4] J. de Kleer, "An Assumption-based TMS," *Artificial Intelligence,* 28, pp.127-162 (1986).

[5] R. Aibara, "An Architectural Study on Massive Multiprocessor Systems," Doctoral Dissertation, Hiroshima University (1986).

[6] K. Kurokawa and H. Aiso, "Three-Dimensional IC," *IPS Japan,* 27, 7, pp.718-729 (July 1986), in Japanese.

[7] M. Hasegawa and Y. Shigei, "$AT^2 = O(N\log^4 N)$, T=O(logN) Fast Fourier Transform in A Light Connected 3-Dimensional VLSI," *Proc. 13th ISCA,* pp.252-260 (June 1986).

[8] S. Fujita, et al., "A Template Matching Algorithm Using Optically-Connected 3-D VLSI Architecture," *Proc. 14th ISCA,* pp.64-70 (June 1987).

[9] Y. Inoue, et al., "A Three-Dimensional Static RAM," *IEEE Electron Device Lett.,* EDL-7, 5, pp.327-329 (May 1986).

[10] T. Maemoto, H. Takata and M. Hirose, "Optically-Connected Three-Dimensional Common Memory," *IEICE Japan, Report SIG SDM* 87-168 (1988), in Japanese.

[11] T. Ishida and S.J. Stolfo, "Toward the parallel Execution of Rules in Production System Programs," *Proc.ICPP,* pp.568-575 (Aug.1985).

[12] S.J. Stolfo, "Initial Performance on the DADO2 Prototype," *IEEE Computer,* 20, 1, pp.75-83 (Jan. 1987).

[13] S.J. Stolfo, "Five Parallel Algorithm for Production System Execution on the DADO Machine," *Proc.of AAAI,* pp.300-307 (1984).

[14] A. Gupta, et al., "Results of Parallel Implementation of OPS5 on the Encore Multiprocessor," *CMU-CS-87-146* (Aug. 1987).

[15] J. Miyazaki, et al., "A Shared Memory Architecture for MANJI Production System Machine," *Database Machines and Knowledge Base Machines (Ed. by M. Kitsuregawa and H. Tanaka),* pp.517-531, Kluwer Academic Publishers (1988).

[16] R. Aibara and T. Ae, "An Implementation of Sort/Search Engine on a Multiprocessor," *Trans. IPS Japan,* 26, 2, pp.349-355 (Mar. 1985), in Japanese.

THE BRAUNSCHWEIG RELATIONAL DATABASE MACHINE PROJECT RESULTS

H. Herzog, F. Hildebrandt, H.-O. Leilich,
P. Mertinatsch, G. Stiege, H.Ch. Zeidler

Institut für Betriebssysteme und Rechnerverbund
Institut für Datenverarbeitungsanlagen

Technische Universität Braunschweig
Postfach 3329
D - 3300 Braunschweig, FRG

Abstract

Within the scope of a university research project the Braunschweig Relational Database Machine RDBM was implemented. The project closed with the evaluation of the machine. This article sums up the most important research results. After describing the measurement and modeling methodology, the results will be discussed and compared to those of other systems.

Keywords

architectural evaluation, benchmarking, modeling, monitoring, multiprocessor system, performance measurement, relational database machine

1 Introduction

Database machines are computer systems specially dedicated by hardware structure to a database system, so that specific operations can be executed faster than in a general purpose computer system. If one attempts to implement the full access flexibility of a relational database system (i.e. in not using a predefined index) conventional computers are very inefficient, because even primitive search operations lead to overload in substantial parts of the hardware (CPU, buses, I/O system).

On the basis of work in associative memories and the search processor project (SURE, /LSZe 78/) the RDBM concept was developed since 1979. The heterogeneous multiprocessor system with functionally specialized processors has been developed and implemented as a research vehicle in order to evaluate the merits and problems of this kind of special-purpose computer systems. Since various sorting and searching components have been proposed or even been implemented with the claim of phantastic performance improvements, we dared to put together a "complete system" with entirely new hardware and software in order to put these components into an environment as realistic as possible in a university project. It was a joint project of the computer science department and electrical engineering department of the Technical University of Braunschweig, supported by the Federal German Ministry of Defense and the Ministry for Research and Technology.

In the final phase of the project, the emphasis was to obtain quantitative results as the basis of the evaluation, the main topic of this publication. We also shall mention some evaluation work done with simulation models and analytical models. The presented problems of such an evaluation and the experiences gained should be transferable to other multiprocessor systems.

Since the overall principle of our database machine and many aspects of it have been published before, e.g. /SZHL 83, TeZe 83 and ZeAu 85/, we merely summarize the general architecture as follows.

RDBM physically consists of three major components (see Fig. 1); these are firstly a general-purpose minicomputer (DABS) to control the different components and to perform all the database functions which are not supported by specialized hardware, secondly a content-addressable mass storage device (CAM) with the secondary memory (SEM) and its own memory manager (SEMM) and data filters (restriction and update processor, RUP), and thirdly the multiprocessor system with the main memory (MAM) and its manager (MAMM), the sort processor (SOP), the data conversion processor (COP) and an interrecord processor (IRP). All processors are interconnected via a threefold bus system.

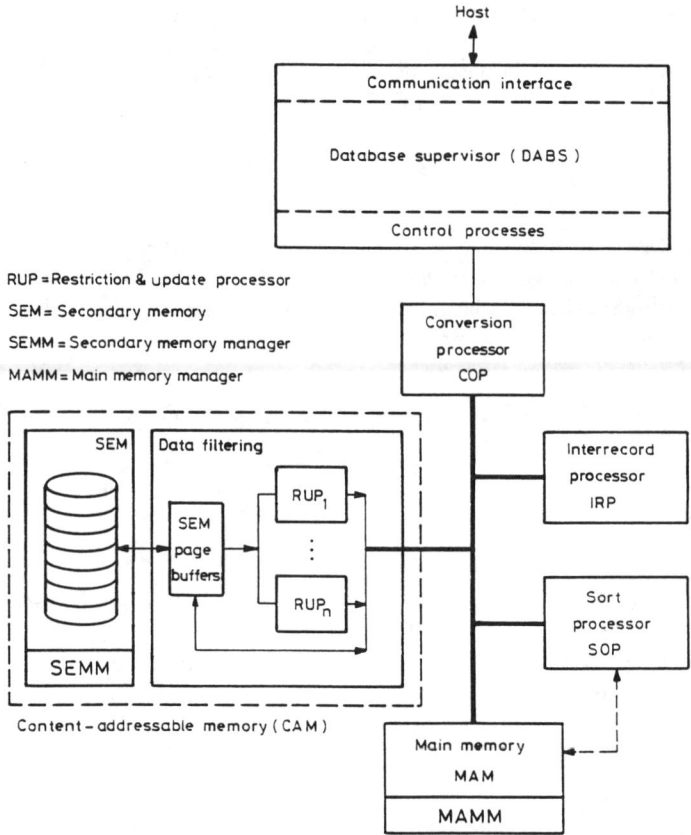

Fig. 1: The RDBM system configuration

2 Measurement Methodology

2.1 Measurement Concepts

The evaluation of RDBM had two targets. First, a comparison to other database machines and database systems should be possible and, on the other hand, an evaluation of the architectural concept at the basis of a bottleneck analysis was to be done. The representation of a user task in RSQL (a RDBM specific SQL derivate) and the decomposition of such a database function into a sequence of multiprocessor system operations suggested the orientation of the measurement concept to this hierarchy. There are two possible causal chains for the explanation of the gained measurement results: *top-down* and *bottom-up* /Brun 85/.

The *top-down* method determines the externally visible system performance (execution times, throughput). The *bottom-up* method tries to get performance parameters on the lowest level to synthesize the results of the higher levels.

Both methods were used within the evaluation of RDBM. From the total times investigated by using the *top-down* method the time portions that are needed to transform the RSQL-formulated user queries into processor programs and parameter sets and to control the database functions could be derived. On the next lower level one could gain (apart from the times spent in the multiprocessor system) the execution times for the controlling and preparation of the execution by the database supervisor (management overhead) and the execution times for the communication between database supervisor and special hardware (communication overhead). Using the *bottom-up* method, first of all a multitude of measurements at the processor level was carried out. The results were used for the synthesis of more global measurement results.

The Wisconsin-Benchmark /BDTu 83/ is the widest used comparison standard for relational database systems and database machines. Therefore it was used as a basis for the evaluation of RDBM. The benchmark consists of a synthetic database with relations containing up to 10,000 tuples. The attribute values are selected especially for a simple modification of query selectivity factors.

2.2 Measurement Tools

For measuring the performance of the database machine, three types of monitors were used: *software and firmware monitors* integrated into the RDBM control software for the registration of durations and events concerning the hierarchical measurement concept, and a *hardware monitor* for the observation of the bus traffic on the three buses of the multiprocessor system with regard to bus load and source/drain-relations between the processors.

While the hardware monitor has no influence on the measured processes, a certain interference of the other two monitor types cannot be avoided. To keep the reactions as small as possible, the measurement code sequences of the software monitor were written in assembler. Because time measurements are done by counting clock cycles, the microcode of the firmware monitor was constructed such that during the execution of the monitor program the counting is suppressed.

Within the measurement process the data of all three monitors were merely collected; the preparation happened offline with the help of special evaluation and representation programs. In the hardware monitor, a special measurement microcomputer was used for this /Mert 88, MAZe 87 and RDBM 88/.

3 Global Measurement Results

3.1 Measurements of Global Execution Times

At this measurement level, the time elapsed between sending a user task at the screen and the presentation of the ready message of the system on the user terminal was measured.

The following tables show the comparison of the average values measured in RDBM with the results of other systems and current investigations (e.g. /DeWi 88, NaKa 88, NaKi 88/), where in contrast to RDBM data distribution and substantial parallelism is being used. Only the results of selection and join queries shall be presented here.

	Selectivity Factor	
System	1%	10%
U-INGRES	53.2 s	64.4 s
C-INGRES	38.4 s	53.9 s
ORACLE	194.2 s	230.6 s
IDMnodac	31.7 s	33.4 s
IDMdac	21.6 s	23.6 s
DIRECT	43.0 s	46.0 s
RDBMRUPas	32.5 s	34.0 s
RDBMRUPmi	13.07 s	13.5 s
Teradata	6.86 s	15.97 s
Gamma	1.63 s	2.11 s
HDMnocache	5 s	4 s
HDMcache	3 s	2 s
MACH1	0.8 s	0.9 s

Table 1: Execution times of selection queries without indices (integer attributes)

Table 1 shows that RDBM with machine programmed data filters (RDBMRUPas) reaches selection query response times being within the scope of the results in /BDTu 83/. On the other hand, microprogrammed data filters (RDBMRUPmi) require distinctly less time than those systems.

	Selectivity Factor			
	Clustered Index		Non-Clustered Index	
System	1%	10%	1%	10%
U-INGRES	7.7 s	27.8 s	59.2 s	78.9 s
C-INGRES	3.9 s	18.9 s	11.4 s	54.3 s
ORACLE	16.31 s	130.0 s	17.3 s	129.2 s
IDMnodac	2.0 s	9.9 s	3.8 s	27.6 s
IDMdac	1.5 s	8.7 s	3.3 s	23.7 s
DIRECT	43.0 s	46.0 s	43.0 s	46.0 s
RDBMRUPmi	13.07 s	13.5 s	13.07 s	13.5 s

Table 2: Execution times of selection queries with indices (integer attributes)

Table 2 shows the results for systems working with index tables. Even here RDBM can compete especially at the results with a selectivity factor of 10%. Of course, parallelism in large database machines (see lower part of Table 1) leads to considerable speed up.

Level overlapping measurements within the meaning of the *top-down* method could not be performed completely because of hardware problems. This made it necessary to synthesize measurement results on higher measurement levels using the *bottom-up* method.

System	Query	
	joinAselB	joinABprime
U-INGRES	10:12 min	9:36 min
C-INGRES	1:48 min	2:36 min
ORACLE	> 300 min	> 300 min
IDMnodac	> 300 min	> 300 min
IDMdac	> 300 min	> 300 min
DIRECT	10:12 min	9:30 min
RDBMas−	4:18 min	7:35 min
RDBMmi−	2:17 min	4:17 min
RDBMmi0	2:57 min	4:57 min
RDBMmi+	3:39 min	5:38 min
Teradata	0:356 min	0:349 min
Gamma	0:051 min	0:065 min
MACH1	0:019 min	0:012 min
HDM	0:044 min	0:044 min

Table 3: Execution times of join queries without indices (integer attributes)

Starting from the sum of individual time measurements collected in the multiprocessor system (RDBM−), Table 3 additionally presents two values representing an upper (RDBM+) and an expected (RDBM0) limit for reasons of software overhead. This method is to balance measurement tolerances at the measurement result synthesis. In the following an operation mode of RDBM, in which all processors are machine-programmed, is denoted *RDBMas*, and a mode, in which all processors are microprogrammed (some of them partly) is called *RDBMmi*. It becomes obvious that the RDBMmi mode performs the join operation in an acceptable amount of time, in spite of the fact that especially at the join operation the low data rate of the secondary memory influences the result considerably. In RDBM, the join operation is preceded by sorting the relations using a sort-merge-algorithm. Because of the limited capacity of the main memory, the intermediate results of this procedure have to be swapped onto the secondary memory. In a following merge process, they have to be transferred back to the main memory. In case of the query type 'joinAselB' (see /BDTu 83/), four additional swaps to the secondary memory and, in case of query type 'joinABprime', eight additional swaps are necessary.

The lower part of Table 3 summarizes the execution times published in /DeWi 88/, /Naka 88/ and /NaKi 88/. The considerable improvement of the execution times of these DBMs is partly due to the shortcomings of the RDBM implementation, and partly the result of data partitioning in this class of parallel machines.

3.2 Measurements on the Level of Database Functions

The execution of a DML database function can be partitioned into three steps: preparation of the operation, execution of the data manipulation and closing procedures.

The preparation as well as the closing procedures comprise operations in MAMM and/or SEMM and software overhead. Therefore, both the corresponding time measurements will be merged to a single value. The real data manipulation comprises (e.g. at the selection operation) the time that is needed by the data filters for the selection and a small software overhead for the communication of the control software with the processors (results in Section 4). Fig. 2 shows the time portions of both measured steps for the selection. This leads to a specification of the part, called DBF, of the total execution time of a selection.

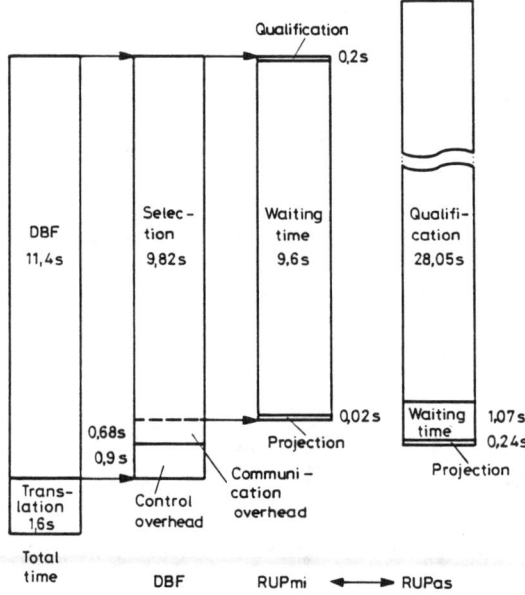

Fig. 2: Total execution time of a selection (breakdown)

Figure 2 shows the execution time breakdown of Table 1 for a selection query with a selectivity of 1%. The overhead of translation and control software of 13% appears to be very large. But if more data had to be processed, this portion would be reduced because it is query dependent (not data dependent).

In practical applications of database machines more data are likely to be handled.

4 Detailed Measurements in the Multiprocessor System

The measurements in the lowest level should show whether the task allocation between the processors is properly solved.

The scope of the detailed measurements shall be demonstrated by means of the results concerning data filters and secondary memory, sort processor, and bus system. Similar evaluations have been done for the other processors of RDBM /Mert 88/.

4.1 The Data Filters (RUPs)

According to investigations in /Mert 88/, acceleration factors of about 10 to 300 (depending on operation types and parameters) are the result of arithmetic operations in micro- instead of machine-programming of the data filters. Processing character strings, improvement factors of about 20 to 30 are reached, independent of the selected internal data format.

The comparison measurements in Fig. 2 done with micro- and machine-programmed data filters show clearly that the machine-programmed version is restricted by its CPU, while the microprogrammed version is waiting for more than 90% of the total time for data transfer from the secondary memory. Looking at the mere execution times of a data filter and neglecting the waiting times, an increase in performance of a factor of about 128 results from the above described selection query by microprogramming kernel functions. This is a strong example that special hardware can drastically improve efficiency. In contrast to the examples VERSO and IDM investigated by Boral /Bora 86/ where an improvement on the performance with a factor of about 1.14 to maximal 7 was given, the microprogrammed data filters of RDBM exceed these performance improvement figures by more than one order of magnitude.

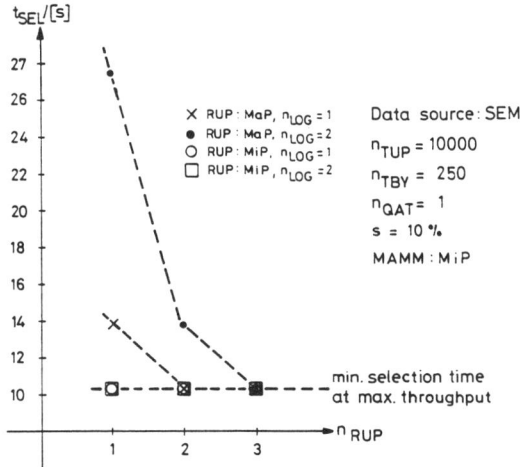

Fig. 3: Selection execution times at different numbers of data filters
(data transfer from secondary memory)

In Fig. 3, the selection time in case of a selectivity of 10%, dependent on the number of data filters (n_{RUP}) and the influence of RUP-machine- (MaP) and microprogramming (MiP), is shown. The measurement results regarding different numbers of logical operations (n_{LOG}) in the qualification expression are given, too. In the case of increasing the number of microprogrammed data filters there will be only a negligible reduction of selection time, caused by further reduction of the qualification and projection times. In case of machine-programmed data filters a second processor will reduce the selection time significantly, because of the relative large execution times of the qualification and projection. Thereby this implementation alternative reaches the bottleneck of the transfer rate of the secondary memory, too. More complex qualification queries with several logical operations would require an increasing number of data filters.

The secondary memory of the implemented Braunschweig RDBM is the limiting factor for a performance improvement of the microprogrammed data filter. From the volume of data and the measured execution time of a segment list command in SEMM a transfer rate of only about 240 KByte/s can be calculated. Conceptionally, RDBM allows a transfer rate of 8 MByte/s. For the investigation of the efficiency of RDBM at such a high data rate a segment buffer was built. The buffer stores segments of a relation to be loaded from SEM. After the loading procedure it acts like a SEM and transfers the stored data with maximum data rate to the data filters.

Using the semiconductor segment buffer with a high selectivity factor the main memory manager (not the secondary memory) is the bottleneck. With low selectivity (e.g. 1%) the data filters are the bottleneck. The obtainable total throughput in the segment buffer mode was about 5.4 MByte/s (see Fig. 4).

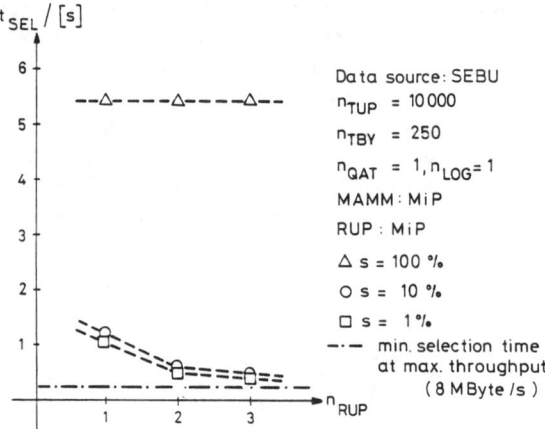

Fig. 4: Selection execution times at different numbers of data filters (data transfer from segment buffer)

The central point of the investigations on the different data filter hardware implementations is the comparison of execution times of the basic operations important for the data filter tasks. In this context it becomes obvious that the necessary number of cycles for the given commands using the less expensive data filter version based on a 8X300 microprocessor is hardly higher than that of the bitslice implementation. On the other hand, a compare operation between strings will take twice as long.

Especially the results concerning the join and selection queries, where extensive in- and outputs to the secondary memory are done, have to be interpreted in the RDBM context.

The results of the join operation were recalculated at a basis of a transfer rate of 3 MByte/s. The assumed transfer rate is typical for today's disk units.

Operation	RDBMsem– 3 MByte/s	RDBMsem0 3 MByte/s	RDBMsem– 8 MByte/s	RDBMsem0 8 MByte/s
Selection 1% (without indices)	1.04 s	3.54 s	0.55 s	3.05 s
Selection 10% (without indices)	1.13 s	3.63 s	0.68 s	3.18 s
joinAselB	1.19 min	1.86 min	1.16 min	1.83 min
joinABprime	2.26 min	2.93 min	2.17 min	2.84 min
Projection 100/10000	10.02 s	17.52 s	9.95 s	17.45 s
Projection 1000/1000	1.13 s	8.63 s	1.09 s	8.59 s
Aggregation	16.35 s	22.45 s	16.35 s	22.45 s

Table 4: Results of detailed measurements at different disk transfer rates

The synthesis of the results made possible by detailed measurements are presented in Table 4. Here, *RDBMsem–* represents a value where all individual time portions measured in RDBM are summarized. The value *RDBMsem0* considers additionally the software overhead already described in Section 3.1. Additionally, the table includes results for the peak processing rate of 8 MByte/s.

4.2 The Sort Processor

Sort operations are executed by a processor controlled microprogrammed sequential network (SOP) which performs the address table list sort. The physical reordering of the target tuples is managed by the main memory manager (MAMM). Therefore, the total sorting time is composed of the respective execution times. We distinguish between micro- and machine-programmed versions of MAMM. The measurement results demonstrated that the reordering time of the tuples in micro- as in machine-programmed MAMM is much larger than the sorting time in SOP (complexity of $O(n\ ld\ n)$); therefore, the total sorting time t_{SOP} of RDBM is approximately proportional to the number of the tuples to be processed. By using the microprogramming of the main memory manager, the internal sorting is being accelerated by the factor 3.3 compared to machine-programming. More details are given in /TeZe 83/.

4.3 The Bus System

Looking at the data bus histogram of the hardware monitor (Fig. 5) for a selection operation with a selectivity of 100%, the pauses in tupel transfer caused by page transfer waiting times of the secondary memory can be observed and the resulting average data bus load is rather low.

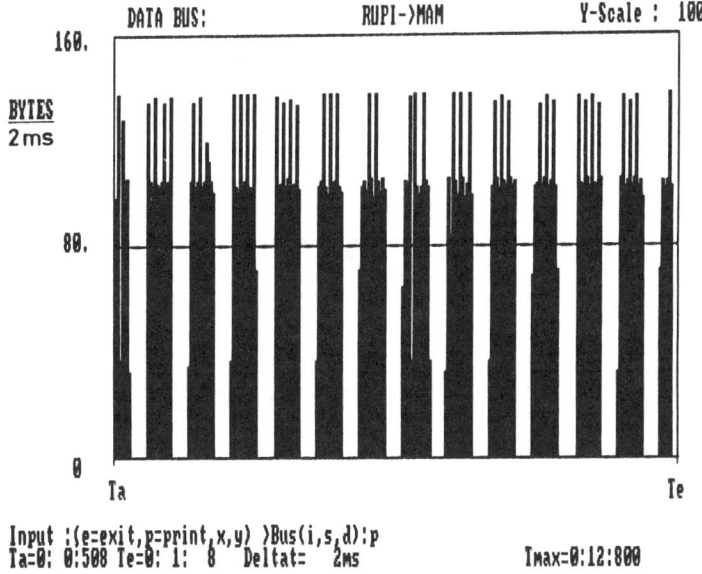

Fig. 5: Data bus histogram of an interrecord operation

This is also true for the instruction transfers between data filter and main memory manager. The measurements of further DB operations /Mert 88/ showed similar results.

4.4 Factors Influencing the Measurement Results

Regarding the evaluation results of Sect. 3 the influence of the database supervisor (NORD 100) is of prime importance. Its efficiency for the version used was given as about 0.3 MIPS which is low compared to current processors like Motorola 68020 (about 2 MIPS). The inefficient implementation of the PEARL compiler on the supervisor was identified as a further limiting factor. With the help of a profiler the frequency of single program constructs was ascertained. Based on comparative measurements with FORTRAN /KIHi 84/ a reduction of the total software overhead from 2 s (selection) to 1.8 ... 1.5 s (using a different programming language) is estimated.

5 Evaluation of RDBM by Modeling

Apart from measurements, modeling techniques were used for an evaluation of RDBM, too /LiSt 88/. At the beginning, we did not yet realize the necessity and the advantages of supporting the system design and system implementation by modeling and model based evaluation did not become clear. Therefore, most of the simulation programs written for parts of RDBM were restricted to function validations. A relatively extensive simulation program (/Arlt 82/, /Sche 85/) was used during the system design to estimate performance parameters. In retrospective, estimations appear to have been too optimistic.

In a later phase of the project, RDBM was analytically modeled and evaluated in two major activities. Ockenga /Ocke 85/ chose a two level approach for modeling. He followed the command flow determined by the control software and chose a tandem waiting queue system (Fig. 6) for his main model.

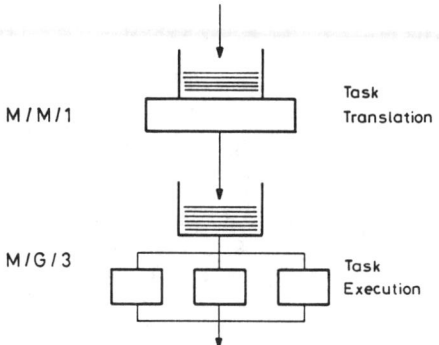

Fig. 6: Main model of the RDBM, according to Ockenga

The communication layer of the control software was regarded as a task source. Considering the number of user programs communicating with RDBM, the assumption of an infinite source with Poisson arrivals seemed justified. Service in the first station was done in FIFO sequence and with negative exponentially distributed service times. The latter was decided on primarily to make the model mathematically tractable by obtaining Poisson arrivals to the second station. In that station, a M/G/3 model was used, where the servers in the model corresponded to the three real servers in the control software. The strategy was again FIFO. The main difficulty was to determine the service time distribution in the servers. The service time distribution was calculated from the service time distributions of database function calls of this same task. The duration of a database function call was expressed as a function of the duration of the multiprocessor calls necessary for this database function. This required a careful analysis of the implementation details. The duration of a database function call was modeled as a server network of the processors to be called consecutively. Thereby, locking times resulting in certain processors from parallel work of three servers had to be considered, using parallel paths in the network with static branch probabilities and different locking nodes. For details see the bibliography. Due to the lack of measured data at the time of his work, Ockenga was forced to use rough estimates for service time distributions. Within these limits his calculated results were confirmed by later measurements.

Lie /Lie 87/ followed another modeling approach. She modeled the multiprocessor system of RDBM, using the conrol software of DABS simply as a source and sender of tasks. A server network representing the processor configuration was used as a basis for the model (Fig. 7).

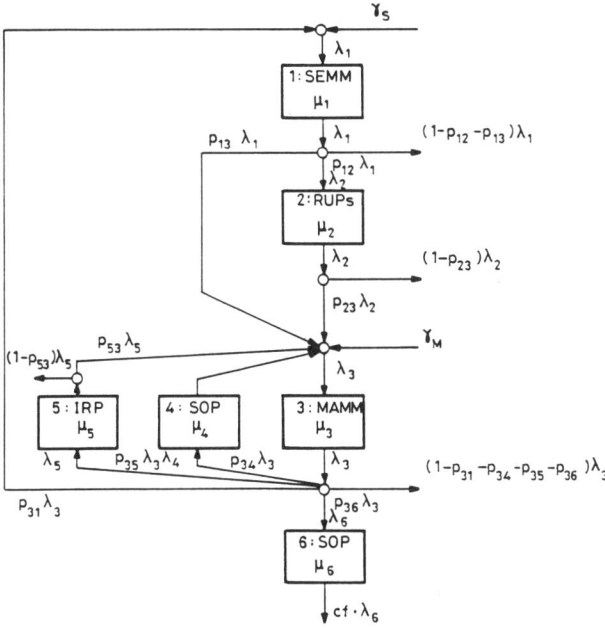

Fig. 7: Network model of the RDBM, according to /Lie 87/

The tasks in the model were the data segments themselves, not the real database tasks. Fixed transition probabilities resulting from analyzing carefully the real system and assumptions about the load profiles were used. An extensive investigation of the operation modes of the special processors was necessary to obtain the service times. With those assumptions, the target values, namely the data flow in the network, were calculated by using Jackson's theorem. For the details of the model we would like to refer to the original literature, too.

Lie applied her model to three load profiles (i.e. query intensive, query and update intensive, tasks with small data amounts) and examined especially the load and throughput of the special processors. The interrecord processor and the data converter turned out to be bottlenecks. In the same model, Lie also assumed an enhanced version of RDBM avoiding these bottlenecks. Of special interest was a further model variation without MAM and a sufficiently big local memory capacity in every special processor. Quite surprisingly, this change did not lead to significant improvements.

Whereas Lie's results concerning the existing RDBM were roughly confirmed by the measurements described elsewhere in this paper, the main results of her work was the discussion of two design alternatives, especially the insight that a pure dataflow approach with local memory would not do better.

6 Conclusions

Concluding this paper which is a concluding report on a rather large university research project, has different faces.

We might comment on the usefulness of the evaluation methods mentioned in a general and on the way they are applied on our specific research vehicle, where we had the chance to implement a rather wide variety of hardware, firmware and software monitors.

Instead, we shall conclude on the object of these evaluations, namely database machines, specifically on the architectural approach taken with the Braunschweig RDBM. Although the detailed performance figures compare quite well with those of several other database machines - most of them being research vehicles or prototypes of may-be industrial products - the real result of the project is what one could learn from the project itself. This is the reason for our thriving to obtain quantitative results and giving a report of them, although we yield ourselves open to criticism.

There is no doubt that a multiprocessor system like our RDBM can be put to useful work by tuning and redesigning some details. There is no doubt either that an industrial product would never be a "chinese copy" of a university research vehicle. Most of the boards would have to be redesigned for better production and testing. The number of parts would have to be reduced drastically.

In the course of the years technology has evolved dramatically, so that nowadays one could make the main and the local memories much larger, use much more powerful microprocessors, controllers, ASICs for most of the special circuitry, and special VLSI circuits supporting relational operations /BLLM 85, LeHe 88/.

On the other hand, in a highly competitive computer world, each architectural and technological generation has its own set of optimization rules. The question is, what we can learn from the Braunschweig RDBM configurational concept and from its implementation of the research vehicle in a university environment with non-redesigned units and only partially up-to-date technology.

Dedicated processors for special tasks have proved to be very efficient for the job profile considered (Wisconsin Benchmark), especially if they are microprogrammed (speed-up factors 10...300). Projecting this result into the future brings up the question how high-performance modern general purpose microprocessors match up with modern special purpose (semi custom) ASICs in terms of effective performance, including manufacturing and testing aspects for the entire system. If special hardware and microprogramming would be entirely replaced by general purpose microprocessors with a specific task allocation then, of course, the entire architecture would have to be reconsidered. In this case there would be little resemblance to RDBM.

The RDBM bus system (with 8 MByte/s) turned out to be adequate, although a 16-bit wide bus could easily be implemented. The number of dedicated processors could even be increased, e.g. multiple interrecord processors executing the join operation in parallel /SJJo 84/. The bottleneck in communication is the main memory manager, a special microprocessor. It would perform better in a fully microprogrammed mode. The data converter is another bottleneck. The duplication of this unit would help to increase the throughput if mass data are inserted.

RDBM was originally designed as a *small system* (Minicomputer) with a single disk. The hardware available was a 64 MByte disk with an 806 KByte/s transfer rate, and we never had the chance to update the mass memory periphery. We used an available HP 2100 minicomputer as an emulator for a secondary memory manager (SEMM) which further reduced the data rate. A special memory manager /Bala 83/ was designed to avoid this bottleneck.

If there had been a mass memory with multiple disks, adequate to the performance of the RDBM multiprocessor system, then we would have thought to attach certain search and management logic to each unit, commensurate with our general concept to structure logic, memory and communication according to the system requirements. In this case our system would probably resemble *clustered processing* systems like GAMMA /DeWi 88/, HDM /NaKa 88/ or MACH /NaKi 88/, for which we have given the corresponding measurement results (Table 1 and 3).

The performance of the special sort processor was much lower than originally conceived because of the large memory access times and the physical reordering in the main memory. Various refinements for a drastic speed-up of the join procedure have been suggested, including studies on hardware supported hash procedures (/Adi 87/; see also /DeGe 88/ and /KiTa 88/).

7 Acknowledgements

The authors would like to thank all participants of this large university project. Many students of electrical engineering and computer science contributed to its success within the scope of their theses by solving partial problems (in altogether over 250 papers). During several "generations" the following researchers applied their creativity and endurance for the joint project: W. Adi, H. Auer, J. Bartram, Ch. Dieter, R. Großjohann, A. Hahlweg, W. Hartwig, W. Hell, H. v. Kleist-Retzow, J.S. Lie, S. Seehusen, H. Schweppe, W. Teich, J. Thornton and H. Winoto.

8 References

/Adi 87/	Adi, W.: Design Criteria and Complexity Evaluation of a Hashbased Join Processor, Habilitationsschrift, TU Braunschweig, 1987
/Arlt 82/	Arlt, V.: Simulationssystem zur Leistungsmessung und -bewertung des RDBM-Multiprozessorsystems, Diplomarbeit, Institut für Betriebssysteme und Rechnerverbund, TU Braunschweig, 1982
/Bala 83/	Balasus, R.: Entwicklung eines mikroprogrammierbaren 16-Bit Bitslice-Prozessors unter Einhaltung der Abwärtskompatibilität zu den Kleinrechnern der Serie HP 1000 von Hewlett Packard, Diplomarbeit, Institut für Datenverarbeitungsanlagen, TU Braunschweig, 1983
/BDTu 83/	Bitton, D.; DeWitt, D.; Turbyfill, C.: Benchmarking Database Systems - A Systematic Approach, Proc. 9th VLDB, Florence, 1983
/BLLM 85/	Bonuccelli, M.A.; Lodi, E.; Luccio, F.; Maestrini, P.; Pagli, L.: VLSI Algorithms and Architecture for Relational Operations, Calcolo (Italy), Vol.22, No.1, 1985
/Bora 86/	Boral, H.: Design Considerations for 1990 database machines, Proc. COMPCON, Spring 1986, San Francisco, 1986
/Brun 85/	Brunk, M.: Bewertung des RDBM-Multiprozessorsystems anhand interner Messungen, Diplomarbeit, Institut für Betriebssysteme und Rechnerverbund, TU Braunschweig, 1985
/DeGe 88/	DeWitt, D.J.; Gerber, R.: Multiprocessor Hash-Based Join Algorithms, Computer Sciences Department, in: /KiTa 88/
/DeWi 88/	DeWitt, D. et al.: A Single User Evaluation of the GAMMA Database Machine, in: /KiTa 88/
/Herz 88/	Herzog, H.: Synchronisation kooperierender Aktivitäten in Nicht-Standard-Datenbanksystemen, Dissertation, TU Braunschweig, 1988

/KiTa 88/ Kitsuregawa, M.; Tanaka, H. (ed.): Database Machines and Knowledge Base Machines, 5th International Workshop on Database Machines, Karuizawa, Japan, 1987; Kluwer Academic Publishers, Boston/Dordrecht, Lancaster, 1988

/KlHi 84/ von Kleist-Retzow, H.; Hildebrandt, F.: Steuerung einer Relationalen Datenbankmaschine mit PEARL, in: K. Regensberg (Hrsg.): Proc. PEARL-Tagung, Düsseldorf, 1984

/Krey 88/ Kreyßig, J.: Hardware zur Unterstützung einer Transaktionsorientierten Datenverwaltung, Dissertation, TU Braunschweig, 1988

/LeHe 88/ Lee, K.C.; Herman, G.: A High Performance VLSI Data Filter, in: /KiTa 88/

/Lie 87/ Lie, J.S.: Analytische Bewertung relationaler Datenbankmaschinen, Dissertation, TU Braunschweig, 1987

/LiSt 88/ Lie, J.S.; Stiege, G.: Analytic Performance Evaluation of Relational Database Machines, in: /KiTa 88/

/LSZe 78/ Leilich, H.-O.; Stiege, G.; Zeidler, H.Ch.: A Search Processor for Data Base Management Systems, Proc. VLDB, Berlin, 1978

/MAZe 85/ Mertinatsch, P.; Adi, W.; Zeidler, H.Ch.: Ein Hardware Monitor zur Messung der Busbelastungen in einer Multiprozessoranordnung, Informatik-Fachbericht 110, Springer, Berlin 1985

/Mert 88/ Mertinatsch, P.: Messungen der Leistungsfähigkeit des Multiprozessorsystems einer Datenbankmaschine, Dissertation, TU Braunschweig, 1988

/Naka 88/ Nakamura, S. et al.: A High Speed Database Machine - HDM, in: /KiTa 88/

/NaKi 88/ Nakano, R.; Kiyama, M.: MACH: Much Faster Associative Machine, in: /KiTa 88/

/Ocke 85/ Ockenga, H.: Modellierung des Softwaresystems der Relationalen Datenbankmaschine (RDBM), Diplomarbeit, Institut für Betriebssysteme und Rechnerverbund, TU Braunschweig, 1985

/RDBM 88/ RDBM: Die Bewertung der Braunschweiger Relationalen Datenbankmaschine RDBM, Informatik-Bericht 88-09, TU Braunschweig, 1988

/Sche 85/ Scheller, T.: Messungen am Simulationssystem zur Leistungsmessung und -bewertung des RDBM-Multiprozessorsystems, Studienarbeit, Institut für Betriebssysteme und Rechnerverbund, TU Braunschweig, 1985

/SJJo 84/ Staunstrup, J.; Jespersen, J.O.; Johansen, O.V.: Physical Datarepresentation in a Multiprocessor Database Machine, Computer Science Department, Aarhus 1984

/SZHL 83/ Schweppe, H.; Zeidler, H.Ch.; Hell, W.; Leilich, H.-O.; Stiege, G.; Teich, W.: RDBM - A Dedicated Multiprocessor System for Database Management, in: Database Machine Architecture (ed. D. Hsiao), Prentice Hall Inc. 1983

/TeZe 83/ Teich, W.; Zeidler, H.Ch.: Data Handling and Dedicated Hardware for the Sort Problem, in: H.-O. Leilich, M. Missikoff (Hrsg.): Database Machines, Third Int. Workshop, Springer Berlin, 1983, (Proc. IWDM-83)

/ZeAu 85/ Zeidler, H.Ch.; Auer, H.: On the Development of Dedicated Hardware for Searching, in: D.J. DeWitt, H. Boral (eds.): Database Machines, Fourth Int. Workshop, Springer New York, 1985

The Development of the CROSS8 and HC16-186 Parallel (Database) Computers

Kjell Bratbergsengen and Torgrim Gjelsvik
Division of Computer Systems and Telematics
The Norwegian Institute of Technology, N-7034 Trondheim

Abstract

The development of the database computer HC16-186 is a follow up on the CROSS8 database computer. HC16-186 has a hypercube communication topology where dual port RAM modules play an important role. They are used in communication between nodes and for communication between nodes and the host computer. Each node is complete with a disk for storing database relations. Each node is programmed as if it was an independant machine. However, everything is controlled from the host computer which has a special program for controlling parallel systems.

CROSS8 and HC16-186 are used for testing methods and algorithms used in database systems on tightly coupled multicomputer systems. It has not been the goal to develop a complete new product. The first area of research was methods for doing parallel relational algebra operations. The first results from these experiments was reported in [BRAT87]. This paper is a follow up. The first experiments were run on CROSS8, the same programs have been ported to HC16 and the new results are presented here. A description of the HC16 architecture is also included. A load model is used for finding bottlenecks and for being able to develop balanced systems in the future.

Introduction

Our work on database computers dates back to 1974, when we proposed to build a database computer for the company Kongsberg Vaapenfabrik. We had by then finished the development of RA2, a database system which ran on PDP-11 computers. There were several motives for the ideas of isolating the database management system in a separate computer: The address space of the micros of those days was tiny, 32 KB - so separation of functions gave more room for the application programs. Processing capacity and speed was another reason. Better speed could also be achieved because the operating system could be dedicated. And last, but not least, the functions of a database system were well defined, giving a clear interface between application programs and the DBMS. However, the idea did not catch on then, mostly because of lack of development funding.

The ideas of a database computer was revitalized and further developed during the years from 1977 to 1980 in the ASTRA project [BRAT80, SCHM83]. The ideas of ASTRA were many and one was to execute relational algebra operations in parallel on a system of connected

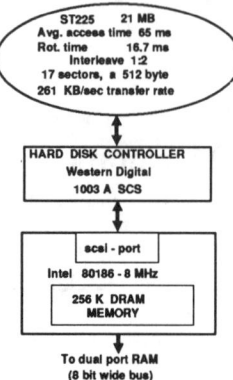

Fig. 1
The node computer of CROSS8

computers. Another idea was that memory was going to be so inexpensive that the entire database was to be held in memory. The cost of memory did follow the predictions, but the price of magnetic disks also fell, and the appetite of storing data grew.

The methods for doing relational algebra were relatively well understood already at that time. Hashing and the need for redistribution of data was part of the method. The main problem with the new hardware was to find a system with no absolute limit on data redistribution capacity. We searched through several connection topologies [Brat80] and ended up at multidimensional connected rings. One type of this structure, the ring with only two nodes in it, is the hypercube. No computer was built in this period, although several architectures were discussed. The main obstacle was the interconnection network.

Although the ASTRA project was abandoned in 1980 the work on relational algebra and interconnection networks continued at The Department of Computer Science. In 1983 the new methods for doing relational algebra was put to work in TECHRA [TECH84], the DBMS developed by KVATRO A/S in Trondheim. The performance of TECHRA was quite up to expectations, and TECHRA is probably still the most efficient relational database system on the market running on one processor.

Just after TECHRA was designed we saw a chance for testing the parallel version of our algorithms. In October 1984 we got aware of some new memory chips which could be used from two separate buses, dual port RAM. The first parallel computer was three PCs connected together in a triangle. Data was exchanged between PCs via 3 1K dual port RAMs. This first experiment was done as a student project work, and the results were encouraging [SOLB85]. We applied to NTNF, the government research agency - for research money in 1985, and we got enough to start work the fall of 1985. It took 18 months to complete the first parallel computer. CROSS 8 was running the so called DeWitt (see later in this paper and also [Bitt83]) test for the first time on March, Friday 13th 1987. It had also been heard some warning voices. In [DeWi83a] it was said that more nodes than 4 would only give negative contributions to the systems processing power.

CROSS8

CROSS8 consists of 9 computers, 8 slaves or nodes and one master or host computer. The master is an IBM-compatible PC/ XT. The master is directly connected via dual port RAM to all nodes. Every node on CROSS8 is also directly connected to all other nodes, the system

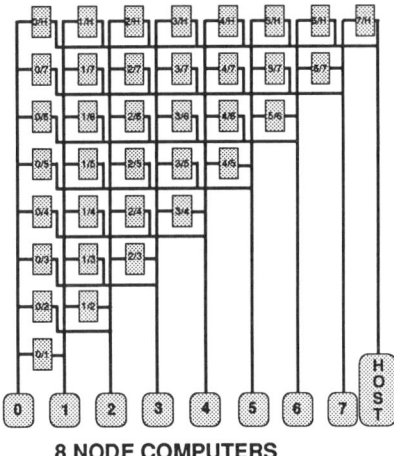

Fig. 2
The CROSS8 interconnection scheme. Each dual port RAM module has 1 K bytes.

8 NODE COMPUTERS

is completely cross connected, hence the name. Each node in CROSS8 is a complete single board computer with a Winchester disk attached. The processor is Intel 80186 running at 8 MHz, giving a computing capacity of about one MIPS and a bus capacity of 4 MB/second. The main memory is 256 KB dynamic RAM with no wait states. The disks are Seagate ST225 PC disks with 21 MB storage capacity and 65 ms average access time.

Each dual port RAM chip has 1 KB of memory. The bus width to the dual port memory system is 8 bits, only half the system bus width. The cross connected network requires 36 memory modules, and the smallest possible memory module is one dual port RAM chip. At that time each chip cost more than 600 Kr (approximately 100 US$), a fairly good reason for having only 8 bit words in the dual port memory. Todays price is about one tenth pr. KiloByte!

Dual port RAMs are a very flexible communication medium. In the same program the DPR (Dual Port RAM) may be used in several different ways. One basic communication mode between processes (processors) are the Send/Receive primitives. They also imply process synchronization. One DPR can contain many software FIFOs at the same time. One pair of FIFOs constitute a communication channel between two processes. Two cells of the DPRs are special. When the processor on one side writes into this cell, the processor on the other side receives an interrupt. The interrupt is removed when the interrupted processor reads the same cell. The other cell works similarly in the other direction. These two cells are used for calling functions on the other processor. The cell is written with a function code, and the function code is used to index a vector of function entries.

We have also used the DPR as normal main memory for regular variables which have been shared by the two nodes. A program for parallel computing of heat transfer has been written to demonstrate this feature [TORB88c].

To move data from one node to another, three or four bus accesses are required: The sender reads data in main memory and writes it in the DPR. The receiver reads the DPR. If the data do not have to be saved by the receiver, the transmission is completed. If they must be saved; they also have to be written into receivers main memory. One bus cycle on CROSS8 takes 500 ns, hence the transfer of one byte from one node to another takes 2000 ns. The combined relocation capacity of all nodes in CROSS8 is 4 MB/s. The relocation time constitutes a major part of relational algebra operation time. The DeWitt test implies relocation of nearly all operand records which is 2 MB. CROSS8 is able to relocate these data in minimum 0.5 seconds.

The usage of dual port RAM for communication has several advantages. The flexibility of usage is already mentioned. DPRs are RAM and will follow the general development of RAM in capacity, speed and price. The speed of communication will also follow the processor speed as long as the DPR is fast enough. State of the art is 16 KB chips with access times as low as 30 ns. This is fast enough for todays fastest micro processors.

Programming

The CROSS8 has the same processor as IBM compatible PCs. Programs are completely developed at the PCs with the ordinary PC development tools. In this way we avoid the heavy burden of developing all software from the ground and up. Even linking is done on the PC. Absolute modules (EXE - modules) are then loaded by a special loader from the host to each node. This can be done in broadcast mode, then all nodes are loaded with the same program simultaneously, or each node can be loaded separately. The "operating" system on each node is a small monitor. System calls to MSDOS BIOS is not supported, this is the only restriction using high level languages like Pascal, FORTRAN or C. Features which result in BIOS system calls, like read, write and file I/O must be avoided. Instead we have developed a similar set of subroutines which can be used [TORB88b].

We have a policy decision of using C as our main programming language. It is developed a suite of C routines which substitutes for the ordinary C routines regarding file I/O and basic input/output. We have also developed routines for communication between nodes, presentation of graphics, and parallel process control. The monitor contains a debugger which is used for low level debugging. Our experience is that it is not difficult to develop programs and get them running, but testing can be more tricky. The most used tool for program debugging is write statements. The program behavior can be followed via executed write statements. It is not wise to stop one program, since the programs in the other nodes would go on. Having write statements in the code may have consequences. The programs are interacting in real time and write statements slows down the execution. It has happened several times that programs have executed correct *with* write statements, but when they are *removed* "unexplainable" errors have occurred.

CROSS8 has been used for relational algebra, sorting, matrix multiplication and image processing and storage.

The Second Prototype

Having finished the tests on CROSS8 we had to decide what to do next. We knew that using a fully cross connected network was not viable for a large number of nodes. We originally wanted a hypercube network, but there was very little to save on only 8 nodes, and considering the added complexity in the software, a fully connected network was chosen. However, we wanted to test the scalability of our methods, and through the development of CROSS8 we got plenty of ideas on how to improve a new computer. Each node on CROSS8 had a small main memory, only 1/4 MB. Main memory is one of the most valuable resources for reducing operation time for sorting and relational algebra. Having experienced the very encouraging results from the experiments on CROSS8, we were anxious to build a prototype closer to a production database computer. It was important to be quite sure that the hypercubic interconnection network served its purpose, because the hypercube network had to be used for a large number of nodes.

HC16-186

The work on HC16-186 was started in the spring of 1987. Each node is connected to 5 modules of shared or dual ported RAM, 4 neighbors and the host, see fig. 4. We could make one large Printed Circuit Board with all the interconnection lines, but that would cost a lot of money. The other approach was to to use lot of flat cables and connectors. This design could alsogive a very compact construction. Short signal lines are important for reducing noise, but a PCB

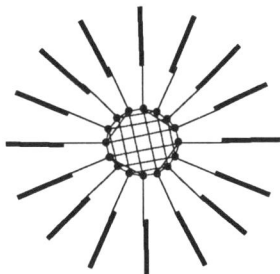

Fig. 3
Top view of the HC16. The center contains the hypercubic interconnection network, then comes the dual port RAM modules, and the outer ring holds the node computers. The complete computer is placed on top of the PC/AT host computer, which again stands on top of the 16 element disk battery.

gives better quality lines than cable and connectors. The cable/connector approach was chosen. HC16 is built as a three layered cylinder. The center holds the hypercubic interconnection system realized with flat cables. Diameter is 10 cm. Then comes the the cards holding shared RAM. This layer is 9 cm. The outer layer is the node processors themselves. They are also about 9 cm wide. All cards are mounted vertically and there is no fans for ventilation. The total height of the cylinder is about 40 cm.

We chose to use the same processor on HC16 as on CROSS8 because the software could be transferred with a minimum of problems. Other reasons were price, complexity and

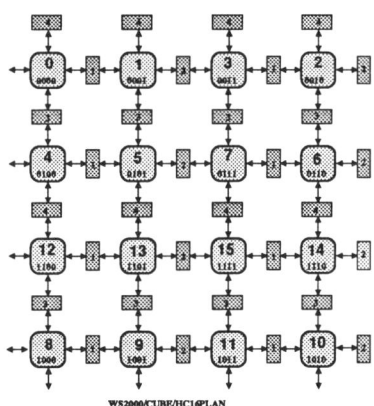

Fig. 4
The topology of the HC16 hypercube interconnection network. The node computers are symbolized with rounded squares, and the dual port RAMs with rectangles. Each dual port RAM module contains 2 KB. The dimension number is written into all DPRs. All nodes are in addition connected to the host. This is not shown on the figure.

availability. CROSS8 had only 1/4 MB of RAM, this was quadrupled on HC16. At this time, disks with integrated SCSI controller were readily available. This would save the disk controller card for each node. The clock frequency was increased by 25% to 10 MHz. Each module of shared RAM is 2 KB, but the main difference is that there is full bus size - 16 bits to the shared RAM modules. This gives a maximum transfer rate of 2.5 MB/second between any two neighbors in the network and a combined transfer rate of 20 MB/second for all nodes when they exchange data with neighbor nodes. The combined general relocation capacity is 13.33 MB/second because some transfer capacity is used for transit records, i.e. records which must pass one or more nodes to reach their destination node.

Each disk stores 65 MB, giving a total storage capacity in the cube of 1040 MB. The transfer rate is 7.5 Mbit/second, the theoretical transfer rate is 798 KB/sec. There are 26 sectors of 512 bytes on each track. A cylinder has 6 tracks and track to track positioning time is 8 ms. The average access time is 40 ms. The disks are relatively slow, but again price was important. Similar disks are available with average access time of 16 ms and 2 times higher transfer rate. The disks are formatted with interleave 1:1. Effective disk transfer rate and positioning time is very important in database systems. Lost rotations will degrade effective transfer rate significantly. With interleave 1:1 one rotation is lost between commands for sequential reads. This favors using large blocks. Our database tests have been run with block size 31 sectors. Sequential read gives 1 lost rotation for each block read. There are 5 blocks on one cylinder with 6 tracks. Even when the next block is on the next cylinder only one rotation is lost. The effective transfer rate is then:

$$(31*512*5)/((6+5)*0.01667) = 432786 \text{ bytes/second},$$

or slightly more than half the nominal transfer rate. Rotations may be lost due to positioning over several tracks, and for random read, rotational delay must also be counted for.
All features of HC16-186 are controlled from the host. Even starting and stopping disks is done under program control. The disks are started with 0.5 seconds interval to reduce the peak load of the power supply. During start up, the disks draw 3 to 4 times more power than during normal operation. Each node can get a hardware reset from the host. On CROSS8 these functions required an operator to push buttons. The HC16 is prepared to be operated from remote workstations connected to the local Ethernet.

Relational Algebra

In a relational database systems the user specified operations are almost universally translated into a sequence of relational algebra operations. CROSS8 and HC16 are relational algebra engines. The fundamental operation in any algebra operations except selection is to find matching records.
- **selection**, find records with certain values in certain fields, this is not a matchmaking operation, and is not considered further in this paper.
- **projection**, delete given fields of all records in the table. Duplicate records may result and duplicates must be deleted.
- **union**, two tables are put together and duplicates which may result, must be deleted.
- **difference**, delete records in first operand which also is found in the second operand.
- **intersection**, retain one copy of records which is found in both operands.
- **join**, construct result records from records in both operands which have the same value in some given field(s).

- **aggregate**, records with the same value(s) in given fields are grouped together.

Selection, projection and aggregation are "one operand operations", the others have two input relations. The basic method of finding equal records is based on hashing. A hash formula is applied to the operation key. If two records really have equal keys they would hash to the same value.

Records in one relation is spread out on all nodes. A hash formula on the primary key gives the node number. When one single record is updated and the primary key is known, only the correct node is activated. This is exploited every time a new record is inserted when checking for duplicates.

When a relation is searched, all nodes are reading their share of the relation. Selection is easily distributed. Finding equal records is based on repeatedly use of hashing. This method is described in [BRAT84], [DeWi85], and several later papers. Only records having the same hash value are candidate pairs. This fact is used in CROSS8 and HC16. The first hash application is for relocating records between nodes. Records which potentially have the same key are gathered in the same node. After this redistribution of records the completion of the operation is done locally. And again the hashing technique can be used for reducing search length. Records are put into a number of linked lists, which list is again determined by the hash value. In this way the search length can be brought down close to one.

The algorithm for doing relational algebra operations in parallel is:
- Read records from disk.
- Relocate operands according to a hash value computed from the operation key.
- Complete algebra operation locally on each node.
- Write result records to disk.

After the result records are formed locally they are also stored at the same node. If the result records are to be included in a permanent table they may have to be redistributed according to their primary key. This is not counted for in our tests.

Limits on Performance.

There are obviously three possible bottlenecks in the system: the disk transfer, the relocation, and the local system bus. The local system bus is used in all steps: disk transfer, relocation and record handling locally (CPU). To determine the lower limit of the time consumption for the different algebra operations we will compute the bottleneck values based on an operand volume of one megabyte.

Disk transfer.

The effective disk transfer rate is earlier found to be 432786 bytes/second on each disk. Transferring 1 MB in parallel takes:

$$1000000/(432786*16)= \mathbf{0.144 \text{ seconds or } 144 \text{ ms}}.$$

62500 bytes on each node also has to be transferred over the system bus, and will add to bus load.

Relocation

The hypercube network is not fully connected and records must do several hops to reach their destination node. When all records are moved randomly from one node to another the average number of dimension crossed is $D/2$, where D is the dimension of the cube. To cross $D/2$ dimensions $D/2+1$ moves are necessary, see fig. 5. Each move require one read and one write

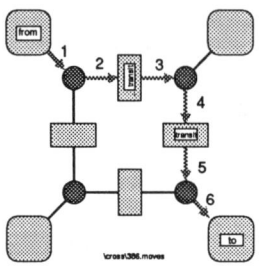

Fig. 5
The path of data between nodes. The local bus is used for moving records in transit to other nodes. The relative amount of work for moving data will increase with increasing number of nodes, however - not very fast. . The number of hops is $D/2+1$, and the number of nodes in the network is $N = 2^D$

of each word. Relocation of one megabyte takes:

$$1000000*(D/2+1)*2*t/2^D = \underline{1000000*(D/2+1)*t/2^{D-1}}$$

t is the time for writing or reading one byte in dual port RAM or main memory. For HC16 t is 200 ns (when writing word by word), and D is 4.

$$T_{relocate} = 1000000*(4/2+1)*0.0002/2^{(4-1)} = \underline{75 \text{ ms/MB}}.$$

We have taken into account that data are moved word by word. Reading or writing one word takes 400 ns on HC16.

Bus load
The bus is loaded by disk transfer, relocation and local record handling. Disk transfer is controlled by the DMA channel, and because the SCSI port is only 8 bits wide, the bus transfer is done byte by byte. Transfer of 1 MB takes:

$$1000000*s*2/2^D = 1000000*0.0004*2/2^4 = \underline{\mathbf{50 \text{ ms/MB.}}}$$

s is bus cycle time which is 400 ns.

The bus load from relocation has already been found to be 75 ms.

The last factor is harder to determine, the local record handling. There is also a record handling involved in relocation which is not counted for so far. The main contribution to record handling is believed to stem from computing hash values (2 or 3 times for each record), storing records in work space or comparing records with records in work space. This time is estimated on a per record basis:

Relocation (D/2+1)*100	= 300 µs
Hash computation 2*100	= 200 "
Work storage operations	= 300 "
Record handling	800 µs.

Relocation in this context is overhead for each record, not the actual time for transferring each record, which is already counted for. The share from record handling depends on the number of records. Let L be record length and we get:

$$T_{handling} = 1000000*0.8/(L*16).$$

When L is 182 bytes we get $T_{handling}$ = **275 ms/MB**.

Adding all contributions together we get for bus load:

Disk transfer	75 ms/MB
Relocation	50 "
Record handling	275 " (L = 182)
Total	400 ms/MB

This calculation is not counting the effect of writing result records back to the disk. For this record size the effect on total result is small, only 7.5 ms has to be added. The more correct estimate for execution time would then be **407.5 ms/MB of input operand volume.**

The actual disk transfer can run in parallel with CPU operations. From these calculations it is clearly seen that CPU or bus capacity is the bottleneck. Next comes disk transfer which takes 140 ms. A different CPU could change this picture entirely. An Intel 80386 with 20 MHz clock would in general be about 4 times faster then the Intel 80186 on HC16-186. Bus capacity is 8 times larger and that will reduce the load from disk transfer and relocation with a factor 8. So with Intel 80386 in the nodes, disks are again the limiting factor at least for medium sized records and a similar disk.

The DeWitt Test.

The DeWitt test or the Wisconsin benchmark is a number of performance tests developed by professor David DeWitt [BITT83]. The test is run against an artificial database which is well described an easy to reconstruct. This database and the tests run against it has been used by several researchers and companies to assess the performance characteristics of different database systems. The tests are run on an empty computer, i.e. no other programs are competing for resources. We have chosen to use the join test because it is generally the most representative test. DeWitts original join test was on two tables, A with 1000 records and B with 10000 records. Records were 182 bytes long. All records in A had one matching record in B, hence the result table also contained 1000 records. Both tables were unordered.

Table 1 contains results from several performance tests on different systems. For CROSS8 and HC16-186 there is no parsing or query optimization involved as it is the direct execution of relational algebra routines which is tested. The same is at least true for HDM as they have quoted both times, with and without query processing overhead. As explained in [DeWi88] the Teradata machine has a special handicap in this comparison. The result records are inserted

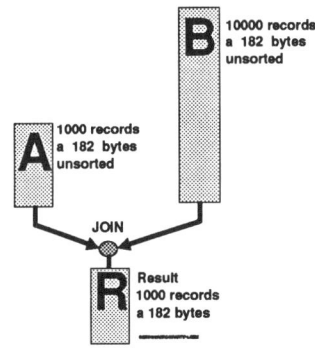

Fig. 6
The Wisconsin join benchmark. This benchmark executes in 1.8 seconds on CROSS8 and 0.8 seconds on HC16-186.

HC16-186	16 disks,	16 Intel 80186	(10 MHz, 1 MB)	0.8 seconds
CROSS8	8 disks,	8 Intel 80186	(8 MHz, 0.25 MB)	1.8 seconds
HDM	5 disks,	5 Motorola 68020	(16 MHz, 4 MB)	4.4 seconds
GAMMA	8 disks,	17 VAX 11/750		6.5 seconds
TechRa	1 disk,	1 ND 500		17.0 seconds
TechRa	monoprocessor system		VAX 11/750	32.0 seconds
Teradata DBC/1012	40 disks,	20 Intel 80286		34.9 seconds
Oracle	monoprocessor system		VAX 11/750	87.0 seconds
Ingres	monoprocessor system		VAX 11/750	156.0 seconds

Table 1 Reported results on the DeWitt join test. The numbers for Oracle and Ingres are reported in [BITT83], Data on Gamma from [DEWI88], data on Teradata from [DEWI87] and data on HDM from [NAKA87].

into an (in principle) existing relation, and Teradatas DBC/1012 consequently logs all updates to the result table. This explains to some degree the Teradata results. No logging is performed on the other computers as the result tables are regarded as new.

We have also run the join with larger operand volumes. In fig. 7 and 8 these results are summarized and compared to some recent results reported in [DeWi88]. HC16-186 is almost 10 times faster than Gamma, which has the best results of the other two contenders. For Gamma and Teradata we have results for three different sizes: 10000, 100000 and one million tuples. The operand volumes are accordingly: 2 MB, 20 MB and 200 MB. HC16-186 has a break on its curve at about 100 MB. The reason for this is working storage overflow. The

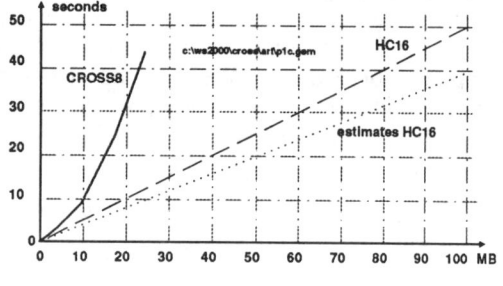

Fig. 7
Join of large operand volumes. B is 1o times larger than A. Solid line on CROSS8, dashed line on HC16-186 and dotted line is estimates on HC16-186. Data on Gamma from [DEWI88].

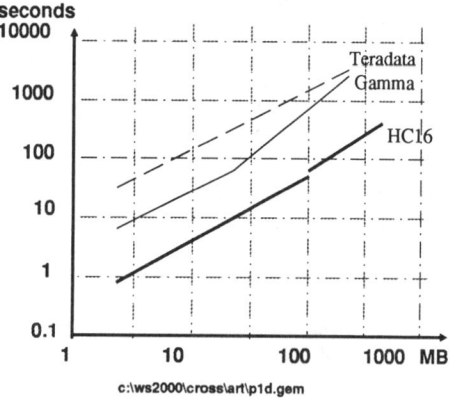

Fig. 8
Join of very large data volumes. Solid thick line is HC16-186, dashed line is Teradata and thin solid line is Gamma. Data on Teradata and Gamma are taken from [DEWI88]. Join of **400 MB** takes 460 seconds on HC16-186. Join of **200 MB** takes 2938 seconds on Gamma and 3419 seconds on Teradata

A-operand is so large that it does not fit into workspace. The consquences are that both operands must be stored on disk locally. This means an extra pass of the operands. However filters are used to get rid of tuples which are clearly not candidates for a matching couple, see [BRAT84].

The conclusions from these tests are that relational algebra can be executed on parallel computers with impressive performance improvements. The methods used, scale well and at least operations with large amounts of data will benefit from more parallelism.

Ongoing Research.

Several projects are in process. Jarle Greipsland and Bjørn Arild Baugstø worked on sorting large volumes of data during spring 1988 using CROSS8. They managed to sort 70 MB in about 20 minutes They have continued this work and transferred the programs to HC16. They are now sorting 100MB in slightly less than 3 minutes. The record length is 100 bytes , i.e. one million records. Again the system has shown to be deeply CPU bound. The initial sort phase, pulling records in sorted order out of a "tree of losers" takes almost 90 seconds of the total 175. Sorting the same amount of data, but half the number of records, 200 bytes long - takes approximately 40 seconds less. A paper describing this project is presented at this conference [BAUG89].

Fault tolerance and recovery after failures is a very important subject on parallel computers. The resources to continue after failures are available, principally - only when the last node fails, the system must stop. The problem is to prepare for failures in such a way that one has the information necessary for continued execution available. Øystein Torbjørnsen has worked on the communication problem when nodes are failing [TORB88d].

Kjetil Gudmundsen has worked on methods for database recovery when nodes storing parts of the database is failing. He has described and analyzed several distribution strategies for duplicate records of the database. Records have to be found in at least two nodes. All records on a failed node are unavailable. After a failure, records on the failed node are available only in one copy. The time until these are reduplicated is a vulnerable window, and the database can not handle another failure in this period [GUDM88].

We are at this time setting up an experiment to measure the transaction processing capacity of HC16-186. We will run the so called bank transaction test. Each transaction will update three registers and necessary files for logging and recovery [NYMO88].

Acknowledgments.

The HC16-186 was built with assistense from Jan Grønsberg. Øystein Torbjørnsen has written the major part of the C Library and other test programs in C, and not least; he has in all ways guided users of the system.

We are very gratefull to all users of the system, project-, diploma- and Dr.Ing.-students, they have taken the risk of being dependant on our equipment, one of a kind and not always perfect.

The project has been supported by NTNF, The Norwegian Research Council since 1985, and would not have been possible without it. The project has also had support from Norsk Data A/S in 1988.

References, Related Papers and Project Reports

/BAUG89/ Bjørn Arild W. Baugstø and Jarle Greipsland: "Parallel Sorting Methods for Large Data Volumes on a Hypercube Database Computer", The Sixth International Workshop on Database Computers, France, June 1989.

/BITT83/ D.Bitton, D. DeWitt and Turbyfill "Benchmarking Database Systems. A Systematic Approach", The 9th International Conference on Very Large Data Bases, Florence Oct. 1983.

/BRAT80/ Kjell Bratbergsengen, Rune Larsen, Oddvar Risnes and Terje Aandalen "A Neighbor Connected Processor Network for Performing Relational algebra Operations" Paper presented at 5th Workshop on Computer Architecture for Non-Numeric Processing, March 11-14, 1980 Pacific Grove, Ca.

/BRAT81/ Kjell Bratbergsengen "Design of a VLSI-Chip for Moving Data in a Hypercube Network", Report, Department of Computer Science, The Norwegian Institute of Technology, June 20, 1981.

/BRAT83/ Kjell Bratbergsengen "The Hypercube as a Line Switching Network", Report, Department of Computer Science, The Norwegian Institute of Technology, March 1983.

/BRAT83/ Kjell Bratbergsengen "Data Base Management Systems for Engineering Applications. Requirements Specification", Kongsberg Vaapenfabrikk, avd. Trondheim, July 1983.

/BRAT84/ Kjell Bratbergsengen "Hashing Methods and Relational Algbra Operations", The 10th Conference on Very Large Data Bases, Singapore Aug. 1984.

/BRAT86b/ Kjell Bratbergsengen "Use of DMA and the SASI Port on SBC SLICER", Working Paper No. 6, 8 pp, Department of Computer Science, The Norwegian Institute of Technology, August 10, 1986.

/BRAT86c/ Kjell Bratbergsengen "Hyperkuben -, det perfekte kommunikasjonsnett for flermaskinsystemer" Rapport nr.7, Department of Computer Science, The Norwegian Institute of Technology, August 1986, 14 pp (in Norwegian).

/BRAT87a/ Kjell Bratbergsengen "Design of the Hypercube Interconnection Network and the SBC186 Single Board Computer", Working Paper No. 10, Revision 2, Department of Computer Science, The Norwegian Institute of Technology, March 12 1987. 32 pp.

/BRAT87b/ Kjell Bratbergsengen "Relational Algebra Operations. A Systematic Realization and System Documentation", Working paper no. 11, revision 4, Department of Computer Science, The Norwegian Institute of Technology, May 1987. 53 pp.

/BRAT87d/ Kjell Bratbergsengen "Parallel Matrix Multiplication on the CROSS8 and $HC2^D$ Database Computers" Working Paper No. 13, Department of Computer Science, The Norwegian Institute of Technology, March 1987. 7 pp.

/BRAT87e/ Kjell Bratbergsengen "Algebra Operations on a Parallel Computer - Performance Evaluation" Dept. of Computer Science Report No. 14, May 1987. The 5th International Workshop on Database Machines, Oct 5-8 1987 Karuizawa Japan. 8 pp.

/BRAT87i/ Kjell Bratbergsengen "Algebra Operations on a Parallel Database Computer - Performance Evaluation" The 3rd Workshop on Hypercube Machines, Jet Propulsion Laboratory, January 19-20, 1988. Poster session.

/BRAT88a/ Kjell Bratbergsengen "Performance Analysis of the Hypercube Line Switch", Department of Computer Science, for the Conference Proceedings "The 3rd Workshop on Hypercube Machines", Jet Propulsion Laboratory, January 19-20, 1988.

/DeWi83/ David DeWitt: "Database Computers, an Idea Whose Time Has Passed", The Second International Workshop on Database Machines, 1983.

/DEWI85/ David DeWitt and Robert Gerber "Multiprocessor Hash-Based Join Algorithms", The 11th Conference on Very Large Data Bases, Stockholm Aug. 1985.

/DEWI88/ David DeWitt, Shahram Ghandeharizadeh and Donovan Schneider :"A Performance Analysis of the Gamma Database Machine", SIGMOD Proceedings, Vol. 17, No. 3 Sept. 1988.

/GJEL88a/ Torgrim Gjelsvik: "Bruksanvisning for HC16 parallell databasemaskin", Hyperkubegruppen, Rapport nr. 39, IDT July 1988 (in Norwegian).

/GJEL88b/ Torgrim Gjelsvik: "HC16 teknisk dokumentasjon", Rapport IDT July 1988 (In Norwegian).

/GJEL86/ Torgrim Gjelsvik "DeWitt Test", Arbeidsnotat nr 8, Dec. 1986, Institutt for databehandling (in Norwegian).

/GOOD81/ J.R. Goodman "An Investigation of Multiprocessor Structures and Algorithms for Database Management", Technical Report UCB/ERL M81/33 Electronic Research Lab., College of Engineering, UCB, May 1981.

/GUDM88/ Kjetil Gudmundsen: "A Non-Stopping Database Management System", Division of Computing Systems and Telematics, The Norwegian Institute of Technology, Oct. 1988, paper prepared for The 6th International Workshop on Database Machines.

/KITS83/ M. Kitsuregawa, H. Tanaka and T. Moto-oka " Application of Hash to Data Base Machine and Its Architecture" New Generation Computing, Vol. 1, No. 1, 1983.

/JOHA86a/ Tor Eivind Johansen og Kjell Bratbergsengen "CROSS 8 Hardware Documentation", Report No. 1, April 1986, 24 pp.

/JOHA86b/ Tor Eivind Johansen "Testing of the CROSS8 Board" Report No. 2, IDB, April 1986, 12 pp.

/NAKA87/ Shun-ichiro Nakamura, Harumi Minemura, Tatsuo Minohara, Kuniji Itakura, Masakazu Soga : "A High Speed Database Machine HDM", The 5th Workshop on Database Machines, Karuizawa Oct. 1987, Proceedings: "Database Machines and Knowledge Base Machines", edited by Masaru Kitsuregawa and Hidehiko Tanaka, Kluwer Academic Publishers 1988.

/NYMO88/ Knut Nymoen: "Concurrecy Control in a Parallel Database System", Division of Computing Systems and Telematics, The Norwegian Institute of Technology, Oct. 1988.

/MENO86/ Jai Menon: "Sorting and Join Algorithms for Multiprocessor Database Machines" Database Machines, Modern Trends and Applications, Springer-Verlag 1986.

/QADA85/ G. Z. Qadah "The Equi-join Operation on a Multiprocessor Database Machine: Algorithms and the Evaluation of Their Performance" Fourth International Workshop on Database Machines, Grand Bahama Islands 1985, Conference Proceedings, Springer Verlag New York 1985.

/SCHM83/ Joachim W. Schmidt and Michael Brodie, Eds. : "Realational Database Systems. Analysis and Comparison.", Springer Verlag, 1983.

/SOLB85/ Svein-Arne Solbakk og Tor Eivind Johansen "DELTA databasemaskin for relasjonsdatabaser", Prosjektarbeider i databehandling ved IDB, NTH, May 1985 (in Norwegian).

/SOLB86a/ Svein Arne Solbakk "Software for the CROSS8 Database Computer", Parallel Database Computer, Report No. 4, NTNF ED 0221.18614, Teknisk notat 38/86 IDB, June 1986, 81 pp.

/SOLB86b/ Svein Arne Solbakk "The CROSS8 Programming Environment",Parallel Database Computer, Report No. 3, Teknisk notat 37/86 IDB, June 1986, 77 pp.

/SOOD86/ A.K.Sood, M. Abdelguerfi and W. Shu "Hardware Implementation of Relational Algebra Operations". Database Machines, Modern Trends and Applications, Springer-Verlag 1986.

/STON76/ Stonebraker M. et al. "The Design and Implementation of INGRES", TODS 2, Sept. 1976.

/TECH84/ TECHRA User Manual. Kongsberg Vaapenfabrikk avd. Trondheim, 1984.

/TORB88a/ Øystein Torbjørnsen "Turbo-C for the CROSS8 Computer", Division of Computing Systems and Telematics, The Norwegian Institute of Technology, January 1988.

/TORB88b/ Øystein Torbjørnsen: "Turbo-C for the HC-16 Computer", Working Paper no. 43, Division of Computing Systems and Telematics, The Norwegian Institute of Technology, August 1988.

/TORB88c/ Øystein Torbjørnsen: "Heat Transfer. An Example Program Demonstrating the Finite Element Method on HC-16", Working Paper no. 44, Division of Computing Systems and Telematics, The Norwegian Institute of Technology, August 1988.

/TORB88d/ Øystein Torbjørnsen "Communication in a Failsoft Hypercube Database Machine", Division of Computing Systems and Telematics, The Norwegian Institute of Technology, Oct. 1988, presented at NIK - Norsk Informatikk Konferanse, Sundvolden Nov. 1988.

/VALD84/ P.Valduriez and G.Gardarin "Join and Semi-Join Algorithms for a Multiprocessor Database Machine", ACM Transactions on Database Systems 9, No 1, March 1984

Analysis of Some Experimental Results for the TDM

Liming Meng

Dept. of Computing Science
University of Alberta
Edmonton
Canada T6G 2H1
E-Mail: meng@alberta.UUCP

ABSTRACT

So far, most results reported for multiprocessor database machines (DBMs) have been simulation results, and very few results are from a real database machine implementation. In this paper, we present some experimental results obtained from our real prototype: TDM (Tree-structured Database Machine). Analysis based on these results is given in detail. For three types of basic database operations: selection, sort, and join, we have obtained 9.96, 7.62, and 7.63 fold speed-ups respectively as the number of SPs (Slave Processors) increases from one to three. Analysis of an I/O throughput and a load balancing property is also presented. From these analysis, we believe that our TDM system is able to support a large database application with a better performance improvement.

1. Introduction

Many database machine researchers around the world have been working on exploring alternative ways to design and implement a database machine with a high parallelism to support large database systems. Some efforts focus on the multiprocessor architectures, like MBDS [HeH83], SM3 [BrS86], and GAMMA [DGG86], some others focus on parallel operation algorithms [KTM83] [Bra84] [DeG85], still some efforts focus on the architecture with a special hardware, such as Delta [KMS85] and GRACE [FKT86] or with a special database storage structure, like SABRE [Gaa83], and RDBP [Men84]. However, our TDM implementation focuses on both a parallel multiprocessor architecture and parallel operation algorithms [Men87].

So far, most results reported for multiprocessor database machines are simulation results, very few results come from a real database machine implementation. In this paper, we present some experimental results obtained from our TDM prototype, which has been implemented in May, 1987 in HIT, China [MXC87] [XCM87]. Analysis based on the experimental results indicates that the TDM architecture design is reasonable and is able to achieve significant speed-up in three types of basic database operations: selection, sort, and join, as well as better I/O and load balance properties. A major goal of the TDM design is to overcome both I/O and complex database operation bottlenecks and solve load balance issues in multiprocessor database machines. The experimental results we report here show that the TDM architecture has satisfied our initial design requirements.

In this paper, we first give an overview of the TDM architecture, then present analysis and a discussion of some experimental results obtained from the TDM prototype with respect to throughputs (tuples/second) of I/O operations, time properties of selection, sort, and join database operations as well as properties of load balance, respectively. Finally, we summarize the analysis results obtained.

2. TDM Architecture

2.1. TDM Hardware Architecture

The TDM is a multiprocessor database machine in a tree-structured form, which it consists of several Sub-Tree Element(STEs). The TDM architecture is shown in Figure 1. For overcoming the I/O and complex database operation bottlenecks and solving load balance problems in a multiprocessor database machine system, following factors are considered in the TDM hardware architecture design:

1). A general-purpose microprocessor as processing element;

2). A tree-structured architecture;

3). A distributing tightly-coupled interconnection;

4). A multiple processor-disk-pair I/O structure;

5). A two-level Sub-Tree-Element(STE) as the TDM sub-architecture;

6). A STE as a sub-structure of the TDM architecture.

These features show that the TDM is a MSIMD multiprocessor system and has the ability not only to execute database operations simultaneously and independently within each STE, but also to perform multiple query operations in parallel.

There were several tree-structured database machines proposed recently, such as, HYPER-TREE [GoD80], DBC1012 [Nec84], REPT [ShZ84], and NON-VON [Sha85]. However, there were many differences between the TDM and those tree-structured database machines in respects to the hardware architecture. One is the TDM employs two-level multiple-branch tree-structured architecture but not a binary tree architecture. Another is that the TDM architecture is composed of many STEs so that its architecture is more flexible and extensible than that of the other tree-structured database machine architectures. Still another is that the technique of distributed tightly-coupled interconnection is effective in supporting a large amount of data movement between processors, it is also efficient in reducing the overhead and the conflict of accessing shared-memory.

2.2. STE Structure

The STE is a hardware sub-structure in the TDM architecture, it is a two-level multiprocessor architecture in tree-structured form, as shown in Figure 2. It consists of three basic components as follows:

1). Backend Controller/Processor (BCP), which is responsible for controlling all slave processors in the STE to perform basic database operations and communicating with the Backend Controller (BC). Each BCP runs a sub-management-system resident in the STE and completes its functions, like data processing, local database management, query task execution control, and communication between processors in the STE;

2). Slave Processor (SP), which is responsible for execution of all basic database operations, local memory management, and I/O data accesses;

3). Switchable Working Memory (SWM), which is specially designed for supporting fast and large amounts of data movement in multiprocessor architecture during data processing. Each SWM can be accessed both by the BCP and by a SP in a STE. This is a distributed shared memory structure which can reduce access conflicts and support the architecture extensibility.

The distributing shared memory technique used in each STE, as shown in Figure 3, is suitable for parallel database operations and effective for the architecture extension. Also, this technique can reduce memory access conflicts, shared memory costs, and control overheads. From above discussion, we can find that the TDM architecture provides a highly parallel processing environment and is able to overcome both I/O and complex database operation bottlenecks and solves load balance issues effectively at its hardware architecture level, which will be proved by an analysis of the some experimental results from the TDM prototype in next section.

3. Analysis of Some Experimental Results

The TDM prototype with one STE (three SPs and one BCP) and a HOST has been implemented in May, 1987. Many experimental results have been carried out based on our TDM prototype. Here, only a few experimental results are given: throughputs of I/O data access, time properties of selection, sort, and join database operations, and a property of load balance, because of limited space.

3.1. Analysis of throughput of I/O operations

All relations in our testing database are horizontally partitioned into several data segments and these data segments are uniformly distributed and stored on all disks in a STE in the TDM. So, the execution process of an I/O operation in the TDM is: when all SPs in a STE receive the I/O operation command, they start to access the data segments from disks to memories in parallel, then send to the BCP. As soon as the BCP receives data segments from all SPs, it moves these data segments to the Host computer through its own SWM. Figure 4 shows some I/O experimental results of the TDM prototype. From Figure 4, we determine that:

1). The throughput of I/O operations is able to be improved as the number of parallel I/O channels (processor-disk-pairs in our case) increases. For a large database application, the more the number of parallel I/O channels, the better the throughput of I/O operations (see Table 1);

Table 1. Throughputs of I/O operations from the TDM prototype (TL=100 bytes)

No. of Tuples (bytes)	1000	3000	5000	7000	9000	10000
1 Slave Processor (sec.)	2.4	4.2	9.1	16.8	26.2	40.1
2 Slave Processors (sec.)	2.3	3.2	4.4	5.1	6.8	8.7
3 Slave Processors (sec.)	2.2	2.8	3.4	4.0	4.5	4.8

2). The time of I/O operations is not always linear as the database size increases. When the time property becomes non-linear, we call it "I/O Bottleneck". As an example, consider a query with many I/O data accesses in a case of the 10000 tuples in a disk. To overcome such an I/O bottleneck, we can extend the linear range of an I/O time property by use of parallel I/O channels for parallel data transferring. Based on this idea, we can choose a different number of I/O channels for different database applications so as to make the I/O time property stay in a linear range. Table 2 lists some experimental results about the linear ranges for different number of I/O channels from the observation of the Figure 4 (here TN is the number of tuples and TL is a tuple length);

Table 2. Linear ranges (tuples) for different number of SPs (TL=100 bytes)

SP=1	TN≤2000	SP=2	TN≤7500	SP=3	TN≤10000

3). For a very large database application, the I/O bottleneck is quickly reached although a parallel I/O channel structure was used. This is because, in most cases, a large amount of data irrelevant to a query has to be moved through the parallel channels. To avoid the I/O bottleneck, a data dictionary should be built to minimize the data moved, i.e., to extend the linear ranges of an I/O time property.

3.2. Analysis of simple database operation: Selection

Execution of selection operations is roughly same as that of the I/O operations mentioned previously, i.e., when all SPs in a STE receive operation commands, they first load the data relevant to the query into memory and then do selection operations in parallel. Finally, the BCP collects the results from all SPs and sends them back to the host computer. Time properties of a selection operation with two simple selection conditions are shown in Figure 5. From Figure 5, we see that:

1). As the number of parallel processors increases, the time properties of simple database operations can be improved. Obviously, the larger the database, the more dramatic the improvement of the time property (see Table 3);

Table 3. Time properties of selection (TL=100 bytes)						
No. of Tuples (bytes)	1000	3000	5000	7000	9000	10000
1 Slave Processor (sec.)	3.5	5.1	10.3	19.6	30.4	48.2
2 Slave Processors (sec.)	2.6	3.4	4.8	7.3	8.7	10.6
3 Slave Processors (sec.)	2.21	2.82	3.425	4.03	4.53	4.84

2). The time property of simple database operations is dependent on the I/O time property directly. This means that if a database machine architecture has a better I/O time property, it also has a better time property for simple database operations (see Table 4);

Table 4. I/O vs. selection for three SPs (TL=100 bytes)						
No. of Tuples (bytes)	1000	3000	5000	7000	9000	10000
I/O operation time (sec.)	2.2	2.8	3.4	4.0	4.5	4.8
Select operation time (sec.)	2.21	2.82	3.425	4.03	4.53	4.84

3). Similar to the case of the I/O time property, a linear range of simple operations exists for a fixed database size and fixed number of parallel processors. From Figure 5, we can see that for the different number of parallel processors, there are different linear ranges (i.e. different number of tuples in our case). Experimental results to this issue are listed in Table 5;

Table 5. Linear ranges of selections (TL=100 bytes)					
SP=1	TN≤2000	SP=2	TN≤5500	SP=3	TN≤10000

4). As the database becomes larger and larger, the time property of simple operations will move into a non-linear area. In this case, a data index technique should be used to overcome simple operation bottlenecks. Otherwise, the performance of database machines will become poor for simple database operations due to the irrelevant data movement, although a parallel hardware architecture is used, like DIRECT [DeW79].

3.3. Analysis of sort operation time property

In a complex database operation, multiple scans on tuples in a relation are involved, so the time property of complex database operations becomes non-linear easily in comparison with that of simple database operations. For an initial measure of sorting performance of the TDM prototype, a simple n^2 sorting algorithm was used. Figure 6 shows time properties of sort operations that are carried out from the TDM prototype.

1). It is obvious that the time property of sort operations has been improved as the number of processors increases. Table 6 shows some results for the cases of sort operations on different database sizes. When the number of tuples is 1000, 5000, and 10000, we have obtained about 4.81, 3.64, and 3.6 fold speed-ups as the number of SPs increases from one to two and 7.56, 8.17, and 8.13 fold speed-ups from one to three, respectively. Hence, the multiprocessor architecture is one of key approaches to improve performance of database machines in sort operation;

Table 6. Sorting times for different SPs (TL=100 bytes, including $T_{I/O}$)

No. of Tuples (bytes)	1000	3000	5000	7000	9000	10000
1 Slave Processor (min.)	3.9	28.1	72.1	136.5	221.3	268.2
2 Slave Processors (min.)	0.83	7.2	19.8	39.8	60.8	74.4
3 Slave Processors (min.)	0.51	3.2	8.82	17.5	28.5	35.2

2). Similarly, for a certain number of parallel processors, there is a linear range for a sort operation (see Figure 6). But this linear range is much shorter than that of simple database operations. Table 7 lists our experimental results of linear ranges for a sort operation;

Table 7. Linear ranges of sorting for different SPs (TL=100 bytes)

SP=1	TN≤1500	SP=2	TN≤2500	SP=3	TN≤4000

3). Because the linear range in sort operation is shorter than that in simple operations, the bottleneck problem appears sooner, especially in a large database system with less parallel processors. In this case, a data index should be used for overcoming operation bottleneck, otherwise, performance of database machines in sort operation will become poor although a parallel processor architecture is used. Also, fast sorting algorithms should be developed.

3.4. Analysis of join operation time property

Execution of a join operation in the TDM is based on sort-merge-join algorithm and parallel sort operation, so the time property of join operations depends directly on the time property of sort operations. The execution process of a join operation on the TDM is as follows: First, when all SPs receive join operation commands, one relation, say R, is accessed from disks and sorted in memory in parallel. Then relation S is loaded and sorted in the same way as the relation R. After both relation R and S are sorted, they are merged and joined by the BCP and final results are sent to host computer. The time equation for the join algorithm on the TDM can be represented as following:

$$T_{join} = t_{I/O(R)} + t_{sort(R)} + t_{I/O(S)} + t_{sort(S)} + t_{merge-join(RS)}$$

Figure 7 shows some experimental results of join operations based on the sort-merge-join algorithm. They are also listed in Table 8 (here, we assume both relations joined have the same tuples). From Table 8, we know that:

Table 8. Join time properties for different SPs (TL=100 bytes)						
No. of Tuples (bytes)	1000	3000	5000	7000	9000	10000
1 Slave Processor (min.)	7.9	57.4	150.6	271.2	443.6	543.5
2 Slave Processors (min.)	1.9	14.6	38.9	80.8	121.4	149.3
3 Slave Processors (min.)	1.2	6.5	17.5	35.4	57.5	71.2

1). The time complexity of join operations increases rapidly as the database size (the number of tuples in our case) increases. Also the time complexity of join operations can be decreased as the number of parallel processors increases. When the number of tuples is equal to 1000, 5000, and 10000, we have obtained about 4.16, 3.87, and 3.64 fold speed-ups as the number of SPs increases from one to two and 6.58, 8.61, and 7.63 fold speed-ups from one to three, respectively. So, the parallel processor technique is an effective method to improve the join efficiency and overcome join bottlenecks.

2). Based on an observation of Figure 7, linear ranges for join operations can be found, as shown in Table 9. They show that join operations are CPU intensive and extra CPU capability is required for speed-up join operations.

Table 9. Linear ranges for join operations (TL=100 bytes)					
SP=1	TN≤1500	SP=2	TN≤2300	SP=3	TN≤3500

3). A data index in join operations plays an important role for reducing join operation complexity, i.e, it is possible for a data index to reduce the join complexity as the multiprocessor did. In other words, we can use data index techniques to achieve a better performance but with a smaller number of processors. For example, if the number of tuples can be reduced from 9000 to 3000 by use of a data index, then, we can use one SP to achieve almost same performance as three SPs without a data index.

3.5. Analysis of load balance issues

Load balance is an important issue in multiprocessor database machines to obtain a better utilization of processor resources and a higher throughput of query processing. There have been some strategies for solving this issue [BaF87]. Here, we consider how a load imbalances can occur and how it is solved in our TDM system. Table 10 shows experimental results for the cases of evenly-uniformed data partitioning and not in a sort operation. The last row gives the difference between the two cases. We found that the maximum difference between the two cases is 0.9 minutes. This means that the BCP will have to wait 0.9 minutes for some SP in the case of uneven-data distribution. Our experimental results attempt to show that there are two major reasons: a balanced data partitioning and distribution and a balanced configuration (symmetry of hardware and software structures), to overcome load imbalances in the TDM system. When the hardware symmetry and the software symmetry of multiprocessor database machiines are well considered, the uneven data distribution is the major factor in producing load imbalances. Figure 8 shows the TDM load balance experiments in the cases of even-distributed data and uneven-distributed data on disks.

Table 10. Load balance experiments of the TDM on a sort operation (TL=100 bytes)

No. of Tuples (bytes)	500	1000	2000	3000	4000	5000
load balance (min.)	0.2	0.3	1.3	2.9	5.1	7.2
load imbalance (min.)	0.4	0.6	2.1	3.8	5.8	7.8
difference (min.)	0.2	0.3	0.8	0.9	0.8	0.6

4. Summary

We have analyzed some experimental results from our TDM prototype. Obviously, the results we obtained reveal that the performance of database operations has indeed been improved and a high speed-up has been obtained in our TDM prototype, especially for very large database applications. Comparison of the performance of database operations: selection, sort, and join as the number of SP increases from one to three is about 9.96, 7.62, and 7.63 fold speed-ups respectively when the tuple count is 10000 and the tuple length is 100 bytes. In addition, three observations have been obtained through the analyses. The first observation is that it is essential to employ the multiple processor-disk-pair structure and the multiple level processor-memory structure in database machine architectures for eliminating both I/O and complex operation bottlenecks, especially in large database systems.

The second observation is that it is important to trade-off parallel processors and database applications. The experimental results suggest that it is possible for us to choose an architecture with an optimal number of processors for a given database application. In other words, for a particular database application, we can determine the number of processors in database machine architectures so as to keep time properties of most database operations within the linear ranges. In this way, we not only can overcome bottlenecks of I/O and complex database operations, but also can achieve a better performance cost ratio of the database machines.

The third observation is that it is necessary to build a database dictionary and database index into database machines. The multiprocessor technique in database machines is efficient but not effective because it can not avoid movement of data segments irrelevant to the query and reduce the times and ranges of comparisons. But, a data dictionary and a data index can solve these problems perfectly. A data dictionary can "filter" irrelevant data segments and a data index can reduce times of comparisons. This is why the performance of some database operations on a software database system will be better than that on a database machine system in some cases. If these *software techniques* and *multiprocessor techniques* are incorporated in database machines, the linear ranges of time properties of all data operations can be extended, so the bottlenecks mentioned in this paper can be overcome efficiently and effectively. For the same data size and the same query, on the other hand, the number of processors can be reduced after data dictionary and data index are introduced, Therefore, the database machine with data dictionary and data index and parallel processors can work efficiently and effectively. Its performance, in this case, will become much better [Men87].

The TDM system research work is not yet finished, current work on the TDM prototype focuses on the implementation of query processing and management software system as well as the improvement of parallel algorithms. All these results will be reported in future. We are pursuing our investigation along several directions. We plan to implement a complete TDM system with at least two STEs, each having 8 SPs, and put it into a practical database application with a large data size, so the real performance of the TDM system can be tested. We will examine the TDM architecture in order to seek the best performance cost ratio and study a new software database structure on the TDM and see how they are combined can work well. Finally, we plan to incorporate an additional reasoning machine into the TDM to develop the TDM to support Knowledge Base processing in future. We are encouraged by the results and hope that they may be useful to other database machine designs.

5. Acknowledgement

The TDM prototype has been implemented at the Harbin Institute of Tech., China. Author would like to acknowledge the effort and cooperation of the TDM research team which consisted of Prof. Chen Guangxi, Prof. Hu Mingzeng, Prof. Li Sheng, Dr. Xu Xiaofei, Dr. Chang Huiyou, Mr. Nie Hongxiang, and Mr. Xu Dunbao. Author would also like to thank Prof. T.A. Marsland for his helpful commends on this paper.

References

[BaF87] C.K. Baru and O. Frieder, Implementing Relational Database Operations in a CUBE-CONNECTED Multiprocessor System, *Proc. of the 1987 Intel. Conf. on Data Eng.*, Los Angeles, February, 1987, 36-43.

[Bra84] K. Bratbergsengen, Hashing Methods and Relational Algebra Operations, *Proc. of the 1984 VLDB Conference*, Singapore, August, 1984, 323-333.

[BrS86] C.K. Brau and S.Y.W. Su, The Architecture of SM3 : a Dynamically Partitionable Multicomputer System, *IEEE Trans. on Computers*, C-35(9), (1986), 790-802.

[DeW79] D.J. DeWitt, DIRECT A Multiprocessor Organization for Supporting Relational Database Management Systems, *IEEE Trans. on Computers*, C-28(6), (1979), 395-406.

[DeG85] D.J. DeWitt and R.H. Gerber, Multiprocessor Hash-Based Join Algorithms, *Proc. of the 1985 VLDB Conference*, Stockholm, August, 1985, 151-164.

[DGG86] D.J. DeWitt, R.H. Gerber and G. Graefe, GAMMA A High Performance Dataflow Database Machine, *Proc. of the 1986 VLDB Conference*, Tokyo, August, 1986, 228-237.

[FKT86] S. Fustimi, M. Kitsuregawa and H. Tanaka, An Overview of the System Software of a Parallel Relational Database Machine: GRACE, *Proc. of the 1986 VLDB Conference*, Tokyo, August, 1986, 209-219.

[Gaa83]   G. Gardarin and et al., Design of Multiprocessor Relational database System, *Proc. of the 1983 IFIP Conference*, Paris, 1983, 363-367.

[GoD80]   J.R. Goodman and A.M. Despain, A Study of Interconnection of Multiple Processors in a Data Base Environment, *Proc. of the 1980 International Conf. on parallel procesing*, Harber Springs, August, 1980, 269-278.

[HeH83]   X. He' and D. Hsiao, The Implementation of a Multibackend Database Systems (MBDS), in Advanced Database Machine Architecture, David Hsiao, ed., Prentice-Hall, 1983, 327-385.

[KMS85]   T. Kakuta, N. Miyazaki, S. Shibayama and H. Yokota, The Design and Implementation of relational Database Machine: Delta, in Database Machine: Proc. of the 1985 Int. Workshop on DBMs, D.J. DeWitt and H. Boral, eds., March, 1985.

[KTM83]   M. Kitsuregawa, H. Tanaka and T. Moto-oka, Application of Hash to Data Base Machine and Its Architecture, *New Generation Computing*, 1(1), (1983), 63-74.

[Men84]   L. Meng, Relational Data Base Processor: RDBP , Master Thesis (in chinese), Dept. of Computer Sci. HIT, June, 1984.

[MXC87]   L. Meng, X. Xu, H. Chang, G. Chen, M. Hu and S. Li, Tree-structured Database Machine for Large Relational Database Systems, *Journal of Computer Sci. & Tech.*, 2(4), (1987), 265-276.

[Men87]   L. Meng, Basic Issues in the Design and Implementation of a Tree-structured Database Machine (TDM), in Ph.D Dissertation (in Chinese), Computer Sci. Dept. Harbin Institute of Tech., May, 1987, 1-211.

[Nec84]   P. Neches, Hardware Support for Advanced Data Management Systems, *Computer*, 17(11), (1984), 29-40.

[Sha85]   D.E. Shaw, Relational Query Processing on the NON-VON Supercomputer, in Query Processing in Database Systems, W. Kim, D. Triner and D. Batory, eds., Springer-Verlag, 1985, 248-258.

[ShZ84]   R.K. Shultz and R.J. Zingg, Response Time Analysis of Multiprocessor Computers for Database Support, *ACM Transactions on Database Systems*, 9(1), (1984), 100-132 .

[XCM87]   X. Xu', H. Chang and L. Meng, Design and Implementation of a Tree-structured Database Machine, *Proc. of the 1987 IEEE Int. Conf. on Computer Applications*, Beijing, June, 1987, 432-439.

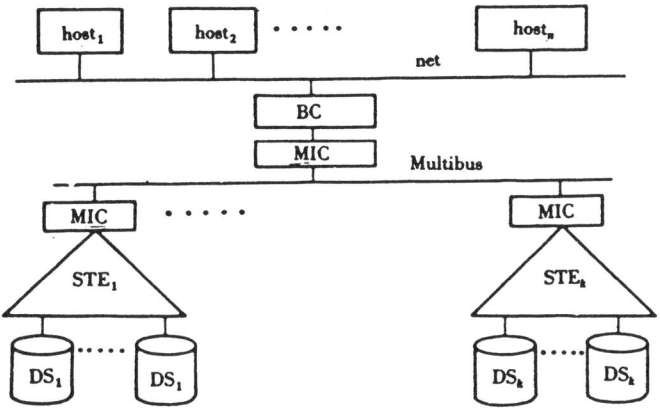

Figure 1. Tree-structured Database Machine (TDM) Architecture

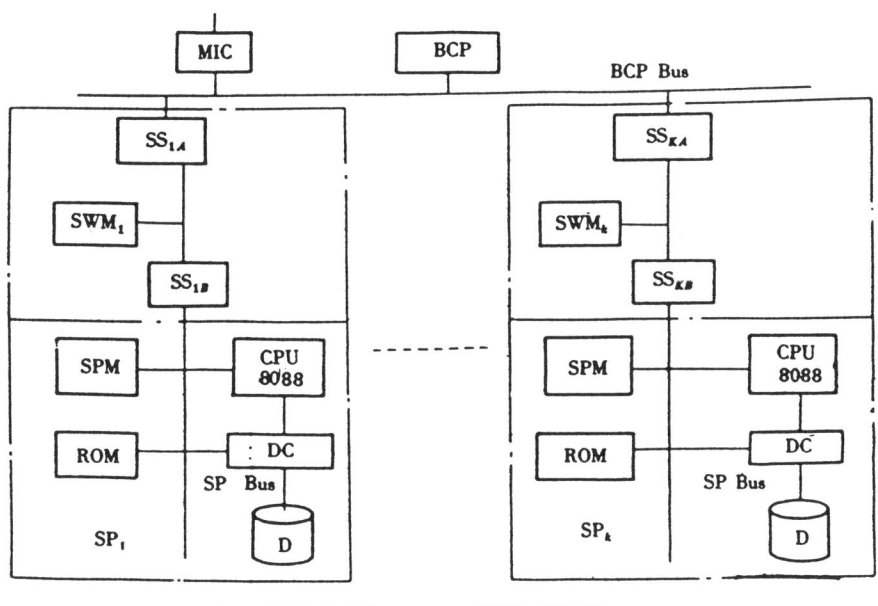

SS: SWM Switch   SPM: SP Memory
DC: Disk Controller   D: Disk

Figure 2. Sub-Tree Element (STE) structure

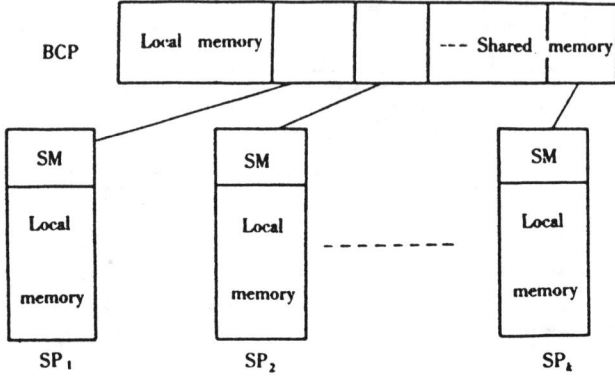

Figure 3. Switchable Working Memory (SWM) structure

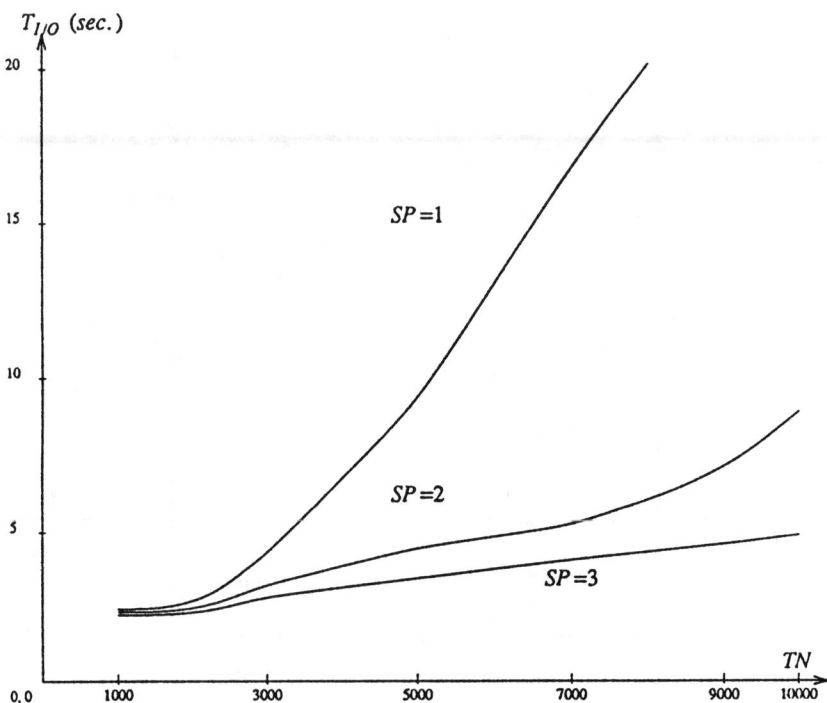

Figure 4. Throughput of I/O operations of the TDM

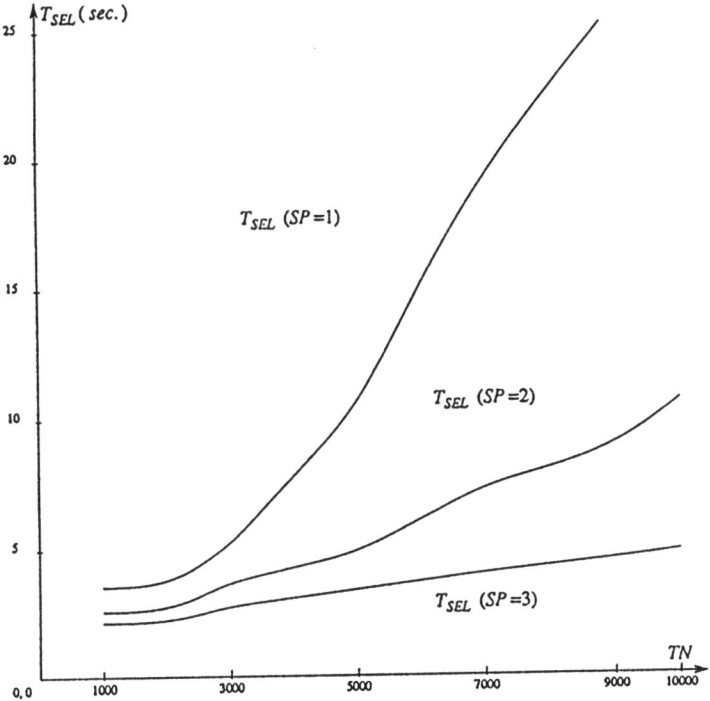

Figure 5. Time properties of selection operations of the TDM

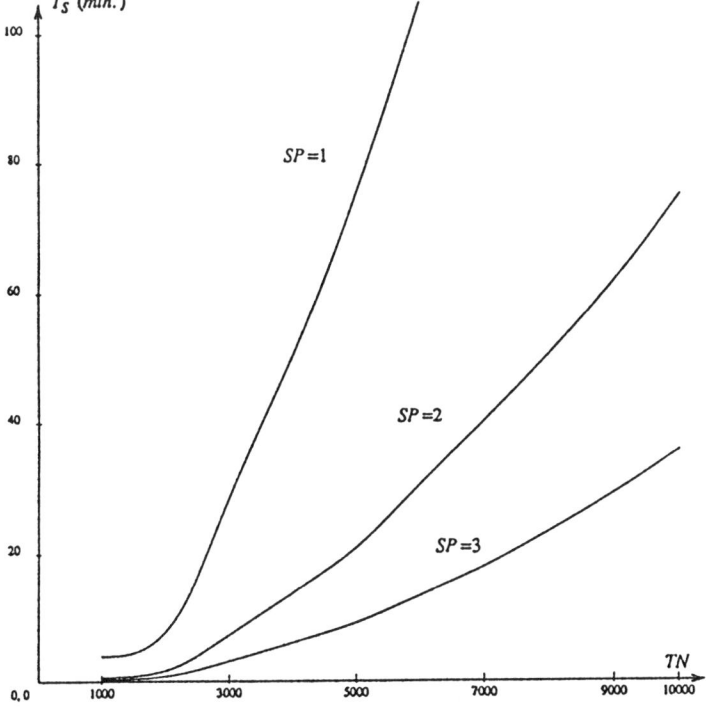

Figure 6. Time properties of sort operations of the TDM

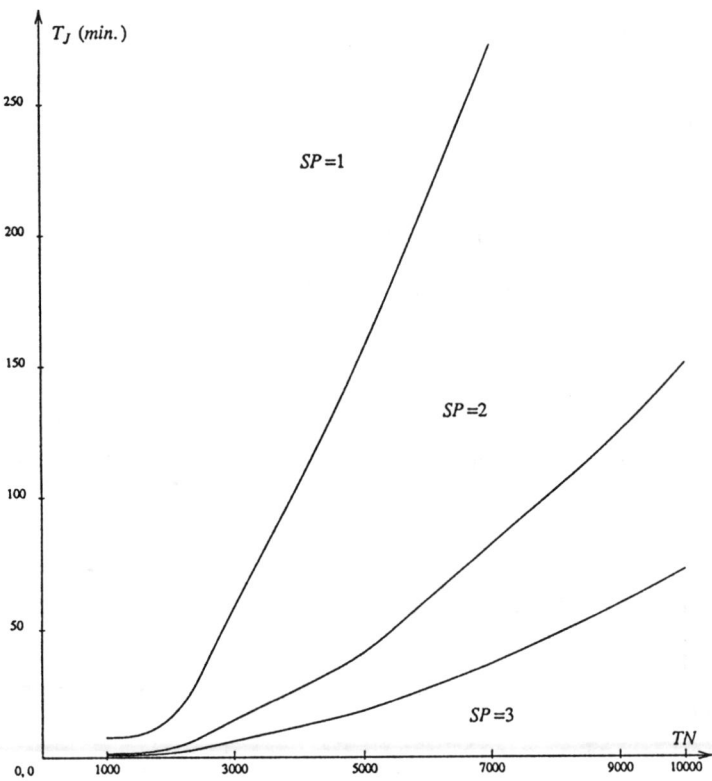

Figure 7. Time properties of join operations of the TDM

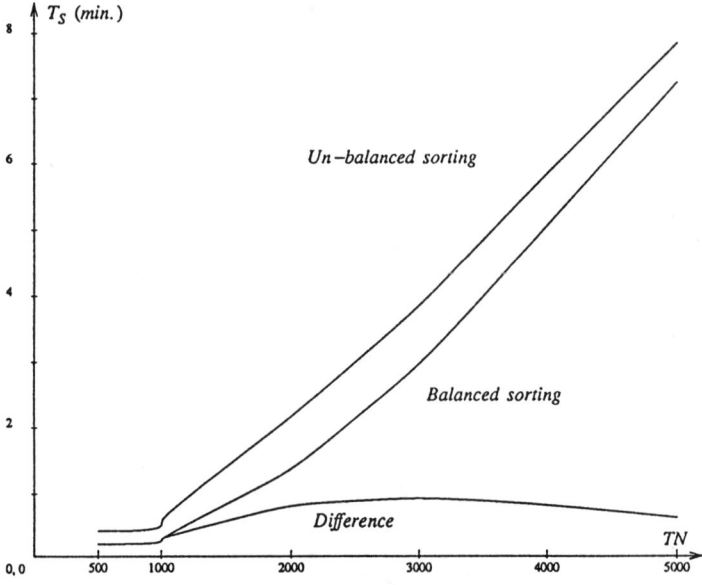

Figure 8. Experimental results of a load balance of sorting in the TDM

Author Index

Abdelguerfi, Mahdi	187
Ae, Tadashi	331
Agrawal, Rakesh	269
Aibara, Reiji	331
Aiso, Hideo	317
Alexander, Bill	34
Amano, Hideharu	317
Apers, Peter M. G.	97
Asthana, Abhaya	286
Baugstø, Bjørn Arild W.	127
Bergsten, Björn	58
Boral, Haran	34
Bratbergsengen, Kjell	359
Cheiney, Jean-Pierre	301
Choi, C. H. Ben	202
Copeland, George	34
Couprie, Michel	58
de Maindreville, Christophe	301
Dittrich, Klaus R.	18
Eich, Margaret H.	251
Fujita, Satoshi	331
Gjelsvik, Torgrim	359
González-Rubio, Rubén	58
Grefen, Paul W. P. J.	97
Greipsland, Jarle Fredrik	127
Hallmark, Gary	171
Herzog, Holger	345
Hildebrandt, Frank	345
Iochpe, Cirano	269
Jagadish, Hosagrahar V.	269
Jagadish, Hosagrahar V.	286
Kerherve, Brigitté	58
Keller, Tom	34
Kersten, Martin L.	97
Khoshafian, Setrag	156
Kim, Myoung Ho	112
Kitsuregawa, Masaru	142
Knauer, Scott C.	286
Kramer, Ralf	18
Lam, Herman	1
Lee, Chiang	1
Lee, Dik L.	202
Lee, Kuo Chu	215
Leilich, Hans-Otto	345
Liedtke, Rolf-Peter	18
Lockemann, Peter C.	18
Mak, Victor W.	215
Meng, Liming	373
Mertinatsch, Peter	345
Miyazaki, Jun	317
Ozkarahan, Esen	230
Penaloza, Manuel	230
Pramanik, Sakti	112
Pucheral, Philippe	73
Schryro, Michael	18
Schwetman, Herb	34
Smith, Marc	34
Stiege, Günter	345
Su, Stanley Y. W.	1
Takeda, Kenji	317
Thevenin, Jean-Marc	73
Valduriez, Patrick	156
von Bültzingsloewen, Günter	18
Wilschut, Annita N.	97
Yamashita, Masafumi	331
Yang, Weikang	142
Young, Chii-Ren	34
Ziane, Mikal	58
Zeidler, Hans Christoph	345

AUG 1 5 1989